THE BOATS OF THE ENGLISH MAN OF WAR "BORSE" CUTTING OUT THE FRENCH SHIP "LA CHEVRETTE"

GRATIS with No. 1 of EDWIN J. BRETT'S "NAVAL HISTORY OF GREAT BRITAIN."

TORY OF GREAT BRITAIN."

E FRENCH SHIP "LA CHEVRETTE."

RETT'S

ILLUSTRATED NAVAL HISTORY

OF

REAT RITAIN,

FROM THE EARLIEST PERIOD TO THE PRESENT TIME.

A RELIABLE RECORD OF THE MARITIME RISE AND PROGRESS OF ENGLAND.

LONDON:
PUBLISHING OFFICE, 173, FLEET STREET, E.C.

MDCCCLXXI.

PREFACE.

THE object of the work now offered to the public is to furnish a concise history of the growth and services of the British Navy, with narratives of the most exciting events in which our brave sailors have participated.

Such deeds as those performed by Blake, Benbow, Anson, Nelson, Howe, Duncan, Jervis, Exmouth, Dundonald, and others of her naval heroes, have tended to raise the fame and the influence of England far above all nations. In every quarter of the globe, on every sea, her flag has been triumphant; and innumerable acts of valour and enterprise, of emulation and daring, invest the doings of the British Navy with an interest not belonging to any other portion of our National History.

Our work has been to relate these deeds of daring, and to place before the public, in a cheap and accessible form, a faithful record of the prowess of Britain's naval heroes. Of the manner in which the task has been performed, modesty forbids us to speak. The reader shall judge for himself.

CONTENTS.

	PAGE
INTRODUCTION	2

CHAPTER I.
FROM THE ROMAN INVASION OF BRITAIN TO THE REIGN OF ALFRED THE GREAT 2

CHAPTER II.
FROM ALFRED TO THE ACCESSION OF EDWARD THE CONFESSOR 7

CHAPTER III.
FROM THE NORMAN CONQUEST TO THE REIGN OF EDWARD I.—SHIPS OF THE THIRTEENTH CENTURY—ORIGIN OF THE WARS BETWEEN FRANCE AND ENGLAND 15

CHAPTER IV.
TO THE ACCESSION OF HENRY IV. 22

CHAPTER V.
FROM HENRY IV. TO HENRY VII.—NAVAL EVENTS AND IMPROVEMENTS—THE "GRACE DIEU" . . . 27

CHAPTER VI.
DISCOVERIES OF COLUMBUS—GREAT IMPROVEMENTS IN NAVAL ARCHITECTURE—ORIGIN OF THE NAVY BOARD AND TRINITY HOUSE—THE "GREAT HARRY" . 32

CHAPTER VII.
FROM THE ACCESSION OF ELIZABETH TO THE WAR WITH SPAIN—SIR FRANCIS DRAKE AND HIS ADVENTURES 40

CHAPTER VIII.
TRIUMPHANT ADVANCE AND SIGNAL DEFEAT OF THE SPANISH ARMADA 48

CHAPTER IX.
EXPEDITION TO PORTUGAL—HEROIC DEATH OF SIR RICHARD GRENVILLE 53

CHAPTER X.
EXPEDITIONS UNDER ESSEX AND RALEIGH—BOMBARDMENT AND DESTRUCTION OF CADIZ . . . 58

CHAPTER XI.
THE FIRST DUTCH WAR, 1652—BLAKE AND VAN TROMP—CAPTURE OF JAMAICA 68

CHAPTER XII.
THE NAVY OF THE RESTORATION—SECOND DUTCH WAR 77

CHAPTER XIII.
THE THIRD DUTCH WAR, 1672—MEMOIR OF THE DUKE OF ALBEMARLE 85

CHAPTER XIV.
FROM THE CONCLUSION OF THE THIRD DUTCH WAR TO THE DEATH OF ADMIRAL BENBOW . . . 93

CHAPTER XV.
CAPTURE OF GIBRALTAR—PEACE OF UTRECHT . 101

CHAPTER XVI.
OPERATIONS IN THE BALTIC—ADMIRAL VERNON AT PORTOBELLO—TREATY OF AIX-LA-CHAPELLE . . 107

CHAPTER XVII.
LOSS OF THE ISLAND OF MINORCA—TRIAL AND EXECUTION OF ADMIRAL BYNG 116

CHAPTER XVIII.
ALLIANCE BETWEEN FRANCE AND THE AMERICAN STATES—RODNEY'S ACTION WITH COUNT DE GRASSE—LOSS OF THE "ROYAL GEORGE" 125

CHAPTER XIX.
NAVAL EVENTS CONNECTED WITH THE OUTBREAK OF THE FRENCH REVOLUTION—COMMENCEMENT OF NELSON'S CAREER 135

CHAPTER XX.
CHIEF EVENTS OF THE YEAR 1795 . . . 140

CHAPTER XXI.
CONTINUATION OF THE WAR—PRINCIPAL NAVAL ACTIONS OF THE YEAR 1796 143

CHAPTER XXII.
NAVAL VICTORIES IN 1797—BATTLE OF CAPE ST. VINCENT—BATTLE OF CAMPERDOWN—MUTINY AT THE NORE 147

CHAPTER XXIII.
CONTINUATION OF THE WAR IN 1798—BATTLE OF THE NILE 161

CONTENTS.

CHAPTER XXIV.
CONTINUATION OF THE WAR IN 1799—EXPEDITION TO HOLLAND 171

CHAPTER XXV.
NAVAL ACTIONS DURING THE YEAR 1800—DESTRUCTION OF THE "QUEEN CHARLOTTE" BY FIRE . 180

CHAPTER XXVI.
BOMBARDMENT OF COPENHAGEN—DESTRUCTION OF THE BOULOGNE FLOTILLA—TREATY OF AMIENS . 183

CHAPTER XXVII.
RENEWAL OF THE WAR IN 1803 194

CHAPTER XXVIII.
ALARMS OF INVASION IN 1804—ACTION OF ADMIRAL LINOIS WITH A FLEET OF ENGLISH MERCHANTMEN 199

CHAPTER XXIX.
EVENTS OF 1805—NELSON IN PURSUIT OF THE FRENCH FLEET—SIR R. CALDER'S ACTION WITH VILLENEUVE—NELSON'S LAST VICTORY AND DEATH . . 206

CHAPTER XXX.
ACTIONS FOUGHT IN 1806—WRECK OF THE "ATHÉNIENNE" 225

CHAPTER XXXI.
DOINGS OF THE NAVY IN 1807—ADMIRAL DUCKWORTH AT CONSTANTINOPLE—WRECKS AND DISASTERS 235

CHAPTER XXXII.
1808. ACTION WITH THE RUSSIANS IN THE BALTIC . 252

CHAPTER XXXIII.
1809. LORD COCHRANE ON THE FRENCH COAST . 262

CHAPTER XXXIV.
NAVAL DOINGS IN 1810—DEATH OF ADMIRAL LORD COLLINGWOOD 275

CHAPTER XXXV.
NAVAL ACTIONS IN 1811 282

CHAPTER XXXVI.
WAR DECLARED WITH THE UNITED STATES IN 1812. 288

CHAPTER XXXVII.
1813. ACTIONS ON THE AMERICAN COAST—THE "SHANNON" AND "CHESAPEAKE" . . . 295

CHAPTER XXXVIII.
CONTINUATION OF THE AMERICAN WAR IN 1814—CAPTURE OF THE U.S. SHIP "PRESIDENT" . . 303

CHAPTER XXXIX.
1815. END OF THE FRENCH WAR 311

CHAPTER XL.
PARTICULARS OF SHIPS. 313

CHAPTER XLI.
1816—1827. BOMBARDMENT OF ALGIERS—BATTLE OF NAVARINO 315

CHAPTER XLII.
THE FIRST CHINESE WAR 317

CHAPTER XLIII.
OPERATIONS ON THE COAST OF SYRIA, 1840. . . 319

CHAPTER XLIV.
VOYAGES OF DISCOVERY 320

CHAPTER XLV.
THE RUSSIAN WAR, 1854 322

CHAPTER XLVI.
THE RUSSIAN WAR, 1855 324

CHAPTER XLVII.
THE SECOND CHINESE WAR, 1856—1860 . . . 325

LIST OF PORTRAITS IN THIS VOLUME.

	PAGE
PORTRAIT OF SIR F. DRAKE	52
" SIR WALTER RALEIGH	61
" JOHN HAWKINS	69
" ADMIRAL BLAKE	76
" JAMES, DUKE OF YORK	84
" PRINCE GEORGE OF DENMARK	101
" CLOUDESLEY SHOVEL	108
" ADMIRAL VERNON	116
" LORD ANSON	124
" LORD ST. VINCENT	133
" LORD HOOD	141
" LORD DUNCAN	149
" LORD NELSON	157
PORTRAIT OF LORD COLLINGWOOD	164
" SIR SIDNEY SMITH	173
" LORD BRIDPORT	180
" LORD KEITH	189
" SIR THOMAS TROWBRIDGE	196
" ADMIRAL DUCKWORTH	205
" SIR W. HOSTE	228
" LORD COCHRANE	264
" ADMIRAL COCKBURN	277
" LORD EXMOUTH	285
" ADMIRAL CODRINGTON	293
" ADMIRAL SIR M. SEYMOUR	301
" SIR THOMAS BRISBANE	317

BRETT'S ILLUSTRATED NAVAL HISTORY OF GREAT BRITAIN

BEING A RELIABLE RECORD OF THE

Maritime Rise and Progress of England.

NAVAL BATTLE BETWEEN KING ALFRED AND THE DANES IN THE YEAR 898.

INTRODUCTION.

NOAH'S ARK, THE EARLIEST RECORDED VESSEL.

AT what remote period of the world's history man's natural skill and temerity first induced him to construct a float, and finally to venture his body on the uncertain deep, is a question that must ever remain a subject of vague conjecture.

That those members of the human family dwelling on the banks of lakes and rivers, or those inhabiting the sea coasts, early possessed some means, however rude, of crossing estuaries and reaching remote headlands, there can be no possible question or doubt.

Without a raft or a boat to enable him to reach deep water, of what benefit to man would have been the teeming myriads with which a beneficent Providence had stocked the lake, the river, and the sea?

From the fisherman's primitive craft, whatever it was, the transition to ships of size and burthen must have been a natural sequence; and here, for our very first idea of a vessel, we must turn to the book to which, as a record of God and the world, we refer for all real information and good instruction—the Bible.

In the sixth chapter of Genesis we read of God's command to Noah to construct a floating house, or Ark, in which Noah, his wife, and family, with all the animals necessary to replenish the earth, might be safely lodged for six months, the duration of the Deluge.

The Ark, we are told, was 300 cubits long, 50 broad, and 30 cubits high. The interior was divided into rooms, and subdivided longitudinally into three floors or decks. Finally, the Ark had a window, a door at the side, and a covering or roof.

From these few but very significant facts it is not difficult to picture both the size and the shape of the Ark. Taking the Hebrew *cubit* to measure five feet, the actual dimensions of the Ark were 1,500 feet in length, 250 feet beam, or wide, and 150 feet in height, irrespective of the roof.

These dimensions would give us a vessel only a little shorter than the first Crystal Palace in Hyde Park, but with more than its greatest altitude.

The great interest, however, which we derive from these few facts is the knowledge that the secret of naval architecture, which men have been striving to obtain for the last eight hundred years, is to be found in these very figures.

The difficulty of every ship-builder, since ship building became a high class profession, has been the solution of the problem — *What proportion should the length of a craft bear to its width or beam?*

Modern science has at length decided that, according to her sailing or carrying capabilities, a ship should be between six and seven times the length of her breadth. The length of the Ark was *exactly six times* that of her beam!

Leaving for a time Holy Writ, we must return to the antique world, as peopled by the descendants of Noah and his three sons, and briefly trace the origin of ship-building down to the epoch when the Roman galleys first met the gaze of the astonished Britons.

CHAPTER I.

FROM THE ROMAN INVASION OF BRITAIN TO THE REIGN OF ALFRED THE GREAT.

BEFORE we enter on the actual Naval History of England, it will be necessary to give the reader some account, however brief, of the ships used in the ancient world, and which formed the prototype of those in vogue for nearly a thousand years after the Christian era.

The ships of the ancients consisted, in general, of two kinds—galleys, propelled solely by oars, and galleys with both sails and oars, the latter description being generally employed as ships of burthen or as transports. Vessels freighted with merchandise were generally of this class, or, more properly speaking, rig.

Our readers will be astonished to hear that two of the latest and most celebrated inventions in naval warfare were in common use centuries before the Christian era. We refer to the *Ram* and the *Turret*.

The Roman ships, which were at best only a slight improvement on the Carthagenian vessels, varied in length from 90 to 120 feet, by a breadth of from 10 to 13 feet. The stem, or prow, was high, sharp, and long, armed with iron, and, propelled with force, could cut an enemy's galley in two. The stern was also high, broad, and strong, to resist the force of the waves. Different woods were employed in the construction of the galleys, oak being always selected for the hull, on account of its strength.

In the time of Trajan, A.D. 109, if not much earlier, the war galleys seem to have been sheathed with lead, and riveted with bolts of copper; while in some of the larger Roman galleys, of the Carthagenian date, large towers or *turrets* were erected.

In these turrets the Romans placed their archers and slingers, and their heavy engines of war, such as their battering rams and catapults, machines that threw scores of immense javelins and huge stones.

The usual war galley was propelled by a great number of oarmen or rowers, who sat on benches or banks, raised one behind the other, like the seats in the gallery of a theatre.

Upon the size and weight of the galley depended the number of banks or benches, or in other words, the number of rowers.

Of war galleys there seem to have been three kinds or sizes, named after their banks, such as the triremes, quadriremes, and quinquiremes, or ships with three, four, and five banks or rows of rowers.

The naval tactics of the Romans appear to have been very simple, and may be said to have resolved themselves literally into a hand-to-hand encounter, an engagement of ship to ship and man to man.

If the first attempt to sink or cut the enemy's ship in two, by means of the sharp prow or ram, failed, the ships grappled together, broadside to broadside, and then, each man singling out an antagonist, the work of death was continued till all opposition ceased, or one or both vessels sank with their freight of living and dead.

It was in these close encounters with the enemy that the courage and military training of the Romans made them so formidable, and rendered abortive even the nautical superiority of the Carthagenians, often snatching victory from those whose naval skill and experience should have commanded success.

This system of sea fighting continued from the very earliest ages, down to the period when gunpowder and cannon were first used aboard ships.

Of the frightful sacrifice of human life that usually attended ancient sea-fights it is almost impossible to form anything like an approximate opinion.

The antique sword was an awful weapon; short, broad, double-edged, and heavy, its thrust was mortal. Consequently every stab was a death, and the wounded after a battle formed but a miserable minority in proportion to the slain.

Of the utter disregard of human life displayed by the kings and leaders of ancient fleets and armies, an instance is shown in the clever and heroic stratagem of Artemisia, the Queen of Xerxes, the Persian monarch, at the memorable battle of Salamis.

This shrewd and dauntless woman, seeing that the utter ruin of her husband's fleet must follow its flight down the Ægean Sea, if followed by the excited Athenians, at once conceived a stratagem that might have immortalised a general.

Springing into one of the swiftest of the Persian ships, she hung out a Greek flag, and boldly passing the enemy, attacked one of the largest Persian ships she could meet, fought and sank it, and then continued her seeming pursuit of the others.

The weary Greeks, seeing, as they believed, one of their own ships so gallantly pursuing the foe, gladly gave up the chase, and allowed Artemisia to lead the rest of the Persian fleet into a harbour of refuge.

Cæsar, having brought the Gauls to a state of temporary subjection and peace, and anxious to employ his army in further conquests, turned his eyes to Britain, and giving orders to augment his fleet, in the summer of the year of the world, 3761, or forty-five years before the birth of Christ, put in practice his intention.

Embarking two legions, or about 15,000 men, in his principal vessels, and leaving the cavalry belonging to the legions—600 strong—to follow in the larger transports, Cæsar took advantage of a favourable wind to leave the coast of Gaul, and set sail on the evening of the 24th of August for Britain.

By the morning of the 25th the Roman fleet was close under the cliffs of Dover; the wind, however, failing, the Roman galleys were obliged to skirt the coast in search of a beach where the troops could be landed. On reaching the Downs, the shore was found to be lined with the armed and determined natives.

Disregarding this hostile demonstration, Cæsar decided on landing, and at once testing the bravery of the natives.

Fortunate it was for Cæsar that the greater part of the painted warriors who confronted him had followed their chief, Cassevalanus, from the inland counties of Buckingham, Bedford, and Herts, then known as the Catieulani; men who had never seen, or probably heard of a ship before, and whose astonishment at sight of the Roman galleys far exceeded their dread of the invader's arms.

The greater portion of Cassevalanus's army fled from those monsters of the deep; and to the men of Kent and Sussex, then Cantii and Regni, was left the task of disputing the Roman landing.

These, however, fought with such determined bravery, as to force from the pen of their historian and conqueror terms of the highest praise.

The disaster attending Cæsar's transports with his cavalry, and the ruin of his fleet by tempests and the fury of the natives, are matters of history, with which we have nothing directly to do.

The Britons were probably as ignorant of ships

and naval matters when the Romans invaded this country as the natives of the South Sea Islands were when discovered by Captain Cook.

The rivers, lakes, and estuaries of this country abounded in fish, and these the natives could easily capture in their *Coracles*, oblong wicker baskets covered with hides.

Seated in these skiffs, which were carried on the shoulders to the water, the fisherman could paddle where he pleased.

If anything larger than a coracle existed among the natives in Cæsar's time, it was probably only a log-canoe to hold a party of hardy fishermen who ventured beyond hail but not out of sight of shore.

The Phœnicians had, for ages, ceased to trade with Cornwall; and, perhaps, only to those inhabitants dwelling on the south-eastern coasts of Britain was the occasional sight of a trading galley from Gaul familiar.

Bearing these facts in mind, the astonishment of the natives on first seeing a large fleet of Roman galleys is much less remarkable than it would otherwise appear.

That vast fabric that had spread civilization and slavery over so large a portion of the known world was fast hastening to its ruin; and Rome, threatened in its very capital by the barbarians they had so often scorned and conquered, was compelled to call in her outlying forces to save, for a few months or years longer, the fall of her tottering empire.

In the year 445, or about 490 years from the first invasion of Julius Cæsar, the Romans, threatened on all sides by the triumphant Goths, were forced to leave Britain, and desert for ever one of her most favoured and valuable colonies.

In taking their final leave of this country the Romans not only carried with them all the ships and portable engines of war, but at the same time drained the island of all its youth and martial blood, swelling its reduced legions with the vigour and strength of the country.

Without defenders and without ships, the remaining inhabitants, long unaccustomed to arms, and, by that time, inured to the softening arts of peace, presented a tempting prize to the first hardy adventurer.

Passing over the troubles and misfortunes endured by the Britons in their vain attempts to resist the Picts and Scots, and of their after calamities under their allies and conquerors, the Saxons, we must come to a new and still more formidable enemy of the country.

The Scandinavians, or the people inhabiting the extreme north-western portions of Europe, the Danes and Norwegians, living in a cold and unproductive country, inured to a life of toil and privation, and to whom the surrounding and tempestuous seas were familiar, and almost cherished, objects, early gave vent to their daring and roving propensities.

The Norwegians seem, as far as the half poetical annals of Scandinavia permit us to form an opinion, to have been the first to merit the appellation of sea kings and rovers, another name for pirates and murderers.

Living on a coast lined with iron-bound rocks eternally washed by the vast waves of the Atlantic, and visited at times by overwhelming and fearful storms, it is natural to suppose that the vessels the Norwegians built, though they might have the shape of the universal galley, were of a construction much stronger and more seaworthy than the adorned and graceful vessels used on the Mediterranean, or to skirt the coast of Spain and Gaul.

BRIDGE OF BOATS, TIME OF JULIUS CÆSAR.

In fact, they were built to resist the force of the Atlantic, and to contain as many men and as much plunder as possible; or, in other words, utility and strength, not elegance, were the objects aimed at.

The Orkney and Shetland Islands were probably the first places visited by these piratical rovers, whose excursions soon spread to the eastern coasts of Scotland and England.

The success of these early voyages seem to have incited the Danes to a similar course of action, till, from solitary adventurers with one or two ships, whole fleets were fitted out under the command of the king in person, or one or more of his principal officers.

In the course of years it became the general custom of either the Danes or the Norwegians to put to sea in the summer and sail to some southern shores on their predatory excursions, when, having found some favoured spot, they ran their ships aground, landed their forces, and having pillaged the country far and near, murdered all who opposed them, and then loaded their ships with the plunder, and returned home to enjoy the winter in peace and plenty.

To the peaceable inhabitants of Britain and France the aspect of these Norsemen, or Sea Kings, was more alarming than their rude arms, uncouth gestures, and savage courage.

Of almost gigantic stature—few of these invaders being under six feet in height—with long, yellow hair, and grizzly beards, and possessed of herculean strength, their very appearance inspired terror in the hearts of their unaccustomed enemies.

How long these roving and piratical adventurers had existed before the Danes or Norwegians conceived the idea of conquest and settlement, we have no authentic knowledge.

The first reliable information we possess on this subject is that abuot the end of the ninth century, the Norwegian fleet, passing through the channel, and giving the harassed Saxons a brief respite, shaped its course for Neustria, that portion of France long after known as Normandy; and there Rollo, their king, landed, and, what is more, made so good his landing that he could never afterwards be expelled from the country.

Other chieftains, but of less importance than Rollo, quickly followed to support and share the good fortune of their hardy countrymen, till one of the most fertile and beautiful provinces of Gaul became permanently settled by these northern barbarians.

This brief digression may, to the hasty and inconsiderate reader, appear irrelevant to our "Naval History of Great Britain;" such, however, is by no means the case, as will be fully evident as we proceed.

The whole history of the world probably presents no instance of so perfect and radical a change of an entire people, in so short a time, as that effected in the bearded pirates of Norway, who possessed themselves of the fertile province of Neustria.

In a space of time little exceeding 150 years, those rude and shaggy giants, who had seized on the lands and homes of the peaceable Gauls, and whose greatest happiness consisted in daily pillage and nightly carousal, became the most accomplished, most elegant, and most refined nation in Europe.

The country was covered with beautiful and opulent cities, where letters, and many of the arts, reached their highest excellence, and the people themselves were not only brave, but courteous.

Giving the Norse appellation to the new country, we shall for a time leave *Normandy* and the Normans, and return to our own country of Britain.

A SHIP-BUILDER'S YARD, TIME OF KING ALFRED.

Scarcely had the Saxons, who first landed in the Isle of Thanet about the middle of the fifth century, firmly established their dominion in this country, and begun to realise the luxury of their home, when their dominion was threatened by an enemy as persevering as he was formidable.

About the year 790, a small band of Danes, or Norsemen, in a fleet of some 50 ships, made their first incursion into England.

Landing somewhere on the coast of Devon, the invaders were encountered on their march inland by a general of the then King of Wessex.

The Saxon general having demanded their business, commanded them to follow him to the presence of his royal master.

Instead of complying with this demand, the Danes fell on the Saxon chief and his retinue, and, having put them all to the sword, retreated to their ships, and, with what booty they could secure, returned home.

From that time scarcely a year passed without bringing some band of these dauntless rovers to the shores of England.

Sometimes their depredations were effected by the armed crews of only a few ships; at others, the dreaded foe appeared in fleets, comprising from 100 to 200 ships, from which they spread like a devastating swarm over the land.

From north to south, from east to west, no portion of the kingdom was free from their inroads, and so sudden was their appearance, so rapid their incursions and retreat, that they shipped their plunder and put to sea before the troops of the country could overtake them.

So intolerable had become this state of incessant murder and pillage, that the people, in despair, neglected the cultivation of their land, and the inhabitants of one county dreaded to stir to the relief of another, lest the foe, in their absence, should invade their unprotected homes. When the Danes, Norwegians, and Swedes, who usually comprised these roving armies, had reduced their piratical excursions into an organized system, they altered the size of their ships, the better to suit their predatory purposes, and built them shorter and lighter. With these vessels, which, in reality, were little better than fishing-boats, they run aground on the first sandy beach that offered, or, sailing up rivers, drew their ships high and dry on the banks.

In either case they seem to have followed the Roman example, and having securely entrenched their boats or galleys, and left nearly a third of their force to guard them, advanced with the rest on their freebooting excursions.

It may be here necessary to give our readers some idea of the *reason* of these constant visitations of the sea kings, and why they waged a war on their neighbours, so unlike all similar incursions of barbarian hordes on civilised nations.

The Goths and Vandals, and those myriads of the populous north who desolated and destroyed the Roman empire, even down to the time of the Huns under Attila, were all naturally of a migratory habit; and when they invaded a fertile country, they poured into it in swarms like locusts.

They came, too, with their wives and children, with their cattle, tents, and household gods, meaning to settle; and, in their rude way, cultivate the soil they overspread.

When they had destroyed the military prestige of Rome, and overthrown her power, they intermarried with the peasantry; and, in time, became a new people, considering the land their fathers had acquired by rapine as their lawful property.

In time, however, other tribes of these rude Scythians, having exhausted all the pasturage of their barren steppes, and looking out for fresh food for their starving cattle, fell on the original invaders, and acted again on the Goths and Vandals all those horrors of war and rapine which they had perpetrated on the civilized Romans; always in the end making good their footing in some portion or other of Gaul or Italy.

The tactics of the Norsemen, or sea kings, on the contrary, were very different.

The Scandinavians were never a pastoral people.

Surrounded on three sides by water, with a rocky and tempest-beaten coast and a mountainous country covered with dense forests of pine, and for nearly half the year shut in by snow and ice, they possessed neither herds nor pasturage for the support of cattle.

The small patches of country in the three nationalities of Denmark, Sweden and Norway, at that time under cultivation, hardly deserved the name of arable land, at best only yielding small and uncertain crops of oats or barley.

So small, indeed, and inadequate to the wants of the people were these annual harvests, especially in Norway, that the suffering natives were often driven to the direst extremity to economise their scanty crops of grain, and spread their few measures of oat or barley meal over the tedious stretch of twelve months.

So seldom were our rude progenitors of the north blessed with an abundant harvest, or a sufficiency of food that, to eke out their scanty supply, the people dried and ground the inner bark of the fir and larch, that grew so abundantly on their mountains, and, mixing it with their meal, made the whole into bread.

The bread, a species of cake, of the hardy Norsemen, consisted, in fact, of about two parts of meal to one of sawdust, or ground bark; the resin and turpentine of the wood serving as a sort of spice to the cold and cludgy bannock.

Unsavory and coarse as this kind of wood and oaten cake may appear to our modern and fastidious taste, which repudiates anything short of the best wheaten bread, it was, in those days, a luxury which the dreaded warriors of Scandinavia and their families could not always indulge in.

So scarce, indeed, was even this description of food, that it was only partaken of at particular times, and then in limited quantities.

In the case of a people like the Norwegians and the Danes, living almost entirely on fish—fish from the ocean, and fish from the lakes and rivers—it will naturally be asked, grain being so scarce, what did they substitute for bread or vegetables?

The surprise of the youthful reader will be still greater when we reply that the corrective for all the fresh and salted fish of lake, stream, and ocean, on which the northern barbarian feasted from spring to winter and from winter to spring, was still fish.

Stock-fish, a species of ling cut open, washed in the sea, and dried in the frosty nights of winter, and then cut into pieces, formed the substitute for vegetables at every meal of the sea kings or their followers.

Modern civilization and the spread of agriculture has not yet overcome the necessity for this raw food; and, *at the present day*, after a lapse of more than twelve centuries, over all the northern portion of

Norway, the stock-fish still does duty at every meal for bread and potatoes.

To a people whose food consisted almost exclusively of fish, oatmeal, and pine-dust, it need cause no surprise if the better filled larders of their neighbours presented a temptation too powerful to be resisted.

The truth is, the Norsemen were first driven to their piratical habits by want of food, and the absolute poverty of their country.

In their piratical excursions, however, they went alone, and, with their swords and war implements by their sides, took leave of their wives and families, and, for the time, committed themselves to the dangers of the deep, and the protection of their gods.

It was not till after repeated descents on the coast of England, and when the invaders had made themselves well acquainted with all the maritime parts of the island, that they seem to have brought over their wives and made up their minds to settle here.

It was, perhaps, the knowledge of this fact, and that their household gods and families were at their back, that made them fight with such obstinate fury during the entire reign of Ethelred, and the first years of his brother Alfred, when peace was at last only obtained by allowing them to settle in the northern counties of the island.

Having thus briefly run through the early history of the construction of sea-going vessels, and brought our readers to a period at which the NAVAL HISTORY OF ENGLAND really commences, we will close our introductory chapter, and address ourselves to the task of showing the rise and progress of that branch of our national power, whose deeds have excited the admiration of the world, and—until the modern age of iron set in—has always been proudly called "the wooden walls of Old England."

CHAPTER II.

ALFRED, TO THE ACCESSION OF EDWARD THE CONFESSOR.

T is a singular fact, that though this country had been almost annually infested by the Danes for nearly a century, no attempt had ever been made to meet and resist the national enemy on the sea, the pirates being allowed to land, murder, pillage, and destroy with impunity, till a force could be collected to pursue, and, if possible, overtake them; too often, however, a vain and futile attempt.

This lamentable state of ignorance and neglect was now to cease, and the sea kings to find that the people they had begun to despise only wanted a leader to convert them into a formidable foe.

Alfred the Great, after his signal victory over Guthrum, the Danish king, and his solemn compact with him and his people to settle as peaceable inhabitants in East Anglia and Northumberland, turned his attention to the settlement and defence of his distracted kingdom.

The whole eastern coast of England had become so completely depopulated in consequence of the incessant depredations of the Danes, that Alfred, about the year 880, unable to obtain ships along that maritime coast, was obliged to order the immediate construction of such an armament as might be fit to confront any fresh adventurers who should have the daring to threaten his country.

At the same time he ordered all the ship-builders and merchants on the south and western coasts to supply a certain number of their vessels to join those which he was constructing under his own eye and authority.

To man these vessels with brave and hardy seamen, he collected the most expert sailors from every part of the country, and, these not being sufficient for his purpose, he sent to Friesland, and the countries on the North Sea, now known as Hanover and Holland, and having hired the most experienced mariners he could find, put them aboard his newly-constructed fleet.

Like a politic king and wise commander, Alfred was not content with manning a certain number of ships, and sending them out to meet the enemy on a new battle ground, and in a style of warfare with which his people were totally unfamiliar, but he himself personally led his fleet of 120 ships.

Having fully supplied his vessels with warlike stores, and all the engines of destruction then in use, he took them out to sea, and, by reviews and sham fights, drilled the crews of his ships as he would have done his soldiers in all the then known tactics of naval warfare.

After satisfying himself of the competency of his fleet to meet and engage an enemy, he landed, and, dividing his ships, sent a division south, east, and west, to protect the coast, fully believing they would give a good account of the enemy if they encountered him.

Alfred had no reason to be disappointed in his hopes, for several bands of Danes and Norsemen, ignorant of the total ruin of Guthrum's army, and the defeat of the last year's hordes, put to sea in the spring, and appeared nearly at the same time on several parts of the eastern coast.

The English, hardly allowing the Danes time to recover from their astonishment at finding a hostile fleet presuming to dispute their landing, and burning with a desire to meet their hated enemies on their own element, fell on the different squadrons with such fury, and fought so well, that not a ship's crew escaped to record the disaster.

A few more of such naval actions completely cleared the seas of this no longer invulnerable foe, and for some years not a hostile prow was to be seen off the coast of England.

In all the excursions of these idolatrous barbarians they had invariably made towards the nearest cities as offering the richest plunder; though the special objects of their cupidity were the abbeys, cathedrals, and all religious houses.

In these, after outraging the nuns, murdering the monks, and carrying off the gold and silver vessels of the altar, they always made themselves free of the abbot's cellar, and finally regained their ships loaded with booty.

Alfred had barely time to effect his contemplated improvements and repairs, when danger threatened him in a new and unexpected quarter.

Hastings, another Danish prince, and the confederate of Guthrum, after ravaging the French coast, suddenly appeared off the southern shores of Kent with a fleet of 330 ships.

Leaving the greater part of his army and fleet at Appledore, in the river Rother, Hastings himself, with eighty sail, directed his course towards the Thames; but, suddenly running his ships aground at Milton, near Sittingbourne, landed his men, and, having firmly entrenched his forces, sent out parties to ravage the country in all directions.

The almost superhuman exertions that Alfred made to protect his country, so suddenly threatened from the south and east, are matters of military history with which our subject has nothing to do.

Having almost annihilated the Danes at Appledore, Alfred hastened to protect London and meet Hastings, who had crossed to Shoeburyness, leaving a body of Danes who had escaped him at Appledore to the militia of the country.

This body of the enemy, having cut its way through the English army, sacked and burnt the city of Chichester; and, for a time, committed their usual ravages; but the troops Alfred had left fell on them when loaded with spoil, recovered all the booty, and, after a sanguinary action, drove the defeated Danes back to their ships.

Not satisfied with this achievement, the English folowed up their success by again attacking the enemy before he could put to sea; and ended the prolonged contest by taking or destroying nearly the whole of his fleet.

Reviewing the naval and military history of our country as we now do, in the broad light of universal knowledge, civilization, and peace, we can form no conception of the horrors endured by our Saxon ancestors, or of the difficulties and troubles suffered by that noblest and best of English sovereigns, Alfred, most justly surnamed the Great.

Alfred had ever shown the greatest magnanimity to his vanquished foes, had conferred on Guthrum and his people the most sterling marks of his kindness and friendship, and had resigned to them nearly a fifth part of his kingdom; and all he demanded in return was the duty of peaceable citizens.

No sooner, however, did Hastings appear on the coast, than the treacherous Danes of Northumbria and East Anglia rose in insurrection, and while the latter spread themselves over the heart of England, the Northumbrians put to sea in a fleet of 240 ships, and, sailing down the coast, appeared in full strength before the city of Exeter.

After dispersing his enemies in the west of England, Alfred returned to complete, if possible, the destruction of Hastings, the head and leader of the insurrection and war.

In their attack on the Danish camp at Shoeburyness, the English had the good fortune to capture the wife and two sons of Hastings.

These Alfred generously restored to his enemy, on Hastings' promise to return instantly to Denmark and forbear all future incursions.

No sooner had Hastings and his followers quitted the kingdom, than Sigefert, an influential noble of Northumbria, collected most of the roving bands of that country and the Danes who had escaped from Alfred's vengeance, and began to plot a new rebellion on his own account.

To carry out his piratical schemes with the greater success, and to be more than a match for the English, Sigefert built a number of ships higher, longer, and swifter than those of the Saxons.

With this powerful fleet he put to sea, and immediately began the customary depredations.

Alfred, however, had not been idle during these preparations; and having heard of Sigefert's intentions, built ships still higher out of the water, longer in the keel, sharper in the bows, and still swifter than those of the Northumbrians.

With a fleet of such vessels, Alfred, to the intense astonishment of Sigefert, fell suddenly on his revolted Danes, while engaged in their interesting occupation of murder and robbery. The action was short, severe, but undecisive.

ANCIENT WEAPONS USED BY THE ROMANS.

Sacrificing his plunder and a portion of his fleet to the fury of the English, Sigefert put to sea with all the ships able to follow him, bearing away for some part of the island where his presence was less expected, and where there was a better prospect of pillage.

Alfred, however, had no intention of allowing his enemy to escape him so easily, and followed the flying Danes so rapidly, that, after cutting off and destroying many of his straggling ships, he finally overtook the main body off the coast of Dorsetshire in the autumn of the year 898.

In this battle, one of the last naval actions of his life, Alfred was triumphantly successful; the defeat of the enemy was complete. Sigefert, it is true, escaped, but his power was completely broken; while the king, who had taken twenty of his ships, was determined to make such an example as should for a long time to come deter the Danes from repeating their buccaneering expeditions in England.

Alfred had tried clemency and every form of kindness, in the hope of inspiring a friendly feeling in the breasts of the native Danes, and in the belief that in time he could make good subjects out of them. But in vain. Their natural love of blood and plunder was unconquerable; and on the appearance of the first roving ship on the coast all the naturalised Danes in Northumbria, East Anglia, and other parts of England, were instantly up in arms, and, making common cause with the invaders, covered the whole country with desolation and murder.

Alfred, now determined to strike a vigorous blow

"THE DANE, RAISING HIS CLUB, WOULD HAVE DISPATCHED THE KING."

at this internal treason and rapine, proceeded to Winchester, ordering the entire crews of the twenty ships he had taken to be brought after him.

Here, probably, for the first time in England, Alfred's law (borrowed from the Danes) of TRIAL BY JURY was put in practice to try these revolted Danes.

That they were tried we have indisputable evidence; and, arraigned as pirates, the common enemies of mankind, were found guilty, and condemned to death, a sentence which Alfred had carried out to the letter, and every man found on board those twenty ships was hanged as an enemy to the human species.

This terrible but necessary measure struck such terror into the minds of the East Angles and Northumbrians, that they made the most abject submission, and once more took an oath of allegiance.

After the death of Alfred, the Danes again attempted their invasions and revolts; and the twenty-four years of his son's reign, Edward the Elder, were spent in a constant, though successful war, chiefly naval, with the rovers of Denmark and Northumbria.

So wise had been the regulations established by Alfred, and so ably did his immediate successors carry out his views, especially with regard to the naval strength of the country, that after the death of his son Edward the Elder, for a period of nearly seventy years the country remained almost free from both foreign tumult and domestic broils.

This long period of comparative quiet led to the neglect of those precautions on which the safety of the kingdom mainly depended, and when Ethelred the Unready came to the throne, the kingdom was almost defenceless.

The Danes having sent two small squadrons of seven and eight vessels to the south and west of England to look into the state of the land, the Scandinavians, on the return of those ships, loaded with plunder, prepared to renew their incursions; and the next year fitted out a large fleet, and, landing in the south, soon spread all the horrors of war over the kingdom.

Instead of attempting to check their incursions, the weak and unready Ethelred listened to the advice of some of his craven courtiers and churchmen, and actually bribed the Danes by a gift of £10,000 to quit the country.

This, as might have been expected, only brought them back the next year in greater numbers, when a still larger ransom was paid to induce them to return to their homes.

On one of these occasions, Ethelred had a conference with the Danish leaders, and still further to make them friendly, in addition to the stipulated ransom, betrothed a Saxon princess to Leofric, the eldest son of the Danish leader.

In the hope more effectually to conciliate his rude enemies, he feasted the whole army for some weeks, not forgetting to supply them with plenty of strong liquor.

The night before the Danes were to embark for their own country, Ethelred gave a grand entertainment to the Danish chiefs, especially to honour young Leofric and his bride.

In the midst of the enjoyment and carouse of the guests, a sudden commotion was heard without, mingled with shouts of—

"Treason! murder! treason!"

The next moment, the doors were burst open, and a crowd of the treacherous Danes, who hated the Saxons so much as even to disapprove the alliance, rushed into the hall, led on by a tall, powerful chief, flourishing an enormous club armed with iron spikes.

Leofric, ignorant of the plot which his father and the leaders of the invaders had conceived, sprang to his feet, and drawing his sword, held his bride to his side, and then stood, prepared to sell his life dearly, or to force his way from the scene of strife.

All was in an instant noise and confusion, and a deadly struggle ensued between the Saxons and the Danes.

The leader, striking down all before him, rushed to the throne, and raising his club, would have despatched the king at the first blow, had not Leofric, who refused to take part in the treacherous assault, taken advantage of the raised arm, and buried his sword in his side.

The fight was short, but bloody; the Saxons, enraged at the treachery of the Danes, drove them from the hall, and finally forced them on board their ships; the only booty they were enabled to secure being the young bride of their chief's son, Leofric the Dane.

The enemy instantly put to sea and returned home; but only to fit out a more powerful fleet than had ever yet left their shores, and in the year 993 appeared unexpectedly on the eastern coast of England.

This immense armament was commanded in person by Sweyn, King of Denmark, and Olave, King of Norway, but the infatuated Ethelred took no steps to arrest the progress of the destroyers, and the whole country became, in a short time, a scene of rapine and desolation.

Nearly all the fortified towns and cities, with the exception of London, had fallen into their hands, and against the opulent capital of the kingdom they now directed their attention.

Sailing up the Thames with a fleet of 95 of their largest ships, they at once began the siege of London.

The rich merchants and inhabitants, however, although deserted by their king, had no mind to share their wealth and homes with the invaders, and had made such energetic efforts to resist him that the enemy, after losing more than half his ships, and unable to gain a foot of ground, suddenly raised the siege.

Then, with his shattered force, he dropped down the river, and, in revenge for his defeat, landed in Essex and carried fire and sword into the heart of the kingdom.

As we must here take leave of the sea kings, the rest of the long record of Danish innovation under Canute and his successors being rather matters of political and military than naval history, we shall conclude this chapter with a few paragraphs explanatory of the manner in which Ethelred the Unready for a time cleared the country of these northern barbarians.

Finding the whole kingdom at the mercy of the invaders, the vacillating Ethelred once more resorted to the cowardly offer of a bribe, and promised the two kings a sum of sixteen thousand pounds if they would be content with their plunder and quit the country.

Sweyn and Olave at once agreed to the terms, and as a proof of their good faith instantly discontinued their raids and marauding excursions. Sweyn then summoned all his Danes around him, and took up a peaceable position at Southampton.

King Olave, who, with his Norwegians, was in the West of England, visited Ethelred at his palace at Andover, and entered into such friendly relations with him that he was not only confirmed by the bishops in attendance on the English king, but took a solemn oath that neither he nor any of his subjects should ever again molest the English people.

This wise and good man, long after canonised, and known in the Romish calendar as St. Olave, was in every respect as good as his word; taking an affectionate leave of Ethelred, he called his Norwegians about him, and, going aboard his ships, set sail from England.

Sweyn, finding himself so unceremoniously deserted by his ally, was obliged to fulfil his promise also, and, giving a pledge never to return, set sail with his plunder for Denmark.

From the death of Edmond Ironside, in the year 1017, to the accession of Edward the Confessor, in 1041, the intervening time may more properly be called Danish than English history; while during the twenty-five years that the saintly Edward reigned as the last representative of a long line of Saxon kings, there is little to record in connection with naval matters in this country.

Before, however, taking a final leave of Dane and Norwegian, we purpose devoting a brief space to the history of one of the most extraordinary families that ever flourished within the British Isles, and to the career of one of whom the memory of every Englishman clings with a feeling of pride and romance, unequalled in English history—Harold, our last Saxon King.

After one of the battles between the Danes and the English, near the end of the tenth century, a Danish chief, or nobleman, seriously wounded, dragged himself from among the dead and dying, and, to save himself from the infuriated English, contrived to secrete himself in a neighbouring thicket.

In this retreat he was found by a humane swineherd, named Godwin, who, taking him to his hut, carefully tended him till health and opportunity enabled him to return to Denmark.

The wounded Dane was not unmindful of the swineherd's kindness, and subsequently amply rewarded him for his humanity and good faith.

This reward was the first step in the ladder of that extraordinary fortune that ultimately advanced his grandson to a throne.

Godwin, the son of the swineherd, assisted by his father's wealth, embraced a military career, and soon rose to considerable distinction among the military leaders of his country.

On the accession of the Danes to power, Canute took notice of Godwin's capabilities, and bestowed on him many favours.

When subsequently, Canute sailed for Scandinavia to subdue the King of Sweden, he took a body of the young nobility of England with him, giving the command of them to young Godwin, who soon found an opportunity of greatly distinguishing himself, and of so promoting the object Canute had in view, that he was not only advanced to posts of great honour, but became by marriage son-in-law to Canute.

By this marriage Godwin had six sons, who were each provided with important posts under the crown, so that when Edward the Confessor came to the throne, the power of the family equalled that of the sovereign himself.

The old earl was the trust and hope of the nation, while his son, Harold, was their idol.

Though Edward the Confessor, on his succeeding Hardicanute, felt a natural antipathy to Godwin and his family, such was the influence the earl possessed, that he, in a measure, compelled the young king to espouse his daughter.

With a family so all-powerful as the Godwins, causes, real or imaginary, were never wanting to harass and annoy the king with open or threatened revolt. The cause, however, which led to the last and most serious rebellion was an umbrage which Godwin took to Edward, in consequence of a supposed neglect of his daughter Edith, the queen.

In this quarrel all the sons took part, as they believed their sister had been most cruelly wronged; and the people taking part with the Godwins, the king was compelled to exert all his authority to avert the threatened danger, and not only confiscated the estates of the whole family, but banished them the kingdom.

He little knew, however, the character of the faction he had to do with.

The Godwins, when expelled from England, spread themselves in Flanders, Denmark, Norway, and Ireland, and, collecting from each a supply of ships and men, returned with a powerful fleet and sailed direct for London. At the same time, having excited all his dependents and partizans in different parts of the kingdom, and induced them to support his cause, the whole country was at once thrown into confusion, and threatened with the horrors of a civil war.

Edward, having disbanded his army and fleet, was, in a measure, at the mercy of Godwin.

At this extremity the parties came to terms; the earl said he only wished to clear the country of the Normans, who preyed on the people, and, assured of that, he would lay down his arms.

Edward agreed to the conditions demanded,

banished the Normans, and restored the earl and his sons to all their lands, offices, and privileges.

On the death of Godwin, about 1052, men's eyes were turned on Harold, as the representative of the family dignity and the upholder of the national honour.

As the king's years and infirmities increased, the ambitious views of Harold on the crown became every day more sure and demonstrative, and, assured of the love and devotion of the people in his favour, he was only kept in check by the uncertainty of the king's mind, and the doubt as to whom he might at the last moment bequeath his throne and sceptre.

At the reconciliation which had taken place between the king and the late earl, Godwin had been compelled to give up one of his sons as a hostage of his good faith.

This hostage Edward sent, for better security, to his friend, William, Duke of Normandy there to be kept in captivity.

INTERVIEW BETWEEN KING ETHELRED AND THE DANISH CHIEFS.

Harold, who had a secret antipathy to Duke William, used all his influence to induce Edward to recall the banished hostage, and rest satisfied with the loyalty and devotion of Harold and his brothers, for whose good faith he became responsible.

Edward, who had become in a measure attached to Harold, and afraid to refuse so powerful a noble so small and natural a boon, consented, and despatched Harold on an embassy, with a princely retinue, to the court of Normandy to bring home his brother.

Harold, agreeable to his rank and importance, embarked and set sail for Normandy; but a heavy storm arising, drove his ships on the territories of Guy, Count of Ponthieu.

This noble no sooner heard of the quality of the stranger than, in the hope of making him pay a heavy ransom, he made prisoner of Harold and his entire company.

At the same time William, hearing of the arrest of Edward's ambassador, and anxious to make a friend of so influential a noble as Harold, ordered Count Guy instantly to set his prisoner free, and treat him with every honour.

The reception Harold met at the Court of Normandy was of the most cordial and friendly description, the duke taking him completely into his confidence, and, to the utter astonishment of Harold, telling him that Edward had made him his heir, and bequeathed the crown of England to him, Duke William.

Completely taken by surprise, and feeling that both he and his brother were in the hands of the crafty William, Harold assured the duke he might depend on his co-operation and support.

Upon this William induced Harold to take a solemn oath at the altar that he was sincere, and would be the duke's devoted friend.

No sooner had the artful Norman extracted this reluctant oath, than, uncovering the altar, he exposed a number of mouldering bones, the holy relics of some long forgotten saint. Deceived and horrified by the ghastly sight, Harold recoiled from the altar, and though promising to observe his vow, he secretly swore to be even with the duke.

No sooner did Harold find himself safely back in England, than he made preparations to resist the storm he foresaw was destined to break on his country.

His first preparations were directed to the navy of the kingdom, and he gave directions at once for the building of large and powerful ships.

The army next commanded his attention, and his active and vigorous mind was turned in every direction that could secure the peace and safety of the land.

Scarcely had Harold effected his necessary measures, and prepared men's minds for his assumption of royal power, when Edward, worn out by bodily infirmities, was seized with a mortal malady, and expired on the 5th of January, 1066.

Nearly all the great nobles had been summoned to the monarch's deathbed, each eager to know to whom the king would bequeath his crown.

In his last moments one of the officiating prelates asked the dying king on whom he wished to bestow his sceptre.

"Give it," cried Edward, with his last breath, "give it to the most deserving among you!"

SAXON YOUTH, 12TH CENTURY.

Every eye was instantly turned on Harold, who was, by universal acclaim, hailed King of England, and the next day was crowned by the Archbishop of York.

The same messenger who told William of Edward's death, apprised him of Harold's coronation, and of the prudent measures he had taken to defend his kingdom.

Of the steps which William of Normandy took to establish his more than doubtful claim to the kingdom of England, we have nothing here to do, except as it affected Harold, the representative of the Godwins.

Tostig, one of the earl's sons, had, through the influence of his brother, been created Earl of Northumberland a few years before Edward's death, but, proving a cruel, tyrannous, and execrable wretch, the people rose in rebellion against him, and, by force of arms, drove him out of his earldom.

Upon this, Harold was sent to reduce the Northumbrians to obedience, and reinstate his brother, but, finding on his arrival that Tostig's conduct had been even worse than represented, he banished his brother from the kingdom, gave the Northumbrians an earl of their own choice, and returned to Edward with the thanks and blessings of the people.

Harold's universal vigilance, and his wise and provident preparations, both by sea and land, were sources of profound trouble and anxiety to Duke William, but none of his enemy's warlike preparations gave him so much trouble as the formidable fleet the English king had so proudly sent to sea, and which, boldly sailing up and down the channel, defied the approach of any hostile armament.

William, however, had ransacked Europe for soldiers, and collected one of the finest and best appointed armies that a Christian monarch had ever commanded, and he was resolved not to endanger the success of his enterprise by any preventable means.

In spite of the fact that he could bring ten ships to every one of the English, he saw that, with such a fleet sweeping the channel, it would be an act of simple madness to attempt to cross the narrow sea that parted Normandy from England.

SAXON ARCHER, 9TH CENTURY.

What strength and daring could not do, perhaps cunning and treachery might achieve. So thought Duke William; and sending for Tostig, who had found shelter in Flanders, he represented the conduct of Harold, both to Tostig and himself, as abominable and unnatural in the extreme.

At the same time he promised not only to restore him to his earldom of Northumberland, but to bestow on him all the governments which Harold had possessed as Duke of Wessex if he would assist him in his descent on England.

The unnatural and depraved Tostig at once closed with the wily duke's terms, and, swearing eternal friendship to his new ally, departed to put in practice his portion of the contemplated programme.

Hastening to Norway, Tostig induced the king of that country, Harold Halfagar, to espouse his cause and assist William in the subjugation of England.

SHIP, TIME OF KING ALFRED.

While the Norwegian prince was collecting his army and fleet, Tostig, with sixty ships, suddenly appeared off the eastern coast, and, to a limited extent, began the usual depredations along the sea-coast. Harold, who well knew that the object of this piratical expedition was to distract his attention and induce him to weaken his channel fleet by sending a part of his navy against his brother, appeared quite unmoved by his appearance in the Downs, and, in fact, left Tostig to his fate.

The banished earl, enraged that he could not induce Harold to attack him, sailed direct to Northumbria, meaning to punish his refractory people. Before he could put in practice his revengeful intention he was joined by the Norwegian king, with a powerful army and a fleet of 300 sail.

Joining his friend, the united force sailed south, and entering the Humber, Harold Halfagar landed his army, and the allies advanced into the heart of Yorkshire, where, having met the army of the Earls of Mercia and Northumbria, and totally defeated it, the exultant Norwegian sent to Harold to order him to give up to him the land he had conquered, and do homage for the rest of the island.

The English king, who with his army was encamped in the south, waiting the advent of his mortal foe, was both grieved and surprised at the news of this new danger.

Sending the Norwegian king—a perfect giant, standing six feet six—a message that he would give him seven feet of English soil for a grave, and not an inch more, he broke up his camp, and, by forced marches, hastened to Yorkshire, where he encountered his rebel brother and his ally near Stamford Bridge.

In the dreadful battle that followed the invaders were utterly defeated, Harold Halfagar and his friend, Tostig, being among the slain. Harold is reported, with his own hand, to have struck down the giant King of Norway, and faithfully gave him the seven feet of English earth for a grave which he had promised.

Leaving a sufficient force to bury the dead and attend to the embarkation of the Norwegians who had laid down their arms, the king hastened back to the south with a part of his army, and, receiving a large reinforcement of troops from London, again posted onwards towards the coast.

During Harold's absence in the north the Normans had repeatedly put to sea; but, being met by contrary winds, had to put back with the loss of several of their ships. These frequent disasters induced the English to believe that William had quite abandoned his intention of invading the country, at least for that season.

But a worse evil than the negligence that such a belief inspired arose from a natural cause. While Harold was hastening back from his great victory at Stamford Bridge, a sudden storm in the channel had scattered his fleet as it cruised before the Isle of Wight, compelling it to fly for shelter and repairs to the nearest ports along the coast.

Before the ships could refit and return to their rendezvous, a change of wind took place, and Duke William again put to sea and brought his immense armament to a safe anchor off the coast of Sussex.

Landing his army of 60,000 horse and foot from a fleet of 3,000 sail, William entrenched himself at Pevensey, and calmly awaited the arrival of Harold.

For an account of the great and fatal battle of Hastings, a battle that terminated the reign and life of Harold, and extinguished the liberties of Saxon England, the reader is referred to the general history of the country.

With the death of Harold and his brothers on the field of Hastings, expired the family of the Godwins.

In taking leave of this subject it would ill become us to omit mention of so important a place in the maritime history of this country as the Downs.

This large expanse of sea, extending between the North and South Forelands off the coast of Kent, lies between the most dangerous and dreaded quicksands in the kingdom.

The Godwin, or Goodwin Sands, consist of about 4,000 acres of what once was fertile land and part of the Kentish estate of the great Earl Godwin.

Some time in the early part of the eleventh century the earl, anxious to be on good terms with the Church, made a gift of these 4,000 acres to the Abbot of St. Augustine's monastery at Canterbury upon the understanding that the abbot would attend to the safety of the sea-wall, or embankment, that protected that part of the county from the storms and encroachments of the sea.

The clerical authorities of Canterbury cathedral having at that time a pet church in the course of erection at Tenterden, and being rather straightened for means, spent the money which should have gone to repair the sea-wall in finishing the steeple of the new church.

Not long after a terrific storm broke on the coast, the sea burst in all the barriers, and, in one night the whole land between the two Forelands was submerged, and the princely estate given to the Church became a dangerous shoal, a source of constant fear to the merchant and of peril to the mariner.

From this circumstance arose the popular saying, "That Tenterden steeple was the cause of the Goodwin Sands."

CHAPTER III.

FROM THE CONQUEST TO EDWARD I.—SHIPS OF THE THIRTEENTH CENTURY—ORIGIN OF THE WARS OF FRANCE AND ENGLAND.

THOUGH during his reign of twenty-one years, William had no direct use for a navy, he was by no means unmindful of the importance of such a valuable arm, both as a protection and a defence.

Harold, both from interest and inclination, had devoted much attention to the navy of the country, and, building ships on the best and most approved models, had carried naval architecture to the highest point it was probably then capable of reaching.

William, we may be sure, did not allow any good military work to fall into abeyance, and the belief is that he encouraged the art of ship building, and, in a measure, insisted on the construction of large and useful vessels.

His frequent voyages from England to Normandy, sometimes with his troops, and always with an extensive court, prove that he was often in need of safe and swift ships; and we may take it for granted that the Conqueror would not a second time trust himself or his followers to the fishing-boats and herring-busses, in which, in the hope of a crown, he braved the dangers of the Channel.

Besides, in order to form a nucleus at all times for a national navy, and support a small fleet at the smallest possible cost, he established by charter the corporation known as the Cinque Ports.

This corporation, as the name implies, originally consisted of five ports, or towns, namely, Dover, Hastings, Romney, Hythe, and Sandwich; to which were added, Rye, Winchelsea and Seaford.

According to their wealth, population, and commercial importance, these five havens, or seaports, were obliged to supply the king on all occasions of emergency with a certain number of ships, fully manned and armed, and commissioned for forty days.

Some idea of the comparative trade and importance of these towns may be gathered from the number of ships each port had to supply, namely, Dover and Hastings, twenty-one ships each, and Romney, Hythe and Sandwich, five each; in all fifty-seven ships, all of the same size and armament.

In return for this service, the several towns were exempt from certain taxes, feudal restrictions and imposts; the inhabitants were granted special honours and privileges; and their chief, or warden, held a foremost rank in the kingdom, was rated as an admiral, and made perpetual Constable of Dover Castle.

Though the service formerly demanded of these towns has long been abolished, and the British Navy now consists of vessels infinitely more formidable than the half-decked sloops of the eleventh century, the Cinque Ports still enjoy many of their ancient privileges, and their jurisdiction is still entrusted to the highest and noblest personage in the land.

Some authors state William's fleet to have consisted of nine hundred ships; but this number seems evidently erroneous, when we remember that every species of vessel were forced into the service, and collected from all the adjoining states, and many of them were little better than open boats.

Again, when it is recollected that each ship or boat had, according to its size, an efficient crew of mariners to navigate it, it is clear that, bearing in mind the size of the vessels then in use, nine hundred ships could hardly have transported the sixty thousand heavy armed soldiers whom William landed on the beach at Pevensey.

No doubt the largest and best ships were appropriated for this purpose; but when it is borne in mind there were at least five thousand horses to be transported, with their provender, and all the military material, commissariat and baggage of an immense army, the number we have given will not appear unnecessarily large or exaggerated.

That William did not expect to find a land of milk and honey, or provisions ready at hand to feed such a host as he commanded, is incontestibly shown by the immense accumulation of stores he had provided for the expedition.

Indeed, to this great abundance of food, is in a great measure to be attributed the good order and discipline that existed in his camp in Normandy, and during the many disappointments and trials endured by the army in their several attempts to put to sea.

Had we a doubt remaining on this subject, it would be set at rest by that monument, even more veracious than history, the Bayeux Tapestry, an immense surface of needle-work executed by and under the direction of Matilda, the wife of William the Conquerer.

This extraordinary piece of female skill, patience, and genius, is still, though eight hundred years old, in excellent preservation in the Abbey of Bayeux in Normandy.

It represents, in a series of worked pictures, the whole history of the Conquest.

It shows us Harold, setting out with hawk and hound on his embassy to bring home his captive brother; his arrest by the treacherous Guy of Ponthieu, his friendly reception by William, his oath on the hidden relics, and his departure.

More than this, however, it shows us the embarkation of William and his army, with the costume of the invading Normans, the size and form of their best ships, ending with a woman's idea of the battle of Hastings, and the fall of Harold with an arrow in his head.

Setting aside all the naval and military facts which this authentic tapestry affords us, we advert to one point, as specially bearing out our assertion, that William had paid particular attention to what we now call the commissariat, or the food of his army.

In the tapestry we see not only provisions taken aboard, but pipes of wine swung on the shoulders of sturdy vintners carried from the shore to the ships.

A convincing proof that the number of transports to carry such an army and all its necessaries must have been immense.

Indeed, at this time, and probably for a considerable period later, the tonnage of a ship was estimated by the quantity of wine she could carry as cargo, as a vessel of sixty tons was calculated by sixty tons (wine measurement.)

But to return to the Cinque Ports.

However considerable the advantages conferred on them might be, the corporation of the five ports had no sinecure office.

Not only were they called upon on every occasion of war, or foreign invasion, to supply their quota of ships armed and provisioned for service, but they were subsequently expected, in fact, commanded, to attend the king on every occasion of his leaving the country; and when we remember that the early Norman kings were in the repeated habit of visiting their hereditary possessions, this tax on the Cinque Ports became a rather serious infliction.

It was not alone the expense of arming, clothing, and feeding so many men for so long a period as their charter compelled them to keep at sea, but the serious injury it must have been to trade, especially to the merchants who owned the ships that made up the complement of fifty-seven vessels, especially as the ships demanded were the largest and best the several ports possessed.

So onerous, in fact, appears to have become this part of the contract, that after a time the Cinque Ports were only compelled to maintain the expense of the armament for fifteen days, instead of the original six weeks, the king guaranteeing to be at all the charge if the ships were detained over the fifteen days.

A few further particulars about the Cinque Ports and an insight into the free and easy manner in which the early Plantagenets disposed of their subjects' property and collected a royal navy, may be gleaned from the following extracts from the old chronicles.

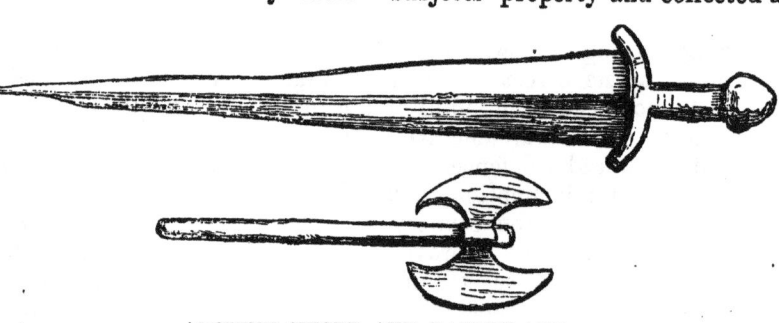

ANCIENT SWORD AND BATTLE-AXE.

According to Hakluyt, in the year 1278, it was stipulated—

"That whenever the king goes beyond sea, the Cinque Ports ought to attend him with fifty-seven ships, each having twenty armed soldiers, and to maintain them at their own cost for the space of fifteen days."

In the year 1297, King Edward I. directed a precept, "To the barons and good men of the port of Hastings, that, on account of certain urgent affairs relating to us and to our faithful subjects, you get ready, and send to our port of London, your whole service of shipping, well supplied with arms, &c., so as our service be by no means retarded."

The number of ships, and the ports by which they are to be sent, are then specified, and the precept proceeds—

"We also desire of you, that over and above the before-named service which you are bound to us, you do send to us all your other shipping as well of forty tons as of upwards of forty tons of wine (meaning tons by wine measure) well furnished as aforesaid, which last demand, however, above your wonted service, shall not be drawn into consequence hereafter."

In the year 1304, King Edward I. let to Philip of France, for an expedition against the Flemings, twenty ships, to be assembled at Sandwich, and to be picked out from amongst the best and largest of those of the several ports of London, Sandwich, Winchelsea, Romney, Hythe, Rye, Faversham, Hastings, Southampton and Portsmouth; each of which ships were to be manned with at least forty stout men, and well furnished with all requisites of war.

EARLY BRITISH CANOE, NOW IN BRITISH MUSEUM.*

* The canoe represented in our engraving was dug up on the seashore at Deal. These early British canoes were of very rough formation, being first burnt out, and then fashioned into shape with rude knives and axes.

The small complement of men for each of these ships sufficiently demonstrates the small size of ships of war in the early days of our history.

At this period, and for two hundred years afterwards, the kings of England had no ships of war that were properly their own.

The ships now mentioned appear to have been hired of their owners, and were doubtless the best and largest that could be procured in England.

In 1335, a precept, directed from King Edward II. to the mayor and sheriffs of London, directed them to "take up all ships in their port, and of all other ports of the kingdom, of the burden of *forty tons* and upwards, and to furnish the same with armed men, and other necessaries for war against the Scots."

In 1394, a mandate of Richard II. again commanded the subsidies of the Cinque Ports. The previous subsidy was to reconnoitre the coast of Berwick, in consequence of a war with Scotland. Upon this occasion, as the king expresses it in his mandate—

"We have ordained a great naval armament for our present voyage to Ireland; we therefore direct the said Cinque Ports to attend us at Bristol."

The object of the "great naval armament" was to suppress a rebellion in the sister country. This royal mandate set forth the pay to be given to the different classes of mariners:—

"1. The master of each ship shall have sixpence (or fifteenpence of our money) per day. 2. The Constable the like wages. 3. Each of the other men threepence (or sevenpence halfpenny of our money) per day."

The ships and men were to be at the expense of the Cinque Ports for the first fifteen days, and at the expense of the crown after that time.

William the Conqueror seems to have made few,

RICHARD I. EMBARKING HIS TROOPS FOR PALESTINE.

if any, demands on the people for a fleet; for, except going and coming from Normandy, as we have before mentioned, in which he was attended by the Cinque Port ships, he seems to have had no special need for a naval armament.

His son, Rufus, however, apprehending the resentment of his brother, Robert, who had only been left Normandy, while William had been bequeathed the kingdom of England, was for a time compelled to keep a fleet at sea to resist any attempt to invade the country.

The usurpation of Henry Beauclerk, on the death of William, while his elder brother, Robert, was in the Holy Land, rendered it imperative on the young king to maintain a fleet in the channel to resist Duke Robert, who, on his return to Normandy, made vigorous efforts to recover his crown from his young and crafty brother.

Such was the love generally entertained both in England and Normandy for the brave Duke Robert, who had won so much glory in the Holy Land, that he found himself not only at the head of a large army, but in command of the whole of Henry's fleet, which deserted to him, thereby affording him the means of transport for his forces.

The only other event of interest in respect to Naval History which occurred in this reign, was the disastrous wreck of one of the king's ships in the voyage from Harfleur to Southampton, in the autumn of 1120.

By this grevious calamity King Henry lost his eldest and most beloved son, Prince William, and two other children, a son and daughter, while all the great nobles of Normandy and England, to the number of nearly a hundred and fifty, had to mourn the loss of a son and heir, the companions and body guard to the future hope of England and Normandy, the unfortunate Prince William.

The prince's ship, the "Blanche Neuf," being driven through the ignorance or mistake of the pilot or captain on a dangerous reef of rocks, called the Caskets, off the island of Alderney, the vessel soon became a hopeless wreck.

In the height of the confusion and dismay, Prince William was seized, and being forced into the ship's long-boat, the crowded craft was pushed off as far from the sinking vessel as possible.

That the prince and many of his nobles might have escaped, there can be no doubt; for the sturdy mariners had taken to the oars, and would soon have been beyond the sight of the foundering ship, when the shrieks of his sister from the wreck fell on the prince's ear.

Drawing his sword, he commanded the unwilling crew to return to the ship to save his sister. Scarcely, however, had the boat touched the vessel's side, and the prince bounded on deck in search of his sister, when the usual catastrophe occurred.

The struggling crew left behind flung themselves in crowds into the already overloaded boat, which instantly sank, while at the same moment the wreck went down in deep water, dragging the few struggling swimmers into the fatal vortex.

At midnight one survivor alone was to be seen clinging to the ship's mast, and fighting with the waves for life.

Fitz-Stephen, the captain of the ill-fated ship, had been swimming about the spot where the wreck went down, in the hope of seeing the boat in which he believed the prince to have been safely placed.

Seeing the solitary tenant of the mast, Fitz-Stephen raised himself to his side, and began to question the man—a butcher from Rouen—as to what had become of the prince and the long-boat.

When informed of the final disaster, Fitz-Stephen declared he would not survive so fearful a calamity, and, plunging head foremost into the waves, never rose again.

The butcher eventually reached the English coast, and, as the sole survivor of that unfortunate disaster, gave the only authentic record of a misfortune that plunged the whole kingdom in sorrow.

During the rest of Henry's life, and, indeed, through the entire reigns of his successors, Stephen and Henry II., there seems to have been no necessity for a fleet, excepting voyages of state to and from the continent.

But, though he had little use for his ships, Henry paid considerable attention to maritime affairs, and the nucleus of an English *Royal* Navy had been formed.

We do not possess much information on the subject, but, from the hints left by old historians, we are inclined to think that some of his vessels must have been of considerable size; at all events "one of the chiefest and newest" of these ships was capable of containing 400 men.

Some little time before his death he began to prepare ships for an expedition to Palestine; and when Richard succeeded to the throne these preparations were very far advanced.

When the second Crusade was declared, in which Philip of France and Richard I. joined with such seeming friendship and determination, the two great western powers, profiting by the experience and disasters that befel the first, which had marched overland to Palestine, resolved on prosecuting their undertaking by sea.

For this purpose both nations made great preparations to collect a fleet proportionate to their military arrangements. Richard, as we have seen, was pretty well supplied with shipping.

The allies of France and England assembled their army of 100,000 men on the borders of Burgundy; and on the 29th of June, 1190, breaking up their camp, the two hosts separated, and marched to the ports where their fleets had been ordered to rendezvous.

Philip led his troops to Genoa, where they embarked; Richard, with the English army, embarked at Dover under circumstances of great pomp, and marched through France, to Marseilles, where his fleet was in waiting.

Richard, when he started on this expedition to the Holy Land, had in his train thirteen *buccas*, which were ships with triple sails, besides 100 ships of burthen, and 50 galleys, each having a triple bank of oars.

The *buccas* appear to have been vessels of the largest size; and in the greatest fleets described by the Norman writers, we meet with not more than twenty or thirty at most, which always took the lead. The *buccas* had three sails, the other vessels but one.

The ships of burthen, distinguished by the names of *carikes* or *mulks*, were also large vessels. The *galleys* were of two sorts, some sailed and rowed, others rowed only.

The larger galleys were of a size to carry sixty men in armour, besides one hundred and four men who rowed, and the sailors; some of them had triple banks of oars, one over the other.

The *buccas* were flat-bottomed boats, used chiefly to convey troops to the shore in shallow waters.

It is evident, by the account of these vessels, and also by the number of the ships employed, that considerable improvement had taken place in shipbuilding, and especially in the size of the vessels themselves. Though some of the ships given in the above catalogue carried three sails, it must not be supposed that the *buccas* mentioned had three masts, one being the orthodox number for a considerable time subsequent to Richard's reign.

That the ships of that period were heavy, clumsily built craft, and very slow sailers, may be inferred from the fact, that though the fleet had the best of the summer for the voyage, Richard was obliged to winter at Sicily, having accomplished little more than half the sea journey to Palestine.

For the next quarter of a century we hear of no English fleet; which, under the weak and distracting reign of John, seems to have dwindled, like every other national institution, into insignificance and decay.

So defenceless, in fact, does the country seem to have been in this respect, that when the revolted barons invited over the Dauphin Louis, making him a tender of the crown and their allegiance, a French army, with several subsequent reinforcements, was allowed to land with impunity.

But although King John allowed the naval power of this country to decay, it should be remembered that it was he who first claimed for England THE SOVEREIGNTY OF THE SEAS, and declared, though he was not in a position to enforce his declaration, that all ships belonging to foreign nations which should refuse to strike their flag to the British standard should be fair and lawful prizes.

On the death of John, and the appointment of the Earl of Pembroke as Lord Protector, for the young King Henry III., a bold and vigorous line of conduct was at once pursued, an army was collected, a fleet prepared, the revolted barons brought back to their duty, and the French in the kingdom reduced to the last extremity.

To save his son and the remnant of the French army from total ruin, Philip sent a fleet with reinforcements to relieve the Dauphin.

To intercept this armament, the English fleet put to sea, and the following is Hume's account of the action that ensued—an action that led to the immediate departure of the French and the tranquillity of the kingdom:—

"A French fleet, bringing over a strong reinforcement, had appeared on the coast of Kent, where they were attacked by the English under the command of Philip d'Albiney, and were routed with considerable loss.

"D'Albiney employed a stratagem against them, which is said to have contributed to the victory. Having gained the wind of the French, he came down upon them with violence, and throwing in their faces a great quantity of quick-lime, which he purposely carried on board, he so blinded them that they were disabled from defending themselves."

Henry III., like Richard I., had some vessels of his own, for in the exchequer rolls of the tenth year of his reign, we find the following order:—

"Henry by the grace of God, &c., &c. Pay out of our treasury to Reynold de Bernevall, and Brother Thomas, of the Temple, twenty-two marks and a half for repairs of our great ship; also pay to the six masters of our great ship, to wit, Stephen le Vel, one mark; Germanus de la Rie, one mark; John, the son of Sampson, one mark; Colmo de Warham, one mark; Robert Gaillard, one mark; and Simon Westlegrie, one mark. Witness ourself at Westminster, in the tenth year of our reign. For the mariners of the great ship."

From Madox's "History of the Exchequer," we learn that the name of the great ship was the "Queen;" and that in the year 1232, Henry lent or chartered it to a merchant named John Blancbally for life, for an annual payment of fifty marks.

It is also very interesting to learn that about this period the mariner's compass began to come into general use.

An Italian, Gioia, of Amalfi, is supposed to have been the first who attached a card to the needle; but his card had only eight points upon it instead of the thirty-two now described upon the mariner's compass.

During the long and stormy reign of Henry III. very great and material improvements were made in the build and rig of all ships, whether meant for merchandise or war.

The somewhat rapid and distinctive alteration in the trim and size of the ships which were built in England at this period (about 1240), is said to have been caused by a circumstance of which tradition rather than history thus speaks.

When nearing the coast of Syria, some of the late king Richard's fleet had fallen in with a very large Turkish or Saracenic ship, called a *dromo*, a Greek word signifying a caravel, or a swift-sailing ship of war.

This vessel—which, it is needless to say, Richard took—is said to have contained *fifteen hundred men*, with an ample supply of provisions, and a full cargo of military stores, was, we suppose, after the custom of the time, cleared, by the destruction of her crew, and then sent home with the fleet to England.

That such a vessel arrived is all very probable, and that she was put away in some dockyard and forgotten till the time of Henry III. is also extremely likely, when, under different auspices, she was made, in a measure, a model for a larger and better class of ships, such as undoubtedly came into vogue towards the latter part of the thirteenth century.

The two most important facts that strike us in the ships of Henry III.'s reign—for mere size is of no reign or age—are that, for the first time, we find a vessel with *two* masts; one, as we should now say, rising from the forecastle, the other from the poop.

The next important improvement is that the shrouds which support the masts are fastened to the outsides of the bulwarks, giving a purchase and security which did not exist before, as well as affording more room and convenience on deck.

The rudder is the same clumsy contrivance we have seen attached to the ancient galleys, a long peel-like oar secured by some kind of swivel to the port and starboard quarters of the gunwale.

There are other marked and special differences observable in these new-built ships; the sharp, ram-like bows giving way entirely, and the prow being round and bulging, after the fashion of a north country surf or shore boat.

The high, hooked stern has also entirely disappeared, and for the first time we find a short, strong bowsprit, with two stays but no sail.

These ships carried two square sails, one on each mast, brailed up or loose from the yard; each mast, too, was crowned by a circular box or basket for the look-out or watch, while the whole was surmounted by a flag on the foremast and a pennon on the mizen.

Independent of these changes, there is yet another and still more striking alteration.

The house abaft the mast seen in the Saxon and Anglo-Saxon ships of the Conqueror's time, has totally disappeared, and we find two castellated buildings rising many feet above the deck; one, the smaller, placed in the bows, the other at the stern of the vessel.

The buildings were called the fore and the after castle, or, as those parts of a ship would be now denominated, the forecastle and the poop.

THE DEATH OF PRINCE WILLIAM.

These castles, though ostensibly serving as cabins for the crew and officers, in time of war were filled with archers and slingers, and used for the service of such warlike engines as were then in use in naval actions.

At this time also we, for the first time, meet with blocks aboard ship. The first use made by Henry's son and successor, Edward I., of his ships was to take the Isle of Anglesey from the Welsh, in which expedition the mariners of the Cinque Ports distinguished themselves.

The other events in the reign of Edward Longshanks are so important, both in a naval and military light—particularly as this was the beginning of that hereditary warfare and animosity that has existed for nearly six hundred years between England and France — that we consider ourselves justified in giving some account of the cause which led to Edward's invasion of France, and the origin of the national animosity that has so long existed.

At the same time it is interesting to observe from what absolute trifles two great nations may be provoked to murder and destroy the happiness of one another.

The violence, robberies, and disorders, to which that age was so subject, were not confined to the licentious barons and their retainers on land; the sea was equally infested with piracy; the feeble execution of the laws had given license to all orders of men, and a general appetite for rapine and revenge, supported by a false point of honour, had also infected the merchants and mariners, and it pushed them, on any provocation, to seek redress by immediate retaliation upon the aggressors.

A Norman and an English vessel met off the coast near Bayonne, and both of them having occasion for water, they sent their boats to land, and the several crews coming at the same time to the same spring, there ensued a quarrel for the preference.

A Norman, drawing his dagger, attempted to stab an Englishman, who grappled with him, threw his adversary on the ground, and the Norman, as was pretended, falling on his own dagger, was slain.

This scuffle between two seamen about water soon kindled a bloody war between the two nations, and involved a great part of Europe in the quarrel.

WAR VESSEL, 13TH CENTURY.

The mariners of the Norman ship carried their complaints to the French king.

Philip, without inquiring into the facts, without demanding redress, bade them take revenge, and trouble him no more about the matter.

The Normans, who had been more regular than usual in applying to the crown, needed but this hint to proceed to immediate violence. They seized an English ship in the Channel, and hanging along with some dogs several of the crew on the yard-arm in the presence of their companions, dismissed the vessel and bade the mariners inform their countrymen that vengeance was now taken for the blood of the Norman killed at Bayonne.

This injury, accompanied with so general and deliberate an insult, was resented by the mariners of the Cinque Ports, who, without carrying any complaint to the king, or waiting for redress, retaliated, by committing like barbarities on all French vessels without distinction.

The French, provoked by their losses, preyed on the ships of all Edward's subjects, whether English or Gascon; the sea became a scene of terrible slaughter between the nations; the sovereigns, without either seconding or repressing the violence of their subjects, seemed to remain indifferent spectators; the English made private associations with the Irish and Dutch seamen; the French with the Flemish and Genoese, and the animosities of the people on both sides became every day more violent and barbarous.

A fleet of two hundred Norman vessels set sail to the south for wine and other commodities, and in their passage seized all the English ships which they met with, hanged the seamen, and seized the goods.

The inhabitants of the English sea-ports, informed of this incident, fitted out a fleet of sixty sail, stronger and better manned than the others, and awaited the enemy on their return.

After an obstinate battle they put them to rout, and sunk, destroyed, or took the greater part of them.

No quarter was given; and it is said that the loss of the French amounted to fifteen thousand men, which is accounted for by this circumstance, that the Norman fleet was employed in transporting a considerable body of soldiers from the south.

* * * *

In 1294, when King Edward was preparing for war with France, he divided his navy into three fleets, over each of which he placed an admiral, this being the first time that the title is used in English naval history. Many of the ships in these three fleets were merchant vessels.

In King Edward's attack on the town of Berwick, in the course of his war

WAR VESSEL, 12TH AND 13TH CENTURIES.

against Scotland (A.D. 1296), we learn that operations were commenced simultaneously by sea and land; but three of his ships were burnt and the others compelled to retire.

CHAPTER IV.

FROM THE END OF EDWARD THE FIRST, TO THE ACCESSION OF HENRY THE FOURTH.

HE incident mentioned in the last chapter in regard of the retaliation of the Normans on the English, for the accidental murder of a mariner at the watering party, is differently reported by different historians.

It may appear strange and inexplicable to many of our younger readers why the Normans who, in the Conqueror's time, and that of his successors, William, Henry, Stephen, and down to Richard, were fellow subjects of the English, should now of a sudden have become their deadly enemies; but the fact is, the whole of Normandy and all the English possessions in France, except those belonging to the Dowager Queen Eleanor, had been overrun and taken possession of by Philip of France, in the reign of John, and incorporated into the French king's dominions more than seventy years before this date.

During the remainder of the reign of Edward I. no naval event of any national importance occurred.

As regards the state of the English navy during the reign of Edward II. the following is a list of his ships mentioned by name, though we are not to suppose that he had no other vessels :—

THE PETER.   THE BERNARD.
THE MARION.   THE MARY.
      THE CATHERINE.

All of Westminster.*

When Edward III. came to the throne, and styled himself King of France as well as of England, the state of naval affairs was very materially altered.

The French, highly incensed at this unwarrantable assumption of sovereignty over their country by Edward, made a national matter of the occasion, and, from the king to the meanest peasant, took natural umbrage at the appropriation of a title to which Edward could offer no valid justification.

This, with the rumour of Edward's intended second invasion of their country, roused the people to the highest pitch of indignation; and a resolve, not only to meet their insular invaders hand to hand in the field, but to wrench from England the boasting title of mistress of the sea, settled in their hearts.

As Philip was apprised, from the preparations which were making both in England and the Low Countries, that he must expect another invasion from Edward, he fitted out a great fleet of 400 vessels, manned with 40,000 men, and he stationed them off Sluys, with a view of intercepting the king in his passage.

The English navy was much inferior in number, consisting only of 240 sail; but whether it were by the superior abilities of Edward, or the greater dexterity of his seamen, they gained the wind of the enemy, and had the sun in their backs, and with these advantages began the action.

The battle was fierce and bloody; the English archers, whose force and address were now much celebrated, galled the French on their approach, and when the ships grappled together, and the contest became more steady and furious, the example of the king, and of so many gallant nobles who accompanied him, animated to such a degree the seamen and soldiery, that they maintained everywhere a superiority over the enemy.

The French also had been guilty of some imprudence in taking their station so near the coast of Flanders, and choosing that place for the scene of action.

The Flemings descrying the battle, hurried out of their harbours, and brought a reinforcement to the English, which, coming unexpectedly, had a greater effect than in proportion to its numbers; 230 French ships were taken, and 30,000 Frenchmen were killed, with two of their admirals. The loss of the English was inconsiderable compared to the greatness and importance of the victory.

None of Philip's courtiers, it is said, dared to inform him of the event till his fool or jester gave him a hint by which he discovered the loss he had sustained.

The French fleet in this action consisted in a great measure of what were called Genoese mercenaries.

The battle commenced at eight o'clock in the morning and lasted until seven in the evening, and was contested with great bravery on both sides.

In this battle the French fleet fought in four divisons, with several ships chained together to prevent their line from being broken. Only 30 French ships escaped, all the others being captured or destroyed.

No galleys are mentioned in the account of this battle; and as an evidence of the slaughter, there were found on one of the captured vessels, the " James of Dieppe," taken by the Earl of Huntingdon, 400 men lying dead.

There are two facts to be gleaned from the above account of the battle of Sluys. First, that ships had very considerably increased in size since Henry III.'s time, as shown by the number of dead found in one of the captured vessels; and, secondly, that the

---

* The editor of "Issues of Exchequer," says :—"The names of other ships are mentioned;" but does not give their names.

useless galley, as a vessel of war, had completely gone out.

In the year 1341, we first hear of cannon being used at sea; some of the largest trading ships carrying one or more of those then dreaded engines of war to protect them from the pirates, who, of all nations, then infested the seas.

At Easter, 1342, we learn (from Holinshed):—The Countess of Mountfort, with the English army appointed to attend her, took the seas, and at length met with Louis of Spain and his fleet, "where betwixt them was fought a sore battell."

The English had six and forty vessels of all kinds, but the Spaniards had nine great ships, and of more force than any of those which the English-men had, and three galleys beside.

They began to fight "about evensong time," and continued till darkness parted them. Next morning they would have renewed the fight but for a tempest that arose about midnight and scattered them.

It seems that the Spaniards and Genoese took away with them four provision ships of the English; and Holinshed also tells us that they were better able to abide the sea than the Englishmen, by reason of their great ships. They kept the main sea, but the English were advised by their mariners to draw unto the land, and so they did.

The next year (1343), a truce having been concluded between England and France, our army was sent home by the narrow seas (Straits of Dover), but the king himself and a few others taking ship "to return by long sea," i.e., to sail up the channel, were marvellously tormented by tempest so that their ships were scattered and driven to land at divers havens.

The Duchess of Bretagne with her son landed in Devonshire; three knights were drowned in a ship which foundered at sea, and the king himself landed at Weymouth in Dorsetshire, glad to have escaped.

One of the greatest naval armaments that England had ever at one time brought against an enemy was in the year 1347, as the following extract from the roll of the English naval force will show:—

"King Edward III.'s fleet when engaged in the siege and blockade of Calais, which lasted about eleven months, consisted of 738 English ships, carrying 14,965 mariners, being but twenty men to each ship on an average, each having fourpence per day for their pay, being about twelvepence in value of our modern money.

"There arrived also by way of aid, fifteen ships and 459 mariners from Bayonne, which is but 30 men to each ship on an average. Seven ships, and 184 men came from Spain, being on an average 26 sailors per ship; one ship and 25 men from Ireland, and one ship and 24 men from Guelderland; in all, 38 ships and 805 mariners from foreign parts."

This affords a pretty good clue to the dimensions of the largest ships of the fourteenth century. It also shows that the English navy was, as indeed it continued to be for 200 years afterwards, a sort of naval militia, each British port being compelled to contribute according to certain conditions; and that when external aid was required, ships were hired wherever they could be obtained.

Only 25 of the ships mentioned in this roll belonged to the king, the others were furnished by his subjects, and most of them were much superior to those belonging to the crown.

The merchantmen attached to this navy were divided into the South and the North fleet, according as they belonged to the ports north or south of the Thames. London supplied 25 ships with 662 men, Sandwich 22 ships with 504 men, Winchelsea 21 ships 596 men, Plymouth 26 ships 603 men, Bristol 24 ships 608 men, Southampton 21 ships 572 men, Yarmouth 43 ships 1,095 men, and other seaports in proportion. Liverpool, now the second port in England, is not mentioned, and probably at that time did not contain a vessel larger than a fishing-boat.

The South fleet consisted of 493 vessels, the North of 217; while the Earl of Warwick, with a number of "tall ships" swept the channel.

From the beginning of this war many date the formation of a regular Royal Navy of England, although, long afterwards, the sovereign's ships were often chartered by merchants. Notwithstanding the number and strength of the English fleet, Edward's navy saw but little severe fighting. Its principal work was that of blockading the port of Calais, carrying aid to the Countess of Mountfort, and destroying some Spanish pirates.

In one engagement with the Spaniards, which took place on the 29th of August, 1350, Edward commanded in person, and greatly distinguished himself by his bravery. Twenty-six of the enemy's ships were captured and many hundreds of the Spaniards were slain.

This battle gained for Edward the title of "King of the Sea." Edward the Black Prince and young John of Gaunt also obtained great reputation this day for the bravery they displayed.

In 1355 the king caused forty ships to be provided, rigged, and made ready at Rotherhithe with provisions for three months, and every one of the said ships had principal streamers of the Duke of Lancaster's arms, "who was appointed with great power of men to pass to the sea with such ships; but few or none of his company knew whither."

This great expedition was detained a very long time by contrary winds, and on reaching the Isle of Wight was broken up, both men and ships returning homewards.

We now come to the year 1372, when the Earl of Pembroke was carrying reinforcements to the Duke of Lancaster (then with the Black Prince in Spain.)

Off Rochelle he was encountered by a Spanish fleet larger than his own, and carrying engines, probably cannon.

Pembroke was either unable or unwilling to avoid the combat; he fought desperately one whole day, rested at night, and renewed the conflict in the morning; but his ship being grappled by four Spanish vessels at once, and boarded by them, he was taken prisoner.

Not a sail of all his fleet escaped, though many of them went down with their colours flying, amongst them being one that carried the military chest with £20,000 in it.

This defeat was a heavy blow to the whole nation.

In the year 1365, a ship of Aberdeen, in Scotland, belonging to the bishop of that city, laden with merchandise, was driven by a storm from her anchors in the roads of Aberdeen as far as Great Yarmouth.

The people on the coast seized on the ship and goods as a wreck, although there were two men left alive and on board. Upon the Scottish ambassador's claiming the ship and cargo, King Edward directed that if there were any living creature found in the said ship, the vessel and all its cargo should be delivered to the owners; "this," said the king, "being agreeable to the laws and customs of our kingdom."

The above circumstance affords a favorable instance of Edward's sense of justice and strict impartiality, even in the case of an enemy.

The actual weakness not only of the navy but of mercantile shipping at this period is shown by the fact that Edward III. found it necessary to direct "all the ships in the several ports—east, west, north, and south—to be taken up, of the burthen of twenty tons and upwards." These were "to repair to Portsmouth and Southampton to join the expedition against France."

In 1377, the year of Edward's death, one Mercer, a Scotch pirate, joined the French, and committed many depredations on the English coast. As the government apparently had not sufficient force or energy to protect the country, John Philpott, a London merchant, fitted out a small fleet at his own cost, with which he engaged Mercer's squadron, defeated and captured it.

With the crown of England Richard II. inherited all the wars and continental quarrels in which his grandfather Edward III. had contrived to embroil the country.

Within six or seven days after Richard II. succeeded to the throne, a French fleet ravaged the Isle of Wight, whence they sailed to Hastings, which they burnt. Winchelsea, however, offered a stout resistance, and at Southampton the invaders were beaten off with loss. The commerce of the country, however, suffered very great loss.

So, while the remembrance of these insults and injuries was fresh in every one's mind, a Parliament was assembled, supplies were voted, and by borrowing great sums of the merchants, Government was enabled to send out a considerable fleet under the command of the Earl of Buckingham.

But in the next year (1387) John of Gaunt, Duke of Lancaster, obtained command of this fleet.

He sent off a portion under the Earls of Arundel and Salisbury, with instructions to take possession of the town and port of Cherbourg. While crossing the channel, these lords encountered a Spanish fleet, which inflicted considerable loss upon them; nevertheless the English seem to have succeeded in their enterprise.

And about the same time nine large ships, which the duke had hired, being on their way from Bayonne to England, fell in with a fleet of Spanish merchantmen, and captured fourteen vessels, very richly laden with wine and other valuable goods.

In June the same year the Duke of Lancaster himself put out to sea with a great power, and laid siege to the French port of St. Malo, an undertaking in which he was not successful.

However, the Duke of Brittany—the son of the Countess of Mountfort—ceded to him the well-fortified and important harbour of Brest, which ahd been one of the ports from which came those frequent attacks on England which had so aroused the Parliament and the nation.

These wars, in accordance with the spirit of procrastination universal in those days, were prosecuted in the most tardy and unsatisfactory manner; sometimes great armaments were fitted out, and formidable demonstrations made against the enemy, which, after putting the state to great expense and inconvenience, often returned home, if not in dishonor, without effecting any noteworthy action.

Of this character were nearly all the naval adventures undertaken in the reign of Richard.

In the reign of Richard II. the Earls of Arundel and Nottingham were admirals in the English navy, and in the spring of 1387 they put to sea with a large fleet, and made many captures among the French, Spanish, and Flemish merchantmen.

Subsequently they sailed for Brest, and relieved that port, which was besieged by the Duke of Bretagne.

The success these commanders achieved aroused the jealousy of Richard's ministers,

DEAD!

and not being rewarded or praised for their able services, they resigned their commissions. Their successors were careful not to excite any envy by gallant exploits, and for many years following the deeds of the English navy are not worth recording.

During the reign of Henry IV., the English navy seems to have been in a very poor condition. inhabitants repulsed him, and he then sailed away to avoid being taken by an English fleet.

This system of irregular warfare, of course, led to reprisals.

English sailors associated together and made war on the French coast, capturing ships and burning towns; many fleets of merchantmen, richly laden

THE FRENCH LANDING ON THE ISLE OF WIGHT.

The French made many descents on our coast, and captured nearly every English merchantman they could find at sea.

Just about the time that the king's son (afterwards Henry V.) was fighting with Hotspur, at Shrewsbury, they landed in force at Plymouth, plundered the whole neighbourhood, and burnt the town; but on hearing the result of the battle they sailed away in great haste.

The same year a commander, named Waleran de St. Pol, landed on the Isle of Wight, but the with wine and other valuable commodities, were brought into English ports, and much mischief was done to the enemy.

Most of these expeditions were organised by men who held no regular commission from the king; but on some occasions Henry granted to enterprising men what we now call "Letters of Marque," thus founding the system of privateering, which has, in later years, proved so destructive to the commercial prosperity of the world.

Some two or three years after Shrewsbury fight,

the Duke of Orleans encouraged the Flemings, Easterlings, or East Germans, and other dwellers on the coast of the German Ocean, to send out cruisers to prey on the English mercantile marine. King Henry on this fitted out a fleet himself, the command of which was given to his second son, Thomas, Duke of Clarence, who fulfilled his mission in the most sanguinary manner, sinking ships, burning towns, and destroying people without any distinction or favour.

But Henry never had sufficient maritime power to thoroughly protect his own coasts from insult.

In the reign of Richard II. was written an elegy on the death of Edward III., in which the deceased monarch is likened to a ship of the period. The poem is too long to be printed in full, but the following lines will give an idea both of the poetry and naval architecture of the period :—

> "Sum tyme an Englisch schip we had,
>   Noble it was, and heih of tour,
> Thorw al Cristendam it was drad,
>   And stif wold stande in such a stour,
>   And best dorst byde a scharp schour,
>   And other stormes smale and grete.
> Now is that schip that bare the flour
>   Seldom sege and sone forgete.
>
> That schip had a ful siker mast,
>   And a sayle strong and large,
> That made the gode schip never agast,
>   To undertake a thing of charge.
> And to that schip there longed a barge—
> * * * * * *
> * * * * *
> The routher* was nouther ok ne elm—
> It was Edward the Thridde, the noble kniht.†

Early in the fifteenth century, the Spanish carraques or carracks, were found to be much superior to English vessels. This fact probably led to the sale of the king's ships at Southampton in May, 1423. They were all sold on condition that none of them should be disposed of to foreigners. History says but little about this shameful suppression of the English navy, and it was not till nearly twenty years afterwards that another royal navy was even commenced.

Sir Robert Umfraville, Vice-Admiral of England, sailed with ten ships of war in the year 1411, and ravaged the coasts of Scotland, landing every day and capturing prisoners or treasure.

Also he burnt (we quote from Holinshed), "the galliott of Scotland, being a ship of great account, with manie other vessels lieing over against Leith. At his return from thence, he brought with him fourteene good ships, and manie other great prizes of cloathes, bothe linen and woollen; pitch, tar, flower, meale, wheat, and rie: which, being sold abroad, the markets were well holpen therewith."

From this circumstance Sir Robert acquired the nickname of Robert Mendmarket.

In the same year, Sir John Prendergast and William Long scoured the seas so effectually that "no pirate durst appear," but merchant and passenger vessels might go to and fro in safety.

But after a time these very men were accused of practising piracy themselves; Prendergast was compelled to take sanctuary at Westminster, where he set up a tent in the porch of St. Peter's church, and had his servants to guard him day and night for fear of being killed by his accusers.

Long kept out at sea till "the lord admiral, having prepared certaine vessels, went to the sea himselfe in person to fetch him; but yet he could not catch him until he had promised him pardon; yet, notwithstanding all promises upon his surrender, he was shut up fast in the Tower, and so remained in durance for a season."

About the middle of July, 1412, Sir John Prendergast contrived to make his peace with the king, and ventured out of sanctuary.

Having collected thirty ships he again set sail and scoured the seas, taking many rich prizes of wine and provisions, which (according to Holinshed) "releeved the commons greatlie."

Among other enterprises performed by this worthy freebooter, we may mention the following.

He landed suddenly at the town of Craal on the fair day, captured the town, took away all the goods that had been brought to the fair, and then sailed off, "so as they that were come thither to sell their wares had quick utterance and slow payment."

The following account from an old chronicle gives us a good idea of the tyrannous exactions of the early English monarchs whenever they conceived a project of attacking an enemy; what it might cost their subjects to make a warlike display, or fulfil an idle boast, never gave the sovereigns of those days a moment's consideration.

In the eighth volume of Rymer's "Fœdera" we find an account of "further preparations for war" by King Henry IV. The king issues mandates to a number of towns to build and fit out certain vessels for sea service, called *barges* and *ballingers*. The first, which appear to have been the largest and most costly, were to be supplied by the larger towns, and the ballingers by the smaller ones. Inland towns were commanded to unite with sea-ports, and jointly fit out one barge, or one ballinger.

---

* Routher means rudder.
† The poem is to be found in what is called the Vernon Manuscript, Bodleian Library, Oxford.

CHAPTER V.

FROM HENRY IV. TO HENRY VII.—NAVAL EVENTS AND IMPROVEMENTS OF THE PERIOD—THE GRACE DIEU CARRACK.

HOUGH the whole period of the Fifth Henry's reign was one continued scene of foreign warfare, but beyond merely transporting his armies to and from the continent, this heroic prince seems to have had little use for a navy.

King Henry V., for his invasion of France, hired ships from Holland and Zealand.

He also directed all English vessels of twenty tons burthen and upwards to attend him. His fleet numbered fourteen hundred sail of ships, hulks, barges, &c.

The national enemy at that time was too hotly pressed on land to think of making reprisals at sea, and, beyond a few audacious pirates, who plundered the ships of all nations alike, there was no enemy to be met with or dreaded on the high seas.

In 1415, the town of Harfleur, then held by the English, was besieged by the French by land, while at the same time the Viscount Narbonne, vice-admiral of France, brought the whole of the French navy and endeavoured to enter the town from the waterside; but the Earl of Exeter, the English commander, defeated his intentions and defended the town manfully.

King Henry V., on hearing this, authorised the Duke of Bedford, with two hundred sail, to go to the relief of the town. These vessels were assembled at Rye, and very quickly made sail across the channel.

As soon as the French commander saw them coming, he formed his line of battle across the mouth of the harbour, and then sailed a little way out to meet his foes.

The Duke of Bedford, observing this, sent forward a few of his strongest ships, which at the first encounter captured two French vessels, "the captains whereof were too rash and forward."

It seems that this trial of strength satisfied the duke that his men and ships were of the right kind, for he then gave command for his whole line to advance.

The fight was long and desperate, but at length victory fell to the English, and almost all the navy of France, in which were many ships, hulks, carricks and other small vessels, was taken or sunk. Amongst the captured vessels were "three great carikes of Genoa, a citie of Italie, which were sent into England."

In this conflict so many Frenchmen were slain that for many days afterwards the harbour was full of their dead bodies, floating about the English ships.

The Duke of Bedford then sailed up to the town of Harfleur and compelled the French to raise the siege.

It is to be supposed that after the siege was raised, many of these vessels were discharged, for we find that in the year 1418, when Henry was besieging Rone (or Rouen), the English navy, to the number of "an hundred sails," besieged it on the waterside, while the king's cousin-german, the King of Portugal, sent a large fleet to the mouth of the Seine to stop French vessels from proceeding up the river.

Henry V. had built at Southampton some large ships of war such as were never seen in the world before; to match which the French obtained ships from the Genoese and Castilians.

Three of Henry's ships were named respectively "The Trinity," "The Grace de Dieu," and "The Holy Ghost."

A writer of the period mentions two other vessels, which we may imagine were for Henry's own use; one being called the "King's Chamber," the other the "King's Hall," both of which were fitted up in the most sumptuous manner.

That called "The King's Chamber" is said to have carried a sail of purple silk, with the royal arms of England and France embroidered on it.

During the distracted reign of Henry VI., and the War of the Roses, the English having lost France, appear to have been for a very long period free from all foreign enemies.

But though during this long reign the country was not called upon for the support of naval armaments, and an English fleet ready for action and their crews burning to meet a foe was an unknown and almost forgotten sight to the people, ship-building, both in this country and in every maritime state of Europe, was undergoing a great and almost radical change.

The Portuguese, by their discoveries along the western coast of Africa, and that, then considered, wonderful triumph of naval daring and enterprise, doubling the Cape of Good Hope, had given an impetus to naval research and adventure that led at once to the construction of larger and infinitely superior vessels.

England, of course, was not slow in adopting what was so self-evidently good in the ships of other nations; and, though the government did not then, as now, take the lead in whatever improved the navy of the country, the merchants, from motives of interest, were not backward in adopting whatever was likely to be profitable.

When we consider that the English merchant and ship-builder received no encouragement whatever from the state, and the ship on which he had lavished time and money, and on whose successful voyage all his hopes were centred, might be impounded for the king's use, as she was leaving the harbour, the enterprise of the merchants of those days is every way worthy of our highest praise.

What should we think of the government of the country at the present time, if a fleet of pirates, after capturing our East and West India merchantmen, insolently threatened the coast, and the State, too indolent to punish the robbers, allowed another John Philpott to fit out a squadron, at his own cost, to destroy the common enemies of society?

From an illustration, still extant, of Earl of Warwick embarking on what we should call a brig, having only two masts, we are enabled to form a very tolerable opinion of her capabilities.

Her lines, as a sailor would say, are much more ship-like and graceful than formerly, and she has a long jib, as well as bowsprit, with a main and mizen mast, and regular shroudings to the former. She carries two sails; her main-sail, very large, is attached aloft to a yard, while the two corners are secured to the port and starboard gunwale below.

WAR SHIP AND BARGE. A.D. 1400.

This sheet is covered with heraldic devices, while an immense pennon, with a St. George's Cross, floats from her mast-head.

The forecastle has been given up altogether, while the aftercastle, or poop, is a kind of palatial structure, divided into two stories.

The most interesting feature, however, in this ship of the early part of the fifteenth century, is the rudder, which, for the first time, we see attached to the stern posts like a modern helm; in addition, she is reported to have carried eight small deck-guns, called *bombards*, four on each side.

This is the earliest drawing on record of a two-masted ship.

The largest ship upon record down to 1455 appears to have been a Swedish vessel, to the captain of which King Henry VI., at the request of Charles, King of Sweden, granted a license for a ship of the burthen of 1,000 tons or under, laden with merchandise, and having 120 persons on board, to come to the ports of England, there to dispose of her lading, and to relade back with English merchandise, paying the usual customs.

Thus the people of the Hanseatic ports had obtained vessels of great dimensions prior to either the English or the French.

The following account of the largest ship which, up to that time, had been built in England, is highly interesting.

About the year 1449, one John Taverner, of Hull, "built a ship as large as a great carrack, or larger." King Henry VI. granted that "the said ship, then lying in the river Thames on account of its unusual largeness, shall be called the '*Grace Dieu Carrack*,' with a license to the said John Taverner to lade thereon and export wool, tin, skins, leather, and other merchandise from the ports of London, etc., belonging either to English or foreign merchants, and to carry the said merchandise through the Straits of Morocco into Italy, he paying alien's duty for the same, and upon firm expectation that he would, in return, bring home such merchandise of other nations as were most wanted in England, such as bowstaves, wax, etc., whereby a great increase of the duties and customs to the crown would ensue, and much gain to the subjects."

"By the grace of God, and the help of some of our loving subjects!" so runs the pious King Henry's charter to John Taverner, "we have built this mighty carrack," a term first used in England about this time, and meant to convey the idea of a first-rate ship, one equally capable of carrying heavy merchandise or of resisting an enemy.

The following narrative affords us a good idea of the easy, indifferent way in which our old kings could compound a felony, and perform sundry illegal acts, for which the offender would in these days have to do his seven years' hard labour.

One William Canning, of Bristol, who forfeited the king's peace by having committed piracies upon the high seas, had at a previous date obtained, either by purchase or robbery, from the Hanseatics, ships of much larger burthen than were common to the British seas. He had obtained in all "2,470 tons of shipping, among which there was one ship of 900 tons burthen, another of 500 tons, one of 400 and the rest smaller." Being condemned to pay 3,000 marks as a fine for his piratical exploits, King Edward IV. took his ships in lieu of the fine, and forgave the offence.

In 1470, seven Spanish vessels, laden with iron, wines, fruits, wool, &c. bound for Flanders, were captured by certain English ships. The Spanish owners complained to Henry VI., and moved for redress. They deposed upon oath the burthen and value of their ships, and the prices which the merchandise would have realised in Flanders. The particulars are interesting and suggestive:—

"One ship of 100 tons and her furniture valued at . £107 10
"One of 120 tons at 110 0
"One of 110 tons at 140 0
"One of 120 tons at 180 0
"One of 40 tons at 70 0

So that the highest value of any one of these ships was but thirty shillings per ton, cargo included.

King Edward IV. narrowly escaped being captured at sea in the year 1470.

The great Earl of Warwick, after a brief exile, had returned to England and landed on the coast of Devonshire, his standard being joined by most of the English people; thus supported, the earl marched northward till he reached the river Trent.

The news that those he had looked upon as his friends were continually joining the king-maker, seems to have induced Edward to fly without any attempt at a fight.

So he left his station on the river Welland in Lincolnshire, and proceeded to the town of Lynn, where he found one of his own ships and two Dutch vessels ready to make sail.

He, his brother Clarence, Lord Scales, and their followers, to the number of seven or eight hundred people, embarked without anything except the clothes they wore, and the arms they carried. Money they seem to have been entirely unprovided with; nevertheless they sailed towards the coast of Holland.

The Easterlings, or inhabitants of the coasts of the German Ocean, were at this time both privateers and merchants, and seem to have been as lawless and cruel as any pirates of more recent date. They were then at war with both French and English, and had inflicted great injuries on English commerce in the narrow seas.

Eight of their vessels, described as gallant ships, descrying the king's squadron, began to chase him. But Edward's ship was a fast sailer, and gained so much on the Easterlings that he was enabled to gain the shore near the small town of Alkmaar, the governor of which place saved the whole company from captivity by sending down an armed force, for the Easterlings had brought their ships as close to land as possible, and only waited the turn of the tide to board the three vessels.

According to Philip Comines, the historian, King Edward, having no money, was forced to give the master of his vessel a gown, lined with martens' fur, and a promise to do better for him another time, but the governor of that district seems to have behaved most liberally to the mariners.

THE EARL OF WARWICK EMBARKING.

But the following year (1471) Edward was furnished with four great ships belonging to the Duke of Burgundy, and fourteen of the Easterling vessels, with which he made an attempt (and a successful one) to regain the crown he had lost. As Warwick sent no ships to oppose him, it may be supposed that our National or Royal Navy was then in a very weak state.

This opinion is confirmed when we find it is stated that Thomas Neville, son of Lord Falconbridge, had been sent to sea by the Earl of Warwick, and had turned freebooter, having collected a great number of mariners from England and other countries, till at last he was grown so powerful that he actually contemplated sailing up the Thames, and attacking London, and conveying all the riches of the English metropolis on board his ships, which were anchored at Ratcliffe, between St. Katherine's and Blackwall.

Certain pieces of artillery thwarted this design; and Neville, after encamping for a short time on Blackheath with his friends, the Kentish men, drew his ships off towards the coast.

It has been already stated that, for a considerable time after the use of cannon, ships were not provided with portholes, but that the guns were carried upon deck, and appear to have been elevated to obtain a range over the bulwarks. So long as, from the defective rigging of ships, oars were necessary to their propulsion and steerage, it was impossible to occupy their sides with anything but the platforms upon which the rowers stood.

But even after rigging had improved, when two masts were adopted instead of one, and a bowsprit added, by which they could work closer to the wind, and be more independent of the assistance of oars, guns were still carried upon deck, and no port-holes were provided. Subsequently the bulwarks appear to have been *hatched*, portions being made moveable, to take away or let down, and the guns were run out through the openings thus made.

These openings must have been prejudicial in naval engagements; and in the early part of the sixteenth century they were abandoned for regular port-holes, which were invented by a French builder at Brest, and afterwards adopted by the English. Some of the holes were round, others square, and they were usually so small as to interfere with the training of the gun. Port-holes were not only adopted in newly-built ships, but old vessels had their sides pierced. However, they could carry only a very small number of guns, their construction being ill adapted for the weight of ordnance, which in heavy seas caused numerous disasters.

That the guns originally introduced were not very effective weapons is apparent from the fact that the cross-bow and sling remained in use long after the introduction of cannon and hand-guns, and were used in ships simultaneously with the latter.

From several incidents mentioned in the account of Magalhaen's voyage, it may fairly be inferred that the range of the ships' guns was very short, and thus the savages were rather frightened than harmed by their effects.

Cannon appear to have consisted at first of two kinds, a large one for discharging stones, called a bombard, and a smaller sort for discharging darts or quarrels. The following order proves this distinction:—

In 1377, in the time of Richard II., Thomas Norbury was directed to provide from Thomas Restwold, of London, two great and two less engines, called cannons, 600 stone-shot for the same, and saltpetre, charcoal, and other ammunition, for stores to be sent to the Castle of Bristol.

Soon after the invention of cannon, darts and bolts were shot from them, but before these, stones were used instead. In 1388, a stone ball, which weighed 195 lbs., was discharged from a bombard, called the Trevisan.

These stone balls continued long in use. There is preserved an order of Henry V., 1418, addressed to the clerk of his ordnance, commanding him to arrest artificers in stone for the purpose of making cannon-balls.

This order is so curious that we shall give a literal translation of it. What the poor fellows were to do whom the king ordered his beloved John Louth to arrest, and take away from their other work, never seems to have entered his majesty's head; and as the subject is too speculative, and might lead us into a digression, we shall not inquire.

"*The King to his beloved John Louth, Clerk of the Works of our Ordnance, and to John Benet, of Madeston, Mason, greeting*—

"Know you that we have assigned to you to arrest and take as many artificers and workmen as will be found necessary for the making of 7,000 stones for the several sorts of guns, and of a sufficient *stuffura* of stone for the same, both from the quarries of Madeston, Hithe, and such other places as you may think proper; and to place and retain the said workmen in the said our works till the said stones be quite constructed and finished.

"Also to take and to provide as many cars, boats, and vessels with their seamen and workmen as will be found necessary for the carriage or transport of the said stones from the places where they are into our kingdom of Anglia, or to places beyond the sea.

"Therefore we command you to attend with diligence to the above, and to do and to execute everything in due form.

"And we command to all and every viscounts, majors, bailiffs, constabularies, ministers, and to all our other faithfuls and subjects, both within and without the liberties, by these presents that they help and advise you in these things as best as possible.

"Witness the said *Custos* of Westminster, 10th of February, 1418.

"FOR THE COUNCIL."

The mention of "*stuffura* of stone" suggests the inference that not only were stone balls employed, but that broken fragments of stone were cemented into balls, and this inference is supported by the terms of another order of the same reign.

A point of great nautical interest, upon which some light can be thrown, though the question involved cannot be definitively settled, is the time of the invention of the modern rudder, of which great doubt has long existed; and no English antiquary has traced it to an earlier date than the middle of the reign of Edward III. or about 1350. It appears, however, that the old plan of steering ships by a paddle on each side was not abandoned until long after the rudder was invented.

In a manuscript of probaby about the year 1400, two drawings of ships are given, in both of which the rudder appears at the stern, and a man is seen steering with a tiller.

In another manuscript of the middle of the fourteenth century, there are two delineations of Noah's Ark, represented by ships having large houses on their decks; both of these have rudders at the stern, with two pentles and gudgeons, and a tiller. From the perfect manner in which the rudder appears in these drawings, it is highly probable that though not then, nor until a much later period, in general use, yet that it had long been applied to large vessels, whose height and size, out of the water, must have rendered it extremely inconvenient to steer with the ancient paddles.

The prejudice which seamen of all ages and all countries have shown against innovations, accounts, however, for the tardy adoption of even the most obvious improvements in nautical science.

Sheathing of ships is, according to facts stated in Locke's "History of Navigation," a practice of greater antiquity than might be imagined. Leo Baptisti Alberti, in his book of architecture, has these words, "But Trajan's ship weighed out of the lake of Riccia by this time, while I was compiling this work, where it had lain sunk and neglected above 1300 years; I observed that the pine and cypress of it had lasted most remarkably. On the outside it was built with double planks daubed over with Greek pitch caulked with linen rags, and over all a sheet of lead fastened on with little copper nails."

Raphael Volaterranus, in his geography, says this ship was weighed by order of Cardinal Prospero Colonna. Here we have caulking and sheathing together above 1600 years ago; for, "I suppose (says Mr. Locke) no man can doubt that the sheet of lead nailed over the outside with copper nails was sheathing, and that in great perfection; the copper nails being used rather than iron, which, when once rusted in the water with the working of the ship, soon lose their hold and drop out."

But the sheathing of ships does not appear to have been general prior to the sixteenth century. The longer voyages which had then become common rendered every improvement in the construction of ships a matter of the utmost importance. The Spaniards appear to have introduced this in those of their ships which sailed to their western colonies, and the English took the example from them. The protection of ships' bottoms was not, however, generally sought by the application of metallic sheathing, but more commonly by planks of wood, within which was placed a thick composition of pitch and other materials.

It is our wish to make the present history perfect in every respect, so as to enable the reader to follow, step by step, the progress of ship-building in Great Britain, from the rude coracle of the Briton till England's march across the deep was attended by fleets, the perfection of human ingenuity, and her naval armaments became both the pride of the nation and the admiration of the world.

To carry out this purpose fully we must here pause a few moments to make some remarks on the facts recorded in the last page.

Though, by the statements given above, collected from ancient authorities, the fixed rudder was attached to vessels somewhat earlier than the date we have assigned to its invention in the text, it is evident that, though applied to ships of burthen, it was hung more for ornament than use, the oar or paddle being still employed as a steering apparatus.

The earliest instance in which we see a large ship at sea with the rudder, unaided by the paddles, is in a royal vessel in the time of Edward IV.

These ships, as we have already stated, were armed with eight bombards, or small deck cannon, protruded through moveable shutters in the gunwale. These small mortars, not much unlike the Tower and Park guns, were unable to fire point blank, and had to be elevated to a certain height before being discharged.

The account given of the shot required for these and guns of larger calibre is curious, not because the shot consisted of masses of rounded stone, but from the fact that the chips and debris of the masons' yard were also cemented into concrete globes that were made to do duty for solid shot.

If the gunpowder then in use was of any strength, these missiles must have broken into thousands of fragments when they struck a ship or a wall; and, though they probably did little injury to either, their fragments, in all likelihood, spread among the enemy, much after the style of the grape and canister in modern use.

We had already referred generally to the sheathing of ships' hulls, and instanced the antiquity of its use; the fuller account we have just given of Trajan's ship when raised from the Lake of Riccia, after being submerged for thirteen centuries, quite sets that point at rest.

Of port-holes we shall have to speak in fuller detail when we come to the next epoch of our Naval History.

Caulking, at all times a self-evident necessity both in galleys and ships, appears to have been greatly improved on by modern ingenuity, for instead of filling up the seams of a vessel with pitch and linen rags, we chop up our old ropes and hawsers, and setting our criminal population to pick or teaze them, supply our dockyards with an abundance of a much more manageable article, called oakum.

Of the strength and quality of the government gunpowder in use in those days we may form a pretty shrewd opinion by the contents of a transport sent to Bristol with military stores towards the end of the fourteenth century.

Independent of six hundred stone shots, the vessel was freighted with charcoal, saltpetre and other ammunition for the use of that castle. From this it is plain that "the other ammunition" here alluded to was sulphur, and that the garrison of Bristol was expected to make its own gunpowder.

No wonder, then, if the government powder was uncertain and bad, when there was no established manufactory for the article; nor need we be surprised to find, that long after the introduction of artillery, the sailors and soldiers depended more on their catapults and old engines of war than on the doubtful efficacy of cannon and stone shot.

About this time all the maritime nations of Europe began making great improvements in ship building. The Portuguese, Dutch and Venetians, had about the latter half of the fifteenth century upon the seas fleets of very large vessels.

While the Spaniards were making their dis

coveries in one part of America, the Portuguese were equally busy in investigating another.

These great enterprises awakened great interest in all commercial quarters, and there grew a sudden demand on all maritime nations for large navies, for the furtherance and protection of a rapidly growing commerce.

For a period of many years, more eventful to other nations, there is but little worthy of notice in the Naval History of England till the next reign.

CHAPTER VI.

DISCOVERIES OF COLUMBUS—GREAT IMPROVEMENTS IN NAVAL ARCHITECTURE—ORIGIN OF THE NAVY BOARD AND TRINITY HOUSE—THE "GREAT HARRY."

E are now approaching the most important epoch not only of the Naval History of this country but of every maritime nation in the world; that time when the discoveries of Columbus were about to effect such a wonderful change in the tastes and manners of every nation in Europe.

From the time of King Alfred to the year 1360, there appear to have been no attempts on the part of the English to discover new territories. There is a vague historical mention only of one Nicolas de Lerina, a friar, of Oxford, who was a great astronomer, and who is said to have made several voyages to the most northerly islands of the world, the draughts of which he presented to King Edward III.; but the records of those voyages have been lost, and it is conjectured that they extended only to Ireland and the coasts of Norway, and were made for astronomical purposes.

In the reign of Henry VII., Bartholomew Columbus came to England to present to the king some new maps of the world, and also charts for navigation, which, up to that time, had not been employed. He also laid before his majesty the views of his brother, Christopher Columbus, respecting the existence of a vast continent across the waters of the Atlantic Ocean.

But these views met with no encouragement from the English Court; with the king the invasion of a neighbouring nation was a higher object than the discovery of a new world. Bartholomew, therefore, rejoined his brother in Spain; and England lost the honour of being the patron to the greatest geographical discovery recorded in the pages of history. An attempt was subsequently made to prove that America had been discovered three hundred years previously by the Welsh, under Prince Madoc. The futile claims of this pretension are thus examined by Captain Pinkerton:—

EMBARKATION OF TROOPS FOR FRANCE. FROM AN OLD MS.

"When America was first made known, it occasioned abundance of inquiries, and, as it was natural, recalled to many people's remembrances and considerations stories which had before been deemed scarce worthy of notice; amongst the rest, our nation put in its claim; and the tale told in favour of us, as it is the earliest in point of time, seems to merit relation.

"This story asserts that Madoc, Prince of Wales, was the first discoverer of America, and the detail of his expedition ran thus:—He flourished in the twelfth century, and was son of Owen Guyneth, Prince of North Wales. His brethren raising a civil war about the division of his father's dominions, he chose rather to go to sea, with a few of his friends, and seek out a new habitation, than run the hazard of what might happen. Accordingly, about the year 1170, steering due west, and leaving Ireland on the north, he came to an unknown country, where he settled a colony, and returning thence into Wales for a second supply of people.

WESTWARD HO!

This expedition is supposed to have sailed, but Madoc was never heard of afterwards.

That the country he went to was really America, is more than can be thoroughly proved; but that this tale was invented after the discovery of the country, on purpose to set up a prior title, is most certainly false. Meredith ap Rees, who died in

But with submission to these great men, this story does not answer their purpose, for it is evident the course does by no means agree, since, if he had sailed to that country, he could not have left Ireland to the north. There is a very ingenious discourse upon this subject, in which it is suggested that Prince Madoc landed in some part of Florida

THE DEATH OF SIR EDWARD HOWARD.

1477, was a famous Welsh poet, and composed an ode in favour of this Madoc, wherein was contained an account of his new discoveries.

Now, as this was several years before Columbus made his first voyage, we may be sure that the tale was really a British tradition, and no invention of a later contrivance. Some critics have endeavoured to prove that it was not America, but Greenland, to which our Welsh prince sailed. In proof of which they have observed that this country was well known in the ninth and tenth centuries, though the knowledge of it was afterwards lost.

that in process of time the colony he planted there proceeded round by land, and reached the northern parts of Mexico, which country they conquered, and were those foreign ancestors of the Mexicans of whom we have heard so much from those Spanish writers, who recorded the adventures of Cortes; and it is remarkable that several British words are still to be found in the old Mexican tongue.

The sudden accession of wealth, honour, and political importance gained by Spain on the discovery of the new world by Columbus, placed her at once at the head of every nation in Europe.

Of all the maritime states, to which, a few years before, the despised Columbus had submitted his plans and solicited the aid of a few ships, England, perhaps, had now the most cause to repent her parsimony and indifference.

Scarcely had the first Spanish fleet returned, loaded with specimens of the wealth and vegetable wonders of the new world, than Henry VII. was filled with vexation and chagrin for having lost an opportunity that would have made him the first monarch in Europe, and his country the leading state of the old world. As soon as he saw his mistake he tried to rectify it.

On the 5th of March, 1496, Henry granted a patent to John Cabot and his three sons (Venetians, who had settled in Bristol), authorising them to navigate the Eastern, Western, and Northern Seas, with five ships under the English flag, manned by as many men as they should judge fit, *at their own sole cost and charges* (the king, it should be known, was as great a miser as ever lived), to discover the countries of Infidels or Gentiles in any part of the world which had hitherto been unknown to Christians.

This patent or commission gave the voyagers power (to use the words of the document itself) "to set up our banners in any town, castle, island, or continent, of the countries so to be discovered by them; and such of the said towns, castles, or islands so found out and subdued by them, to occupy and possess as our vassals, governors, lieutenants, and deputies; the dominion, title, and jurisdiction thereof, and of the *terra firma* or continent so found out remaining to us."

The king, giving way to the avaricious spirit we have before mentioned, added a provision to the effect that the Cabots should, after each voyage, pay over to him one-fifth of the profits of their discoveries, either in money or goods, a stipulation which takes away all the credit which would otherwise have been his for promoting this expedition, and makes him appear as anxious to take the lion's share of the profits, without contributing to the expense.

The Cabots sailed from Bristol in the beginning of May, 1497, in their ship named the "Matthew." At the end of June they discovered Labrador, which they supposed to be an island. Then they sailed northward, in hopes of discovering a passage to India and China; but, from an entry in the records of Henry's privy-purse expenditure of a donation of £10 "to him that found the new isle," it is to be presumed they failed in their project, and returned to England.

The passage to India which they hoped to discover is the same that Sir John Franklin, in our own time, tried to explore, and lost his life while so doing; but had he been successful it is probable that he would have received a much larger reward than the ten pounds that Henry bestowed on "him that found the new isle."

Other expeditions were started; but the king's niggardly spirit was very discouraging to the adventurers, who were not able to carry out their projects without assistance.

It was not to be supposed that the English people would quietly look on while Spain was monopolising all the commerce and riches of the new world; and a number of large ships—large for that day—were built by the merchants of England to enable their owners to share, in some degree, a part of the inexhaustible treasures of America.

To protect these larger ships of his subjects, and at the same time to lay the foundation of a national navy, Henry VII. built the largest ship then known; at all events, the largest vessel of war that had ever been built in England—"The Great Harry."

This ship had four masts, with all the clumsy contrivances of a fore and after castle, and was pierced for two tiers, or rows, of guns. But, ungainly as we should call such a vessel now, she was decidedly superior in all sea-going and warlike qualities to the ship built by his son and successor several years later.

In the completion of this large line of battle-ship, which was launched in 1502, the king expended fourteen thousand pounds, a very large sum in those days.

But, before this, during the reign of Henry VII. the English Navy received rather a severe defeat from the Scots.

A great deal of bad feeling had existed between the two nations for a long time, and many skirmishes had occurred on the borders.

It would be a difficult matter to prove who were the aggressors in this irregular warfare, but without attempting to argue on that point we will relate the facts of the case.

Soon after the accession of James IV. of Scotland, and, according to Scottish accounts, during a time of peace or truce, five English vessels sailed up the river Clyde, and, after plundering various places and committing many depredations, gave chase to a vessel belonging to the Scottish monarch, greatly injuring her.

King James, who appears at that time to have been encouraging the construction of a Scottish naval force, called upon Sir Alexander Wood, of Largo, who is reported to have been a brave, skilful seaman, and had served with distinction in the previous reign, to avenge these insults and chastise the marauders. Sir Alexander obeyed the command and prepared to give battle to the English.

He had two vessels, named "The Flower" and "The Yellow Carvel," both large ships and well manned. With these he sailed to Dunbar, off which port the English were then lying; a fierce action took place, resulting in the capture of the invaders, who were brought in triumph to Leith by the conquerors.

A man named Stephen Bull, an enterprising

merchant of London, undertook to retrieve this disgrace, being encouraged (as the Scottish historians say) by King Henry, who, in spite of all representations to the effect that the five captured vessels were little better than pirates, and had been guilty of illegal proceedings, permitted some English knights, with various companies of crossbowmen and pikemen, to embark on board the three vessels which Bull fitted out for the expedition.

This force sailed from London, and in due time arrived at the Frith of Forth, where Bull lay to behind the Isle of May, waiting for the appearance of the Scottish fleet, under Sir Alexander Wood; that brave knight having put out to sea to escort some merchant vessels to Flanders.

After waiting for some time Bull saw the "Flower" and the "Yellow Carvel" coming round a point known as St. Abb's Head, whereupon the English ships were immediately cleared for action.

The Scot had the advantage of what seamen call the weathergage, and, like a good seaman as he was, kept it.

The firing commenced, and all that day the battle continued in the sight of a great number of spectators who crowded all the highlands along the coast. It was early in the day when the battle began, and at night the combatants separated, neither party seeming to show a disposition to retreat.

Next morning they recommenced the combat, when after a few shots had been fired, the ships grappled with each other, and a hand-to-hand conflict commenced, which was kept up with such fury, that the vessels were allowed to drift into shallow water at the mouth of the river Tay, where Bull was compelled to surrender.

The captured vessels were taken to Dundee, the wounded carefully attended to, and soon afterwards Bull was taken before the Scottish king, who, after remonstrating against such practices, allowed all the prisoners to be set at liberty without ransom.

In the reign of Henry VIII. the nation became still more awakened to the fact that something must be done for the improvement of the navy, and during his reign the dockyards at Deptford, Woolwich, and Portsmouth were built, and the Admiralty and Navy Boards established.

According to some historians, English Naval History should commence here, as they claim that the Royal Navy was only established in the early part of Henry VIII.'s reign. Such, however, is not our belief, for, whatever may be the opinion of those who have constituted the Boards of Admiralty for years past, we believe it fully possible for a navy to exist without being under their peculiar management.

The question of "How could there be a navy without a board of management?" is no evidence that there was no navy previous to the formation of such a board.

Henry VIII. also established the Corporation of the Trinity House for examining, licensing, and regulating pilots, for ordering and directing the erection of beacons and lighthouses, the placing of buoys and landmarks.* To this corporation he afterwards added subordinate establishments of the same kind at Newcastle, Hull, and other ports.

Bluff King Hal also built the first pier at Dover (about A.D. 1525), and also had an Act of Parliament passed for amending and maintaining the ports of Plymouth, Falmouth, Fowey, and Tynemouth. The preamble of the statute stated that whereas in times past these ports had been the most safe and convenient in the realm for the preservation of shipping, having a good depth of water wherein the largest ships might lie in safety—no matter how the wind blew—they were now so choked up by certain tin works, called stream works, that a ship of 100 tons could scarcely enter at the half-flood. The Act prohibited the working of such stream works for the future, except under certain specified regulations, but did not make any other provision for amending the harbours. Sandwich was, and is at the present time ruined, through an accumulation of sand.

After the dockyard at Portsmouth was completed, Henry prepared a fleet of twenty-five ships, to be employed in an expedition against the French. Previous to the sailing of this fleet, Henry went to Portsmouth, and gave a banquet to the officers.

To meet these vessels, the French fitted out a fleet of thirty-nine ships at Brest, one of them being an immense carrack, called the "Cordeliere." The fleets met in the Bay of Brittany, and a long and severe engagement followed between the large French carrack and the English ship "Regent," assisted by another.

The two vessels got locked together, when the carrack blew up, and both were burnt. Aboard the French ship there were eight hundred men, and on that of the "Regent" seven hundred, all of whom perished. This, for a time, ended the war, but without deciding the victory for either side.

The following is an historical statement of this indecisive action:—

"There happened this summer an action at sea, which brought not any decisive advantage to the English. Sir Thomas Knevet, master of horse, was sent to the coast of Brittany with a fleet of forty-five sail, and he carried with him Sir Charles Brandon, Sir John Carew, and many other young courtiers who longed for an opportunity of displaying their valour.

"After they had committed some depredations, a French fleet of thirty-nine sail issued from Brest, under the command of Primauget, and began an engagement with the English. Fire seized the ship of Primauget, who, finding his destruction inevitable, bore down upon the vessel of the English

---

* Henry VII. hanged a great number of the followers of Perkin Warbeck on the coasts of Kent, Sussex, and Essex, "for sea-marks or light-houses, to teach Perkin's people to avoid the coast."

admiral, and grappling with her, resolved to make her share his fate.

"Both fleets stood some time in suspense as spectators of this dreadful engagement, and all men saw with horror the flames which consumed both vessels, and heard the cries of fury and despair which came from the miserable combatants. At last the French vessel blew up, and at the same time destroyed the English. The rest of the French fleet made their escape into different harbours."

About the year 1513, Henry VIII. equipped another fleet for the invasion of France, and placed Sir Edward Howard in command of it. After cruising about the Channel for a considerable time, Sir Edward sailed to Brest.

On learning that the French fleet, under the command of Prejeant de Bidoux, had departed for Conquet, a pors a few milet from Brest, Howard determined to follow and attack him.

MAGALHAEN'S SHIP THE "VICTORIA."

Sir Edward found the French ships securely moored under the protection of some batteries, and in a place nearly inaccessible to the English fleet. Regardless of the difficulties of the situation, Howard resolved to attack the enemy where he lay, and, with only two light galleys, issued the order to give way, and gallantly led the attack, ably followed by Sir William Sidney, in command of a few barges.

In an engagement so rashly and inconsiderately commenced, the English were repulsed with considerable loss, and the gallant Howard killed. The last act of this noble was to take off his gold chain, whistle, and other badges of his office, and throw them into the sea.

"The French," said he, "shall never possess such trophies of England's loss."

This defeat enabled the French to leave their own shores and make an attempt at invading the coast of Sussex, an undertaking, however, in which they were remarkably unsuccessful.

The following brief account affords a more detailed and graphic description of this unfortunate action:—

"The French admiral, who expected a reinforcement from the Mediterranean of some galleys under the command of Prejeant de Bidoux, kept within the harbour, and saw with patience the English burn and destroy the country in the neighbourhood. At last Prejeant arrived with six galleys and put into Conquet (April 25th), a place within a few leagues of Brest, where he secured himself behind some batteries, which he had planted on rocks that lay on each side of him.

"Howard was, notwithstanding, determined to make an attack upon him; and as he had but two galleys, he took himself the command of one, and gave the other to Lord Ferrars. He was followed by some row-barges and some crayers, under the command of Sir Thomas Cheyney, Sir William Sidney, and other officers of note. He immediately fastened on Prejeant's ship, and leaped on board of her, attended by one Carroz, a Spanish cavalier, and seventeen Englishmen. The cable, meanwhile, which fastened his ship to that of the enemy, being cut, the admiral was thus left in the hands of the French; and as he still continued the combat with great gallantry, he was pushed overboard by their pikes. Lord Ferrars, seeing the admiral's galley fall off, followed with the other small vessels; and the whole fleet was so discouraged by the loss of their commander, that they retired from before Brest."

The French navy then came out of harbour, and even ventured to invade the coast of Sussex. They were repulsed, and Prejeant, their commander, lost an eye by the shot of an arrow. Lord Howard, brother to the deceased admiral, succeeded to the command of the English fleet; and little memorable passed at sea during this summer.

In the thirteenth volume of the "Fœdera" there is an indenture in English, between King Henry VIII. and his admiral, Sir Edward Howard, which affords an insight into the manner of fitting out fleets of war in those times (1512). There were to be three thousand men "armed for sea war," and were allotted to seven hundred soldiers, mariners, and gunners, in King Henry's ship the "Regent." The three thousand men consisted of the captains of the eighteen English ships, seventeen hundred and fifty soldiers, and twelve hundred and thirty-two mariners and gunners.

The admiral was to have for the maintaining of himself in diet, and for wages and reward, ten shillings daily pay during the voyage, and each captain one shilling and sixpence per day, or about two and tenpence of our modern money. The soldiers, mariners, and gunners to have per month of twenty-eight days five shillings wages and five shillings more for victuals.

The ships are specified to consist of the "Regent," 1,000 tons burthen; the "Mary Rose," 500 tons; the "Peter Pomegranate," 400 tons; "John Hopton's Ship," 400 tons; the "Nicholas Reede," 400 tons; and the Mary George, 300 tons. The rest of the eighteen ships were from 140 tons down to one of 70 tons burthen.

VIEW OF THE OLD ENTRANCE TO SANDWICH (ONE OF THE CINQUE PORTS.)

It was about this time that ships first began to be reckoned by their strength in guns as well as by tonnage, gunners being now first mentioned. We find a mention in "Rapin's History of England" that in 1512 James IV. of Scotland equipped a fleet *in which was the largest ship that had yet been seen on the sea.* This ship is said to have been 240 feet in length, by 56 in breadth.

In the same year, King Henry VIII. built the largest ship ever known in England. She was named the "Regent," of 1,000 tons, and her capacity has been already indicated by reference to the number of soldiers, mariners, and gunners she was appointed to carry. The Scottish writers affirm that the "Regent" was but a copy of the great ship of James IV. of Scotland.

Our English naval historians think that, down to the year 1545, ships had not port-holes, but that they only carried a few guns, which were placed on deck.

It is certain, however, that King Harry's ship, the "Grace Dieu," had regular port-holes; and there is mention, by Father Daniel, of a French ship, about the same period, which carried a *hundred* large brass cannon.

Among the great explorers or discoverers of this period, we must not forget to mention Ferdinand Magalhaen, or Magellan, who, in 1520, discovered the straits at the southern extremity of America which bear his name, and thence sailed round into the Pacific Ocean. On the opposite side we give a representation of the good ship "Victoria," in which he made these discoveries.

A notorious Scotch pirate of the name of Barton created about this time much annoyance to the commerce of England. This man, having suffered injuries from the Portuguese, for which he could obtain no redress, had procured letters of marque against that nation; but he had no sooner put to sea than he was guilty of the grossest abuses, committed depredations upon the English, and much infested the narrow seas. Lord Howard, son of the Earl of Surrey, sailing out against him, fought him in a desperate action, where the pirate was killed, and he brought his ships in triumph into the Thames.

Only few other events of any naval importance occurred during the remainder of this reign; the first was the fitting out a fleet of nearly two hundred ships, carrying an army of ten thousand men, which Henry, in 1544, sent against Scotland.

On the 4th of May, 1544, this armament arrived off Leith, and the English landed, their intention being to capture Edinburgh; but eventually they were obliged to retire, the army marching along shore towards Berwick, while the fleet kept as near the shore as possible.

The fleet carried off with them two large ships, and burnt and destroyed all the other craft they could find, scarcely leaving even a fishing-boat on the coast.

The old historian Holinshed, in speaking of the prizes taken in this war, says—

"Among other ships which the Englishmen had in Leith haven, there were two of notable fairness, the one called the 'Salamander,' given by the French king at the marriage of his daughter, into Scotland;

the other called the 'Unicorn,' made by the late Scottish king.

"The ballast of these two ships was cannon shot, which they found in the town to the number of four score thousand. The rest of the Scottish ships, being taken away, together with their own ships, which they brought with them, were for the more part pestered with the spoil and booties of the soldiers and mariners."

The Scottish war was not over, when Henry thought it necessary to quarrel with the French, and a fleet was sent out under the command of Lord Lisle, Admiral of England, who sailed to the mouth of the river Seine, and appeared before Newhaven, where the French fleet had assembled.

The enemy was estimated to number 200 ships and 26 galleys; twenty well equipped vessels having been sent to the aid of the French king by the Pope.

Lord Lisle had with him 160 vessels, and determined not to attack the French as they lay at anchor, but, if possible, draw them out to sea.

Accordingly, some few ships were sent forward with instructions to fire at the French, who moved their galleys to the front (with ours) and replied. But, while this firing was going on, there suddenly arose a violent tempest, and the English, to avoid being driven on the sands and shoals at the mouth of the river were obliged to put out to sea, and eventually returned to Portsmouth, where the king was staying.

It seems that Henry had received intimation that the French intended to make a landing on the Isle of Wight, and had gone down to the South coast to see that proper measures for defence were taken.

The information Henry had received proved to be correct, for, in the month of July, 1545, the French admiral, after burning several villages on the coast of Sussex, cast anchor off St. Helen's Point in the Isle of Wight, and sent some of their smaller vessels to the very mouth of Portsmouth harbour.

To quote Holinshed again—"the English navy laying there in the same haven, made them ready, and set out towards the enemies; but the wind was so calm that the king's ships could bear no sail, which greatly grieved the minds of the Englishmen, and made the enemies more bold to approach with their gallies, and assail the ships with their shot even within the haven."

In the days of Henry VIII. many ships that otherwise might have been very efficient in naval warfare, were rendered nearly useless through having their port-holes made too low.

The "Mary Rose," the third ship in Henry's navy, sank in this action with the French from this cause, namely, by the entry of the sea through the lower port-holes, which were then but sixteen inches above the water. In 1840, some brass cannon were obtained from this wreck by Mr. Deane, the celebrated diver.

The "Mary Rose," contained four hundred soldiers under Sir George Carew, and, we may presume, a number of mariners to work the vessel; not more than forty persons were saved.

The French certainly made a landing on the island, but were driven back again with loss. Afterwards, finding they could not obtain a permanent footing there, they weighed anchor, and sailed once more along the coast of Sussex, making two or three other unsuccessful attempts to land; but, finding everywhere the people in arms ready to receive them, "they turned stern and so gat them home again."

That this was really a serious attempt at invasion may be guessed from the fact that nearly sixty thousand prisoners remained in the hands of the English.

We are reminded, by the perusal of an ancient Norwegian document, of the privations endured, and the fearful ravages to which the crews of ships were exposed in those ages, before matters of marine hygiene became properly understood, and which in small ships, which were slow sailers, difficult of management, and carrying a very limited number of men, must have produced thousands of disasters that have never been recorded:—

"Being betwixt three and four degrees of the equinoctial line, my company within a few daies began to fall sicke of a disease which seamen are apt to call the scurvie, and seemeth to be a kind of dropsie. * * * * And I wish that some learned man would write of it, for it is the plague on the sea, and the spoyle of mariners; doubtless, it would be a worke worthy of a worthy man, and most beneficial for our countrie, for in *twenty years* (since I have used the sea) I dare take upon me to give account of *ten thousand men consumed with this disease!*"

About A.D. 1546 some French sailors made a voyage to Brazil in a ship called the "Ager," which had been captured from English owners. On their way they met with a much smaller craft, of which one Golding was master, "a proper man and hardie." The Frenchmen, perceiving that this small vessel was English, fired at her, doing great damage, and then ran alongside; six or seven of the Englishmen, with "Maister Golding" at their head, leaped on board the "Ager," and, while the Frenchmen were watching their little adversary as she sunk, found a great number of lime-pots, and threw them at the Frenchmen so thick that some were obliged to jump overboard, and others to take refuge in the hold. Thus the English regained possession of the bark "Ager."

On the 18th of May, 1546, four of the king's ships and four pinnaces were cruising in the neighbourhood of Boulogne, when they met with eighteen French galleys. The only particulars we have of this fight are that "there was great shooting between them, and at length one of their gallies was taken, in which were fourteen score soldiers and seven score rowers; the rest of their gallies packed away."

In course of time King Henry VIII. died, and Edward VI. succeeded to the throne.

This Boy Monarch had not long been seated on

the throne when England again became embroiled with Scotland, and Lord Protector Somerset deemed it necessary to send both an army and a fleet to reduce the Scots to reason.

The fleet consisted of "the great galley," and four-and-twenty tall ships, well furnished with men and munitions of war, besides many merchant ships and other small vessels carrying stores.

Lord Edward Clinton was admiral of the fleet, and Sir William Woodhouse, Knight, his vice-admiral.

These vessels for some time lay off Leith and Edinburgh; but on Tuesday, the 13th of September, 1547 (according to Holinshed), the smaller vessels of the English fleet burned Kinghorn and a town or two standing on the north shore of the Forth.

Two days afterwards Lord Clinton took with him "the galley whereof Richard Brook was captain," and four or five smaller vessels, with which he proceeded up the Forth to a haven on the south shore, called Black Ness, where the Scots had stationed three vessels—the "Mary Willoughby," and the "Anthony," which had been taken from the port of Newcastle, and another large vessel called the "Bosse," with seven smaller craft. Black Ness was defended by a castle as well as these ships; but Lord Clinton, after a severe conflict, "by fine force, won from them those three ships of name, and burnt all the residue before their faces."

We have no recollection of any other event of importance in which the Navy was concerned, and as peace was soon afterwards proclaimed, it had no further opportunity of gaining distinction during Edward's reign.

When Edward died in July, 1553, the tonnage of the Royal Navy is supposed to have been 11,065 tons; the number of ships, galleys, pinnaces, and row-barges, being 53, of which only 28 were above 80 tons burden.*

While the country was in a state of doubt as to whether Lady Jane Grey or the Princess Mary would reign, the Lord Protector sent six ships to Yarmouth to prevent the last named lady from escaping to France.

Master Jerningham, who was raising forces on behalf of Mary, persuaded the crews to give them up to him, thus, no doubt, expediting the overthrow of the power of poor Lady Jane Grey.

When Philip of Spain was coming to England to espouse the queen of this country, the lord admiral, with 28 ships and other small vessels, was sent to meet him, and escort him to the shore with due honour. Stone shot were still used, and in 1556 caused no little consternation at Greenwich, where one of them, fired from a vessel passing up the river, passed through the wall of the palace, but fortunately did no harm to the inmates.

In the year 1558, when Mary embroiled England in her husband's quarrel with France, the money granted by Parliament enabled the queen to fit out a fleet of 140 sail, which, being joined by 30 Flemish ships, and carrying 6,000 land forces on board, was sent to make an attempt on the coast of Britanny.

The fleet was commanded by Lord Clinton; the land forces by the Earls of Huntingdon and Rutland. But the equipment of the fleet and army was so dilatory that the French got intelligence of the design, and were prepared to receive them.

The English found Brest so well guarded as to render an attempt on that place impracticable; but landing at Conquet they plundered and burnt the town, with some adjacent villages, and were proceeding to commit great disorders when Kersimon, a Breton gentleman, at the head of some militia, fell on them, put them to rout, and drove them to their ships with considerable loss.

But a small squadron of ten English ships had subsequently an opportunity of amply revenging this disgrace upon the French. The Mareschal de Thermes, governor of Calais, had made an irruption into Flanders with an army of 14,000 men, and having forced a passage over the river Aa, had taken Dunkirk and Berg St. Winoc, and had advanced as far as Newport; but Count Egmont coming upon him suddenly with superior forces, he was obliged to retreat, and being overtaken by the Spaniards near Gravelines, and, finding a battle inevitable, he chose very skilfully his ground for the engagement.

He fortified his left wing with all the precautions possible, and posted his right along the river Aa, which he reasonably thought gave him full security from that quarter.

But these English ships, which were accidently on the coast, being drawn by the noise of the firing, sailed up the river, and flanking the French, did such execution by their artillery, that they put them to flight, and the Spaniards gained a complete victory.

During this reign, history records the loss of the "Great Harry," which was pronounced the "goodliest ship in England, being of the burden of one thousand tons." She was accidentally burnt at Woolwich, on the 27th of August, 1553, through the carelessness of her crew.

This ship was built at Erith, in 1515, and is supposed to be the first English ship built with *port-holes*.

Port-holes were invented by M. Descharge, a Frenchman of Brest, early in the sixteenth century.

A doubtful account is to be found in some histories about this time of an attempt of the French on the island of Guernsey, and of a squadron under Commodore Winter, who was sent to defend the island. The French, it is said, with a large fleet and a land force of two thousand men, were besieging the island, when they were attacked and defeated with a loss of half their number.

The rest escaped, leaving the greatest part of their fleet, which was burnt by the English.

---

* Vide Burchett's Memoirs of the Royal Navy.

CHAPTER VII.

FROM THE ACCESSION OF ELIZABETH TO THE WAR WITH SPAIN—SIR FRANCIS DRAKE AND HIS ADVENTURES.

BEFORE proceeding to give a faithful narrative of the heroic achievements of Elizabeth's reign, we must afford the reader a brief glimpse of the strength and power of the English navy in the time of Mary, only ten years previous to the opening of this chapter.

The naval power of England was in the year 1548 so inconsiderable, that £14,000 being ordered to be applied to the fleet, both for repairing and victualling, it was computed that £10,000 a year would afterwards answer all necessary charges.

In entering on the reign of Queen Elizabeth, we approach the most illustrious epoch of the Naval History of Great Britain.

Prior to the accession of this courageous woman, the title that England had assumed of Mistress of the Seas had been more tolerated than acknowledged by surrounding states.

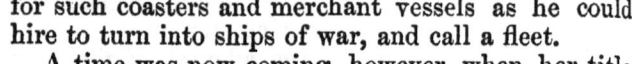

ANCIENT SHIP'S GUN.

To support the arrogance of such a title the country should have maintained a fleet of sufficient strength always to support her vaunted right to be so regarded, and one strong enough at any time to crush the hostile power that might question the right to the sovereignty she had assumed.

From what we have already shown of the Naval History of England, it will be evident to the youngest capacity that this country never had the means, and was never in a position to compel obedience to her title, or even to enforce permanent respect to her flag.

That Englishmen knew how to fight, both on land and sea, no country had the hardihood to dispute; but, though she had won great victories on both elements, she was not always victorious, and had no more right to call herself Mistress of the Seas than she would have had to style herself King of the Earth.

Indeed, if we are to speak honestly, she had still much less right to do so, with a national navy that at the opening of the sixteenth century consisted of only *one* ship; and so late as 1545 embraced no more than *fifteen* vessels, the sovereign being dependent on his subjects, or foreigners, for such coasters and merchant vessels as he could hire to turn into ships of war, and call a fleet.

A time was now coming, however, when her title of Ruler of the Waves was no longer an idle or unsubstantial boast, but a fact maintained by the thunder of her cannon on every sea of either world.

The navy, however, which Elizabeth left at her death, compared to that of her sister, appears considerable when we reflect only on the number of vessels, which was forty-two; but when we consider that none of these ships carried above forty guns, that four only came up to that number, that there were but two ships of a thousand tons, and twenty-three below five hundred, some of fifty, and some even twenty tons, and that the whole number of guns belonging to the fleet was seven hundred and twenty-four, we must entertain a contemptible idea of the English navy, compared to the force which it has now attained.

In the year 1588 there were not above five vessels fitted out by the noblemen and sea-ports which exceeded two hundred tons.

At this period England was—not without reason, it seems—jealous of the French maritime power, and in the state papers of the period we find our ambassador in France, Sir Nicholas Throckmorton, making constant reports as to seafaring matters. Writing from Paris, on July 1st, 1559, he says—

"There is great inquiry made by the French here where our ships lie at moor, whether any of them be to be rigged to the seas, and in what readiness they be; also in what case the great new ship * and how near she is to perfection, and what shall become of her." And on the 4th of the same month he says, "We have great cause to suspect the French meaning towards us, and the suspicion doth daily increase."

Also on the same day, writing to the Lords of the Privy Council, he informs them that "the French

* On the 3rd July, the Queen went to Woolwich to the launching of a new ship named after her. This most probably is the great new ship alluded to.

do increase the number of their ships to be set forth upon the seas, and that they do, within these fourteen days, despatch to the number of five thousand men to the sea-coast."

This Sir Nicholas Throckmorton was one of the most industrious and watchful ambassadors we ever had at a foreign court, and advised our home Government of everything that passed. On the first of August, 1559, he wrote to the queen, to inform her that the admiral of France and De Labross had gone to Calais; the admiral being instructed to provide ships for the other, who had been appointed to command an expedition fitting out for Scotland. At the same time he adds that the French "are in very great fear on all sides, and suspect much the preparation and readiness of your majesty's ships;" which is a very good proof that reforms and improvements in the navy were taking place.

Soon after this a French army was for some time in occupation of Edinburgh, and Elizabeth was induced to sign a treaty with the Lords of the Convocation by which she undertook to assist them, and never to lay down her arms till the French should be entirely driven out of Scotland. These Lords of the Convocation, it should be understood,

ARRIVAL OF FLEMING, THE PIRATE, AT PLYMOUTH.

were promoting, by everything in their power, the religious views of Knox and Calvin against the Catholic party, at the head of which stood Mary Queen of Scots and her French husband.

In accordance with the terms of this treaty, an English fleet, consisting of thirteen large ships of war, besides transports, appeared in the Frith of Forth, in March, 1560, at a time when they were little expected on account of the roughness of the weather. The commander of the French, who had been checked in an attempt to ravage the county of Fife, was highly delighted at the sight of this gallant navy, and burnt a considerable quantity of gunpowder in firing a general salute; but his joy was turned into sorrow when Winter, the English admiral, hoisted the flag of Old England.

Winter's part of the campaign was to blockade the port of Leith, and also to watch for the arrival of French reinforcements under the Marquis D'Elbœuf, for whose fleet, it seems, the English ships had been mistaken by the salute-firers.

But D'Elbœuf's transports were scattered by a storm, and either wrecked on the coast of Holland or driven back to France, so that the English fleet had no opportunity of distinguishing itself in battle. The siege was converted into a blockade, and our sailors performed their duty so well that not an ear of corn could be carried into the garrison at Edinburgh, and the French were even prevented from gathering shell-fish on the beach as they had been accustomed to do. In July the garrison made terms of surrender, and thus this brief war came to an end.

The following account of Elizabeth's navy, being the opinion of a contemporary, is not only interesting but instructive, as showing us what our ancestors thought of a fleet that a modern Englishman would regard as a paltry squadron of clumsy frigates and gun-boats.

Harrison, in his "Description of Britain," printed in 1597, has the following passage, chap. xiii:—"Certes, there is no prince in Europe that hath a more beautiful sort of ships than the Queen's Majesty of England at this present; and those generally are of such exceeding force, that two of them, being well appointed and furnished as they ought, will not let (hesitate) to encounter with three or four of them of other countries, and either bowge them or put them to flight, if they may not bring them home.

"The Queen's highness hath at this present already made and furnished to the number of one-and-twenty great ships, which lie for the most part in Gillingham Road. Beside these, her grace hath others in hand also, of whom hereafter, as their turns do come about, I will not let to leave some further remembrance. She hath likewise three notable galleys, the 'Speedwell,' the 'Tryeright,' and the 'Black Galley,' with the sight whereof, and the rest of the navy royal, it is incredible to say how marvellously her grace is delighted, and not without great cause, sith by their means her coasts are kept in quiet, and sundry foreign enemies put back, which otherwise would invade us."

After speaking of the merchant ships, which he says are commonly estimated at seventeen or eighteen hundred, he continues:—

"I add, therefore, to the end all men should understand somewhat of the *great masses of treasure* daily employed upon our navy, how there are few of these ships of the first and second sort (that is, of the merchant ships), that being apparelled and made ready to sail, are not worth £1,000, or 3,000 ducats at the least, if they should presently be sold. What shall we, then, think of the navy-royal, of which some one vessel is worth two of the other, as the shipwright hath often told me?

"It is possible that some covetous person, hearing this report, will either not credit at all, or suppose money so employed to be nothing profitable to the queen's coffers; as a good husband said once, when he heard that provisions should be made for armour, wishing the queen's money to be rather laid out to some speedier return of gain unto her grace; but if he wist that the good keeping of the sea is the safeguard of our land, he would alter his censure, and soon give over his judgment."

Speaking of the forests, this author says:—

"An infinite deal of wood hath been destroyed within these few years, and I dare affirm, that if wood do go so fast to decay in the next hundred years of grace as they have done, or are like to do, in this, it is to be feared that sea coal will be good merchandise, even in the City of London."

Harrison's prophecy was fulfilled in a very few years; for about 1615 there were 200 sail employed in carrying coal to London. But to proceed with the actual events of this period.

Simultaneously with the accession of Elizabeth and the restoration of the Protestant religion, there broke out over the land a perfect epidemic for deeds of daring and adventure; and as the hateful peace with Spain no longer existed, that country's immense and wealthy possessions in America became the magnet towards which every adventurous spirit in England was irresistibly drawn.

Though no war at the time existed between Spain and England, yet noblemen, gentlemen, merchants, and corporations in every part of the kingdom, fitted out single ships or small squadrons, and sent them, like a swarm of pirates, to win glory and wealth on the Spanish main, as the West Indian Islands and the eastern coast of Mexico were then generally called.

Such was the enthusiam of the people to engage in this permitted violation of the territories of a neutral power, that adventurers put to sea even in pinnaces and craft totally unfit to contend with the dangers and storms of the Atlantic.

Undeterred, however, by the smallness of the vessels, their insufficiency, or the certain privations and even horrors of the voyage—horrors, the result of crowded ships, insufficient food and water, that fatal scourge of the sailor, scurvy, and tropical fever—the people flocked from all quarters to the ports, in the hope of not being too late for acceptance.

Never did Englishmen so prodigally offer up their blood and lives in the hope of wealth and glory, than during the whole term of this queen's long reign.

Elizabeth seemed too delighted to witness this daring spirit among her subjects, a courage that despised all danger and death, to think of checking the warlike bent of the people; and so long as they avoided implicating herself or government in her subjects' buccaneering exploits, she remained perfectly indifferent to the injury they inflicted on her late brother-in-law.

Indeed, as we shall presently see, in regard to her reception of Drake, she openly encouraged it.

It is not to be supposed, however, that Philip could quietly bear this constant swarm of hornets on his American shores, killing his subjects, burning his towns, and robbing him and them of treasure with total impunity and calmness.

Nor is it likely he cared to have his exchequer yearly drained to keep a strong fleet to convoy home the annual treasure ships from Peru and Mexico.

Philip did, however, endure the loss occasioned by this swarm of English privateers, and tolerated this open insult to himself and crown as long as his Castilian blood could stand it; then he made civil remonstrances to Elizabeth on the ungentlemanly conduct of her subjects.

But as Elizabeth treated all his remonstrances with evasion or indifference, the Spanish king was for a time compelled to put up with the daily loss and hourly humiliation.

Though rebuffed, Philip was not deterred, but, locking the memory of his wrongs in his gloomy mind, he made a vow to all the saints in his calendar one day to take a terrible vengeance on Elizabeth and her heretical people.

How he meant to execute this vow we shall see when we come to speak of the Armada.

As we have already stated, the wealth and fame which Spain and other nations, especially the Portuguese, were daily acquiring by their discoveries both in the east and the west, awoke among the aspiring adventurers of this country such dauntless spirits as Drake, Gilbert, Frobisher, Raleigh, Hawkins, and a host of others, equally bold and daring.

It is of the exploits of these men that we are now about to speak; men whose great deeds and utter contempt of death in their aspirations after honour and glory have added such lustre to the Naval History of this country.

In this necessarily brief account of the doings of the celebrated men who contributed so much to England's greatness, we shall commence with Sir Martin Frobisher.

The date of this man's birth is uncertain, but at all events we know that he was of Yorkshire parentage, and was born at Doncaster. Being sent to sea when he was young, he soon displayed all the talents of a great sailor.

He was the first Englishman who attempted the northwest passage to China.*

For fifteen years he made constant proposals to English merchants; but meeting little encouragement from them, he applied to Dudley, Earl of Warwick, and other noblemen, who enabled him to fit out three small vessels—two barks of twenty-five tons each, and a pinnace of ten tons.

With these he sailed from Deptford on the 8th of June, 1576, and, the Court being then at Greenwich, the queen beheld them as they passed by, "commended them, and bade them farewell, with shaking her hand at them out of the window."

Frobisher bent his course northward. On the 24th June he saw the Shetland Islands, and on the 10th August, went on shore at a desert island three miles from the main land of Greenland, but only stayed there a few hours. The next day he entered a strait, called Frobisher's Strait, which name it still bears.

On the 18th they again went on shore, but a number of his men having been captured by the natives, he set sail for England, and, in spite of a terrible storm, reached Harwich on the 2nd of October.

He had, however, formally taken possession of the lands he touched in the name of the Queen of England; and in token of such possession, had ordered his men to bring away whatever they could find. One man brought a piece of black stone, like sea coal, but very heavy.

Having, on his return, distributed fragments of it among his friends, the wife of one of the adventurers threw a portion of it on the fire, and this piece, on being taken out again and quenched in vinegar, sparkled like gold, and being tried by some refiners in London, was found to contain a portion of that rich metal. This circumstance raised the most extravagant expectations in the minds of the people of England; and great numbers of very influential persons pressed Frobisher to undertake another voyage in the spring. This Frobisher readily consented to do, more especially as the queen lent him a vessel of 200 tons burden,* with which, and two other barques of about 30 tons each, they sailed from Harwich on the 31st May, 1577, and proceeded to Frobisher's Straits.

The commander's commission for this voyage directed him to search for ore only, leaving the discovery of the north-west passage till another time. Frobisher sailed about and gave names to various bays, headlands and isles, one of which was named after the Countess of Warwick. In this island Frobisher found a large quantity of ore with which he sailed home on the 23rd of September, and was very graciously received by the queen.

Commissioners having been appointed to examine the ore, a very favourable report was given, and preparations were made to work the mines; England expected to find large quantities of gold in these newly discovered regions.

---

* Cabot, mentioned in a preceding chapter, was a Venetian, it should be remembered.

* Our authority is Chalmer's Biographical Dictionary; but, on turning to the list of royal ships for 1578, as given by Derrick, we do not find *any* ship of 200 tons. The nearest, in point of size, are the "Aid," 240 tons, manned by 160 men; and the "Bull," 160 tons.

Workmen were selected for the business, and soldiers were enlisted for their protection; but the third voyage was not so successful as the former, and the expedition returned in October, 1577.

* * * * * *

A list of the Royal Navy in 1578, given by Derrick, shows twenty-four ships, burthen 10,506 tons, manned by 6,570 men, of whom 3,760 are classed as mariners, 630 as gunners, and 1,900 soldiers; it must be presumed that they had 280 officers.

In an estimate in the Ordnance office, dated 1578, the number of guns on board the queen's ships are computed to be 504.

We shall next speak of another renowned sailor.

Francis Drake was a nephew of Captain John Hawkins, the first Englishman who sailed from Africa with a cargo of slaves. It is stated that Drake made one voyage in the trade with his uncle, but was so disgusted with the whole business that he would never again engage in such a revolting traffic.

The rest of his youth and much of his early manhood seems to have been passed in prosecuting adventures on his own account, and supported at first evidently by very slender means. All the attacks were made upon the Spanish possessions in the Gulf of Mexico.

These adventures appear to have resulted in the acquisition of immense wealth, though in amassing this treasure there is very little doubt that Drake and his companions committed many acts of wanton depredation, far beyond even those which were then considered as justifiable even by other piratical leaders.

Indeed, so atrocious were some of these depredations of Drake's, that historians, in memory of his after great and signal services, have kindly drawn a veil over his early career, or attributed to the passion and heat of youth crimes his countrymen would fain forget altogether.

In 1570 he made his first expedition with two ships, and the next year with only one.

The year 1572 saw him as busy as ever against the Spaniards, being assisted by a nation of Indians, whose chief was named Pedro. Drake presented this chief with a cutlass, and received in return four large wedges of gold, which he threw into the common stock, saying that he thought it but right and just that those "who bore the charge of so uncertain a voyage on his credit should share the utmost advantages that voyage produced."

His success in this expedition was great, and the reputation he gained was increased when he afterwards fitted out three vessels at his own expense, and with them proceeded to Ireland, where he served as a volunteer under Walter, Earl of Essex, father of the earl who was afterwards beheaded by order of Queen Elizabeth.

The next national and important service this dauntless navigator performed, and to which history is proud to point, was undertaken in the year 1577. To the success of this adventure Francis Drake owed all his subsequent honour and renown.

By means of Sir Christopher Hatton, then vice-chamberlain, a great favourite of the queen's, he obtained her consent and approbation, and set sail from Plymouth in 1577 with four ships and a pinnace, on board of which were one hundred and sixty-four able sailors. He passed into the South Sea by the Straits of Magellan, and attacking the Spaniards, who expected no enemy in those quarters, took many rich prizes, and prepared to return with the booty which he had acquired.

Apprehensive of being intercepted by the enemy if he took the same way homewards by which he had reached the Pacific Ocean, he attempted to find a passage by the north of California; and failing in that enterprise, he set sail for the East Indies, and returned safely this year (1580) by the Cape of Good Hope.

He was the first Englishman who sailed round the globe, and the first commander-in-chief; for Magellan, whose ship executed the same adventure, died in his passage. His name became celebrated on account of so bold and so fortunate an attempt; but many, apprehending the resentment of the Spaniards, endeavoured to persuade the queen that it would be more prudent to disavow the enterprise, to punish Drake, and to restore the treasure.

But Elizabeth, who admired valour, and was allured by the prospect of sharing in the booty, determined to countenance that gallant sailor; she conferred on him the honor of knighthood, and accepted of a banquet from him at Deptford, on board the ship which had achieved so memorable a voyage.

When Philip's ambassador, Mendoza, exclaimed against Drake's piracies, she told him that the Spaniards, by arrogating a right to the whole new world, and excluding thence all other European nations who should sail thither even with a view of exercising the most lawful commerce, naturally tempted others to make a violent irruption into those countries.

Elizabeth, by her countenance of these yearly expeditions to the Spanish Main, and by openly espousing the cause of the revolted Flemings, at last so exhausted the patience of Philip, that in 1586 he declared war against England.

By no means daunted by Philip's immense naval and military preparations, Elizabeth resolved to take the initiative in the coming struggle, and strike a blow at Spain where she was most vulnerable—in her American colonies.

For this purpose a fleet of twenty sail was equipped to attack the Spaniards in the West Indies, and two thousand three hundred volunteers, besides seamen engaged on board; Sir Francis Drake was appointed admiral, Christopher Carlisle, commander of the land forces. Frobisher sailed with his fleet in command of a ship called the "Aid."

They took St. Iago, near Cape Verde, by surprise, and found in it plenty of provisions, but no riches. They sailed to Hispaniola (January, 1586), and easily making themselves masters of St Domingo by assault, obliged the inhabitants to ransom their houses by a sum of money. Carthagena fell next into their hands, after some more resistance, and was treated in the same manner. They burned St. Anthony and St. Helen's, two towns on the coast of Florida.

Sailing along the coast of Virginia they found the small remains of a colony which had been planted there by Sir Walter Raleigh, and had gone extremely to decay.

This was the first attempt of the English to form such settlements, and though they have since surpassed all European nations, both in the situation of their colonies and in noble principles of liberty and industry on which they are founded, they had here been so unsuccessful that the miserable planters abandoned their settlements, and prevailed on Drake to carry them with him to England.

He returned with great riches, which encouraged the volunteers, and with such accounts of the young adventurers, who hoped to rival the great navigator.

It was while engaged in this expedition, that Drake first heard from some of his indignant prisoners that their master, Philip, was fitting out a fleet of such strength and size as would not only subjugate the whole kingdom, but sweep the detested flag of England for ever from the seas.

The hope, indeed the belief, in the accomplishment of this threat, seemed to soothe the feelings of the robbed and insulted Spaniards in America, and made them endure more complacently the daily wrongs to which they were subjected by the English.

The execution of Mary Queen of Scots, a Catholic, and a princess for whom the Spanish monarch entertained a warm friendship, so enraged Philip, that he threw aside all reserve and dissimulation with regard to his immense prepartions, and seemed to pant for the moment when his priest-blessed and invincible Armada should put to sea, to execute the vengeance of man and Heaven on the heretic Queen of England and her people.

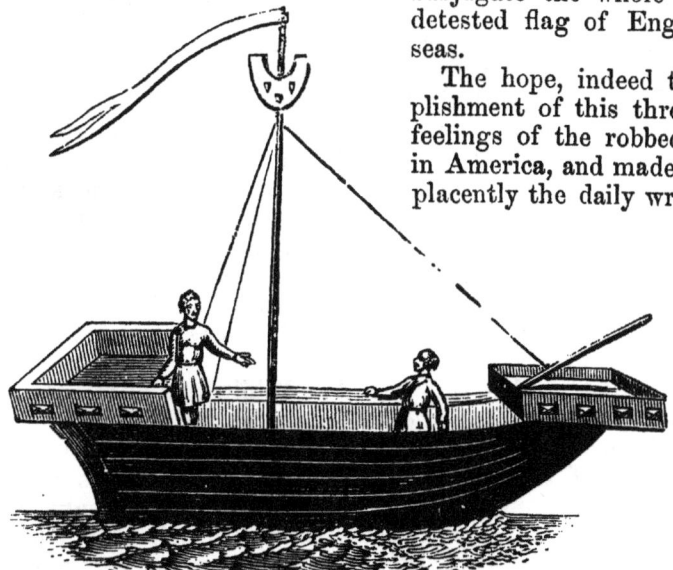

MERCHANT VESSEL, TIME OF HENRY VI.

This news, though it did not in the least disconcert Drake, induced him probably to return home earlier than he otherwise would have done, believing that he and every man would be wanted to beat off

QUEEN ELIZABETH KNIGHTING FRANCIS DRAKE.

Spanish weakness in those countries as served to inflame the spirits of the nation to future enterprises.

The great mortality which the climate had produced in his fleet was, as is usual, but a feeble restraint on the avarice and the sanguine hopes of the invader, should Philip indeed attempt to carry out his threat.

The very motive that had induced Drake to hasten home, seems to have acted in a like manner on those roving adventurers, such as Hawkins, Frobisher, Raleigh, and others, all who, though eager after wealth, were so anxious to meet the Spaniard in fair battle, that they resigned with pleasure the chance of acquiring more treasure for the satisfaction of participating in the expected fight.

The Spanish armament was so formidable, and danger of an invasion so imminent and near, that Elizabeth could no longer delay her preparations to meet the coming storm.

Though news at that time travelled slowly, and the intercourse of nations was confined to a few individuals, the whole of Europe rang with the fame of Philip's preparations, and the English were excited to a degree of enthusiasm to meet the audacious enemy, quite unusual with a nation generally so apathetic.

Elizabeth, considering prevention better than cure, after having placed the country in a posture of defence, and hearing that Philip's navy was nearly ready to make an attack, sent Sir Francis Drake with a fleet to intercept his supplies, to pillage his coast, and to destroy his shipping. Drake carried out four capital ships of the queen's and twenty-six great and small with which the London merchants, in hopes of sharing in the plunder, had supplied him.

Having learned from two Dutch ships, which he met with in his passage, that a Spanish fleet, richly laden, was lying at Cadiz, ready to sail for Lisbon, the rendezvous of the intended Armada, he bent his course to the former harbour, and boldly, as well as fortunately, made an attack on the enemy. He obliged six galleys which made head against him to take shelter under the forts, he burned about a hundred vessels laden with ammunition and naval stores, and he destroyed a great ship of the Marquis of Santa Croce.

Thence he set sail for Cape St. Vincent, and took, by assault, the castle situated on that promontory, with three other fortresses. He next assaulted Lisbon, but, finding that the merchants of London, who had engaged entirely in expectation of profit, were discontented at these military enterprises, he set sail for the Terceras with the intention of lying in wait for a rich carrack which was expected in these parts. Drake, who was something of a wag, termed this "singeing the King of Spain's beard."

He was so fortunate as to meet with his prize; and by this short expedition, in which the public bore so small a share, the adventurers were encouraged to attempt further enterprises, the English seamen learned to despise the great unwieldy ships of the enemy, the naval preparations of Spain were destroyed, the intended expedition against England was retarded a twelvemonth, and the queen thereby had leisure to take more secure measures against that formidable invasion.

This unexpected disaster occurring at the moment his fleet was about to put to sea, was a source of the deepest mortification to Philip.

It was not the slaughter of a few hundred of his soldiers or mariners, or the loss of naval stores, that gave him a moment's uneasiness; it was being thwarted in his revenge, and compelled to endure for another year the insults of his insular foe; this was the feeling that made the disaster at Cadiz so terribly galling.

There is no doubt the Spanish fleet might have put to sea directly after this attack of Drake's, and with nearly as much probability of success as was expected to attend its great advent; but Philip was determined that when he did launch his thunderbolt, it should be perfect in all its powers of destruction and conquest.

For this purpose, all the resources of his vast empire and enormous wealth were instantly employed in repairing the damage Drake had inflicted; but in despite of prodigal means and unwearied labour, the rest of that season was lost, and it was spring of the following year before Philip heard the joyful news that his Armada was again ready for sea.

While the Spaniards are repairing the damage inflicted by that detested freebooter, Drake, for whose punishment special vials of wrath were being shipped, with heaps of pincers, whips and racks, and sundry holy monks, who knew well how to use them, we shall take a few moments' respite to contemplate more closely the nature and character of this Spanish armament.

For three years, every dockyard and seaport in Sicily, Naples, Spain and Portugal, resounded with the din of labour; swarms of galley slaves and skilled workmen hourly vieing with each other who should do the most work in this service of God—the building of the Armada, heaven's scourge against schism and heresy.

At the same time naval stores were bought at a great expense, provisions amassed, armies levied and quartered in the maritime towns of Spain, and plans laid for fitting out such a fleet and embarkation as had never before been witnessed in Europe. The military preparations in Flanders were no less formidable. Troops from all quarters were every moment assembling to reinforce the Duke of Parma. Capizuchi and Spinelli conducted forces from Italy; the Marquis of Borgaut, a prince of the house of Austria, levied troops in Germany; the Walloon and Burgundian regiments were completed or augmented, the Spanish infantry was supplied with recruits, and an army of thirty-four thousand men was assembled in the Netherlands, and kept in readiness to be transported into England.

The Duke of Parma employed all the carpenters he could procure, either in Flanders or in Lower Germany, and the coasts of the Baltic, who built at Dunkirk and Newport, but especially at Antwerp, a great number of boats and flat-bottomed vessels for the transporting of his infantry and cavalry.

The most renowned nobility and princes of Italy and Spain were ambitious of sharing in the honor of this great enterprise. Don Amadeus of Savoy,

Don John of Medicis, Vespasian Gonzaga, Duke of Sabionetta, and the Duke of Pastrana, hastened to join the army under the Duke of Parma. About two thousand volunteers in Spain, many of them men of family, had enlisted in the service.

No doubts were entertained but such vast preparations, conducted by officers of such consummate skill, must finally be successful. And the Spaniards, ostentatious of their power and elated with vain hopes, had already denominated their navy the *Invincible Armada*.

Elizabeth had foreseen this invasion, and finding that she must now contend for her crown with the whole force of Spain, made great preparations for resistance; nor was she dismayed with that power by which all Europe apprehended she must of necessity be overwhelmed. Her force, indeed, seemed very unequal to resist so potent an enemy.

The size of the English shipping was in general so small, that except a few of the queen's ships of war, there were not four vessels belonging to the merchants which exceeded four hundred tons. The royal navy consisted only of thirty-four sail, many of which were of small size; none of them exceeded the bulk of our largest frigates, and most of them deserved rather the name of pinnaces than ships.

The only advantage of the English fleet consisted in the dexterity and courage of the seamen, who, being accustomed to sail in tempestuous seas, and expose themselves to all dangers, as much exceeded in this particular the Spanish mariners, as their vessels were inferior in size and force to those of that nation.

All the commercial towns of England were required to furnish ships for reinforcing this small navy, and they discovered on the present occasion great alacrity in defending their liberty and religion against those imminent perils with which they were menaced. The citizens of London, in order to show their zeal in the common cause, instead of fifteen vessels which they were commanded to equip, voluntarily fitted out double that number.

The gentry and nobility hired, armed, and manned forty-three ships at their own charge, and all the loans which the queen demanded were frankly granted by the persons applied to.

The entire number of ships collected on this occasion, amounted to 191, manned by 17,400 men. The "Triumph" was the largest, being 1,100 tons burthen, with 500 men on board and 42 guns; next was the "White Bear," 1,000 tons, with also 500 men on board; the "Elizabeth Jonas," of 900 tons, carried 500 men; while the "Ark Royal" and the "Victory," each 800 tons, carried respectively 425 and 400 men, with 55 and 42 guns.

The Dutch had been applied to for assistance; and, according to Stowe, they "came roundly in with three score sail, brave ships of war, fierce and full of spleen, not so much for England's aid, as in just occasion for their own defence, foreseeing the greatness of the danger that must ensue if the Spaniards should chance to win the day and get the master over them."

This fleet was stationed at various points along the coast, for it could not be known where the enemy would land.

Lord Howard of Effingham, a man of courage and capacity, was admiral, and took on himself the command of the navy; Drake, Hawkins, and Frobisher, the most renowned seamen in Europe, served under him. The principal fleet was stationed at Plymouth. A smaller squadron, consisting of forty vessels, English and Flemish, was commanded by Lord Seymour, second son of Protector Somerset, and lay off Dunkirk, in order to intercept the Duke of Parma.

The land forces of England, compared with those of Spain, possessed contrary qualities to its naval powers; they were more numerous than the enemy, but much inferior in discipline, reputation, and experience. An army of twenty thousand men was disposed in different bodies along the south coast, and orders were given them, if they could not prevent the landing of the Spaniards, to retire backwards, to waste the country around, and to wait for reinforcements from the neighbouring counties, before they approached the enemy.

A body of twenty-two thousand foot, and a thousand horse, under the command of the Earl of Leicester, was stationed at Tilbury in order to defend the capital. The principal army consisted of thirty-four thousand foot and two thousand horse, and was commanded by Lord Hunsdon. These forces were reserved for guarding the queen's person, and were appointed to march whithersoever the enemy should appear.

The fate of England, if all the Spanish armies should be able to land, seemed to depend on the issue of a single battle, and men of reflection entertained the most dismal apprehensions, when they considered the force of fifty thousand veteran Spaniards, commanded by experienced officers, under the Duke of Parma, the most consummate general of the age, and compared this formidable armament with the military power, which England, not enervated by peace, but long disused to war, could muster up against it.

On the 20th of May, 1588, the Armada sailed from the Tagus, after appointing Cape Finisterre as a general rendezvous, where the ships from Naples and Sicily were to join company.

Nearly every vessel met at the appointed place and time, but had scarcely assembled when they encountered a violent gale. The storm raged with such fury that many of the largest ships were driven into collision with each other, suffering fearfully both in hull and rigging.

Sails were torn to shreds, masts sprung or lost, spars carried away, rigging damaged, and such serious injuries sustained, that the Armada was compelled to put back to port and refit.

The news of this disaster spread like wildfire, not

only to England, but over all Europe; and the general belief was that the Armada had been so far disabled as to render an invasion of England impossible.

Though neither Elizabeth nor the English people believed in so serious an injury of the Spanish fleet as had rendered it unfit for service, it was fully thought by many that it had suffered so severely that for another year, at least, Philip would be unable to execute his threat against this country.

The queen, fully believing that her kingdom was safe from all attack for another year, and being always ready to lay hold on every pretence for saving money, she made Walsingham write to the admiral, directing him to lay up some of the larger ships, and discharge the seamen; but Lord Effingham, who was not so sanguine in his hopes, used the freedom to disobey these orders, and begged leave to retain all the ships in service, though it should be at his own expense.

He took advantage of a north wind, and sailed towards the coast of Spain, with the intention of attacking the enemy in their harbours; but the wind changing to the south, he became apprehensive lest they might have set sail, and by passing him at sea, invade England, now exposed by the absence of the fleet.

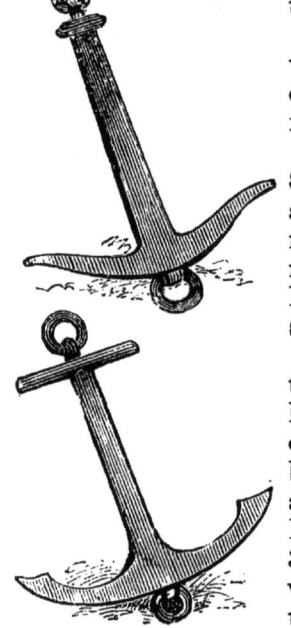

ANCIENT ANCHORS.

He returned, therefore, with the utmost expedition to Plymouth, and lay at anchor in that harbour.

Meanwhile, all the damages of the Armada were repaired, and the Spaniards with fresh hopes set out again to sea in prosecution of their enterprise.

The fleet consisted of 130 vessels, of which near 100 were galleons, and were of greater size than any ever used before in Europe.

It carried on board 19,295 soldiers, 8,456 mariners, 2,088 galley slaves, and 2,630 great pieces of brass ordnance. It was victualled for six months, and was attended by twenty lesser ships called caravels, and ten salves, with six oars apiece.

Philip's plan of operations was that the Armada, after beating off the English fleet, and taking possession of the channel, should land the troops on board, near the mouth of the Thames, and there wait till the Duke of Parma, with the main army of 34,000 men, crossed from Dunkirk, when the united force should proceed to London, supported by the fleet in the river. Such was the enemy's plan of intended operations.

We shall now proceed to show how all his hopes were frustrated, and his scheme of conquest and triumph defeated.

CHAPTER VIII.

TRIUMPHANT ADVANCE AND SIGNAL DEFEAT OF THE ARMADA.

T was late in the day of the 19th of July; Drake, Hawkins, Frobisher, and some others of England's doughty captains, were ashore at Plymouth, playing a game at bowls, when a fast-sailing craft, with every stitch of canvas spread, entered Plymouth Sound, and, threading her way through the English fleet, brought the startling, but welcome, news that the Armada was at sea and in full sail for the channel.

The bearer of this important piece of intelligence was a Scotch pirate of the name of Flemming.

"Finish the game!" cried the fiery Drake, as his messmates seized their hats and swords in their haste to get aboard.

"Finish the game, and let the Don and his blessed crew wait for their thrashing till we have finished our score," said the others.

All was now bustle and action where so late had been silence and repose; boats in myriads flocked from shore to the fleet, ships were unmoored, sails set, and the forest of masts, so lately stationary, were now all in motion; and, in obedience to the signals from the admiral, the ships were forming into squadrons and divisions.

In a short time they were all ready to meet the enemy.

While these manœuvres were taking place at sea, the gloom of evening was suddenly illumined by the blaze of a hundred watch-fires.

From every crag, hill, cliff and promontory, flared up an instant sheet of flame, till from Dungeness to Berwick, and from the Lizard to the Solway, the red beacon of alarm glanced meteor-like through the land.

When the sun rose on the following morning, one of the most imposing sights of naval grandeur that the eye of an Englishman had ever seen, lay out like a map before his gaze;—slowly advancing through the chops of the Channel, propelled by a gentle breeze, was seen the Armada, majestically surging ahead.

The Spanish fleet, consisting of 150 of the largest

RALEIGH BOARDING THE "ADMIRAL GALEASS."

The shepherd on his lonely wolds held tighter to his crook, the hardy fisher in his storm-beat boat grasped with harder grip the oar, and set his teeth with firmer clench as that red sign flashed lightning-like across the sky, then, hastening to his hut, looked to the edge and temper of his long-neglected brand.

Ere midnight, through every vale and nook in England, that fiery banner had drawn each man from his couch, and roused the martial spirit of the land to arms.

ships in the world, with the sun flashing on their long lines of brazen guns, was seen advancing in a semi-circle, extending seven miles from horn to horn of the crescent.

With regal and measured grandeur the stately pageant swept slowly up the Channel, seeming, in its majestic course, to subjugate the water over which it glided so imposingly.

In this manner, more like a triumphant procession than a hostile armament, the Armada proceeded onwards till the 21st, when, having got well into

Channel, and past the Ram's Head, Lord Effingham gave his orders to attack the enemy.

The English admiral knew well that the only advantage he possessed over those leviathans, crowded with troops and sailors, lay in the better seamanship of his men and the ease with which his small ships could be manœuvred; and, anxious not to come to close quarters with the foe till his crews had made themselves better acquainted with the kind of enemy they had to deal with, he advised his captains to avoid boarding, and be content with cannonading the Armada from a distance.

Lord Effingham, having divided his fleet into three divisions, and instructed them to hang on the enemy's wing and rear, the admiral in the "Royal Ark," led the attack, while Drake, in the "Revenge," Hawkins in the "Victory," and Frobisher in the "Triumph," at once bore down on the Armada.

Drake and Frobisher, with their usual intrepidity, at once began the action by cannonading the rear of the enemy's line.

Having kept up a running fire for some time, these enthusiastic captains, becoming each moment more indifferent to the size and number of their antagonists, approached still closer to the foe, and by their quick manœuvres and rapid firing, soon produced considerable disorder among the heavy sailing Spanish ships.

In the midst of this confusion one of the immense galleons, commanded by Don Pedro Valdez, was so injured that she fell out of the line, to the rear of the rest of the fleet.

No sooner did Drake perceive what had happened than he at once laid the "Revenge" alongside the Spaniard, and, after a sharp contest, boarded and took her.

While Drake was thus hotly engaged, one of the great ships of the Armada, on board of which all the treasure was embarked for the pay of the land and sea service of the fleet, took fire, creating immense alarm and confusion among the rest of the Spanish line.

By great exertion and the assistance of the other ships the fire was extinguished, and her treasure removed to another vessel.

The ship herself, however, was so disabled or badly worked, that she, like the galleon, being unable to keep the line, fell astern; then Frobisher bore down on her, and, despite the opposition of the rest of the fleet, who strove to save her, she was run into by the "Triumph," boarded, and taken by her gallant captain.

The capture of these two ships concluded the achievements of that day. Drake sent his prize into Dartmouth, and then followed the enemy.

While this spirited affair was taking place in the rear of the Armada, Lord Effingham and the others were not idle, but followed the enemy and harassed his flank with a constant and damaging cannonade.

The result of this day's action showed the English that they had little to dread from the Spaniards as mariners, and that the size of their ships was no protection to them, as in close action the greater portion of their shot flew over the heads of the English, while every discharge from the British guns told on their antagonists.

The following day passed without any special incident, the English still hanging on and annoying the enemy as he swept slowly up the channel.

On the 23rd, however, the wind having veered to the north, the Spanish admiral resolved to change his tactics; and probably irritated by the persistent cannonading of the English, resolved to bear down on his enemy, and give him battle or drive him off.

The Armada's course was accordingly altered; and, sailing direct on the English fleet, the Spaniards began the action off Portsmouth.

In the sharp and desperate engagement that followed, and which lasted for several hours, the Spaniards, despite their immense superiority in ships and men, were signally repulsed.

In this indecisive but sanguinary action, the Spaniards learnt that they had a very different enemy to deal with than had been represented to them, and began to respect, if not to dread, the heretics they had been taught to despise. At the same time the size and unwieldiness of their ships forced itself unpleasantly on the minds of all.

Meanwhile, the small English ships, manned by experienced sailors, were enabled to stand on and off with the greatest ease, and, delivering one broadside, sail round their adversaries and pour in the contents of the other battery before the Spaniard was prepared or expected a repetition of the assault.

Every day Don Medina Sidonia, the Spanish admiral, had sent one of his despatch-boats to Dunkirk, to beseech the Duke of Parma to put to sea, and join him at once that they might make a descent on the English coast and land the army.

Lord Seymour, however, with his English and Dutch fleet, kept so close a watch over Dunkirk and Newport that, though Parma had built a powerful flotilla for the purpose of crossing the Channel, he was afraid to embark his troops, and remained totally inactive.

In the hope of giving the Duke of Parma assistance, and covering his transports with the Armada, the Spanish admiral, after the action with Lord Effingham's fleet on the 23rd, drew off from the English coast and sailed for Calais, pursued all the way by Effingham, Drake, and others.

On the afternoon of the 27th of July, the Armada reached the roads before Calais, and here Don Medina Sidonia moored his fleet in four deep lines, with their bows pointing seaward.

From this anchorage the Spanish admiral made a last and earnest appeal to Parma to brave all risk and put to sea, but Philip's great general either could not, or would not, embark.

Lord Effingham, with his fleet, having followed the enemy to his moorings, anchored his ships in front of the Armada, and just within gunshot, with the seeming intention of blockading it where it lay.

Scarcely had Lord Effingham reached Calais when he was joined by a squadron of queen's ships, by the lords of Oxford, Northumberland, Cumberland, Lord Thomas Cecil, Sir Walter Raleigh, and a number of other lords and gentlemen, all volunteers, with well-manned ships, and who, at the first signal of danger, had put to sea from all parts of the coast.

On this occasion the Lord High Admiral knighted the Lords Howard and Sheffield, Roger Townsend, John Hawkins, and Martin Frobisher, for their gallant conduct in the late actions.

As the night of the 27th was very dark and favourable for a daring enterprise, Lord Effingham resolved to put in practice a stratagem he had been waiting for an opportunity to attempt.

He filled eight vessels with pitch, oil, gunpowder, and other inflammable materials, and had them silently towed in front of the enemy, when, firing the train of each, he sent them down the long lines in which the Armada was moored.

The consternation of the Spaniards when, roused from their slumbers, they found themselves on all sides surrounded by fire-ships, amounted to a perfect panic.

In the first moment of their alarm, they cut their cables, and, in their haste to put to sea, ran their ships foul of each other, inflicting the most serious damage, while the terror inspired by the hazard of their situation, the darkness of the night, and the shouting of the horrified crews, created a scene of the wildest discord and ungovernable confusion.

As soon as the light of day enabled him to comprehend his situation, the Duke of Medina saw at a glance the full and irreparable nature of his disaster.

As far as his eye could reach east and north, the whole sea to the horizon was covered with the scattered Armada.

Some of the finest of his ships, with rent sails and flapping rigging, with stove-in bows and sprung masts, lay helpless and wallowing in the trough of the sea, or were vainly striving to wear off the Flemish coast, on whose treacherous and fatal flats the rising breeze was fast driving them.

Having signalled to his scattered fleet to put back to their late moorings as soon as possible, the Spanish admiral was obliged for a time to run before the breeze, having no anchors to make good his position off Calais.

When the sun rose, the English saw the sea covered with the wreck of masts and spars, the boasted Armada scattered in all directions and struggling in the rising sun for very existence, while two of their largest galleons the "Sans Felipa" and "Matteo," were caught on the Dutch Flats, and a prey to the Zealanders.

Before the English could bear down to take advantage of their disabled enemy, one of their monster ships, the "Admiral Galeass," commanded by Hugo de Moncada, which had lost her stern posts and rudder, was seen drifting and rolling about at random, alone, and the apparent sport of every wave.

No sooner was her situation understood by the English, when from every direction ships of all size and rig were seen dashing through the water in the hope of capturing so rich a prize.

Raleigh and Frobisher laid their ships alongside the Spaniard at the same time, and, without pausing to fire a shot, boarded her from the opposite bows.

Moncada, irritated by the ill success of the expedition, and enraged by the helpless state of his ship, became maddened by the insolence and audacity of the English in daring to board his ship without a previous bombardment, and called on his crew—the "Galeass" was swarming with men—to stand by him for the honour of Castile and manhood, and teach these heretics that Spain was not to be trifled with.

A thousand voices shouted a glad response to the courageous Moncada's appeal, and the next moment the murderous contest began.

Inch by inch the Spaniards disputed their deck, leaving a line of dead to mark their slow retreat. At length the heroic Moncada fell; then the crew at once threw down their arms, and the "Admiral Galeass" became an English prize.

The action on board this ship was one of the most sanguinary and obstinate in the whole expedition.

While this brief, but sharp, conflict was taking place on board the "Galeass," the rest of the English fleet were not idle, but each ship selecting an enemy began a running fight, the weather alone, which was hourly becoming more boisterous, preventing the English from boarding.

By this time it had become apparent that the intention for which these preparations were made by the Spaniards was entirely frustrated. The vessels provided by the Duke of Parma were made for transporting soldiers, not for fighting; and that general, when urged to leave the harbour, positively refused to expose his flourishing army to such apparent hazard, while the English were not only able to keep the sea, but seemed even to triumph over their enemy.

The Spanish admiral found, after these rencontres, that while he lost so considerable a part of his own navy, he had destroyed only one small vessel of the English, and he foresaw that by continuing so unequal a combat he must draw inevitable destruction on all the remainder.

He prepared, therefore, to return homewards; but as the wind was contrary to his passage through the Channel, of which the English fleet was in possession, he resolved to sail northwards, and making the tour of the island, reach the Spanish harbours by the Atlantic Ocean.

The English fleet followed him for some time, and had not their ammunition fallen short, by the negligence of those who should have supplied them, they would have obliged the whole Armada to surrender at discretion. The Duke of Medina had once taken that resolution, but was diverted from it by the advice of his confessor.

This conclusion of the enterprise would have been more glorious to the English, but the event proved almost equally fatal to the Spaniards. A violent storm overtook the Armada after it passed the Orkneys; the ships had already lost their anchors, and were obliged to keep to sea; the mariners, unaccustomed to such hardships, and not able to govern such unwieldy vessels, yielded to the fury of the storm, and allowed their ships to drive either on the western isles of Scotland, or on to the coast of Ireland, where they were miserably wrecked.

Not a half of the navy returned to Spain; and the seamen as well as soldiers who remained, were so overcome with hardships and fatigue, and so dispirited by their discomfiture, that they filled all Spain with accounts of the desperate valour of the English, and of the tempestuous violence of that ocean which surrounds them.

Seven hundred of the soldiers and mariners, who had escaped to land in the King of Scotland's dominions, were sent to the Duke of Parma with Elizabeth's consent; but all those who were wrecked and got ashore in Ireland were either slaughtered or hanged, the lord-deputy, by whose orders it was done, fearing they would join with the rebels; at least, this was a pretence to excuse his barbarity.

Of the Armada were taken and destroyed in July and August fifteen great ships, and 4,791 men in the fight between the English and the Spanish navies in the Channel; and on the coast of Ireland in September, seventeen ships, and 5,394 men. In all, 32 ships, and 10,185 men.

The following anecdote connected with the wreck of one of the Spanish ships on the eastern coast of Scotland, as it shows in a good light the humanity of King James to an enemy he had almost as much reason to fear as Elizabeth, is worthy of a place in this history, especially when we remember that only a year had passed since the execution of his mother by order of the woman whose interest he now supported by closing his ports to her enemy.

"After the dispersion and destruction of the Spanish Armada in 1588, Joan Comes de Medina, who had commanded twenty ships, was, with about 260 men, driven in a vessel to Anstruther in Scotland, after suffering great hunger and cold for six or seven days.

"Notwithstanding the object for which this fleet had been sent, and the oppresive conduct of the Spaniards to the Scottish merchants who traded with them, these men were most humanely treated. Mr. James Melvil, the minister, told the Spanish officer first sent on shore that they would find nothing among them but Christianity and works of mercy. The Laird of Anstruther, and a great number of the neighbouring gentlemen, entertained the officers, while the inhabitants gave the mariners and soldiers kail pottage and fish; the minister having addressed his flock as Elijah did the King of Israel in Samaria, "Give them bread and water."

PORTRAIT OF SIR FRANCIS DRAKE.

Such was the miserable conclusion of an enterprise which had been preparing for three years, which had exhausted the revenue of Spain, and had long filled all Europe with anxiety or expectation.

Philip, who was a slave to his ambition, but had an entire command over his countenance, no sooner heard of the mortifying event which blasted all his hopes, than he fell on his knees, and, rendering thanks for that gracious dispensation of Providence, expressed his joy that the misfortune was not greater. The Spanish priests, who had so often blessed this holy crusade, and foretold its infallible success, were somewhat at a loss to account for the victory gained over a Catholic monarch by excommunicated heretics and an execrable usurper; but they at last discovered that all the calamities of the Spaniards had proceeded from their allowing infidel Moors to live among them.

There can be no doubt that up to the time the Armada anchored in Calais Roads, the Spaniards believed they had effected a triumph, as on that day the Duke of Medina despatched a vessel with such information to the Court at Madrid; and the news spread generally that the Armada had been crowned with victory.

The rejoicing in England for so signal a deliverance was profound and universal. Elizabeth went in state to St. Paul's to return thanks; Lord Effingham received a pension for life, and all the chief officers of the fleet were rewarded with honours, or received the thanks of the queen.

Several pieces of money were coined to com-

memorate this victory. On one piece was a representation of a fleet flying under full sail, and the words—
"*Venit, vidit, fugit*"—"It came, it saw, it fled."

The Dutch on the occasion had a large medal struck, on which was represented the Spanish fleet with the words—
"*Flavit Jehovah, et dissipati sunt*, 1588"—"Jehovah blew and they were scattered."

CHAPTER IX.

EXPEDITION TO PORTUGAL—HEROIC DEATH OF SIR RICHARD GRENVILLE.

AS Elizabeth, freed for the present from all apprehension on the side of Spain, as far as an invasion of her dominions was concerned, had no idea of letting an enemy who had caused her so much anxiety, escape with one disaster, however crushing

granted a commission to Sir Francis Drake and Sir John Norris to raise soldiers and sailors, and to equip a fleet at their own expense, to war on the Spaniards wherever they could find them, insuring herself a royalty out of the plunder they were expected to bring home.

THE SPANISH ARMADA (*from tapestry destroyed in the old House of Lords*).

that might have been, she resolved to attack him where he was most vulnerable, and where the spoil, if not the glory, would be infinitely greater, namely, on the Spanish Main.

With her usual prudence and forethought, Elizabeth saw that by carrying on a desultory war with Philip in the West Indies, and intercepting his annual treasure-ships, or plate-fleets, as they were then called, she might not only greatly benefit her own exchequer, but enrich, while she employed, her subjects.

Having once conceived this idea, she carried it out with a spirit of frugality and economy that we can hardly regard at this time without a smile. Her first act was to let loose on the Spaniards all the fiery and adventurous spirits of her kingdom, armed with roving commissions to burn, pillage, and destroy the enemy and his property wherever found.

Then, to give a national importance to these expeditions, in which, without incurring any expense, she insured herself a share of all the gains, she

Volunteers, both in men and ships, flocked in to Drake from all parts the moment the news of his intended expedition got wind, and he soon found himself in command of a flotilla of a hundred sail, vessels of all size.

A design was formed among these adventurers, though not with the sanction of Elizabeth, to conquer from Spain the kingdom of Portugal for Don Antonio, one of the royal line of that country; and, with this object in view, the expedition set sail in the April of 1589.

Sir Francis Drake and Sir John Norris were the leaders of this romantic enterprise; near twenty thousand volunteers enlisted themselves in the service, and ships were hired, as well as arms provided, at the charge of the adventurers. The queen contributed sixty thousand pounds to the expense, but only allowed six of her ships of war to attend the expedition.

There was more spirit and bravery than foresight or prudence in the conduct of this enterprise. The small capital of the adventurers did not enable them to buy provisions or ammunition sufficient for such an undertaking; they even wanted vessels to stow away the numerous volunteers who crowded to them, and they were obliged to seize by force some ships of the Hanse Towns which they met with at sea, an expedient which set them somewhat more at ease in point of room for their men, but did not remedy the deficiency of their provisions.

Had they sailed directly to Portugal, it is believed that the good-will of the people, joined to the defenceless state of the country, might have ensured them success; but, hearing that great preparations were making at the Groine for the invasion of England, they were induced to go there and destroy this new armament of Spain.

They broke into the harbour, burned some ships of war, particularly one commanded by Recalde, vice-admiral of Spain; they defeated an army of four or five thousand men which was assembled to oppose them; they assaulted the Groine, and took the lower town, which they pillaged, and they would have taken the higher, though well fortified, had they not found their ammunition and provisions beginning to fail them.

The young Earl of Essex, a nobleman of promising hopes, fired with the thirst of military honour, who had, unknown to the queen, stolen from England, here joined the adventurers, and it was then agreed by common consent to make sail for Portugal, the main object of their enterprise.

The English landed at Paniche, a sea-port town twelve leagues from Lisbon, and Norris led the army to that capital, while Drake undertook to sail up the river, and then attack the city with their united sea and land forces.

By this time the Court of Spain had leisure to prepare against the invasion. Forces were thrown into Lisbon; the Portuguese were disarmed, all suspected persons were taken into custody, and thus, though the inhabitants bore great affection to Don Antonio, none of them durst declare in favour of the invaders.

The English army, however, made themselves masters of the suburbs, which abounded with riches of all kinds; but as they desired to conciliate the affection of the Portuguese, and were more intent on honour than profit, they observed a strict discipline, and abstained from all plunder.

Meanwhile they found they had no siege artillery to make a breach in the walls; the admiral had not been able to pass some fortresses that guarded the river; there was no appearance of an insurrection in their favour, sickness from fatigue, hunger, and intemperance in wine and fruits, had seized the army, so that it was found necessary to make all possible haste to re-embark.

They were not pursued by the enemy, and finding at the mouth of the river sixty ships laden with naval stores, they seized them as lawful prizes, though they belonged to the Hanse Towns, a neutral power. They sailed thence to Vigo, which they took and burned, and having ravaged the country around, returned to England.

Above half of these gallant adventurers perished by sickness, famine, fatigue, and the sword, and England reaped more honour than profit from this extraordinary enterprise. It is computed that eleven hundred gentlemen embarked on board the fleet, and that only three hundred and fifty survived.

When these ships were on their voyage homewards, they met with the Earl of Cumberland, who was outward bound with seven sail, all equipped at his own charge, except one ship of war which the queen had lent him.

That nobleman supplied Sir Francis Drake with some provisions, a generosity which saved the lives of many of Drake's men, but for which the others afterwards suffered severely.

Cumberland sailed towards the Terceras, and took several prizes from the enemy; but the richest, valued at a hundred thousand pounds, perished in her return with all her cargo near St. Michael's Mount, in Cornwall.

Many of these adventurers were killed in a rash attempt at the Terceras; a great mortality seized the rest, and it was with difficulty that the few hands which remained were able to steer the ship back into harbour.

Philip was now the sole enemy Elizabeth had to fear, and to secure herself from all surprise, she took just, though very expensive, precautions.

She had constantly a stout and well-conditioned navy ready to put to sea on the shortest notice. The fortified towns and maritime ports were also in good condition, and this cost her as much as if she had been at actual war with Spain; but she supplied all by her excellent economy, expending no money but what was absolutely necessary.

We are now about to narrate one of the most chivalrous and determined feats of bravery ever recorded in the annals of Naval History, and to show our readers how their ancestors, despising overwhelming odds, would sooner embrace death than strike to an enemy.

In the year 1590, Elizabeth still directed much of her naval strength against Philip, and this year exerted all her power to intercept his West Indian treasures, the source of that greatness which rendered him so formidable to all his neighbours.

She sent a squadron of seven ships, under the command of Lord Thomas Howard, for this service; but the King of Spain, informed of her purpose, fitted out a great force of fifty-five sail, and despatched them to escort the Indian fleet.

They fell in with the English squadron, and by the courageous obstinacy of Sir Richard Grenville, the vice-admiral, who refused to make his escape by flight, they took one vessel, the first English ship of war that had yet fallen into the hands of the Spaniards.

Grenville had been engaged alone with the whole Spanish fleet of fifty-three sail, which had ten thousand men on board; and from the time the fight began, which was about three in the afternoon, to the break of day the following morning, he repulsed the enemy fifteen times, though they continually endeavoured to board with fresh men.

In the beginning of the action he received a wound, but he continued doing his duty on deck till eleven at night, when receiving a fresh wound, he was carried below to have it dressed. At this time he had lost all his spars and rigging, the ship was riddled with shot, and rocked like a sheer hulk on the water.

During the dressing of his wounds he received a shot in the head, and the surgeon was killed by his side.

The English began now to want powder; all their small arms were broken or become useless, and out of the men, who at first numbered but a hundred and three, forty were killed, and almost all the rest wounded; all their masts were shot away, their tackle cut in pieces, and nothing was left but a hulk, unable to move one way or the other.

In this situation Sir Richard proposed to the ship's company to trust to the mercy of God, not to that of the Spaniards, and by snapping a pistol in the magazine destroy the ship with themselves rather than strike to the enemy.

The master gunner and many of the seamen agreed to this desperate resolution, but others opposed it, and obliged Grenville to surrender himself a prisoner.

He died a few days after, and his last words were—

"Here die I, Richard Grenville, with a joyful and quiet mind, for that I have ended my life as a true soldier ought to do, fighting for his country, queen, religion, and honour, my soul willingly departing from this body, leaving behind me the lasting fame of having behaved as every valiant Englishman is in his duty bound to do."

The Spaniards lost in this sharp but unequal action four ships, and about a thousand men. Grenville's vessel, the "Revenge," foundered soon after with a prize crew of two hundred Spaniards on board.

The rest of the squadron returned safely into England, frustrated of their expectations; but pleasing themselves with the idea that their attempts had not been altogether fruitless in injuring the enemy.

The Indian fleet had been so long detained in the Havanna through fear of the English, that they were obliged at last to set sail in an improper season, and most of them perished from shipwreck ere they reached the Spanish harbours. The Earl of Cumberland made a like unsuccessful enterprise against the Spanish trade. He carried out one ship of the queen's and seven others equipped at his own expense, but the prizes which he made did not compensate the charges.

Occasional disasters seemed rather to stimulate than depress the appetite of the nation for deeds of excitement and daring; and the spirit of these expensive and hazardous adventures was very prevalent in England.

Sir Walter Raleigh, who had enjoyed great favour with the queen, finding his interest decline, determined to recover her good graces by some important undertaking, and as his reputation was high among his countrymen, he persuaded great numbers to engage with him as volunteers in an attempt on the West Indies.

The fleet was detained so long in the channel by contrary winds that the season was lost. Raleigh was recalled by the queen, Sir Martin Frobisher succeeded to the command, and made a privateering voyage against the Spaniards.

He took one rich carrack near the Island of Flores, and destroyed another.

About the same time Thomas White, a Londoner, took two Spanish ships, which, besides fourteen hundred chests of quicksilver, contained about two millions of Papal bulls for indulgences, a commodity useless to the English, but which had cost the King of Spain three hundred thousand florins, and would have been sold by him in the Indies for five millions.

Though Elizabeth, at a considerable expense of blood and treasure, made war against Philip in France and the Low Countries, the most severe blows which she gave him were by those naval enterprises which either she or her subjects scarcely ever intermitted during one season.

In 1594, Richard Hawkins, son of Sir John, the famous navigator, procured the queen's commission, and sailed with three ships to the South Sea, by the Straits of Magellan; but his voyage proved unfortunate, and he was taken prisoner on the coast of Chili.

James Lancaster was supplied the same year with three ships and a pinnace by the merchants of London, and was more fortunate in his adventure. He took thirty-nine ships of the enemy; and, not content with this success, he made an attack on Pernambuco in Brazil, where he knew great treasures were at that time lodged.

As he approached the shore, he saw it lined with great numbers of the enemy; but, nowise daunted at this appearance, he placed the stoutest of his men in boats, and ordered them to row with such violence on the landing place as to split them in pieces.

By this bold action he both deprived his men of all resource but in victory, and terrified the enemy, who fled, after a short resistance. He returned home with the treasures which he had so bravely acquired.

In 1595, Sir Walter Raleigh, who had again forfeited the queen's friendship by an intrigue with a maid of honour, and who had been thrown into prison for this misdemeanour, no sooner recovered his liberty, than he was pushed by his active and enterprising genius to attempt some great action.

The success of the first Spanish adventurers against Mexico and Peru had begotten an extreme avidity in Europe, and a general idea prevailed that in the inland parts of South America, called Giuana, a country as yet undiscovered, there were mines and treasures far exceeding any which Cortes or Pizzaro had met with.

Raleigh, whose turn of mind was somewhat romantic and extravagant, undertook, at his own charge, the discovery of this wonderful country. Having taken the small town of St. Joseph in the isle of Trinidado, where he found no riches, he left his ship and sailed up the river Oronoko, in pinnaces, but without meeting with anything to answer his expectations.

On his return he published an account of that country, full of the grossest and most palpable lies that were ever attempted to be imposed on the credulity of mankind.

We now approach the period when two of the most illustrious men of the Elizabethan era were about to close their long and glorious career, the success that had gilded their early years of adventure being clouded in shadow and disappointment.

In the year 1595 Sir Francis Drake and Sir John Hawkins undertook a more important expedition against the Spanish settlements in America; and they carried with them six ships of the queen's and twenty more, which either were fitted out at their own charge or were furnished them by private adventurers. Sir Thomas Baskerville was appointed commander of the land forces, which they carried aboard.

Their first design was to attempt Porto Rico, where they knew a rich carrack was at that time stationed, but as they had not preserved the requisite secresy, a pinnace having strayed from the fleet was taken by the Spaniards, and betrayed the intentions of the English.

Preparations were made in that island for their reception, and the English fleet, notwithstanding the brave assault which they made on the enemy, was repulsed with loss. Hawkins soon after died, and Drake pursued his voyage to Nombre-di-Dios on the isthmus of Darien, where, having landed his men, he attempted to pass forward to Panama, with a view of plundering that place, or, if he found such a scheme practicable, of keeping and fortifying it.

But he did not meet with the same facility which had attended his first enterprises in those parts. The Spaniards, taught by experience, had everywhere fortified the passes, and had stationed troops in the woods, who so infested the English by continual alarms and skirmishes, that they were obliged to return, without being able to effect anything.

Drake himself, from the intemperance of the climate, the fatigues of the journey, and the vexation of his disappointment, was seized with a distemper of which he soon after died.

A contemporary poet wrote of his funeral:—

"The waves became his winding sheet,
The waters were his tomb,
But for his fame the ocean sea
Was not sufficient room."

Sir Thomas Baskerville took the command of the fleet, which was in a weak condition; and after having fought a battle near Cuba, with a Spanish fleet, of which the event was not decisive, he returned to England. The Spaniards, it is true, suffered some loss, but the English reaped no profit.

Hawkins, as we have seen, had been in the African slave trade, and is said to have been the first who introduced African slaves into an English colony. There was nothing at that time considered dishonourable in this unnatural traffic; indeed, Sir John Hawkins, who, we have shown, was knighted for his gallant services against the Armada, was rather proud of his achievement, and had a crest granted for this performance, namely, a crest with deminegro, manacled.

Sir John possessed much personal courage and great presence of mind, was submissive to those above him, and courteous to his inferiors. He died in 1595, it is said from grief and mortification at his want of success in the expedition with Drake against the Spanish West Indies.

The following account of the commencement of the slave trade is taken chiefly from Hakluyt, and, as showing the unscrupulous conduct of those engaged in this abominable pursuit, with the perils and difficulties of the undertaking, is, at this date, fully worthy of record.

"A small squadron was fitted out in 1562 by Captain John Hawkins, with which he sailed to the coast of Guinea, and commenced the inhuman traffic in slaves."

The following note upon his first expedition is from Hakluyt:—

"He departed from the coast of England in the month of October, 1562, and in his course touched first at Teneriffe, where he received friendly entertainment. From thence he passed to Sierra Leone upon the coast of Guinea, which place by the people of the country is called Tigarin, where he stayed some good time, and got into his possession, partly by the sworde, and partly by other means, to the number of 300 negroes at the least, besides other merchandises which that country yieldeth.

"With this praye, he sayled over the ocean sea, unto the land of Hispaniola, and arrived first at the port of Isabella; and there he had reasonable utterance of his English commodities, as also of some part of his negroes, trusting the Spaniards no further than that by his own strength he was able still to master them.

"From the port of Isabella he went to Puerto de Plata, where he made like sales, standing always upon his guard; from thence also he sailed to

Monte Christi, another port on the north side of Hispaniola, and the last place of his touching, where he had peaceable traffique, and made vent of the whole number of his negroes, for which he received in those three places, by way of exchange, such quantity of merchandise, that hee did not only lade his own 3 shipps with hides, ginger, sugars, and expedition which commenced that awful traffic, which will ever remain as a dark spot upon our history, was named the "Jesus," and of this vessel Hawkins was the captain. In his own account of the second expedition, which sailed in 1564, he frankly says—

"In this island we stayed certaine daies, going

INTERVIEW BETWEEN KING JAMES AND THE SPANISH AMBASSADOR.

some quantities of pearles, but he freighted also two other hulks with hides and other like commodities, which hee sent into Spaine.

"And thus leaving the island, hee returned and disembarked, passing out by the islands of the Laycos, without further entering into the bay of Mexico in this his first voyage to the West India. And so, with prosperous successe, and much gaine to himselfe and the aforesayde adventurers, hee came home, and arrived in the month of September, 1563."

It is remarkable that the principal ship of the every day on shore to take the inhabitants with burning and spoiling their towns."

In his account of "the third troublesome voyage made with the 'Jesus,' and foure other ships," he says—

"But even in that present instant there came to us a negro, sent from a king oppressed by other kings, his neighbours, desiring our aide, with a promise that as many negroes as by these warres might be obtained as well of his part as of ours, should be at our pleasure.

"Whereupon we concluded to give aide, and sent

120 of our men, which the 15th of Januarie assaulted a towne of the negroes of our allies' adversaries, which had in it 8,000 inhabitants, being very strongly impaled and fenced after their manner, but it was so well defended that our men prevailed not, but lost five men and fortie hurt, so that our men sent forthwith to me for more help.

"Whereupon, considering that the good success of this enterprise might highly further the commoditie of our voyage, I went myselfe, and with the help of the king of our side, assaulted the towne both by land and sea, and very hardly with fire (their houses being covered with dry palm leaves) obtained the towne and put the inhabitants to flight. We tooke 250 persons, men, women, and children and by our friend the king on our side, there were taken 600 prisoners, whereof we hoped to have our choise; but the negro (in which nation is seldom or ever found truth) meant nothing less, for that night he removed his camp and prisoners, so that we were faine to content us with those few which we had gotten ourselves."

CHAPTER X.

EXPEDITIONS UNDER ESSEX AND RALEIGH—BOMBARDMENT AND DESTRUCTION OF CADIZ.

IF we were to attempt to give an account of all the daring adventurers, who, in the reign of Queen Elizabeth, fitted out expeditions at their own expense, and on their sole responsibility waged war against the common enemy, we should swell our work to a weary and unbecoming length.

Of these adventurers, after Drake, Hawkins and Frobisher, the most illustrious were Raleigh, Carew, James Lancaster, Sir Conyers Clifford, Sir Francis Vere, and Lord Thomas Howard.

Several of these piratical adventurers on the Spanish main and the coasts of Chili and Peru, having signally failed, the speculators in some instances not realising their expenses, Elizabeth resolved to take the matter into her own hands.

It was evident the enemy was now fully on his guard, and on the watch for his unprincipled and persistent foe.

This was so much the case that for the last two seasons the English had been signally unfortunate in all their expeditions.

Elizabeth accordingly resolved to attack the Spaniards where they least expected an enemy, namely, in their homes in Europe.

Accordingly she fitted out a fleet of over 150 ships, of which 17 were vessels of the Royal Navy, 22 Low Country ships (*i.e.* from Holland), the rest provision ships, transports and pinnaces. On board these vessels were embarked 6,360 soldiers in pay, 1,000 volunteers willing to serve for glory, and perhaps plunder, 6,772 seamen, besides a number of Dutchmen.

Robert Earl of Essex, and Charles Lord Howard, Lord Admiral of England, were commanders-in-chief of this expedition, having been at great expense in procuring men and ships. Their authority was equal, yet so arranged that Howard should have principal rule at sea, while Essex governed the land forces.

These had associated with them as a military and naval council, Lord Thomas Howard, Sir Walter Raleigh, Sir Francis Vere, Sir George Carew, and Sir Conyers Clifford.

The fleet was divided into four squadrons, the first being commanded by the Lord Admiral Howard, the second by the Earl of Essex, the third by Lord Thomas Howard, and the fourth by the world-renowned Sir Walter Raleigh.

The Dutch vessels were commanded by Lord Van Duyvenvoord, a naval officer of some renown; while the soldiers from the Low Countries were under the orders of Count Louis of Nassau.

The whole number of soldiers, English, Dutch, and volunteers amounted to 10,000; Essex having under him Robert Earl of Sussex, Sir John Wingfield, Sir Christopher Blunt, and many other noted leaders.

Sir Edward Wingfield, brother of the above, was captain of the volunteers, and Anthony Ashley (ancestor of the present Earl of Shaftesbury), was secretary at war, in which capacity he accompanied the expedition.

When all was ready some fainted-hearted politicians objected to the departure of the fleet lest England should be attacked in its absence; but Elizabeth was not to be turned aside from her purpose.

She had a special form of prayer prepared for use on board; but the chaplains being mostly Puritans, did not make much use of it.

The fleet set sail on the 1st June, 1596; and meeting with a fair wind, bent its course to Cadiz, at which place, by sealed orders delivered to all the captains, the general rendezvous was appointed.

They sent before them some armed tenders, which intercepted every ship that could carry intelligence to the enemy, and they themselves were so fortunate when they came near Cadiz, as to take an Irish vessel, by which they learned that the inhabitants of Cadiz felt perfectly secure, that not a word had been heard there of the coming of the English fleet, and that there were no forces there except a small garrison. He then went on to tell his hearers—who little cared what number of Spaniards might be opposed to them—that in the bay were twenty galleys, and about fifty sail of other ships, four or five of which were of the set of great galleons known as the Twelve Apostles; there were also two galleasses, three frigates, two Levantine vessels, described as huge hulks, two ships of Biscay, and many merchant vessels richly laden, some bound for the Indies, and some for other places.

The Earl of Essex, who had come on board the "Ark" (the lord admiral's vessel) to hear what the Irishman had to say, is reported by an old historian to have been "eager to come up with this booty;" so the lord admiral immediately hoisted the standard of Old England on board his ship, and the fleet made the best of its way to Cadiz, where it arrived on the 26th of June in the morning to the great surprise of the Spaniards, who had retired to rest the previous night without the least expectation of receiving such a visit.

The English commanders cast anchor near St. Sebastian's chapel, on the west side of the island of Leon, and the impatient Essex was for landing at once; but Lord Admiral Howard and Sir Walter Raleigh did not deem it prudent.

However, after some discussion, they yielded to his wishes, and an attempt was made which did not succeed through the sea beating so violently on the shore.

Then the earl urged an immediate attack on the Spanish men-of-war and merchant ships, but this was also deemed hazardous, as they were under the protection of some powerful land fortifications; so nothing was done that day.

The next morning, as the tide came in, the Spaniards removed their men-of-war to a point of land called the Puntal, the merchant ships being sent more forward towards Port Royal.

The English immediately weighed anchor, and shifted into the position just vacated by the Spaniards, and were subjected to a furious cannonade from Fort St. Philip on the one side, and the enemy's galleys on the other. A brief consultation among the leaders resulted in a resolution to attack the Spanish ships, which so delighted the fiery Earl of Essex, that he threw his hat in the air for joy.

The officers selected for this task, were Lord Thomas Howard, Sir Francis Vere, Raleigh and Sir George Carew; Captain Alexander Clifford in the "Dreadnought," the "Alcedo of London," and some smaller vessels, the commanders not deeming it prudent to risk their large vessels in the narrow shallow channel that had to be passed.

Raleigh led the way in the "Warspite," and in the middle of the channel directed the prow of his vessel against the Spanish men-of-war, who fell back, while Sir Francis Vere directed his guns against the Spanish galleys, which, being protected by the town forts, returned the fire till Essex came to his assistance, when they fled, keeping along the shore till they came to the bridge which joined the island of St. Leon with the mainland. On this bridge stood some powerful engines which hoisted the galleys over into the open sea.*

Sir John Wingfield in the "Vanguard," succeeded in stopping two or three of the vessels about to be hoisted thus.

The Spanish men-of-war at the Puntal kept their broadsides towards the English ships, which were prevented from getting very near by the lowness of the water.

However, when the tide was nearly at flood, they pushed forward. Essex thrust himself into the thick of the fight, according to his usual custom, and the lord admiral, with his son, Lord William Howard of Effingham, passed from the "Ark" into a smaller vessel to take part in this action.

From nearly break of day till noon the fight continued furiously, when the Spaniards, finding that they were getting the worst of it, resolved to run their ships aground and burn them. This being done, their sailors began to jump overboard; some of them were fortunate enough to reach shore, but many of them were drowned, and others were saved and taken prisoners by Howard, who sent boats to pick them up.

The Spanish admiral's ship, the "St. Philip," of 1,500 tons, was burnt, with one or two other vessels which happened to be near her. Two of the Twelve Apostles, namely, the "St. Matthew" and the "St. Andrew," were taken and sent to England, while the English fired the "St. Thomas" and the "St. Juan," and many other vessels of less renown.

Sea fighting was now nearly at an end for lack of enemies to dispute the progress of the English fleet, so the Earl of Essex landed with 800 men at the Puntal, about a league from the town of Cadiz.

As soon as the soldiers were safely on shore, Sir Christopher Blunt marched to the bridge before mentioned (the Puente de Suaco) to stop the Spaniards from sending reinforcements to the Isle of St. Leon, and also to destroy the engine that had so greatly aided the escape of their galleys; Essex drove back a force of 500 cavalry and 600 foot, and pursued them so rapidly that they had not time to close the gates of the town, so that the English entered with the fugitives, while some of the Spaniards, by climbing over the walls, showed the English the way to do the same.

In the meantime Lord Admiral Howard had landed 1,200 more men, and hastened to the assistance of Essex, who was fighting in the streets of Cadiz; but as soon as Howard entered the place, the Spaniards fled to the castle and the Civalda, or town-hall, adjoining.

About this time Sir John Wingfield received a shot in the head which killed him almost instantly. Before night the Civalda was taken, and there the

---

* So says Stowe, who professes to have been told so by a gentleman who served in the action.

admiral and Essex lodged that night. Next morning the castle and Fort St. Philip surrendered, and thus the English became masters of the city.

The terms on which the civic authorities yielded were that they should be spared their lives and their wearing apparel, and pay for ransom 520,000 ducats, the rest of their goods and wealth to be spoil and pillage for the soldiers.

Forty of the chief inhabitants were delivered up to the English, who sent them to England and kept them as hostages till the ransom was paid.

Then Essex sent away a number of boats, barges, and pinnaces filled with the better class of inhabitants. The ladies were permitted to take their jewels and as much clothing as they could wear; and, to make sure that no insult was offered by the English or Dutch, Essex and Howard themselves stood at the water-gates and saw them safely embarked.

The Bishop of Cusco was among those who thus departed; no ransom was demanded for him, as he had promised to send the lord admiral a fine horse—which promise, however, he forgot to perform.

Howard then ordered the smaller ships of his fleet to sail to Port Royal to capture or destroy such of the Spanish vessels as had escaped.

The Spaniards offered two millions of ducats to be allowed to keep those ships and their cargoes; an offer which Essex was inclined to accept, for it seemed that such a great treasure would be of far greater advantage than the mere wanton destruction of shipping; but Howard thought to the contrary, being willing to take ransom for the cargoes, but not for the ships.

The Duke of Medina Sidonia, the Spanish admiral, put an end to this controversy by ordering all the ships to be burned. However, the English hastened to the spot so quickly that, although they were not in time to preserve the vessels, they saved a large quantity of merchandize and many guns.

Thus the whole of the Spanish fleet in Cadiz and the neighbouring ports was either taken, sunk, or burnt.

An immense quantity of treasure was taken; but the losses that touched the King of Spain most were 1,200 pieces of artillery either captured or sunk, and arms for 6,000 men were taken from his arsenal. Three well-informed men, Don Pedro de Castilla, the king's judge, Don Juan de Sola, a sea officer, and Signor Fantanco, a Florentine merchant residing at Cadiz, estimated the treasure captured at twenty millions of ducats.

THE "GREAT HARRY."

On Sunday, June 27, the chiefs of the army and navy went to the church of San Francesco and heard a sermon, which was probably the first Protestant sermon preached in Spain till the English became masters of Gibraltar many years later.* Afterwards, the honour of knighthood was conferred upon several of the gentlemen of the army and navy who had distinguished themselves; Count Louis of Nassau, Anthony Ashley, and Van Duyvenvoord, the Dutchman, being among those so honoured.

The city of Cadiz, having been thoroughly sacked, was set on fire, the forts were blown up, and then, an agreement for exchange of prisoners having been executed between the English and Spanish admirals, the invading fleet sailed away, and next cast anchor before a place called Faro (probably Ferrol). Howard sent Sir Francis Preston, Sir William Mounson, or Monson,† and Captain William Morgan, to ascend

---

* Vide Oldmixon's History of England.

† Monson was one of the newly-made knights. To his account of this war we are indebted for much of the information now laid before the reader.

the river in boats, and find out if possible what forces were opposed to them.

Faro was found to be deserted, so Essex landed some men, and marched into the town, where the only plunder of value he could discover was the library in the bishop's palace, valued at 1,000 marks.

Captain Priest was sent with a strong detachment to scour the country; he burnt a village about seven miles from Faro, and brought away a hundred head of cattle, a supply of fresh food very acceptable to all.

Then they hoisted sail again, and reached Cape St. Vincent (many years afterwards the scene of a great English victory), where they were overtaken by a furious north wind, which drove them a great distance out to sea; a council of war was then held to consider a proposition made by Essex that they should sail to the Azores, and there wait for the South American plate fleet.

Finding the others opposed to this, Essex volunteered to take two of the queen's ships, and ten others, and perform the exploit by himself; but again he was overruled. He then prevailed on them to go to the Groyne, where he would have landed and assaulted the town, but that was not agreed to.

The other leaders, finding it almost impossible to drag this fiery warrior away from the foe, eventually left him on the Spanish coast with a very slender force.

The fleet reached Plymouth on the 7th and 8th of August, not having been more than three months engaged in this great enterprise, which, for a second time, completely smashed the maritime power of Spain. Essex was soon glad to follow them.

He complained much to the queen of their want of spirit in this enterprise; nor was she pleased that they had returned without attempting to intercept the Indian fleet; but the great success in the enterprise of Cadiz had covered all their miscarriages; and the queen, though she admired the daring bravery of Essex, could not forbear expressing an esteem for the other officers.

The admiral was created Earl of Nottingham, and his promotion gave great disgust to Essex. In the preamble of the patent it was said that the new dignity was conferred on him on account of his good services in taking Cadiz and destroying the Spanish ships, a merit which Essex pretended to belong wholly to himself, and he offered to maintain this plea by single combat against the Earl of Nottingham, or his sons, or any of his kindred.

Another powerful fleet was fitted out the following year, the supreme command of fleet and army being this time conferred on Essex, with Lord Howard and Sir Walter Raleigh to act as his vice-admirals.

This expedition had two objects in view; the destruction of the enemy's shipping in the ports of Spain, and the capture of the Indian fleet with all the treasure ships on its homeward voyage.

PORTRAIT OF SIR WALTER RALEIGH.

This fleet set sail from Plymouth early in July, but was no sooner out of harbour than they met with a furious storm, which shattered and dispersed them, and before they could be refitted, Essex found that their provisions were so far spent that it would not be safe to carry so numerous an army along with him.

He dismissed, therefore, all the soldiers, except the thousand veterans under Vere, and, laying aside all thoughts of attacking Ferrol or the Groyne, he confined the object of his expedition to the intercepting of the Indian fleet, which had at first been considered as the second enterprise which he was to attempt.

The Indian fleet in that age, by reason of the imperfection of navigation, had a stated course as well as season both on their going out and in their return; and there were certain islands, at which, as at fixed stages, they always touched, to take in water and provisions.

The Azores being one of these places where about this time the fleet was expected, Essex bent his course thither, and he informed Raleigh that he, on his arrival, intended to attack Fayal, one of these islands.

By some accident the squadrons were separated, and Raleigh, arriving first before Fayal, thought it more prudent, after waiting some time for the general, to begin the attack alone, lest the inhabitants should, by farther delay, have leisure to make preparations for their defence.

He succeeded in the enterprise; but Essex, jealous of Raleigh, expressed great displeasure at his conduct, and construed it into an intention of robbing the general of the glory that attended that action;

he therefore cashiered Sydney, Berry, and others, who had concurred in the attempt, and would have proceeded to inflict the same punishment on Raleigh himself.

Lord Thomas Howard, however, interposed with his good offices, and persuaded Raleigh, who was high spirited, to make submissions to the general. Essex, who was placable as well as hasty and passionate, was soon appeased, and both received Raleigh into favour, and restored the other officers to their commands.

This incident, however, though the quarrel was seemingly accommodated, laid the first foundation of that violent animosity which afterwards took place between these two gallant commanders.

Essex next made a proper disposition for intercepting the Indian galleons, and Sir William Monson, whose station was the most remote of the fleet, having fallen in with them, made the signals which had been agreed on.

That able officer, in his memoirs, ascribes Essex's failure, when he was so near attaining so mighty an advantage, to his want of experience in seamanship, and the account which he gives of the errors committed by that nobleman appears very reasonable as well as candid.

The Spanish fleet, finding that the enemy was upon them, made all the sail possible to the Terceras, and got into the safe and well-fortified harbour of Angra before the English fleet could overtake them.

Essex intercepted only three ships, which, however, were so rich as to repay all the charges of the expedition.

This was the last naval enterprise of any importance that occurred during the few remaining years of Elizabeth's reign.

Private adventures, or, more properly speaking, piratical speculations, were still carried on by the English against the Spanish possessions in America, and to the last days of Elizabeth's life ships were coming home from thence loaded more or less with plunder.

Queen Elizabeth, sensible how much the defence of her kingdom depended on its naval power, was desirous to encourage commerce and navigation, but as her monopolies tended to extinguish all domestic industry, which is much more valuable than foreign trade, and is the foundation of it, the general train of her conduct was ill calculated to serve the purpose at which she aimed, much less to promote the riches of her people.

The exclusive companies also were an immediate check on foreign trade. Yet notwithstanding these discouragements the spirit of the age was strongly bent on naval enterprises; and besides the military expeditions against the Spaniards, many attempts were made for new discoveries, and other new branches of foreign commerce were opened by the English.

Sir Martin Frobisher undertook three fruitless voyages to discover the north-west passage; Davis, not discouraged by this ill-success, made a new attempt, when he discovered the straits which pass by his name.

In the year 1600 the queen granted the first patent to the East India Company; the stock of that company was seventy-two thousand pounds, and they fitted out four ships under the command of James Lancaster for this new branch of trade. The adventure was successful, and the ships returning with a rich cargo, encouraged the company to continue the commerce.

On the death of Queen Elizabeth, however, this state of things suddenly ceased, and during the whole term of James's inglorious reign the Navy of Great Britain was under a nearly total eclipse.

The most important expedition of the first James's reign was that undertaken by Sir Walter Raleigh to Guiana in search of a gold mine.

But before giving an account of his last exploit, it will only be proper to say something of the early career of this great man, whose name has already frequently been mentioned in this work, though it cannot be expected that every event of his life will be noted in this necessarily brief biography of

SIR WALTER RALEIGH.

This distinguished courtier, soldier and historian was born near Hayes, in Devonshire, in 1552. At the age of eighteen he was sent to Oriel College, Oxford, to complete his education, but in the following year he left his studies for the more dazzling acquirements of military fame, and proffering his services, with many other English gentlemen, embarked for France to assist the Queen of Navarre in defending the Protestants in the year 1571.

He continued in the service five or six years, distinguishing himself by his valour and undaunted courage. Soon after his return to London he joined the expedition of General Norris in the Netherlands, in aid of the cause of the Prince of Orange. He subsequently engaged with his brother-in-law, Sir Humphrey Gilbert, in a voyage to America, whence they returned in 1579.

The next year he was in Ireland, where he distinguished himself against the rebels of Munster, and on his return to England introduced himself to the queen by a romantic piece of gallantry.

Her majesty, while walking, stopped at a muddy place, hesitating whether to proceed or not, upon which Raleigh took off his new plush cloak and spread it on the ground; the queen trod gently over it, and soon rewarded the sacrifice of a cloak with a handsome suit to the owner.

Raleigh, being still intent upon making discoveries, in 1584 fitted out a squadron, and endeavoured to establish the colony called, in honour of Elizabeth, Virginia, but at most the only fruits of the expedition were bringing tobacco and the potato to England.

After expending forty thousand pounds in an unsuccessful attempt to found a colony, he abandoned the scheme to a mercantile community. Meanwhile he had been created a Knight, Captain of the Queen's Guard, Lord Warden of the Stannaries, and Lieutenant-General of Cornwall.

In the defeat of the Spanish Armada in 1588, Sir Walter bore a glorious part, for which he received distinguished marks of favour from the queen. In 1591 he sailed on an expedition against the Spanish fleet, but without success, and about the same time incurred the queen's displeasure by an intrigue with one of her maids of honour, whom he afterwards married.

In 1595, he sailed to Guiana, and destroyed the capital of Trinidad, and in the following year took a distinguished part in the taking of Cadiz. Honors were lavished in abundance on him, and he obtained the Lordship of St. Germains in Cornwall.

Sir Walter was one of those who brought about the fall of Essex, and remained in the favour of the queen till her death, but with the succeeding reign his fortunes changed.

He was stripped of his preferments, tried, and condemned for high treason on the most frivolous charge, and without the least evidence, and was sent to the Tower, where he remained for thirteen years, which time he occupied in writing many works, historical, philosophical, poetical, and political, the best of which, however, is his "History of the World," which was published in 1614.

The following year he was released, occasioned by a flattering account he gave of gold mines in Guiana, in search of which pretended mines he directly sailed, but which instead of discovering, he burnt the Spanish town of St. Thomas and returned to England, where, in consequence of the complaint of Gondomar, the Spanish ambassador, he was apprehended, and, in a most unprecedented manner, beheaded on his former sentence at Westminster, in 1618.

Aubrey has sketched the character of this poet, courtier, navigator, statesman, and military and naval commander, as a tall, handsome and bold man, with a most remarkable aspect, and exceeding high forehead and long face, and altogether one of the most remarkable men of a remarkable age.

The annexed quaint account of the circumstance to which Raleigh owed all his after honour and fortune, is taken from Fuller, who, in his "Worthies," gives the following account of Sir Walter Raleigh's first rise in life.

"This Captain Ralegh," he says, "coming out of Ireland into the English court in good habit, his clothes being then a considerable part of his estate, found the queen walking, till, meeting with a dirty place, she seemed to scruple going over it.

"Presently Ralegh cast and spread his new plush cloak on the ground, whereon the queen trod gently, rewarding him afterwards with many suits for his so free and seasonable tender of so fair a foot-cloth.

"An advantageous admittance into the first notice of a prince is more than half a degree of preferment.

When Sir Walter found some hopes of the queen's favour reflecting on him, he wrote on a glass window obvious to the queen's eye—

"'Fain would I climb, but fear I to fall.'

"Her majesty, either espying or being showed it, did under write—

"'If thy heart fail thee climb not at all.'

"How great a person in that court this knight afterwards proved to be is scarcely unknown to any."

* * * * * *

In dispatching Sir Walter on the expedition to Guiana, James intended it should be one in which the newly cemented peace with Spain should not be broken.

The following account of the last of those piratical expeditions and the last public service on which that great and unfortunate man was employed, is extracted from "Hume."

At the time when Sir Walter Raleigh was first confined in the Tower, his violent and haughty temper had rendered him the most unpopular man in England, and his condemnation was chiefly owing to that public odium under which he laboured.

During the thirteen years' imprisonment which he suffered, the sentiments of the nation were much changed with regard to him. Men had leisure to reflect on the hardship, not to say injustice of his sentence; they pitied his active and enterprising spirit which languished in the rigours of confinement; they were struck with the extensive genius of the man, who, being educated amidst naval and military enterprises, had surpassed in the pursuits of literature even those of the most recluse and sedentary lives; and they admired his unbroken magnanimity, which, at his age, and under his circumstances, could engage him to undertake and execute so great a work as his "History of the World."

To increase these favourable dispositions on which he built the hopes of recovering his liberty, he spread the report of a golden mine which he had discovered in Guiana, and which was sufficient, according to his own representation, not only to enrich all the adventurers but to afford immense treasures to the nation.

The king gave little credit to these mighty promises, both because he believed no such mine as the one described was anywhere in nature, and because he considered Raleigh as a man of desperate fortunes, whose business it was by any means to procure his freedom, and to reinstate himself in credit and authority.

Thinking, however, that he had already undergone sufficient punishment, he released him from the Tower, and when his vaunts of the golden mine had induced multitudes to engage with him, the king gave them permission to try the adventure, and, at their desire, he conferred on Raleigh authority over his fellow adventurers.

Though strongly solicited, he still refused to

grant him a pardon, which seemed a natural consequence when he was entrusted with power and command. But James declared himself still diffident of Raleigh's intentions, and he meant, he said, to reserve the former sentence as a check upon his future behaviour.

Raleigh well knew that it was far from the king's purpose to invade any of the Spanish settlements, he therefore firmly denied that Spain had planted any colonies on that part of the coast where his mine lay.

When Gondomar, the ambassador of that nation, alarmed at his preparations, carried complaints to the king, Raleigh still protested the innocence of his intentions; and James assured Gondomar that he durst not form any hostile attempt, but should pay with his head for so audacious an enterprise.

The minister, however, concluding that twelve armed vessels were not fitted out without some purpose of invasion, conveyed the intelligence to the Court of Madrid, who immediately gave orders for arming and fortifying all their settlements, particularly those along the coast of Guiana.

When the courage and avarice of the Spaniards and Portuguese had discovered so many new worlds they were resolved to show themselves superior to the barbarous heathens whom they invaded, not only in arts and arms, but also in the justice of the quarrel; they applied to Alexander VI., who then filled the papal chair, and he generously bestowed on the Spaniards the whole western, and, on the Portuguese, the whole eastern part of the globe.

The less scrupulous Protestants, who acknowleged not the authority of the Roman Pontiff, established the first discovery as the foundation of "their" title, and if a pirate or sea adventurer of their nation had but erected a stick or a stone on the coast as a memorial of his taking possession, they concluded the whole continent to belong to them, and thought themselves entitled to expel or exterminate as usurpers the ancient possessors and inhabitants.

It was in this manner that Sir Walter Raleigh, about twenty-three years before, had acquired to the crown of England a claim to the continent of Guiana, a region as large as the half of Europe, and though he had immediately left the coast, yet he pretended that the English title to the whole remained certain and indefeasible.

But it had happened in the meantime that the Spaniards, not knowing or not acknowledging this imaginary claim, had taken possession of a part of Guiana, had formed a settlement on the river Oronoko, had built a little town called St. Thomas, and were there working some mines of small value.

To this place Raleigh directly bent his course, and remaining himself at the mouth of the river with five of the largest ships, he sent up the rest to St. Thomas under the command of his son, and a Captain Keymis, a person entirely devoted to him.

The Spaniards, who had expected this invasion, fired on the English at their landing, were repulsed and pursued into the town. Young Raleigh, to encourage his men, called out—

"That this was the true mine, and none but fools looked for any other."

And advancing upon the Spaniards, received a shot of which he immediately expired.

This dismayed not Keymis and the others. They carried on the attack, got possession of the town, which they afterwards reduced to ashes, and found not in it anything of value.

Raleigh did not pretend that he had himself seen the mine which he had engaged so many people to go in quest of; it was Keymis, he said, who had formerly discovered it, and had brought him that lump of ore which promised such immense treasures; yet Keymis, who owned that he was within two hours' march of the mine, refused, on the most absurd pretences, to take any effectual step towards finding it, and he returned immediately to Raleigh with the melancholy news of his son's death, and the ill-success of the enterprise.

Sensible to reproach, and dreading punishment for his behaviour, Keymis, in despair, retired into his cabin, and put an end to his own life.

The other adventurers now concluded that they were deceived by Raleigh—that he never had known of any such mine as he pretended to go in search of—that his intention had ever been to plunder St. Thomas; and having encouraged his company by the spoils of that place, to have thence proceeded to the invasion of the other Spanish settlements.

They accused him of endeavouring to repair his ruined fortunes by such daring enterprises, and that he trusted to the money he should acquire for making his peace with England, or if that view failed him, that he purposed to retire into some other country, where his riches would secure his retreat.

The small acquisitions gained by the sack of St. Thomas discouraged Raleigh's companions from entering into those views, though there were many circumstances in the treaty and late transactions between the nations which might invite them to engage in such a piratical war against the Spaniards.

But as there appeared a great difference between private adventurers

in single ships, and a fleet acting under a royal commission, Raleigh's companions thought it safest to return immediately to England, and carry him along with them to answer for his conduct.

It appears that he employed many artifices, first to engage them to attack the Spanish settlements, and, failing of that, to make his escape into France; but, all these proving unsuccessful, he was delivered

He might have been tried either by common law for this act of violence and piracy, or by martial law for breach of orders; but it was an established principle among lawyers that as he lay under an actual attainder for high treason, he could not be brought to a new trial for any other crime.

To satisfy, therefore, the Court of Spain, which raised the loudest complaints against him, the king

THE ELECTOR OF THE RHINE LANDING AT GRAVESEND.

into the king's hands, and strictly examined, as well as his fellow adventurers, before the Privy Council.

The Council, upon inquiry, found no difficulty in pronouncing that the former suspicions with regard to Raleigh's intentions were well grounded; that he had abused the king in the representations which he had made of his projected adventure; that, contrary to his instructions, he had acted in an offensive and hostile manner against his majesty's allies, and that he had wilfully burned and destroyed a town belonging to the King of Spain.

made use of that power which he had purposely reserved in his own hands, and signed the warrant for his execution upon his former sentence.

In the third year of the reign of James I. we find that he issued a proclamation relative to the flags to be borne by British ships. All vessels were to carry at their maintops the *red*, commonly called the St. George's Cross; and the *white*, commonly called the St. Andrew's Cross, joined together; while on their foretops the ships of South Britain should carry the red cross, and those of North Britain the white cross. In the year 1604 certain treaties of peace and commerce were signed at London between Austria and England. These seem to have given offence to the Dutch, who, accordingly, ceased to pay the usual marks of respect to the English flag.

Such behaviour was represented to King James as an indignity which could not be submitted to; accordingly, a fleet was fitted out, the command of which was given to Sir William Monson, who sailed in the spring of 1605 to compel the Dutch to do as other nations did. Monson's own account of what he did has been preserved.

"On my return from Calais," he says, "with the Emperor's ambassador, as I approached Dover Roads I observed an increase of six ships more than I observed three days before. As I drew near them the admiral struck his flag thrice and advanced it again.

"His coming from the other coast at such a time caused me to make another construction than he pretended—viz., to let the ambassador see it, that he might spread the news throughout Europe; as also of the Spaniards, that they might have the less esteem of his majesty's prerogatives in the narrow seas. I hastened the ambassador ashore, and despatched a gentleman to the admiral.

"I ordered the gentleman to tell him to take in his flag; he answered that he had struck it thrice, which he thought a sufficient acknowledgment, and that it was more than the former admiral had required at his hands. The gentleman replied that it was such an answer as he expected, and therefore that he was prepared to acquaint him with the reason why that toleration was indulged, and that the case was really altered.

"The admiral then said that he was well acquainted with me, and had reason to expect more favour from me than from other admirals. I sent him answer that he might in a friendly manner comply with my demand, if not I should weigh anchor and come near him, and that the force of our ships must determine the question; for rather than suffer his flag to be worn in the view of so many nations I would bury mine in the sea.

"The admiral, it seems, upon better advice, took in his flag and stood immediately off to sea, firing a gun for the rest of the fleet to follow him. This passage was observed from the shore, and upon my landing I met with Sciziago, the general of the Spaniards, who told me, if the general of the Hollanders had worn their flag, times had been strangely altered in England since his old master, King Philip was shot at by the Lord Admiral of England for wearing his flag in the narrow seas when he came to marry Queen Mary."

Monson had one or two slight skirmishes with the Dutch afterwards, and thus we have the commencement of that spirit of rivalry which afterwards led to desperate war.

The year 1609 is remarkable for the fact that Hudson made a voyage for the purpose of discovering the north-west passage, and gave his name to the great inland bay in the northern part of America.

In 1610 the East India Company sent out an expedition of four ships under Sir Henry Middleton, who, on his arrival at Mocha, delivered some letters from the King to the Aga and Bashaw of the place. The English were treated with the greatest apparent kindness till the 10th of November, when the Mahometans suddenly fell upon them, killed eight men, wounded fourteen others, and imprisoned the admiral, threatening him with death unless he surrendered his ship.

Sir Henry refused to comply with this demand, and was thrown into a dungeon, where he remained for six months. In May, 1611, he found means to escape to his ships, which then lay off the coast of Abyssinia. He immediately returned and sent word to the Aga of Mocha that unless the remainder of his men were released, and ample satisfaction made for the damages he had received, he would burn all the native shipping in the harbour and batter the town to pieces. This threatening message had the desired effect: the prisoners were restored, and eighteen thousand rials paid by way of compensation.

Sir Henry then continued his voyage to India, but found a large Portuguese fleet assembled near Surat to prevent his trading there, or anywhere else on that coast. He very bravely attacked them, but being greatly outnumbered both in ships, men, and guns, was obliged to return without accomplishing his purpose.

Improvements in cables and anchors also took place; 120 fathoms of cable being allowed to each anchor instead of about 80, and the sheet anchor of a twenty-four gun-ship (of about 1,651 tons burden) was increased to 6,700 pounds, whereas the sheet anchor of the first "Royal Sovereign" weighed only 4,400 pounds.

The masts and yards were decreased in size; the mainmast of the "Prince" was 102 feet long, and three feet three inches in diameter. It was also established that the lower tier of ordnance in a vessel of war should stand at least four feet clear above the water when all the ship's lading was in.

During the reign of Elizabeth and James, there were several improvements made in naval architecture, and it is to this period that we are indebted for the introduction of chain pumps, the capstan, the striking of the topmast, and the invention of studding and sprit sails.

Another circumstance connected with the Royal or National Navy during this, was the building of a full-sized sixty-four gun vessel, called the "Prince," the largest vessel of war at that time in the navy.

Of the launching of the "Prince" we have the following account:—

"The King caused a famous ship-builder to build a most goodly ship for warre, the keel whereof was

114 feet in length, and the cross-beam 44 feet in length; she will carry 64 pieces of great ordnance, and is of the burden of 1,400 tons. This Royal ship is double built, and is most sumptuously adorned within and without with all manner of most curious carving, painting and gilding, being, in all respects, the greatest and goodliest ship that ever was builded in England; and this glorious ship the King gave to his son Henry, Prince of Wales; and the 24th of September the King, the Queen, the Prince of Wales, the Duke of York, and the Lady Elizabeth, with many great lords, went unto Woolwich to see it launched, but because of the narrowness of the dock it could not then be launched; whereupon the Prince came the next morning by three of the clock, and then, at the launching thereof he named it after his own dignity, and called it the 'Prince.'"

The master ship-builder was Phineas Pett, Master of Arts, of Emanuel College, Cambridge.

In a MS. life of Mr. Pett, a vessel is spoken of which is worthy of note from its size and purpose.

Mr. Pett mentions that in January, 1603-4, he was "ordered by the Lord High Admiral to build a vessel at Chatham with all speed for the young Prince Henry to disport himself in above London Bridge. This little ship was in length by the keel 28 feet, in breadth 12 feet. I laid her keel on the 19th January, and launched her on the 6th of March: set sail with her on the 9th of March, and on the 14th anchored right against the Tower. On the 18th anchored right against the Privy stairs (Whitehall). On the 22nd, the Prince, with the Lord High Admiral, &c., &c., came on board, when we weighed and dropped down as low as Paul's wharf, where we anchored; and there, His Grace, with a great bowl of wine, christened the ship, and called her the 'Disdain.'"

In 1612 the Elector Palatine of the Rhine came to England to espouse the Princess Elizabeth, daughter of King James. On his landing at Gravesend he was received with great honour by the British fleet; and the naval parade seems to have been very grand, and worthy of the nation in every respect.

After this there is no naval event of importance in James's reign, except a pretence of going to war with Spain. On this occasion the command of the fleet was given to the Duke of Buckingham, but nothing was done worth recording.

The ships added to the Royal Navy by James were nine in number, viz.:—

Reformation	250	men
Happy Entrance	160	,,
Garland	160	,,
St. George	250	,,
Mary Rose	120	,,
Triumph	300	,,
Swiftsure	250	,,
Bonaventure	160	,,
St. Andrew	250	,,

King James seems to have been tolerably liberal to his seamen, and inclined to do them honour. In his reign the contractors for victualling the Royal Navy were allowed eightpence per day for the diet of each man when in harbour, and sevenpence halfpenny at sea.

Every man's allowance was one pound of biscuit, one gallon of beer, two pounds of beef with salt, four days in the week; or else, instead of beef, for two of those four days, one pound of bacon or pork, and one pint of peas, according to the custom before established; and for the other three days of the week one quarter of stock-fish, half-a-quarter of a pound of butter, and a quarter of a pound of cheese; excepting on Fridays, when they were to have a quantity of fish, butter and cheese, but for one meal, or, instead of stock fish, a quantity of herrings, or other fish, as the time of year shall afford.

The contractors were to have the use of all his majesty's brewhouses, bakehouses, mills, and other storehouses at Tower Hill, Dover, Portsmouth and Rochester, paying the same rent as former contractors.

These contractors were Sir Allen Apsley and Sir Sampson Darrel, who were to enjoy during life the title and office of Purveyors General of the victuals of his Majesty's Navy.

Nothing was accomplished in the reign of Charles I. that added in the least degree to the renown of the Royal Navy.

In 1626, it is true, a large fleet was despatched for the ostensible purpose of attacking the Genoese, who were then the allies of Philip III. of Spain.

The crews of the English fleet, having a suspicion that they were destined to attack Rochelle, at that time besieged by the French under Cardinal Richelieu, and where the leaders of the Protestant party had fixed their head quarters, mutinied, and swore they would not assist the Catholics; the fleet was consequently compelled to return, in defiance of the government order.

This is certainly only one account; another, and perhaps a truer statement, is that the fleet was fitted out for the express relief of the Protestants at Rochelle, but, having encountered a heavy storm at sea, was compelled to return into harbour without effecting anything.

The English people were very indignant at this un-English management, so another fleet was fitted out, and the Duke of Buckingham went to Portsmouth to take command of it. But, before he could get on board his ship he was killed by a man named Felton. The fleet sailed in spite of this, under the command of Earl Lindsay, but did nothing.

From this time the French again began to affect a maritime power, and to be jealous of the growth of the English Navy. This was part of Richelieu's plans for increasing the power of France, and, to carry it out, he spared neither pains nor expense in procuring the services of persons skilful in all the arts and sciences connected with navigation.

Although there was a war with Spain during the reign of the first Charles, Spanish vessels, laden with valuable merchandise, went to and came from America with very little or no molestation.

Another fleet was fitted out in 1635, and placed under the command of the Earl of Lindsay, for the protection, as it was alleged, of English commerce, and particularly the North Sea fisheries. This fleet consisted of forty sail; but, as their instructions were to commit no hostilities, they simply fired a few guns to frighten away the Dutch fishermen, and then, having been saluted by Admiral Van Drop, who lowered his topsails, and struck his flag, they returned.

About the year 1636 the King (Charles) ordered Phineas Pett to build, at Woolwich, a vessel called the "Sovereign of the Seas," which, when completed, surpassed in force as well as tonnage, any that had been built in Britain before that time. She was the first genuine three-decker, and her dimensions were:—

THE SOVEREIGN OF THE SEAS.

Length from stem to stern, all over 232 feet.
Length of the keel . . . 128 „
Breadth of beam . . . 48 „
Tonnage . . . . . 1,637 tons.

She was pierced for a great number of guns. Her lower tier had 30 ports for cannon and demi-cannon; her middle tier 30 for culverins and demi-culverins; third tier, 26 for other ordnance; forecastle, 12; two half-decks, 13 or 14 ports more within board, besides 10 pieces of chace ordnance forward, and 10 right aft. She carried eleven anchors, one of which weighed 4,400 pounds. On the lower part of the stern, either side of the helm, was this inscription:—

"He who seas, winds and navies doth protect,
Great Charles thy ship in her course direct."

In 1638 it was ordained that 6d. per month was to be deducted from the pay of officers, and 4d. per month from the pay of men of all ships sailing from London, to form a fund, managed by the Trinity House Corporation, for the widows and children of shipwrecked mariners. East India Company's seamen were not included in this, having a fund of their own.

In 1640 we find that Peter Pett (son of Phineas) built the first English frigate, which was called the "Constant Warwick."

On the first breaking out of the Civil War, the English navy was divided, one siding for the king, the other for the Parliament; but both portions remained very inactive. Captain Butten, formerly vice-admiral under the Earl of Warwick, at last succeeded in placing a part of the fleet under the command of the Prince of Wales, who, with Prince Rupert and others, were trying to assist the king, but they accomplished nothing of the slightest importance.

Charles I. had but little opportunity to augment his navy; he added, however, at least 22 vessels of various classes to the navy. In his reign vessels were first rated, or classed, and the following is an abstract of the state of the Royal Navy when the Civil War broke out: there were 5 ships of the 1st rate; 12 of the 2nd rate; 8 of the 3rd rate; 6 of the 4th rate; 2 of the 5th rate; and 9 of the 6th rate.

So, it appears, that although the king had added vessels, a greater number had gone to decay, as in 1633 the navy is reported to have consisted of fifty ships.

CHAPTER XI.

THE FIRST DUTCH WAR 1652—BLAKE AND VAN TROMP—CAPTURE OF JAMAICA.

E are now approaching a period in the Naval History of Great Britain when, for the first time, she met on her native element an enemy worthy of her power and dignity.

The unsatisfactory, and often indecisive actions between single ships and ill-appointed squadrons, that for the last century and a half, with but one exception—that of the Armada—had comprised the naval warfare of this country, was now to give way to long, protracted, and pitched battles at sea. The piratical expeditions of the Raleighs, Drakes, and Frobishers, gave way at once to the wealth and strength of two powerful nations, whose immense fleets embattled on the ocean, fought for the supremacy and national existence of one or the other.

England has since the time we are now writing of, fought, single-handed, against the united fleets of France, Holland, and Spain, and after a day of desperate toil and slaughter, rode mistress among her vanquished foes.

In the Dutch wars, however, to which we are now coming, so infuriated were the antagonists and so determined was each to be master, that almost every naval battle between the two states was so prolonged and obstinately contested that they were continued for two, three, and, on one occasion, for four entire days.

Up to the time of Henry VIII. almost the whole of the foreign commerce of this country had been carried on with the Spanish Netherlands, as the kingdom now known as Holland was then called.

The Dutch at that time, and for half a century after, were the general carriers for the rest of Europe.

The greater part of our trade with Central Europe was at this time carried on through Holland.

When the Netherlands threw off their allegiance to Spain, and openly defied the power of Philip II., it was to England they looked for aid and sympathy, and for the means to establish their independence.

Though Elizabeth refused the crown they offered her, she yearly supplied them with vast sums of money to pay their soldiers and carry on the war.

Nor was it by money only that Elizabeth aided the Dutch; she garrisoned their frontier towns, and sent over horse and foot to support their cause, and never ceased her good offices till the Netherlands became a free and independent state.

Owing thus, as it were, their very liberty and national prosperity to England, her closest, longest, and best friend, it will be naturally asked what wrong on the part of this country could, in a few months, convert our steady-going Dutch traders into inveterate foes?

Where two commercial nations are jealous of each other's power, or interference in their trade, it is not difficult to find or make a cause of quarrel.

The Dutch had now become a wealthy and important nation, and were daily growing more and more jealous of the English, who had lately established their East India Company, and were fast competing with the Dutch, as the carriers from both Indies to Europe.

They first began by sending their fishing, or herring busses on our best grounds, and robbing the English of the fish out of their own waters.

PORTRAIT OF CAPTAIN JOHN HAWKINS.

This, with some real or imaginary insults, offered to St. John, our ambassador, so enraged the Council, that they demanded an explanation.

The Dutch minister at London, in his attempt to explain away all mistakes, foolishly said that Holland had a hundred and twenty sail of the line, ready to vindicate her honour.

This reply the English Council at once interpreted as a threat, and to avenge their present wrongs, and the still rankling injury inflicted at Amboyna, at once declared war against the United Provinces.

To give our readers a clear insight into this war, we must refer to an event that had occurred thirty years before, in the time of James; and which that monarch, to the disgust of the nation, quietly put up with.

James, as we have already seen, was not the man to uphold England's dignity, and the Dutch knew it.

But there was now no longer a weak James, or an unfortunate Charles on the throne, but a hand grasped the truncheon of State that knew how to defend the honour of its country: the Protector Cromwell.

Amboyna is the richest and most important of all the Spice Islands in the Indian Ocean; from this island the Dutch, having shaken off the Spanish yoke, expelled by fire and sword the Portuguese, at that time the subjects of Philip.

Having got rid of their rivals, the Dutch assumed the sovereignty of the whole island, and sought to secure the entire monopoly of the spice trade.

The English, however, in 1615, some ten years subsequent to this event, not acknowledging the Dutch supremacy of the island, had, though not without strong opposition on the part of the malignant and crafty Dutch, succeeded in establishing a trading colony in Amboyna, a branch of the then newly chartered East India Company.

This company, anxious to share in the lucrative spice commerce—the whole European trade in which, as had been foreseen by the expulsion of the Portuguese, having fallen into the hands of the Dutch,—had built a vessel of twelve hundred tons, the largest merchant ship that had ever been floated, and despatched her to the East to take up her position on the new line.

But the Netherlanders, forgetful of the treaties of amity between the two nations, or the lasting debt of gratitude they owed to the English for the blood and treasure so freely expended in their cause during the war of independence, resolved to free themselves from a rival whom they both feared as an opponent in trade and detested as a nation.

As it was impossible to find any valid reason for a quarrel, or just cause for their expulsion, they consummated their purpose by a deed of such treachery, murder, and cruelty, that must to the end of time remain as an enduring disgrace on the name of Holland, and can only be paralleled by the shame of allowing such an outrage to pass unpunished; but, unfortunately for the honour of this country, the nation was at that time governed by a pedant and a coward.

In the year 1622, the Dutch, under the semblance of the purest friendship and neighbourly hospitality, invited the governor, officers, men, women, and children—in fact, the entire infant community of the English factory—to the Dutch factory, on the plea of celebrating some national event, in which both nations were supposed to feel an interest.

In the midst of their confidence and rejoicing, and following, on a small scale, the example of Ethelred's massacre of the Danes, the Dutch suddenly fell upon the unsuspecting English, brutally murdered a great number, and made prisoners of all who escaped the first savage onslaught.

Had they completed their savage deed at once, and put old and young, women and children, to the sword upon the spot, horrible and revolting as the act would have been for a civilised people to perpetrate on men of their own faith, it would have been mild compared with the atrocities which marked the sequel of this fearful tragedy.

With a malignity of feeling and a refinement of cruelty only worthy the worst days of the Inquisition, the prisoners, loaded with chains, were thrown into cells and dungeons, where, from the heat and dearth of water, they suffered dreadful tortures, being brought forth singly to endure all the agony that racks, pincers, and other implements of torture could inflict on their naked flesh.

In this manner, with every conceivable suffering, the Dutch gloated over the total extermination of their rivals, the women being subjected to double torture, their dying moments agonised by the sight of their butchered children—for these Christian savages left not one of that unhappy colony alive to tell the tale of murder; and it was by strangers and natives the nation heard of this outrage on its honour.

As the first action with the Dutch arose out of an alleged disrespect to the English flag, in the refusal of Van Tromp to strike to Blake's ensign, we must pause for a moment to give our readers some idea of what this perpetual source of heart-burning to all foreign nations consisted.

England had for some centuries arrogated to herself the title of Mistress of the Seas, and compelled every foreign ship, whether at peace or war with her, to drop her topsails, wherever the British standard was displayed in a king's, or government ship.

This reverence, or curtseying, as it was sometimes called, was a prolific source of humiliation to foreigners; but down to the end of the last war England constantly insisted on this homage being paid.

Tromp, an admiral of great renown, received from the States the command of a fleet of forty-two sail, in order to protect the Dutch navigation against the privateers of the English. He was forced by stress of weather, as he alleged, to take shelter in the Road of Dover, where he met with Blake, who commanded an English fleet much inferior in number.

Who was the aggressor in the action which ensued between these two admirals, both of them men of such prompt and fiery dispositions, it is not easy to determine, since each of them sent to his own State a relation totally opposite in all its circumstances to that of the other, and yet supported by the testimony of every captain in his fleet.

Blake pretended that having given a signal to the Dutch admiral to strike, Tromp, instead of complying, fired a broadside at him. Tromp asserted that he was preparing to strike, and that the English admiral, nevertheless, began hostilities.

It is certain that the Admiralty of Holland, who are distinct from the Council of State, had given Tromp no orders to strike, but had left him to his own discretion with regard to that vain, but much contested ceremonial. They seemed willing to introduce the claim of an equality with the new Commonwealth, and to interpret the formal respect paid the English flag, as a deference due only to the monarchy.

This circumstance forms a strong presumption against the narrative of the Dutch admiral. The whole Orange party, it must be remarked, to which Tromp was suspected to adhere, were desirous of a war with England.

Blake, though his squadron consisted only of fifteen vessels, reinforced, after the battle began, by eight, under Captain Bourne, maintained the fight with bravery for five hours, and sunk one ship of the enemy and took another. Night parted the combatants, and the Dutch fleet retired towards the coast of Holland.

The populace of London were enraged, and would have insulted the Dutch ambassadors, who lived at Chelsea, had not the Council of State sent guards to protect them.

After this action, the Dutch declared war, upon which Blake sailed northwards, with a numerous fleet, and fell upon the herring busses, which were escorted by twelve men-of-war. All these he either took or dispersed. Tromp followed him with a fleet of above one hundred sail. When these two admirals were within sight of each other, and preparing for battle, a furious storm attacked them. Blake took shelter in the English harbours. The Dutch fleet was dispersed and received great damage.

Sir George Ayscue, though he commanded only forty ships, according to the English accounts, engaged, near Plymouth, in August of the same year, the famous De Ruyter, who had under him fifty ships of war, with thirty merchantmen. The Dutch ships were indeed of inferior force to the English.

De Ruyter, the only admiral in Europe who has attained a renown equal to that of the greatest general, defended himself so well, that Ayscue gained little advantage over him. Night parted them in the greatest heat of the action. De Ruyter next sailed off with his convoy, one of his ships having been captured. The English fleet had been so shattered in the fight that it was not able to pursue, and three or four of the Dutch sank afterwards.

A few days after this a small English fleet in the Mediterranean (sent there by the Commonwealth to protect trade) was attacked near Leghorn by a vastly superior force; but after a most desperate encounter the Dutch withdrew, not having gained any advantage.

Many other encounters took place, and, although it cannot be pretended that the English seamen were invariably successful, yet they certainly vindicated their old reputation, which had become somewhat tarnished since the stirring times of Drake, Essex, Hawkins and Raleigh.

About this time the King of Denmark formed an alliance with the States of Holland, and laid an embargo on the British merchant vessels in the Baltic. He also ordered the channel known as the Sound to be closed to the British fleet, and sent five of his great ships to join the Dutch. At the same time ships of various nations, but all bearing the French flag, were cruising almost everywhere.

Near the coast of Kent, Blake, seconded by Bourne and Pen, met a Dutch fleet on the 28th of October, commanded by De Witte and De Ruyter. A battle was fought, much to the disadvantage of the Dutch. Their rear-admiral was boarded and taken. Two other vessels were sunk, and one blown up. The Dutch, next day, made sail towards Holland.

The English were not so successful in the Mediterranean on a second occasion. Van Galen, with much superior force, attacked Captain Badily and defeated him. He bought, however, his victory with the loss of his life.

Sea fights are seldom so decisive as to disable the vanquished from making head in a little time against the victors. Tromp, seconded by De Ruyter, met, near the Goodwins, with Blake (29th November), whose fleet was inferior to the Dutch, but who resolved not to decline the combat.

A furious battle commenced, in which the admirals on both sides, as well as the inferior officers and seamen, exerted great bravery. In this action the Dutch had the advantage. Blake himself was wounded.

The "Garland" and "Bonaventure" were taken. Two ships were burned and one sunk, and night came opportunely to save the English fleet. After this victory, Tromp, in bravado, fixed a broom to his masthead, as if he were resolved to sweep the sea entirely of all English vessels.

Great preparations were made in England to wipe off this disgrace.

The Parliament, with great diligence and energy, repaired their shattered fleet, and fitted out another with such rapidity as to amaze all Europe.

On the 8th of February, 1653, Blake again hoisted his flag, having under him sixty men-of-war, with Dean and Monk, who had been summoned from Scotland, for his vice-admirals.

Sailing from Queenborough (near Sheerness), Blake proceeded to Portsmouth, where he was joined by twenty more men-of-war.

Then he made sail towards Portland, "half-seas over, to call Van Tromp to account for passing the Parliament's leave."

When the English arrived off Portland, they descried, near break of day, the Dutch fleet of seventy-six vessels, sailing up the channel, along with a convoy of three hundred merchantmen, who had received orders to wait at the Isle of Rhe, till the fleet should arrive to escort them. This was on the 18th of February.

Tromp and, under him, De Ruyter, commanded the Dutch.

Blake very speedily commenced the action, at first with only thirteen of his ships. Blake and Dean were both on board the "Triumph," which received 700 shots in her hull, but was bravely relieved by the vessel commanded by Captain Lawson; the remainder of the fleet being for some time prevented from coming up by contrary winds.

When they did at length arrive, a most furious fight took place, wherein the Dutch lost six men-of-war captured or sunk; the English not losing one vessel.

Night separated the combatants, but on the morning of the 19th Blake again brought Van Tromp to action off Weymouth. The Dutch admiral, after the first encounter, put his merchant-vessels before him, and retreated fighting towards the port of Boulogne; but the English frigates took many of his merchantmen, while Captain Lawson boarded and captured one of the Dutch men-of-war.

Again night stopped the terrible fight, but on the morrow—which was the Sabbath—Blake once more commenced action with his stubborn foe, and fought him with advantage till four in the afternoon, when the wind proved contrary.

The Dutch admiral made a skilful retreat to Calais, and saved all the merchant ships, except thirty. He lost, however, eleven ships of war, had 2,000 men slain, and near 1,500 taken prisoners. The English, though many of their ships were extremely shattered, had but one sunk. Their slain were not much inferior in number to those of the enemy.

All these successes of the English were chiefly owing to the superior size of their vessels, an advantage which all the skill and bravery of the Dutch admirals could not compensate.

But the misfortunes which the Dutch met with in battle were small in comparison to those which their trade sustained from the English. Their whole commerce by the Channel was cut off; even that to the Baltic was much infested by English privateers. Their fisheries were totally suspended. A great number of their ships (above 1,600) had fallen into the hands of the enemy.

All this distress they suffered, not for any national interest or necessity; but from vain points of honour and personal resentments, of which it was difficult to give a satisfactory account to the public. They resolved, therefore, to gratify the pride of the Parliament, and to make some advances towards peace. They met not, however, with a favourable reception; and, it was not without pleasure that they learned the dissolution of that haughty assembly, by the violence of Cromwell; an event from which they expected a more prosperous turn to their affairs.

The Dutch now made the most strenuous overtures for peace, and these were, for a time, favourably received by the English Government; in order, however, to obtain better terms, the Dutch resolved to have one more and final trial for victory.

For this purpose Van Tromp was again sent to sea with ninety-five vessels, still leaving behind thirty more, which were to follow under De Witt.

The English fleet consisted of a hundred sail, and commanded by Monk and Deane, and, under them, by Penn and Lawson, met, near the coast of Flanders, with the Dutch fleet, equally numerous, and commanded by Van Tromp.

The two republics were not inflamed by any national antipathy, and their interests very little interfered; yet, few battles have been disputed with more fierce and obstinate courage than were those many naval combats which were fought during this short but violent war. The desire of remaining sole lords of the ocean animated these States to an honourable emulation against each other.

After a battle of two days, in the first of which Deane was killed, the Dutch, inferior in the size of their ships, were obliged, with great loss, to retire into their harbours. Blake, towards the end of the fight, joined his countrymen with eighteen sail. The English fleet lay off the coast of Holland, and totally interrupted the commerce of that republic.

Deane, the distinguished commander, and military companion of Monk, who fell at the first broadside of the Dutch in this action, was instantaneously cut in two by a chain-shot. Monk, who was standing close to Deane's side when he fell, calmly took off his cloak, and covering the mangled body of his friend, continued his orders perfectly unmoved to the close of the battle.

The States, maddened at their defeat, made every effort to recover their injured honour, and never, on any occasion, did the power and vigour of that republic appear in a more conspicuous light.

In a few weeks, they had repaired and manned their fleet; and they equipped some ships of a larger size than any which they had hitherto sent to sea. Tromp issued forth, determined again to fight the victors, and to die rather than yield the contest.

He met with the enemy, commanded by Monk, and both sides immediately rushed into the combat. Van Tromp, gallantly animating his men, with his sword drawn, was shot through the heart with a musket ball. This event alone decided the battle in favour of the English. Though near thirty ships of the Dutch were sunk and taken, they little regarded this loss compared with that of their brave admiral.

After this signal disaster, the Dutch again negotiated for peace, which, after a short delay, was ratified, and peace with Holland proclaimed on the 26th of April, 1654. In every part of the world where the ships of the two nations traded, this destructive war extended; and in different places there were actions with single ships and squadrons, while many of the colonial towns and forts of both parties were bombarded.

In this short, but disastrous war, which lasted only twenty-three months, the Dutch lost 1,700 prizes, valued by the owners at 6,000,000 sterling. At the same time, the States, to satisfy Cromwell's demands, at once allowed the supremacy of the British flag, bound themselves to treat as enemies all the enemies of England, to pay £87,000 as compensation to the East India Company, and to punish all the survivors, if any, of the massacre at Amboyna.

The following year, Cromwell, excited as much by ambition as interest, resolved to employ the immense force at his disposal in demanding reparation from foreign states, for some real or imaginary wrongs inflicted on subjects of the English nation.

For this purpose he declared war against Spain, principally in the hope of intercepting her annual Plate fleets, and crushing the detested idolators, as he termed the Spaniards and other Catholic nations. Actuated equally by these bigoted, ambitious, and interested motives, the Protector equipped two considerable squadrons, and while he was making those preparations, the neighbouring States, ignorant of his intentions, remained in suspense, and looked with anxious expectation on what side the storm should discharge itself.

DESTRUCTION OF THE VICEROY OF PERU'S SHIP.—(*See page* 75.)

One of these squadrons, consisting of thirty capital ships, was sent into the Mediterranean under Blake, whose fame was now spread over Europe.

Blake appeared before Leghorn, to demand from the Duke of Tuscany reparation for some losses which the English commerce had formerly sustained from him. As soon as he had anchored, Blake sent his secretary to the Grand Duke of Tuscany to demand the sum of £100,000. It seems that the great complaint against the duke was this:—

Towards the end of the reign of Charles I., when

the fortunes of that monarch were at their lowest ebb, Prince Rupert had escaped to sea with a few ships, and had captured several merchant vessels belonging to citizens of the English commonwealth. These prizes he had taken to Leghorn, and sold to the grand duke's subjects.

The duke offered to pay part of the money, but wished for time to consult the Pope about payment of the rest; to which Blake replied that the Pope had nothing to do with it.

Eventually, the British admiral consented to take £60,000, which was paid, and he sailed away—having proved the truth of a saying of Cromwell's, that a ship of the line was the best ambassador.

He next sailed to Algiers, and compelled the Dey to make peace, and to restrain his piratical subjects from further violences on the English.

He presented himself before Tunis, and having there made the same demands, the Dey replied to the effect that he would very willingly release all his English prisoners, provided the Knights of Malta would set at liberty all the Moors they held in captivity.

Blake answered that he could not concern himself about the Knights of Malta, but that unless the English were sent he should capture all vessels he could find belonging to the Dey of Tunis. To prove that he was in earnest, he cruised off the town and captured a fleet of provisions; then, having thoroughly put his ships in order, he repeated his demands.

The Dey was a spirited man, and sent for answer: "Here are our castles, Guletta and Porto Firmo—do what you please; we do not fear you."

Blake needed not to be roused by such a bravado; he drew his ships close up to the castles, and tore them in pieces with his artillery. He sent a numerous detachment of sailors in their long boats into the harbour, and burned every ship that lay there. This bold action, which its very temerity perhaps rendered safe, was executed with little loss, and filled all that part of the world with the renown of English valour.

The Dey sent to beg for peace, and delivered up all the English slaves he had; after which Blake left a consul in the town to look after British interests.

The inhabitants of Algiers were by this time so fond—*or fearful*—of Blake, with whom, as we have seen, a treaty had been concluded, that whenever they met with any other Moorish vessels that had English prisoners on board, they compelled them to deliver them up to the English admiral.

Altogether, Blake sent home sixteen vessels richly laden with goods and money he had received for satisfaction and compensation, and these were ordered to sail up the river Thames in procession, "to make a grateful spectacle to the people, who were told that such ships were coming, and with rich freight." *

---

* Oldmixon. History of England.

The other squadron was not equally successful. It was commanded by Penn, and carried on board four thousand men, under the command of Venables. About five hundred more joined them from Barbadoes and St. Christopher's. Both these officers were inclined to the king's service, and it is pretended that Cromwell was obliged to hurry the soldiers on board in order to prevent the execution of a conspiracy which had been formed among them in favour of the exiled family.

The ill success of this enterprise may justly be ascribed as much to the injudicious schemes of the Protector, who planned it, as to the bad execution of the officers by whom it was conducted.

The soldiers were the refuse of the whole army; the forces enlisted in the West Indies were the most profligate of mankind; Penn and Venables were of incompatible tempers; the troops were not furnished with arms fit for such an expedition; their provisions were defective both in quantity and quality; all hopes of pillage—the best incentive to valour among such men—were refused the soldiers and seamen; no directions, nor intelligence were given to conduct the officers in their enterprise, and, at the same time, they were tied down to follow the advise of commissioners, who disconcerted them in all their projects.

It was agreed by the admiral and general to attempt St. Domingo, the only place of strength in the island of Hispaniola. On the approach of the English, the Spaniards, in a fright, deserted their houses, and fled to the woods.

Contrary to the opinion of Venables, the soldiers were disembarked without guides, ten leagues distant from the town. They wandered four days through the woods without provisions, and, what was still more intolerable in that sultry climate, without water.

The Spaniards recovered spirit and attacked them. The English, discouraged with the bad conduct of their officers, and, scarcely alive from hunger, thirst, and fatigue, were unable to resist. An inconsiderable number of the enemy put the whole army to rout, killed six hundred of them, and chased the rest on board their vessels.

The English commanders, in order to atone as much as possible for this unprosperous attempt, bent their course to Jamaica, which was surrendered to them without a blow. Penn and Venables returned to England, and were both of them sent to the Tower by the Protector, who, though commonly master of his fiery temper, was thrown into a violent passion at this disappointment.

He had made a conquest of greater importance than he himself was at that time aware of: yet was it much inferior to the vast projects which he had formed. He gave orders, however, to support it by men and money; and that island has ever since remained in the hands of the English; the chief acquisition which they owe to the enterprising spirit of Cromwell.

So disgusted were many of the captains and superior officers of the fleet, at what they regarded as an unjust, cruel, and tyrannous war, that they sent a protest to the Protector, and, in a body, threw up their commissions.

Unmoved by their dissatisfaction, Cromwell soon filled up the vacancies, and Blake was ordered to prepare for sea.

This renowned admiral set sail early in 1656, and lay some time off Cadiz, in expectation of intercepting the Plate fleet, but was at last obliged, for want of water, to make sail towards Portugal.

Captain Stayner, whom he had left on the coast with a squadron of seven vessels, came in sight of the galleons, and immediately set sail to pursue them. The Spanish admiral ran his ship ashore: two others followed his example: the English took two ships valued at near two millions of pieces of eight.

The Marquis of Badajos, Viceroy of Peru, with his wife and daughter, betrothed to the young Duke of Medina-Celi, were destroyed.

The marquis himself might have escaped; but, seeing these unfortunate women, astonished with the danger, fall into a swoon, and perish in the flames, he rather choose to die with them than drag out a life embittered with the remembrance of such dismal scenes. When the treasures gained by this enterprise arrived at Portsmouth, the Protector, from a spirit of ostentation, ordered them to be transported by land to London.

The next action against the Spaniards was more honourable, though less profitable to the nation. Blake, having heard that a Spanish fleet of sixteen ships, much richer than the former, had taken shelter in the Canaries, immediately made sail towards them.

He found them in the bay of Santa Cruz, disposed in a formidable posture. The bay was secured with a strong castle, well provided with cannon, besides seven forts in several parts of it, all united by a line of communication, manned with musketeers.

Don Diego Diagues, the Spanish admiral, ordered all his smaller vessels to moor close to the shore, and posted all the larger galleons farther off at anchor, with their broadsides to the sea, sending out word by a Dutch merchant, "Let Blake come if he dares."

Blake was rather animated than daunted by this challenge—and come he did with a vengeance; but, finding that it was not practicable to carry off the galleons, he resolved to burn them all. He sent the gallant Captain Stayner, in the frigate "Speaker," to stand into the bay with a squadron.

About eight in the morning the fight commenced. Blake admirably seconded Stayner, and, with his large vessels, battered the forts till he had silenced them.

The Spanish vessels continued the fight for four hours, but the English ships delivered their broadsides so fast that at last they were obliged to abandon their galleons, the least of which was bigger than Blake's largest vessel.

The sailors then quitted the smaller ships that had taken refuge under the forts, and Stayner burnt every one of them, while Blake did the same with the larger one. The whole Spanish fleet of sixteen ships was thus destroyed, the English loss having been only forty-eight men killed and one hundred and twenty wounded.

Then, the wind suddenly shifting, carried them out of the bay, where they left the Spaniards in astonishment at the temerity of their audacious victors.

This action is considered by many as equal to anything performed by Nelson, for Blake fought at once with foes on sea and land.

The news of this great victory reached England before the Parliament was adjourned, and the House, to mark its sense of Blake's gallant conduct, voted him a diamond ring worth £500.

Any present which seemed to him a public recognition of his services, would, it was well known, be acceptable to him; but he had an extreme contempt for empty titles.

This was the last and greatest action of the gallant Blake. He was consumed with a dropsy and scurvy, and hastened home, that he might yield up his breath in his native country, which he had so adorned by his valour. As he came within sight of Plymouth he expired.

The Government bestowed on his remains honors due to such an illustrious naval hero.

His body was conveyed by sea from Plymouth to Greenwich, where it remained for some time; but was conveyed (on the 4th September, 1657) in a barge of state to Westminster.

Captain Humphrey Blake, brother of the deceased, several of his relatives and servants, in mourning, were chief mourners; and the melancholy procession was accompanied by the members of the Privy Council, the Lords of the Admiralty, the Commissioners of the Navy, the Lord Mayor and Aldermen of London, the field officers of the army, and a great many of the most celebrated men of the time.

On landing, the corpse and the mourners proceeded through a guard of several regiments of foot soldiers to Westminster Abbey, where the mortal remains of the great admiral were deposited in a vault in Henry VIIth's chapel.

* * * * * *

We will now proceed to condense, if possible, the historical events of many years into a brief—

BIOGRAPHY OF ROBERT BLAKE.

Robert Blake was born at Bridgewater, in Somersetshire, in the year 1599.

In 1617 he took his first degree at Oxford, and at the age of forty-one was returned to Parliament for his native town of Bridgewater. Two years later he was sent by the Parliament to assist Lord Say and his son in the defence of Bristol, which, however, soon after had to surrender to Prince Rupert.

A few months after this misfortune he assisted in the reduction of Taunton, when, for the gallantry he had displayed in the siege, he was appointed its governor.

While in this capital, he twice sustained a siege from the Royalists, and defended the town with such skill and heroism, that he received the unanimous thanks of the Parliament for his meritorious services.

In the year 1649 he was, without any previous knowledge of nautical affairs, removed from the army, entrusted with the command of a squadron of ships, and sent, with Dean and Popham, to destroy that portion of the fleet which, under Prince Rupert, had declared for the king.

After a long search, Blake at last found the prince and his ill-appointed squadron in Kinsale harbour, in Ireland; but being too strongly defended by the town and forts, Blake was obliged to content himself by a close blockade of his enemy.

This blockade soon became so rigorous and oppressive, that Prince Rupert resolved, at all hazards, to break through, and if possible escape.

PORTRAIT OF ADMIRAL BLAKE.

Taking advantage of a favourable night for his purpose, he contrived to work his ships out of the harbour, and, passing Blake's line in the dark, stood out to sea.

Daylight showed the new admiral that the enemy had not only escaped him, but made so good a use of the darkness and wind, that, when the sun rose, not a sail was to be seen on the horizon.

Determined not to allow the prince to escape so easily, Blake crowded all sail, and followed in pursuit, tracking him from port to port, till the fugitive reached the Tagus, up which he sailed, as high as Lisbon.

Scarcely had the prince taken shelter under the guns of the Portuguese capital, when Blake appeared in the Tagus; and, making every disposition to attack the Royalist ships, sent one of his officers on shore to request permission of the king to destroy the enemies of the Republic.

Such, however, was the sympathy with royalty, that in the face of all the danger of a war with the Commonwealth, the King of Portugal had the courage to refuse the demand of the fiery Blake.

The English admiral, enraged at the refusal, set sail from the Tagus, and, standing out to sea, fell in with the Portuguese Plate fleet, bound from the Brazils to Lisbon, and, in revenge, at once attacked it, and made several valuable prizes.

Prince Rupert, taking advantage of Blake's absence, immediately weighed anchor, and directed his course to the Mediterranean; but his determined foe was on his track again in a few days, and followed so quickly, that Rupert had only time to enter the harbour of Malaga to escape his pursuer.

In this haven Blake, without any further delay, attacked the weakened squadron with such fury that he destroyed nearly two-thirds of his enemy's armament.

Prince Rupert at last, by an act of desperate bravery, forced his way out, and entered a friendly port, when, seeing the utter hopelessness of further resistance, he disbanded his crews, and sold his ships and stores.

Blake now set sail for England with his prizes, when he received the thanks of Parliament for his services, and, as some reward, was made Warden of the Cinque Ports.

His next public service was reducing the Scilly and Channel Islands to obedience to the Commonwealth; for this duty he was again publicly thanked, and promoted to the dignity of one of the Council of State.

On the breaking out of the Dutch war, Blake was created sole admiral of the fleet, and, as we have shown in our narrative of that event, performed great and important services.

For his victory at Santa Cruz, and the destruction of the Spanish Plate fleet, he was once more voted the thanks of the Parliament, and a diamond ring.

Returning soon after to his old station off Cadiz, his health suddenly gave way, and his system, being weakened by scurvy, the vicissitude of hot climates, and fatigue, was so broken down, that, feeling his end approaching, he was seized with a strong desire to end his days in his native country; and, setting sail for England, arrived in Plymouth Sound on the 27th of August, 1658, when he expired as his ship entered the harbour.

Never man so zealous for a faction was so much respected and esteemed, even by the opposite party. He was by principle an inflexible republican; and the late usurpations of Cromwell, amidst all the trust and caresses he received from the ruling powers, were thought to be very little grateful to him.

"*It is still our duty,*" he said to the seamen, "*to fight for our country, into what hands soever the Government may fall.*"

Disinterested, liberal, generous; ambitious only of true glory; dreadful only to his avowed enemies; Blake forms one of the most perfect characters of the age, and the least stained with those errors and violences which were then so predominant.

The Protector ordered him a pompous funeral at the public charge; but the tears of his countrymen were the most honourable panegyric on his memory.

His body on this occasion was interred in Henry VII.'s chapel, Westminster Abbey; but, on the Restoration, it was dragged from its resting place, and, with the remains of Admiral Dean and Popham, thrown, without any ceremony, but with a great deal of insult, into a pit in the neighbouring churchyard of St. Margaret.

CHAPTER XII.

THE NAVY OF THE RESTORATION.—SECOND DUTCH WAR.

AFTER the death of Blake, Admiral Lawson was appointed to command the channel fleet, which was reinforced, and continued in command till after Cromwell's decease, when General Monk, who designed the restoration of the Stuart family, proposed that Montague should be appointed admiral.

Afterwards, when Monk's plans were ripe, Montague was ordered to proceed to Holland, and place his fleet at the disposal of Charles the Second. This was done on the 23rd of May, 1660. Charles embarked at Schevelin, with his brothers, the Dukes of York and Gloucester, and on the 25th they arrived at Dover. Monk received the king as he landed on the beach, was embraced by him, and acted as his escort.

For this service Montague was created Earl of Sandwich and a Knight of the Garter, receiving as well the appointment of Vice-Admiral of England. Lawson and Stayner were knighted, and the seamen in general received special marks of the new king's favour. The Duke of York received the appointment of High Admiral.

His Royal Highness also received the appointment of Warden of the Cinque Ports; while General Monk, through whom this change in the Government had been effected, was made Duke of Albemarle.

LANDING OF KING CHARLES II. AT DOVER.

Several historians have been of opinion that at the time of the Restoration the English navy consisted of only 65 vessels; but in a letter written by Mr. Secretary Coventry, it is mentioned that there were, at this period, "divers ships left without care, being neither of the 36 His Majesty pays, nor the 65 the commissioners pay." So here we have at once a force of 101 vessels in pay, besides those "left without care."

It seems very probable indeed that there was little difference between the strength of our fleet when Cromwell died and when Charles was restored.

At Cromwell's death England had—

3 first-class ships with 250 guns and 1,600 men.
12 second „   „   694   „   3,930 „
16 third   „   „   776   „   4,010 „
42 fourth „   „ 1,476   „   6,630 „
38 fifth   „   „   873   „   4,080 „
34 sixth   „   „   321   „   1,660 „
8 hulks.
4 building.

Total... 157 ships.   with 4,390 guns and 21,910 men.

Sixty-four of these were foreign built, mostly taken from the Dutch and Spaniards.*

In September, 1660, the Earl of Sandwich was sent to Holland, with a squadron of nine men-of-

---

* Derrick's Memoirs of the Royal Navy.

war, to bring over the Princess of Orange, the king's sister. On the 24th of the same month the fleet returned, and the king, with the Duke of York, went on board the admiral's ship, the "Resolution," where they slept that night, and the next day inspected the squadron.

In June, 1661, the earl was ordered to sail, with a numerous and well-equipped fleet, under pretence of convoying the infanta Catherine of Portugal, to whom Charles was betrothed; also to take possession of Tangier, which was part of her dowry. The armament of this fleet greatly exceeded the requirements of mere escort duty, and people soon saw that it had been appointed another task.

This was to compel the Algerines to confirm the treaty Blake had exacted from them.

On the 19th of June the fleet sailed, after having been visited by the Duke of York. Sandwich sailed in the first place to Lisbon, and from thence to Tangier, which was formally delivered up to the English on the 31st January, 1662, when the Earl of Peterborough marched into the town with an English garrison, and received the keys from the Portuguese commander.

On the 29th July, Sandwich, with Sir John Lawson as vice-admiral, arrived before Algiers, and sent Captain Spragge with the king's letter to the governor of the town, also with orders to bring off Mr. Brown, the consul, both of which commissions the captain executed. The same evening a council of war was held, and the next morning certain propositions were sent to the regency then holding power there.

Spragge and Brown were again the messengers, and at eleven o'clock returned to the ship of the admiral, with an Algerine officer of rank, who informed Lord Sandwich that the government of Algiers would not consent to any treaty by which they were deprived of *the right of searching our ships*.

In the meantime those on shore had with very great difficulty brought a great mortar from the mole head to the opposite corner of the harbour, by the help of which, and several new fortifications, they hoped to be able to defend the city.

Lord Sandwich attempted to sail in and burn their shipping, but found it a difficult task. After a great deal of firing on both sides, which did far more damage to the city than to the ships in the harbour, the English admiral sailed away to Lisbon, and soon afterwards took the Portuguese princess on board.

Sir John Lawson was left with a strong squadron to harass the foe, and protect British commerce, which he did with such effect that he compelled the Algerines to renew the treaty. After this, Lawson himself was recalled, and the Moors once more showed a disposition to break the peace, but Captain Allen, who had been left behind with a very small squadron, reduced them to such distress that they were glad to accept any terms of peace.

It was about this time that a judge advocate, with a salary, was first appointed to the English navy.

* * * * * *

Very early in the reign of Charles II. the former popular jealousy against Holland began to manifest itself.

This feeling soon showed itself in many overt acts, on the part of captains of ships and merchants, till at last, assuming a tangible form, the State was obliged to take cognizance of the popular feeling.

As we have given the grounds on which the Commonwealth based its reasons for the FIRST DUTCH WAR, it is right that we should be equally explicit as regards the motives that led to the SECOND.

Trade was beginning, among the English, to be a matter of general concern; but notwithstanding all their efforts and natural advantages, their commerce seemed, hitherto, to stand upon a footing which was somewhat precarious.

The Dutch, who by their industry and frugality were enabled to undersell them in every market, retained possession of the most lucrative branches of commerce; and the English merchants had the mortification to find that all attempts to extend their trade were still turned, by the vigilance of their rivals, to their loss and dishonour.

Their indignation increased when they considered the superior naval power of England; the bravery of her officers and seamen; and, above all, her favourable situation, which enabled her to intercept the whole Dutch commerce.

By the prospect of these advantages, and from motives less just than political, England resolved to make war upon the States, and at once to ravish from them, by force of arms, what they could not obtain, or could obtain but slowly, by superior skill and industry.

Downing, the English minister at the Hague, a man of an insolent, impetuous temper, presented a memorial to the States, containing a list of those depredations of which the English complained.

It is remarkable that all the pretended depredations preceded the year 1662, when a treaty of league and alliance had been renewed with the Dutch, and these complaints were then thought either so ill-grounded, or so frivolous, that they had not been mentioned in the treaty.

Two ships alone, the "Bonaventure" and the "Good-Hope," had been claimed by the English; and it was agreed that the claim should be prosecuted by the ordinary course of justice. The States had consigned a sum of money, in case the cause should be decided against them, but the matter was still in dependence.

Cary, who was entrusted by the proprietors with the management of the law-suit for the "Bonaventure," had resolved to accept of thirty thousand pounds, which were offered him, but was hindered by Downing, who told him that the claim was a matter of State between the two nations, not a concern of private persons. These circumstances give us *no favourable* idea of the justice of the English pretensions.

Charles confined not himself to memorials and remonstrances. Sir Robert Holmes was secretly dispatched with a squadron of twenty-two ships to the coast of Africa. He not only expelled the Dutch from Cape Corse, to which the English had some pretentions, he likewise seized the Dutch settlements of Cape Verde, and the Isle of Goree, together with several ships trading on the coast.

Having sailed to America, he possessed himself of Nova Belgia, since called New York; a territory which James I. had given by patent to the Earl of Sterling, but which had never been colonised but by the Hollanders. When the States complained of these hostile measures, the king, unwilling to avow what he could not well justify, pretended to be totally ignorant of Holmes's enterprise. He, likewise, to give colour to his assertion, confined that admiral to the Tower, but some short time after released him.

The Dutch, finding their applications for redress were likely to be eluded, and that a ground of quarrel was industriously sought for by the English, began to arm with diligence. They even exerted with some precipitation an act of vigour, which hastened on the rupture.

Sir John Lawson and De Ruyter had been sent with combined squadrons into the Mediterranean, in order to chastise the piratical States on the coast of Barbary, and the time of their separation and return was now approaching.

The States secretly dispatched orders to De Ruyter that he should take in provisions at Cadiz; and, sailing towards the coast of Guinea, retaliate on the English, and put the Dutch in possession of those settlements from whence Holmes had expelled them.

De Ruyter, having a considerable force on board, met with no opposition in Guinea. All the new acquisitions of the English, except Cape Corse, were recovered from them. They were even dispossessed of some old settlements, and such of their ships as fell into his hands were seized by De Ruyter. That admiral then sailed to America, when he attacked Barbadoes, but, being repulsed, afterwards appeared before New York, and committed hostilities in Long Island.

Meanwhile, the English preparations for war were advancing with vigour and industry. The king had received no supplies from Parliament; but by his own funds and credit, he was enabled to equip a fleet.

The city of London lent him a hundred thousand pounds: the spirit of the nation seconded his armaments: he himself went from port to port inspecting with great diligence, and encouraging the work: and in a little time the English navy was put in a formidable condition. Eight hundred thousand pounds are said to have been expended on this armament.

When Lawson arrived, and communicated his suspicion of De Ruyter's enterprise, orders were issued for seizing all Dutch ships; and a hundred and thirty-five fell into the hands of the English. These were not declared prizes till afterwards, when war was proclaimed.

The Dutch saw with the utmost regret a war approaching, whence they might dread the most fatal consequences, but which afforded no prospect of advantage. They had tried every art of negociation before they would come to extremities.

Their measures were at this time directed by John de Witte, a minister equally eminent for greatness of mind, for capacity, and for integrity. Though moderate in his private deportment, he knew how to adopt in his counsels that magnanimity which suits the minister of a great state.

It was ever his maxim, that no independent government should yield to another any evident point of reason or equity; and that all such concesssions, so far from preventing war, served no other purpose than to provoke fresh claims and insults. By his management a spirit of union was preserved in all the provinces, great sums were levied, and a navy was equipped, composed of larger ships than the Dutch had ever built before, and such as were able to cope with the fleets of England.

As soon as certain intelligence arrived of De Ruyter's enterprises, Charles declared war against the States (February 22nd, 1665). His fleet, consisting of a hundred and fourteen sail, besides fire-ships and ketches, was commanded by the Duke of York, and, under him, by Prince Rupert and the Earl of Sandwich. It had about twenty-two thousand men on board.

Obdam, who was admiral of the Dutch navy, of nearly equal force, declined not the combat. In the heat of the action, when engaged in close fight with the Duke of York, Obdam's ship blew up. This accident much discouraged the Dutch, who thereupon fled to their own coast.

Van Tromp alone, son of the famous admiral killed during the former war, bravely sustained with his squadron the attacks of the English, and protected the rear of his countrymen. The vanquished had nineteen ships sunk and taken; the victors lost only one. Sir John Lawson died soon after of his wounds.

The Dutch admiral's ship that blew up in this engagement, entered the action with a crew of five hundred men, and out of that number only *five* were known to have been saved.

It is affirmed, and with an appearance of reason, that this victory might have been rendered more complete, had not orders been given to slacken sail, by Brounker, one of the duke's bedchamber, who pretended he had authority from his master. The duke disclaimed the orders; but Brounker was never sufficiently punished for his temerity.

It is allowed that the duke behaved with great bravery during the action. He was long in the thickest of the fire. The Earl of Falmouth, Lord Muskerry, and Mr. Boyle were killed by one shot at his side, and covered him all over with their brains and gore. And it is not likely that in a pursuit, where even persons of inferior station and of the most cowardly dispositions acquire courage, a commander should feel his spirits flag.

This disaster threw the Dutch into consternation, and determined De Witte, who was the soul of their councils, to exert his naval capacity in order to support the declining courage of his countrymen.

He went on board the fleet, which he took under his command, and he soon remedied all those disorders which had been occasioned by the late misfortune. The genius of this man was of the most extensive nature. He quickly became as much master of naval affairs as if he had from his infancy been educated in them, and made improvements in some parts of pilotage and sailing beyond what men expert in those arts had ever been able to attain.

Though the King of France was resolved to support the Hollanders in that unequal contest in which they were engaged, yet he protracted his declaration, and employed the time in naval preparations, both in the ocean and the Mediterranean.

The King of Denmark, meanwhile, was resolved not to remain an idle spectator of the contest between the maritime powers. The part which he acted was certainly most extraordinary; he made a secret agreement with Charles to seize all the Dutch ships in his harbours, and to share the spoils with the English, provided they would assist him in executing this measure.

In order to increase his prey, he perfidiously invited the Dutch to take shelter in his ports; and, accordingly, the East India fleet, very richly laden, had put into Bergen.

Sandwich, who now commanded the English navy —the duke having gone ashore—dispatched Sir Thomas Tiddiman with a squadron to attack them; but whether from the King of Denmark's delay in sending orders to the governor, or, what is more probable, from his avidity in endeavouring to engross the whole booty, the English admiral, though he behaved with great bravery, failed of his purpose. The Danish governor fired upon him, and the Dutch, having had leisure to fortify themselves, made a gallant resistance.

The Dutch, encouraged by fresh allies, and other favourable circumstances, continued resolute to exert themselves to the utmost in their own defence.

De Ruyter, their great admiral, was arrived from his expedition to Guinea; their Indian fleet was come home in safety; their harbours were crowded with merchant ships; faction at home was appeased; the young Prince of Orange had put himself under the tuition of the States of Holland and of De Witte, their pensionary, who executed his trust with honour and fidelity; and the animosity which the Hollanders entertained against the attack of the English, so unprovoked as they thought it, made them thirst for revenge, and hope for better success in their next enterprise.

Such vigour was exerted in the common cause, that in order to man the fleet, all merchants were prohibited to sail, and even the fisheries were suspended.

The English likewise continued in the same disposition, though another more grievous calamity had joined itself to that of war. The plague had broken out in London; and that with such violence as to cut off in a year near NINETY thousand inhabitants.

By the spring of the following year, 1666, the Dutch having formed the triple alliance with France and Denmark, exerted all their strength and energy to prepare a fleet that should decide the war, and give them a certain victory.

Though terribly overmatched by three such powerful foes as France, Denmark and Holland, England possessed a great advantage in her natural situation, for, lying as she did, between the fleets of her two most important enemies, she might, by well-concerted measures, prevent their junction, and even destroy them in detail.

But such was the jealousy and animosity existing between the English admirals, Prince Rupert, the king's cousin, and Monk, the Duke of Albemarle, or such the want of intelligence in her ministers, that this circumstance turned rather to her prejudice.

Louis had given orders to the Duke of Beaufort, his admiral, to sail from Toulon; and the French squadron under his command, consisting of above forty sail, was now commonly supposed to be entering the Channel.

The Dutch fleet, to the number of seventy-six sail, was at sea, under the command of De Ruyter and Van Tromp, in order to join him.

The Duke of Albemarle and Prince Rupert commanded the English fleet, which did not exceed seventy-four sail. Albemarle, who, from his successes under the Protector, had learned to despise the enemy, pro-

posed to detach Prince Rupert with twenty ships, in order to oppose the Duke of Beaufort.

Sir George Ayscue, well acquainted with the bravery and conduct of De Ruyter, protested against the temerity of this resolution; but Albemarle's authority prevailed. The remainder of the English set sail to give battle to the Dutch, who, seeing the enemy advance quickly upon them, cut their cables and prepared for the combat.

The Dutch fleet on this occasion consisted of 71 He himself was found dead in his cabin, all covered with blood.

The English had the weather-gage of the enemy; but, as the wind blew so hard that they could not use their lower-tier guns, they derived but small advantage from this circumstance. The Dutch shot, however, fell chiefly on their sails and rigging, and few ships were sunk or much damaged.

Chain-shot was, at that time, a nearly new invention, commonly attributed to De Witte.

THE WRECK OF THE UNICORN.

ships of the line, 12 frigates, 14 fire-ships, and 8 yachts, carrying 22,000 men and 4,716 guns.

The battle that ensued is one of the most memorable that we read of in story,—whether we consider its long duration, or the desperate courage with which it was fought. Albemarle made here some atonement, by his valour, for the rashness of the attempt. No youth, in fact, animated by glory and ambitious hopes, could have more exerted himself than did this man, who was now in the decline of life, and who had reached the summit of honours.

On the first day (June 1st) Sir William Berkeley, vice-admiral, leading the van, fell into the thickest of the enemy, was overpowered, and his ship taken.

Van Tromp's ship was disabled, and he was obliged to remove into another; De Ruyter, coming to his assistance, met the same fate, while the magazine of another Dutch vessel exploded, destroying the ship and killing Admiral Stagg-hower.

Later in the day, Sir John Harman, in the "Henry," found himself surrounded by several of the enemy. The Dutch admiral, Evertzen, who commanded on board the "Zealand," hailed, and offered quarter.

"No, sir," replied Harman; "it has not come to that yet."

In the furious cannonade that followed Evertzen was killed. One of the Dutch fire-ships grappled on the starboard quarter of the "Henry," and was for some time unobserved, on account of the dense smoke; but at length the boatswain of the "Henry" perceived it, jumped on board, removed the grappling irons, and instantly regained his own ship.

This brave feat was scarcely accomplished when another fire-ship appeared on the larboard side, and the sails and rigging of the "Henry" caught fire. Destruction seemed inevitable, and several of the crew prepared to jump overboard. On seeing this, Sir John Harman, whose leg had been broken, drew his sword and threatened to kill any man who attempted to leave the vessel. Afterwards, by dint of great exertion, the flames were quenched, and the "Henry," extricated from her perilous position, was compelled to retire to Harwich for repairs.

Darkness coming on, the combat was stopped for a time, and the English commanders held a council of war, during which the Duke of Albemarle uttered the following sentiments:

"To be overcome is the fortune of war, but to fly is the practice of cowards. Let us teach the world that Englishmen would rather be acquainted with death than with fear."

While the chiefs were consulting and deciding on a plan of action for the next day, the sailors were engaged in repairing damages.

The second day the wind had somewhat fallen, and the combat became more steady and more terrible. The English now found that the greatest valour cannot compensate the superiority of numbers, or against an enemy who is well conducted and who is not defective in courage.

De Ruyter and Van Tromp, rivals in glory and enemies from faction, exerted themselves in emulation of each other; and De Ruyter had the advantage of disengaging and saving his antagonist, who had been surrounded by the English, and was in the most imminent danger.

Sixteen fresh ships joined the Dutch fleet during the action; and the English were so shattered that their fighting ships were reduced to twenty-eight, and they found themselves obliged to retreat towards their own coast. The Dutch followed them, and were on the point of renewing the combat, when a calm, which came on a little before night, prevented the engagement.

Next morning, the English were obliged to continue their retreat; and a proper disposition was made for that purpose. The shattered ships were ordered to stretch a-head, and sixteen of the most entire followed them in good order, and kept the enemy in awe. Albemarle himself closed the rear, and presented an undaunted countenance to his victorious foes.

The Earl of Ossory, son of Ormond, a gallant youth, who sought honour and experience in every action throughout Europe, was then on board the admiral's vessel. Albemarle confessed to him his intention rather to blow up his ship and perish gloriously than yield to the enemy. Ossory applauded this desperate resolution.

About two o'clock, the Dutch had come up with their enemy, and were ready to renew the fight, when a new fleet was descried from the south, crowding all sail to reach the scene of action.

The Dutch flattered themselves that the French admiral, Beaufort, had arrived, to cut off the retreat of the vanquished; the English hoped that Prince Rupert had come to turn the scale of action. Albemarle, who had received intelligence of the Prince's approach, bent his course towards him.

Unhappily, Sir George Ayscue, in a ship of 100 guns, the largest in the fleet, struck on the Galloper Sands, and could receive no assistance from his friends, who were hastening to join the reinforcement. He could not even reap the consolation of perishing with honour and revenging his death on his enemies. They were preparing fire-ships to attack him, and he was obliged to strike.

The English sailors, seeing the necessity, with the utmost indignation surrendered themselves prisoners.

Albemarle and Prince Rupert were now determined to face the enemy; and next morning the battle began afresh, with more equal force than ever, and with equal valour.

After long cannonading, the fleets came to a close combat, which was continued with great violence till they were parted by a mist. The English retired first into their harbours.

Though the English, by their obstinate courage, reaped the chief honour in this engagement, it is somewhat uncertain who obtained the victory. The Hollanders took a few ships, and, having some appearances of advantage, expressed their satisfaction by all the signs of triumph and rejoicing.

But as the English fleet was repaired in a little time, and put to sea more formidable than ever, together with many of those ships which the Dutch had boasted of having burned or destroyed, all Europe saw that those two brave nations were engaged in a contest which was not likely to prove decisive.

It was a junction alone of the French that could give a decisive superiority to the Dutch. In order to facilitate this junction, De Ruyter, having repaired his fleet, posted himself at the mouth of the Thames. The English, under Prince Rupert and Albemarle, were not long in coming to the attack.

The English fleet now consisted of 80 men-of-war and 19 fire-ships, divided into three squadrons,—the *Red*, commanded by Prince Rupert and the Duke of Albemarle, with Sir Joseph Jordan as vice-admiral and Sir Robert Holmes rear-admiral; the *White*, with Sir Thomas Allen, admiral, Sir Thomas Teddiman, vice-admiral, and Urthurt or Urquhart, rear-admiral; and the *Blue* squadron, commanded by Admiral Sir Jeremy Smith, Vice-Admiral Sir Edward Spragge, and Rear-Admiral Kempethorne.

The Dutch had, according to their own accounts,

88 men-of-war and 20 fire-ships, also divided into three squadrons, commanded by De Ruyter, Van Tromp, and Evertzen, a brother of the commander slain on the 1st of June.

The valour and experience of the commanders, as well as of the seamen, rendered the engagement fierce and obstinate.

Sir Thomas Allen, who commanded the White Squadron of the English, attacked the Dutch van, which he entirely routed, and killed the three admirals who commanded it. Van Tromp engaged Sir Jeremy Smith, and during the heat of action he was separated from the main body—whether by accident or design was never certainly known.

De Ruyter, with very great valour, maintained the combat against the main body of the English; and though overpowered by numbers, kept his station till night ended the engagement.

Next day, finding the Dutch fleet scattered and discouraged, his high spirit submitted to a retreat, which he conducted with such skill as to render it equally honourable to himself as the greatest victory.

Full of indignation, however, at yielding the superiority to the enemy, he frequently exclaimed—

"My God! what a wretch am I! Among so many thousand bullets, is there not one to put an end to my miserable life?"

Young De Witte, his son-in-law, who stood near, exhorted him, since he sought death, to turn upon the English, and render his life a dear purchase to the victors. But De Ruyter esteemed it more worthy a brave man to persevere to the uttermost, and as long as possible to render service to his country. All that night and the next day the English pressed upon the rear of the Dutch; and it was chiefly by the redoubled efforts of De Ruyter that the latter saved themselves in their harbours.

When the remnant of the Dutch fleet had reached a place of safety behind the shoals and sandbanks of the coast, Prince Rupert sent a little boat, called the "Fanfan," which only carried two small guns. This miniature craft rowed up to De Ruyter's vessel, and, shifting both her cannon to one side, fired broadsides at the huge Dutch ship for the space of at least half-an-hour, to the great amusement of the English and indignation of the Hollanders, till a well-directed ball so damaged the boat, that the crew had to row with all their might to save their lives.

In this great battle the Dutch lost 20 ships, 4 of their admirals (the second Evertzen being one of them), many captains, and 4,000 men killed and 3,000 wounded. The English lost the "Resolution," which was burnt, 3 officers of rank, and about 400 sailors killed.

The loss sustained by the Hollanders in this action was also very considerable; and as violent animosities had broken out between the two admirals, who engaged all the officers on one side or the other, the consternation which took place was great among the provinces.

Van Tromp's commission was at last taken from him; but though several captains had misbehaved, they were so effectually protected by their friends in the magistracy of the towns, that most of them escaped punishment, and many were still continued in their commands.

The English now rode incontestable masters of the sea, and insulted the Dutch in their harbours. A detachment, under Sir Robert Holmes, was sent to Vlie.

The ships appointed for this duty were comparatively small vessels—5 of the fourth-rate, 3 of the fifth-rate, 5 fire-ships, and 7 ketches. On the 8th of August these vessels came to anchor about a league from the buoys, where they met the industrious little "Fanfan," which had ventured nearly into the harbour, and had discovered there two men-of-war and about 150 merchant vessels of over 200 tons burden each, most of them richly laden with merchandize from Russia, Guinea, and the East Indies.

Sir Robert considered an attack by land hazardous, and therefore resolved to commence action with the ships, two of which were ordered to remain at anchor outside the buoys. The rest of the fleet with great difficulty got into Schelling Road, where the "Tiger" came to an anchor. Sir Robert then went on board the "Fanfan," and signalled for the captains, with whom he held a council of war, at which it was resolved that the "Pembroke," being the ship that drew the least water, should lead the way, with the five fire-ships.

Captain Brown, with one of the fire-ships, very bravely and cleverly ran into one of the men-of-war, and burnt her completely. Another fire-ship, at the same time, attacked the second man-of-war, but the captain perceiving his danger backed his sails: by so doing he escaped the fire-ship, but ran his vessel aground, in which condition she was taken and burnt by some of the English long-boats. The three other fire-ships bore down on three of the great merchantmen, which carried flags on their main tops, and burnt them.

This threw the whole fleet into the greatest confusion.

Sir Robert Holmes then again called his captains, and gave orders that Sir William Jennings, with all the boats that could be spared, should go into the harbour to sink, burn, and destroy; but they were strictly commanded not to plunder. This was so well done that only twelve ships escaped.

The next day it was decided that it would be more expedient to land on the Island of Schelling rather than on that of Vlie; so accordingly Sir Robert landed with eleven companies of men, meeting with no opposition. He left one company in charge of the boats, and marched the others to Brandaris, a town containing at least a thousand houses, which he destroyed. The inhabitants had fled.

The Dutch merchants, who lost by this enterprise, uniting themselves to the Orange faction, exclaimed against an administration which they pretended had brought such disgrace and ruin on the country. None but the firm and intrepid mind of John De Witte could have supported itself under such a complication of calamities.

The King of France, apprehensive that the Dutch would sink under their misfortunes, at least that De Witte, his friend, might be dispossessed of the administration, hastened the advance of the Duke of Beaufort. The Dutch fleet of 79 men-of-war likewise was again equipped, and, under command of De Ruyter, cruised near the Straits of Dover.

Prince Rupert, with the English navy, now stronger than ever, came full sail upon them. The Dutch admiral thought proper to decline the combat, and retired into St. John's Road, near Boulogne. Here he sheltered himself from the English and from a furious storm that arose.

Prince Rupert, too, was obliged to retire into St. Helen's, where he stayed some time in order to repair the damages which he had sustained.

Meanwhile, the Duke of Beaufort proceeded up the Channel, and passed the English fleet unperceived; but he did not find the Dutch, as he expected. De Ruyter had been seized with a fever, many of the chief officers were attacked with sickness, a contagious distemper was spread through the fleet, and the States thought it necessary to recall them into their harbours before the enemy could be refitted.

The French king, anxious for his navy, which, with so much care and industry, he had lately built, despatched orders to Beaufort to make the best of his way to Brest. That admiral had again the good fortune to pass the English. One ship alone, the "Ruby," fell into the hands of the enemy.

More tired of a war which he had unjustly provoked than the Dutch, who had been such serious losers by it, Charles was the first to throw out hints of his desire for peace. These were readily acted on by the allies, and preliminaries for that purpose were opened at Paris.

Charles had but one chief object to achieve in effecting a peace with France and Holland—namely, to secure for the use of the Court, and his own personal expenses, the large sums granted by the Parliament for the prosecution of the war.

The expenses of the different armaments, however, had hitherto been so imperative and pressing, that he had been compelled to employ a very large portion of the sums granted to their legitimate use, much to the disgust of himself and his importunate courtiers.

After the late victory, the Parliament, delighted at the success of the national arms, and further to enable Charles to strengthen the fleet, secure the defences of the country, and pay the seamen their arrears, granted him an immediate advance of *one million eight hundred thousand pounds*.

PORTRAIT OF JAMES, DUKE OF YORK, LORD HIGH ADMIRAL OF ENGLAND.

This immense sum of ready money was too tempting to be resisted, and Charles resolved, if possible, to retain it in his own hands, or, at all events, to fill the privy purse before he thought of his public disbursements.

The motives that induced the French king to desire a suspension of hostilities were twofold. He wanted to keep the balance of power equally divided between England and Holland; and, as his ally had already endured loss enough, he had no desire to see her further humiliated, either by the loss of prestige or of commerce.

Another, and more powerful, motive was, that Louis was proud of his navy, a hobby on which he had expended such vast sums, and of whose safety he was in constant dread. For these reasons the French king was anxious to bring the war to a speedy conclusion.

The desire for peace on the side of the Dutch was much more natural and simple. They had suffered the mortification of a defeat, and severe loss in their ships, besides enduring an incalculable injury in their trade; and, finally, in addition to all, they had incurred great debts to equip their fleet.

Charles, who thought the Dutch to be much more crippled than they really were, and that after their late defeat they would gladly accede to any offers of peace, remitted all his preparations, omitted to refit or augment the fleet, and leaving the country undefended and the seamen unpaid, quietly awaited the ratification of peace.

The Dutch, however, who seemed to be well informed on English affairs, and had already discovered in many ways that Charles II. had no attribute in common with the once resistless Cromwell, were resolved to make the most of the short time taken up in the negotiations for peace.

Anxious, therefore, to get the best terms they could before the suspension of the war, they took advantage of Charles's neglect and folly to strike a blow at the national honour of this country, that should at least enable them to maintain their own at the conclusion of hostilities.

We have now to record one of the greatest and most humiliating insults that Great Britain ever had to endure from an enemy—a degradation which she owed solely to the wanton extravagance and carelessness of her own sovereign.

De Witte protracted the negotiations at Breda, and hastened the naval preparations. The Dutch fleet appeared in the Thames under the command of De Ruyter, in June, 1667, and threw the English into the utmost consternation.

The first ships De Ruyter saw were eight or nine outward-bound merchantmen, convoyed by a man-of-war. On perceiving the Dutch fleet these tacked, and were chased nearly as far as Gravesend, when the wind dropped, and the Dutch were obliged to anchor. Then a storm arose, succeeded by a strong north-east wind, favoured by which De Ruyter sailed to the Isle of Sheppey, where he bombarded and took the fortress of Sheerness, as well as an English man-of-war.

BOMBARDMENT OF SHEERNESS BY THE DUTCH.

The next day they sailed up the river Medway.

Fears were entertained that London would be visited by these daring invaders, to prevent which nine ships were sunk at Woolwich and four at Blackwall, many batteries of artillery being stationed near the obstacles.

A chain had been drawn across the river Medway; some fortifications had been added to Chatham and Upnor Castle, but all these preparations were unequal to the present necessity.

Having the advantage of a spring-tide and an easterly wind, the Dutch pressed on and broke the chain, though fortified by some ships which had been sunk there by orders of the Duke of Albemarle. They burned the three ships which lay to guard the chain, the "Matthias," the "Unity," and the "Charles the Fifth."

After damaging several vessels, and possessing themselves of the hull of the "Royal Charles," which the English had burned, they advanced with six men-of-war and five fire-ships as far as Upnor Castle, where they burned the "Royal Oak," the "Loyal London," and the "Great James."

Captain Douglas, who commanded on board the "Royal Oak," perished in the flames, though he had an easy opportunity of escaping. "Never was it known," he said, "that a Douglas had left his post without orders."

The Hollanders fell down the Medway without receiving any considerable damage, and it was apprehended that they might next tide sail up the Thames, and extend their hostilities even to London Bridge.

Defences of various kinds were prepared for their reception; platforms were raised in many places, furnished with artillery; the train-bands were called out; and every place was in a violent agitation.

The Dutch sailed next to Portsmouth, where they made a fruitless attempt; they met with no better success at Plymouth; they insulted Harwich, and sailed again up the Thames as far as Tilbury, where they were repulsed.

The whole coast was in alarm; and had the French thought proper at this time to join the Dutch fleet and to invade England, consequences the most fatal might have been justly apprehended.

But Louis had no intention to push the victory to such extremities. His interest required that a balance should be kept between the two maritime powers,—not that an uncontrolled superiority should be given to either.

Great indignation prevailed among the English to see an enemy whom they regarded as inferior—whom they had expected totally to subdue, and over whom they had gained many honourable advantages—now of a sudden ride undisputed masters of the ocean, burn their ships in their very harbours, fill every place with confusion, and strike terror into the capital itself.

The cause of all these disasters could be ascribed neither to bad fortune, to the misconduct of admirals, nor to the bad behaviour of seamen, but solely to the avarice—at least, to the improvidence —of the Government.

Many acts of heroism and devotion were performed, alike by officers and men, on board the English ships on that day of national disgrace.

One of these we have already recounted, in the

case of Captain Douglas, who, having received orders to defend his ship to the last extremity, but none to retire, preferred death to what he considered a breach of duty.

The following anecdote shows, in a remarkable manner, the coolness of the English commander under such trying and humiliating circumstances.

The famous Duke of Albemarle, who was equally distinguished in naval and military exploits, possessed personal courage in the highest degree. When the Dutch fleet approached Chatham, the duke, apprehending they would land, exposed himself to the hottest of their fire, that his example might keep others to their duty, and defeat the design of the enemy.

When a person of distinction expostulated with him on the danger to which he exposed himself, and would have persuaded him to retire, he answered, very coolly—

"Sir, if I had been afraid of bullets, I should have quitted this trade long ago."

On the 10th of July, 1667, peace with Holland was signed at Breda, the English being compelled to forego most of their former claims, and only retaining the—at that time considered insignificant —settlement of New York, in America.

Among the minor actions of this war must be recorded the spirited engagement with the enemy off St. Kitts, or Christopher.

Sir John Harman, cruising in the West Indies with a squadron of twelve frigates, fell in with a combined fleet of Dutch and French to the number of twenty-two ships, many of them line of battle, the Dutch being under Admiral Evertzen, the third of the family, and the French commanded by M. de la Bume.

Harman's small fleet was almost surrounded by the enemy, nearly every ship having two antagonists at once, but with such determination did the English keep up the fight that the French, as if afraid of injuring their ships, gradually dropped out of action, leaving the Dutch to carry on the fight.

After an obstinate engagement of some hours, Admiral Evertzen was obliged to sheer off, and sailed away with the wreck of his fleet, leaving the French to their fate.

In this short but glorious action, five of the combined fleet were burnt, or blown up, and several others sunk.

The French admiral, finding himself deserted by the Dutch, bore up for an anchorage in the island of St. Christopher, off which the battle had taken place, and where he believed himself in safety.

Sir John Harman, after seeing his gallant enemy fairly beyond recall, cleared his deck for a second action, and bearing down on the French ships, attacked them with such fury, that every ship was either captured or destroyed.

On his passage home, the brave admiral met with a mishap that nearly deprived the country of his valuable services.

His ship, the "Unicorn," was wrecked on the rocky shore of Bermuda, and totally destroyed. Only a few of the crew escaped to land;—happily the gallant admiral was among them. However, in a few hours they were rescued by the other vessels.

CHAPTER XIII.

THE THIRD DUTCH WAR, 1672.

TO second the French king's ambitious views of conquest in the Netherlands, Charles entered into a secret treaty with Louis, not only not to oppose his unprincipled aggressions on the Dutch, but actually to assist him in his undertaking, by declaring war on the Hollanders, and engaging their fleets, while Louis burst into their country with an overwhelming army.

The better to secure the goodwill and co-operation of the English government, the French king took special care, not only to bribe all Charles's most influential ministers, but actually allowed the king himself a yearly pension to insure his good offices in this infamous scheme of tyranny and injustice.

Still further to bind the pleasure-loving Charles to his interest, he sent him over a very beautiful and accomplished French lady, whom Charles subsequently created Duchess of Portsmouth, and who, for the rest of the king's life, kept him faithful to his alliance with France.

The reasons Charles assigned for his meditated breach with Holland, and for plunging two countries into a war, ruinous to the interests of both, and repugnant alike to the English as to the Dutch, were almost too contemptible for record.

Reasons more unjust and frivolous were probably never employed to justify a flagrant violation of treaty.

The following are some of the chief alleged grievances:—

Some complaints that were made of injuries done to the East India Company, which yet that company disavowed. The detention of some English in Surinam is mentioned, though it appears that these persons had voluntarily remained there; the refusal of a Dutch fleet on its own coasts to strike to an English yacht is much aggravated; and to piece up all these pretensions, some abusive pictures are mentioned and represented as a ground of quarrel.

The Dutch were long at a loss what to make of this article, till it was discovered that a portrait of

Cornelius De Witte, brother to the pensionary, painted by order of certain magistrates of Dordt, and hung up in a chamber of the town-house, had given occasion to the complaint.

In the perspective of this portrait, the painter had drawn some ships on fire in a harbour. This was construed to be Chatham, where De Witte had really distinguished himself and had acquired honour; but little did he imagine that, while the insult itself committed in open war had so long been forgiven, the picture of it should draw such severe vengeance upon his country.

The yacht in question had been despatched to bring home from the Hague Lady Temple, the wife of the late minister together with his effects. The captain sailed through the Dutch fleet, which lay on their own coasts, and he had orders to make them strike, to fire on them, and to persevere till they should return his fire.

The Dutch admiral, Van Ghent, surprised at this bravado, came on board the yacht and expressed his willingness to pay respect to the British flag, according to former practice; but that a fleet on their own coast should strike to a single vessel, and that not a ship of war, was, he said, such an innovation, that he durst not, without express orders, agree to it.

The captain, thinking it dangerous as well as absurd to renew firing in the midst of the Dutch fleet continued his course, and for that neglect of orders was committed to the Tower.

An attempt, before the declaration of war, was made on the Dutch Smyrna fleet (March 13) by Sir Robert Holmes.

This fleet consisted of 70 sail, valued at a million and a half, and the hopes of seizing so rich a prey had been a great motive for engaging Charles in the present war, and he had considered that capture as a principal resource of supporting his military enterprises.

Holmes, with nine frigates and three yachts, had orders to go on this expedition, and he passed Sprague in the Channel, who was returning with a squadron from a cruise in the Mediterranean.

Sprague informed him of the near approach of the Hollanders; and had not Holmes, from a desire of engrossing the honour and profit of the enterprise, kept the secret of his orders, the conjunction of these squadrons had rendered the success infallible.

When Holmes approached the Dutch, he put on an amicable appearance and invited the admiral, Van Ness, who commanded the convoy, to come on board of him; one of his captains gave a like insidious invitation to the rear-admiral.

But these officers were on their guard. They had received an intimation of the hostile intentions of the English, and had already put all the ships of war and merchantmen in an excellent posture of defence. Three times were they valiantly assailed by the English, and as often did they valiantly defend themselves.

In the third attempt one of the Dutch ships of war was taken, and three or four of their most inconsiderable merchantmen fell into the enemy's hands. The rest, fighting with skill and courage, continued their course, and, favoured by a mist, got safe into their own harbours.

This attempt is denominated perfidious and piratical by the Dutch writers, and even by many of the English. It merits, at least, the appellation of irregular; and as it had been attended with bad success, it brought double shame upon the contrivers.

The English ministry endeavoured to apologise for the action, by pretending that it was a casual encounter, arising from the obstinacy of the Dutch in refusing the honours of the flag; but the contrary was so well known, that even Holmes himself had not the assurance to persist in this asseveration.

After this flagrant act the Dutch could no longer doubt of the hostile intentions of the English, and Charles having declared war, the Dutch at once prepared to meet this unexpected danger, and De Ruyter was sent to sea with a formidable fleet, consisting of 91 ships of war and 44 fire-ships. Cornelius de Witte was on board as deputy from the States.

They sailed in quest of the English, who were under the command of the Duke of York, and had already joined the French, under Mareschal d'Etrees.

The combined fleets lay at Solebay in a very negligent posture; and Sandwich, being an experienced officer, had given the Duke warning of the danger, but received, it is said, such an answer, as intimated that there was more of caution than of courage in his apprehensions.

Upon the appearance of the enemy, everyone ran to his post with precipitation, and many ships were obliged to cut their cables in order to be in readiness. Sandwich commanded the van; and though determined to conquer or perish, he so tempered his courage with prudence, that the whole fleet was visibly indebted to him for its safety.

He hastened out of the bay, where it seemed easy for De Ruyter with his fire-ships to have destroyed the combined fleets, which were crowded together, and by this wise measure gave time to the Duke of York, who commanded the main body, and to Mareschal d'Etrees, admiral of the rear, to disengage themselves.

He himself, meanwhile, rushed into the battle with the Hollanders, and by presenting himself to every danger, drew upon him all the bravest of the enemy.

He killed Van Ghent, a Dutch admiral, and beat off his ship. He sunk another ship, which ventured to lay him aboard. He sunk three fire-ships which endeavoured to grapple with him; and though his vessel was torn in pieces with shot, and of a thousand men she contained nearly six hundred were laid dead upon the deck, he continued still to thunder with all his artillery in the midst of the enemy.

Another fire-ship, more fortunate than the preceding, having laid hold of his vessel, her destruction was now inevitable. Warned by Sir Edward Haddock, his captain, he refused to make his escape, and bravely embraced death as a shelter from that ignominy which a rash expression of the duke's, he thought, had thrown on him.

During this fierce engagement with Sandwich, De Ruyter did not remain inactive. He attacked the Duke of York, and fought him with such fury for above two hours, that of two-and-thirty actions in which that admiral had been engaged, he declared this combat to be the most obstinately disputed.

The duke's ship was so shattered that he was obliged to leave her, and remove his flag to another. His squadron was overpowered with numbers, till Sir Joseph Jordan, who had succeeded to Sandwich's command, came to his assistance; and the fight being more evenly balanced, was continued till night, when the Dutch retired, and were not followed by the English.

The loss sustained by the two maritime powers was nearly equal, if it did not rather fall more heavy on the English. The French suffered very little, because they had scarcely been engaged in the action; and as this backwardness is not their national character, it was concluded that they had received secret orders to spare their ships, while the Dutch and English should weaken each other by their mutual animosity.

Almost all the other actions during this war tended to confirm this suspicion.

The gallant Earl of Sandwich, then in his seventy-seventh year, deeply grieved by the inconsiderate answer made by the Duke of York to his prudent suggestion concerning the negligent position of the fleet, had vowed never to outlive what he considered an imputation on his honour, but die in the action.

When he perceived that it was impossible to save the vessel, he begged his captain, Sir Edward Haddock, who was almost his only surviving officer, and the crew to get into the boats and save themselves, declaring that he would be the last man to quit the ship.

Many of the seamen, however, with a noble disdain of death, that ought never to be forgotten, refused to leave their admiral, and, the ship blowing up soon after, perished with him.

The English officers, and especially the seamen, were highly indignant at the remarkable backwardness on the part of their French allies; and if they had not known them to be a brave and chivalrous nation, and beyond the imputation of cowardice, such repeated acts of timidity as were shown by the French fleet might have been interpreted as unworthy pusillanimity or fear.

The English officers, however, did not know the secret orders of the French admiral, to let the Dutch and English injure one another as much as possible, but save his own ships by all possible means. Not knowing this, the English were naturally indignant at having all the fighting to do, while their allies claimed quite half the honour of every victory.

Prince Rupert was resolved that on the first possible opportunity his French allies should do something more than merely smell the battle from a distance.

As we shall have occasion to show in the present chapter, the prince kept his promise; and in the fight off the Dutch coast, contrived to place D'Etree's squadron in the van of the battle, and where his ships were exposed for a time to the hottest and most destructive fire of the enemy.

After a time, when some English ships took fire,

CRESTS OF VESSELS IN THE ROYAL NAVY (A.D. 1870).

the English sailors expressed unequivocal signs of delight at the catastrophe, and at seeing the *Mounseers*, as they called their allies, get so good a thrashing.

One tar in particular was so elated at the sight, that though his ship, which had taken the place of a disabled Frenchman, was rocking under a terrific broadside of a Dutch seventy-four, he thrust his head out of one of the port-holes, and pointing to his crippled ally, cried out—"Well done, little

from the precarious operations of winds and tides, as well as from the smoke and darkness in which everything is there involved.

No wonder, therefore, that accounts of those battles are apt to contain uncertainties and contradictions, especially when delivered by writers of the hostile nations, who take pleasure in exalting the advantages of their own countrymen and depressing those of the enemy.

All we can say with certainty of this battle is

THE SHIP "BRITON" OVERTAKEN BY A WATERSPOUT.

breeches." A term of derision applied to the immense trunk-hose at that time worn by the Dutch.

The money granted by Parliament sufficed to equip a fleet, of which Prince Rupert was declared admiral; for the Duke of York was set aside by the Test Act. Sir Edward Sprague and the Earl of Ossory commanded under the prince. A French squadron joined them, commanded by D'Etrees.

The combined fleets set sail towards the coast of Holland (28th May), and found the enemy lying at anchor within the sands at Schonvelt.

There is a natural confusion attending sea-fights, even beyond other military transactions, derived

that both sides boasted of the victory, and we may thence infer that the event was not decisive. The Dutch, being near home, retired into their harbours. In a week they were refitted, and presented themselves again to the combined fleets.

A new action ensued (4th June), not more decisive than the foregoing. It was not fought with great obstinacy on either side; but whether the Dutch or the allies first retired seems to be a matter of uncertainty.

The loss in the former of these actions fell chiefly on the French, whom the English, diffident of their intentions, took care to place under their own squadrons, and they thereby exposed them to all the fire of the enemy. There seems not to have been a ship lost on either side in the second engagement.

It was sufficient glory to De Ruyter, that, with a fleet much inferior to the combined squadrons of France and England, he could fight them without any notable disadvantage, and it was sufficient victory that he could defeat the project of a descent in Zealand, which, had it taken place in the present circumstances, would have endangered the total overthrow of the Dutch commonwealth.

Prince Rupert was also suspected of not favouring the king's projects for subduing Holland or enlarging his authority at home, and, from these motives, he was thought not to have pressed so hard on the enemy as his well-known valour gave reason to expect.

It is, indeed, remarkable that, during this war, though the English, with their allies, much overmatched the Dutch, they were not able to gain any advantage over them; while in the former war, though often overborne by numbers, they still exerted themselves with the greatest courage, and always acquired great renown, sometimes even signal victories.

But they were disgusted at the present measures, which they deemed pernicious to their country; they were not satisfied of the justice of the quarrel, and they entertained a perpetual jealousy of their confederates, whom, had they been permitted, they would with much more pleasure have destroyed than even the enemy themselves.

If Prince Rupert was not favourable to the designs of the Court, he enjoyed as little favour from the Court—at least, from the Duke of York, who, though he could no longer command the fleet, still possessed the chief authority in the Admiralty.

The prince complained of a total want of everything: powder, shot, provisions, beer, and even water, and he went into harbour that he might refit his ships, and supply his numerous necessities.

After some weeks he was refitted, and again put to sea. The hostile fleets met at the mouth of the Texel, and fought the last battle (11th August) which during so many years these neighbouring maritime powers had disputed with each other.

De Ruyter and, under him, Van Tromp, commanded the Dutch in this action, as in the two former; for the Prince of Orange had reconciled these gallant rivals, and they retained nothing of their former animosity, except that emulation which made them exert themselves with more distinguished bravery against the enemies of their country.

Brankert was opposed to D'Etrees; De Ruyter to Prince Rupert; Van Tromp to Sprague. It is to be remarked that in all actions the brave admirals last mentioned had still selected each other as the only antagonists worthy each other's valour, and no decisive advantage had as yet been gained by either of them. They fought in this battle as if there were no medium between death and victory.

D'Etrees and all the French squadron, except Rear-Admiral Martel, kept at a distance; and Brankert, instead of attacking them, bore down to the assistance of De Ruyter, who was engaged in furious combat with Prince Rupert.

On no occasion did the prince acquire more deserved honour; his conduct, as well as valour, shone out with signal lustre. Having disengaged his squadron from the numerous enemies with whom he was everywhere surrounded, and having joined Sir John Chichley, his rear-admiral, who had been separated from him, he made haste to the relief of Sprague, who was hard pressed by Van Tromp's squadron.

The "Royal Prince," in which Sprague first engaged, was so disabled that he was obliged to hoist his flag on board the "St. George," while Van Tromp was for a like reason obliged to quit his ship, "The Golden Lion," and go on board "The Comet."

The fight was renewed with the utmost fury by these valorous rivals, and by the rear-admirals, their seconds. Ossory, rear-admiral to Sprague, was preparing to board Tromp, when he saw the "St. George" terribly torn, and in a manner disabled. Sprague was leaving her, in order to hoist his flag on board a third ship, and return to the charge, when a shot, which had passed through the "St. George," struck his boat and sunk her. The admiral was drowned, to the great regret of Van Tromp himself, who bestowed on his valour deserved praise.

Prince Rupert found affairs in this dangerous situation, and saw most of the ships in Sprague's squadron disabled from fight. The engagement, however, was renewed, and became very close and bloody.

The prince threw the enemy into disorder, and to increase it, he sent among them two fire-ships, at the same time making a signal for the French to bear down, which, if they had done, a decisive victory must have ensued.

But the prince, when he saw that they neglected his signal, and observed that most of his ships were in no condition to keep long at sea, wisely provided for their safety by making easy sail towards the English coast.

The victory in this battle was as doubtful as in all the actions fought during the present war.

The extreme unpopularity of the Dutch war in England, conjoined with the disgust the people had taken to the king's brother—the Duke of York—on account of his open adoption of the Roman Catholic religion, rendered Charles's situation at this time extremely unpleasant.

The Parliament, too, began to show a stubborn spirit of economy, and not only found fault with the king's measures, but compelled him to remove from his councils some of his favourite, but most obnoxious ministers.

This, however, owing to the easy temper of Charles, caused him but little annoyance; but as it was utterly impossible to carry on the war against such a determined enemy as the Dutch without money, and as neither of his allies would give any, he resolved to come to terms with Holland; and after a brief negotiation with the States, peace between the two countries was concluded on the 28th of February, 1674.

Thus, to the great delight of both nations, one of the most unprovoked and unjustifiable wars ever waged between two civilized States, was brought to a conclusion.

Nearly all the paltry excuses urged by Charles for this attack on Holland were waived or ignored, the Dutch, however, agreeing to pay the English a sum of eight hundred thousand patacoons—about three hundred thousand pounds sterling—as compensation for damage sustained by certain colonists.

Our gallant tars, though victorious in action during this period, suffered many losses from the fury of the elements, the dangers of unknown or imperfectly surveyed coasts, and the other evils which continually threaten those that go down to the sea in ships.

Two vessels, the "Sandwich" and the "Briton," were cruising in the West Indian seas, when they were overtaken by a terrible storm, in the midst of which a waterspout appeared.

Both received terrible damage, more than half their crews were washed overboard, and the remainder, being insufficient to work the vessels properly, and having been compelled to throw nearly all their stores overboard, suffered great privations before they could make land.

English sailors, however, were not to be daunted by such sufferings.

In concluding this chapter of our history, we must give here a brief narrative of two brave and illustrious men, who about this time closed their earthly career. The first of these is

SIR EDWARD SPRAGUE.

This gallant admiral and experienced seaman entered the navy early, and closed his career in the last battle fought between the Dutch and English.

In the second Dutch war (1665) he commanded a ship called the "Royal Charles," when, for his gallant conduct, he was knighted by the king on board the "Royal Charles."

He attracted the particular notice of the Duke of Albemarle in the four days' battle in 1666; and in the following year he burnt a number of Dutch fire-ships when they came up the Thames, which threw their whole fleet into confusion, and caused them to retreat.

In 1671 he destroyed in the Mediterranean seven Algerine men-of-war.

He was drowned just before the close of the action (August, 1673) by a round shot sinking his boat as he was removing his flag for the second time; both his previous ships, the "Royal Prince" and the "St. George," being in a foundering condition.

The body was subsequently found and interred with all honour in Westminster Abbey.

Next we must give a biographical memoir of

GEORGE MONK, DUKE OF ALBEMARLE.

George Monk, created Duke of Albemarle, was the second son of Sir Thomas Monk, an impoverished baronet, and was born in Devonshire in 1608. His father, having been publicly arrested for debt before all the country gentlemen assembled at Plymouth to meet the young King Charles I., his son George, who was present, was so indignant at the insult that he assaulted the officer, whom he caned so severely, that, to escape the consequences of his rash act, he was compelled to quit the country, joining an expedition, under Sir Richard Greville, against the Spaniards.

On his return, he volunteered to serve in the Low Countries, where he rose to the rank of captain, and for the next ten years continued in the army, taking part in all its operations and acquiring considerable professional experience.

Upon his return, on the breaking out of the Civil War, he attached himself to the royal cause, receiving the rank of colonel. Being accused of treason, he was deprived of his command, but, hastening to Oxford, he so justified himself to the king, that Charles restored him to favour, with the rank of major-general, and in 1644, sent him to besiege the town of Nantwich.

Here, however, he was made prisoner, and suffered a signal defeat from Fairfax, who sent him to the Tower, where he remained in captivity for two years.

Through the influence and persuasion of his friends, and, as it is alleged, through a large bribe, he was induced to join the Parliamentary party, upon which his liberation immediately followed, and he was entrusted with considerable powers, and sent to Scotland, where, as well as in Ireland, and subsequently in command of a fleet, both against the Royalists and in the war with Holland, he displayed great military talents, and rose to the highest grade in the army—that of general.

On the breaking out of the first Dutch war in 1652, Cromwell, wanting a trusty and valiant officer to aid Blake, recalled Monk from his post in Scotland, and gave him the command of a fleet.

Of his conduct in that war, we have already spoken in our history.

On the ratification of peace, Monk returned to his government in Scotland, where he remained till the death of Oliver Cromwell.

In all his commands, whether as general or governor, Monk had the good fortune to secure the entire affection and devotion of his troops, and to conciliate the feelings of both Scotch and Irish over whom he had to exercise authority; and though the inhabitants of both countries detested the cause and the principles he upheld, their respect and esteem for himself were earnest and profound.

His former loyalty made him an object of suspicion to Cromwell, even to the hour of his death, while it kept the king's party in constant hope of his returning to his allegiance; but so cautiously and prudentially did Monk act through all the attempts made to compromise him on the one hand, and to obtain a declaration of support on the other, that Cromwell himself, though to the last suspicious, could find nothing but open and conscientious conduct in the general, nor could the Royalists obtain any confirmation, one way or the other, as to his intended actions or secret feelings.

On the death of the Protector, Monk was the first to proclaim Richard his successor; and though Richard Cromwell endeavoured to win him to his side by saying his father had told him to be guided by Monk in all things, he replied so carefully that no one could fathom his future intentions.

His brother was sent to him from the king's party, to endeavour to get from him a promise of support; but though he treated the ambassador with every mark of affection and regard, he refused to entertain or even enter upon the secret subject with which he came charged.

Perfectly conscious that Richard Cromwell would be unable to maintain his authority, Monk soon after put his army in motion, and, by easy stages, advanced from Scotland to the metropolis, everywhere being met on his march by the most influential inhabitants, and petitions, urging on him the necessity of establishing a permanent and equitable government.

On his arrival in London, Monk quartered his army and established his head-quarters at Westminster, where, for a time, he affected a blind obedience to the orders of the Parliament, and executed without a murmur all its odious decrees.

At length, throwing off the mask, he complained of the degrading work they gave him to execute, and ordered them immediately to issue writs for a new Parliament. This was the death-blow to the Long, or Rump Parliament, which was compelled to yield, and General Monk became by universal consent the head of authority; the Puritan party, in the hope of maintaining their own influence, offering him the protectorate, which Richard had surrendered.

This, and all similar offers, he declined with firmness; and sending his old friend, Sir John Grenville, with a message to the king, with assurances of his devotion and loyalty and advice how to act, awaited the meeting of the new Parliament.

In the meantime Sir John returned from Charles with the letters Monk had suggested to the new House. These were immediately laid before Parliament, May 1st, 1660, and, backed by the declaration of the general, resulted in the immediate acknowledgment of the royal authority, and the restoration of the king, unfettered by conditions, and absolute in all prerogative.

Monk met Charles at Dover, and was received by both brothers with the distinction and favour his eminent services justified.

He was soon after created a knight of the garter, admitted into the privy council, made master of the horse, gentleman of the bedchamber, first commissioner of the treasury, commander-in-chief of the forces, and created Baron Monk, Earl of Torrington, and Duke of Albemarle, with the gift of a landed estate of the value of £7,000 per annum, besides many rich presents and princely rewards.

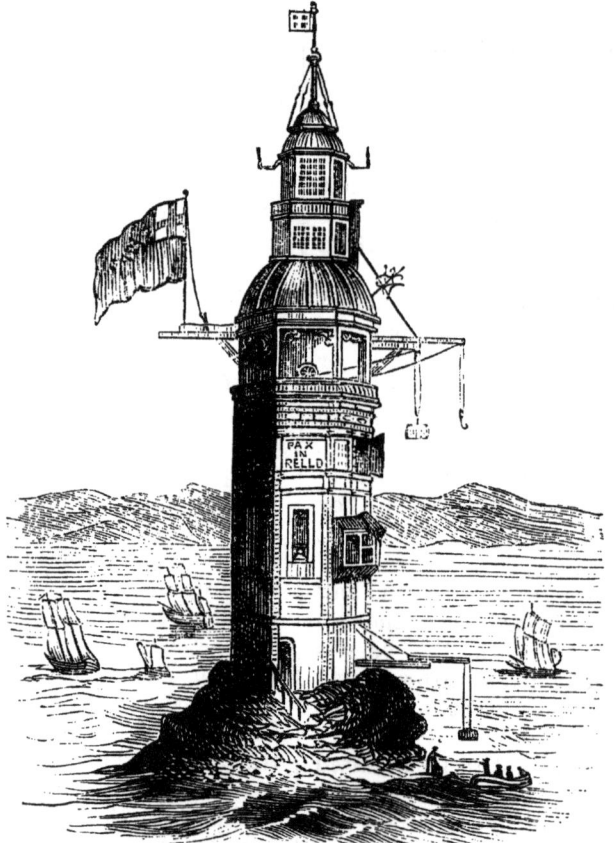

THE FIRST LIGHTHOUSE.

Nor did his honours stop here. The whole body of peers met him at the door of the House, and respectfully conducted him to his seat. He was made lord lieutenant of the counties of Devon and Middlesex, first lord of the admiralty, and, with Prince Rupert, was given the command of the fleet in the Dutch war.

Monk amassed a large property, and, besides, a noble landed estate worth £15,000 a-year, he left a fortune of above £60,000 in money, the proceeds of a life of frugality and economy.

The fatigues of a long and active life brought on an attack of asthma and dropsy, of which he died on the 3rd day of January, 1674, in the sixty-second year of his age, at the Cock Pit House, which had been given him by the king, and was soon after interred in Westminster Abbey with great pomp.

He married a milliner of Drury Lane, the daughter of a blacksmith, and left one child, a son, who at the age of sixteen years and two days, was, before his father's death, married in his parent's bedroom to the daughter of Lord Ogle. He died, however, without issue, in his thirty-fourth year, and the title became extinct in that family, the estate and property going to Lord Bath, the son of Sir John Grenville, Monk's kinsman.

CHAPTER XIV.

FROM THE LAST DUTCH WAR TO THE DEATH OF ADMIRAL BENBOW.

THE rest of the events of Charles's reign as regards naval affairs resolve themselves into mere matter of detail.

Some of our readers no doubt would like to know the titles and duties of the various naval officers of this period, so we will endeavour to supply the information.

The officers on board each ship were the captain, his lieutenant, the corporal, the master and his mates, the pilot, the master gunner and his mates, the master carpenter and his mates; and in great ships the joiner, the coxswain and his mate, the master cook and his mate, the purser, the steward, the quartermasters, and lastly, the swabber. At least, so says Captain Nathaniel Boteler in his "Six Dialogues on Sea Services," first published in 1685.

Commencing at the lowest rank, he tells us that the duties of the swabber were to see the ship kept clean, to which end he was to have the ship well washed very day, if possible or at least twice a week, and for prevention of infection to burn pitch, "or the like wholesome perfume," between the decks. He was also to have a regard to each private man's sleeping place, and to admonish them all in general to be cleanly and handsome.

The duties of the quartermasters were to "rummage in the hold of the ship, to accompany and overlook the steward in the delivery of the victuals to the cook, and in his pumping and drawing of the beer, and to take care that there be no abuses nor wastes committed."

The steward had to receive the full supply of provisions from the purser, and see them properly

FIRST-RATE MAN-OF-WAR, REIGN OF CHARLES II.

stowed away; the purser having received the said supplies from the victualling yard. The purser had also to keep a roll or list of the ship's company, on which was to be put down the date of each man's admittance to pay. The duties of the cook were of course to prepare the food, and see it properly distributed.

The coxswain was supposed to have care of the barge or shallop, and the implements belonging thereto, and be ready with his boat company to man the boat on all occasions. The boatswain had care of the rigging, sails, cables, and anchors; and also of the ship's flags, colours, and pendants. He was "to call up the several gangs and companies of men belonging to the ship to the due execution of their watches, works, and spells;" and, lastly, to see that punishment was properly executed on offenders.

The duties of the carpenter, too, are expressed by his title. The master gunner had charge of all the ordnance, and also of the magazine; he had to keep an account, as nearly as possible, of the expenditure of powder and shot. The corporal took charge of small arms and their ammunition, and was supposed to drill the men to the use of the musket.

A pilot was employed to conduct ships into strange harbours. It was the master's duty to "take the general conduct of the way and sailing of the ship, and to shape all such courses as may safest and soonest bring her to her designed port, to which end he is to take account of all the ways that the ship hath made, and upon what points of the compass she hath been steered, to take a view of the traverse board, to consider all the dead reckonings, and by his observations to take the height of the sun or stars with his astrolabe, backstaff, or Jacob-staff, and accordingly to prick his card."

The lieutenant was then, as now, *locum tenens*, in the absence of the captain, who had supreme command of the ship, and all it contained.

The duties of the officers have, since Captain Boteler wrote, been somewhat modified, but in all essential particulars they are the same.

In the year 1675, the king, having applied to the Parliament for money to put the country in a posture of defence, the House, jealous of his majesty's real intentions, and afraid to trust him with too large a sum of ready money, took time to consider his necessities.

After some days' delay, the Commons granted the king the sum of £300,000 for the express purpose of building new ships.

To prevent the king, however, from applying this sum to his own use, the House strictly confined the grant to the use of the dockyards, and only paid it in small sums, and at long intervals.

The events of this year are made memorable by the death of one of England's bravest and noblest enemies.

In the summer of 1675, the Sicilians having revolted against their French masters, Louis despatched a fleet to reduce them to obedience.

A Dutch fleet, meeting the French ships in the Mediterranean, an obstinate action ensued, in which the renowned Dutch admiral, De Ruyter, was killed.

The French, though they lost the battle, thought they had gained a great victory by the death of so celebrated an enemy.

The French, who, twelve years before, had scarcely a ship of war in any of their harbours, had raised themselves, by means of perseverance and policy, to be, in their present force, though not in their resources, the first maritime power in Europe.

The Dutch, while in alliance with them against England, had supplied them with several vessels, and had taught them the rudiments of the difficult art of ship-building.

The English next, when in alliance with them against Holland, instructed them in the method of fighting their ships, and of preserving order in naval engagements.

Louis availed himself of every opportunity to aggrandise his people, while Charles, sunk in indolence and pleasure, neglected all the attributes of government; or if at any time he roused himself from his lethargy, that industry, by reason of the unhappy projects he embraced, was often more pernicious to the public than his inactivity itself. He was as anxious to promote the naval power of France as if the safety of his crown depended on it; and many of the plans executed in that kingdom were first, it is said, digested and corrected by him.

The progress of the French arms in the Netherlands, during the next campaign, so alarmed the English for the safety of their old friends, the Dutch, that on Charles's yearly appeal for more money to put the country in a posture of defence, the Commons granted him an immediate sum of upwards of half a million.

As, however, the amount granted last year for naval expenses had been squandered without any apparent result, the House, on this occasion, was resolved to leave nothing to chance or mistake, and therefore ordered estimates to be supplied for the building and arming of the thirty new ships of war ordered to be laid down.

When this new fleet was fully equipped, it was found that the estimates had fallen short of the £586,000, granted by Parliament, by at least a hundred thousand pounds.

Such was the dread of the English Parliament at the progress of the French arms, and their anxiety to save their Dutch neighbours from the absolute ruin that threatened them, that a fleet of ninety sails, and an army of thirty thousand men, was instantly voted.

At the same time, to enable the king to put this power in motion, and compel Louis to suspend the war against Holland, the House granted him a million sterling for immediate necessities.

At the demise of Charles II. on the 6th of February, 1685, the navy consisted of 179 ships, 5 of which carried 100 guns, 4 others 96 guns each, and 10 of 90 guns.

During the three eventful years of James the Second's reign, the fleet, though kept in an admirable state of strength and efficiency, had little or nothing to do, till the rumours of the Prince of Orange's preparations for an invasion of England filled the king with dread and the people with delight.

The universal suspicion of the English with regard to the king's intention of converting the whole kingdom to his own religious persuasion, spread at this time both to the army and navy.

In fact, the fleet had begun to mutiny, because Strickland, the admiral, a Roman Catholic, introduced the mass aboard his ship, and dismissed the Protestant chaplain.

It was with some difficulty the seamen could be appeased, and they still persisted in declaring that they would not fight against the Dutch, whom they called friends and brethren, but would willingly give battle to the French, whom they regarded as national enemies.

The king had intended to augment his army with Irish recruits, and he resolved to try the experiment on the regiment of the Duke of Berwick, his natural son; but Beaumont, the lieutenant-colonel, refused to admit them, and to this opposition five captains steadily adhered.

They were all cashiered, and had not the discontent of the army on this occasion become very apparent, it was resolved to have punished those officers for mutiny.

As the designs of the Prince of Orange were very evident, a squadron was appointed to observe the movements of the Dutch fleet. Two ships were to cruise continually off the East coast, Orfordness being their rendezvous; others were to ply between the Goodwin Sands and Calais, while fishing smacks from Barking were sent over to the coast of Holland to watch. Sir Roger's squadron consisted of 26 vessels, 35 fire-ships, and 6 tenders.

Having consulted with some of his captains, Strickland resolved to sail to the Gunfleet buoy, near Harwich, that being a place where he could learn what the Dutch were doing better than by remaining in the Downs. But James was displeased at this, and ordered him to continue between the North Land head and the Kentish Knock (at the mouth of the Thames).

When the danger became greater he was ordered to repair to the buoy at the Nore, and Lord Dartmouth was sent to sea with 40 men-of-war. These vessels being at the Gunfleet a council of war was held, and Sir William Jennings proposed to steer over to the Dutch coast; but this proposition was overruled, and the fleet remained inactive.

The Dutch fleet appointed to bring over the Prince of Orange consisted of about 50 sail and 500 transports conveying the soldiers. The captains were Hollanders, but the chief admiral, Herbert, was an Englishman. After many delays they sailed on the 1st of November, 1688, Admiral Herbert leading the van, and Vice-Admiral Evertzen bringing up the rear.

The same wind which brought William to the English coast kept James's fleet from sailing; and the day was foggy, another advantage to the invaders, who thus passed the British ships in safety, and proceeded to Torbay, where the army landed.

As soon as possible the English fleet pursued, but was overtaken by a storm, and compelled to put into Portsmouth Harbour.

Although the people of England were flocking to the Prince of Orange's standard, Lord Dartmouth, the admiral, was desirous of serving James. But finding most of his officers opposed to this, he yielded to necessity, and sailing back to the Downs, held a council of war, which resulted in the dismissal of all Roman Catholics from the navy and the presentation of a loyal address to William III.

The ships which most needed repair were then sent into dock, the others being kept on service.

The administration of the Admiralty under Pepys during James's reign, is still regarded as a model for order and economy.

The fleet at the revolution consisted of one hundred and seventy-three vessels of all sizes, and required forty-two thousand seamen to man it.

One of the first events in King William's reign, in which the navy had an opportunity of displaying its zeal, was for the relief of Londonderry, besieged by the partisans of the deposed monarch. This was in the year 1689.

On arriving off the town of Londonderry, Major-General Kirk, the commander of the expedition, saw that he had a very difficult task to perform.

So completely had James's army invested the place, that the banks of the river were lined with batteries mounting heavy guns, and strongly protected on both sides by lines of musketeers.

Still further to protect the town on the water side, a boom of strong timber fastened together by heavy chains was stretched across the narrowest part of the river, and additionally strengthened by a cable twelve inches thick twisted round it.

When Kirk heard that the besieged inhabitants had been reduced by hunger to eat all the horses, dogs, and even rats they could find, and were just on the point of sacrificing their Catholic fellow citizens to assuage their famine, he determined to make a desperate and bold attempt to relieve them.

He sailed up the river with some of his strongest ships, and although opposed to a terrible fire from the shore, he succeeded at last in reaching the obstruction.

The foremost ship, with all sails set, was three times driven on the timber barriers. At the third effort, the boom gave way, and such was the force of the shock that the ship was driven so far back by the recoil, that she grounded near one of the enemy's batteries.

The shock of her broadside, however, when she replied to the shore guns, shook her free, actually driving her into deep water.

The ships then passed the boom in triumph, drove back the besiegers, and relieved the garrison of the town when on the brink of stavation, nine lean horses, and a pint of meal for each man, being all the provisions left in the place for a garrison of five thousand men.

At this period there was much jealousy in England at the growing power of France, and owing to the assistance that the French king gave to the deposed James the Second, preparations were being made for a declaration of war.

Before the proclamation, however, Admiral Herbert heard that a French fleet had left Brest with supplies for King James in Ireland, when he instantly sailed to intercept, and if possible, destroy it.

The cruelties and tyranny practiced by the abdicated James and his French troops in Ireland, were equally as fatal to his popularity among the Catholics as the Protestant inhabitants of that kingdom.

Indeed, all the revenues of Ireland, and all the schemes contrived to bolster up the credit of the base coin, would have proved insufficient to support the expenses of the war, had not James received occasional supplies from the French monarch.

After the return of the fleet, which had conveyed

him to Ireland, Louis sent another strong squadron, commanded by Chateau Renault, as a convoy to some transports, laden with arms, ammunition, and a large sum of money for the use of King James.

Before they sailed from Brest, Admiral Herbert had put to sea with twelve ships of the line, one fireship, and four tenders, in order to intercept the enemy. He was driven by stress of weather into Milford Haven, from whence he steered his course to Kinsale, on the supposition that the French fleet had sailed from Brest, and that in all probability he should fall in with them on the coast of Ireland.

On the first of May, he discovered them at anchor in Bantry-Bay, and stood in to engage them, though they were greatly superior to him in number.

They no sooner perceived him at daybreak, than they weighed, stood out to windward, formed their line, bore down, and began the action, which was maintained for two hours with equal valour on both sides, though the English fleet sustained considerable damage from the superior fire of the enemy. Herbert tacked several times, in hopes of gaining the weather-gage, but the French admiral kept his wind with uncommon skill and perseverance.

At length the English squadron stood off to sea, and maintained a running fight till five in the afternoon, when Chateau Renault tacked about, and returned into the bay, content with the honour he had gained. The loss of men was inconsiderable on both sides, and, where the odds were so great, the victor could not reap much glory.

Herbert retired to the Isles of Scilly, where he expected a reinforcement; but being disappointed in this expectation, he returned to Portsmouth in very ill humour, with which his officers and men were equally infected.

The common sailors still retained some affection for James, who had formerly been a favourite among them; and the officers complained that they had been sent upon this service with a force greatly inferior to that of the enemy.

King William, in order to appease their discontent, made an excursion to Portsmouth, where he dined with the admiral, on board the ship "Elizabeth," declared his intention of making him an earl, in consideration of his good conduct and services, conferred the honour of knighthood on the captains, Ashby and Shovel, and bestowed a donation of ten shillings on every private sailor.

In the following spring, the English fleet being thoroughly refitted, and joined by a strong squadron of Dutch ships, the whole, under the command of Admiral Herbert, now created Earl of Torrington, put to sea, and entering St. George's Channel, bore up for Cork.

This important town, at the time, was not only strongly garrisoned by James's partisans, but further protected by a large number of French troops and several ships of war.

The earl, however, made preparations for attacking and reducing the place, partly by bombardment and partly by blockade.

In this undertaking the English fleet was singularly unfortunate; a fatal endemic broke out among the crews, and great numbers of men and officers perished.

Though much of this sickness was attributed to the bad provisions supplied to the navy, the result was equally fatal to the enterprise; the "Dartmouth" ship-of-war fell into the hands of the enemy, and the Earl of Torrington was reduced to the humiliation of abandoning the siege, and returning with his weakened fleet to England.

What added to the bitterness and national vexation at this failure was the fact, that at the time the English and Irish channels were swarming with French ships of war and privateers, which were

CRESTS OF SHIPS IN THE ROYAL NAVY (A.D. 1870).

daily harassing and destroying the commerce of the kingdom.

In June of the year 1690, while King William was taking the field in Ireland against the French and Irish army, news reached the English court of another French armament destined to aid the dethroned James.

Advice being received that a fleet was ready to sail from Brest, Lord Torrington hoisted his flag in the Downs, and sailed round to St. Helen's in order to assemble such a number of ships as would enable him to give them battle.

The Dutch squadron which composed the van began the engagement at nine in the morning; in about half-an-hour the blue division of the English were close engaged with the rear of the French; but the red, which formed the centre, under the command of Torrington in person, did not fill the line till ten o'clock, so that the Dutch were almost surrounded by the enemy, and, though they fought with great valour, sustained considerable damage.

At length the admiral's division drove between them and the French, and in that situation the fleet

ACTION BETWEEN THE ENGLISH AND FRENCH FLEETS, OFF MALAGA.

The enemy being discovered off Plymouth on June 20th, the English admiral, reinforced with a Dutch squadron, stood out to sea with a view to intercept them at the back of the Isle of Wight, should they presume to sail up the Channel; not that he thought himself strong enough to cope with them in battle.

Their fleet consisted of seventy-eight ships of war, and two-and-twenty fire-ships; whereas, the combined squadrons of England and Holland did not exceed six and fifty; but he had received orders to hazard an engagement if he thought it might be done with any prospect of success.

After the hostile fleets had continued five days in sight of each other, Lord Torrington bore down upon the enemy off Beachy-Head on the 13th of June at daybreak.

anchored about five in the afternoon, when the action was interrupted by a calm.

The Dutch had suffered so severely that Torrington thought it would be imprudent to renew the battle; he, therefore, weighed anchor in the night, and with the tide at flood retired to the eastward.

The next day the disabled ships were destroyed, that they might not be retarded in their retreat. They were, however, pursued as far as Rye. An English ship of seventy guns, being stranded near Winchelsea, was set on fire and deserted by the captain's command.

A Dutch ship, of sixty-four guns, met with the same accident, and some French frigates attempted to burn her, but the captain defended her so vigorously that they were obliged to desist, and he afterwards found means to carry her safely to Holland.

In this engagement the English lost two ships, two officers, and about four hundred men; but the Dutch were more unfortunate, six of their great ships were destroyed, Dick and Brackel, rear-admirals, were slain, together with a great number of inferior officers and seamen.

Torrington retreated without further interruption into the mouth of the Thames, and, having taken precaution against any attempts of the enemy in that quarter, returned to London, the inhabitants of which were overwhelmed with consternation.

To such a height had popular indignation risen at these repeated failures of the fleet, that the ministry felt bound to interfere, and, if possible, pacify the public mind.

The Queen, who, during William's absence in Ireland, had been left absolute sovereign, at once committed Lord Torrington to the Tower, and he was ostentatiously conducted through the city to his prison.

At the same time, the people were made to believe that every disaster was the consequence of the spies and traitors in the pay of the dethroned James II.

During the whole of this reign, and that of William's successor, Queen Anne, the friendly relations that existed between this country and Holland were shown by the active part the latter took in all our naval enterprises, always doing their share, and sometimes a great deal more, of the fighting.

The French and Irish having laid down their arms, King William took the opportunity of returning to Holland, to make ready for the next campaign with the French in the Low Countries.

Admiral Russell at the same time received orders to put to sea, to engage, and, if possible, destroy the French fleet.

About the middle of May, 1692, being joined by the squadrons of Delaval and Carter, and reinforced by the Dutch squadrons, commanded by Allemonde, Callemberg and Vandergoes, Russell set sail for the coast of France on the eighteenth day of May, with a fleet of ninety-nine ships of the line, besides frigates and fire-ships.

Next day, about three in the morning, he discovered the enemy, under the Count de Tourville, and threw out the signal for the line of battle, which, by eight o'clock, was formed in good order, the Dutch in the van, the blue division in the rear, and the red in the centre.

The French fleet did not exceed sixty-three ships of the line, and as they were to the windward, Tourville might have avoided an engagement, but he had received a positive order to fight, on the supposition that the Dutch and English squadrons had not joined. Louis, indeed, was apprised of their junction before they were descried by his admiral, to whom he despatched a countermanding order by two several vessels, but one of them was taken by the English, and the other did not arrive till the day after the engagement.

Tourville, therefore, in obedience to the first mandate, bore down alongside of Russell's own ship, which he engaged at a very small distance. He fought with great fury till one o'clock, when his rigging and sails being considerably damaged, his ship, the "Rising Sun," which carried one hundred and four guns, was towed out of the line in great disorder.

Nevertheless, the engagement continued till three, when the fleets were parted by a thick fog. When this abated, the enemy were descried flying to the northward; and Russell made the signal for chasing.

Part of the blue squadron came up with the enemy about eight in the evening, and engaged them half-an-hour, during which Admiral Carter was mortally wounded. Finding himself in extremity, he exhorted his captain to fight as long as the ship could swim; and expired with great composure.

At last the French bore away for Conquet Road, having lost four ships in this day's action.

Next day, about eight in the morning, they were discovered crowding away to the westward, and the combined fleets chased them with all the sail they could carry, until Russell's foretopmast came by the board. Though he was retarded by this accident, the fleet still continued the pursuit, and anchored near Cape La Hogue.

On the twenty-second of the month, about seven in the morning, part of the French fleet was perceived near the Race of Alderney, some at anchor, and some driving to the eastward with the tide of flood. Russell, and the ships nearest him, immediately slipped their cables, and gave chase.

The "Rising Sun," having lost her masts, ran ashore near Cherbourg, where she was burned by Sir Ralph Delaval, together with the "Admirable," another first-rate, and the "Conquerant," of eighty guns.

Eighteen other ships of their fleet ran into La Hogue, where they were attacked by Sir George Rooke, who destroyed them, and a great number of transports laden with ammunition, in the midst of a terrible fire from the enemy, and in sight of the French and Irish camp.

Sir John Ashby, with his own squadron, and some Dutch ships, pursued the rest of the French fleet, which escaped through the Race of Alderney by such a dangerous passage as the English could not attempt without exposing their ships to the most imminent hazard.

This was a very mortifying defeat to the French king, who had been so long flattered with an uninterrupted series of victories; it reduced James to the lowest ebb of despondence, as it frustrated the whole scheme of his embarkation, and overwhelmed his friends in England with grief and despair.

The battle of La Hogue was so galling to the French king's pride, and, at the same time, so disastrous that, to the end of this long war, Louis never again risked a naval action with the English.

The queen was so pleased with the victory, that she ordered thirty thousand pounds to be distributed among the sailors. She caused medals to be struck in honour of the action, and the bodies of Admiral Carter and Captain Hastings, who had been killed in the battle, to be interred with great funeral pomp.

In the following year the English were signally unfortunate in all their naval enterprises. Sir George Rooke had to desert his convoy off the coast of Spain, and return with shame and vexation to Ireland to refit.

In the same summer, 1693, Sir Francis Wheeler was equally unsuccessful in the West Indies, and returned in the autumn with his crippled squadron, also to refit.

Some slight success of Admiral Benbow, however, closed the year with a small glimmer of éclat.

In November, Benbow sailed with a squadron of twelve capital ships, four bomb-ketches, and two brigantines, to the coast of St. Maloes, and, anchoring within half a mile of the town, cannonaded and bombarded it for three days successively. Then his men landed on an island, where they burnt a convent.

On the nineteenth, they took the advantage of a dark night, a fresh gale, and a strong tide, to send in a fire-ship of a particular contrivance, styled the "Infernal," in order to burn the town; but she struck upon a rock before she arrived at the place, and the engineer was obliged to set her on fire and retreat.

She continued burning for some time, and at last blew up, with such an explosion as shook the whole town like an earthquake, unroofed three hundred houses, and broke all the glass and earthenware for three leagues round.

A capstan that weighed two hundred pounds was hurled into the place, and, falling upon a house, levelled it to the ground; the greatest part of the wall towards the sea fell down, and the inhabitants were overwhelmed with consternation, so that a small number of troops might have taken possession of the town without resistance; but there was not a soldier on board. The sailors, however, took and demolished Quince Fort, and did considerable danger to the town of St. Maloes, which had been a nest of privateers that perpetually harassed the English commerce.

The French, having augmented their navy by the purchase of ships from all the surrounding nations, contrived to amass so immense a fleet that Louis resolved again to put to sea, and send a powerful force to attack the Spaniards.

Upon this, the English fleet put to sea, but too late to intercept the enemy, and after a brave but fruitless attempt to land at Camaret Bay the commanders contented themselves by bombarding all the towns on the western coast of France, and creating an immense amount of damage to the enemy.

Admiral Russell, however, with part of the fleet, sailed to the Mediterranean and compelled the French to retire to their own harbours, and in the end effectually relieved Barcelona.

While Admiral Russell supported the honour of his country in the Mediterranean in this and the following year, the English and Dutch squadrons again insulted the French coast, bombarded and nearly destroyed St. Maloes, and carried destruction all along its western sea board.

A small expedition to the West Indies ended, however, in mortification and failure, the squadon having scarcely a sufficient crew to bring it home, so fatal had the climate and scurvy proved to those on board.

With the exception of an occasional bombardment of the French sea-ports, the sending of a fleet to the Baltic to watch the King of Sweden, and another unsuccessful expedition to the West Indies, there was nothing further of note to record in naval affairs up to the death of William in 1701.

The first memorable enterprise of the next reign was that undertaken by Admiral Rooke.

In the month of July, 1702, an English and Dutch fleet sailed for Cadiz, to carry out a plan of the late King William for the invasion of Spain.

The fleet, which consisted of fifty English and twenty Dutch vessels, sailed on the 1st of July, under the chief command of Sir George Rooke. The fleet at the same time conveyed a large number of transports, conveying troops under the command of the Duke of Ormond.

The troops were landed at the bay of Toros, and, after they had captured Port St. Mary and Fort St. Katherine, they became insubordinate, got drunk, and commenced plundering the people they were sent to relieve. This was the principal cause of the unsuccessful result of the expedition, for none of the Spaniards would join them as expected.

The garrison of Cadiz, being found too strong for an attack to be made upon it, the fleet embarked the insubordinate soldiers, and sailed for England, the officers suffering under shame and indignation at the disgraceful result of the enterprise.

On the passage back, they heard of a large fleet of merchant ships at Vigo, and immediately sailed for that place, where they anchored on the 11th of October, 1702.

A land force, under the Duke of Ormond, landed first, and captured a fort, after a severe fight. Vice-Admiral Hopson then broke the boom across the river, and entered the harbour.

The other ships followed to support him, but, unfortunately, struck on the boom, when Hopson was attacked by the enemy's entire fleet.

A fire-ship, at the same time, was sent down upon him, which, setting fire to his vessel, several of his crew were compelled to jump overboard.

Fortunately for the admiral, the fire-ship was a merchant vessel, laden with snuff. It blew up, and the snuff extinguished the fire.

The other vessels soon after extricated themselves from the boom, and came up to his relief, though only one at a time.

Seeing that he should be now attacked by the fleet, as well as by the batteries the English had captured on shore, the French admiral commenced burning his vessels, to prevent them from falling into the hands of his enemies.

The English and Dutch now set to work to save as much booty as possible; and, in this pursuit, they were by no means unsuccessful. They managed to save from the fire ten men-of-war and nine galleons.

An immense amount of property and money was also obtained, although it is supposed the French carried away and destroyed the greater part of the most valuable cargoes of the merchant ships.

The ships finally returned to England, their success at Vigo atoning in a measure for their failure at Cadiz.

In many of the late unsuccessful adventures Admiral Benbow, either as captain or commodore, had taken an active part, always proving himself an able seaman and a courageous officer.

The cases of misadventure had all proceeded, either from the badness of his ships, the mutinous state of his crews, or from sickness, and never from want of heroism or good seamanship.

As the last of Benbow's actions gives a good idea of the trials he had often to endure in his career, we have omitted many of his other adventures to close his history with his last naval action.

On the 19th of August, 1702, Admiral Benbow, of the "Breda," in command of the West India fleet of seven ships, encountered the French fleet, under Du Casse, off the Isle of Santa Martha.

The French immediately bore away, the English fleet pursuing, and a running fight followed for several days, until Benbow, deserted by his captains, was compelled to give up the chase.

During the pursuit and fight, on the 24th, Benbow had his leg broken by a chain shot. Of this wound he died in Jamaica, on the 4th of the following November.

While in Jamaica, dying of his wounds, Benbow received from Vice-Admiral Du Casse the following letter:—

"CARTHAGENA, AUG. 22, 1702.

"SIR,—I had little hopes on Monday last to have supped in your cabin, but it has pleased God to have ordered it otherwise. I am thankful for it. As for those cowardly Captains who deserted you, hang them up, for they deserve it.
"Yours,
"DU CASS."

The remains of this brave sailor were taken to England and buried in Deptford churchyard, and the following brief

MEMOIR OF ADMIRAL BENBOW,

VIEW OF LONDONDERRY DURING THE SIEGE.

will give the reader a concise view of his many important services.

Admiral John Benbow, one of the plain, brave seamen of the old school, whose name is held in deserved honour by his country, was descended from a respectable family in Shropshire, which, espousing the cause of Charles the First, on his rupture with the Parliament, suffered both in person and estate.

It is stated that he first began his career as a waterman's boy. He first attracted public attention by his gallantry in the Mediterranean, when in command of a merchant-vessel of his own, which he had named "The Benbow Frigate."

Among his other exploits, the repulse of a Sallee rover of superior force in the year 1686, attracted the notice and admiration of the King of Spain, who invited him to his court, and strongly recommended him to his own monarch, James II.

The story told of Benbow's conduct on the occasion of this victory over the Moorish pirate, is characteristic of the man and of the times.

Thirteen of the Moors had been left dead on the deck of the English vessel, which, trusting to their superiority of numbers, they had vainly endeavoured to carry by boarding; Benbow ordered their heads to be cut off and barrelled up.

On arriving at his port of destination, Cadiz, he at first refused to allow the custom-house officers to examine the barrel, then burst into a pretended passion, as if enraged at being suspected of wishing to pass contraband goods.

"They are salt provisions," he exclaimed, "for

my own use. Cæsar, throw them on the table; and, gentlemen, if you like them, they are at your service!"

The tale flew to the Spanish court, with the result just stated; and the undaunted seaman, on his return to England, was at once admitted into the Royal navy, and appointed to the command of a ship.

After the revolution of 1688, his merits did not escape the notice of the sagacious William III. He was kept in constant employment, bombarding or blockading the French ports, and opposed with success the renowned Admiral Du Bart, whose fiery dashes from Dunkirk, to the great loss of our merchants, were often rendered abortive by the English admiral's valour and vigilance.

He subsequently distinguished himself in the West Indies in 1697, receiving the thanks of the merchants for his services.

Five years afterwards, the state of affairs calling for a strong squadron in that quarter, Benbow, who had been made Vice-Admiral of the Blue, was fixed upon by the minister for the command.

King William, however, objected to the unfairness of despatching the veteran to so unhealthy a station, and where, too, it was likely he would be detained a considerable time, and the names of several other officers were brought forward for the appointment, but on its being proposed they all managed to find reasons for declining it.

The naval service, it must be explained, had not at that period become the well-disciplined and regularly established arm of war, which at a later day would admit of no such shrinking from the post of duty.

In this dilemma, the king said jocularly—

"Well, I find we must spare our beaux, and send honest Benbow."

On the latter being offered his option to go or stay, he bluntly replied that he did not understand compliments of that kind, but was willing to go wherever ordered; to the West Indies, or to the devil and to do his duty.

His rough manners and strict discipline offended the captains under him, and when on the 19th of August, 1701, he, with six ships of war, fell in with a French squadron of ten sail, he was left with but one vessel of his own to engage it, the rest having deserted him by a preconcerted arrangement.

For this disgraceful conduct the captains were tried by court martial; two, Kirby and Wade, were sentenced and shot. Captain Hudson died before his trial, and Captain Constable was cashiered.

The gallant old admiral, who had one of his legs shattered by a chain shot during the engagement, sank under the combined effects of fever from his wounds, grief at his miscarriage, and outraged feelings. He died on the 4th of November, 1701, his last words being, "I would sooner have lost both legs than have witnessed such a disgrace on my country."

PRINCE GEORGE OF DENMARK, LORD HIGH ADMIRAL.

CHAPTER XV.

THE TAKING OF GIBRALTAR TO THE PEACE OF UTRECHT.

THE 10th of April, 1703, the 50-gun ship "Salisbury," Captain Cotton, in company with the "Adventure," 44 guns, met a squadron of seven French ships, under M. St. Paul.

The "Salisbury" was deserted by her consort, and obliged to encounter the whole fury of the enemy, and after a long and gallant action of more than two hours she was compelled to strike. The "Salisbury" had eighteen men killed and forty-five wounded. The "Adventure" was then pursued and captured by the same squadron. It is supposed that had the two fought together the French squadron in all probability would have been beaten off.

On the 26th of July the boats of a squadron, under Rear-Admiral Thomas Dilks, cut out fifteen French merchant vessels, burnt six, and sunk three in the port of Granville, France. During the same month Captain Norris, of the "Orford," 70 guns, captured the French 36-gun ship "Philippeant," and which in the action had not less than fifty men killed and wounded.

About the same time the "Chatham," 50 guns, Captain Bokenham, captured the French 54-gun ship "Auguste," with some slight assistance from her consorts of the squadron under Sir Cloudesley Shovel.

The next enterprise we shall have to describe is one of the most glorious in the naval annals of Great Britain.

Early in the year Sir George Rooke put to sea with a combined Dutch and English fleet, and a number of transports with troops and marines.

His orders were to land Charles, King of Spain, at Lisbon, and then proceed to Barcelona, and there disembark his troops, to annoy Philip, the rival King of Spain.

Having landed Charles in the Tagus, and captured three Spanish ships of war, Rooke sailed for the Mediterranean to execute the rest of his orders.

On reaching Barcelona the troops under the command of the Prince of Hesse Darmstadt were landed, but the inhabitants both of the city and province were resolved to adhere to King Philip, and made a desperate resistance.

So obstinate was the defence, and, finding that none of the Spaniards joined them, the enterprise at last was abandoned, and the troops re-embarked, when the admiral was compelled to give up the most important part of the expedition.

Immense sums had been voted by Parliament for this enterprise, and the country looked for great results from its successful accomplishment.

But, in the month of November, 1703, one of the most fearful tempests ever known took place, and the British Navy suffered severely; the following vessels being totally lost:—

Vanguard *	90 guns	Northumberland	70 guns
Stirling Castle	70 „	Restoration	70 „
Resolution	70 „	Mary	64 „
York	60 „	Newcastle	54 „
Reserve	48 „	Lichfield Prize	32 „
Arundel	32 „	Mortal	12 „
Suffolk (Hospital Ship)	10 „	Eagle	10 „
Vesuvius	8 „	Canterbury	8 „

Admiral Sir Cloudesley Shovel, who commanded in the Downs, had a narrow escape, and was missing for some days; 1,519 seamen and many officers were lost.

To repair these losses orders were immediately issued for building more vessels, and Queen Ann, by several bounties, gave relief to the widows and families of those who had been drowned.

A few months after Rooke's departure with King Charles of Spain, Sir Cloudesley Shovel was sent with a strong squadron to watch Brest harbour, and prevent the putting to sea of a French fleet that was supposed to be intended for the Mediterranean.

The French, however, had contrived to escape from Brest before Sir Cloudesley Shovel could reach his destination.

Upon this the admiral gave chase, and followed the enemy into the Mediterranean.

---

* The Vanguard was at Chatham, and, luckily, had neither men nor guns on board.

In the mean time, Rooke, smarting with shame at the failure of his enterprise, and dreading to return to England without achieving anything memorable, came to the sudden resolution of attacking Gibraltar.

Calling a council of war, and finding that all his officers approved the scheme, he immediately bore up for the rock.

On the 21st day of July, 1704, the British fleet anchored before that impregnable fortress, as it was then regarded.

On the following morning the Prince of Hesse Darmstadt, with eighteen hundred English and Dutch marines, landed to the north of the town, cutting off all communication from the country.

The next day, Rear-Admirals Byng and Vanderduffen, who were to bombard the town, took up their positions.

Captain Hicks, of the "Yarmouth," commanded the vessels that were to bombard the South-Mole Head.

Captain Whitaker, with all the boats, was ordered to attack the fortifications.

After the attack commenced, it is estimated that in less than five hours more than fifteen thousand shots were fired at the town and fortifications.

The South-Mole Head was destroyed, and the Spaniards driven from their guns.

The party under command of Captain Whitaker now rushed forward to storm the Mole, actually standing over a mine prepared by the Spaniards, and which was instantly fired.

A terrible explosion followed, which killed and wounded upwards of a hundred men; but this did not prevent the Mole from being taken, when the gates were thrown open to admit the Prince of Hesse and the marines under his command.

Gibraltar, the key of the Mediterranean, was then in the possession of the English, and only at the cost of sixty-three men killed, and two hundred and twenty-five wounded.

The Rock of Gibraltar projects about three miles into the sea. Its northern extremity is inaccessible, owing to the precipitous and perpendicular face of the rock; its southern and eastern sides are also very rugged and steep, affording many natural means of defence not often found; but that which makes its possession most valuable is, that it commands an important highway of the sea.

Gibraltar was captured on the 24th of July, 1704, and many hard-fought battles, attended with far greater loss of life, the English have had with their enemies for possessions not one hundredth part of the importance of Gibraltar.

The marines were left to guard the town, and the confederate fleets again put to sea.

A sufficient garrison being left with his Highness the Prince of Hesse, the admiral returned to Tetuan to take in wood and water, and when he sailed on the 9th of August, he descried the French fleet, to which he gave chase with all the sail he could spread.

On the 13th, he came up with it, as it lay in a line off Malaga, ready to receive him, to the number of fifty-two large ships, and twenty-four galleys, under the command of the Count de Thoulouse, High Admiral of France, with the inferior flags of the white and blue divisions.

The English fleet consisted of forty-five ships of the line, six frigates, and eighteen smaller craft, but they were inferior to the French, in number of guns and men, as well as in weight of metal.

A little after ten in the morning, the English fleet bore down in order of battle, but when within half gunshot, the enemy at once set all their sails, as though intending to weather us. Seeing this, Sir George Rooke at once signalled to commence action, which was continued with very great fury on both sides.

But about two in the afternoon, the enemy's van began to give way to ours, and, later in the day, the Dutch squadron forced back the French rear.

The Dutch being better provided with ammunition than the English, were enabled to continue firing longer than our sailors, and several of the English ships were compelled to fall out of the line of battle for want of shot.

This caused the enemy's fire to fall very heavily upon the "Royal Catherine," the admiral's own ship, as well as on the "St. George" and the "Shrewsbury" by which she was supported.

This being observed by Sir Cloudesley Shovel, who commanded the white squadron, he immediately backed astern, and endeavoured to reinforce Sir George, which act of valour and good seamanship had two useful effects; first, it drew several of the enemy's ships from our centre, which had been hardly pressed by them in superior force, and drove them at length out of the line; secondly, finding the force of this assistance, they found it unsafe to advance along Sir Cloudesley's broadside, but set their sprit-sails, and, with their boats ahead, towed away from him.

Though the Count de Thoulouse was supported by the best ships in the French fleet, he suffered the same fate as his vanguard, and about seven o'clock was obliged to tow away out of danger to leeward.

The wind shifting before morning, the French gained the weather-gage, but they made no use of this advantage; for two successive days the English admiral endeavoured to renew the engagement, which the Count de Thoulouse declined, and at last, he disappeared.

Though not a single ship was taken or destroyed by either side, the honour of the day certainly remained with the English.

Over and above the disadvantages we have enumerated, the bottoms of the English fleet were foul, and several of the large ships had expended all their shot long before the battle ceased; yet the enemy were so roughly handled, that they did not venture another engagement during the whole war.

In a letter, written by Sir Cloudesley Shovel directly after the action, is the following description of the share his squadron took in it:—

"The ships that suffered most in my division were the 'Lennox,' 'Warspight,' 'Tilbury,' and 'Swiftsure'; the rest escaped pretty well, and I the best of all, though I never took greater pains in my life to have been soundly beaten; for I set all my sails, and rowed with three boats ahead, to get alongside with the admiral of the white and blue. But he, outsailing me, shunned fighting, and lay alongside the little ships. Notwithstanding, the engagement was very sharp, and I think the like between two fleets has never been in any time. There is hardly a ship that must not shift one mast, and some must shift all; a great many have suffered much, but none more than Sir George Rooke and Captain Jennings in the 'St. George.'"

The English lost 687 men killed, and 1,632 wounded; the Dutch loss in killed and wounded being 400, making a total of 2,719 men *hors de combat*.

The loss in officers killed is thus stated:—Captain Sir Andrew Leake, Captain Crow, four lieutenants, and two warrant officers; Captains Mynge, Baker, Jumper, Mighells, Kirkson, thirteen lieutenants, and thirteen warrant officers were wounded.

On the French side a rear-admiral, five captains, six lieutenants, and five sea-ensigns were killed; Count de Thoulouse was wounded in the forehead, shoulder, and thigh, Count de Relignes had his leg shot off. The Marquis de Herbault, intendant of the fleet, was also wounded, as were Commodore du Casse, M. de Chateau Regnault, Count de Phelipeaux, Count de Cominges, and M. de Valincourt, with seven captains, eight lieutenants, and about one hundred and fifty other officers, while of seamen the total loss in killed and wounded amounted to 3,048.

Leaving Sir John Leake with a squadron at Gibraltar, Admiral Rooke, as soon as his fleet had refitted, returned to England in triumph.

To show the value set upon this action by the Queen and ministry, it was thought proper that His Royal Highness Prince George of Denmark, the Lord High Admiral of the Fleet, should introduce such officers as had most distinguished themselves; accordingly, on the 9th of October, he presented first Sir Cloudesley Shovel, who kissed Her Majesty's hand, then Captains John Jennings, George Byng, and Thomas Dilkes, who were knighted.

In the Parliament, on the 7th of November, the following resolutions were carried, viz.:—That forty thousand seamen should be allowed for the year 1705, including eight thousand marines. And on the 9th, they voted that one hundred thousand pounds should be allowed for the ordinary expenses of the navy for the same period, and that forty thousand pounds should be given to the ordnance office for the sea service, over and above the usual provision.

This last sum appears to have been expended on ordnance stores and carriages for eight new ships.

Such was the disposition of the country at this time, that every step towards increasing its naval forces became very popular, and therefore it continually *was* increased.

The following abstract of the Royal Navy on the 13th of December, 1706, will show the force then possessed by the country:—

First-rate ships 7, second-rate 14, third-rates 47, fourth-rates 61, fifth-rates 35, sixth-rates 27, with 86 smaller vessels described as brigantines, bombs, fire-ships, smacks, advice boats, store-ships, yachts, hoys, and hulks. Total of all classes, 277.

Philip of Spain, being obstinately bent on retaking Gibraltar, sent Mareschal de Thesse to renew the siege, while De Pointis was ordered to block up the place by sea with his squadron.

These French officers carried on the siege with such activity, that the Prince of Hesse dispatched an express to Lisbon with a letter, desiring Sir John Leake to sail immediately to his assistance. This admiral having been reinforced from England by Sir Thomas Dilkes with five ships of the line and a body of troops, set sail immediately, and on the 10th of March, 1705, descried five men-of-war hauling out of the Bay of Gibraltar.

These were commanded by De Pointis in person, to whom the English admiral gave chase. One of them struck, after having made a very slight resistance, and the rest ran ashore to the westward of Marbella, where they were destroyed.

The remaining part of the French squadron had been blown from their anchors, and taken shelter in the bay of Malaga, but now they slipped their cables, and made the best of their way to Toulon.

The Mareschal de Thesse, in consequence of this disaster, turned the siege of Gibraltar into a blockade, and withdrew the greater part of his forces.

While Sir John Leake was employed in this expedition, Sir George Byng, who had been ordered to cruise in soundings for the protection of trade, took a ship of war from the enemy, together with twelve privateers, and seven vessels, richly laden, from the West Indies.

The following is a list of the vessels which fell into his hands:—

Thetis, man-of-war,	44 guns	250 men	
Desmaria, privateer	36 ,,	240 ,,	
Phillipo -	22 ,,	220 ,,	
Constable -	30 ,,	210 ,,	
Voler -	28 ,,	210 ,,	
Royal -	26 ,,	200 ,,	
Beringhen -	24 ,,	160 ,,	
Sansparcil -	20 ,,	135 ,,	
Minerve -	16 ,,	92 ,,	
Merveilleux -	14 ,,	85 ,,	
Postboy -	10 ,,	70 ,,	
Bonaventure -	10 ,,	70 ,,	
Admirable -	12 ,,	75 ,,	

This victory gave such a blow to the French privateers, that they scarce ventured into the Channel all the year after, but preferred to sail northwards in hopes of meeting some of our homeward-bound ships from the Baltic.

Sir Cloudesley Shovel, with his subordinate admirals, Sir John Leake and Sir Thomas Dilkes, aided, as usual, by a squadron of Dutch ships, for the next two years were actively though not memorably employed against the enemy.

Two further attempts were made in Catalonia, and a demonstration in favour of King Charles was attempted in the Tagus, while a projected invasion of France was abandoned.

The year 1705 was remarkable for a very signal instance of naval discipline. Captain Cross, commander of the "Elizabeth," meeting with the French fleet in the Channel, struck after a very slight re-

CRESTS OF VESSELS IN THE ROYAL NAVY (A.D. 1870).

sistance, for which he was tried by a court-martial on the 25th of August. It appeared in evidence that he had exhibited signs of fear, and that if he had behaved as he ought the enemy might have been repulsed and the ship saved.

After a full hearing he was declared guilty of neglect of duty, and sentenced to be cashiered and rendered incapable of serving Her Majesty, to forfeit all his arrears of pay, and to be kept a close prisoner for life. The Queen permitted this sentence to be executed without any mitigation, except as regards the imprisonment, in order to deter others from being guilty of the like offence.

In July, 1707, Sir Cloudesley Shovel, who commanded the Mediterranean fleet, accompanied by a squadron of Dutch ships, sailed from Toulon, and commenced bombarding that town.

So fierce was the attack that within twenty-four hours half of the town, with nearly all the magazines and naval stores, and the best part of the shipping in the harbour, were destroyed. Eight ships of war were burnt, some of which mounted from fifty-four to ninety guns, with many of the merchantmen.

Sir Cloudesley Shovel, having left a squadron with Sir Thomas Dilkes for the Mediterranean service, set sail for England with the rest of the fleet, and was in soundings on the 22nd of October. About eight o'clock at night his own ship, the "Association," struck upon the rocks at Scilly, and perished with every person on board.

This was likewise the fate of the "Eagle" and the "Romney;" the "Firebrand" was dashed in pieces on the rocks; but the captain and four-and-

THE WRECK OF THE SHIP "AUGUST," A.D. 1715.

twenty men saved themselves in the boats; the "Phœnix" was driven on shore; the "Royal Anne" was saved by the presence of mind and uncommon dexterity of Sir George Byng and his officers; the "St. George," commanded by Lord Dursley, struck upon the rocks, but a wave set her afloat again.

The admiral's body being cast ashore, was stripped and buried in the sand, but afterwards brought into Plymouth, from whence it was conveyed to London, and interred in Westminster Abbey.

Some naval historians say that there is good evidence for believing that Admiral Shovel reached the shore alive, and was murdered by a female wrecker.

BIOGRAPHICAL MEMOIR OF SIR CLOUDESLEY SHOVEL.

This gallant and distinguished British admiral, whose untimely fate was so deeply mourned, was born of poor and humble parents, in the year 1650, and, being early sent to sea, commenced his nautical career as a cabin-boy.

When a boy, Cloudesley Shovel was on board a ship commanded by Sir John Narborough, who, during an action, expressed a very earnest wish to have some orders of consequence conveyed to a ship at a considerable distance. Shovel, hearing this, immediately undertook to convey it; and this he actually performed, by swimming through the enemy's line of fire, with the despatches in his mouth.

From the mercantile, while yet a lad, he passed to the Royal Navy, and, as early as 1674, was engaged in the Mediterranean, where, in several dashing cutting-out expeditions, he so greatly distinguished himself that, before he left the station, he obtained a captain's commission.

His encounters with the French also added largely to his reputation as a bold, skilful officer; while, for his conduct in Bantry Bay, he was subsequently knighted.

The next important services of Sir Cloudesley were the bombardment of Dunkirk, and afterwards of Calais, which latter town was almost reduced to a heap of ruins.

He was subsequently entrusted with a fleet, with orders to sweep the Mediterranean of the enemy; and, after participating in several gallant actions, in 1705 took Barcelona, and, though the French fleet had been annihilated in the Mediterranean, this action, the reduction of Barcelona, was regarded as the most important service of the year.

In 1707, Rear-Admiral Sir Cloudesley Shovel set sail with a large fleet to the aid of the Spanish monarch, Charles, and, having landed the troops and stores in Spain, and effected his orders, returned to England with one squadron of his fleet, and while in soundings, on the night of October the 22nd, got involved in the Scilly Islands, and, before the leading ships could be worked off, the flagship and three others were flung on the rocks, and instantly broke up.

The Admiral sank, with every soul on board, and only twenty-four men and one officer escaped out of the crew of the other three.

Sir Cloudesley's body being washed on shore, was sent to Portsmouth, and subsequently to London for interment in Westminster Abbey, where a monument was raised over his tomb.

* * * * *

The other naval events of this reign are so insignificant as scarcely to merit notice.

One or two unprotected convoys had been attacked by the enemy in force, a few heavy frigates destroyed or taken, and prizes made of a few merchantmen.

An expedition to Quebec and Canada had terminated most ingloriously; indeed, the chief duty of the fleet, during the last years of Queen Anne's life, was confined to sweeping the channel of the privateers which then infested our waters.

The following is one of the most memorable of these detached and unimportant actions.

On the 28th of May, 1708, Commodore Wager, in the "Expedition" of 60 guns, with the "Kingston" and "Portland," each of the same size, had an engagement in the West Indies with a Spanish fleet of seventeen vessels.

When the action had been continued for little more than an hour the Spanish admiral's ship took fire and blew up.

The Spanish rear-admiral's ship was captured soon after, and the others escaped in the night.

The country was called upon about this time to lament the loss of another well-tried officer, in the unexpected death of Admiral Sir George Rooke, a name that will be ever associated with the capture of Gibraltar, as long as one of the most valuable possessions of the British crown can be appreciated by the people of England.

MEMOIR OF ADMIRAL SIR GEORGE ROOKE.

This celebrated English admiral was born in Kent, in 1650, and very early showing a predilection for the sea, was entered in the navy when but a child. His enthusiasm in his profession, however, soon advanced him into notice, and his promotion was so rapid that he gradually attained the first honours of his profession.

He gave eminent proofs of his skill and courage in many expeditions, particularly at Vigo and La Hogue, at which latter place he burnt thirteen French ships.

In 1704, he took Gibraltar by bombardment, after which important service he encountered the French fleet off Malaga, and in a desperate engagement obtained a decided victory, the English losing two thousand, and the French three thousand men in the conflict.

Notwithstanding the great services he had rendered to the state, he was obliged to resign his command, through the influence of the Whig party, and retiring to his estate in Kent, died in 1709.

CHAPTER XVI.

TO THE PEACE OF AIX-LA-CHAPELLE.

At the death of Queen Anne, in 1714, the state of the navy was as follows: we had—

| 7 ships of the 1st rate, carrying 100 guns |
| 13 „ „ 2nd „ „ 90 „ |
| 16 „ „ 3rd „ „ 80 „ |
| 26 „ „ 3rd „ „ 70 „ |
| 19 „ „ 4th „ „ 60 „ |
| 50 „ „ 4th „ „ 50 „ |
| 24 „ „ 5th „ „ 40 „ |
| 18 „ „ 5th „ „ 30 „ |
| 24 „ „ 6th „ „ 20 „ |

We had also 1 vessel carrying 10 guns (not rated in the statement), 7 sloops, 4 bomb vessels, 1 fireship, 1 store-ship, 15 yachts, 13 hoys and lighters, and 8 hulks, making altogether 247 vessels, being 25 less than at Her Majesty's accession; though there was an increase in the tonnage of the navy to the extent of 8,199 tons.

At the accession of George I. the fleet was considerably in want of repair, as might have been expected, after so long a war as that which had only recently been brought to a conclusion, in the course of which nearly every vessel had gone through a lengthened course of active service.

In the year 1715 a general survey was taken of all the stores in His Majesty's dockyards, and the following is an account of the value thereof on the 31st of July:—

	£
At Deptford	90,544
Woolwich	60,174
Chatham	186,855
Sheerness	35,246
Portsmouth	182,076
Plymouth	109,833
Total	664,728

A new parliament had been summoned in March, 1715, which on the 1st of April resolved to allow 10,000 seamen, at £4 per month, and on the 9th of May granted £135,574 3s. 6d. for the half-pay of sea officers; £197,896 17s. 6d. for the ordinary pay of the navy, and £237,277 for extraordinary repairs and rebuilding of ships.

During the early part of the reign of the first George, the time of the ministry was chiefly taken up on domestic matters and theological disputes, and in suppressing the rebellion of 1715 in favour of the son of James II., Charles Stuart, commonly called the Chevalier de St. George.

There soon came a serious prospect of active employment for the navy, however, for the Swedes had fitted out a number of privateers, which captured many of our merchant vessels, on the pretence that, contrary to our treaties with the crown of Sweden, we supplied the Czar of Russia and his subjects with ships, arms, and ammunition.

Our minister at Stockholm presented several memorials to the Swedish Government, without receiving any satisfactory reply, so it was resolved to send a strong force to the Baltic.

Accordingly, a squadron of twenty sail was appointed for this purpose, the command being given to Sir John Norris, who had under him Sir Thomas Hardy.

The admiral hoisted his flag on board the "Cumberland," a third rate, having ten ships of the line in his division.

Sir Thomas Hardy sailed in the "Norfolk," also a third rate, and had under his immediate command eight ships of the line, the "Mermaid," frigate, 32 guns, and the "Drake," sloop, 16.

On the 18th of May, 1715, this fleet sailed from the Nore, and arrived in the Sound on the 10th of June, when it joined a Dutch squadron.

On the 14th June, the commanders held a council, which ended in their resolving that the combined squadrons should proceed, together with several English and Dutch merchant vessels, to the respective ports for which the latter were bound.

Sir John Norris first despatched a messenger to the Court of Stockholm, to know whether the Swedes were resolved to continue their practice of seizing English vessels, or whether they felt inclined to enter into negociations with a view to a peaceful solution of the difficulty; but the reply to his message was so vague that he determined at once to act according to the instructions he had received from his own government.

At this time, forty-six merchantmen, which had not been ready to sail from England with Sir John, arrived at Copenhagen, under the convoy of two men-of-war.

These ships remained till the fleet of Denmark (in alliance with England, Russia, and Holland) was ready to sail, in order to take advantage of the convoy.

About the middle of August it was resolved that the combined squadrons of England, Holland, Denmark, and Russia should sail up the Baltic, and as the Czar of Russia was then at Copenhagen, intending to command his own ships in person, it was determined, after several conferences, that the nominal command of the combined forces should be given to him, though, at the same time, it was arranged that Sir John Norris should command the vanguard, the Czar the body of the line of battle, and the Danish admiral the rear; while the Dutch admiral, with his squadron and five British men-of-war, proceeded with the traders of all nationalities to the various ports in the Baltic.

According to the terms of this resolution, the

Czar, on the 16th of August, hoisted his flag as admiral on board one of his finest ships, and, after the usual salutes, gave the signal for sailing. They proceeded towards Bornholm, when, receiving intelligence that the Swedish fleet had returned to Carlscrona, the British and Dutch merchantmen proceeded on their voyages, and the Czar sailed for the North German coast. On the 28th of October, Sir John Norris, with his own squadron and the Danish men-of-war, arrived at Bornholm, and the same night two swift cruisers were sent to hasten the traders who intended to return to England under protection of the fleet.

On the 31st, some British merchantmen, with their convoy, sailed from Dantzic, and on the 9th of November they joined Sir John Norris with traders from other Baltic ports, and on the 10th they all entered the port of Copenhagen, where, two days afterwards, they were joined by the Dutch merchant and war vessels. A few days afterwards they sailed for home, and, though the fleet was surprised by a violent storm which dispersed them, and in which the "August," 60 guns, and the "Garland," 24, were lost, the remainder arrived home in safety.

Sir John Norris left seven ships of war under Commodore Cleveland, to act in conjunction with the Danes for the further security of British trade in the Baltic.

This expedition, though it led to no very daring exploits, was of great benefit to the mercantile community of England, and it was fancied that the display of our fleet in Swedish waters would free us from all apprehension of danger from that country.

The King of Sweden, however, had a strong desire to assist the French in aiding the Pretender, and in consequence of his threats to invade England, Admiral Byng was sent in 1717 up the Baltic, with a fleet of thirty-three sail.

After the admiral's departure the public were under no alarm about the King of Sweden's boast of invading England.

In 1718, some Spanish troops were sent to Sardinia. By a treaty made in the previous reign, England had concluded a peace with Italy; consequently, Admiral Byng was recalled from the Baltic, and ordered to proceed to Cadiz.

On remonstrating with the Spanish Government upon the course it was pursuing, he was haughtily told to follow the instructions he had received, as the Spanish Court declined to notice his remonstrance. This answer left Byng no alternative but to seek the Spanish fleet and engage it.

He then sailed for the Mediterranean, and fell in with the Spaniards off the Island of Sicily on the 31st of July, 1718.

The insolence of the Spaniards induced them to commence hostilities, and fire the first shots, and that before they had been in any way molested.

This indignity, however, was not resented by the English, who were determined to have as much cause of complaint on their side as possible.

After the second broadside from the Spanish ships, the English ports were thrown open, the guns run out, and the battle commenced in earnest.

PORTRAIT OF CLOUDESLEY SHOVEL IN YOUTH.

The English fleet mounted fourteen hundred guns—the Spanish, twelve hundred and eighty-four. Considering the insolent and haughty manner in which the latter had acted, they made but a weak resistance when attacked in earnest, for in the engagement twenty-three vessels were either captured, sunk, or burnt.

Admiral Byng did not lose a ship, and only one, the "Grafton," was severely damaged.

Captain Watson was sent in pursuit of some of the Spanish vessels, which became detached from the flying fleet; on his return, he made to Admiral Byng the following brief and simple report.

"Sir, we have taken and destroyed all the Spanish ships which were upon the coast, the number as per margin." In all, eight ships of the line.

Admiral Byng immediately despatched his son to England to inform the Court of this victory. He was received with great honour by King George I., who wrote to the admiral, *in French*, the following letter :—*

SIR GEORGE BYNG,—

Although I have received no news from you directly, I have heard of the victory gained by the fleet under your command, and would not therefore delay giving you that satisfaction which must result from my approbation of your conduct. I give you my thanks, and desire that you will testify my satisfaction to all the brave men who distinguished themselves on that occasion. Mr. Secretary Craggs has instructions to inform you more fully of my intentions, but I was myself willing to assure you that I am

Your good friend,
GEORGE R.

Hampton Court, August 23rd, 1718.

The admiral also received an autograph letter of thanks from the Emperor Charles VI., of

* The King could not speak English very well.

Austria, whose viceroy at Naples presented Sir George with a sword set with diamonds, and a costly staff of command.

After the presentation, Sir George Byng and the principal officers of his fleet were splendidly entertained at a banquet, and then lodged in the palace of the Duke de Matelona, which had been magnificently fitted up for the purpose.

The viceroy also sent provisions to the fleet, consisting of 100 oxen, 300 sheep, 600 pounds of sugar, 70 hogsheads of brandy, and many other articles.

On the 3rd of December, 1718, war was formally declared against Spain, yet, for nearly a year afterwards, there was literally nothing done by the navy. Sir John Norris remained with a large fleet in the Baltic, and Admiral Sir George Byng cruised with his fleet on and off the Island of Sicily.

On the 21st of September, 1719, an English squadron sailed from Spithead for the coast of Spain. It conveyed 4,000 troops, under Lord Cobham, which were landed at Vigo, a place where the Duke of Ormond, who had been assisting the Pretender, had collected many military stores.

EXECUTION OF ADMIRAL BYNG.

The citadel was captured after a siege of a few days, and 2,000 barrels of powder, with 8,000 muskets, were taken as spoil.

In February, 1720, the Spanish king agreed to the quadruple alliance, and England was again for a time at peace.

In May, 1726, the English Government, having reason to believe that the Court of Russia was engaged in some intrigues for the restoration of the Stuart family to this country, as also was the Court of Spain, it was resolved to fit out three squadrons: one to proceed to the Baltic, to overawe the Czarina; one to cruise in the neighbourhood of Gibraltar, and intimidate his Catholic Majesty; and one to proceed to the West Indies, to pounce on the Spanish possessions there if war broke out.

The Russians were much nettled at the appearance of an English fleet before St. Petersburgh, and the Spaniards indulged in a little skirmishing near Gibraltar; but neither power was in a position to do much in the way of fighting, so the English demands were acceded to.

At the death of George I., in June, 1727, our navy consisted of a total of 273 vessels, manned by 68,652 seamen, and carrying 11,018 guns and 166 swivels. Seven of these ships were of the first rate, carrying 100 guns each, and thirteen of the second rate, carrying 90 guns.

Early in the reign of George II. serious difficulties arose with the Spanish Government, principally in regard to the conduct of English merchants trading with the Spanish colonies of America. It was alleged that the merchants trading to those colonies were constantly breaking the treaties of commerce that had been ratified between the two nations some few years before.

There is not the slightest doubt but that the Spaniards were justified in their complaints, and England seems to have commenced a war against them for not submitting patiently to these open violations of national treaties.

War was declared against Spain in October, 1739, and a fleet was prepared to act against the enemy in America. The chief reasons for attacking the enemy in his American colonies were; first, the well known riches of those possessions; and secondly, they were by no means strongly fortified; and thirdly, there was a much better chance of maintaining a successful war against the Spaniards there than in Europe.

A squadron, under the command of Commodore Anson, was ordered to sail round Cape Horn to the western coast of America; another, under Admiral Vernon, was to attack Porto-Bello, and some other places on the Atlantic sea-board.

This war may be said to have been almost instigated by the taunts and boastful speeches of Admiral Vernon, while in his place in the House of Commons.

He so assailed the Government with reproaches for neglecting the commercial welfare of the country in not allowing our merchants to share some of the Spaniards' wealth, and gave such glowing accounts of the riches of Central America—

showed how weak were the enemy's defences, and how easy it would be to rob them, that the House became excited to the highest pitch of enthusiasm.

When he subsequently told them that with *six ships* he would sweep the whole coast, capture the enemy's largest towns, and secure millions of treasure, the House became almost ungovernable.

The ministry was reproached for neglecting such opportunities of gain, and taunted with purposely ignoring such a man as Admiral Vernon from base party motives.

The country soon took up the cry, and the public indignation, or rather, the public appetite for plunder and buccaneering adventure, grew so strong, that the Government was compelled to give way.

Admiral Vernon was appointed to the South American station, and supplied, not with the six ships with which he was to do such wonders, but with a large and well-appointed fleet.

Walpole devoutly prayed that he might never return to England, to annoy him and his ministry again.

Admiral Vernon sailed with his fleet in July, 1739, and in the November of the same year anchored off Porto-Bello.

On the 21st of July he attacked the fort called the Iron Castle. The men scaled the lower buttresses by mounting on each other's shoulders, when the fort was taken without much loss of life. The next day Fort Castellio de Gloria surrendered.

From this place Vernon took on board sixty pieces of cannon, spiked the remainder, and used the powder he found in the magazine for blowing up the fortifications.

A fast sailing ship was instantly despatched to England with the intelligence that Admiral Vernon had taken Porto-Bello, and, remarkable to say, he had effected this adventure with only six ships.

But as regarded the spoil, or the treasure he was to take, not a word was said, or the slightest evidence of either sent home.

The fact, however, that Vernon had taken Porto-Bello with only six ships, quite intoxicated the people. The thanks of the nation were voted to the admiral, and merchants and ship-owners began to fit out privateers, to harass and destroy the enemy's commerce.

A large armament was immediately fitted out, and several thousand troops embarked on board, for the double purpose of intercepting the Plate fleet, before it could reach Spain, and of reinforcing Vernon in the West Indies.

Having wasted the whole summer in trying to blockade a Spanish fleet and convoy, bound for Central America, and, having allowed the treasure ships to pass them, the fleet at last stood away for the West Indies.

On the arrival of Sir Chaloner Ogle, with his reinforcements, Admiral Vernon had a fleet under his command of one hundred and fifteen ships of war, thirty of which were line of battle, and the rest frigates, bomb-ketches and fire-ships.

This fleet was manned by fifteen thousand men, and carried a land force of twelve thousand marines and soldiers, which, on the death of General Carteret, were under the command of General Wentworth.

With this force Admiral Vernon determined to attack Carthagena.

The harbour of this city could only be entered by a long, narrow inlet called "Boca Chica," or the little mouth, across which was a heavy boom, guarded on either side by strong buttresses.

Within the harbour was the Castillo Grande, a large fort protecting a channel in which several ships had been sunk to impede the passage of an enemy's vessels.

The ramparts of Carthagena mounted three hundred guns, it had a garrison of four thousand regular troops, and was commanded by an experienced and capable officer. Such were the difficulties that encountered the English when they appeared off the place on the 4th of March, 1741.

The "Boca Chica" was first attacked and captured, after an obstinate defence of fifteen days, but with a loss of four hundred men.

When the English eventually forced an entrance into the harbour, the Spaniards deserted the "Castillo Grande," and retreated to the inner defences, resolved to hold the city to the last.

So satisfied was Admiral Vernon that Carthagena was now in his hands, that that very evening a ship was despatched to England to inform the Government that all difficulties had been at last surmounted, and Carthagena was actually within his grasp. So sanguine was his tone, so certain was he of success, that a medal was actually struck in London to celebrate the capture of Carthagena.

The medal represented Vernon on one side and on the other this legend—"The Avenger of his Country."

This is the only instance of bombast and inflated folly to which this country can plead guilty.

Instead of attacking the town directly they got into the harbour, and securing victory when it was in their reach, the two commanders began to quarrel, and set their personal dignity above their duty to their country. Admiral Vernon wanted to monopolise all the honour and glory, while General Wentworth thought it only fair that he and his soldiers should have a share in the honour of an enterprise in which both army and navy bore an equal proportion of the danger.

After giving the enemy full time to make ample preparations for resistance, an attack was made upon the town.

Twelve hundred men, led by General Guise, made a night assault upon Fort San Lazaro, a strong outwork of the city defences.

The English lost their way in the dark, the scaling ladders were too short, and after a long and desperate fight, the assault resulted in a complete failure, with the loss of nearly eight hundred men. General Guise was killed, and the remainder of the force was embarked with the greatest expedition.

Fatigue, salt and bad provisions, with the usual diseases of the climate, now suddenly attacked the troops and crews of the fleet, and in less than two days more than three thousand men were placed on the sick list. Under these circumstances a council of war was called, and acting, under its decision, the fleet sailed for Jamaica.

After the re-embarkation of the troops, the distempers peculiar to the climate and season began to rage with redoubled fury; and great numbers of those who escaped the vengeance of the enemy, perished by a more painful and inglorious fate. Nothing was heard but complaints and execrations, the groans of the dying and the service for the dead. Nothing was seen but objects of woe and images of dejection. The conductors of this unfortunate expedition agreed in nothing but the expediency of a speedy retreat from this scene of misery and disgrace.

The miscarriage of this expedition, which had cost the nation an immense sum of money, was no sooner known in England than the kingdom was filled with murmurs and discontent, and the people were depressed in proportion to that sanguine hope by which they had been elevated.

Admiral Vernon, instead of undertaking any enterprise which might have retrieved the honor of the British arms, set sail from Jamaica with the forces in July, and anchored at the south-east part of Cuba, in a bay, on which he bestowed the appellation of Cumberland Harbour.

The troops were landed, and encamped at the distance of twenty miles farther up the river, where they remained totally inactive, and subsisted chiefly on salt and damaged provisions, till the month of November, when, being considerably diminished by sickness, they were put on board again, and reconveyed to Jamaica.

He was afterwards reinforced from England by four ships of war, and about three thousand soldiers; but he performed nothing worthy of the reputation he had acquired; and the people began to perceive that they had mistaken his character.

In the course of the following year, Vernon and General Wentworth made another effort in the West Indies. They had in January received a reinforcement from England, and planned a new expedition, in concert with the governor of Jamaica, who accompanied them in their voyage. Their design was to disembark the troops at Porto-Bello, and march across the isthmus of Darien, to attack the rich town of Panama.

They sailed from Jamaica on the 9th day of March, and on the 28th arrived at Porto-Bello. There they held a council of war, in which it was resolved, that as the troops were sickly, the rainy season begun, and several transports not yet arrived, the intended expedition was become impracticable. In pursuance of this determination the armament immediately returned to Jamaica, exhibiting a ridiculous spectacle of folly and irresolution.

In August, a ship of war was sent from thence, with about three hundred soldiers, to the small island of Rattan, in the Bay of Honduras, of which they took possession.

In September, Vernon and Wentworth received orders to return to England with such troops as remained alive; these did not amount to a tenth part of the number which had been sent abroad in that inglorious service. The inferior officers fell ignobly by sickness and despair, without an opportunity of signalising their courage, and the commanders lived to feel the scorn and reproach of their country.

Preparations for a naval expedition had been for a long time in progress in the French ports of Toulon and Brest, and in 1744, a French squadron, having been joined by another from Spain, contrived to put to sea about February. They were overtaken, however, by an English fleet, off Toulon, on the 22nd of February.

On this occasion the English fleet of forty-eight ships, twenty-seven of them being line-of-battle, was superior to the combined squadrons of France and Spain. Under such circumstances a victory was almost certain; yet such was the petty feud and jealousy existing between Admirals Mathews and Lestock, and their subordinate officers, that though the crews of a few ships fought bravely, the enemy escaped almost uninjured, and the battle was unworthy and indecisive.

The feeling in England on the receipt of this news was one of ungovernable indignation; the nation felt it had been betrayed by its incompetent officers, and the Commons, in an address to the throne, desired that a court-martial might be appointed to try the delinquents.

By this time Lestock had accused Mathews, and all the captains of his division who misbehaved on the day of battle. The court-martial was constituted and proceeded to trial. Several commanders of ships were cashiered; Vice-Admiral Lestock was honourably acquitted, and Admiral Mathews rendered incapable of serving in future in His Majesty's navy.

All the world knew that Lestock kept aloof, and that Mathews rushed into the hottest part of the engagement. Yet the former triumphed on his trial, and the latter narrowly escaped the sentence of death for cowardice and misconduct. Such decisions are not to be accounted for, except from prejudice and faction.

Mathews died in 1751, Lestock on the 12th of December, 1746. It is said that he expired without a friend, the victim of mortified pride and disappointment.

An expedition to the island of Cape Breton, in the Gulf of St. Lawrence, had been crowned with success in the previous year, and a great number of the enemy's privateers had been destroyed or captured in the channel, and six hundred and forty-four prizes made in the course of one year.

The French, in the meantime, were actively employed in fitting out two squadrons, meant to annoy British commerce, one squadron being designed to act in the East and the other in the West Indies.

The ministry of Great Britain, being apprised of these measures, resolved to intercept both squadrons, which were to set sail together. For this purpose Vice-Admiral Anson and Rear-Admiral Warren took their departure from Plymouth with a formidable fleet, and steered their course to Cape Finisterre, on the coast of Gallicia.

On the 3rd of May they fell in with the French squadrons, commanded by La Jonquiere and St. George, consisting of six large ships of war, as many frigates, and four armed vessels, equipped by their East India Company, having under their convoy thirty ships laden with merchandise. Those prepared for war immediately shortened sail, and formed a line of battle; while the rest, under the protection of the six frigates, proceeded on their voyage with all the sail they could carry.

The British squadron was likewise drawn up in line of battle; but Admiral Warren, perceiving that the enemy began to sheer off, now their convoy was at a considerable distance, advised Admiral Anson to haul in the signal for the line, and hoist another for giving chase and engaging, otherwise the French would, in all probability, take advantage of the darkness and escape.

The proposal was embraced; and in a little time the engagement began with great fury, about four o'clock in the afternoon. The enemy sustained the battle with equal conduct and valour, until they were overpowered by numbers, and then they struck their colours. The admiral detached three ships in pursuit of the convoy, nine sail of which were taken; but the rest were saved by the intervening darkness.

About seven hundred of the French were killed and wounded in this action. The English lost about five hundred; and among these Captain Grenville, commander of the ship "Defiance." He was nephew to the Lord Viscount Cobham, a youth of the most amiable character and promising genius, animated with the noblest sentiments of honour and patriotism.

Eager in the pursuit of glory, he rushed into the midst of the battle, where both his legs were cut off by a cannon ball. He submitted to his fate with the most heroic resignation, and died universally lamented and beloved.

The success of the British arms in this engagement was chiefly owing to the conduct, activity, and courage of the rear-admiral.

A considerable quantity of bullion was found in the prizes, which was brought to Spithead in triumph; and the treasure being landed, was conveyed in twenty waggons to the Bank of England. Admiral Anson was ennobled, and Admiral Warren honored with the Order of the Bath.

Rear-Admiral Hawke sailed from Plymouth in the beginning of August, with fourteen ships of the line, to intercept a fleet of French merchant ships bound for the West Indies. He cruised for some time on the coast of Bretagne, and at length the French fleet sailed from the Isle of Aix, under convoy of nine ships of the line, besides frigates, commanded by Monsieur de Letendeur.

On the 14th of October the two squadrons were in sight of each other in the latitude of Belle Isle. The French commodore immediately ordered one of his great ships and the frigates to proceed with the trading ships, while he formed the line of battle, and waited the attack.

At eleven in the forenoon Admiral Hawke displayed the signal to chase, and in half-an-hour both fleets were engaged. The battle lasted till night, when all the French squadron, except the "Intrepide" and the "Tonant," had struck to the English flag. These two capital ships escaped in the

CRESTS OF VESSELS IN THE ROYAL NAVY (A.D. 1870).

dark, and returned to Brest in a shattered condition.

The French captains sustained the unequal fight with uncommon bravery and resolution, and did not yield until their ships were disabled. Their loss in men amounted to eight hundred; the number of English killed in this engagement did not exceed two hundred, including Captain Saumarez, a gallant officer, who had served under Lord Anson in his expedition to the Pacific Ocean.

From the beginning of this war, to the peace of Aix-la-Chapelle, there were several unimportant actions with squadrons of the enemy, both at sea and off the coast; but none of them are deserving of special mention.

At the same time there were many naval duels fought between ships of the line, frigates and privateers, in which the crews behaved in a manner that did honour to their country, and covered them with deathless fame.

The following are a few of the most memorable of these desperate exploits.

In the year 1745, his Majesty's ship the "Lion," of 58 guns, commanded by Captain Brett, engaged with two French vessels; one a man-of-war of 64 guns, and the other a ship of 16 guns.

The "Lion" ran alongside the large ship, and fought her within pistol shot for five hours, when her rigging being cut to pieces, and her masts shot away, so that she lay muzzled in the sea, and could do nothing with her sails, the French ship escaped.

Every person quartered at the guns was killed on the spot, except two men and a boy. Forty-five of the "Lion's" men were killed, and a hundred and seven wounded. Captain Brett was wounded in the arm, in the foot, and was knocked down with

DUTCH FISHERMEN PUTTING OFF TO RESCUE THE CREW OF THE "BRANCAS" PRIVATEER.

splinters several times. His lieutenants were all wounded two hours before the close of the action, but still would not leave the deck, but continued to encourage the men to the last.

It is singular that, with such examples of bravery, a coward could be found in the vessel; but yet this was the case. The captain of marines, though called for several times during the action, could not be found. At last one of the midshipmen discovered him concealed under a large bag of hay, with one of his corporals with him.

The charge which this recreant so basely deserted, was taken by the Rev. Mr. Leach, the chaplain, who bravely put himself at the head of the corps, rallied them thrice on the poop of the ship, and encouraged them to behave like Englishmen, until he was shot dead on the spot.

An English sailor being on the foretop, and having one of his legs carried away by a shot, with the heart of a lion, he let himself down by a rope, saying at the same time, "he should not have cared for the accident, if he had done his duty; but it gave him pain to think he should die without having done anything for his country."

In this action the French man-of-war, the "Elizabeth," lost sixty-four men killed, and one hundred and forty wounded. The smaller vessel, after one or two broadsides, sheered off.

The next instance, was an action fought between an English coaster or small merchant ship, trading between Norfolk and Holland, and a French privateer, and is perhaps one of the most remarkable examples of courage and determination to be found in the annals of any maritime nation.

Mr. Richard Hornby, of Stokesly, was master of a merchant ship, the "Isabella," of Sunderland, in which he sailed from the coast of Norfolk for the Hague, June 1st, 1744, in company with three smaller vessels recommended to his care. Next day they made Gravesant Steeple, in the Hague; but while they were steering for their port, a French privateer, that lay concealed among the Dutch fishing boats, suddenly came against them, singling out the "Isabella" as the object of attack, while the rest dispersed and escaped.

The strength of the two ships was most unequal; for the "Isabella" mounted only four carriage guns and two swivels, and her crew consisted of only five men and three boys, besides the captain; while the privateer, the "Marquis de Brancas," commanded by Captain Andre, had ten carriage guns and eight swivels, with seventy-five men, and three hundred small arms.

Captain Hornby, nothing daunted, having animated his little crew by an appropriate address, and obtained their promise of standing by him to the last, hoisted the British colours, and with his two-swivel guns returned the fire of the enemy's chase guns. The Frenchmen, in abusive terms, commanded him to strike. Hornby coolly returned an answer of defiance, on which the privateer advanced, and poured such showers of bullets into the "Isabella," that the captain thought it prudent to order his brave fellows into close quarters.

While he lay thus sheltered, the enemy twice attempted to board him on the larboard quarter, but by a dexterous turn of the helm he frustrated both attempts, though the Frenchman kept firing upon him, both with guns and small arms.

At two o'clock, when the action had lasted an hour, the privateer, running furiously in upon the larboard of the "Isabella," entangled her bowsprit among the main shrouds, and was lashed fast to her.

Captain Andre now bawled out, in a menacing tone—

"You English dog, strike!"

Captain Hornby challenged him to come on board, and strike his colours if he dared.

The exasperated Frenchmen instantly threw in twenty men on the "Isabella," who began to hack and hew into the close quarters; but a general discharge of blunderbusses forced the assailants to retreat as fast as their wounds would permit them.

The privateer, being now disengaged from the "Isabella," turned about, and made another attempt on the starboard side, when the valiant Hornby and his mate, shot each his man, as the enemy were again lashing the ships together.

The Frenchman once more commanded him to strike; and the brave Englishman returning another refusal, twenty fresh men entered, and made a fierce attack on the close quarters with hatchets and pole-axes, with which they had nearly cut their way through in three places, when the constant fire kept up by Captain Hornby and his crew, obliged them a second time to retreat, carrying their wounded with them, and hauling their dead after them with boat-hooks.

The "Isabella" continuing still lashed to the enemy, the latter with small arms, fired repeated and terrible volleys into the close quarters; but the fire was returned with such spirit and effect, that the Frenchmen repeatedly gave way.

At length Captain Hornby seeing them crowding behind their mainmast for shelter, aimed a blunderbuss at them, which being by mistake doubly loaded, containing twice twelve balls, burst in the firing, and threw him down, to the great consternation of his little crew, who supposed him dead.

In an instant, however, he started up again, though greatly bruised, while the enemy, among whom the blunderbuss had made dreadful havoc, disengaged themselves from the "Isabella," to which they had been lashed an hour and a quarter, and sheered off with precipitation, leaving their graplings, and a quantity of pole-axes, pistols, and cutlasses behind them.

The gallant Hornby now exultingly fired his two starboard guns into the enemy's stern. The indignant Frenchman immediately returned and renewed the conflict, which was carried on yard-arm and yard-arm, with great fury, for two hours together.

The "Isabella" was shot through her hull several times, her sails and rigging were torn to pieces, her ensign was dismounted, and every mast and yard damaged; yet she still bravely maintained the combat, and at last, by a fortunate shot, which struck the "Brancas" between wind and water, obliged her to sheer off and careen. While the enemy were retiring, Hornby and his little crew sallied out from their fastness, and erecting their fallen ensign, gave three cheers.

By this time both vessels had driven so near the English shore, that immense crowds had assembled to be spectators of the action.

The Frenchman having stopped his leak, returned to the combat, and poured a dreadful volley into the stern of the "Isabella," when Captain Hornby was wounded by a ball in the temple, and bled profusely.

The sight of their brave commander streaming with blood somewhat disconcerted his gallant companions; but he called to them briskly to keep their courage and stand to their arms, for his wound was not dangerous. On this their spirits revived, and again taking post in their close quarters, they sustained the shock of three more tremendous broadsides, in returning which they forced the "Brancas," by another well-aimed shot, a second time to sheer off and careen.

The huzzas of the "Isabella's" crew were renewed, and they again set up their shattered ensign, which was shot through and through into horrible rags.

Andre, who was not deficient in bravery, soon returned to the fight, and having disabled the "Isabella" by five terrible broadsides, once more summoned Hornby, with dreadful menaces, to strike his colours.

Captain Hornby turned to his gallant comrades— "You see yonder, my lads," pointing to the shore, "the witnesses of your valour!"

It was unnecessary to say more; they, one and all, assured him of their resolution to stand by him to the last; and finding them thus invincibly determined, he hurled his final defiance at the enemy.

Andre immediately ran his ship upon the "Isabella's" starboard, and lashed close alongside; but his crew murmured, and refused to renew the dangerous task of boarding, so that he was obliged to cut the lashings and again retreat.

Captain Hornby resolved to salute the privateer with one parting gun, and this last shot, fired into the stern of the "Brancas," happening to reach the magazine, it blew up with a tremendous explosion, and the vessel instantly went to the bottom.

Out of seventy-five men thirty-six were killed or wounded in the action, and all the rest, together with the wounded, perished in the deep except three, who were picked up by the Dutch fishing boats.

This horrible catastrophe excited the compassion of the brave Hornby and his men; but they could unfortunately render no assistance to their ill-fated enemies, the "Isabella" having become unmanageable, and her boat being shattered to pieces.

Mr. Hornby afterwards received from his sovereign a large gold medal in commemoration of his heroic conduct on this occasion; conduct, perhaps, not surpassed by anything in the annals of British naval prowess.

The next anecdote, though equally glorious, was unhappily, less fortunate in its result.

In the month of December, 1756, the "Terrible," privateer, of twenty-six guns, and two hundred men, commanded by Captain William Death, engaged the "Grand Alexander," a French vessel of four hundred tons, twenty-two guns, and one hundred men, and after a smart fight of two hours and a half, in which Captain Death's brother, and sixteen of his men were killed, he took her, and put forty men on board.

A few days after, the "Vengeance," privateer, of St. Maloes, thirty-six guns, and three hundred and sixty men, bore down upon her and retook the prize.

The "Vengeance" and the prize then both attacked the "Terrible," which was between them, and shot away her mainmast at the first broadside.

One of the most desperate engagements ever recorded took place, which lasted an hour and a-half, in which Monsieur Bourdas, the French captain, his lieutenant, and two-thirds of his crew on one side, and Captain Death, almost all his officers, and the greatest part of his crew on the other side, were killed.

The "Terrible" was ultimately taken and carried into St. Maloes, in a shattered and frightful condition, having no more than twenty-six of the crew alive, sixteen of whom had lost legs or arms, and the other ten were all wounded.

As soon as this heroic feat was known in England, a subscription was set on foot, which produced a very handsome sum for the widow of Captain Death, and for the surviving seamen of the gallant crew.

In the summer of 1748 the "Magnanime," a French ship of seventy-four guns, was taken after a short but fierce action in the Channel, by the "Nottingham," of sixty guns, and carried in triumph into Portsmouth, where, under her English name of the "Magnanimous," she became one of the British fleet.

In the West Indies, two British frigates fell in with the "Glorioso," a Spanish treasure-ship of eighty guns. She had reached the latitude of the Azores in safety when the English ships descried her.

Captain Erskine, in the "Warwick," instantly bore down and attacked her, yard-arm and yard-arm, with such fury, that if his consort had assisted him, the ship and her immense treasure must have become their spoil.

As it was her consort bore away, and the "Warwick" was left almost a wreck, and the "Glorioso" escaped into Ferole, where she landed her treasure, and again put to sea.

Two days afterwards she was overhauled by the "Dartmouth," corvette of 40 guns, Captain Hamilton, who, regardless of the size of his enemy, her number of guns, or the strength of her crew, began a fierce action, which he continued, till a shot reaching the magazine blew the ship, crew, and gallant captain into the air.

Once more the "Glorioso" pursued her homeward voyage, had nearly sighted Cadiz, and began to think all her dangers over, when an 80-gun British line-of-battle came athwart her hawse, and after half-an-hour's sharp fighting made her strike.

Before the end of the month she was safely moored at Spithead as a prize.

On the 30th of October, 1747, Admiral Vernon died suddenly at his residence in Suffolk. He was in his sixty-third year, having been born in 1684.

Vernon is said to be the first naval commander who compelled seamen to drink their spirits mixed with water. This new beverage was called grog, for the reason that the admiral wore a grogram waistcoat.

In this year the British cruisers and privateers captured from the French five hundred and fifty-six vessels, and from the Spaniards ninety-one. The French captured from the English four hundred and twenty vessels, and the Spaniards took from them one hundred and thirty-one. Those, however, which were captured from the English were of little value compared with those taken by them.

CHAPTER XVII.

THE LOSS OF MINORCA AND THE TRIAL OF ADMIRAL BYNG.

A SHORT time after the peace of Aix-la-Chapelle had been concluded it was imagined or observed by English statesmen that the French were inclined to act with treachery towards them, and not with the good faith expected from them, and that they were busy making warlike preparations for no apparent cause.

A French fleet, under M. De la Motte, was hovering about the British North American possessions, and there were no honest reasons why such should be the case.

In 1755, Admiral Boscawen was sent with eleven ships-of-the-line to follow a French fleet to America, with orders to attack it, should it attempt to enter the Bay of St. Lawrence.

Having taken on board two regiments at Plymouth, the fleet sailed from thence, on the 27th of April, for the banks of Newfoundland, and in a few days after his arrival there the French fleet from Brest came to the same station.

The thick fogs which prevail upon these coasts, especially at that time of the year, kept the two armaments from seeing each other, and part of the French squadron escaped up the river St. Lawrence, while another part of them went round, and got into the same river by the straits of Belle Isle, by a passage which was never known to be attempted before by ships of the line.

However, whilst the English fleet lay off Cape Race, the southernmost point of Newfoundland, and which was supposed to be the most proper position for intercepting the enemy, two French ships, the "Alcide," of sixty-four guns, and four hundred and eighty men; and the "Lys," pierced for fifty-four guns, but mounting only twenty-two,

PORTRAIT OF ADMIRAL VERNON.

with troops on board, became separated from the rest of their fleet in the fog.

They fell in with the "Dunkirk," Captain Howe, and the "Defiance," Captain Andrews, two sixty-gun ships of the English squadron; and, after a smart engagement, which lasted some hours, and in which Captain (afterwards Lord) Howe behaved with the greatest skill and intrepidity, were both taken, with several officers of rank, and engineers, with about eight thousand pounds in money.

Though the capture of these ships, from which the commencement of the war may, in fact, be dated, fell greatly short of what was hoped for from this expedition, yet, when the news of it reached England, it was of infinite service to the public credit of every kind.

It animated the whole nation, who were now convinced that the Government was determined to keep no further measures with the French, but to repel force by force, and put a stop to their sending more men and arms to invade the property of the English in America, as they had hitherto done with impunity.

The French, who for some time did not even attempt to make reprisals on our shipping, would gladly have chosen to avoid a war at that time, and to have continued extending their encroachments on our settlements, till they had executed their grand plan of securing a communication from the Mississippi to Canada by a line of forts, many of which they had already erected.

On the 15th of July, an express arrived from Admiral Boscawen, with an account of his capture of the two French ships, mentioned above, and orders were soon after given to all our ships of war to attack the French, and take their ships wherever they should meet them.

Sir Edward Hawke sailed from Portsmouth on the 21st of July, with eighteen ships of war, to watch the return of the French fleet from America, which, however, escaped him, and arrived at Brest on the 3rd of September.

Commodore Frankland also sailed from Spithead for the West Indies, with four ships of war, with orders to commit hostilities, as well as to protect our trade and sugar islands from any insult that the French might offer.

Though the English continued to make reprisals upon the French, not only in the seas of America, but also in those of Europe, by taking every ship they could meet with, and detaining them, their cargoes and crews, yet the French, whether from a consciousness of their want of power by sea, or that they might have a more plausible plea to represent England as the aggressor, were far from returning these hostilities.

This was shown in the fact that their fleet which escaped Sir Edwd. Hawke, having on the 13th of August, taken the "Blandford" ship of war, with Governor Lyttleton on board, going to Carolina, they set the governor at liberty as soon as the court was informed of the ship's being brought to Nantes, and shortly after released both the ship and crew.

In England the preparations by sea became greater than ever; several new ships of war were put into commission, and many others taken into the service of the Government, the exportation of gunpowder was forbid, the bounties to seamen were continued, and the number of those that either entered voluntarily, or were pressed, increased daily, as did also the captures from the French, among which was the "Esperance," of seventy guns, taken as she was going from Rochfort to Brest to be manned.

The strength of the English navy, so early as the month of September of this year, consisted of one ship of a hundred and ten guns; five of a hundred guns each; thirteen of ninety; eight of eighty; five of seventy-four; twenty-nine of seventy; four of sixty-six; one of sixty-four; thirty-three of sixty; three of fifty-four; twenty-eight of fifty; four of forty-four; thirty-five of forty; and forty-two of twenty; four sloops of war, of eighteen guns each; two of sixteen; eleven of fourteen; thirteen of twelve; and one of ten; besides a great number of bomb-ketches, fire-ships, and tenders.

This was considered a force sufficient to oppose the united maritime strength of all the powers in Europe; while that of the French, even at the end of this year, and including the ships then upon the stocks, amounted to no more than six ships of eighty guns; twenty-one of seventy-four; one of seventy-two; four of seventy; thirty-one of sixty-four; two of sixty; six of

DESTRUCTION OF THE "BRANCAS" PRIVATEER.

fifty; and thirty-two frigates.

In 1756, the French determined to take possession of the Island of Minorca, which had been captured by the English in 1708.

In the beginning of the year advice was received that a French squadron would soon be in a condition to sail from Toulon, and this was confirmed by repeated intelligence from English ministers and consuls residing in Spain and Italy.

They affirmed that the Toulon squadron consisted of twelve or fifteen ships of the line with a great number of transports; that they were supplied with provisions for two months only, consequently could not be intended for America; and that strong bodies of troops were on their march ready to be embarked.

Notwithstanding these particulars of information, which plainly pointed out Minorca as the object of the expedition; notwithstanding the extensive and important commerce carried on by the subjects of Great Britain in the Mediterranean, no care was taken to send thither a squadron of ships capable of protecting the trade, and frustrating the designs of the enemy.

That great province was left to a few inconsiderable ships and frigates, which could serve no other purpose than that of carrying intelligence from port to port, and enriching their commanders by making prizes of merchant vessels.

Little or no regard was paid to the repeated remonstrances of General Blakeney, deputy-governor of Minorca, representing the weakness of the garrison in St. Philip's Castle, the chief fortress on the island. Far from strengthening the garrison with a proper reinforcement, the Ministry did not even send thither the officers belonging to it, who were in England upon leave of absence, until the French armament was ready to make a descent upon the island.

The destination of the French fleet being at last universally known, measures were taken with hurry and precipitation.

Instead of despatching a squadron that in all respects should be superior to the French fleet in the Mediterranean, and bestowing the command of it upon an officer of approved courage and activity, they allotted no more than ten ships of the line for this service, and gave the command to Admiral John Byng, the second son of the Admiral George Byng, already mentioned in this history.

Admiral Byng had never met with any opportunity to signalize his courage, and his character was not very popular in the navy; but Rear-Admiral West, the second in command, was universally respected for his ability and resolution.

The ten ships destined for this expedition were but in very indifferent order, poorly manned, and unprovided with either hospital or fire-ship. They sailed from Spithead on the 7th of April, having on board as part of their complement a regiment of soldiers, to be landed at Gibraltar, with Major-General Stuart, Lord Effingham, and Colonel Cornwallis, whose regiments were in garrison at Minorca, and a reinforcement for St. Philip's fortress.

The admiral set sail from Gibraltar on the 8th of May, and was joined off Majorca by his Majesty's ship "Phœnix," under the command of Captain Hervey, who confirmed the intelligence he had already received touching the strength and destination of the French squadron.

When he approached Minorca, he descried the British colours still flying at the castle of St. Philip's, and several bomb-batteries playing upon it from different quarters, where the French banners were displayed. Thus informed, he detached three ships ahead with Captain Hervey to reconnoitre the harbour's mouth, and land, if possible, a letter for General Blakeney, giving him to understand the fleet was come to his assistance.

Before this attempt could be made, the French fleet appearing to the south-east, and the wind blowing strong off shore, he recalled his ships, and formed the line of battle.

About six o'clock in the evening, the enemy, to the number of seventeen ships, thirteen of which appeared to be very large, advanced in order; but about seven tacked, with a view to gain the weather-gage. Admiral Byng, in order to preserve that advantage, as well as to make sure of the land-wind in the morning, followed their example, being then about five leagues from Cape Mola.

At daylight, the enemy could not be descried; but two tartanes appearing close to the rear of the English squadron, they were immediately chased. One escaped, but the other being taken, was found to have a reinforcement on board for the enemy's squadron. This soon re-appearing, the line of battle was formed on each side, and, about two o'clock, Admiral Byng threw out a signal to bear away two points from the wind and engage.

At this time his distance from the enemy was so great, that Rear-Admiral West, perceiving it impossible to comply with both orders, bore away with his division seven points from the wind, and closing down upon the enemy, attacked them with such impetuosity, that the ships which opposed him were in a little time driven out of the line.

Had he been properly sustained by the van, in all probability the British fleet would have obtained a complete victory; but the other division did not bear down, and the enemy's centre keeping their station, Rear-Admiral West could not pursue his advantage without running the risk of seeing his communication with the rest of the line entirely cut off.

In the beginning of the action, the "Intrepid," in Admiral Byng's division, was so disabled in her rigging that she could not be managed, and drove on the ship that was next in position, a circumstance that obliged several others to throw all aback, in order to avoid confusion, and for some time retarded the action.

Certain it is, that Admiral Byng, though in command of a noble ship of ninety guns, made little or no use of his artillery, but kept aloof, either from an overstrained observance of discipline or from timidity. When his captain exhorted him to bear down upon the enemy, he very coolly replied, that he would avoid the error of Admiral Mathews, who, in his engagement with the French and Spanish squadrons off Toulon, during the preceding war, had broke the line by his own precipitation, and exposed himself singly to a fire that he could not sustain.

Admiral Byng, on the contrary, was determined

against acting except with the line entire; and, on pretence of rectifying the disorder which had happened among some of the ships, hesitated so long, and kept at such a wary distance, that he never was properly engaged, though he received some few shots in his hull.

M. de la Galissoniere, the French admiral, seemed equally averse to the continuance of the battle; part of his squadron had been obliged to quit the line, and, though he was rather superior to the English in number of men and weight of metal, he did not choose to abide the consequences of a closer fight with an enemy so expert in naval operations; he, therefore, took advantage of Admiral Byng's hesitation, and edged away under easy sail to join his van, which had been already discomfited.

The English admiral gave chase, but the French ships having the advantage, he could not come up and close with them again, and they retired at their leisure.

He then put his squadron on the other tack, so as to keep the wind of the enemy, and next morning they were altogether out of sight.

While he lay to with the rest of his fleet at the distance of ten leagues from Mahon, he detached cruisers to look for the missing ships, which, having joined him, he made an inquiry into the condition of the squadron.

The number of killed amounted to forty-two, including Captain Andrews, of the "Defiance," and about a hundred and sixty-eight were wounded.

Three of the largest ships were so damaged in their masts that they could not keep the sea, with any regard to their safety; a great number of the seamen were ill, and there was no vessel which could be converted into an hospital for the sick and wounded.

In this situation Admiral Byng called a council of war, at which the land officers were present. He represented to them that he was much inferior to the enemy in weight of metal and number of men; that they had the advantage of sending their wounded to Minorca, from whence at the same time they were refreshed and reinforced occasionally.

Under such circumstances it was in his opinion impracticable to relieve St. Philip's fort, and therefore they ought to make the best of their way back to Gibraltar, which might require immediate protection.

They unanimously concurred with his sentiments, and thither he directed his course accordingly.

So exasperated was the public mind against Byng, for what was called his cowardice, that the severest measures were determined on against him; and, on the 16th of June, Sir Edward Hawke and Admiral Saunders sailed from Spithead to Gibraltar to supercede both him and Admiral West in the command of the Mediterranean squadron.

Directions were soon after dispatched to Sir Edward Hawke to send Admiral Byng home under arrest, and he immediately embarked in the ship that had carried out his successor, accompanied by Rear-Admiral West.

When they arrived in England, Mr. West met with a most gracious reception from his majesty, but Admiral Byng was committed close prisoner in an apartment in Greenwich Hospital.

After a most determined and gallant defence, which continued from the middle of April till the end of June, Minorca was compelled to surrender to the French, though they obtained the most honourable conditions, General Blakeney and his brave garrison marching out with all the honours of war.

A few days after the surrender of the fort, Sir Edward Hawke's fleet, augmented by five ships of the line which had been sent from England when the first tidings arrived of Minorca's being invaded, now made its appearance off the island; but by this time Galissionniere had retired, and the English admiral had the mortification to see the French colours flying upon St. Philip's Castle.

Sir Edward Hawke, being disappointed in his hope of encountering the French admiral and relieving the English garrison at St. Philip's, at least asserted the empire of Great Britain in the Mediterranean by annoying the commerce of the enemy, and blocking up the squadron in the harbour of Toulon.

Understanding that the Austrian government at Leghorn had detained an English privateer, and imprisoned the captain on pretence that he had violated the neutrality of the port, he detached two ships of war to insist in a peremptory manner on the release of the ship, effects, crew, and captain; and they thought proper to comply with this demand without waiting for orders from the court of Vienna.

The person in whose behalf the admiral thus interposed, was one Fortunatus Wright, a native of Liverpool, who, though a stranger to a seafaring life, had in the last war equipped a privateer, and distinguished himself in such a manner by his uncommon valour, that had he received a command suitable to his genius, he would have gained an honourable place in the annals of the navy.

An uncommon exertion of spirit was the occasion of his being detained at this time.

While he was at anchor in the harbour of Leghorn, commander of the "St. George," privateer, of Liverpool, a small ship of twelve guns and eighty men, a large French xebeque, mounted with sixteen cannon, and nearly three times the number of his complement, chose her station in view of the harbour, in order to interrupt the British commerce.

The gallant Wright could not endure this insult; notwithstanding the enemy's superiority in metal and number of men, he weighed anchor, hoisted his sails, engaged him within sight of the shore, and after a very obstinate action, in which the captain, lieutenant, and above three score of the men belonging to the xebeque were killed on the spot, he obliged them to sheer off, and returned to the harbour in triumph.

This brave man would doubtless have signalized himself by many other exploits, had he not been overtaken in the midst of his career by a dreadful storm, in which the ship foundering he and all his crew perished.

No action of great importance distinguished the naval transactions of this year.

In the beginning of June, Captain Spry, who commanded a small squadron, cruising off Louisbourg, in the island of Cape Breton, took the "Arc en Ciel," a French ship of fifty guns, having on board near six hundred men, with a large quantity of stores and provisions for the garrison.

He likewise made prize of another French ship, with seventy soldiers, two hundred barrels of gunpowder, two large mortars, and other stores.

On the 27th July, Commander Holmes, being in the same latitude with two large ships and a couple of sloops, engaged two French ships of the line and four frigates, and obliged them to sheer off, after an obstinately contested action.

A great number of privateers were equipped in this country, as well as in the West India islands belonging to the crown of Great Britain; and as those seas swarmed with French vessels, their cruises proved very advantageous to the adventurers.

The most remarkable transaction that distinguished this year was the trial and execution of Admiral Byng, the son of that great officer who had acquired such honor for his naval exploits, and who was generally esteemed one of the best officers in the navy, when he embarked in his last unfortunate expedition to Minorca.

The court-martial at which Byng was tried assembled at Portsmouth, on board the "Saint George," on the 28th of December. He was accused of cowardice, in not engaging the French fleet, and doing his utmost to raise the siege of Minorca, which, in consequence, was compelled to surrender to the French.

He was sentenced to be shot, but the sentence was accompanied by a strong recommendation to mercy, as the evidence in his behalf proved that he evinced neither fear nor confusion during the action, but gave his orders coolly and distinctly, and with no seeming want of personal courage.

The admiral behaved throughout the whole trial with great composure, seemingly the effect of conscious innocence, on which, perhaps, he too much relied. He was evidently surprised at the sentence, having confidently expected an acquittal, but he betrayed no marks of fear when it was pronounced.

No heed was taken of the unanimous recommendation to mercy. The nation was annoyed at, and ashamed of, the loss of Minorca, and demanded a victim. The new party in power wished to please the people, and the late ministry thought that Byng's condemnation would be some vindication of themselves. There was no one but Pitt, and a few personal friends, to intercede for poor Byng.

His own friends and relations exerted their influence and interest for his pardon, and, as the circumstances appeared so strong in his favour, it was supposed that mercy would be extended to him.

But the cry of vengeance was loud throughout the land, and infamous arts were used to whet the savage appetite of the populace for blood, and the king was assured that the execution of Byng was absolutely necessary to appease the fury of the people, and the warrant was accordingly issued for his execution.

The unfortunate admiral prepared himself for death with resignation and tranquility. He maintained a surprising cheerfulness to the last; nor did he, from his condemnation to his execution, exhibit the least sign of impatience or apprehension.

CRESTS OF VESSELS IN THE ROYAL NAVY (A.D. 1870).

During the interval, he had remained on board the "Monarque," a third-rate ship of war, anchored in the harbour of Portsmouth, under a strong guard, in custody of the Marshal of the Admiralty.

On the 14th of March, the day fixed for his execution, the boats belonging to the squadron at Spithead being manned and armed, containing their captains and officers, with a detachment of marines from each ship, attended in the harbour, which was crowded with boats and vessels filled with spectators.

Throwing his hat on the deck, he knelt on a cushion, tied one white handkerchief over his eyes, and dropped the other as a signal for his executioners, who fired a volley so decisive, that five balls passed through his body, and he dropped dead in an instant. The time in which this tragedy was acted, from his walking out of the cabin to his being deposited in the coffin, did not exceed three minutes.

Thus fell, to the astonishment of all Europe, Admiral John Byng, who, whatever his errors and indiscretions might have been, seems to have been

DESTRUCTION OF THE "KENT" MAN-OF-WAR.

About noon, the admiral having taken leave of a clergyman and two friends who accompanied him, walked out of the great cabin to the quarter-deck, where two files of marines were drawn up, ready to execute the sentence.

He advanced with a firm, deliberate step, a composed and resolute countenance, and refused to have his eyes covered.

Some officers represented to him that the soldiers might not like to fire at a man who was looking at them, and it would prevent their taking proper aim.

"If it will frighten them," he said, "let it be done. They would not frighten me."

rashly condemned, meanly given up, and cruelly sacrificed to vile considerations.

Byng was not a coward—he was only weak-minded, and wanted capacity. The only thing he feared was responsibility.

A short time before his execution, one of his friends, standing beside him, said, "Which of us is the tallest?"

"Why this ceremony?" exclaimed Byng. "I know what it means; let the man come and measure me for my coffin."

Admiral Byng proved by the way he died that he did not lack physical courage. Had he known that the English people will always forgive an officer for a rash act, whether successful or not, and that they never show the least sympathy for one who gives the slightest suspicion of cowardice, he would not have died by the verdict of his country.

John Byng, second son of Admiral George Byng, Viscount Torrington, was born in Kent in the year 1704. He served under his father in most of his expeditions, having from his earliest youth been trained to the naval profession, and was always esteemed a good seaman and a brave man.

Early in September, 1757, a powerful fleet was ordered to get in readiness to put to sea on the shortest notice, and ten regiments of infantry were marched to the Isle of Wight.

The naval armament consisted of eighteen ships-of-the-line, besides frigates, fire-ships, bomb-ketches, and transports, under the command of Sir Edward Hawke, an officer whose faithful services recommended him above all others to this command, and Rear-Admiral Knowles was appointed his subaltern.

Sir John Mordaunt was preferred to take the command of the land forces, and both strictly enjoined to act with the utmost unanimity and harmony.

The destination of the armament was kept a profound secret. Various impediments obstructed the departure of the fleet for several weeks, one of which was the absence of the transports which were to form part of the expedition. At last they arrived, and the fleet got under sail on the 8th of September.

On reaching the open sea orders were read, and the men learnt that the expedition was designed for the invasion of France, by the attempted capture of Rochefort.

On the 20th the fleet made the island of Oleron, and Sir Edward Hawke sent an order to Vice-Admiral Knowles to stand in as near to the island of Aix as the pilot would take him, with such ships as he thought necessary for the service, and to batter the fort till the garrison should either abandon or surrender it.

The immediate execution of this order was frustrated by a French man-of-war standing into the very middle of the fleet, and continuing in that station for some time before she discovered her mistake, or any of the captains had a signal thrown out to give chase.

Admiral Knowles, when too late, ordered the "Magnanime" (Captain Howe) and the "Torbay" (Captain Keppel) on that service, and thereby retarded the attack upon which he had been immediately sent, and by the delay he gained time to assure himself of the strength of the fortifications of Aix before he commenced the attack.

On the 23rd the van of the fleet, led by Captain Howe, in the "Magnanime," stood towards Aix, a small island, situated in the mouth of the river Charente, leading up to Rochefort, the fortifications half finished, and mounted with about thirty cannons and mortars, the garrison composed of six hundred men, and the whole island about five miles in circumference.

As the "Magnanime" approached, the enemy fired briskly upon her; but Captain Howe, regardless of their faint endeavours, kept on his course without flinching, dropping his anchors close to the walls, and pouring in so incessant a fire as soon silenced their artillery.

It was, however, near an hour before the fort struck, when some forces were landed to take possession, with orders to demolish the fortifications.

Inconsiderable as this success might appear, it greatly elated the troops, and was deemed a happy omen of further advantages; but instead of embarking the troops that night, several successive days were spent in councils of war, soundings of the coast, and other matters.

Eight days had elapsed since the first appearance of the fleet on the coast, and the enemy had taken the alarm. Propositions were made to attack Fouras and Rochelle, but nothing was done. It was at length determined in a council of war to make a descent, and attack the forts leading to, and upon the mouth of the river Charente.

An order was immediately issued for the troops to be ready to embark from the transports in the boats precisely at twelve at night. Accordingly the boats were prepared and filled with the men at the time appointed, and they remained, beating against each other and the sides of the ships, for the space of four hours, while the council was determining whether, after all the trouble, they should land.

At length an order was given to the troops to return to their respective transports, and all thoughts of a descent were apparently abandoned.

After blowing up the fortifications of Aix, the military officers, in a council of war, took the final resolution of returning to England without any further attempts, choosing rather to encounter the murmurs of an incensed nation, and the contempt of mankind, than fight a handful of militia.

Such was the issue of an expedition that raised the expectations of all Europe, threw the coasts of France into the utmost confusion, and cost the people of England little less than a million of money.

Besides the descent on the coast of France, several means were employed to annoy the enemy, as well as to protect the trade of the kingdom. On the 9th of February, Admiral West sailed with a squadron of men-of-war to the westward, as did Admiral Coates, with the fleet under his convoy, to the West Indies, and Commodore Steevens to the East Indies, in the month of March.

Admiral Holbourn and Commodore Holmes, with eleven ships-of-the-line, a fire-ship, and fifty transports, sailed from St. Helen's for America, in April, with a large number of land forces for that colony.

Besides the success which attended a great number of other privateers, the lords of the Admiralty published a list of above thirty ships-of-war and privateers taken from the enemy in the space of four months, by English sloops and ships-of-war, exclusive of the "Duke d'Aquitaine," Indiaman, taken by the "Eagle" and "Medway;" the "Pondicherry," Indiaman, valued at a hundred and sixty thousand pounds, taken by the "Dover," man-of-war, and above six privateers brought into port by the brave Captain Lockhart.

The naval transactions in America at this time were most unfortunate. Admiral Holbourne set sail for Louisbourg with fifteen ships-of-the-line, one ship of fifty guns, three small frigates, and a fire-ship. There seems to have been no object in this cruise, unless it was the admiral's desire to ascertain the enemy's strength, or the hope of drawing the French admiral into an engagement, though he was superior, both in number of ships and weight of metal.

Be this as it may, the British squadron appeared off Louisbourg on the 20th of August, and, approaching within two miles of the batteries, saw the French admiral make the signal to unmoor. Admiral Holbourne was greatly inferior in strength, and not wishing to fight the enemy, he immediately made the best of his way to Halifax.

About the middle of September, being reinforced with four ships-of-the-line, he again proceeded to Louisbourg, with the intention, if possible, to force the enemy into an engagement, but he found De la Mothe too prudent to hazard an unnecessary battle, the loss of which would have greatly exposed all the French colonies.

The English squadron continued cruising here until the 25th, when they were overtaken by a terrible storm. When the hurricane began the fleet were about forty leagues distant from Louisbourg, but were driven, in twelve hours, within two miles of the rocks and breakers of that coast, when the wind providentially shifted.

The ship "Tilbury" was wrecked upon the rocks, and half her crew drowned. Eleven ships were dismasted, others threw their guns overboard, and all returned in a very shattered condition to England at a very unfavourable season of the year.

In this manner ended the expedition to Louisbourg, more unfortunate to the nation than the preceding designs upon Rochefort; less disgraceful to the commanders, but equally the occasion of ridicule and triumph to our enemies.

On the 29th of April, 1758, a battle was fought between an English fleet of seven ships and a frigate, under the command of Admiral Pocock, and a French fleet under the Comte d'Ache.

In this action the French, after inflicting considerable injury on the English fleet, although at severe loss to themselves, their killed and wounded amounting to nearly six hundred, escaped through the bad conduct of some of the English captains.

For this affair Captains Legge, Vincent, and Brereton were tried by a court-martial, and dismissed the navy.

On the 1st of June in this year, a large fleet, consisting of eighteen ships of the line, thirteen frigates, and a number of transports, carrying an army of 14,000 soldiers and 6,000 marines, sailed for the French coast.

Howe was first appointed to command the fleet, but upon this Sir Edward Hawke, his senior in the service, resigned. Finally the dispute was arranged by Lord Anson undertaking the command himself.

It was a long time before this mighty armament did anything worth recording, but after cruising about for some time, and occasionally destroying a coast battery, the men were landed at Cherbourg, where they destroyed the forts and dockyard basin, on which the French had expended vast sums, levied a "requisition" to the amount of £3,000 sterling, and then re-embarked, taking with them some brass cannon and mortars, which were afterwards exhibited in Hyde Park as trophies of victory.

They afterwards landed near St. Maloes, but performed no exploit worth recording.

In the month of November, Captain Lockhart, a young gentleman who had already rendered himself a terror to the enemy as commander of a small frigate, now added considerably to his reputation by defeating the "Melampe," a French privateer, of Bayonne, greatly superior to his own ship in number of men and guns.

This exploit was seconded by another of the same nature, in his conquest of another French adventurer; and a third large privateer, of Bayonne, was taken by Captain Saumarez, commander of the "Antelope." In a word, the narrow seas were so well guarded, that in a little time scarce a French ship durst appear in the English Channel, which the British traders navigated without molestation.

In 1759 the French made some show of preparing to invade England. A squadron was to sail from Dunkirk and make an attempt on the Scottish coast, where support was expected from the Jacobite party. A second flotilla was to land in Ireland; while on Havre and other Norman coasts, a great number of flat bottomed vessels were fitted out to convey an army over to the coast of Kent.

To prevent the enemy from carrying out these designs, Commodore Boys was sent to blockade the port of Dunkirk. Rodney bombarded Havre with great success, and Hawke kept strict watch upon Brest and Vannes, where the squadron that was intended for Ireland had assembled.

A great French fleet was also assembled at Toulon, the destination of which was not known; so Admiral Boscawen proceeded to keep a strict blockade at that port till bad weather compelled him to proceed to Gibraltar to refit. The French took advantage of his absence and sailed out on the 14th of August.

They had very nearly reached Gibraltar before Boscawen heard of their approach, but such great exertions were then used in completing his preparations, that in *two hours* after the news arrived the ships were able to weigh anchor.

The English fleet was greater in number of vessels than the French, but carried fewer guns and men. Boscawen overtook them off Cape Lagos, in Portugal. A sharp engagement took place, in which two of the enemy's ships were run ashore and burnt, and two others captured.

The remains of the fleet, with difficulty, got into Cadiz.

The French forces at Brest also stole out during a storm which drove Sir Edward Hawke off the coast; but they were overtaken at Quiberon Bay, not far off, attacked by Hawke, and dispersed with great loss.

The Dunkirk division sent out four or five frigates, under Thurot, who sailed for Carrickfergus, on the Irish coast—a defenceless town, which he took after the inhabitants had resisted his men for some time with stones and brickbats. But three English ships from Kinsale overtook the invaders in the Irish Channel. A desperate fight took place, which resulted in the death of Thurot and the capture of his ships.

In 1760, King George II. died. At the time of his death, the English Navy consisted of 127 ships of the line, carrying from 60 to 100 guns each, and 285 vessels of smaller size, frigates, &c., making, in all, a navy of 412 vessels.

PORTRAIT OF LORD ANSON.

Soon after the accession of George III. Pitt determined that another attack should be made on the French coast; so an expedition under Commodore Keppel, carrying land troops, under General Hodgson, was sent to Bellisle, on the coast of Brittany, where the troops attempted to land (on the 8th of April, 1761).

In spite of the furious cannonade from the ships, they were repulsed; but a second attempt was more successful, and, after a rather tedious siege of the forts, we became masters of the isle.

Many naval skirmishes took place during the year 1761, but no other action of importance.

The French were beginning to weary of the war, and, knowing that Pitt's influence was declining, they had hopes of obtaining better terms than he would have granted.

The year 1761 had not closed, however, before the ministry found that a war with Spain must be undertaken.

The Spanish minister replied very insolently when questioned as to the intentions of Charles III., but did not commit himself openly till the Plate fleet had arrived from South America.

Then he told Lord Bristol, our ambassador, that he might leave Madrid as soon as he pleased, and, at the same time, issued an order for the detention of any English ships that might be found in Spanish ports.

Of course, a formal declaration of war was the immediate result.

An expedition was sent out from Portsmouth, consisting of nineteen ships of the line, with eighteen frigates and smaller vessels.

This force arrived at Havanna, and, after a siege of forty-four days, captured the Castle of Moro. Soon afterwards, the town capitulated, with 180 miles of the country to the westward.

Nine Spanish ships of the line, ready for sea, and three frigates, were taken in the harbour, other vessels had been previously destroyed, and some that were building were pulled to pieces.

The booty captured was estimated at £3,000,000 sterling.

After this an attack was made upon the Manilla Islands, and two millions of dollars were exacted as ransom for the lives and property of the inhabitants. Added to this, the "Hermione," a ship with nearly a million pounds sterling on board, was taken by two English frigates when very near the end of her voyage.

All these things convinced the Spaniards that the English fleet was something like a hornet's nest broke loose, and could sting in fifty places at once; and the unpopularity of the war gave rise to a celebrated Spanish saying, "Peace with England, and war with all the world."

In November, 1762, the preliminaries of peace were discussed, and for some time afterwards our navy had little to do. So let us see what had been done in the way of increasing our maritime strength.

In November, 1762, we had 141 ships of the line —that is, ships of the 1st, 2nd, 3rd, and 4th rates, carrying from 60 up to 100 guns each, and 291 ships of lesser size, being altogether twenty more than in October, 1760, when George II. died.

Thirty-four of these had been taken from the enemy, while on the other hand we had lost nine ships of 50 guns and under.

From 1755 to 1762 the sum of £200,000 annually was voted for building and repairing, and during the same time twenty-six sail of the line and eighty-two smaller vessels were built in private yards, against twenty-four sail of the line and twelve smaller craft launched in the Royal dockyards.

During the same period we took or destroyed no

less than 111 ships, as appears by the following statement in "Beatson's Naval and Military Memoirs":—

	French.	Spanish.	Total.
Of 60 guns and above	29	13	42
Of 50 guns and under	64	5	69
Total ...	93	18	111

At the time the war concluded we had seventeen ships building in the Royal yards, and sixteen in private establishments.

The first naval uniform dress was established by Lord Anson in 1748. The *Gazette* of July 1, 1767, orders a new one, after patterns to be seen at the office of the Navy Board. Before this period our gallant tars seem to have dressed just as they pleased.

CHAPTER XVIII.

THERE was an interval of seven years of peace, after which the English people again began to hear of the doings of the Admiralty Board.

Four French ships sailed from Toulon without their destination being declared, and Commodore Proby's squadron in the Mediterranean was immediately reinforced.

IN THE YEAR 1770 HORATIO NELSON FIRST WENT TO SEA.

In September, 1770, press warrants were issued, and many men were taken from merchant ships.

A proclamation was issued, encouraging seamen to enter the Navy.

On the 30th of December a very "hot press" took place on the River Thames, and more than seven hundred men were seized and dragged by force into the captivity of serving in the navy.

One press-gang that day boarded the ship "Glatton," but the gang was beaten off by the crew, who escaped to the shore. Another Spanish difficulty was expected.

By referring to the chronological records of the time, we learn that, on the 15th of January, 1771, the grand dock of Plymouth was opened; that on the 17th the fleet at Spithead, under command of Admiral Buckle, numbered twenty-six ships of the line; and that on the 18th the "Orford" man-of-war of 74 guns was docked at Chatham to have her sheathing fitted, and that 14,000 superficial feet was filled with nails in one night, sixteen tons of nails being used.

In the year 1773, in consequence of a petition presented by Lord Howe, the captains of the navy received the following rates of half-pay:—

The 30 Senior Captains	10s. per day.
Next 50 do. do.	8s. ,, ,,
The rest	6s. ,, ,,

ACTION BETWEEN THE "QUEBEC" AND THE "SURVEILLANTE."

On the 4th of July, 1774, the "Kent," 74 guns, was destroyed off Plymouth through firing a salute, the wadding from some of the guns having set fire to some powder on the poop, which, in turn, communicated with the magazine. About fifty men were killed, and many more wounded.

On the 25th of January, 1775, thirty men-of-war and frigates were put in commission to blockade the ports of the American colonies, to prevent the people from being supplied with European goods. The same year, a squadron of American privateers captured the brig "Bolton," 12 guns, commanded by Lieut. Edward Sneyd.

On the 29th of June, 1775, His Majesty issued letters patent for constituting one body, politic and corporate, called the Hibernian Marine Society in Dublin, for maintaining, educating, and apprenticing the orphans of deceased seamen in the Navy and Merchant services.

In 1776, a small squadron was sent, under Commodore Sir Peter Parker, to capture Charleston, in South Carolina.

After finding much difficulty in getting the largest ships over the bar, it was determined to attack the fortress of Sullivan's Island with the ships, and a land force under General Clinton.

The attack was commenced on the 28th of June,

and resulted in the English being repulsed with much loss.

After an incessant cannonading of nearly ten hours, Sir Peter Parker ordered the ships to make the best of their way out of the harbour.

No men could have behaved better than the officers and crews of the different vessels on this occasion; but they were unassisted by the land force, which was unable to ford a river.

The fort attacked only mounted twenty-six guns, but they were 18 and 26-pounders, and against them the 180 guns of the fleet, few of which could throw a shot or shell to the fort, were of no avail.

In this action, the brave Captain Morris, commander of the "Bristol" man-of-war, was killed.

He fought his vessel after his arm was amputated, and received two other severe wounds before he relinquished the command.

The loss of the English in this unfortunate attack was 64 killed and 143 wounded. The Americans had 36 killed and wounded.

The squadron afterwards assisted in the reduction of Fort Miffin, and in obtaining command of the Delaware River.

During the year, several engagements between small vessels of the revolted colonies and English cruisers took place, without any great advantage to either party.

Amongst these engagements may be mentioned that of the English frigate "Fox," Captain Fotheringham, of 28 guns, which was captured by the American vessels "Handcock" and "Boston," Captains Manly and M'Niel, off Newfoundland.

The English captain was tried by a court-martial, at Portsmouth, for the loss of the "Fox," and was honourably acquitted.

This was soon after followed by the capture of the "Handcock," the finest vessel in the American service, by the "Rainbow," of 44 guns, Captain Sir George Collier, on the 8th of July, 1777.

During a greater part of the year 1778, Lord Howe, with an English fleet, was employed in watching the French fleet, under D'Estaing, sent out by the French king to assist the Americans.

Much to the astonishment of Howe and his officers, and to the disgust of the Americans, D'Estaing avoided an action, and the two fleets never met in a combat.

It is said that D'Estaing was made a prisoner before Madras, in 1758, and that he broke his parole. He was guillotined in the revolution of 1794.

* * * *

Early in 1778 an alliance was concluded between France and America, and war was declared against Great Britain.

The French king immediately issued an order to seize all English ships found in its ports.

Admiral Keppel had command of the Channel fleet, which at that time was much less in number than usual.

Early in the summer he sailed from Portsmouth, and meeting two French frigates, the "Licorne" and "Belle Poule," he captured the former and ran the latter on to some rocks.

In July the French fleet of thirty-two vessels, under Count D'Orvilliers, sailed from Brest, and was met by the English fleet of thirty sail on the 27th, when an engagement took place, which ended by the fleets being separated by a squall.

Not a ship was lost or captured on either side, and Admiral Keppel and Sir Hugh Palliser were both much blamed by the public for this engagement, and a warm dispute arose between them. Keppel demanded a court-martial, which was granted, and after a sitting of thirty-two days he was honourably acquitted.

The dispute between Keppel and Palliser, and the prosecution of the two before different courts-martial, was seized on by politicians, who cared nothing about either, as capital to be used in their controversies. A majority of the people sided with Admiral Keppel, and he became a great favourite amongst them.

Palliser was also acquitted by the court-martial that investigated the course he had taken during the action, and the language he had used afterwards in reference to it; but to him was generally ascribed the blame of a victory not being obtained over the French.

There were no public-houses named after him all over the kingdom, as there were after Admiral Keppel.

Sir Charles Hardy succeeded Keppel in command of the Channel fleet, in 1779, and was threatened by a combined French and Spanish fleet, much superior to his own. Hardy succeeded, however, in avoiding a general engagement and in protecting the English coast.

About this time David Paul Jones, a Scotchman, who held a commission in the navy of the revolted American colonies, with three small ships and one armed brigantine, was cruising off the north coast of Britain.

Off the coast of Yorkshire he attacked the Baltic fleet of merchant vessels, convoyed by the "Serapis," Captain Pearson, and the "Scarborough," Captain Piercy.

Both of these ships were captured by Jones and taken to Holland. In this affair the "Bon Homme Richard," Jones's principal vessel, was so much injured that it sank two days after the action.

Jones captured several other ships after this, nearly all of which were so severely injured that they went down before he could get them into port, and this is said to be the reason why the sea is often called "Davy Jones's Locker."

The "Serapis" and "Scarborough," at the time they were captured, were convoying the Baltic fleet of merchantmen; and, owing to the gallant resistance made by the officers and crews of those vessels, the merchantmen were enabled to escape.

Captains Pearson and Piercy were rewarded by the London Assurance Company for preserving the fleet, and the services of both officers were also duly acknowledged by the government.

Count d'Estaing, on leaving the coast of America, went to the West Indies, where a fleet was sent under Lord Byron to look after him, and recapture the island of Grenada, which had surrendered to the French.

The two fleets met on the 6th of June, 1779, off St. George's Bay.

They merely passed each other, exchanging broadsides, when the French sailed off, avoiding a general engagement, although their force was superior to the English.

In the partial combat that took place on this occasion the English had ninety men killed, and about two hundred wounded.

Several ships were injured and the "Monmouth" was wholly disabled. During most of the year 1779 the English squadrons in America were engaged in sailing up the bays and rivers and destroying the towns and villages of the revolted colonists. At this work the vessels under the command of Sir George Collier achieved the most fame; and on the James and Elizabeth (since called the Piscataqua) rivers in Virginia, their visits were the most destructive.

Sir George was very active in despatching small expeditions for the destruction of property, the result of which only exasperated the colonists, and throughout the whole country provoked a more determined opposition to English rule.

At New Haven, Fairfield, Norwalk Bay, and several other places, General Tyron and others engaged in these expeditions could find no property but what, in their opinion, could be used in the war, and they had it destroyed.

On the 6th of October, 1779, the English frigate "Quebec," Captain Farmer, while in company with the "Rambler" cutter, cruising off Brest, met the French frigate, "Surveillante," of 40 guns, and a sharp action commenced between them, while the "Rambler" at the same time encountered the French cutter "Expedition."

The two frigates fought until both were dismasted.

The "Quebec's" mizen-mast, as it fell over the side, hung a sail in front of the muzzle of a gun as it was about to be discharged.

The sail was instantly in flames, which were communicated to other parts of the vessel.

The "Rambler" tried to come up to the assistance of the frigate's crew, but was unable, owing to light winds. Her boats arrived in time, however, to save a part of the crew.

Captain Farmer and eighty of the crew were either killed or severely wounded before the fire. The vessel burnt until she blew up, and 150 men were lost—most of them by the explosion.

On the 24th of October, the French frigate "Alcmène" was captured off Martinique by a squadron, under Captain Edwards.

On the 20th of December, two French frigates, the "Blanche" and "Fortune," and on the 23rd, the frigate "Ellis," all belonging to D'Estaing's fleet, were captured by the squadron under Sir Hyde Parker. The first two were added to the English navy.

On the 12th of December, the 50-gun ship "Salisbury," Captain Charles Inglis, captured the Spanish 50-gun privateer, "San Carlos." On board the "Salisbury," four men were killed, and fourteen wounded—five of them mortally. Most of the guns of the "San Carlos" were brass, and, besides those mounted, she had on freight twelve brass 24-pounders. Besides these, she carried 5,000 stand of arms.

Early in the month of January, 1780, Admiral George Rodney was ordered with a fleet to the West India Islands to protect English commerce and possessions against the Spaniards, who had again declared war against England.

On the 16th of January, while on his voyage, he met a Spanish fleet, under Admiral Langara, off Cape St. Vincent.

A sharp action ensued, in which four Spanish ships were captured—four others were sunk or driven ashore. The victory of the English was complete, and Rodney, after calling at Gibraltar and relieving the garrison there, which was besieged by a land force of Spaniards, proceeded to the West Indies.

On reaching his "cruising ground," Rodney commenced blockading the French fleet, under Comte de Guichen, in Fort Royal Bay, Martinique.

On the night of the 15th of April the French squadron escaped, and the next morning Rodney got under weigh and pursued them. He overtook them on the 17th, but owing to a misunderstanding of the signals on the part of some of his officers, a general engagement was not brought on. Owing to this mistake the French were allowed to escape after a brief action, in which the English lost 120 men killed and 360 wounded. The French had 158 killed and 820 wounded.

On the 1st of July, the English ship "Romney," 50 guns, Captain Rodman Home, captured the French frigate "Artois," of 40 guns; the "Artois" had 20 men killed and 40 wounded; the "Romney," 2 wounded. The "Artois" was the finest frigate afloat, and was added to the English navy under the same name.

On the 4th July, the "Prudente," 36 guns, under Captain Waldgrave, and the "Licorne," 32 guns, Captain Cadogan, captured the French frigate "Capricieuse," 40 guns, off Cape Ortagal. The "Capricieuse" was so much injured that she could not be taken to port, and was destroyed.

On September 30th, the frigate "Pearl," off Bermuda, captured the French frigate "Espérance," 28 guns, which was added to the English navy under the name of "Clinton." The "Pearl" had 6 men killed and 10 wounded in the action. The "Espérance" had 20 men killed and 24 wounded.

On the 2nd of November, the 14-gun brig "Zephyr," Commander John Ingles, captured the French 18-gun brig "Senegal," on the river Gambia. The French had 12 killed and 22 wounded; the "Zephyr," 2 killed and 4 wounded. The "Senegal" was once the English brig "Racehorse." She took fire and blew up on the way home, and Lieutenant Crofts and 22 others perished.

During the first half of the year 1781 there was but very little severe fighting between the ships of the English navy and those of France, Spain, and Holland, with whom England was then at war.

On the 4th of January, the English recaptured off Brest the 32-gun frigate "Minerva," which had been taken by the French some time before.

On the 5th of the same month, the Dutch ship "Rotterdam," 50 guns, was captured by the 50-gun ship "Warwick," Captain Elphinstone. The "Rotterdam" was added to the English navy under the same name.

On the 26th, the 36-gun frigate "Prudente" captured the French privateer the "American," of 32 guns and 245 men.

On the 25th February, the "Cerberus," 32-gun frigate Captain Robert Mann, captured, the Spanish frigate "Grana," of 28 guns, which had 6 men killed and 17 wounded in the action.

On the 16th of March, Vice-Admiral Abuthnot, who relieved Sir George Collier with his squadron, off the Chesapeake, a few leagues from Cape Henry, had a brief engagement with the French squadron of seven sail of the line, one 64-gun ship and two frigates.

The forces were about equal: nevertheless, the fleet separated without either suffering much injury. On the English squadron there were 30 killed and 64 wounded. Admiral Abuthnot returned to Lynn Haven Bay to repair damages.

Rear-Admiral Sir Samuel Hood, on the 29th of April, 1781, met the French fleet under Comte de Grasse, off Fort Royal Bay, Martinique.

Having the wind in his favour, it was in the power of De Grasse to avoid a general action, which he did, although his force was superior to that of the English.

By the distant cannonading which took place the English lost 36 men killed, and 161 wounded—the French 119 killed, and 150 wounded.

Two of the English ships, the "Russel" and "Centaur," were much injured.

On the 27th of May, the 16-gun ship "Atlanta" and the 14-gun brig "Trespassey," Commanders Edwards and Smith, gave chase to the American 40-gun frigate "Alliance," Captain Barry, who allowed them to overtake him, and then captured them.

The two vessels were gallantly defended, and half the crew of the "Atlanta" were either killed or wounded. The attack on the frigate should not have been made by so small a force.

On the 5th of August, the British squadron, under Vice-Admiral Sir Hyde Parker, while off the Dogger Bank, convoying the Baltic fleet on its return to England, met the Dutch fleet, under Admiral Zoutman, also guarding a fleet of merchant ships.

Admiral Parker's squadron consisted of seven ships of war, six frigates, and six sloops and cutters.

The Dutch squadron was comprised of seven ships, six frigates, and two cutters.

Vice-Admiral Parker placed the convoy under the care of Captain Sutton, of the "Tartar," with orders to make the best of his way to England, and commenced making preparations for battle.

At 8 o'clock in the morning the battle commenced, and continued, without ceasing, for three hours and forty minutes.

In the beginning of the action, owing to the

CRESTS OF VESSELS IN THE ROYAL NAVY (A.D. 1870).

falling of some spars on an English ship, there was a little disorder in the ships taking their stations, and many of them were not equally matched; and, not being satisfied with the way the battle was going, Parker struck the signal for battle, and the fleet hove to for repairing damages.

In this encounter the English had 109 killed, and 362 wounded—many of them mortally.

The Dutch lost 142 killed, and 403 wounded. One of their ships, the "Hollandia," of 64 guns, was so much damaged that she sank the same night. Her flag was saved, and was the only trophy the English could show.

This affair is claimed by some historians as an English victory. The Dutch have also advanced the same claim, and there can be no doubt but that they are more fairly entitled to it than the English, who were the first to leave off the combat.

During the remainder of the month of August, there were several engagements between single ships, principally with French or Americans, nearly all of which resulted in favour of the English.

On the 2nd of September, the "Chatham," of 50 guns, Captain Douglass, captured, in Boston Bay, the French 32-gun frigate, "Magicienne," which was added to the English navy. She had 30 men killed and 54 wounded in the combat.

On the 5th of September, Rear-Admiral Graves, with nineteen ships, seven frigates, and one 50-gun vessel, attacked the French fleet of twenty-four sail of the line, under Comte de Grasse, at anchor in Lynn Haven Bay. Only the English van and centre were able to engage, and as the rear could not be brought into action, after about two hours of cannonading, the English fleet was hauled to the wind and the combat terminated.

A few days later the Comte de Grasse was reinforced by eight ships of the line from Rhode Island. These vessels, in their passage to join De Grasse, captured two English frigates, the "Iris," Captain Dawson, and the "Richmond," Captain Charles Hudson.

The French fleet being now too strong to be engaged the second time, Admiral Graves destroyed the "Terrible," which was too much damaged to take with him, and sailed for New York to refit.

On the 6th of September, the 14-gun sloop "Savage," Captain Stirling, was captured by the United States' ship "Congress," Captain Geddes, of 24 guns.

LOSS OF THE "ROYAL GEORGE," AT SPITHEAD.

When the English first observed the stranger bearing down towards them, they supposed her to be a privateer which Captain Stirling had been instructed to look out for; but he soon found out his mistake, and endeavoured to make off.

At half-past ten in the morning, the "Congress" commenced firing, and the battle continued till three in the afternoon, when Captain Stirling was obliged to strike.

As the "Congress" mounted ten guns more than the "Savage," this victory cannot be considered as adding very much to the glory of the United States' navy.

On the 3rd of December, the 40-gun frigate "Artois," Captain McBride, in the North Sea, captured two Dutch schooners, the "Mars" and "Hercules," both of which were added to the English navy.

These vessels carried twenty-four 9-pounders each, and were commanded by two men, named Hogenboom—father and son.

The father was well known by the nickname of "Hardapple," and had done a great deal of mischief to our merchant navy.

Rear-Admiral Kempenfelt, on the 12th of September, captured fifteen French merchant ships, convoyed by a fleet superior to his own, without suffering any loss from the enemy's ships of war guarding them, which he managed to avoid.

Lord Edward Hawke died in this year.

He was the son of a barrister, was early sent to sea, and passed through all the inferior grades until appointed captain of the "Wolfe," in 1734.

He first distinguished himself in an action off Toulon, where he commanded the "Herbert," and compelled a Spanish ship of 60 guns to strike.

Hawke first discovered and avoided the folly of ever losing time to keep a fleet in order or line of battle.

In 1776 he was made a peer.

He was one of the best characters of the many who adorn the history of the English navy.

He died at Shepperton, in Middlesex, October 14, 1781.

After the fall of St. Kitt's, in 1782, Great Britain retained, of all her former West India possessions, only the islands of Jamaica, Barbadoes, St. Lucie, and Antigua; and of the preservation of these great doubts were entertained. Jamaica, in particular, which had been frequently threatened, now appeared to be in greater danger than ever; for, whilst the Count de Grasse was riding superior in the Carribean Sea, the Spaniards were in great strength at Cuba and Hispaniola; and the fleets of the two nations, if combined, would have consisted of sixty ships of the line, while their land forces would have constituted a powerful army.

In this state of things, Sir George Rodney arrived at Barbadoes, on the 19th day of February, with twelve sail of the line, and made a junction with Sir Samuel Hood's squadron. He was soon after reinforced by three ships of the line from England; so that his fleet consisted of thirty-six vessels of the line. His first object was to intercept a French convoy, which had sailed from Brest on the 11th of February, with naval stores, artillery, ammunition, and other supplies for the Count de Grasse; but being disappointed in this, he put into St. Lucie, while the count was lying at Martinico with thirty-four ships of the line, studious to avoid an engagement till he had effected a junction with the Spaniards. For that purpose, he sailed from Fort-Royal Bay on the 8th of April, with a large convoy, keeping close under the islands. Intelligence of this movement being directly conveyed to the British admiral, a pursuit was instantly begun, and the fleets came in sight of each other the same night, off Dominica. So sudden a pressure was as little expected by the French admiral as it was welcome; but he lost no time in accommodating himself to the emergency, and early in the morning of the 9th, formed the line of battle to windward, to afford his convoy an opportunity of proceeding on its course.

On the other hand, Sir George Rodney had thrown out signals, soon after five in the morning, for forming his line; but the fleet was long becalmed under the highlands of Dominica, while the enemy, who were farther advanced towards Guadaloupe, had sufficient wind for their movements. The breeze at length reaching the van of the British fleet, they began to close with the French centre, whilst their own centre and rear were still becalmed.

The action commenced about nine o'clock; the attack being led by the "Royal Oak," Captain Burnet, and seconded by the "Alfred" and "Montague," with the most impetuous bravery. The whole division was in a few minutes closely engaged, and for upwards of an hour was exceedingly pressed by the great superiority of the enemy. The "Barfleur," Sir Samuel Hood's own ship, had at one time seven, and generally three, ships firing upon her, and none of the division escaped the encounter of a very disproportionate force.

At length the leading ships of the centre were gradually enabled to come up to the assistance of the van, and these were soon followed by Sir George Rodney in the "Formidable," with his two seconds, the "Namur" and "Duke," all of ninety guns, who maintained a most tremendous fire. The gallantry of a French captain of a seventy-four in the rear, who having backed his main-topsail, readily received and bravely returned the fire of these three great ships in succession, without in the least flinching from his station, excited the highest admiration and applause of his enemies.

The coming up of the Admiral, with part of the centre division, rendered the fight less unequal; and De Grasse, to prevent its now becoming decisive, availed himself of his command of the wind, and the connected state of his fleet, to keep such a cautious distance during the remainder of the engagement, as he thought would enable him to do much execution without any considerable hazard on his own side. This sort of firing, which was extremely well supported on both sides, was continued for an hour and three-quarters longer: during all which time the rest of the fleet was held back by the calms and baffling winds under Dominica. About twelve o'clock the remaining ships of the centre came up, and the rear was closing the line; upon which De Grasse withdrew his fleet, and evaded all the efforts of the English commander for its renewal. The enemy failed entirely in his object; for his ships received much more damage than they produced to their opponents, and two of them were so much disabled, that they were obliged to quit the fleet, and put into Guadaloupe. Some of the British ships suffered greatly, but still kept the line. Captain Bayne, of the "Alfred," gallantly fell in this action.

On the 11th, the enemy had gained such a distance that the body of their fleet could only be descried from the mast-head of the British centre, when two of their damaged ships were perceived about noon to fall off from the rest to leeward. The pursuit now became so vigorous that they would necessarily have been cut off, had not De Grasse borne down with his whole fleet to their rescue; and the result was to bring on that general engagement which had been the object of the British commander. The hostile fleets met upon opposite tacks, and in the course of the battle, which commenced about seven in the morning of the 12th, and was continued with unremitting fury till sunset, Sir George Rodney first practised the manœuvre, since attended with such signal success, of breaking the enemy's line. In the early part of the engagement, Admiral Drake, whose division led to action, gained the highest honour, by the gallantry with which he received, and the effect with which he returned, the fire of the whole French line.

His leading ship, the "Marlborough," Captain Penny, was peculiarly distinguished. She received and returned at the nearest distances, the the first fire of twenty-three French ships of war, and had the fortune only to have three men killed and sixteen wounded: one proof, among a hundred others, of the ineffectual force of the French system of firing. The signal for close fighting had from the first been thrown out, and was, without a single exception, punctually observed. The line was formed at only a cable's length distance. The British ships as they came up, ranged slowly along the enemy's line, and close under their lee, where they gave and received a most tremendous fire. They were so near that every shot took effect, and the French ships being overcrowded with troops, the carnage in them was prodigious. Some opinion may be formed of the havoc made, from the circumstance of the "Formidable," Sir George Rodney's ship, having fired near four-score broadsides; and it may be believed that she was not singular. The French stood, and returned this fire with equal bravery, and both sides fought as if the fate and honour of their respective countries had been staked upon the issue of that single day. About noon Sir George Rodney made the movement already alluded to, and, supported by three other ships, broke through the enemy's line, about three ships short of the centre, where De Grasse commanded in the "Ville de Paris," of one hundred and twelve guns. Being followed and supported by ships astern of his division, he wore round upon his heel, and completing their separation, threw them into inextricable confusion. This masterly push decided the fortune of the day; although the French continued to fight with great bravery till the darkness, which in those latitudes almost immediately succeeds the setting of the sun, obliged both parties to desist.

The broken state of the French fleet, naturally exposed, in some instances, a few ships to the attack of a greater number; and the extent of the action, with the darkness and uncertainty occasioned by the smoke, afforded opportunities, which might have been less expected, for single combat.

The "Canada," of seventy-four guns, Captain Cornwallis, took the French "Hector," of the same force, singly. Captain Inglefield, in the "Centaur," of seventy-four guns, also came up from the rear, to the attack of the "Cæsar," of seventy-four. Both ships were yet fresh, and had received no injury, and a most gallant action took place; but though the French captain had evidently the disadvantage, he still disdained to yield. Three other ships came up successively. His courage was inflexible; he is said to have nailed his colours to the masts, and the contest terminated only with his death. When she struck, her masts went overboard, and she had not a foot of canvas without a shot-hole. The "Glorieux" also fought nobly, and did not strike till her masts, bowsprit and ensign were shot away. The English "Ardent," of sixty-four guns, which had been taken by the enemy in the beginning of the war, was now re-taken, by the "Belliqueux" or the "Bedford." The "Diadem," a French seventy-four, went down by a single broadside, in an exertion to save her admiral. The Count de Grasse was nobly supported, even after the line was broken, and till the disorder and confusion became unavoidable. His two seconds, the "Languedoc" and "Coronne," were particularly distinguished, and the former narrowly escaped being taken, in her last efforts to extricate the admiral.

The "Ville de Paris," after being much battered, was closely attacked by the "Canada," and in a desperate action of nearly two hours, was reduced almost to a wreck. Captain Cornwallis was so eager in his design upon the French admiral, that without taking possession of the "Hector," he left her to be picked up by a frigate, while he proceeded to the "Ville de Paris." It seemed as if the

Count was determined to sink rather than strike to anything under a flag; though he perhaps also considered the fatal effects which the striking of his flag might produce on his fleet. At length Sir Samuel Hood came up in the "Barfleur," almost at sunset, and poured in a most tremendous fire, which is said to have killed sixty men; but the Count de Grasse, wishing to signalize, as much as possible, the loss of so fine and so favourite a ship, endured the repetitions of this fire for about a quarter of an hour longer. He then struck his flag, and surrendered himself to Sir Samuel Hood. With the "Ville de Paris," were taken four others of the line, one of which, the "Cæsar," afterwards blew up, with a lieutenant and fifty British seamen aboard, and about four hundred prisoners; and another was sunk by a single broadside during the engagement. Not a ship was lost in the British fleet, and its whole loss of men was computed to be less than that on board the "Ville de Paris" alone.

The brave Captain Blair, of the "Anson," who, in the preceding year had most gallantly fought the "Dolphin" against the Dutch, in the North-sea action under Admiral Hyde Parker, fell on this day.

The loss of Lord Robert Manners was universally lamented by the nation as well as the navy.

That gallant young nobleman, in the command of the "Resolution," of seventy-four guns, had been highly distinguished during the war, by a series of the most brilliant actions; and being most seriously wounded in this battle, though with fair hopes of recovery, from the excellence of his constitution, was, to the great loss of his country and the service, carried off by a locked jaw, a few days after, on his passage to England. Thirty-six chests of money, destined for the pay and subsistence of the troops in the intended invasion of Jamaica, were found in the "Ville de Paris;" but that ship had suffered so much in the action, that it was impossible to keep her above water, and she never reached England.

Of the vanquished ships, some were scattered; but the greater part, under Bougainville and Vaudreuil, bore away in a body for St. Domingo; and, in the pursuit, Sir Samuel Hood's division, after some days, came up with and captured two ships of the line and two frigates, in the Mona passage. This decisive victory put an end to all the projects against Jamaica, and Admiral Rodney, after enjoying his triumph at that island as its saviour, returned to England, where he was rewarded with a British peerage. Sir Samuel Hood was created an Irish peer, and Admiral Drake and Commodore Affleck were both honoured with baronetages.

On the same day, the 12th of April, 1782, the fleet, under Sir Edward Hughes (Admiral of the East India fleet) was attacked by the French fleet, under the command of Admiral Suffrein, off the coast of India.

RODNEY'S ACTION WITH COUNT DE GRASSE.

A sharp engagement followed, which lasted for about two hours, when both fleets drew off to refit. No vessel was taken or sunk on either side, yet the loss on board of the English fleet was 137 killed, and over 400 wounded.

During the year 1782 there were several battles fought on the coast of India between these two fleets. They were all indecisive, much damage being sustained by both fleets, which would have to seek port for repairs. In the four actions which were fought between them during the year, the English lost 1,336 men killed, or severely wounded, and amongst them several valuable officers.

On the 20th of April, the 84-gun ship, "Foudroyant," Captain Jervie, after a chase, came up with the French 74-gun ship "Pégase," and boarded it after an action of 45 minutes. The "Pégase," out of a crew of 700 men, had upwards of 100 killed and wounded, while only two or three were wounded in the "Foudroyant." The "Pégase" was a ship of 1,778 tons, and was added to the Royal navy.

Commander Edward Pellew (afterwards Earl of Exmouth) was at this time in command of the "Pelican," 14-gun brig.

As he was cruising off the Isle of Bas, he observed several vessels at anchor, and bore in towards shore, for the purpose of ascertaining what they were, and making an attack, if possible.

Two of these vessels happened to be privateers, each carrying an armament equal in force to that of the "Pelican."

They placed themselves so that their broadsides opposed Pellew; but that undaunted commander drove them both on shore, as well as a third privateer which was there.

Some heavy batteries prevented Pellew from capturing other vessels, but he received a post-captain's commission for the exploit.

Our naval officers of this period seem to have thoroughly entered into the spirit of their instructions, which were "to sink, burn, and destroy" the enemy's shipping, wherever found.

On the 29th of July, the 36-gun frigate "Santa Margaritta," Captain Salter, captured the French 36-gun frigate "Amazone," after a sharp action of one hour and a quarter; but, unfortunately, the captor and its prize were attacked the next morning by a French squadron. Captain Salter again achieved what may be called a victory, for he succeeded in escaping from a force greatly superior to his own. The prize "Amazone," however, was recaptured.

Soon after the arrival at Spithead, after a long cruise, of the "Royal George," a line of battle ship of 108 guns, it was found necessary that she should undergo some repairs before going again to sea.

To save time and trouble of taking the vessel into dock, it was determined to give her a "Parliament heel."

This operation consists in dragging a vessel on one side until nearly half of the bottom is exposed above water.

The vessel was lying in smooth water, and a fine day (the 29th of August, 1782) was chosen for the work, which was commenced early in the morning.

In order to reach the defect in the ship's bottom, it was "heeled" over a little too much, and turned wholly on one side.

The cannons rolled over, or rather fell to the lower side, where the port-holes were open, and the ship instantly filled with water and sunk.

As the "Royal George" was about to proceed again to sea, it was then being visited by many of the wives and children of the petty officers and crew; and, at the time the accident happened, it is supposed that there were more than 1,100 people on board, most of whom were between decks. Of this number it is supposed that about nine hundred perished.

The ship was commanded by Admiral Kempenfelt, who was in his cabin writing at the time, and was lost.

Captain Waghorn, who escaped, was tried by court-martial for the loss of the vessel, and honourably acquitted.

The "Royal George" was in the celebrated action off the coast of Brittany, when the French fleet was defeated by Admiral Hawke. It had been the flag-ship of several distinguished commanders.

In the following spring, a very elegant monument was erected to the memory of Kempenfelt, and the others who perished, in the churchyard at Portsea, with the following inscription:—

PORTRAIT OF LORD ST. VINCENT.

Reader!
With solemn thought
Survey this grave,
And reflect
On the untimely death
Of thy fellow mortals;
And whilst,
As a Man, a Briton, and a Patriot,
Thou read'st
The melancholy narrative,
Drop a tear
For thy Country's
Loss.
On the twenty-ninth day of
August, 1782,
His Majesty's ship, the
ROYAL GEORGE,
Being on the heel at Spithead,
Overset and sunk;
By which fatal accident
About nine hundred persons
Were instantly launched into
eternity;
Among whom was that brave and
Experienced officer,
Rear-Admiral Kempenfelt.
Nine days after,
Many bodies of the unfortunate
Floated;
Thirty-five of whom were interred
In one grave,
Near this monument,
Which is erected by the Parish of
Portsea,
As a grateful tribute
To the memory
Of that great commander
And his fellow sufferers.

The poet Cowper's verses on this melancholy accident must be well remembered:—

"Toll for the brave!
  The brave that are no more!
All sunk beneath the wave,
  Fast by their native shore!
*   *   *   *
Toll for the brave!
  Brave Kempenfelt is gone;
His last sea-fight is fought;
  His work of glory done.
*   *   *   *
His sword was in its sheath;
  His fingers held the pen,
When Kempenfelt went down
  With twice four hundred men.'

This was not the only misfortune that befell the English navy that year.

On the 1st of December, intelligence reached the Admiralty from Captain Inglefield of the loss of the ship "Centaur," of 74 guns.

The vessel foundered in the Atlantic near the Azores. A few of the crew escaped in the boats, and suffered great hardships from hunger and thirst, of which several died.

Out of a crew of 650 men only the captain, twelve men, and a boy lived to reach Fayal, one of the Azores.

It was during the latter part of this year that Lord Howe with 34 ships relieved Gibraltar, which had been besieged for three years.

The besieged Englishmen had before received some assistance from Admirals Rodney and Darby, but Lord Howe found the garrison reduced to great distress. Thistles and dandelions had become the daily food of many.

On the 18th of October, the English 74-gun frigate, "Torbay," Captain Gidoin, after a long running fight, chased the French 74-gun ship "Scipion" ashore when it was totally lost.

The "Scipion," with her consort, the 40-gun frigate "Sibylle," the day before had an engagement with the English 90-gun ship, "London," Captain Kempthorne, from which they escaped. The "London," in her action with the two vessels, had 11 men killed and 92 wounded.

On the 6th of December, the ship "Ruby," 64 guns, Captain John Collins, after an action of 40 minutes, captured the French 64-gun ship "Solitaire," commanded by Chevalier de Boda. The "Solitaire" had twenty men killed and thirty-five wounded. The "Ruby" had but two men wounded.

On the 12th of December, the 44-gun ship "Mediator," Captain John Luttrell, off Ferrol, captured the "Alexander," of 24 guns, a ship in pay of the American Congress.

This was a very gallant exploit, as the "Alexander" was in company of a squadron, the united force of which, if properly brought against the "Mediator," must have captured it.

On the 19th of December, the United States frigate "South Carolina," Captain Joyner, carrying 28 long 36-pounders on the main deck and 12 long 12-pounders on the quarter deck and forecastle, was captured by an English squadron of three frigates.

In the month of June, this year, Sir Hyde Parker, who commanded the English fleet at the battle of Dogger Bank in 1779, sailed for India, in the ship "Juno."

After passing the Cape of Good Hope, he was never more heard of.

On the 22nd of January, 1783, the French 36-gun frigate "Sibylle" was seen dismasted and jury-rigged by Captain Thomas M. Russell, of the 28-gun frigate "Hussar." The "Sibylle" had been compelled to throw some of her main-deck guns overboard and seemed in a defenceless state. She had a signal of distress flying and also the English colours flying over the French. Under these circumstances Captain Russel ran down under her lee to offer assistance.

On coming alongside, however, the "Hussar" received a broadside from the "Sibylle," which, bearing athwart the hawse of the other, sprang her bowsprit.

The crew of the "Sibylle" then attempted to board; but the "Hussar" was backed clear, and the treacherously given broadside returned.

The "Sibylle" then hauled to the wind on the larboard tack and made off. She was overtaken after a two hours' chase and again brought to action.

The magazine was now found to be swamped by the damages she had received from the first broadside of the "Hussar," and she was compelled to surrender.

Commodore Kergarion, the commander of the "Sibylle," on coming aboard the "Hussar," and presenting his sword, saw the blade broken in pieces by Captain Russell, and himself placed in confinement as a state prisoner for having violated the usages of war.

On his return to England, Russell was offered the honour of knighthood, which he declined.

On the 10th of January, the English frigate "Coventry," 28 guns, Captain William Wolseley, after a gallant resistance, was captured in the Bay of Bengal by the French fleet.

On the 18th of January, the frigate "Argo," 44 guns, Captain John Butchart, was captured by the French frigates "Concorde" and "Nymphe," off Sombrero, when on the way to Antigua.

The "Argo" did not remain long, however, in the possession of the enemy, for it was recaptured on the 20th by the "Invincible," 74 guns, Captain Charles Saxon.

On the same day preliminary articles of peace were drawn up at Paris between England, France and Spain.

The war, however, did not close without another engagement between the East India fleets of the two principal powers. It was fought on the 20th of June, 1783, the news of peace not then having reached India.

The English fleet, under Sir Edward Hughes, had been reinforced by five sail of the line under Sir Richard Bickerton, and now consisted of eighteen ships and eleven frigates.

The battle took place off Pondicherry, and lasted for three hours, when the Admiral made off to the windward.

His fleet throughout the war proved much better sailers than the English, and he was at any time able to decline or bring on an action. It is supposed that he allowed an action to take place this day under the belief that a third of the crews of the English fleet were in their hammocks ill with scurvy.

In the battle, the English ships received much injury in spars and rigging, had 99 men killed, and 431 wounded. A few days after news of the peace reached India.

During this long and sanguinary war, the English captured fifty-one French vessels of war, and destroyed six, five others being lost by accident. Total, sixty-two.

The number of Spanish vessels captured was eleven, twelve were destroyed, and one lost by accident. Total, twenty-four.

Six Dutch ships were captured, and two destroyed; and fifty-three American ships captured, and thirty-two destroyed. Total, ninety-three. Thus, one hundred and seventy-nine vessels were lost to the enemies of Great Britain.

During the war, seventy-six English vessels were captured by her enemies, and twelve were destroyed—a less number than was lost to the Navy by accident in the same time—ninety-three vessels being lost, by accident, without any assistance from the enemy.

It appears that, on the 20th of January, 1783, the state of the Royal Navy was as follows:—

We had 174 ships of 1st, 2nd, 3rd, and 4th rates. 443 ships of 56 guns and under.

Total, 617 vessels of all classes.

In 1778, we had only 450 vessels of all classes, so that, in the space of five years, we had added no less than 167 ships to the Royal Navy.

*   *   *   *

During the peace that followed the close of the war, Admiral Augustus Keppel died. He was born April 2nd, 1725, and, entering the service young, accompanied Commodore Anson round the world.

He saw much service in working his way slowly up to the rank of Admiral.

When called upon by the king to take command of the Channel fleet in 1778, he readily consented, but said, "My forty years' service are not marked by any reward from the Crown except that of confidence in time of danger."

He was raised to the peerage in 1782, and died October 3rd, 1786.

Another of England's naval heroes died before the commencement of another war. It was the gallant Rodney.

George Brydges Rodney was born in December, 1717. He was one of the most successful of England's many successful admirals.

He gave, at different times, a severe blow to three of England's most powerful enemies—France, Spain, and Holland.

He was the first admiral who ever captured and took into port a first-rate man-of-war of any nation. The tactics by which he gained the great victory over the French on the 12th of April by breaking through the enemy's line and capturing the "Ville de Paris," is said to have originated with a Mr. Clerk, author of a "Treatise on Naval Tactics."

There is another account that the same plan was taken by an English admiral in a battle with the Dutch more than a century before.

Another English admiral, whose name has often been mentioned in this work—Sir George Pocock—died on the 3rd of April, 1792.

CHAPTER XIX.

NAVAL EVENTS CONNECTED WITH THE OUTBREAK OF THE FRENCH REVOLUTION.

During the peace that followed the events recorded in the last chapter, France was convulsed by the mightiest revolution that ever shattered thrones and dynasties to pieces. The unfortunate king fell a victim, with thousands of nobles and suspected royalists.

As soon as the news reached England that Louis XVI. of France had been beheaded by the revolutionary party, the French ambassador was ordered to leave the country.

On the 1st of February, 1793, eleven days after the execution of the king, the National Convention of France declared war against England and the United Netherlands.

The kingdoms of Spain and Portugal joined with the English and Dutch.

The first vessel captured in this war was the French privateer, "Sans Culotte," of 8 guns, off Scilly, by the English gun-brig "Scourge," of 16 guns, Captain Brisac.

The privateer had nine men killed and twenty wounded when she surrendered.

On the 14th of April, a squadron of five ships under Rear-Admiral Gell, when on the passage to the Mediterranean, captured the French privateer, "General Dumourier," with its prize, the Spanish galleon, "San Iago," which was being taken to some French port.

The galleon was from the West Coast of America, and had on board treasure to the amount of £200,000. Both the privateer and its prize were taken into Plymouth and condemned.

It is generally believed that the keeping of the recaptured galleon was the principal act that led to the war between England and Spain which was afterwards declared.

The "Hyæna," 24 guns, Captain William Hargood, was, on the 27th of May, captured by the "Concorde," a French frigate. Captain Hargood was tried by a court-martial for the loss of his vessel, but honourably acquitted.

On the 17th of June, the "Nymphe," 36-gun frigate, Captain Edward Pellew, started from Falmouth to cruise with the usual object of sinking, burning, and destroying the enemy's marine.

On the following day, when they were off Start Point, the look-out announced a sail to leeward, and the captain determined to bear up towards her. The stranger shortened sail, to await the approach of the "Nymphe."

When Pellew arrived within hailing distance the stranger, then discovered to be the French frigate "Cleopatre," of 36 guns, hailed. The crew of the "Nymphe" responded with three cheers—a noise which the French sailors vainly endeavoured to imitate.

This was about a quarter past six in the morning. A furious cannonade at once commenced, and continued till past seven, when the "Cleopatre" was boarded and the French colours hauled down.

The "Nymphe" and her prize put into Portsmouth on the 21st of the month, and, as a reward for his bravery, Captain Pellew was knighted by George III.

The "Nymphe" had 23 killed and 27 wounded.

The "Cleopatre" had her captain, M. Mullon, killed, and in all 63 killed and wounded.

In the month of August, Vice-Admiral Lord Hood went to Toulon with twenty-one ships of war.

The commander of the French fleet, Comte de Trogoff, being a royalist, and supported by a large party of the fleet, and by many of the inhabitants of the town, Admiral Hood was allowed to take possession of the town without any opposition.

This was done, but so strong was the besieging party that attacked it a few days later that the place had to be abandoned.

Before leaving the harbour, fourteen French ships were burnt or otherwise destroyed, and fifteen were taken away.

On the 24th of October, the 32-gun frigate "Thames," Captain James Cotes, had a long and severe engagement with the French 40-gun frigate "Uranie." When both vessels were in a crippled and nearly helpless state, a French squadron came up, and the "Thames" was compelled to surrender.

On the 25th of November, the French frigate "Inconstante," of 36 guns, was captured in Leogam Bay, St. Domingo, by the English frigates "Penelope," 32, and the "Iphigenia." She was added to the English navy under the same name.

This was the last engagement that took place in the year 1793. During that year the English fleets and cruizers captured and destroyed 140 armed French vessels, 52 of which belonged to the French navy. This was accomplished at the loss of only four vessels.

After leaving Toulon, Lord Hood went with his fleet to Corsica, to assist General Paoli in taking that island from the French. This work accomplished, he undertook the reduction of Bastia, in which he was greatly assisted by Captain Horatio Nelson, of the "Agamemnon." The siege was began on the 11th of April, 1794, and the place surrendered after a siege of thirty-seven days, and the attention of the admiral was then turned to Calvi, which was taken in the month of August, principally by forces acting under the orders of Captain Nelson, who here lost the sight of his right eye.

On the 23rd of April, 1794, a squadron of five frigates, under Captain Pellew, of the "Arethusa," encountered four French frigates off Guernsey. In the engagement the French frigate "Pomone" was compelled to surrender. Possession was taken of her by the boats of the "Arethusa," which had the principal part of the work in her capture. The "Pomone" was added to the British navy under the same name.

CRESTS OF VESSELS IN THE ROYAL NAVY (A.D. 1870).

On the outbreak of hostilities between France and England, Toulon was occupied by a combined British and English fleet. These vessels, however, were after a lengthened siege compelled to give up possession of the harbour and town, which were within range of certain batteries that had been established by Napoleon Bonaparte, afterwards Emperor of France. This occurred about a week before Christmas, 1793.

It appears that the authorities at Malta had received no news of this on the 3rd of January, 1794, for on that day the frigate "Juno," commanded by Captain Samuel Hood, quitted the island, having on board 150 men to fill up any vacancies that might have occurred in the fleet which he expected to find at Toulon.

It was rather late at night and dirty weather when the "Juno" arrived off the port, and Captain Hood determined to run into the port as quickly as possible. He had no pilot or person acquainted with the port on board, so two midshipmen, with night-glasses, were sent forward to look out for the fleet.

For a long time no ships could be seen, and Captain Hood came to the conclusion that the strong east wind had driven them to take shelter in the inner harbour, to which he therefore proceeded, and discerned a vessel, with the lights of several others.

A brig that lay in the frigate's course hailed, but Captain Hood could not hear distinctly what was said. However, supposing they wanted to know the frigate's name he told them, and finding he could not weather the obstructive craft, tacked to

ENCOUNTER OF THE "DIDO" AND "LOWESTOFFE" WITH FRENCH FRIGATES.

pass by her stern. Suddenly a voice on board the brig was heard to exclaim—

"Luff! Luff!"

Hood, dreading shoal water, instantly ordered the helm to be put a-lee. It was too late, however; the frigate was aground, and as the water in the harbour was tolerably smooth, the sails were clewed up. Neither captain nor crew had as yet any suspicion that they were in the midst of the enemy.

A boat was seen to leave the treacherous brig and pull away towards the town, but no one suspected for what purpose.

The crew of the "Juno" had not all left the yards after clewing up and handing the sails, when a sudden flaw of wind drove the ship astern. To encourage this motion, some canvas was hoisted and boats were lowered to endeavour to warp the vessel further out.

The "Juno's" launch and cutter had hardly finished this service when a strange boat appeared alongside and was hailed.

"Aye! aye!" replied those in her, as though an officer had been there, and as soon as they got alongside two persons, apparently officers, hurried up the side and stood on the "Juno's" deck.

One of them informed Captain Hood that, in accordance with a strictly enforced regulation, he must take his ship into another branch of the harbour to perform ten days' quarantine.

The captain of the "Juno" replied by asking where the English admiral's (Lord Hood's) ship lay, and received a vague answer, which seems to have raised some suspicion. And, a moment afterwards, a midshipman, who was standing near, exclaimed—

"They are Frenchmen. They wear national cockades."

The moon happened at that moment to shine out more brightly, and Captain Hood was enabled to perceive the tricolour rosettes on their hats.

A second question relative to the position of Admiral Lord Hood's ship was put, upon which one of the Frenchmen, seeing that they were suspected, replied—

"*Soyez tranquille : les Anglais sont des braves gens ; nous les traitrons bien ; l'amiral Anglais est sorti il y a quelque temps.*"*

Imagine, if you can, Captain Hood's feelings on hearing this, or the feelings of the officers and crew, who began to whisper to each other the ominous words—

"We are prisoners."

But, at that moment, a puff of wind was felt blowing down the harbour, and Lieutenant Webley, who stood near Captain Hood, said—

"I believe, sir, we shall be able to fetch out, if we can get her under sail."

These words decided the fate of the "Juno," for it was immediately resolved that the attempt should be made, and there certainly was just a chance of being able to escape.

The crew were immediately sent to their various stations, and the unwelcome French visitors ordered below.

They did not like it; two or three of them drew their sabres, and made some show of resistance, but a number of marines quickly compelled them to obey orders.

The state of affairs was totally changed. Every man was instantly at his post, and, in something like three minutes, every sail was set.

---

* "Make yourself easy; the English are fine fellows; we will treat them well; the English admiral has been gone some time."

At the same time, the boats were cut adrift, that they might not retard the vessel's progress through the water.

All this seems to have caused some consternation on board the French brig, which commenced firing on the "Juno," as did also a fort on the frigate's starboard bow, and, soon afterwards, all the other forts that could bring their guns to bear.

Captain Hood returned the fire of some of the batteries, with good effect, so far as could be judged; and, finally, about half-an-hour after midnight, the "Juno" was out of the range of the enemy's fire, not a man of her crew having been lost, although the vessel's rigging was much damaged, and two 36-pound shots had lodged in her hull.

Every one must admit that the escape of the "Juno," from a harbour filled with armed vessels (there were at least twenty in Toulon) and flanked by formidable shore batteries, the vessel having been run aground, was an act of cool bravery and skilful seamanship, reflecting the greatest credit on the British navy.

Two days afterwards, the "Juno" joined Lord Hood's fleet in the Bay of Hieres.

On the 7th of February following, the "Juno" took an active part in bombarding a tower in Mortella Bay, Corsica.

CAPTAIN HORATIO NELSON, afterwards England's greatest admiral, served under Lord Hood at this time, being in command of the Agamemnon, a 64-gun ship.

He greatly distinguished himself at the siege of Calvi, in Corsica, being in command of the seamen in the batteries on shore; an unlucky shot from the town forced a particle of stone into his eye, and completely destroyed it.

In the month of May two captures of French vessels were made by the English. One was on the East India station, by the frigate "Orpheus," Captain Newcome, who captured the French frigate "Duguai Trouin" (late "Princess Royal," Indiaman), of 34 guns.

The Frenchman kept up a brave resistance for an hour and a quarter, when having sustained a great loss in killed and wounded, his bowsprit being shot away, and the British ships "Centurion" and "Resistance" only about three miles astern, he hauled down his colours and surrendered. A brig that had been with the "Duguai Trouin" managed to get safely into Port Louis:

On the 7th of the same month the 74-gun ship "Swiftsure," Captain James Charles Boyles, captured the French 36-gun frigate "Atalanta," Captain Linois. The "Atalanta" was added to the navy in the name of "Espion."

The next day the "Swiftsure" and her prize came nearly in contact with three French sail of the line, and were very nearly being captured. On this occasion Captain Boyles is said to have deserved more praise for saving his vessel, than for the perseverance with which he had just pursued and captured his prize.

In May, 1794, a French fleet of twenty-seven sail left Brest to meet a fleet of merchantmen from the West Indies, and convoy them safely into port. Lord Howe, with a fleet of twenty-five sail of the line, was on the watch for the French merchantmen, and anxious to capture them.

For two or three days after meeting the French war-fleet there were several brief engagements, without much injury to either party.

On the morning of the 1st of June, the two fleets met in one of the most sanguinary encounters ever fought upon the sea.

In this battle, which was fought at a greater distance from land than any other recorded in history, Lord Howe's flag-ship, the "Queen Charlotte," of 100 guns, was engaged with the "Montagu," of 130 guns, which was compelled to "give way."

It was soon followed by most of the French fleet, leaving six ships of the line in the hands of the English.

During the battle the "Brunswick," under Captain Harvey, was part of the time engaged with the "Vengeur," a 74-gun ship, and the "Achilles." A fierce battle raged between them for some time, in which there was great slaughter on both sides. The "Ramillies" then came to the "Brunswick's" assistance, and opened a fire on the "Vengeur," which soon after was found to be sinking. She went down with 320 of her crew, more than 400 of them being picked up by the boats of the "Alfred" and "Culloden."

Captain Renaudin, of the "Vengeur," was picked up by a boat, and taken to Portsmouth. While there a prisoner, lamenting the loss of his son, a brave boy twelve years of age, who was on the ship with him, the father and son met in the street.

The boy had been picked up by another boat.

The "Vengeur" is stated by some historians to have gone down with flying colours, all hands shouting "*Vive la Republique!*" till they were choked by the water. This is a pure invention. The crew of the ship fought like brave men, and surrendered like wise ones when they found that resistance was useless. Many of her men on arriving at Portsmouth as prisoners testified their love of republican principles by joining a regiment of royalist Frenchmen which was being formed by the Count d'Hervilly.

Howe's victory was gained by using the greatest part of his force against half of the enemy's vessels. By coming down obliquely on the French, one-half of them were idle spectators of the destruction of the others. In the two or three meetings which resulted in this victory, the English had 1,140 men killed and wounded.

This victory would have been more complete had Howe not thought it necessary to lose time in securing his prizes. Had the captured ships been destroyed, and the retreating French hotly pursued, the destruction of their whole fleet would have been accomplished.

Howe arrived at Spithead on the 13th of June with his six prizes. The news of his victory was received throughout England with great rejoicing. George III. went down to Portsmouth with his family, visited Howe aboard his ship, and presented him with a splendid sword, worth 3,000 guineas.

The ship "Romney," 50 guns, Captain William Paget, on the 17th of June, encountered the French 44-gun frigate "Sibylle," Captain Rondeau, with three merchantmen.

Captain Paget was convoying some British and Dutch vessels; but, on catching a glimpse of the enemy, he directed them to seek the protection of the "Leda" and "Tartar" frigates, which happened to be in sight from the masthead, and resolved to capture the Frenchman.

First of all, he sent a messenger to Captain Rondeau, commanding him to surrender his ship.

Of course, the Frenchman refused to do so, stating that he had taken an oath never to strike his colours, and immediately placed his vessel in such a position that any of the English shot that missed her must fall in the town of Miconi.*

This obliged the "Romney" to shift her position, so that her shot might fall clear of the town.

However, at one in the afternoon, Captain Paget brought the "Romney" abreast of the "Sibylle," and fired a broadside, which Rondeau immediately returned.

A heavy fight lasted for an hour and a quarter, when the "Sibylle" hauled down her flag, and was captured by the English, together with the three merchantmen.

The French vessel mounted six guns less than the English, but carried three hundred and eighty men against the "Romney's" two hundred and sixty-six, the latter vessel being seventy-four able hands short of her proper number.

The "Sibylle" had 46 men killed, and 112 wounded. She was a new frigate, and was added to the English navy.

Sir John Borlase Warren, of the "Flora," having with him the "Arethusa," commanded by Sir Edward Pellew (afterwards Lord Exmouth), the "Diamond," "Artois," "Diana," and "Santa Margarita," frigates, received orders to sail from Falmouth in search of a squadron of French frigates, reported to be crusing off Lands End. The English vessels sailed on the 7th August, 1794, and on the 23rd of the same month discovered the French frigate "Voluntaire," which was chased by three of the English ships, driven on shore, and destroyed.

While this was going on the remainder of the English squadron stood away towards the French coast, in pursuit of two ship corvettes, which eventually came to anchor off the Gamette Rocks,

---

* In the Grecian Archipelago—neutral ground.

in the Bay of Audierne, but perceiving that the English were resolutely pursuing, got under way again and ran aground near some batteries the French had thrown up on shore. These two vessels proved to be the "Alert" and "Espion," both recently taken from the British.

The French batteries commenced firing, and the English frigates replied for a time, but eventually the boats were sent out and the "Alert" was scuttled, after which our ships stood out to sea again.

On the 21st of October, the French 40-gun frigate "Revolutionnaire" was captured by the "Artois," 38 guns, Captain Nagle, with the assistance of the "Diamond," which came up just as the battle was nearly over.

She was also added to the navy.

The English ship "Alexander," of 74 guns, Captain Bligh, was captured on the 6th of November by a French squadron. This was the finest ship that had been captured from the English for many years.

During the year 1794 an English fleet was cruising about the West India Islands, doing good service without much severe fighting.

On the 17th of March, it captured the "Bienventure," in Fort Royal Bay, and Martinique on the 22nd of the same month.

The fleet also captured St. Lucia on the 4th of April.

Guadaloupe was captured by it, but was retaken by the French a few days after.

During the year 1794 the English captured from the French thirty-six vessels; of that number twenty-seven were added to the English navy.

During the same year, England lost seventeen vessels, nine of which fell into the hands of the French.

It was on the 3rd of December in this year that the crew of the "Culloden" mutinied while the vessel was lying at Spithead.

For eight days they held possession of the vessel, defying all efforts to induce them to return to duty.

Five of the mutineers were hanged on the 13th of the following January.

It appears that during the year 1794 we captured thirty-six French war ships, twenty-seven of which were added to the British navy. During the same period we lost seventeen ships of war, nine of which appear to have been captured by the French.

THE "DIAMOND" FRIGATE OFF THE FRENCH COAST.

Many improvements were made in the new vessels built. For instance, they were made longer in proportion to their breadth than hitherto. An improved class of naval guns came into use.

Our navy was officered and manned at the commencement of 1795 by twenty-one admirals, thirty-six vice-admirals, thirty-one rear-admirals, twenty-eight superannuated flag-officers, 425 post-captains, twenty-seven superannuated post-captains, 230 commanders, 1,623 lieutenants, twenty-six superannuated lieutenants, and 361 masters.

The House of Commons voted supplies for 100,000 seamen and marines, for the service of 510 ships of war of all classes then in existence or on the stocks.

CHAPTER XX.

CHIEF EVENTS OF THE YEAR 1795.

N the month of January, 1795, the French fleet, which despite its losses was still very strong, made several attempts to put out to sea, but a succession of violent gales drove it back again.

The squadron mentioned in the last chapter, under the command of Sir J. B. Warren, was sent to watch the harbour of Brest and see what the French were about. On the 3rd of January, 1795, they arrived off the port, and the "Diamond" frigate, commanded by Captain Sir Sidney Smith, was ordered to get as near as possible to the mouth of the harbour, the other vessels remaining some distance off.

While the "Diamond" was working up towards Brest, in the teeth of an east wind, her commander observed three large French ships endeavouring to enter the harbour; this was late in the afternoon of the 3rd, and soon afterwards one of the vessels was observed to drop anchor, evidently unable to get into Brest that night. The "Diamond," however, persevered in her efforts to beat up to the harbour's mouth.

As early as two o'clock in the morning of the 4th, Sir Sidney Smith discovered that the vessel at anchor was a French ship of the line, and half-an-hour afterwards he passed to windward of a French frigate lying at anchor; but still, in order to avoid being suspected by these powerful foes, he kept on towards Brest.

As soon as day broke—that is, about seven o'clock—he perceived two other ships making towards Brest, and also fifteen small vessels anchored in Camaret Bay, an adjacent inlet. The look-out likewise reported a large ship, which appeared to have gone aground, and to have lost her fore and mizen masts.

Almost directly after this, one of the forts on shore made some signals, to which Sir Sidney replied by hoisting the French national ensign; but this did not seem to satisfy a corvette, which had been stealing out to the westward, and now showed her doubts by rapidly signalling to the shore, and seeking shelter under the battery before mentioned.

The English captain seems to have considered that audacity was the best policy, for he directed his course towards the large vessel he had seen at anchor the previous night, and hailing in the French language, demanded what ship it was.

In reply, he received information that it was the "Nestor," and that she had been parted from the remainder of the fleet three days, through having lost her masts in a gale.

This appeared to be true, for Sir Sidney could see that she had rigged jury masts and topmasts, and appeared to have lost her main-deck guns.

The English commander then asked if she required any assistance, and receiving the answer, "no," sailed away, having completely outwitted the enemy by his disguise, his boldness, and the facility with which he spoke the French language.

A few hours afterwards the "Diamond" joined the "Arethusa," which had been sent nearer shore to look out for her daring companion.

Some severe critics have stigmatized Sir Sidney Smith as a foolhardy adventurer, but it was only by dint of such daring exploits that England maintained her naval supremacy against all the world; and it is much to be hoped that England still possesses such gallant dashing sailors.

On the same day the frigates "Pique" and "Blanche" captured the French 32-gun frigate off Guadaloupe.

In this action Captain Faulkner, of the "Blanche," was shot through the heart with a musket ball.

The "Pique" had 76 killed and 110 wounded. She was added to the navy. For this action a naval medal was granted. Captain Conseil fought his ship bravely, and was mortally wounded in the action.

PORTRAIT OF LORD HOOD.

On the 7th of March, the 74-gun ship "Berwick," Captain Littlejohn, was captured, after a long chase, by a French fleet.

The "Berwick," it appeared, had lost her masts while off the coast of Corsica, with the Mediterranean fleet, and was left behind to fit up jury-masts and follow as soon as possible. In the meantime, a French fleet of 15 *sail of the line and* 6 *frigates* put out from Toulon, and on the 7th of March, as beforesaid, discovered the unfortunate "Berwick," making the best of her way towards the port of Leghorn.

The French fleet immediately gave chase—under Spanish colours, a ruse which Captain Littlejohn soon detected; but it was four hours before the foremost of the enemy's frigates came up and opened fire, being soon afterwards joined by two other frigates and two line-of-battle ships.

Captain Littlejohn kept on his course, hoping to fall in with the British fleet; but in a very short time the "Berwick's" rigging was cut to pieces by the French shot, which were purposely aimed high to avoid damaging the hull, which they hoped soon to possess.

Captain Littlejohn gave the first frigate a broadside, which disabled her, but almost at the same moment the brave fellow's head was carried away by a cannon shot.

However, the fight was kept up for an hour, when, seeing the impossibility of escaping, the senior surviving officer ordered the colours to be struck.

On the 13th of March, off Ushant, the 32-gun frigate "Lively," Captain George Burlton, captured the "Tourterelle," of 28 guns. This vessel was fitted with a furnace for heating shot.

During the month of March, Admiral Hotham, who had been for some time lying in Leghorn Roads, had two skirmishes with a French fleet, in which several ships were injured, and, on the English fleet, 74 men were killed and 284 wounded.

Two French ships, the "Ca-Ira" and "Censeur," were captured, for which the naval medal was granted in the meeting that took place on the 14th, the one that came the nearest to being a battle.

On the 30th of March, the ship "Boyne," of 80 guns, caught fire at Spithead, and was burnt; twenty of the crew were lost.

The "Thorn," a 16-gun sloop, Captain Otway, captured the French 18-gun corvette "Courier National," on the 25th of May.

On the 24th of June, the frigate "Dido," 28 guns, Captain George Towry, and the 32-gun frigate "Lowestoffe," Captain Middleton, engaged the French 40-gun frigate "Minerve," Captain Perrée, and the "Artémise," 36 guns.

The "Minerve" attempted to decide the contest by running down the "Dido," but the helm of the latter was put hard a-port, and thus the catastrophe was averted, but the rigging of the two vessels became entangled.

The "Minerve" had 318 men and boys, the "Dido" only 193, and the Frenchman, well aware of his superiority, endeavoured to board, but was gallantly repulsed. After a time the two vessels parted, the little "Dido" being almost a perfect wreck. But the "Lowestoffe" having chased the "Artémise" for some distance, returned, and the "Minerve" soon hauled down her colours.

The "Minerve" mounted 42 guns, but afterwards, when she was repaired and added to the British navy, her armament was reduced to 38 guns, and the command given to Captain Towry, who, with Captain Middleton, received great praise for this gallantly fought action.

During the month of June there were two other meetings of large fleets, at which but little more than a few shots were fired, a few men killed and wounded, and yet the navy medal, for some unexplained reason, was given on each occasion.

The first was for the meeting of the English fleet of eight large ships of war, including the "Royal Sovereign," under Vice-Admiral Hon. W. Cornwallis, with a French fleet under Admiral Joyeuse, off Brest. This affair happened on the 7th of June, and although some merchant vessels were captured, it was not regarded by those who should know best as a victory.

The second was between the same French fleet, and the English Channel fleet under Admiral Lord Bridport, with seventeen ships of war and five frigates, two of the ships being the "Royal George" and the "Queen Charlotte," of 100 guns each.

In this action it is true that three ships were captured by the English, but this achievement was so insignificant to what should have been accomplished, that the navy medal should never have been given for the battle. In this action the English fleet had 39 men killed and 113 wounded.

Admiral Hotham, with a fleet of twenty-five ships, had a brief encounter with the Toulon fleet, on the 13th of July, and the French ship "Alcide," of 74 guns, was compelled to surrender, but caught fire and blew up, without possession being taken of her by the captors. Between 300 and 400 of her crew perished.

The French admiral, thinking his force inferior to the enemy, made off and was allowed to escape without further injury.

It was still the practise of the British Government to hire vessels occasionally, and we find that about this time the cutter "Rose" was for a time in the government employ, being armed with eight 4-pound guns, and commanded by Lieutenant Walker. This brave officer was sailing, in the latter end of the month of September, from Leghorn to Bastia, in the island of Corsica, when three ships, supposed to be French privateers, were discovered.

Though he had only thirteen men and a boy for his crew, was encumbered by three passengers, and had £10,000 in gold on board, Lieutenant Walker determined to attack them, so he cleared for action, bore down towards the nearest privateer, and poured in a raking fire with her little guns, setting fire to the foresail and mizen.

In the heat of the action, one of the crew of the "Rose," William Brown by name, had his foot crushed by a gun carriage, but although Lieutenant Walker urged him to go below, he refused, saying:—

"You can't spare a man, sir. I can sit here and fire a musket as well as anyone."

In a very short time the first privateer struck her flag, and Lieutenant Walker, threatening the skipper that if he attempted to escape he would burn the vessel, with the crew in her, sailed off to privateer number two, which after receiving two well directed broadsides between wind and water, went to the bottom, and all hands were drowned. The third privateer had by this time got off to windward.

The "Rose" then returned to the vessel that had struck, and not being able to spare a man to take charge, fastened the crew down into the hold, and triumphantly towed the prize to Corsica.

It appeared from the statements of the prisoners, who numbered twenty-nine men, that the prize had at the commencement a crew of forty-two men, the vessel that sank fifty-six men, and the one that escaped forty-eight, making a total of 146 men, who were totally discomfited by fourteen brave British sailors.

Lieutenant Walker received great praise for this gallant action from the naval and military commanders in the Mediterranean, but for some cause still unexplained these praises did *not* lead to the rapid promotion of the officer who had so nobly sustained the glory of Old England's flag.

On the 7th of October, 1795, the "Censeur," 74-gun ship (lately captured from the French), Captain John Gore, with the ships "Bedford" and "Fortitude," while convoying a fleet of merchant ships, were attacked by a French fleet of six sail of the line and three frigates, under Rear-Admiral Richery.

The "Bedford" and "Fortitude" escaped, but the "Censeur" and thirty of the merchant vessels were captured.

On the 13th of October the "Mermaid," 32-gun frigate, Captain Ware, captured the French 18-gun corvette "Republicain," after a long running fight and a sharp action of ten minutes. The "Mermaid" had one man killed and three wounded; the "Republicain" had twenty killed.

In the month of September, Vice-Admiral Sir George Elphinstone went to the Cape of Good Hope with seven ships of war, and a land force under General Clarke.

The Dutch governor was requested to place the settlement at the disposal of the King of England, a request which he at once declined; so it was resolved to take it by force; and 800 soldiers and marines were landed, who captured Simons Town on the 14th of August.

A little skirmishing took up the time till early in September, when other ships-of-war and troops having arrived, the English commander resolved to attack Cape Town. The troops marched by land, and the English fleet took up a position to bombard the town from the sea; and these preparations so alarmed the Dutch commander that he sent to request forty-eight hours' armistice to arrange terms of capitulation.

The English general, Clarke, refused to grant more than twenty-four hours; and at the end of that time the colony was given up to the English. The Dutch army amounted to a thousand men; and seven vessels belonging to the Dutch East India Company fell into the hands of the English.

During this year, a force, under Rear-Admiral Rainier, sailed from Madras for the Island of Ceylon.

Trincomalee surrendered to the English on the 18th of August.

Malacca surrendered to Captain Newcome, of the "Orpheus" frigate, on the 17th of August, and Manaar was taken on the 5th of October, and before the year all the remaining Dutch settlements in India surrendered to the English.

The statistics of the British navy show an increase of fifty vessels during the year 1795; twenty-eight of these were taken from the French. Our total loss amounted to twelve ships—two of which were taken by the French.

We had 105 flag officers—*i.e.*, admirals—on the active list, 466 post captains; 241 commanders; 1878 lieutenants; and 404 masters: the number of seamen and marines voted by parliament being 110,000.*

CHAPTER XXI.

CONTINUATION OF THE WAR—PRINCIPAL NAVAL EVENTS OF THE YEAR 1796.

HERE was no event worthy of record transpired in the war during the months of January and February of 1796.

On the 10th of March, the 38-gun frigate "Phaëton," Captain Stopford, and a small squadron, captured the French 20-gun corvette "Bonne Citoyenne," which was added to the navy.

On the 18th of March, Sir William Sidney Smith, in the frigate "Diamond," 38 guns, assisted by the brig "Liberty," and a lugger, attacked the batteries of Port Spergue, on the French coast.

The batteries were stormed by a party led by Lieutenant Pine, of the "Diamond."

The squadron then entered the harbour and destroyed one corvette, four brigs, two sloops, and a lugger.

The naval medal was given for the affair.

On the 13th of April, the frigate "Revolutionnaire," 38 guns, Captain Cole, captured the French 12-pounder 36-gun frigate "Unité."

On the 17th of April, Captain Sir Sidney Smith, of the "Diamond," went into the harbour of Havre, with some boats, to cut out some luggers, and was made a prisoner.

On the 19th of April, Captain Sir Edward Pellew, of the "Indefatigable," while off the Lizard, saw a large frigate to the leeward, and gave chase.

After a chase of 168 miles, he came up with the vessel, which was the French 40-gun frigate "Virginia," Captain Bergeret.

The "Virginia" surrendered after a sharp resistance, having 15 men killed and 27 wounded. She was added to the navy, and the navy medal was given for the action in which she was captured.

On the 25th of April, Commodore Nelson went

---

* In contrast to this we may here quote the navy estimates for the year ending March 31st, 1871, which provide for a force of 61,000 seamen and marines, to man a total of 408 vessels actually afloat, and seventeen building.

in the "Agamemnon," and with three other vessels to Laon Bay, where there was a convoy laden with stores for the use of the French army in Italy.

The enemy's vessels were found lying under the protection of heavy batteries on shore, and the boats were sent in to cut them out.

This was a dangerous and difficult service; but it was gallantly performed, and four store ships were taken.

On the 4th of May, the 16-gun sloop "Spencer," commanded by Andrew Evans, captured the French 12-gun brig "Volcan."

This is not a very important event, but it is one that possibly may be looked for in a Naval History.

On the 12th of May, the 36-gun frigate "Phœnix," Captain Halstead, captured the Dutch frigate "Argo," 36 guns, which was added to the English navy under the name of the "Janus."

On the 8th of June, the frigate "Unicorn," 32 18-pounders, Captain Williams, after a long chase, engaged and captured the French 36-gun frigate "Tribune."

At the same time the 36-gun frigate "Santa Margarita," after an engagement of twenty minutes, captured the "Tamise," of 36 guns, which had formerly, when under the name of "Thames," 32 guns, been captured from the English.

The "Tamise" lost 32 men killed and 19 wounded.

On the 13th of June, the 18-pounder 32-gun frigate "Dryad," Captain Beauclerk, off Cape Clear, captured the French 36-gun frigate "Proserpine," which lost 30 men killed and had 45 wounded. The "Proserpine" was added to the English navy, and called "Amelia."

On the 22nd of June, the "Légère," the last of the French Commodore Moulston's squadron, was captured by the English frigates "Apollo" and "Doris."

On the 9th of June, a very gallant action was fought by the 32-gun frigate "Southampton," one of the fleet of Sir John Jervis, on the coast of France, near Toulon.

The French corvette "Utile," lying under protection of some batteries, after receiving a few broadsides, was boarded from the "Southampton," and captured by a party led by Lieutenant Lydiard, who brought the prize out of the harbour.

On the 15th of July, the 50-gun ship "Glatton," Captain Henry Trollope, fell in with four French frigates and two corvettes off the coast of Flanders, and attacked them all.

After a few broadsides had been exchanged, the French vessels made off; and the "Glatton," being a slow sailer, they were not pursued.

One of the French vessels sank from the injuries it had received, and four others were much damaged in the encounter.

The "Glatton" carried 68-pounders on the lower, and 32-pounders on the upper deck.

For this exploit her captain was presented with an elegant piece of plate by the merchants of London.

On the 23rd of August, the French 36-gun frigate "Andromaque" was run on shore near Arcasson, and destroyed by the squadron under Sir John B. Warren.

On the 28th of August, the 36-gun frigate "Topaze," Captain Church, one of the squadron under command of Vice-Admiral Murray, off Chesapeake, captured the French frigate "Elizabeth," of 36 guns.

Off Carthagena, on the 13th of October, the 12-pounder 32-gun frigate "Terpsichore," Captain Bowen, captured the Spanish 34-gun frigate "Mahonesa," Captain Ayldi.

On the 26th of November, the 28-gun frigate "Lapwing," Captain Boston, off Anguilla, fell in with the French ship "Decius," 20 guns, and the 6-gun brig "Vaillante."

The "Decius" was first captured, and after the

CRESTS OF VESSELS IN THE ROYAL NAVY (A.D. 1870).

prize was secured, the "Lapwing" chased the brig, drove it on shore, and destroyed it.

On the 12th of December, 1796, Captain Bowen, in the "Terpsichore," being on a cruise off Carthagena, discovered a large French frigate lying to on his weather quarter, the wind at the time blowing hard from the south-east, with a heavy short sea.

Captain Bowen instantly made sail, and gave chase to windward.

The Frenchman, who was not equally desirous of

The "Terpsichore, having the day before sprung her main and fore mast, made Captain Bowen fearful he should not be able to close with her before she could effect her escape.

However, by ten o'clock at night, he had the satisfaction of getting alongside of her.

The enemy, finding it impossible to avoid an action, brought to; when a most gallant and spirited battle commenced, and continued with great fury for an hour and a quarter, at which time the enemy,

EXPLOSION ON BOARD THE "AMPHION," AT PLYMOUTH.

fighting, in order to escape, made all the sail he could crowd.

The chase was continued, with much manœuvring on both sides, till two o'clock in the morning of the 13th, both ships working to windward under their courses, when the "Terpsichore," being close in with the land, about Cape Marcus, Captain Bowen wore, gave up the pursuit, and brought to, with the ship's head off shore.

About eight in the morning, the enemy's frigate was again seen from the mast-head; the wind having shifted to the south-west, gave Captain Bowen the weather gauge.

He immediately wore and made sail in chase, the enemy crowding all sail she could set for Cadiz.

being completely dismasted, with her captain and forty men killed and wounded, she struck, and proved to be "La Vestale," of 36 guns and 300 men.

The "Terpsichore" had four killed and eighteen wounded; among the latter, Lieutenant George Bowen, brother to the captain, who was the only lieutenant on board, the two others, with three midshipmen and forty men, being absent either at the hospital or in prizes.

Captain Bowen sent the master with eight men to take charge of the prize, which had drifted by this time into four fathoms water, not an anchor clear for letting go, and most of the surviving Frenchmen intoxicated.

By great exertions and perseverance, the master made shift to bring her up in rather less than three fathoms of water, and rode out the night about a mile or two from the shore.

The conquest was scarcely achieved when the English become sensible of a danger which the ardour of the chase had caused them to overlook.

Both ships were on a dangerous lee shore, close to some shoals, which lie between Cape Trafalgar and Cadiz, and breakers were seen whitening in the moonlight at a small distance.

The masts and bowsprit of the French frigate had gone by the board immediately after her surrender, and her attempting to clear off the shore became impossible.

In this situation, the English captain sent orders to the master, whom he had charged with the prize, to endeavour to anchor her, exhorting him to urge the Frenchmen, whose lives depended on the success of the attempt, to assist him.

This, after great exertions, was accomplished, and the "Terpsichore," in the mean time, with some difficulty, weathered the rocks of St. Sebastian.

As soon as the day dawned, Captain Bowen, who had in some measure repaired the injury this ship had sustained, and enabled her to carry sail with greater security, returned in search of his prize.

After great toil, he nearly succeeded in securing her, when the breaking of his tackle forced him to give up the attempt, as the day had nearly closed upon his labours.

The first thought that occurred to him was to destroy her; but he revolted from this idea, recollecting the number of wounded on board the prize, whom the loss of almost all his boats rendered it impossible to remove. Having, therefore, determined to resume his task in the morning, he made sail during the night, in order to keep clear of the land.

Unfortunately, it fell calm; he was drawn by the current into the entrance of the straits, and the wind, settling towards daylight in the south-east, blew directly fair for Cadiz.

In the utmost anxiety, he returned with all the sail he could carry to the place where he had left the French frigate, and had the mortification of seeing her far advanced in her course towards the Spanish port, with some spars erected for jury masts, and her colours re-hoisted.

Determined to use every effort to prevent her escaping with impunity, he chased her for some time, in the hope of forcing her on shore; but the crippled state of his ship rendered this impracticable, and, on the Frenchman's reaching the back of the town of Cadiz, he reluctantly abandoned the pursuit.

Willing to hope that Mr. Fancauld, the captain of the "Vestale," had been forced into the measures he had taken by the violence of his crew, Captain Bowen sent a message to him at Cadiz, to claim the restitution of the prize, but the French captain returned no answer to his remonstrances.

During this year Colombo in Ceylon was captured by an English squadron, under command of Captain Gardner. Besides the naval stores, merchandize to the value of £300,000 was taken in the place.

Amboyna and Banda were also captured from the Dutch this year, and a large amount of prize money obtained for them.

A most daring action was fought by the British 18-gun brig "Pelican," commanded by Captain J. C. Searle, who, at daybreak, on the 23rd of September, found himself close on the lea beam of a French frigate.

Searle saw that the enemy was a very powerful one, and did not seek an engagement; but the Frenchman was a very fast sailer, so it became necessary to fight.

The "Pelican" was short handed, having only 97 men on board, out of her proper complement of 121; but the brave tars, when they heard that their captain was resolved to fight, gave three cheers, and expressed a resolution to sink with the ship rather than surrender.

So the decks were cleared for action, and the brig shortened sail, no doubt to the great surprise of the enemy, which proved to be the 36-gun frigate "Médée."

At seven in the morning the firing was commenced, at long range, by the frigate; but the "Pelican" reserved her fire till the distance between the two vessels was diminished, when it was commenced, and kept up with great effect till nine o'clock, when the "Médée" seemed to have had enough, and made off to the northward under all sail.

The "Pelican" was so much cut up in her rigging that pursuit was impossible; but, about two hours after the action was over, Captain Searle recaptured the "Alcyon," a British ship which had been taken by the "Médée" about a fortnight before.

Unfortunately, however, at daybreak, on the following day, it was seen that the "Alcyon" had drifted near shore, where the "Médée" was anchored—two other French frigates being at no great distance.

It was impossible to save her, so Captain Searle was obliged to abandon his prize to the French, who were much disgusted when they learned that they had been beaten by a British 18-gun brig.

The "Médeé," though nominally a 36-gun frigate, really mounted 40 guns, and carried a crew of 300 men, of whom 33 were killed and wounded. The "Pelican" had no person killed, and only one slightly wounded.

The last action of the year was on its last day, when the "Polyphemus," 64-gun ship, Captain Lumsdaine, captured the French frigate "Tortue," of 40 guns.

In this year England obtained many vessels from her enemies with but little hard fighting.

On the 17th of August, a Dutch squadron of three ships of the line, three frigates, besides some smaller vessels, under Admiral Lucas, which had been fitted out for the recapture of the Cape of Good Hope, were captured at Saldanha Bay by an English fleet under Admiral Sir G. K. Elphinstone.

The English force being greatly superior, no imputation was cast on Admiral Lucas for yielding without a combat.

Several Dutch ships were also captured without a battle by the surrender of Demerara and other places.

During the year 1796 England lost twenty-three vessels of war. One was captured, thirteen wrecked, six foundered, and three were burnt.

Captain John Afflick, of the " Amethyst," which was lost by striking on a rock near Guernsey, was tried by a court-martial on the 13th of March for the loss of his vessel, and was sentenced to be reduced to the bottom of the list of post-captains, and rendered incapable of being again employed in His Majesty's service.

Amongst the vessels lost that year may be mentioned the " Amphion," Captain Pellew, which blew up at Portsmouth on the 22nd of September.

The captain, first lieutenant, and 15 men were all who were saved out of more than 300 people who were aboard at the time.

Rear-Admiral Sir Hugh Palliser died on the 16th of March this year of wounds received aboard the " Sutherland."

CHAPTER XXII.

NAVAL VICTORIES IN 1797.

THE 44-gun frigate, "Indefatigable," Captain Edward Pellew, and the " Amazon," 36-gun frigate, Captain Reynolds, met the French 74-gun ship " Droits de l'Homme," Commodore La Crosse, off Ushant, on the 13th of January, 1797.

This vessel was one of the unfortunate fleet that sailed from Brest with General Hoche and 17,000 troops, with the intention of landing them on the coast of Ireland.

The " Indefatigable " was the first to begin the action, and was soon after followed by the " Amazon."

The two frigates placed themselves, one on each bow of the French ship, and raked her decks with great effect.

Fortunately for the English frigates, the sea ran very high and the lower tier of the Frenchman's guns could not be used upon them.

About half-past ten o'clock p.m., the mizen mast of the " Droits de l'Homme " was cut away and the frigates then took each a station on opposite quarters and again commenced their destructive raking.

A little later and through the darkness of that night, Lieutenant Bell, of the " Indefatigable," discovered land about two miles away.

This discovery was reported to his captain, and the vessel was immediately hauled to the wind and a signal of the danger given to the " Amazon."

The " Indefatigable " bore away to the south, but the " Amazon," for some reason or other, wore to the northward.

For half-an-hour or more her officers and crew exerted themselves to the utmost to keep their disabled ship off the shore, but were unable to do so.

The " Amazon " struck the ground, but all hands got safely to shore on rafts, with the exception of six men, who stole the cutter and were drowned.

But French soldiers were waiting for the unfortunate sailors, who were made prisoners, and marched off to the town of Audierne, distant about a league from the wreck.

The " Droits de l'Homme " struck nearly at the same time as the " Amazon."

The French vessel was crowded with human beings; her crew consisted of about 700 men; she also carried 1,050 of the troops which had been destined for the landing in Ireland, together with 55 English prisoners who had been captured some time before; making altogether over 1,800 men. As soon as the ship struck, all was dismay and confusion, and many of those on deck were washed away by the merciless waves.

When daylight came, they could see the shore lined with spectators, but the waves ran so high that it was impossible to communicate.

However, when low water came, the Frenchmen set to work to construct rafts, and the boats were got in readiness to make an attempt to get on shore.

But the weather continued so tempestuous that no one dared to venture during the whole of that day, so another night of misery on the wreck closed in.

When the morning again dawned, the poor wretches had suffered so much from hunger and cold—they had been more than thirty hours without food—that it was resolved, at all hazards, to attempt to reach the shore.

So a small boat was lowered, manned by an English officer and eight English seamen, part of the prisoners; and these daring fellows, by dint of tremendous exertions and great skill, succeeded in reaching land.

The Frenchmen then fancied it would be safe to trust to their rafts, and several of them immediately put off; but, lacking the skill and hardihood of the British tars, their rafts were immediately swamped, and the men on them drowned.

Nothing more was attempted that day; but, after another night of misery had passed, it was resolved to construct larger rafts, and, at the same time, the largest of the ship's boats was lowered over the side.

It was intended, if possible, to place on board these rafts, and in the boat, all the females, wounded, and landsmen; but all subordination was gone; one hundred and twenty men leaped over the side, in defiance of their officers' commands, and all were lost.

The boat sank, and nothing was seen of its occupants for nearly half an hour, at the expiration of which time their bodies began to float up to the surface.

By this time, nearly nine hundred men, or one-half of the total number on board, had perished.

The fourth night came, and those who survived began almost to envy those whose corpses floated around the shattered vessel.

They had tasted no food since the "Droits de l'Homme" struck, and the sense of hunger was already lost, though they suffered severely from thirst.

First, they tried wine diluted with salt water, but that only increased their thirst; then a hogshead of vinegar floated up from the hold, and each man had a small quantity, which for a short time gave relief.

More than half of the ship had, by this time, been broken away by the force of the waves.

As the morning of the fourth day of their sufferings broke, it was observed that the sky had cleared, and the sea was subsiding.

But the poor wretches on the wreck were too enfeebled to derive any hope from these symptoms.

They determined that some must die to afford food for the others, and the lots were just going to be drawn, when two French vessels appeared in sight, and soon afterwards anchored close at hand; boats and rafts were sent, which rescued about two hundred souls—all that survived on the wreck of the "Droits de l'Homme."

It is pleasing to quote from the words of Lieutenant Pipon, that the French gave the English prisoners "a rough shift of clothes; and, in consequence of our sufferings, and the help we afforded in saving many lives, a cartel was fitted out by order of the French government, to send us home, without ransome or exchange. We arrived at Plymouth on the 17th of March following."

On the 31st of January, the 32-gun frigate "Andromache," Captain Mansfield, captured an Algerine frigate, of about equal force, off Tangiers.

The Algerine had 65 men killed and 50 wounded. The "Andromache," 9 killed and wounded.

BOMBARDING THE BATTERIES AT ST. LUCIE.

Admiral Sir J. Jervis, of the "Victory," 100 guns, having under his command fifteen ships of war and five frigates, met, on the 14th of February, a Spanish fleet, commanded by Don Jose de Cordova, off St. Vincent.

The Spanish fleet consisted of twenty-seven ships, twelve frigates, and one brig.

Before the glorious action off Cape St. Vincent, early in 1797, the name of Nelson was little known to the English public; but from the activity, talents, and zeal, which he had so eminently and constantly displayed during a long course of services in the Mediterranean, he was feared and respected throughout Italy.

At this time a letter came to him, directed "Horatio Nelson, Genoa." And the writer was asked by a friend, who was gazing over his shoulder and caught sight of the address—

"Is there but one house in Genoa?"

"One house!" repeated the other, with a laugh, "pray what instituted such an ignorant question?"

"The simple fact that this letter, bearing such a vague address as 'Horatio Nelson, Genoa,' would give rise to the supposition that the place could boast of but one residence."

"Genoa has many houses, sir," was the reply; "but there is but one Horatio Nelson in the world!"

We have said that his name was scarcely known in England, but this short anecdote shows that those whom he honoured with his friendship had discovered germs of that bravery, courage, and resolution, which his after actions so bountifully displayed to the world. That he was the greatest hero, the best tactician, and the noblest commander, both in head and heart, that ever trod a ship's deck.

At Genoa, in particular, where he had so long been stationed, and where the nature of his duty first led him to continual disputes with the government, and afterwards compelled him to stop the trade of the port, he was equally respected by the doge and by the people; for, while he maintained the rights and interests of Great Britain with becoming firmness, he tempered the exercise of power with courtesy and humanity wherever duty would permit.

"Had all my actions," said he, writing at this time to his wife, "been gazetted, not one fortnight would have passed, during the whole war, without a letter from me. One day or other I will have a long gazette to myself. I feel that such an opportunity will be given me. I cannot, if I am in the field of glory, be kept out of sight; wherever there is anything to be done, there Providence is sure to direct my steps."

These hopes and anticipations were soon to be fulfilled. Nelson's mind had long been irritated and depressed by the fear that a general action would take place before he could join the fleet.

At length he sailed from Porto Ferrajo with a convoy for Gibraltar, and having reached that place, proceeded to the westward in search of the admiral. Off the mouth of the Straits he fell in with the Spanish fleet; and, on the 13th of February reaching the station off Cape St. Vincent, communicated this intelligence to Sir John Jervis.

He was now directed to shift his broad pendant on board the "Captain," 74 guns, Captain R. W. Miller; and before sunset the signal was made to prepare for action, and to keep during the night in close order.

At daybreak the enemy were in sight.

The British force consisted of two ships of 100 guns, two of 98, two of 90, eight of 74, and one 64; fifteen of the line in all; with four frigates, a sloop, and a cutter.

The Spaniards had one four-decker, of 136 guns; six three-deckers, of 112; two of 84, and eighteen of 74; in all, twenty-seven ships of the line, with ten frigates and a brig.

Their admiral, Don Joseph de Cordova, had learnt from an American, on the 5th, that the English had only nine ships, which was indeed the case when his informer had seen them; for a reinforcement of five ships from England, under Admiral Parker, had not then joined, and the "Culloden" had parted company.

Upon this information the Spanish commander, instead of going into Cadiz, as was his intention when he sailed from Carthagena, determined to seek an enemy so inferior in force; and relying, with fatal confidence, upon the American account, he suffered his ships to remain too far dispersed, and in some disorder.

When the morning of the 14th broke, and discovered the English fleet, a fog for some time concealed their number.

That fleet had heard their signal guns during the night, the weather being fine, though thick and hazy; soon after daylight they were seen very much scattered, while the British ships were in a compact little body.

PORTRAIT OF ADMIRAL VISCOUNT DUNCAN.

The look-out ship of the Spaniards fancying that her signal was disregarded, because so little notice seemed to be taken of it, made another signal, that the English force consisted of forty sail of the line.

The captain afterwards said he did this to rouse the admiral; it had the effect of perplexing him, and alarming the whole fleet.

The absurdity of such an act shows what was the state of the Spanish navy under that miserable government, by which Spain was so long oppressed and degraded, and finally betrayed.

In reality, the general incapacity of the naval officers was so well known, that in a pasquinade, which about this time appeared at Madrid, wherein the different orders of the State were advertised for sale, the greater part of the sea officers, with all their equipments, were offered as a gift; and it was added, that any person who would please to take them, should receive a handsome gratuity.

When the probability that Spain would take part in the war, as an ally of France, was first contemplated, Nelson said that their fleet, if it were no better than when it acted in alliance with us, would "soon be done for."

Before the enemy could form a regular order of battle, Sir J. Jervis, by carrying a press of sail, came up with them, passed through their fleet, then tacked, and thus cut off nine of their ships from the main body.

These ships attempted to form on the larboard tack, either with the design of passing through the British line, or to leeward of it, and thus rejoining their friends.

Only one of them succeeded in this attempt; and

that only because she was so covered with smoke, that her intention was not discovered till she had reached the rear; the others were so warmly received, that they put about, took to flight, and did not appear again in the action till its close.

The admiral was now able to direct his attention to the enemy's main body, which was still superior in number to his whole fleet, and greatly so in weight of metal.

He made signal to take succession.

Nelson, whose station was in the rear of the British line, perceived that the Spaniards were bearing up before the wind, with an intention of forming their line, going large, and joining their separated ships; or else of getting off without an engagement.

To prevent either of these schemes, he disobeyed the signal without a moment's hesitation, and ordered his ship to be wore.

This at once brought him into action with the "Santissima Trinidad," 136, the "San Joseph," 112, the "Salvador del Mundo," 112, the "San Nicholas," 80, the "San Isidro," 74, another 74, and another first-rate.

Trowbridge, in the "Culloden," immediately joined, and most nobly supported him; and for nearly an hour did the "Culloden" and "Captain" maintain what Nelson called "this apparently, but not really unequal contest." Such was the advantage of skill and discipline, and the confidence which brave men derive from them.

The "Blenheim," then passing between them and the enemy, gave them a respite, and poured in her fire upon the Spaniards.

The "Salvador del Mundo," and "San Isidro" dropped astern, and were fired into in a masterly style by the excellent Captain Collingwood.

The "San Isidro" struck; and Nelson thought that the "Salvador" struck also.

"But Collingwood," says he, "disdaining the parade of taking possession of beaten enemies, most gallantly pushed up, with every sail set, to save his old friend and messmate, who was, to appearance, in a critical situation;" for the "Captain" was at this time actually fired upon by three first-rates, by the "San Nicolas," and by a seventy-four, within about pistol-shot of that vessel.

The "Blenheim" was ahead, the "Culloden" crippled and astern.

Collingwood ranged up, and hauling up his mainsail just astern, passed within ten feet of the "San Nicolas," giving her a most tremendous fire, then passed on for the "Santissima Trinidad."

The "San Nicolas" luffing up, the "San Josef" fell on board her, and Nelson resumed his station abreast of them, and close alongside.

The "Captain" was now incapable of farther service, either in the line or in chase. She had lost her fore-topmast; not a sail, shroud, or rope was left, and her wheel was shot away.

Nelson, therefore, directed Captain Miller to put the helm a-starboard, and calling for the boarders, ordered them to board.

The following is his own account of what followed.

"The soldiers of the 69th foot* with an alacrity which will ever do them credit, and Lieutenant Pearson of the same regiment, were almost the foremost on this service.

"The first man who jumped into the enemy's mizen-chains was Captain Berry, late my first lieutenant (Captain Miller was in the very act of going, too, but I directed him to remain). He was supported from our sprit-sail yard which hooked in the mizen rigging.

"A soldier of the 69th having broken the upper quarter gallery window I jumped in myself, and was followed by others as fast as possible.

"I found the cabin doors fastened, and some Spanish officers fired their pistols; but having broken open the doors, the soldiers fired and the Spanish Brigadier (commodore, with a distinguishing pendant) fell as retreating to the quarter-deck.

"I pushed immediately on for the quarter-deck, where I found Captain Berry in possession of the poop, and the Spanish ensign hauling down.

"I passed with my people and Lieutenant Pearson, on the larboard gangway to the forecastle, where I met two or three Spanish officers, prisoners to my seamen; they delivered me their swords.

"A fire of pistols or muskets opening from the stern galley of the 'San Josef,' I directed the soldiers to fire into her stern; and, calling to Captain Miller, ordered him to send more men into the 'San Nicolas,' and directed my men to board the first-rate, which was done in an instant, Captain Berry assisting me into the main-chains.

"At this moment, a Spanish officer looked over the quarter-deck rail, and said they surrendered.

"From this most welcome intelligence it was not long before I was on the quarter-deck; where the Spanish captain, with a most polite bow, presented me his sword and said the admiral was dying of his wounds.

"I asked him on his honour if the ship was surrendered.

"He declared she was, on which I gave him my hand, and desired him to call on his officers and ship's company, and tell them of it, which he did, and on the quarter-deck of a Spanish first-rate, extavagant as the tale may seem, did I receive the swords of vanquished Spaniards, which, as I received, I gave to William Fearney, one of my bargemen, who put them with the greatest *sang froid* under his arm.

"I was surrounded by Captain Berry, Lieutenant Pearson of the 69th, John Sykes, John Thompson,

---

* Some companies of the 69th were then serving as marines.

Francis Cooke, all old Agamemnons, and several other brave men, seamen and soldiers."*

Twenty-four of the "Captain's" men were killed, and 56 wounded; a fourth part of the loss sustained by the whole squadron falling upon this ship. Nelson received only a few bruises.

The Spaniards had still eighteen or nineteen ships, which had suffered little or no injury; that part of the fleet which had been separated from the main body in the morning was now coming up, and Sir John Jervis made signal to bring to.

His ships could not have formed without abandoning those which they had captured, and running to leeward; the "Captain" was lying a perfect wreck on board her two prizes; and many of the other vessels were so shattered in their masts and rigging, as to be wholly unmanageable.

The Spanish admiral, meantime, according to his official account, being altogether undecided, in his own opinion respecting the state of the fleet, inquired of his captains whether it was proper to renew the action; nine of them answered explicitly that it was not; others replied that it was expedient to delay the business. The "Pelayo" and the "Principe Conquistador" were the only ships that were for fighting.

In this engagement, four vessels were taken, two of which carried 112 guns each; one 84, and one 74. On board the English fleet, the loss amounted to about 300, in killed and wounded; while the loss on board the Spanish ships that were taken, amounted to double that number.

As soon as the action was discontinued, Nelson went on board the admiral's ship.

Sir John Jervis received him on the quarter-deck, took him in his arms, and said he could not sufficiently thank him.

For this victory the commander-in-chief was rewarded with the title of Earl St. Vincent.

In the official letter of Sir John Jervis, Nelson was not mentioned.

It is said that the admiral had seen an instance of the ill consequence of such selections, after Lord Howe's victory; and, therefore, would not name any individual, thinking it proper to speak to the public only in terms of general approbation.

His private letter to the first lord of the admiralty was, with his consent, published for the first time, in a "Life of Nelson," by Mr. Harrison.

Here, it is said, that "Commodore Nelson, who was in the rear, on the starboard tack, took the lead on the larboard, and contributed very much to the fortune of the day."

It is also said, that he boarded the two Spanish ships successively; but the fact that Nelson wore without orders, and thus planned as well as accomplished the victory, is not explicitly stated.

---

* This document, which we quote from "Naval Chronicles," Vol. II, is said to have been signed by Horatio Nelson, Ralph Willett Miller, and T. Berry.

Perhaps it was thought proper to pass over this part of his conduct in silence, as a splendid fault; but such an example is not dangerous.

The author of the work in which this letter was first made public, protests against those over-zealous friends, "who would make the action rather appear as Nelson's battle, than that of the illustrious commander-in-chief, who derives from it so deservedly his title."

"No man," he says, "ever has less needed, or less desired, to strip a single leaf from the honoured wreath of any other hero, with the vain hope of augmenting his own, than the immortal Nelson; no man ever more merited the whole of that which a generous nation unanimously presented to Sir J. Jervis, than the Earl St. Vincent."

Certainly Earl St. Vincent well deserved the reward which he received; but it is not detracting from his merit to say, that Nelson is fully entitled to as much fame from this action as the commander-in-chief; not because the brunt of the action fell upon him; not because he was engaged with all the four ships which were taken, and took two of them, it may almost be said, with his own hand, but because the decisive movement, which enabled him to perform all this, and by which the action became a victory, was executed in neglect of orders, upon his own judgment, and at his peril.

Earl St. Vincent deserved his earldom: but it is not to the honour of those by whom titles were distributed in those days, that Nelson never obtained the rank of earl for either of those victories which he lived to enjoy, though the one was the most complete and glorious in the annals of naval history, and the other the most important in its consequences of any which was achieved during the whole war.

Nelson, who, before the action was known in England, had been advanced to the rank of rear-admiral, had the Order of the Bath given him.

The sword of the Spanish rear-admiral, which Sir John Jervis insisted upon his keeping, he presented to the mayor and corporation of Norwich, saying, that he knew no place where it could give him or his family more pleasure to have it kept than in the capital city of the county where he was born.

The freedom of that city was voted him on this occasion.

But of all the numerous congratulations which he received, none could have affected him with deeper delight than that which came from his venerable father.

"I thank my God," said this excellent man, "with all the power of a grateful soul, for the mercies he has most graciously bestowed on me in preserving you. Not only my few acquaintances here, but the people in general, met me at every corner with such handsome words, that I was obliged to retire from the public eye. The height of glory to which your professional judgment, united with a proper degree of bravery, guarded by Providence, has raised you, few sons, my dear child, attain to, and fewer fathers live to see.

"Tears of joy have involuntarily trickled down my furrowed cheeks: who could stand the force of such general congratulation?

"The name and services of Nelson have sounded through this city, from the common ballad-singer to the public theatre."

The good old man concluded by telling him, that the field of glory, in which he had so long been conspicuous, was still open, and by giving him his blessing.

* * * * *

A little before four o'clock in the afternoon, the signal for bringing to was made on the "Victory," and the work of securing prizes and disabled ships began.

Only a few shots were exchanged by any of the vessels afterwards.

The Spanish vessels captured were the "Salvador del Mundo," the "San Josef," the "San Nicolas," and the "Isidro."

In this action 74 men were killed on the English fleet and 227 wounded.

The loss of life on the Spanish ships was much greater; 200 being killed and wounded on the "Santissima Trinidad" alone.

On the 16th of the month, the English fleet and prizes anchored in Lagos Bay, where about 3,000 prisoners were sent ashore.

For this action Admiral Sir John Jervis was created a peer under the title of Earl St. Vincent, and a pension of £3,000 per annum was allowed him.

Notwithstanding Commodore Nelson was not mentioned in Admiral Jervis's letter announcing the victory, he was made a Knight of the Bath.

A few days afterwards the great Spanish ship "Santissima Trinidad," of 130 guns, was trying to regain some Spanish harbour, having escaped from the great fight in rather a crippled condition.

The British frigate "Terpsichore," of 32 guns, Captain Richard Bowen, appeared in sight, and the English captain having heard of the great victory guessed at once what the Spanish vessel was, so he cleared his decks for action, and bore down upon the enemy.

This was on the morning of the 28th of February, and about ten o'clock in the morning the little British frigate began to fire upon the gigantic Spanish vessel.

Captain Bowen knew very well that one broadside from the enemy would blow his little craft out of the water; so he kept crossing the stern of the "Santissima Trinidad," firing and tacking as fast as possible, carefully keeping clear of her broadside.

Bowen kept firing till half-past twelve at night, when he was obliged to leave off in order that his men might fill cartridge cases.

That done, he continued to annoy his gigantic foe till the 2nd of March, when twelve Spanish men-of-war appeared in sight, and Bowen judged it prudent to sail for Tangier Bay.

Had not this reinforcement appeared it is quite possible that the Spanish four-decker would have struck to the English frigate.

On the 17th of February, an English squadron of five ships, two frigates and five sloops, under command of Rear-Admiral John Harvey, in the "Prince of Wales," took possession of the island of Trinidad.

Four Spanish ships of the line and one frigate were burnt in the bay by the Spaniards to prevent them from falling into the hands of the English.

On the 22nd of February, the French 40-gun frigate, "Resistance," and the 22-gun corvette "Constance," were captured off Brest by the English 38-gun frigate "San Fiorenza," Captain Neale, and the 36-gun frigate "Nymphe," Captain Cook. These vessels were two of a fleet that had just been to the coast of England, where they had landed 1,200 men, most of them galley-slaves.

A naval medal was given for the action in which they were captured. On the 16th of April, the French 36-gun frigate "Hermione," was driven on shore and destroyed off St. Domingo by the squadron under command of Vice-Admiral Sir Hyde Parker.

In Conil Bay, on the 26th of April, the "Irresistible," Captain Martin, and the "Emerald," Captain Berkley, after a sharp action, captured the Spanish frigate "Ninfa," and sunk the frigate "Santa Elena."

The "Ninfa" was added to the English navy under the name of "Hamadryad."

The French 14-gun brig "Mutiné," lying in the roads of Santa Cruz, Teneriffe, was attacked by a party of Englishmen in boats led by Lieutenant Thomas M. Hardy of the "Minerva," on the 26th of May, and captured. This exploit was deserving of much praise, and Lieutenant Hardy was promoted to the command of the brig he had captured.

CRESTS OF VESSELS IN THE ROYAL NAVY (A.D. 1870).

During the early part of the month of July, the fleet commanded by Earl St. Vincent was blockading the Spanish fleet at Cadiz. While there, an attack was made by the English on the town of St. Sebastian.

It was led by Rear-Admiral Nelson, who had charge of the in-shore squadron.

In a hand to hand encounter, between the crew of Nelson's boat and that of the Spanish commodore, Nelson's life was saved by John Sykes,* the cox-

"Terror," and "Thunder," mortar vessels, protected by the "Theseus," "Terpsichore," and "Emerald" frigates. Considerable damage was done to the town, with a loss to the English fleet of three killed, and twenty wounded.

On the 16th of July, a frigate squadron under Sir John Warren destroyed the French frigate "Calliope," 28 guns, and burnt several vessels which were under its convoy.

In the destruction of the frigate, the 18-gun

DUNCAN'S FLEET OFF CAMPERDOWN.

swain of the boat, who saved the admiral at the expense of a wound on the head.

The Spanish barge was after a desperate encounter captured, but not till eighteen of her crew had been killed and nearly all the others wounded.

On the English side Captain Freemantle, Lieutenants Selby, Rowe, and Grant, Master's Mate Pearson, Midshipman Tooley, and Coxswain John Sykes, were wounded.

This occurred on the 3rd of July; on the 5th, the place was again bombarded by the "Stromboli,"

* This man was killed on the 1st of May, 1798, by the bursting of a gun. He had been promoted to the rank of gunner on board the "Andromache," and Nelson intended to procure him a lieutenancy when he had served longer. Sykes was a native of Lincoln.

brig "Sylph," Captain White, had the principal share.

About this time, Rear-Admiral Nelson was dispatched with a squadron to attack Santa Cruz, Teneriffe, and arrived off that island on the 20th of July.

The following were the vessels of which the squadron consisted:—

Theseus	74 guns .	{ Rear-Admiral Nelson. { Captain R. W. Miller.
Culloden	74 ,, . .	,, T. Troubridge.
Zealous	74 ,, . .	,, Samuel Hood.
Seahorse	38 ,, . .	,, Thos. F. Freemantle.
Emerald	36 ,, . .	,, John Waller.
Terpsichore	32 ,, . .	,, Richard Bowen.
Fox	. Cutter .	Lieut. John Gibson.

A mortar boat accompanied them, and on the 24th of July, the "Leander," 50 guns, joined the squadron.

About five o'clock in the afternoon of the 24th, the large ships anchored at a distance of six miles to the north-east of the town, the frigates being much nearer. At six the signal was made to prepare the boats.

Nelson then sat down, and wrote to Lord St. Vincent the last letter his *right hand* ever penned.

In it he said—"This night I, humble as I am, command the whole, destined to land under the batteries of the town; and to-morrow my head will probably be crowned either with laurel or cypress."

He was in rather a desponding mood, and called Lieutenant Nisbet, his stepson, into the cabin, to assist in arranging and destroying Lady Nelson's letters.

Young Nesbit was armed, ready to accompany the boats, and Nelson, on perceiving this, entreated him to remain on board.

"Should we both fall, Josiah, what would become of your poor mother? The care of the 'Theseus' falls to you; stay, therefore, and take charge of her."

To this appeal, Nesbit replied—

"Sir, the ship must take care of herself. I will go with you to-night, if I never go again."

After this, he met his captain at supper, on board the "Seahorse," commanded by Captain Freemantle, who had lately been married, and whose wife presided at the table.

About eleven o'clock, the "Fox" cutter, with the boats, stood in towards the shore, in six divisions, as silently as possible.

Till half-past one, all went well, when, being within half gun-shot of the batteries, Nelson ordered the men to give three cheers, and make a dash for the landing-place.

The Spaniards were on the watch, and answered the cheers by opening fire from forty heavy guns.

But that was not likely to stop the British sailors, who bent to their oars and made for land.

The night was so dark that most of them, instead of touching at the mole, were run on the beach in a raging surf.

Nelson's boat, with five or six others, found the mole, which was instantly stormed by the sailors, though defended by something like 400 Spanish sailors.

Nelson himself was in the act of stepping out of the boat, drawing his sword while doing so, when he received a shot in the right elbow.

He fell, dropping his sword, which, however, the next moment, he caught with his left hand, vowing he would never part with it.

Lieutenant Nesbit took the wounded hero in his arms, laid him down in the bottom of the boat, and bound his silk necktie round the arm above the wound, thus, to a great extent, checking the flow of blood, and, in all probability, saving Nelson's life.

A sailor, named Lovell, constructed a sling for the broken limb out of strips of his shirt, and then Nesbit got a few men together, and took the boat close under the battery, that they might be out of the reach of its terrific fire.

About that time, the "Fox" cutter, with 180 men packed on board of her, was struck by a shot and filled.

Only 83 of the poor fellows were saved, many of them being rescued by the exertions of Nelson himself.

But the pain from his wound was so great that he was obliged to be taken on board ship, when it was found necessary to amputate his arm.

The principal forts and defences of the town still remained to be captured, and the troops were now exposed to a fire that threatened to annihilate them.

It soon became doubtful about the majority of them being got off the island, and Captain Freemantle beat a parley. He promised that should the English be allowed to embark, with their arms, they would not attack any other of the Canary Islands.

To this the Spanish governor agreed, and gave each of his enemies a ration of wine and biscuit.

Amongst the killed was Captain Richard Bowen, of the frigate "Terpsichore," who has before been mentioned in this history.

Lieutenant Gibson and several other valuable officers were also lost.

The total loss of the English in killed, wounded, and drowned, was 250 men.

On the 10th of August, the 38-gun frigate "Arethusa," Captain Thomas Wolley, captured the French corvette "Gaieté," which was added to the English navy.

The "Gaieté" made no attempt to escape when chased by the frigate, but fought with great determination for nearly an hour.

Several minor battles between single ships took place. For instance, the "Alexandrian," a 6-gun schooner, commanded by Lieutenant Senhouse, was sent on a cruise to put down French privateers.

The "Alexandrian" captured the "Coq," of 6 guns, after a sharp action, on the 5th of August; the same evening she chased and engaged a second vessel, which escaped.

Again, in the forenoon of October 4th, while cruising off Barbadoes, the "Alexandrian" engaged and captured the French vessel "Epicharis," of 8 guns, and, after a sharp action of fifty minutes, captured her.

The crew of the "Alexandrian" consisted of 40 men, their loss being 1 killed and 4 wounded; the "Epicharis" had 74 men on board, of whom 4 were killed and 12 severely wounded.

Commander John Pulling, of the 16-gun brig "Penguin," also greatly distinguished himself on the 21st of August by an action in the Channel with two brigs.

The sea was so rough that the English sailors were knee deep in water as they worked their guns, but that mattered not; they continued to fire away till both the enemy struck.

One of them was the French 18-gun brig "Oiseau;" the other the 14-gun brig "Express," lately taken from the English by the "Oiseau."

The French government having it in contemplation to make a landing in Ireland, the finely-equipped Texel fleet was sent to sea, under Admiral Duncan, as a powerful division.

But the best fleet that Holland could furnish was incompetent to contend with the inferior ships of our navy; for of such were the fleet of Admiral Duncan composed, with the exception of three or four that were ordered to join him from Portsmouth.

They sailed on the 8th of October, 1797, at which time the admiral was lying at Yarmouth, having left a small squadron, under the command of Captain Trollope, in the "Russell," to cruise off the Texel till his return.

Mr. Hamilton was, however, despatched to the admiral, and on the 10th conveyed by signal, from the back of Yarmouth Sands, to the flag-ship, that the enemy was at sea.

Not a moment was lost to meet them; and early on the 11th, Duncan arrived on his old cruising station, and saw the "Russell" to leeward, with the signal flying for an enemy's fleet.

He instantly bore up, and at eleven o'clock got sight of the object of his anxious wishes, which for two long years he had watched, yet never expected to see outside of the Nieu Diep.

There was no delay, no unnecessary manœuvres in forming lines, or making dispositions; but Duncan dashed at them, like a sea lion on its prey; and at half-past twelve at noon, cut through their line, and got between them and their own coast.

No means of retreat being allowed, a general action shortly ensued, and, by the greatest part of the Dutch fleet, was bravely maintained.

A wish on their part was, however, early shown to withdraw from their antagonists, and they kept constantly edging away for their own shore, until their progress was arrested in nine-fathom water, off the heights or sand-hills of Camperdown, about three leagues from the land.

Vice-Admiral Onslow, in the "Monarch," bore down in the most gallant style on the enemy's rear, broke through his line, and engaged his opponent to leeward, the wind being dead on the land at west-north-west.

Duncan selected the Dutch admiral, De Winter, who had his flag in the "Vryheid," of 74 guns, as his opponent; in running down to her, however, he was opposed by the "States-General," a Dutch 74, whose fire the "Venerable" soon silenced, forced him to quit the line, and then proceeded to the "Vryheid," which he engaged for two hours and a half, until that ship was completely dismasted.

The action had now become general between the fleets, with the exception of two or three ships on either side, whose captains preserved a cautious distance.

De Winter displayed, in his own person, the most undaunted valour, and was well supported by some of his countrymen; but was compelled at length to yield to superior skill—it would be untrue to say superior bravery.

About the same time that Vice-Admiral Onslow had silenced his opponent, the Dutch vice-admiral and the whole of his fleet were thrown into complete confusion, and twelve sail struck their colours, and surrendered; but owing to the bad weather which ensued, and the disabled state of our ships, only nine were secured, and these were in such a wrecked condition, that they could scarcely be got into an English port.

This was one of the severest and most decisive battles ever fought between the two nations, and produced an effect on the maritime powers of Europe, of the highest advantage to the character and interests of Great Britain.

The loss sustained in the British fleet was upwards of seven hundred killed and wounded; that of the Dutch was never correctly known, but in each of the two flag-ships there were two hundred and fifty killed and wounded.

De Winter behaved nobly, and was the only person on board his ship that was not either killed or wounded.

When conducted a prisoner on board the "Venerable," he presented his sword to Admiral Duncan, who gallantly returned it to him with as gallant a compliment.

When the two admirals were seen together it was universally acknowledged that they were the finest-looking men in both fleets.

After the duties of the day were all done, these brave admirals dined together in the most amicable manner, and concluded the evening by *playing a friendly rubber at whist*.

It has been remarked, and with some truth, that the laconic manner in which the gallant admiral first announced his success to the Admiralty board, in no small degree resembled the celebrated letter of Captain Walton, written in consequence of his having attacked, taken, or destroyed a detachment of the Spanish fleet off Syracuse:—

"We have taken and destroyed all the Spanish ships and vessels that were upon the coast, the number as per margin.

"Yours, &c.,
"G. Walton."

That which we bring into comparison with it was to the following purport:—

"'Venerable,' off the coast of Holland, the 12th of October.
"Camperdown, E.S.E. eight miles.

"Sir,
"I have the pleasure to acquaint you, for the

information of the Lords Commissioners of the Admiralty, that at nine o'clock this morning I got sight of the Dutch fleet; at half-past twelve I passed through their line, and the action commenced, which has been very severe. The admiral's ship is dismasted, and has struck, as have several others, and one on fire. I shall send Captain Fairfax with the particulars the moment I can spare him.

"I am, &c.,
"Adam Duncan."

The gallant admiral's address to the officers of his fleet, when they came on board his ship for his final instructions, previous to this memorable engagement, was couched in the following laconic and humorous manner:—

"Gentlemen of my fleet, you see a very severe *Winter* fast approaching; and I have only to advise you to keep up a good fire."

For their meritorious conduct in this engagement, Admiral Duncan, his officers, and seamen, received the thanks of both houses of parliament.

The admiral was honoured by his Majesty with the dignity of a viscount of Great Britain, and a pension of £3,000 per annum for his public services.

Vice-Admiral Onslow was created a baronet.

The City of London presented Admiral Duncan with its freedom, and a sword of the value of 200 guineas; and to Vice-Admiral Onslow the freedom, with a sword of the value of 100 guineas.

His Majesty went in state to St. Paul's Cathedral, to return thanks for the victory, and to deposit there the flags taken on that and other eminent occasions, Lord Duncan carrying the one he had taken in person.

After this victory, the Dutch ceased to be a maritime nation, for their navy was now destroyed, with the exception of four or five ships, which, with Admiral Storey, in the "States General," escaped from the scene of action after having struck, and, getting into the Texel, contrived to make their peace with the Gallo-Batavian government, by proving that their only means of safety was in flight.

The "Delft," one of the ships taken, was in so shattered a state, that, after the greatest exertion for five days to keep her from sinking, all hope of saving her was given up.

The English prize-officer called Mr. Hieberg, who had been first lieutenant of the "Delft," and who remained on board along with the sick and wounded prisoners, who were not in a condition to be removed, and represented that it was impossible to save all; that he intended, at a certain signal, to throw himself, with his men, into the long-boat; and he invited Hieberg to do the same.

"What!" exclaimed Hieberg, "and leave these unfortunate men?" pointing to his wounded countrymen, who it had been necessary to bring on deck, as the hold was already full of water. "No, no; go, and leave us to perish together."

CAPTAIN PELLEW BOARDING THE "HYÆNA."

The English officer, affected by the generosity of Hieberg's answer, replied, "God bless you, my brave fellow! Here is my hand; I give you my word I will stay with you."

He then caused his own men to leave the ship, and remained himself behind to assist the Dutch. The "Russell" soon sent her boats to their assistance, which brought off as many as could leap on board of them.

These boats lost no time in making a second voyage with equal success. The "Delft" was now cleared of all but Hieberg, and the English officer, with three Dutch subalterns, and about thirty seamen, most of them so ill from their wounds as to be unable to move.

While still cherishing the hope that the boats would come a third time, the fatal moment arrived, and on a sudden the "Delft" went down.

The English officer sprang into the sea, and swam to his own ship; but the unfortunate Hieberg perished, a victim of his courage and humanity.

It was in this glorious action that the following instances of daring bravery occurred among the many which so nobly distinguished the character of the British tar.

During the time the "Venerable" was so closely engaged with the "Vryheid," the flag halliards of the former were shot away.

A young man, named John Crawford, instantly

ascended the mast for again hoisting the colours; and to prevent a recurrence of a similar accident, he actually nailed the flag to the maintop-gallant mast-head, declaring that "It should not come down again but with the mast!"

This intrepid youth was a native of Sunderland, which town prepared a medal at its own expense, to be presented to him for his heroic conduct on this occasion.

A marine of the name of Covey, was carried down to the cockpit, deprived of both his legs; and it was necessary, some hours after, to amputate still higher.

"I suppose," said Covey, "those scissors will finish the business of the bullet, Master Mate?"

"Indeed, my brave fellow," cried the surgeon, "there is some fear of it."

"Well, never mind," said Covey, "I've lost my legs, to be sure, and mayhap may lose my life; but we beat the Dutch, my boy, we have beat the Dutch; this blessed day my legs have been shot off, so I'll have another cheer for it—huzza!—huzza!"

Covey recovered, and was cook of one of the ships in ordinary at Portsmouth, where he died, in the year 1805.

* * * *

The following account of the battle of Camperdown was written to the Dutch Government by Admiral Winter:—

PORTRAIT OF NELSON.

With the deepest impressure of grief I inform you, that yesterday morning, October 11, we discovered the English fleet; I immediately formed into a line of battle on the starboard tack, and did everything in my power to keep the ships as close together as possible; but my orders for this purpose could not be completely obeyed, on account of the unsteadiness of the wind, the high sea, and the bad sailing of some of the vessels.

At eleven o'clock the enemy attacked the rear of the line, which they broke through with great resolution.

This I saw with some pleasure, because I always entertained hopes that the rest of the fleet would close up, and therefore I made the signal to the headmost ships to slacken sail: this, however, was of no avail; we came into action successively in an irregular manner: my ship was engaged at one time with two, and afterwards with three: the "Hercules," which was the second in the line from me, took fire and drove towards me, by which means I was obliged to shift my station, and approach a fourth English, being that of the admiral.

All my running rigging was now torn to pieces; and while I was endeavouring to make a signal for some of the ships to come to my assistance, the flag line was shot from my hand.

In the meanwhile the "Waassenaar," by the captain being wounded early, and the loss of a great many people, was obliged to strike; as did also the "Haarlem," the "De Vries," the "Delft," and the "Jupiter," whose mainmast went by the board: this I was in some measure prevented from seeing, by the thickness of the smoke, and the closeness with which I was engaged.

Everything being at length shot away, and having lost a considerable number of men, I nevertheless endeavoured to force my way through the five English ships, with a view of making for port, or of giving an opportunity to some of the fleet not yet disabled to afford me assistance; but my attempt was not successful.

At two o'clock all my three masts went overboard, but I still continued to defend the wreck for half an hour; when, having no further hope, seeing the rest of the ships at a distance, and finding that my flag was shot away, I ordered the people, one half of whom I had already lost, to stop firing; and at three o'clock an English frigate approached me, the captain of which came on board and carried me to Admiral Duncan.

The "Gelykheid" lay to the windward of me; I saw also that she made no longer any resistance, and had ceased firing; her running rigging was all in pieces, but why she struck I know as little as I do of the "Admiral de Vries," the "Delft," and the "Haarlem."

The "Hercules" lost her mizen-mast, and took fire, which brought her, as well as me, into the midst of the English fleet, and she has also been captured.

With the behaviour of my officers and crew I am perfectly satisfied; I recommend them to you, as men who defended themselves to the last, and continued faithful to their admiral.

Both sides fought with fury, and many men have fallen. The English also have sustained great loss.

They had returned to Yarmouth with nine sail of the line, in order to refit.

On Saturday evening, they received intelligence that we were at sea. On Monday they again sailed, having revictualled in twenty-four hours, and having received eight other ships from Portsmouth and the Downs, in the room of the eight which were under repair.

They had altogether sixteen sail of the line, among which there was only one 50, the greater part of the rest being of 74 guns.

Behold, then, the most unfortunate day of my life. Every exertion that depended on manœuvre, or personal courage, was made by myself, and many others, but in vain.

Our enemies respect us on account of the obstinacy of our defence. No action can have been so bloody, for it was fatal to us.

I shall have the honour of sending you a more accurate and minute account as soon as I find an opportunity.

I at present take advantage of a permission from the English admiral to give you this short notice, and to call your care and attention to a number of prisoners, whose bravery and courage deserved a better fate, and particularly to the crew of the "Vryheid."

I recommend to you the poor widows and orphans, and the wife and children of my worthy Captain Van Rossum, whose thigh was shot off at half-past two. He is still alive; but there are little hopes of his recovery.

Two cadets, one of whom is my nephew, have each lost their left leg. The rest of my officers are well. Cranenburg, the lieutenant of marines, only is dead.

Of the state of the other ships I can give no account, nor do I know what loss they have sustained; the English do not know themselves. I am informed, however, that Vice-Admiral Reintjies has been wounded also, and that he is on board Admiral Onslow's ship. Meurer is well; but Captain Holland, of the "Waassenaar," was mortally wounded in the begi n ing of the action, and lost a great many men.

* * * * *

Some time after, Admiral de Winter sent a detailed account of the action to the Batavian government, wherein he relates minutely the situation of his fleet, with the various manœuvres performed before and during the action, and concludes in the following manner:—

"Thus the battle of the 11th of October, 1797, was ended by the ceasing of the fire from the Batavian ship 'Vryheid,' which to the last, nobly contended to preserve what she so honourably lost, the Batavian colours.

"The bad success of this engagement is to be attributed to the following causes:—

"1st. The English force, although equal in number, exceeded that of the Batavians as to ships of the line.

"2ndly. The English ships having been together at sea during the space of nineteen weeks, the particular capacity of all the ships was known to them, with relation to each other, which, it must be allowed, is of the utmost importance and advantage in nautical manœuvres. This was not the case with the Dutch.

"3rdly. The advantage of the attack; and—

"4thly. The early retreat of six Batavian ships from the action; and among those that remained were four very indifferent sailers, to which may be principally attributed the breaking of the line.

"Add to this, that having lost the advantage of the attack, and being partly forsaken, it becomes a matter of less surprise that the victory turned out so decisively in favour of the English.

"Upon the whole, without magnifying Batavian courage beyond what was exemplified in this memorable engagement, and admitting that casual circumstances had been equally favourable to them as to the English, had Admiral de Winter's signals been obeyed and executed with the same promptitude as Admiral Duncan's were, it is no improbable conjecture that some of the British fleet would at this time have been moored in the Texel, as a memento of Batavian prowess, and a monument to the memory of the 11th October, 1797."

Admiral Duncan was descended from an ancient and respectable family long settled at Lundie, in the county of Perthshire, North Britain. He was born on the 1st of July, 1731, and received the rudiments of his education at Dundee.

In his earliest infancy, he is said most strongly to have displayed that mildness and suavity of manners which marked his demeanour in all situations of life.

He entered into the navy in 1746, or the following year, when he was put under the command of Robert Haldane, his relation, who then commanded the "Shoreham" frigate.

After the cessation of hostilities, he entered, in 1749, as a midshipman on board the "Centurion," of 50 guns, which was then equipping to receive the broad pennant of Commodore Keppel, who was appointed commander-in-chief on the Mediterranean station, for the customary period of three years.

From this time his successes were uninterrupted, till he gained for himself the high and honourable name of Admiral.

On the 25th of October, the "Hyæna" was boarded, and, after a severe fight, captured off Teneriffe by the "Indefatigable," 44 guns, Captain Edward Pellew. The "Hyæna" had previously been captured from the English.

On the 20th of December, the 18-pounder 36-gun frigate "Phœbe," Captain Robert Barlow, captured the French 12-pounder 36-gun frigate "Néréide," and, on the same day, the 10-gun brig "Growler" was captured off Dungeness by two French armed luggers.

On the 29th of December, the 20-gun corvette "Daphne" was captured by the 44-gun frigate

"Anson," Captain Durham. The "Daphne" had been captured from the English.

During the year 1797, the English navy lost four ships by being captured by the enemy, and one by being destroyed. Eight were wrecked and five foundered.

The year 1797 was made remarkable in the annals of the British navy by the mutinies at Portsmouth and the Nore.

Regarding the insubordination at Spithead, it seems that as early as the latter end of February, 1797, Lord Howe was petitioned by the seamen of the Channel fleet to use his influence to procure them an increase of wages, but as all the petitions seemed to be written by one hand, while not one of them bore any signature, no notice was taken for some time.

After a while, however, Lord Howe sent Rear-Admiral Seymour to ascertain if any discontent existed among the men; and the reply made by that officer was so favourable, that it was generally considered that some one had been endeavouring to hoax the officials.

In the meantime the seamen, not being aware that their petitions were looked upon as forgeries, imagined that Lord Howe's silence proceeded from indifference, not being aware of the fact that the gallant Lord had, after receiving Admiral Seymour's report, forwarded the documents to the government.

Matters stood thus when Lord Bridport, to whom Howe had just given up command of the Channel fleet, signalled on the 15th of April to prepare for sea.

Then the mutiny broke out; the seamen of the "Royal George," instead of obeying the signal, ran up the rigging and gave three loud cheers, which were answered throughout the fleet, and showed how general was the discontent that prevailed.

Of course the officers of the fleet were utterly astonished at this act of disobedience, especially when they found all their efforts to persuade the men to return to their duty were unavailing.

The next day, two men were appointed from each ship's company to act as delegates, and these men selected, as the place for their deliberations, the state cabin of the "Queen Charlotte."

On the following morning (April 17th), every man in the fleet swore an oath to support the cause. The officers who had distinguished themselves by tyranny were sent on shore, and ropes were fixed at the yard-arms as a warning to the others.

The delegates were all this time very busy on board the "Queen Charlotte," drawing up two petitions, which were signed and sent—one to the Admiralty, and the other to the House of Commons.

From all that can be learnt on the subject, these petitions were framed in very mild and respectful language.

They requested an advance of wages, that the sick should receive better attention, that their food should be of a better quality, and that fresh vegetables should be served out while at anchor.

They also demanded that the weights and measures by which their food was issued should be the same as those used in commerce; for it seems that, before this, the seaman's pound was only fourteen ounces, and the pint considerably less than imperial measure.

The difference between the weights and measures fell to the share of the purser, who received no other remuneration.

A great deal of discussion took place on these terms, and, on the 21st of April, after an interview with the delegates, Admiral Gardner lost his temper. He drew his sword, and threatened one of the delegates with it, vowing he would have all of them hanged, together with every fifth man in the fleet.

The delegates withdrew to their various ships, hoisted the red flag, and loaded their cannon. They also sent most of the officers on shore.

Things went on in this way till the 14th of May, when Lord Howe arrived from London, with powers to grant all the terms demanded.

On the 15th, the delegates went on shore to meet him, and, after the business had been settled, they carried him on their shoulders through the town.

On the 16th, the fleet weighed anchor and stood out to sea.

The mutiny at the Nore also assumed a methodical shape.

Each ship had a committee of twelve men, who governed the vessel, and went to a conference each day at Sheerness.

Every officer was deprived of command.

Concessions were then made to the mutineers which they would not accept, but demanded terms which the Board of Admiralty refused to grant.

Without the knowledge of the officers a vast conspiracy had been organized amongst those from whom the least danger had been expected, and at a time when England was almost entirely depending for a national existence on the exertions of her brave seamen.

For three or four years Lord Howe and other high officers of the navy had received anonymous communications, informing them of what would certainly happen should there not be some change made in the treatment of English seamen; but with the usual heedlessness of those in power to those who are not, no attention was paid to these communications.

The demands for higher pay, more food and civility from officers, and a greater pension, made by the men, was promised by the government, and the mutiny subsided, to the great joy of all.

Admiral Bridport's fleet of twenty-one ships of the line sailed for the blockade of Brest.

This satisfactory state of affairs was of but short duration.

On the 22nd of May, the mutiny broke out in the fleet at the Nore, and assumed a methodical shape. Each ship had a committee of twelve men, who governed the vessel and went to a conference each day at Sheerness.

Every officer was deprived of command, but still the strictest order was maintained in the fleet.

More concessions were made to the mutineers, and refused by them.

They demanded terms which the Board of Admiralty would not give.

The chief mutineer of the fleet was a man named Richard Parker. He had been a small shopkeeper, in Scotland, where he had been confined in Perth gaol for debt.

To regain his liberty, he took the parish bounty of £30, and joined the navy.

He had been in the navy about two years when the mutiny commenced, and had been appointed a petty officer.

On the 6th of June, a proclamation was issued by Government forbidding all intercourse with the mutineers, either personally or by letter, on pain of death.

Several men-of-war and gunboats were manned with volunteers, the batteries of Gravesend and Tilbury were furnished with furnaces for heating shot, and the buoys at the Nore were removed.

A misunderstanding, or controversy, then arose between the mutineers, some of them being more moderate in their demands than others.

The seamen of the "Ajax," "Standard," and "Nassau" then returned to their duty by striking the flag of revolt and hoisting the Union Jack.

The crew of the "Sandwich" then gave up Richard Parker to the authorities, and he was confined in Maidstone gaol.

The other crews soon after surrendered unconditionally.

On the 28th of June, Johnson and Ashley, two of the mutineers, were hanged; and on the 30th, Richard Parker was also executed on board the "Sandwich," lying off Sheerness.

On the 9th of October, a general mutiny broke out in the fleet at the Cape of Good Hope, but it ended three days after on the crews being informed that the seamen at Spithead had gained the concessions they demanded.

On the 30th of November, the ship "La Tribune," 44 guns, was wrecked near the harbour of Halifax, Nova Scotia, and more than 240 persons were drowned.

This year, the 74-gun ship "Blenheim," Vice-Admiral Sir Thomas Troubridge, and the "Java," Captain George Pigot, that had been captured from the Dutch at Batavia under the name of "Maria Riggersbergen," are supposed to have foundered off the island of Roderigue, East India.

On reviewing the actual state of the British navy at this period, we find that very few large vessels were ordered to be built during the year 1797.

The reason for this was, that so many had been taken from the enemy.

For instance, during the year 1797, we took seven ships of the line and two frigates from the Dutch, five ships of the line and one frigate from the Spaniards, and three frigates from the French.

Of these eighteen vessels, seventeen were deemed worthy to be added to the British navy.

During the year, ten vessels belonging to the above nations were wrecked, destroyed, burnt, or driven ashore.

At the end of the year 1797, we had a grand total of 696 vessels of all kinds, either afloat, laid up for repairs, or building.

To man this fleet, supplies were voted for 120,000 seamen and marines, commanded by 24 admirals, 36 vice-admirals, 44 rear-admirals, 518 post-captains, 338 commanders, 2,030 lieutenants, and 492 masters.

We had lost altogether eighteen ships during the year, including five captured and destroyed by the enemy.

CRESTS OF VESSELS IN THE ROYAL NAVY (A.D. 1870).

CHAPTER XXIII.
CONTINUATION OF THE WAR IN 1798.

The year 1798 began with many encounters between single vessels and small detachments, in which the English sailors exhibited all their accustomed bravery, though it sometimes happened that the chances of war were against them.

On the 3rd of January, the English sloop "George," Lieutenant Mackey, was captured on her passage from Demerara to Martinique by two Spanish privateers.

Before surrendering, she had her master and seven men killed, and her commander and sixteen wounded, out of a crew of forty men.

Thirty-two men were killed on the privateers, and a large number wounded.

On the 5th of the same month, the frigate "Pomone," of 40 guns, Captain Reynolds, captured the French privateer "Chéri," off Ushant.

The "Chéri" was commanded by Captain Chassin, and carried 26 long heavy guns and 230 men. She sank soon after her crew had been taken out.

On the 8th of January, the brig "Kingfisher," of 18 guns, captured the French privateer "Betsey," of 16 guns.

The "Betsey" had one man killed and eight wounded.

The 36-gun frigate "Melampus," Captain Moore, captured the French 22-gun corvette

DESTRUCTION OF THE FRIGATE "PIQUE."

"Volage," on the 22nd of January, after a brief and sharp action in which the "Melampus" sustained but little injury, and had but five men wounded.

On the 17th of April, the 10-gun cutter "Recovery," commanded by Lieutenant Ross, captured the French 10-gun schooner privateer "Revanche," in the West Indies, after a cannonade that lasted three-quarters of an hour. The rigging of the "Revanche" was destroyed, three of her men killed, and nine wounded. The "Recovery" had not a man injured.

In 1798, Lord Bridport had the command of the Channel fleet; and on the 21st of April, he threw out a signal for Captain Hood in the "Mars," to give chase to a strange ship, which was evidently keeping near the French coast, for the purpose of endeavouring to escape through the passage Du Raz; it is probable she would have completely and speedily succeeded in this attempt, had not the wind been directly against her, and the tide at the same time setting in from the shore; she was, therefore, obliged to come to an anchor.

Captain Hood took immediate and effectual advantage of this circumstance; and it is difficult to decide, whether the skill which he manifested in laying the "Mars" alongside of the enemy, or the bravery with which he afterwards fought her, is most to be celebrated and commended.

The British captain was resolved to do the business so effectually, as to put it entirely out of the power of the French ship to escape, or even to resist for any length of time; and besides, it was to encourage and *accommodate* his brave crew by coming to close quarters, that he laid the "Mars" so near, that several of the lower deck ports were unshipped.

The enemy on his part was not dismayed by having a British man of war so near him; he fought his ship with great gallantry and coolness, and a most bloody conflict commenced and continued for upwards of an hour and a half; when British bravery received its due and just reward in the surrender of the French ship.

The prize was a valuable one; proving to be a quite new and well-finished ship—the "Hercules" of 74 guns, and 700 men.

She had sailed but a very short time before from L'Orient to join the Brest fleet. Her loss was dreadful: upwards of 400 men were killed or wounded; and on the side where, from being at anchor, she was exposed to the fire of the "Mars," her hull was burnt, and almost torn to pieces.

The loss on board the "Mars" was trifling, if the mere number of men killed and wounded is taken into account; but heavy and lamentable indeed, from the circumstance that the gallant Captain Hood fell in this well fought action.

Just before it terminated, he received a wound in the thigh, that proved mortal; he lived long enough, however, to be gratified in the hour of his dissolution, with the joyful news of the enemy's surrender, which he received with a smile, and expired as a Briton ought to die, whose life is devoted to his country, in the arms of that victory which had been won by his courage.

He had previously called for pen, ink, and paper, and made a short will.

Besides her captain, the "Mars" had 17 killed, 65 wounded, 5 of whom died of their wounds, and 8 missing.

It is probable that the last had fallen overboard during the heat and bustle of this dreadful engagement.

This, though a single action, was one of great importance.

The meeting of two ships of the line is a circumstance of rare occurrence, and its decision in our favour a brilliant ornament to our naval history.

The "Bellona" and "Courageux," the "Foudroyant" and "Pegasse," the "Mars" and "Hercules," the "Victorious" and the "Rivoli," will be recorded as the finest memorials of naval prowess, and a decided proof of our superiority on the ocean.

During the month of May two gallant exploits were performed in cutting out the enemy's vessels when lying in fancied security at anchor. The first was on the 13th, when the boats of the English 36-gun frigate "Flora," led by Lieutenant Russel, took the French 18-gun brig "Mondovi" in the port of Cerigo, in the Archipelago.

The second was on the 31st of May, when the boats of the 38-gun frigate "Hydra," Captain Laforey, burnt the French frigate "Confiante," of 36 guns, which had been chased on shore near Havre, and was under the protection of shore batteries, and a large army which had been assembled on the beach for the purpose of invading England.

On the 26th of June, the 18-pounder 36-gun frigate "Seahorse," Captain Foot, captured, after a chase of twelve hours, and an action of eight minutes, the French frigate "Sensible," of 36 guns, Captain Bourde, from Malta to Toulon. The "Sensible"* had eighteen men killed and thirty-five wounded.

The "Seahorse" had two killed and fifteen wounded. Among the passengers, twenty in number, on board the "Sensible," was the General Baraguay d'Hilliers. As soon as the "Seahorse" brought her prize into the English fleet, Lord St. Vincent sent six men from each of his ships on board the "Sensible," and in the short space of twelve hours had her completely equipped ready for sea.

Three days after this the British 38-gun frigate "Jason," and the 36-gun frigate "Pique," were cruising off the French coast, when they espied a stranger, and at once made chase.

The chase continued throughout the day, and at nine o'clock in the evening the "Pique" was within gunshot of the stranger, which proved to be the French 40-gun frigate "Seine," Captain Julien Gabriel Bigot.

Captain Milne, of the "Pique," ordered his men to open fire with the bow guns, and a constant cannonade was kept up till about eleven o'clock, when the British vessel ranged alongside the French vessel and gave a broadside, receiving one in return.

For two hours and a half the ships ran alongside each other, keeping up a constant exchange of broadsides, but at last the maintopmast of the "Pique" was shot away, and she was obliged to drop astern. But at that moment up came the "Jason," whose captain hailed the "Pique," and

---

* A brass field-piece, once taken from the Turks, and presented by Louis XVI. to the Knights of Malta, and now exhibited in the Tower of London, was found aboard this vessel.

desired her commander to drop anchor, but Captain Milne, who commanded the "Pique," did not thoroughly understand what was said, and pushed on till the ship grounded. Almost at the same instant the "Jason" ran aground, and soon afterwards the enemy was discovered in a similar condition.

A few more shots were fired, when, seeing the British frigate "Mermaid" fast approaching, the Frenchman struck his colours.

After the "Seine" had been taken possession of, the "Jason" was got off into deep water, as was also the "Seine;" but the unfortunate "Pique" was obliged to be destroyed, after her men and stores had been transferred to the prize.

The glory of this action certainly belongs to the "Pique," as that vessel did most of the fighting. The home authorities marked their sense of this by honourably acquitting the officers of blame in losing their vessel, and placing the captain in command of the "Seine," after she had been repaired and purchased into the British navy.

On the 15th of July, the 64-gun ship "Lion," Captain Manley Dixon, captured the Spanish 34-gun frigate "Santa Dorotea," one of a Spanish squadron under Commodore O'Neil, who did all in his power to save his consort from capture.

The "Dorotea" was added to the English navy, and the naval medal was given for the action in which she was captured.

It was well known during the latter part of the year 1797 and the beginning of 1798, that a great French fleet was being fitted out.

Some said that it was destined for an invasion of England, others that it was intended for an attack on our West Indian possessions; while a third party fancied that Buonaparte intended, after conquering Egypt, to pounce down upon our East Indian dominions.

The British Government very naturally wished to know as much as possible about these rumoured preparations, and with that view instructed Earl St. Vincent to send Vice-Admiral Sir Horatio Nelson, with a detachment of the Mediterranean fleet, to obtain information.

Nelson sailed from Cadiz on the 2nd of May, 1798, in the "Vanguard," and on the 4th arrived at Gibraltar, where he took command of the "Orion" and "Alexander," 74-gun ships, the "Terpsichore" and "Emerald" frigates, and the "Bonne Citoyenne" sloop.

On the 9th of April, all these vessels commenced their cruise.

By the 17th of the month they gained information that the French had collected a fleet of nineteen ships of the line at Toulon, in which Buonaparte was expected to embark, with a large army—destination kept a profound secret.

Fifteen of these vessels were already fit for sea, the admiral-in-chief being Brueys, under him Rear-Admirals Blanquet, Decrès, and Villeneuve.

During the French occupation of Milan the preceding year Buonaparte had taken from the great library there all the books he could find on matters connected with Oriental, and particularly Egyptian affairs; these, on arriving at Paris, were found to be plentifully marked with marginal notes, from which it may be guessed that the great general was then meditating the plan for subduing Egypt, which he submitted to the Republican Government early in 1798.

On the 5th of March he was appointed commander-in-chief of the expedition he had planned by Lareveillère, Lépaux, Merlin, and Barras, the military, naval, and financial ministers of the French nation.

But this was not known in England till long afterwards.

The expedition, when it was complete, consisted of seventy-two vessels of war of all kinds, and 400 transports, with 36,000 soldiers on board.

On the 19th of May this great fleet sailed from Toulon; Nelson and his squadron having been driven to take refuge on the coast of Sardinia by a dreadful gale, which damaged his ships considerably.

The French proceeded to Genoa, where more transports joined it, and then proceeded to Malta, which was in the possession of the Knights of St. John of Jerusalem.

A landing was effected on the 10th of June, and on the 12th the island capitulated, and was plundered by the French troops. They only remained a short time, and then re-embarked on the 19th, rather alarmed by the news that Nelson's squadron was in search of them.

The English admiral, with the least possible loss of time, had repaired the damages we have already spoken of, and on the 27th of May had put to sea again.

Nelson sailed for the rendezvous off Toulon, where he heard that the French fleet had sailed, but could learn nothing of its destination.

He was highly pleased, however, when, on the 5th of June, the brig "Mutine," 16 guns, arrived with the news that ten sail of the line and a 50-gun ship were on their way to join his squadron.

The brig also brought Nelson instructions what to do, and those instructions were, among other things, to proceed in quest of the Toulon fleet, "in any part of the Mediterranean, Adriatic, Archipelago, Morea, or even into the Black Sea."

Nothing could have pleased Nelson more than these instructions; for his fleet now consisted of thirteen ships of the line, carrying 74 guns each, one of 50 guns, and a brig.

True the enemy had fifteen ships of the line, one of which carried 120 guns, and three of them 80 guns, the rest being 74's; but the British admiral felt confident of being able to give a good account of his foes if he could only come up with him.

On the 12th June, Nelson sailed, and shaped his course towards Italy.

While off the coast of Tuscany, the "Leander" spoke a Moorish vessel, and received information that the French fleet was at Syracuse; but this proved false.

Nelson then visited Naples and Messina, at which last-named place he heard that the French had captured Malta, so he bent his course for that island.

But, at daybreak on the 22nd of June, an Italian vessel informed them that Admiral Brueys had left Malta.

Nelson immediately guessed that the French meant to invade Egypt, and sailed towards Alexandria.

On the night of the 22nd, the weather being very hazy, the hostile fleets crossed each other's track unperceived.

The British, who were anxious to come up with the enemy, arrived at Alexandria on the 28th of June, and found there only a Turkish ship of the line, four frigates, and some few merchant ships.

The governor of the town was much alarmed when he heard that the British were in search of the French, who were expected to land there, and declared that he would resist the forces of either nation if they attempted to land.

Nelson did not want to land; his object was to find the French fleet.

PORTRAIT OF LORD COLLINGWOOD.

With that object, he sailed over to the coast of Greece, and afterwards to Syracuse, where he took in fresh provisions and water.

On the 28th of July he was again off the Greek coast, where he heard that, some weeks before, the French fleet had been seen steering south-east, i.e., in the direction of Egypt.

The French fleet, in the meantime, after its narrow escape during the fog, had proceeded on its way to Alexandria, where, on the 1st of July, part of the troops landed.

Buonaparte himself had just stepped into a boat, when the look-out vessels signalled that an English ship of war was in sight.

"Fortune, wilt thou abandon me? What, only five days?" he exclaimed, turning very pale.

A few minutes afterwards the great man's mind was set at ease by the news that the approaching vessel was only a French frigate from Malta.

As soon as Buonaparte had landed his troops, he ordered Brueys to anchor in the bay of Aboukir, about twenty miles north-east of Alexandria, as the harbour of that town was not capable of receiving the ships, which was accordingly done.

On the 1st of August, the British fleet caught sight of Alexandria, on the walls of which the French flag waved, while a forest of masts showed that a number of vessels were at anchor.

But great was the disappointment when the "Alexander" and "Swiftsure," which were ahead, signalled that most of the vessels in the harbour were merchantmen and transports.

In a short time, however, the "Zealous" discovered the French fleet at anchor in Aboukir Bay, and the British then steered eastward under topgallant sails, with a fresh breeze from north-northwest.

Before describing the battle itself, we will give the names of the vessels that took part in it.

The British fleet was composed of the "Vanguard" (flagship of Nelson), "Culloden," "Orion," "Minotaur," "Bellerophon," "Alexander," "Defence," "Zealous," "Audacious," "Goliath," "Theseus," "Swiftsure," and "Majestic," 74-gun ships, the "Leander," of 50 guns, and the brig "Mutine," 16 guns.

The French fleet consisted of the "Orient," 120 guns (flagship of Admiral Brueys), the "Franklin," "Guillaume Tell," and "Tonnant," 84-gun ships; the "Aquilon," "Généreux," "Heureux," "Conquérant," "Guerrier," "Mercure," "Peuple-Souverain," "Timoléon," and "Spartiate," 74-gun ships; the "Diane," "Justice," "Artémise," and "Sérieuse" frigates, 36 and 40 guns; two brigs, three bombvessels, and some gunboats, number unknown.

Total, fifteen English ships of all kinds, against twenty-two French, not counting gunboats.

It was about two o'clock, on the 1st of August, when the French fleet saw the English approaching.

The French admiral signalled to prepare for battle, but does not seem to have expected an attack that night.

His fleet was at anchor in line, protected at each flank by shore batteries.

Nelson spent a short time in preparations; his plan was soon formed, and it was to pass between the outermost French vessel and the shore batteries with all his ships, so that seven of the enemy would have an English ship both at bow and stern.

The French broadsides facing the land were not expected to be manned, and this would be another point in favour of the English.

Nelson hailed Captain Hood, of the "Zealous," and asked if he thought there was sufficient water for the English ships to pass between the enemy and the shore.

"I don't know, sir," replied Hood; "but, with your permission, I will stand in and try."

He did so; but, in a short time, the "Goliath" got ahead of him; and, at 6.30 p.m., the action commenced.

This battle was fought with great obstinacy, skill and courage on both sides, and with but little advantage to either, until about nine o'clock, when the large French ship "Orient" was found to be on fire.

After illuminating the horizon for an hour, this ship blew up with a concussion that did much injury to surrounding ships.

For some time after this explosion all firing ceased. It was resumed by the French ship "Franklin," which was soon after compelled to surrender.

The fight was maintained until about eleven o'clock the next morning, when some of the French vessels got under way.

Eight French ships surrendered that morning, and two were destroyed.

Two other French ships were on shore, but with their colours flying.

One was the "Timoléon," which was set on fire and destroyed by her own crew to prevent her being captured.

The other was the "Tonnant," which had borne a large share of the fighting and danger throughout the combat. On the 3rd she surrendered to the "Theseus" and "Leander."

During the engagement Nelson was severely wounded in the forehead by a splinter. He was taken below, and the surgeons were hurrying to his assistance, when he waved them back.

"No!" said he; "I will take my turn with my brave fellows!"

In this great victory there were 218 men killed on the English fleet, and 664 wounded. Amongst the killed was Captain Wescott, of the "Majestic."

The French are supposed to have had about 2,000 men killed and wounded.

Sir James Saumarez was sent off with the prizes, most of which were safely taken to Plymouth.

The "Franklin" was added to the navy, under the name of the "Canopus."

The "Tonnant" and "Spartiate" were also added without change of names.

For this action Nelson was created Baron Nelson of the Nile, and Burham Thorpe in Norfolk, and received a pension of £2,000 per annum.

The East India Company presented him with £10,000.

The Battle of Aboukir was one of the most complete and glorious naval victories ever fought.

The plan of the battle was clearly arranged before the attack was begun; each captain of a vessel was assigned a particular place and duty, and all orders were obeyed.

On the 4th of August the boats of the frigate "Melpomene" and the brig "Childers," led by Lieutenant Shortland, captured the French 14-gun brig "Adventurer," anchored in a port at the Isle of Bas, and protected by batteries on shore.

THE BATTLE OF THE NILE.

The prize was taken out against a fresh gale. The "Adventurer" was added to the navy, and Lieutenant Shortland was appointed her commander.

On the 7th of August, the 44-gun frigate "Indefatigable," Captain Edward Pellew, captured the French 20-gun ship "Vaillante," off the Isle of Rhè.

On the 12th of August, the 18-gun ship "Hazard," Captain Butterfield, captured the French ship "Neptune," which had twenty-seven killed and wounded in the engagement.

On the 18th of August, the 50-gun ship "Leander," Captain Thompson, was captured by the French 74-gun ship "Généreux," off Goza.

During the action the French vessel ran aboard the "Leander," dropped alongside, and her crew made several attempts to board, but were repulsed.

Later in the action the two ships became separated, and the "Généreux" took up a position on the larboard bow of the "Leander," which, having lost her masts, was compelled to surrender.

Possession of the "Leander" was taken by a boatswain and a midshipman, who swam off from the French vessel—neither ship having a boat that could float.

The "Leander" had 35 men killed and 58 wounded.

One lieutenant, a midshipman, and fifty of her crew, were in one of the prizes captured at Aboukir.

Sir Edward Berry, bearing the despatches of the action at Aboukir, was in the "Leander" at the time of her capture.

Captain Thompson and his officers were tried by a court-martial for the loss of the ship, and honourably acquitted.

On the 22nd of August, the French 36-gun frigate "Decade" was captured off Cape Finisterre by the English frigates "Naiad" and "Magnanime," Captains Pierrepoint and De Courcy. She was added to the navy.

On the 7th of September, the French 32-gun frigate "Flora" was captured by the frigates "Phaëton" and "Anson," Captains Stopford and Durham, off the French coast.

In the month of September, a French fleet of nine ships, under Admiral Bompart, sailed from Brest, with 3,000 troops, for the coast of Ireland.

Commodore Sir John Borlase Warren was sent with a fleet of eight ships to look after it. The two fleets met on the 12th of October.

The English squadron was composed of the "Canada," 74 guns, "Robust," 74, "Foudroyant," 80, "Magnanime," 44, "Ethalion," 38, "Anson," 44, "Melampus," 36, and "Amelia," 38.

At ten minutes past seven in the morning the "Robust" sailed down towards the rear of the French line, closely followed by the "Magnanime," and the fight commenced.

Admiral Bompart's ship, the "Hoche," 74 guns, was attacked by the "Robust" so vigorously, that by half-past ten o'clock the rigging of the French vessel was cut to pieces, her masts shattered, her hull damaged so much, that the hold contained five feet of water, twenty-five of her guns dismounted, and a great portion of her crew killed or wounded.

Under these circumstances, her commander considered it necessary to strike his colours, and, accordingly, the "Hoche" was taken possession of by the boats of the "Robust" and "Magnanime," Lieutenant Dashwood, of the latter vessel, receiving the French commander's sword.

About an hour later, the French frigate, "Ambuscade," 36 guns, also surrendered, and the others then made off, some of the English ships having suffered so severely in their rigging, as to be unable to pursue.

In this engagement, the English fleet had 13 killed, and 75 wounded—the French 462 killed and wounded.

On the 14th of October, the "Immortalité" and "Résolute," two others of the French fleet, under Commodore Bompart, were captured by the "Melampus," Captain Moore.

On the 18th of October, the French ship "Loire," of 46 guns, another of the same fleet, was captured by the "Anson" and "Kangaroo." The "Loire" made a gallant resistance, and had 48 men killed, and 70 wounded. The "Anson" had 2 men killed, and 14 wounded.

An event occurred in the year 1798 which, though not exactly a naval victory, was an event much to be rejoiced at. This was the escape of Sir Sidney Smith, whose exploits in the "Diamond" frigate, and capture by the French, we have already spoken of.

So romantic were the circumstances connected with this escape that we prefer relating the whole affair in the words of the gallant officer himself. In an account of his escape, Sir Sidney says:—

"When I was taken at sea I was accompanied by my secretary and Mr. Tr——, a French gentleman, who had emigrated from his country, and who, it had been agreed, was to pass for my servant, in the hope of saving his life by that disguise; nor were our expectations frustrated, for John, as I called him, was lucky enough to escape all suspicion.

"On my arrival in France I was treated, at first, with unexampled rigour, and was told I ought to be tried under a military commission and shot as a spy.

"The government, however, gave orders for my removal to Paris, where I was sent to the Abbaye, and, together with my two companions in misfortune, was kept a close prisoner; meanwhile the means of escape were the constant object on which we employed our minds.

"The window of our prison was towards the street, and from this circumstance we derived a hope sooner or later to effect our object. We already contrived to carry on a tacit and regular correspondence, by means of signs, with some ladies who could see us from their apartment, and who seemed to take the most lively interest in our fate. They proposed themselves to assist in facilitating my liberation, and it is my duty to confess that notwithstanding the enormous expenses occasioned by their fruitless attempts, they have not less claim to my gratitude.

"Till the time of my departure, in which, however, they had no share, their whole employment was endeavouring to save me; and they had the address at all times to deceive the vigilance of my keepers. On both sides we used borrowed names, under which we corresponded, theirs being taken from the ancient mythology, so that I had now a direct communication with Thalia, Melpomene, and Clio.

"At length I was removed to the Temple, where my three muses soon contrived means of intelligence, and every day offered me new schemes for effecting my escape. At first I eagerly accepted them all; but reflection soon destroyed the hopes to which the love of liberty had given birth.

"I was also resolved not to leave my secretary in prison, and much less poor John, whose safety was more dear to me than my own emancipation.

"In the Temple, John was allowed to enjoy a considerable degree of liberty; he was highly dressed like an English jockey, and knew how to assume the manners that corresponded with that character. Every one was fond of John, who drank and fraternized with the turnkeys, and made love to the keeper's daughter, who was persuaded he would marry her; and as the little English jockey was not supposed to have received a very brilliant education, he had learnt by means of study sufficiently to mutilate his native tongue.

"John appeared very attentive and eager in my service, and always spoke to his master in a very respectful manner. I scolded him from time to time with much gravity; and he played his part so well, that I frequently surprised myself, forgetting the friend, and seriously giving orders to the valet.

"At length John's wife, Madame De Tr——, a very interesting lady, arrived at Paris, and made the most uncommon exertions to liberate us from our captivity. She dared not come, however, to the Temple, through fear of discovery; but from a neighbouring house she daily beheld her husband, who, as he walked to and fro, enjoyed alike in secret the pleasure of contemplating the friend of his bosom.

"Madame De Tr—— now communicated a plan for delivering us from prison, to a sensible and courageous young man of her acquaintance, who immediately acceded to it without hesitation.

"This Frenchman, who was sincerely attached to his country, said to Madame De Tr——,

"'I will serve Sir Sidney Smith with pleasure, because I believe the English government intend to restore Louis the Eighteenth to the throne. But if the commodore is to fight against France, and not for the King of France, Heaven forbid I should assist.'

"Charles L'Oiseau (for that was the name our young friend assumed) was connected with the agents of the king when confined in the Temple, and for whom he was also contriving the means of escape. It was intended we should all get off together.

* * * * *

"Everything was now prepared for the execution of our project; the means proposed by C. L'Oiseau appeared practicable, and we resolved to adopt them.

"A hole twelve feet long was to be made in a cellar adjoining to the prison; and the apartments to which the cellar belonged were at our disposal, Mademoiselle D—— rejected every prudential consideration, generously came to reside there for a week, and being young, the other lodgers attributed to her alone the frequent visits of C. L'Oiseau. Thus everything seemed to favour our wishes.

"No one in the house in question had any suspicions, and the amiable little child Mademoiselle D—— had with her, and who was only seven years old, was so far from betraying our secret, that she always beat a little drum, and made a noise while the work was going on in the cellar.

"Meanwhile L'Oiseau had continued his labour a considerable time without any appearance of daylight, and he was apprehensive he had attempted the opening considerably too low; it was necessary, therefore, that the wall should be sounded, and for this purpose a mason was required.

"Madame de Tr—— recommended one, and C. L'Oiseau undertook to bring him, and to detain him in the cellar until we had escaped, which was to take place that very day: the worthy man perceived the object was to serve some of the victims of misfortune, and came without hesitation. He only said—

"'If I am arrested, take care of my poor children.'

"But what a misfortune now frustrated all our hopes!

"Though the wall was sounded with the greatest precaution, the last stone fell out and rolled into the garden of the Temple; the sentinel perceived it; the alarm was given; the guard arrived, and all was discovered: fortunately, however, our friends had time to make their escape, and none of them were taken.

"They had indeed taken their measures with the greatest care; and when the commissaries of the Bureau Central came to examine the cellar and apartment, they found only a few pieces of furniture, trunks filled with logs of wood and hay, and the hats with tri-coloured cockades provided for our flight, as those we wore were black.

"This first attempt, though extremely well conducted, having failed, I wrote to Madame De Tr——, both to console her and our young friend, who was miserable at having foundered just as he was going into port. We were so far, however, from suffering ourselves to be discouraged, that we still continued to form new schemes for our deliverance; the keeper perceived it, and I was frequently so open as to acknowledge the fact.

"'Commodore,' said he, 'your friends are desirous of liberating you, and they only do their duty; I also am doing mine in watching you still more narrowly.'

"Though this keeper was a man of unparalleled severity, yet he never departed from the rules of civility and politeness. He treated all the prisoners with kindness, and even piqued himself on his generosity. Various proposals were made to him, but he rejected them all, watched us more closely, and preserved the profoundest silence.

"One day when I dined with him, he perceived that I fixed my attention on a window, then partly open, and which looked upon the street.

"I saw his uneasiness, and it amused me: however, to put an end to it, I said to him, laughing—

"'I know what you are thinking of; but fear not, it is now three o'clock, I will make a truce with you till midnight, and I give you my word of honour until that time, even were the doors open, I would not escape; when that hour is passed, my promise is at an end, and we are enemies again.'

"'Sir,' replied he, 'your word is a safer bond

than my bars or bolts; till midnight, therefore, I am perfectly easy.'

"When we rose from table, the keeper took me aside, and said—

"'Commodore, the Boulevard is not far; if you are inclined to take the air there, I will conduct you.'

"My astonishment was extreme; nor could I conceive how this man, who appeared so severe and so uneasy, should thus suddenly persuade himself to make me such a proposal. I accepted it, however, and in the evening we went out; from that time forward this confidence always continued.

"Whenever I was desirous to enjoy perfect liberty, I offered him a suspension of arms till a certain hour; this my generous enemy never refused; but when the armistice was at an end, his vigilance was unbounded; every post was examined; and if the government ordered that I should be kept close, the order was enforced with the greatest care: thus I was again free to contrive and prepare for my escape, and he to treat me with the utmost rigour.

"This man had a very accurate idea of the obligations of honour; he often said to me—

"'If you were under sentence of death, I would permit you to go out on your parole, because I should be certain of your return. Many very honest prisoners, and I myself among the rest, would not return in the like case; but an officer, and especially an officer of distinction, holds his honour dearer than his life: I know it to be a fact, commodore, and therefore I should be the less uneasy if you desired the gates to be always open.'

"My keeper was right; while I enjoyed my liberty, I endeavoured to lose sight of the idea of my escape: and I should have been averse to employ, for that object, means that had occurred to my imagination during my hours of liberty.

"One day I received a letter containing matter of great importance, which I had the strongest desire immediately to read; but as the contents related to my intended deliverance, I asked leave to return to my room and break off the truce. The keeper, however, refused, saying, with a laugh, that he wanted to take some sleep; accordingly, he lay down, and I postponed the perusal of my letter to the evening.

"Meanwhile no opportunity of flight offered; but on the contrary the Directory ordered me to be treated with rigour. The keeper punctually obeyed all the orders he received; and he who, the preceding evening, had granted me the greatest liberty, now doubled my guard, in order to exercise a more perfect vigilance.

"Among the prisoners was a man condemned, for certain political offences, to ten years' confinement, and whom all the other prisoners suspected of acting in the detestable capacity of a spy on his companions.

"Their suspicions, indeed, appeared to have some foundation, and I felt the greatest anxiety on account of my friend John. I was, however, fortunate enough soon after to obtain his liberty. An exchange of prisoners being about to take place, I applied to have my servant included in the cartel; and though this request might easily have been refused, fortunately no difficulty arose, and it was granted.

"When the day of his departure arrived, my kind and affectionate friend could scarcely be prevailed upon to leave me, till at length he yielded to my earnest entreaties. We parted with tears in our eyes, which to me were tears of pleasure, because my friend was leaving a situation of the greatest danger.

"The amiable jockey was regretted by every one; our turnkeys drank a good journey to him; nor could the girl he had courted help weeping for his departure; while her mother, who thought John a very good youth, hoped she should one day call him her son-in-law.

"I was soon informed of his arrival in London, and this circumstance rendered my own captivity less painful. I should have been happy also to have exchanged my secretary; but as he had no other dangers to encounter than those which were common to us both, he always rejected the idea, considering it as a violation of that friendship of which he has given me so many proofs.

"On the 4th of September (18th Fructidor) the rigour of my confinement was still further increased.

"The keeper, whose name was Lasme, was displaced. I was again kept close prisoner, and, together with my liberty, lost the hopes of a peace which I had thought approaching, and which this event must contribute to postpone.

"At this time, a proposal was made to me for my escape, which I adopted as my last resource.

"The plan was, to have forged orders drawn up for my removal to another prison, and then to carry me off.

CRESTS OF VESSELS IN THE ROYAL NAVY (A.D. 1870).

"A French gentleman, M. de Phelipeaux, a man of equal intrepidity and generosity, offered to execute this enterprise.

"The order then being accurately imitated, and, by means of a bribe, the real stamp of the minister's signature procured, nothing remained but to find men bold enough to put the plan into execution.

"Phelipeaux and C. L'Oiseau would have eagerly undertaken it, but both being known, and even notorious at the Temple, it was absolutely necessary to employ others. Messrs. B—— and L——, therefore, both men of tried courage, accepted the offer with pleasure and alacrity.

"With this order, then, they came to the Temple, Mr. B—— in the dress of an adjutant, and Mr. L—— as an officer.

"The keeper having perused the order, and attentively examined the minister's signature, went into another room, leaving my two deliverers for some time in the cruellest uncertainty and suspense. At length he returned, accompanied by the registrar of the prison, and ordered me to be called.

"When the registrar informed me of the orders of the Directory, I pretended to be very much concerned at it; but the adjutant assured me, in the most serious manner, that the government were very far from intending to aggravate my misfortunes, and that I should be very comfortable at the place whither he was ordered to conduct me.

"I expressed my gratitude to all the servants employed about the prison, and, as you may imagine, was not very long in packing up my clothes.

"At my return, the registrar observed, that at least six men from the guard must accompany me; and the adjutant, without being in the least confounded, acquiesced in the justice of the remark, and gave orders for them to be called out. But, on reflection, and remembering, as it were, the laws

WRECK OF THE "COLOSSUS."

of chivalry and of honour, he addressed me saying—

"'Commodore, you are an officer—I am an officer, also; your parole will be enough. Give me that, and I have no need of an escort.'

"Sir,' replied I, 'if that is sufficient, I swear, on the faith of an officer, to accompany you wherever you choose to conduct me.'

"Every one applauded this noble action, while, I confess, I had myself great difficulty to avoid smiling.

"The keeper now asked for a discharge, and the registrar gave the book to Mr. B——, who boldly signed it, with a proper flourish, 'L. Oger, adjutant-general.'

"Meanwhile, I employed the attention of the

turnkeys, and loaded them with favours, to prevent them from having time to reflect—nor, indeed, did they seem to have any other thought than their own advantage.

"The registrar and keeper accompanied us as far as the second court, and at length the gate was opened, and we left them, after a long interchange of ceremony and politeness.

"We instantly entered an hackney coach, and the adjutant ordered the coachman to drive to the suburb of St. Germain; but the stupid fellow had not gone a hundred paces before he broke his wheel against a post, and hurt an unfortunate passenger.

"This unlucky accident brought a crowd of people about us, who were very angry at the injury the poor fellow had sustained. We quitted the coach, took our portmanteaus in our hands, and went off in an instant.

"Though the people observed as much, they did not say a word to us, only abusing the coachman. And when our driver demanded his fare, Mr. ——, through an inadvertency that might have caused us to be arrested, gave him a double louis d'or.

"Having separated when we quitted the carriage, I arrived at the appointed rendezvous with only my secretary and M. De Phelipeaux, who had joined us near the prison, and though I was very desirous of waiting for my two friends, to thank and take my leave of them, M. De Phelipeaux observed there was not a moment to be lost.

"I therefore postponed till another opportunity my expression of gratitude to my deliverers, and we immediately set off for Rouen, where Mr. R—— had made every preparation for our reception.

"At Rouen we were obliged to stay several days, and as our passports were perfectly regular, we did not take much care to conceal ourselves, but in the evening we walked about the town, or took the air upon the banks of the Seine. At length, everything being ready for us to cross the Channel, we quitted Rouen."

It so happened that on the 4th of May, 1798, in the afternoon, a small squadron of English frigates, namely, the "Arethusa," 38 guns, the "Niger," 32 guns, and the "Argo," 44 guns, chanced to be cruising off the mouth of the river Seine, when a small fishing boat stood out from shore, and came alongside the "Argo." It was found to contain Sir Sidney Smith, Lieutenant J. W. Wright, and two French gentlemen, one of whom was M. De Phelipeaux.

As soon as Captain Wooley, of the "Arethusa," the commander of the squadron, heard who had come out in the boat, he signalled the "Argo" to part company and return to England, and on the 6th of May, in the evening, Sir Sidney and his friends landed at Portsmouth.

* * * * *

On the 20th of October, the 38-gun frigate "Fisgard," Captain Thomas Martin, fell in with the French 38-gun frigate "Immortalité," on her way to Brest. A sharp action ensued, in which the French frigate had her mizen mast shot away, the other masts damaged, her captain, first lieutenant, and 54 men killed and 61 wounded, when she surrendered.

The "Fisgard" was much injured in her masts and rigging, had five feet of water in her hold, and 10 men killed and 27 wounded.

The "Immortalité" was another of Admiral Bompart's squadron—the last one captured.

On the 24th of October the 18-pounder 36-gun frigate "Sirius," Captain King, off Texel, captured two Dutch vessels, the 36-gun frigate "Furie," and the 24-gun corvette "Waakzaamheid." On first being seen, the Dutch vessels were about two miles apart, and Captain King captured them by attacking one at a time.

On the 3rd of December, the English frigate, "L'Aigle," 38 guns, was wrecked on the coast of Barbary. The vessel was burnt to prevent her from falling into the hands of the enemy.

On the 4th of December, the English 32-gun frigate, "Ambuscade," Captain Jinkins, was captured, after a long and well fought battle, by the French 28-gun ship "Bayonnaise."

During the action, a 12-pound gun on the maindeck of the "Ambuscade" burst, severely injuring eleven men and damaging the vessel.

All the "Ambuscade's" officers were shot down except the purser, when the French vessel ranged alongside, and boarded the English ship.

The English ship, "Colossus," was wrecked on the 10th of December off the coast of Sicily. All the crew, except three, were saved.

On the 11th of December, the English 22-gun ship "Perdrix," Captain Fahie, captured the French privateer, "Armée d'Italie," of 18 guns.

Among other naval incidents connected with the year 1798, we may mention that, on the 13th of January in this year Lord Camelford shot Charles Peterson, first lieutenant of the English ship "Perdrix," for refusing to obey orders. A court-martial was held at Fort Royal Bay, Martinique, for the trial of his lordship, who was acquitted.

Also, that on the 27th of February, a dangerous mutiny broke out in the fleet at the Cape of Good Hope, but was quelled with the assistance of the military. The mutineers delivered up the ringleaders, who were tried, found guilty, and executed.

We should also mention that on the 19th of May, Captain Home Popham, with a fleet carrying a body of troops under command of Major-General Coote, landed at Ostend and burnt a number of boats intended for the invasion of England, and destroyed the locks and basins of the Bourges canal. By the time this work was completed, a heavy storm arose, preventing the English forces from embarking. They took up a position on the sand hills to wait, but the enemy collected in great force, attacked them, and, after some resistance, the English troops were compelled to surrender. This affair is not mentioned in every naval history of England.

In the year 1798 five English vessels of war were captured by the enemy, twelve were wrecked, two foundered, and one was burnt.

The French lost during the same period one ship of 120 guns, two of 80 guns, eleven of 74 guns, three of 40 guns, and nine of 36 guns; altogether, twenty-six vessels, of which twenty-one were captured by the English.

During the same period the Dutch lost two frigates, and the Spaniards one.

CHAPTER XXIV.

CONTINUATION OF THE WAR IN 1799.

THE commencement of 1799 saw us still at war, and the navy still our chief means of offence and defence. For the naval services of the year the following supplies were voted by the House of Commons:—

	£	s.	d.
For pay and maintenance of 100,000 seamen and 20,000 marines	5,850,000	0	0
Wear and tear of ships	4,680,000	0	0
Ordinary expenses, including half-pay officers and cost of ordnance	1,119,063	0	0
Extraordinaries: Building and repairing	693,750	0	0
Transport service and maintaining prisoners of war	1,311,200	0	0
Total	£13,654,013	0	0

At the commencement of 1799 we had 401 cruising vessels in commission, 34 laid up in ordinary or repairing, and 152 stationary harbour vessels, 80 of which were in commission.

In addition to these, 46 were either building or ordered to be built, making the total number of ships to be provided for 633. The English navy had in it no less than 155 foreign built vessels, most of which had been captured from the French, Dutch, or Spaniards.

This great navy was officered by 21 admirals, 36 vice-admirals, 42 rear-admirals, 547 captains, 386 commanders, 2,157 lieutenants, and 535 masters.

French armies had, it is true, overrun nearly the whole of Europe, but Austria was preparing to aid the Italian States in throwing off Bonaparte's yoke, while Russia had united with Turkey to avenge the invasion of Egypt. The French government being well informed of all these things had issued orders in the preceding November for the construction of sixteen ships-of-the-line, eighteen heavy frigates, and twelve corvettes.*

Of course men were wanted to man these vessels, so a proclamation was issued by the French government, promising seamen who would join the navy that their families should be provided for during their absence, and that a third part of the value of all prizes should be paid them immediately, with many other minor inducements, which had the effect of enticing seamen from merchant ships and privateers to the national navy.

The British government as usual received information of these preparations, and several light vessels were sent to watch the coast.

On the 2nd of January, 1799, the "Woolverine," of 12 guns and seventy men, commanded by Captain Mortlock, sailed from the Downs, and, being off Boulogne, on the 4th, she discovered two French luggers, one mounting 16 guns and the other 14, with a complement of 140 men each.

The weather being very thick and foggy, the British ship was close in with the enemy before they could recognise one another. Captain Mortlock knew, if the enemy suspected the "Woolverine" to be a ship-of-war, they would make off; he, therefore, put her head towards them, and hoisted Danish colours. The luggers immediately bore down, and came within hail.

Being hailed by them, Captain Mortlock answered he was from Plymouth, for Copenhagen, reserving his fire till they should come abreast of him. One of the luggers was close upon the starboard quarter, and had her bowsprit between the mizen chains and the side of the "Woolverine."

Captain Mortlock instantly hoisted English colours, and the action commenced with musketry.

The intrepid commander immediately proceeded to lash the bowsprit of the lugger to one of the iron stanchions or mizen chains of the "Woolverine," in order to prevent the escape of the enemy. The other lugger meanwhile shot ahead, and got on the larboard bow of the "Woolverine," running on board of her.

In this position she was boarded by the enemy three times from both the vessels; but every Frenchman engaged in these attempts was killed.

At one time, the crew of the lugger on the larboard bow, made so desperate an attack, that it required the assistance of almost every man on the "Woolverine" to repulse them. At the same time an equally daring effort was made by the lugger on the quarter, and many Frenchmen were actually on board the "Woolverine," but were killed by the

---

* A corvette is a war-sloop, or despatch-boat, carrying less than 20 guns. A frigate is a fast-sailing war-vessel, with *two* gun-decks, and mounting from 20 to 50 guns.

intrepid gallantry of Captain Mortlock and his brave crew.

One Frenchman, in particular, was observed to cheer his men, and force them to come on by beating them with the flat of his sword. This man got on the round-house of the "Woolverine," and gave three cheers to encourage the rest to follow him. He was supposed to be the captain of the lugger.

Captain Mortlock ran up to dispute with him the possession of his post. The Frenchman presented his pistol at Captain Mortlock's face, which fortunately missed fire.

He again cocked his pistol, but Captain Mortlock plunged his half-pike into his body before he could fire, and he fell overboard.

The Frenchmen now threw some leather bags, which were filled with combustibles, from the lugger into the windows of the "Woolverine's" cabin, which immediately set her on fire. The whole crew were obliged to leave the enemy for the purpose of extinguishing the flames; of which circumstance they availed themselves to disentangle their vessels, and made off with all sail set.

In this conflict the "Woolverine" had two men killed and eight wounded; among the latter, her brave commander, who received so desperate a wound from a shot fired from the enemy, while they were going off, that he died at Portsmouth on the 10th.

Captain Mortlock received two or three slight wounds previous to the last fatal one.

On the 6th of February, the 44-gun ship "Argo," Captain James Bowen, captured, off Majorca, the Spanish 34-gun frigate "Santa Teresa," Captain Don Pablo Perez. It was added to the English navy under the same name. A little time after this the "Argo" was sent to Algiers to negotiate for a supply of provisions. Captain Bowen not only succeeded in his mission, but so worked on the feelings of the Dey that he released six British prisoners who had been fourteen years in slavery there.

On the 9th of February, off Cape Natal, the 32-gun frigate "Dædalus," Captain Ball, captured the French 32-gun frigate, "Prudente,"

CUTTING OUT OF THE "HERMIONE."

Captain Le Jolliffe. The French frigate had twenty-seven men killed, and twenty-two wounded. The "Dædalus" had two killed, and twelve wounded. The lieutenant of the "Dædalus" was recommended for promotion by Captain Ball, for his skill and bravery; but as late as the year 1823 he was still a lieutenant.

On the 28th of February, the 38-gun frigate "Sibylle," Captain Edward Cooke, cruising in search of the "Forte," a French frigate that had been very successful in taking prizes from the English in the East Indian seas, met that vessel in company with the "Endeavour" and "Lord Mornington," two prizes that it had just taken. After a long and spirited action the "Forte" surrendered, but not until she was nearly a wreck. On board the "Forte" sixty-five officers and men were killed and eighty wounded. Amongst the killed was Captain Le Long. On the "Sibylle" Captain Cooke was mortally wounded, two officers, and four of the crew were killed and sixteen men wounded. Captain Cooke died, after a painful illness, the following May in Calcutta, where a monument was erected to his memory by the Directors of the East India Company. The "Forte" was the finest frigate afloat, being 1,400 tons measurement. She was added to the English navy, and the navy medal was given to those who assisted in her capture.

In March, Commodore Sir William Sidney Smith, with a squadron in the East, assisted the Turks in defending Acre against the French.

Sir Sidney's old French friend Phelipeaux, who was an engineer officer of some renown, did his best to put the ruined walls in the best possible state of defence; and on the 18th of March the siege commenced.

The next day Sir Sidney was lucky enough to capture seven small vessels which were conveying the French battering artillery. These guns were immediately landed at Acre, and mounted on the walls to repel the attacks of their former owners. A number of English sailors and marines were also sent on shore to increase the garrison.

On the 7th of April it was discovered that the French were endeavouring to mine the forts; a sortie was made; Lieutenant Wright, Sir Sidney's old companion in captivity, succeeded in discovering the mine and destroyed it. The Turks, who also took part in the sortie, brought in the heads of sixty Frenchmen and a great number of muskets.

The French continued the siege till May the 6th, during which time they were repulsed in seven or eight attempts to storm the place. On the 7th, the garrison saw with joy some ships with reinforcements in the offing: the French also perceived them, and made another desperate attempt to gain possession of the place before the new comers could land. They were repulsed with great loss, and the siege was raised soon afterwards.

The total British loss during this siege was twenty-two killed, four accidentally drowned, sixty-six wounded, and eighty-two taken prisoners by the French.

On the 18th of March, the brig "Telegraph," of 18 guns, Lieutenant Worth, captured the French 16-gun brig "Hirondelle" off the Isle of Bas.

On the 8th of June, the 10-gun polacca, "Fortune," Lieutenant Davis, and a gun-boat, were captured off the coast of Syria, by the French 16-gun brig "Salamine."

On the 9th of June, the boats of the frigate "Success" boarded a Spanish vessel of 10 guns and 113 men in the harbour of La Selva, and captured it. This was a very gallant action, for which the navy medal was given to those engaged.

On the 19th of June, Vice-Admiral Lord Keith, off Minorca with a part of his squadron, captured the French 38-gun frigate "Junon," the 36-gun frigates "Alceste" and "Courageuse," and the brigs "Salamine" and "Alert."

All these vessels were added to the English navy under the same names, except the "Junon," which was first called the "Princess Charlotte," and afterwards the "Andromache."

On the 26th of June, the 32-gun frigate "Alcmène," Captain Digby, captured the French privateer frigate "Courageuse," of 28 guns and 250 men.

Holland still supplied France with loans and resources of every kind, by which means the latter country continued to support her own declining credit.

Therefore, in a grand plan of military operations concerted between the confederate courts, it was determined that Great Britain should attempt a powerful diversion of the French arms, by the actual invasion of Holland, aided by a body of about 20,000 auxiliaries, to be furnished by Russia, exclusive of the force employed by the Emperor Paul in Italy and Switzerland.

The benefits to be derived by this expedition were great and obvious; the ancient alliance between the two states would be renewed; the power of France diminished, and the Prince of Orange, at this time in exile on account of his attachment to England, restored to the rank of stadtholder and captain general of the forces by sea and land.

Though apparently of the utmost consequence that this expedition should have been undertaken at an early period of the campaign, the convention of Great Britain and Russia was not signed at St. Petersburgh till the 11th of June, 1799.

PORTRAIT OF SIR SIDNEY SMITH.

By Article IV., it was stipulated, that on the arrival of the corps of 17,593 men at Revel, the sum of £44,000 sterling was to be advanced immediately, and £44,000 more paid in two months. The same sum was also to be furnished at the commencement of every month.

By Article VI., his Britannic Majesty engaged to provide and maintain, at his expense, the necessary number of horses; and by Article VIII., it was agreed, that two months' additional subsidies should be paid for the troops after their return to their own country.

It was agreed, in a separate article, that the emperor should lend his ships, frigates, and transports, on the following conditions, viz.:—

1. Upon their quitting the port of Cronstadt, the sum of £58,927 10s. sterling was to be advanced for the expenses of equipment for three months, over and above the subsidy of £19,642 10s. per month, to be paid always on the first day thereof.

2. As the squadron was already furnished with provisions for three months, the same was to be paid for by estimate.

3. The officers and sailors were to be fed at the expense of Great Britain; and,

4. The officers were to be indemnified for the preparations made for the campaign.

Instead of keeping the object in view a secret, it was publicly known, and a considerable body of troops having been assembled on the coast of Kent, the necessary dispositions were made for effecting a descent.

It was determined that there should be two successive expeditions, by two divisions of the army. The first, under General Sir Ralph Abercromby, an officer of great reputation and experience, sailed from the Downs early in August; and the other, under the Duke of York, whose rank as commander-in-chief, and dignity as a prince of the blood, were calculated to confer splendour on the intended enterprise.

These two divisions were composed of thirty battalions of infantry, besides cavalry and artillery, making, in conjunction with the Russians, an army of 45,000 or 50,000 men.

In the interim, the hereditary Prince of Orange repaired to Lingen, on the Emms, where he assembled all the Stadtholderian party capable of bearing arms; magazines were at the same time formed at Bremen, and an active intercourse kept up with the partisans of his family.

His Serene Highness, the Prince of Orange, who had been driven into exile by the Republican party of his native land, had also prepared a proclamation, dated at Hampton Court, July 28, 1799, in which he informed his "dear countrymen," that the long-wished-for moment had arrived, when they were to be delivered from their several calamities.

He stated, that the troops sent to their assistance did not repair as enemies, but as friends and deliverers, in order to rescue them from the odious oppression under which they were kept by the French government, and to restore to them "the enjoyment of their religion and liberty, those invaluable blessings for which, with divine protection, they and their ancestors had fought and conquered."

The first division of the army embarked on board 140 transports, and on the 13th of August, sailed from Margate, Ramsgate, and the neighbouring ports; after which they proceeded, under the convoy of Vice-Admiral Mitchell, to join Lord Duncan, who was cruising in the North Seas.

Two grand objects were embraced upon this occasion; the first was the possession of the Helder, which would not only confer on the invaders a seaport and arsenal, but contribute greatly to the attainment of the second object, namely, the possession of the Batavian fleet, most of the seamen and some of the officers of which were discontented with the government, while the naval commander himself was supposed not to be wholly averse to the cause of the Stadtholder.

From the first moment of embarkation the weather proved so adverse to the designs of the English, that apprehensions were entertained of a deficiency of water, and a certain period was actually fixed, on the expiration of which it would not have been deemed prudent to hazard an attack.

Five days, however, before this fixed period, the weather became so favourable, that the fleet was enabled to stand in for the Dutch coast.

Notwithstanding a landing could not be immediately effected, General Abercromby seized on this opportunity to disperse the proclamation of the Prince of Orange, as well as another of his own, in which he stated, "that his Majesty, the King of Great Britain, the ancient ally of the United Provinces, had intrusted him with the command of a body of troops," and that it was not "as enemies, but as friends and deliverers, that the English now entered their territories."

At the same time his excellency found means to transmit a summons to the commanding officer of the Dutch troops; while Lord Duncan sent a letter to the admiral of the Batavian fleet, on the supposition that the forces were about to land immediately, stating, that as more than 20,000 men had disembarked at the Helder, "he had now an opportunity of manifesting his zeal to the Prince of Orange, by declaring for him, together with all the ships that might choose to follow his example."

The answers were, however, unfavourable; the former having replied, "that he would oppose the progress of the army with the brave troops under his command;" and the latter, "that the enemy might expect a defence from him worthy of his nation and his honour."

Although the squadron had been once more forced to sea, yet, through unceasing efforts, the shore of the Helder was again descried, and the troops began to disembark by daylight, August 27th, all the bomb-vessels, sloops, and gun-brigs, being stationed so as to open a well-directed fire, in order to scour the beach, and prevent all opposition from the enemy.

General Daendels having assembled a body of infantry, cavalry, and artillery, near Callanstorg, made repeated attempts to dislodge the right of the British, now posted on a ridge of sandhills, stretching along the coast from north to south, and incapable of forming more than a battalion in line of battle; but the narrowness of the position was, upon the whole, favourable to troops entirely destitute of horse and artillery; so that the enemy, instead of being able to make any impression, were, after a sharp but irregular engagement, which lasted for some hours, obliged to retire to another position, six miles in the rear. According to the official accounts the English lost 500 men.

General Abercromby determined immediately to attack the Helder; and the brigades commanded by the Major-Generals Moore and Burrard were accordingly destined for this undertaking.

Late, however, in the evening, the garrison of the fort, consisting of about 2,000 national troops, was withdrawn, and the English took possession of the works next morning, August 28th.

This was but a prelude to the great success which followed.

Having shipped pilots at the Helder, Vice-Admiral Mitchell, who succeeded to the command in the absence of Lord Duncan, got under sail with his squadron, for the purpose of reducing the Dutch fleet, which he was determined to follow to the walls of Amsterdam, unless they surrendered to the

British flag, or capitulated to the Prince of Orange. Accordingly, on August 30th, he formed the line of battle.

At five o'clock in the morning, orders were given to prepare for action; and, notwithstanding two ships and a frigate ran on shore, the English passed the Helder point and Mars Diep, continuing their course along the Texel, in the channel that leads to the Vleiter, the Dutch being then at anchor at a spot called the Red Buoy.

The Dutch government had not been inert in preparing the means of defence and resistance.

Their naval force consisted of nine ships of the line, and a great number of frigates, under the command of Admiral Storey, who had saved himself by an early flight from the battle of Camperdown. Their military did not exceed 20,000 men, to which must be added about 15,000 French, under General Brune, the directory not being able to allow these provinces a larger force.

The English admiral sent Captain Rennie, of the "Victor," with the following summons to the Batavian commander:—

"Sir,—I desire you will instantly hoist the flag of his Serene Highness the Prince of Orange. If you do, you will be immediately considered friends of the King of Great Britain, my most gracious sovereign; otherwise take the consequences.—Painful it will be to me for the loss of blood it will occasion, but the guilt will be on your own head.

"I have the honour to be, Sir,
"Your most obedient humble servant,
(Signed) "Andrew Mitchell,
"Vice-admiral and commander-in-chief of his Majesty's ships employed on the present occasion.
"To Rear-Admiral Storey, or the commander-in-chief of the Dutch squadron."

An hour was allowed, but in less than that time the following answer was returned, the sailors on board the Dutch fleet having mutinied, in consequence (as supposed) of the proclamation of the Prince of Orange and the successful exertions of his adherents:—

"Admiral,—Neither your superiority, nor the threat that the spilling of human blood could be laid to my account, could prevent my showing to you, to the last moment, what I could do for my sovereign, whom I acknowledge to be no other than the Batavian people and its representatives, when your prince's and the Orange flags have obtained their end. The traitors whom I commanded refused to fight, and nothing remains to me and my brave officers but vain rage, and the dreadful reflection of our present situation. I therefore deliver over to you the fleet which I commanded. From this moment it is your obligation to provide for the safety of my officers and the few brave men who are on board the Batavian ships, as I declare myself and my officers prisoners of war, and remain to be considered as such.

"I am, with respect,
"S. Storey."
"To Admiral Mitchell, commanding his Britannic Majesty's squadron in the Texel."

Thus one ship of 74 guns, four of 68, two of 54, two of 44, a frigate, and a sloop of war, were surrendered by Rear-Admiral Storey.

After this the fleet had no opportunity of distinguishing itself, and some time afterwards the troops were withdrawn from Holland.

On the 20th of August, the frigate "Clyde," of 32 guns, Captain Cunningham, captured the French 36-gun frigate "Vestale," Captain Gaspard, after a sharp fight of one hour and fifty minutes. The "Vestale" had ten men killed and twenty-two wounded; the "Clyde" had two killed and three wounded.

On the 26th of August, the English frigate "Tamar," 38 guns, Captain Western, captured the French frigate "Republicain."

On the 30th of August, Admiral Mitchell, with the fleet under his command, captured the whole of the Dutch squadron in the Texel, consisting of one 74, five 68, two 54, two 44, and some smaller vessels.

On the 12th of October, the 16-gun sloop "Trincomalee," Lieutenant Rowe, in the Straits of Babelmandel, attacked the French privateer "Iphigénie," of 22 guns.

After two hours' hard fighting the "Trincomalee" blew up, and only two men were saved. The two vessels were so close together that the French vessel shared the fate of the other, and eighty-five of its crew were lost.

The next event to be commemorated in the present number of our work, is one of the most singular, as well the most gallant, which grace the naval annals of our country.

Our engraving represents the "Hermione," with the assailants in their boats on the instant previous to the commencement of the attack; on the right is seen one of the Spanish forts, between which the vessel in question was moored, the better to ensure her protection from a ship at least one-third inferior in force.

Captain Edward Hamilton, in the "Surprise," a small frigate of 28 guns, having received orders from Sir Hyde Parker, in the month of October, 1799, to cruise between the island of Aruba and Cape St. Roman, near the gulf of Venezuela, in search of the "Hermione," which the Spaniards had fitted out to cruise against us, and which, from information, was said to be on the point of sailing for the Havannah through that channel, he immediately proceeded off Porto Cavallo, and found the intelligence that had been received in every particular correct.

The "Hermione" lay at the entrance of the port, moored between two very strong batteries, so that it became necessary to proceed with more than common precaution; two days were consequently spent in reconnoitring, when Captain Hamilton, having arranged the whole of his plan, carried the attack into execution.

The dishonourable circumstances which threw the ship in question into the possession of the Spaniards, the miserable and lamented fate of the officers, with their commander, and the effects which such a mutiny might produce on the general discipline of the British navy, induced Captain Hamilton and his people to make every possible effort in their power for her recovery.

The whole crew were animated on the occasion with an eagerness and zeal which raised them almost superior to men, and the well-timed harangue made to them by the captain contributed to increase it to so great a height, that many instances occurred of pecuniary offers being made by those who were ordered to remain with the ship, on condition of their exchanging stations with such as had been selected to make the attack.

The boats had reached within sight of the "Hermione" when they were discovered by the guard-boats, at the distance of three-quarters of a mile; the enemy therefore had time to prepare completely for the encounter, and to discharge both their main-deck and forecastle guns, which were considerably depressed and pointed to a centre.

Two of the English boats had in the confusion ran foul of the two guard-boats, but after some scuffle cleared themselves, and united in the attack. The gigs got up on the larboard bow, and came to the assistance of the captain, under the command of the surgeon, Mr. M'Muller; the black cutter, with a sea lieutenant, and an officer of marines, with his party, were beaten off, and could not board on either gangway.

The red cutter, under the orders of the boatswain, shared nearly the same fate. The first lieutenant was to have had the direction of cutting the bower cable in the launch, and the jolly-boat, under the direction of the carpenter, the stern cable; these boats had, besides their proper crews, which were not to move out of the boats, but immediately to go ahead and take the ship in tow, as many people, called boarders, as they could stow.

Captain Hamilton having got up with eight or ten men from his boat, took possession of the forecastle with only one man wounded: he then advanced aft on the starboard gangway, with an intention of getting to the general rendezvous, the quarter-deck; but meeting with a serious opposition, and having several of his people wounded, he left the gunner in charge of the starboard gangway, and finding the surgeon with his party had boarded on the larboard bow, advanced along the larboard gangway to the quarter-deck, and drawing the attention from those that opposed the gunner on the other gangway, got the enemy between the five boarding parties. Great numbers were killed, some got down the after-ladders, and others jumped overboard, and in this part of the affair it was that Captain Hamilton was wounded.

The first lieutenant had now boarded, and shortly after, the acting lieutenant of marines, Mons. de la Tour du Pin, with his small party of marines; and the cables being now cut, the boats under the direction of the second lieutenant, he not having boarded, went ahead, and with their hook-ropes took the ship in tow; the hands that were stationed for that purpose had loosened the sails aloft, and every boat and man betook themselves, in conformity with the orders and arrangements made prior to the attack, to the different services allotted to them.

Immediately after the quarter-deck was taken possession of as above stated, and the force of the assailants increased by the marines and others who had boarded from different boats, no time was lost in making an attack upon the main deck, for which purpose the officer of marines, with his party, and the surgeon, and a small party of sailors (Captain Hamilton and the gunner being at this time too much wounded to make a part of the number), followed the Spaniards down the after-ladder so quickly that they had not time to make any regular defence, and the constant fire which was kept up from those who remained upon deck, enabled those officers to carry their point after a most dreadful slaughter.

The firing that was kept up on board by both parties, made it uncertain to those on shore who had possession of the ship; consequently they did not know when to begin their fire, and before the

CRESTS OF VESSELS IN THE ROYAL NAVY (A.D. 1870).

batteries opened, the "Hermione," by means of the boats towing, and the sails, had increased her distance from the forts half-a-mile.

The batteries commenced their cannonade nearly at the same instant, and the effect was most tremendous, but the lightness of the wind prevented them from pointing the guns direct to the object, the smoke not clearing away for a considerable time after the discharge.

Several shot struck the ship, but being chiefly grape, did little damage, except to the rigging; one 24-pound shot passed through the ship under water, and obliged the captors to rig the pumps immediately, for it was with difficulty the leak was kept under by heeling the ship. The main and springstays being both shot away, made it necessary, from a great head swell, to secure the mainmast directly.

At two o'clock the "Hermione" was completely in possession of the boarding party, after having had 119 of her officers and crew killed, and upwards of 100 wounded, in a conflict which, from beginning to end, did not last longer than an hour and a quarter.

The future historian might doubt the credibility of the fact to be told, were it not so well authenticated, that on this gallant occasion the assailants had no more than one officer killed, and twelve officers and seamen wounded.

Amongst the latter number Captain Hamilton stands first on the list. He was wounded in six places, and bruised all over the body, the principal wound being on the left temple, with the butt-end of a musket, which broke over his head, and knocked him down senseless on the deck; he received also a severe wound by the cut of a sabre on the left thigh, one also in the right thigh by a pike, another

BOAT LEAVING THE "NEMESIS" FRIGATE.

on the right shin-bone by a grape shot; one finger was much cut, and his loins and kidneys so much bruised, as to require the highest medical advice and assistance.

As generosity and humanity are generally allied to true courage and magnanimity, we cannot resist giving a trait of Captain Hamilton's character in that respect. He rewarded the seamen who so much distinguished themselves on the above occasion, by dividing amongst them no less a sum than £500 of his own particular share of the prize-money. Thus setting a noble example of valour and generosity, which has ever its due influence on the minds and hearts of British seamen.

Soon after the exploit of the "Hermione," one of

the seamen belonging to Captain Hamilton's own boat, who distinguished himself in boarding, was taken up as a deserter from the "Swallow" sloop of war, and tried by a court-martial. At his trial it appeared in evidence that he had saved Captain Hamilton's life, when he had been knocked down on the quarter-deck, and was without arms!

The court, in considering the mitigating circumstances in favour of his character, thought proper to recommend that the sentence of 300 lashes ordered to be inflicted should be remitted.

On the 7th November, 1799, Captain Hamilton was voted, by the House of Assembly at Spanish Town, Jamaica, a sword, value 300 guineas, "in testimony of the high sense that House entertained of the extraordinary gallantry and ability displayed by him in attacking and cutting out of Porto Cavallo, his Majesty's late ship 'Hermione,' an enterprise surpassed by none in this glorious war."

His Majesty was graciously pleased to confer upon him knighthood by letters patent, and honoured him with the naval gold medal in reward of his gallant conduct.

On the 6th of March, 1800, the Court of Common Council in London, voted Sir Edward Hamilton the freedom of the city in a gold box, value fifty guineas.

In the month of April, 1800, Sir Edward, returning home in the "Jamaica" packet, for the re-establishment of his health and the cure of his wounds, was captured by a French privateer, and carried into France. He was sent to Paris, where he was taken notice of by Bonaparte, and after remaining there six weeks, was exchanged for four midshipmen.

On the 25th of October, 1800, being the anniversary day of the exploit in which the "Hermione" was cut out by the boats of His Majesty's ship "Surprise," Sir Edward, by special invitation, dined at the Mansion House, and the chamberlain of the city having delivered to him the freedom of the city in the gold box voted, communicated to him, in a very appropriate speech, the thanks of the corporation for his conduct in an action, which, in the emphatic language of his commander-in-chief, Admiral Sir Hyde Parker, "must ever rank amongst the foremost of the gallant actions executed by our navy this war."

On the 9th of October, the ship "La Lutine," of 32 guns, Captain Skynner, was lost on the way to the Texel. She foundered at sea, and only one person was saved. Aboard this vessel were £140,000 sterling, shipped in England to commercial houses in Hamburgh.

An action, which caused much sensation in England, took place about the middle of October, 1799. The British frigate, "Naiad," was cruising on the 25th of the month named, in latitude 44° 1' north, longitude 12° 35' west (that is off, the north of Spain), when two frigates were discovered, and soon found to be enemies.

Captain Pierrepont, regardless of the odds against him, gave chase, and continued the pursuit till half-past three the following morning, when a third ship was seen to the south-west. This, however, proved to be the British frigate, "Ethalion," and joined in the chase, as did a short time afterwards the "Alcmène" and "Triton."

About seven o'clock, in the morning of the 16th, the strangers, now well known to be Spanish frigates, parted company, and made off in different directions. Captain Pierrepont, the senior British officer, signalled the "Ethalion" to pursue the foremost of the enemy's ships.

The commander of the "Ethalion" did as ordered, and, by dint of good sailing, got within shot of the enemy by about eleven o'clock: a running fight commenced, and lasted about an hour, when the Spanish frigate, "Thetis," of 34 guns, Captain Don Juan de Mendoza, surrendered. The "Ethalion" had not a man hurt; the "Thetis" had one man killed and nine wounded.

In the meantime the other Spaniard, the "Santa Brigida," had by her fast sailing succeeded in getting round Cape Finisterre early on the 17th, and was bearing away to the southward, keeping not far from shore.

The "Triton," first of the pursuers, struck upon some rocks, but got off almost immediately. At seven in the morning of the 17th, the "Triton" commenced firing; at eight, the "Alcmène" and "Naiad" had closed in on the Spaniard, whereupon the captain of the "Santa Brigida" (Don Antonio Pillon) struck his colours, after a brave resistance.

So far there had been nothing extraordinary, either in the pursuit or capture of the Spanish ships; but when the English took possession of them, they found they had indeed captured rich prizes.

The "Thetis" had on board a box, containing 4,000 dollars, 2 doubloons, and 90 half-doubloons; 93 boxes of 4,000 dollars each, 333 boxes containing 3,000 dollars each, and 4 boxes of 2,385 dollars each.

The "Santa Brigida" had indigo and cochineal worth £5,000 on board; also 446 boxes of 3,000 dollars each, 59 bags of dollars, 3 kegs of dollars, and many other packages of specie.

The prizes were sent to Plymouth. On the 28th and 29th of October, the cargoes were landed. Sixty-nine artillery waggons, escorted by horse and foot soldiers, armed seamen and marines, with bands of music, conveyed the treasure to the citadel of Plymouth, from which place it was removed a month later, with great pomp and ceremony, to the Bank of England, in London.

Each captain of the lucky crews received £40,730 18s. 0d.; each lieutenant £5,091 7s. 3d.; each warrant officer £2,468 10s. $9\frac{1}{2}$d.; each midshipman £791 17s. $0\frac{1}{4}$d; and each seaman and marine £182 4s. $9\frac{1}{4}$d.

On the 24th of November, the "Solebay"

frigate of 32 guns, Captain Poyntz, off St. Domingo, captured a small squadron of French vessels, consisting of the "Egyptien," 20-gun frigate, the 18-gun corvette "Eole," the 12-gun brig "Sevrier," and the 8-gun schooner "Vengeur."

On the 23rd of November, the 12-gun cutter "Courier," commanded by Lieutenant Searle, captured the cutter "Guerrier," a privateer, after a fierce action of fifty minutes. Lieutenant Searle was soon afterwards promoted for his gallantry in this affair.

On the 11th December, the 74-gun ship "Tremendous" (Captain Osborn), and the 50-gun ship "Adamant," chased the French ship "Prenéuse," ashore on the Isle of France.

She was deserted by her crew, and then burnt by the English.

* * * * *

In the year 1799, an American colony was taken from the Dutch. An expedition, composed of two line-of-battle-ships, four frigates, and two smaller vessels, sailed from the West Indies, and on the 16th of August anchored off the mouth of the Surinam river, in South America.

After some parley with the Dutch governor of the state, a capitulation was signed, and the colony was surrendered to the English.

During this year, Admiral Howe was lost to the navy of his country.

Lord Richard Howe was born in 1725, and after a few months at Eton, he was sent to sea, at the early age of fourteen years, on board the "Severn."

He accompanied Anson as far as Cape Horn in that navigator's celebrated voyage around the world.

At an early age he was raised to the rank of commander, and appointed to the sloop "Baltimore." While in this craft, he encountered two French vessels in the service of the Pretender. Howe ran between the two, and attacked them both, obtaining an advantage over the two in a long and obstinate fight.

Howe, for some time, had command of an English fleet at New York during the time of the American rebellion. His last duty was assisting in quelling the Mutiny of the Nore.

Howe died at his house in Grafton Street, London, August 5th, 1799.

In consequence of a misunderstanding between Admiral Lord St. Vincent and Vice-Admiral Sir John Orde, while they were serving in the Mediterranean, the latter named officer sent a challenge, which was accepted by the earl. This took place early in the month of October, both the disputants being then in town, and the morning of the 7th of the month was fixed upon for the hostile meeting.

The hostile intentions of the two distinguished seamen became known to Mr. Justice Ford, who issued warrants for the apprehension of both. The warrants were entrusted to the famous Bow Street officers, Townshend and Sayers, who apprehended Sir John Orde at his hotel in Jermyn Street, and kept him in custody till ten o'clock, when Mr. Ford bound him over in the penalty of £2,000 to keep the peace, and also compelled him to find two sureties in £1,000 each.

The magistrate then set off express, attended by the two officers, and very quickly reached Lord St. Vincent's residence, near Brentwood, where they found his lordship just about to proceed to the place appointed for the encounter. Mr. Ford informed the earl that the meeting could not be allowed, and bound him over to keep the peace in the same terms as had been imposed on Sir John Orde.

By this magisterial promptness a duel, which most probably would have resulted in the death of one or the other of these distinguished commanders, was prevented.

During the year 1799, the French lost eleven frigates, the Spaniards lost five frigates, and the Dutch lost seven ships of the line, and seventeen frigates, making a total of forty war vessels lost by the three nations we were then at war with; thirty-seven out of the forty were captured by the English navy, two were destroyed, and only a single ship (the French frigate "Charente," 36 guns) lost by accident or stress of weather.

Among the vessels above enumerated was the 50-gun ship "Leander," which had formerly belonged to the British Navy, and had been captured by the French while conveying Nelson's despatches after the battle of the Nile. The "Leander" was taken from the French by the Russians and Turks at the surrender of Corfu on the 3rd of March, 1799, and restored to England by the Emperor of Russia. Twenty-three other ships taken from the enemy were added to the British Navy.

During the same period, the English lost twenty-one ships, three of which were captured by the enemy, one blown up and destroyed in action, and seventeen lost by accident. The three captured vessels were the "Fortune," carrying 10 guns, taken by a squadron of three French frigates and two brigs; the "Dame-de-Grace," of 1 gun, captured at the same time; and the "Musquito," 6 guns, captured by two Spanish frigates.

CHAPTER XXV.

NAVAL ACTIONS DURING THE YEAR 1800.

E commence our account of the seafaring events of the year with a splendid instance of British courage and seamanship.

On the 10th of January, 1800, a singular instance of valour and dexterity occurred in the escape of a pilot-boat from a French privateer. The vessel was the "Amity," belonging to Bembridge, on the look-out for ships.

About ten in the morning, they discovered a lugger privateer about two miles distant, which they could not perceive before, in consequence of the morning being hazy.

There being little wind, the enemy were rowing with thirteen oars on each side, and fast approaching: the master of the pilot-boat thought it best to leave his vessel immediately, there being no other means of escaping; he and another man, therefore, got into their small boat, and desired James Wallis, the boy, to come also; but he bravely answered, "he would remain by the vessel, whatever might be the consequence."

Thus resolved, he gave them his watch and all the little money he had, which he requested they would give to his father; they promised to perform his request, and immediately left him to his fate, when the privateer was only a quarter of a mile distant.

In a few minutes she shot up under his lee quarter, with an intention to grapple the pilot-boat; and having fresh way, lowered her main topsails and lugsail; the lad observing their design, just as they were in the act of heaving their grappling irons, put his helm down and went about, whilst the privateer fired small arms and swivels into her.

This manœuvre obliged them to make sail and tack; when they had made all the sail they could, the young man with great judgment, tacked, and weathered them about the length of the lugger; the privateer having gained his wake, tacked also.

The youth continued to tack every time the privateer set her sails, which was repeated sixteen or seventeen times; they constantly fired when near, and particularly when crossing at a distance, never more than thirty yards.

After manœuvring in this dexterous manner for above two hours, a fresh breeze happily sprang up; the pilot-boat was on the last tack, and about a cable's length to windward, when she crossed the privateer, which, after firing all her swivels and small arms, bore up and left him.

On the 26th of January, the "Brazen," of 18 guns, Captain James Hunson, was wrecked near Brighton. Only one man was saved.

On the 18th of February, the Mediterranean fleet, under Vice-Admiral Lord Keith, captured the French 74-gun ship "Généreux," Captain Perrée, who was killed in the action.

PORTRAIT OF LORD BRIDPORT.

During the same month, the French frigate "Pallas," 38 guns, Captain Epron, was captured, after a long chase, by the English 16-gun corvette "Fairy," and the 18-gun brig "Harpy." In this action, Commander Horton, of the "Fairy," was killed. The prize was a fine new frigate of 1,030 tons, and was added to the navy, under the name of the "Pique."

On the 3rd of March, after a chase of 123 miles, the 36-gun frigate "Neréide," Captain Watkins, captured the French frigate "Vengeance," of 18 long guns.

Lord Keith, having been previously engaged in the blockade of Toulon, entered the Mediterranean with his ship and cruisers, for the purpose of blockading the island of Malta, and in co-operating with the Austrians in their efforts to expel the French from Piedmont and Tuscany.

Lord Keith arrived in the "Queen Charlotte," at Leghorn, on the 16th of March, 1800, where he landed, together with Lieutenant John Stewart, and four other persons, ordering Captain Todd to get under way, and proceed to reconnoitre the Island of Capraia, distant about thirty-six miles from Leghorn, and then in possession of the French; and which island there was some intention of attacking.

Captain Todd had proceeded only from three to four leagues from Leghorn on her way, when on the next morning, the 17th, the "Queen Charlotte" was discovered to be on fire.

Every assistance was immediately forwarded from the shore; but the boats were deterred from approaching the ship, in consequence of the discharge of the guns, which, being at the time all shotted, as they became heated, scattered the destructive metal in all directions.

At the time the fire was discovered, there were eight hundred and forty souls on board; among the survivors on this melancholy occasion was Mr. John Baird, who gives the following account of the affair:—

"At about twenty minutes after six o'clock in the morning, as I was dressing myself, I heard throughout the ship a general cry of *Fire!*

"I immediately ran to the fore ladder to get upon deck, when I found the whole half-deck, the front bulkhead of the admiral's cabin, the crat of the mainmast, and the boat's covering on the booms, all in flames; which, from every report and probability, I apprehend, was occasioned by some hay, which was lying under the half-deck, having been set on fire by a match in a tube, which was usually kept there for signal-guns.

"The mainsail at this time was set, and almost instantly caught fire, the people not being able, on account of the flames, to come to the clew-garnets. I immediately went to the forecastle, and found the Honourable George Heneage Lawrence Dundas (lieutenant) and the boatswain encouraging the people to get water to extinguish the fire.

"Seeing no other officer in the forepart of the ship, being unable to see any one on the quarter-deck from the flames and smoke between, I applied to Mr. Dundas to give me assistance to drown the lower decks, and secure the hatches, to prevent the fire from falling down. Lieutenant Dundas accordingly went down himself, with as many people as he could prevail upon to follow him; and the lower deck ports were opened, the scuppers plugged, the fore and main hatches secured, the cocks turned, water drawn in at the ports, and the pumps kept going by the people who came down, as long as they could stand at them.

"Owing to these exertions, I think, the lower decks were kept free from fire, and the magazines preserved from danger for a long time. Nor did Lieutenant Dundas or myself quit this station until several of the middle deck guns came through the deck.

"At about nine o'clock, finding it impossible to remain any longer below, Lieutenant Dundas and myself went out at the foremast lower deck ports, and got upon the forecastle; on which I apprehend there were about 150 of the people drawing water, and throwing it as far aft as possible upon the fire.

"I continued about an hour on the forecastle, till, finding all efforts to extinguish the flames unavailing, I jumped from the jib-boom, and swam to an American boat approaching the ship, by which boat I was picked up, and put into a tartan, then in charge of Lieutenant Stewart, who had come to the assistance of the ship. Captain Todd, with the first lieutenant, Mr. Bainbridge, remained on deck to the last moment, giving orders for saving the crew, without providing or apparently caring for their own safety.

"This accident, as may be expected, occasioned a dreadful loss of life: out of the crew saved, including 11 left on shore at Leghorn, the number was 167; of these 3 were lieutenants, 2 lieutenants of marines, 1 carpenter or gunner, 3 midshipmen, 1 secretary's clerk, and 146 seamen.

"Those who perished appeared to have been— 1 captain, 3 lieutenants, 1 captain of marines, 1 purser, 1 surgeon, 1 boatswain, 4 master's mates, 18 midshipmen, 1 secretary's clerk, 1 schoolmaster, 1 captain's clerk, 3 surgeon's mates, and about 636 seamen, boys, and marines; making about 673 souls. These, together with the ship, one of the largest class in the service, her guns, stores, and provisions, fell a prey to the devouring element, or were swallowed up in the fathomless abyss of the ocean."

The "Queen Charlotte" was one of those ships included in the mutiny at the Nore, of which circumstance Captain Brenton avails himself to condemn the general discipline of the crew. He says:— "This ship, from the shamefully relaxed state of discipline in which she had been kept, while the flag of Earl Howe was flying on board her, naturally became the focus of all mutiny," a character she maintained until she was burnt off Genoa.

"It will, however," says a contemporary writer, "require higher authority than Captain Brenton to sully the memory of Captain Todd, who, in order to save the lives of his men, with great bravery, perseverance, and self-devotion, sacrificed his own."

On the same day, the ship "Repulse," of 74 guns, was wrecked on the French coast near Ushant. Ten sailors were drowned, and the rest made prisoners by the French.

Captain Frederick Watkins, in the "Néréide," 36 guns, performed a dashing action on the 1st of March. He was cruising off the French coast when, late at night, four ships and a schooner were discovered to windward.

Preparations for battle were at once made, and the "Néréide," bore up for the strangers, which, by daylight on the 2nd of March, were seen to be armed vessels, and seemed willing to risk an encounter. These valorous vessels were the "Bellone," 30 guns; "Vengeance," 18 guns; "Favourite," 16 guns; "Huron," 16 guns; and "Tirailleuse," schooner, 14 guns, so that the commodore of the squadron had sufficient force to justify him in giving battle.

But, just as the British frigate arrived within gunshot, the hearts of these five pugnacious French captains failed them, and they made all sail, on different courses. The "Néréide" gave chase till night, when darkness hid the fugitives from view; when daylight came again, only one of them could be seen, which, after a twelve hours' chase, was captured, and proved to be the "Vengeance," 18 guns and 174 men.

* * * * * *

The British 20-gun ship "Danaé," commanded

by Captain Lord Proby, fell into the possession of the French under very disgraceful circumstances about this time.

It appears that there was on board the ship a man named Jackson, who had been secretary to Parker, the ringleader of the mutiny at the Nore. About half-past nine in the evening of the 15th of March, Jackson, with part of the crew, rushed on the quarterdeck, knocked down the master, wounding him severely in the head, and then threw him down the main hatchway, over which they placed the ship's boats filled with shot, thus preventing the remainder of the crew from retaking the ship.

All the officers, except Lord Proby, the master, and an officer of marines, were in bed when the mutiny broke out, but Lord Proby, on being informed of the revolt, endeavoured to get up the after hatchway, but found it guarded by at least twenty men, one of whom struck him a severe blow on the head. The mutineers were masters of the ship, which, the next morning, anchored under Fort Conquête, in Camaret Bay, near Brest.

Jackson then sent a boat on board a French vessel, and a detachment of soldiers and sailors boarded the " Danaé." Lord Proby was summoned to surrender, and replied—

" I surrender to the French nation, not to mutineers ! "

Next day, both the French and the English vessel proceeded to Brest, where Lord Proby and his officers were treated with great attention by the French officials, while the ship's crew, *including the mutineers*, were marched off to prison in the interior of the country.

On the 20th of March, off Marseilles, the 16-gun sloop " Petrel," Captain Austin, captured the French 16-gun brig " Ligurienne."

On the 30th of March, the French 80-gun ship " Guillaume Tell," Captain Saulnier, was captured by the English 64-gun ship " Lion," Captain Dixon, the 80-gun ship " Foudroyant," Captain Berry, and the 36-gun frigate " Penelope."

This was a long and obstinate fight, in which the French ship was heroically defended against heavy odds. Aboard of the English vessels there were 17 killed and 101 wounded; and on the " Guillaume Tell," there were about 200 killed and wounded.

On the 5th of April, two Spanish frigates were captured by a squadron, under Rear-Admiral Duckworth in the 74-gun ship " Swiftsure." One of the Spanish vessels was the 34-gun frigate " El Carmen," and the other the " Florentina," of 34 guns. Both were added to the navy.

On the same day, and by the same squadron, was captured the Spanish vessel " Los Anglese," of 14 guns and six swivels.

About this time the men of the fleet commanded by Vice-Admiral Lord Keith, used to amuse themselves occasionally by bombarding Genoa, which was then in the possession of the French.

But little damage was done, however, and the maintenance of a fleet at that station, at the time, was a waste of war material for little or no practical purpose.

Several gallant deeds were about the same time performed on the coast of France by the officers and men of the squadron commanded by Rear-Admiral Warren, by expeditions in boats for cutting out the enemy's ships in harbour.

On the night of the 9th of July, 1800, the squadron of frigates, fire-ships, &c., under the command of Captain Inman, of the " Andromeda," made an attempt to take or destroy the French frigates in Dunkirk Road.

The " Dart " sloop of war, of 30 guns, commanded by Captain Patrick Campbell, stood in, in the most gallant manner, and with intrepid bravery, boarded, carried, and brought off, after a desperate resistance, " La Désirée," of 40 guns and 350 men.

The fire-ships followed; but the moment the enemy discovered them to be in flames, they cut their cables, and stood down the inner channel, within the Braak Sand.

The next morning they regained their anchorage, without our ships being able to molest or cut them off.

The loss sustained in this attack, was one man killed, and Lieutenant James, of the " Dart," and seventeen men wounded.

Several of the French officers and men who were taken on board the " Désirée " being very badly wounded, Captain Inman sent them the next morning into Dunkirk, with a letter to the French commodore, who returned a polite answer.

For this heroic achievement, Captain (now Sir Patrick) Campbell, was promoted to the rank of post-captain, and his first lieutenant was made a commander.

The Earl of St. Vincent declared this to have been one of the finest instances of gallantry on record, and the cool and determined bravery of British seamen was never more conspicuous than on this occasion.

The " Désirée " was added to the British navy, under the command of Captain Inman, and after undergoing the necessary repairs, she proceeded to join the fleet destined for the attack on Copenhagen, then at Yarmouth.

In that sanguinary conflict, when victory was uncertain, " La Désirée," in Lord Nelson's own words, " performed the greatest services;" and we are enabled to state, on the authority of an officer of the " Monarch," the ship which suffered most in the action, that her fire was so astonishingly incessant, that the " Monarch's " men kept exclaiming—

" Look at the frigate ! Look at the frigate !"

On the 25th of July, the 28 gun frigate " Nemesis," Captain Baker, with a squadron, fell in with the Danish 40-gun frigate " Freya," Captain

Kabble, in charge of a convoy, in the North Sea.

The Danish captain refused to allow any of the vessels of his convoy to be searched, and fired at a boat sent from the "Nemesis" for that purpose.

The "Nemesis" and the sloop "Arrow" both commenced firing at the Danish frigate, which soon after surrendered.

This affair was the principal cause of the quarrel with the Northern powers.

On the 20th of August, the 18-pounder 38-gun frigate "Seine," Captain Milne, in the Mona Passage (West Indies), captured the French 18-pounder 40-gun frigate "Vengeance," Captain Pichot.

The "Seine" had 13 killed and 26 wounded; the "Vengeance," 30 killed and 70 wounded.

The latter was a fine ship of 1,180 tons, and was added to the navy.

On the 24th of August, the French 40-gun frigate "Diane" was captured by the 32-gun frigate "Success," Captain George Martin.

The prize was a ship of 1,140 tons, and was added to the navy under the name of "Niobe."

On the 29th of August, the Spanish 18-gun privateer "Guêpe" was cut out from Vigo Bay by twenty boats of the squadron under Commodore Warren, led by Lieutenant Burke, of the "Renown."

This was a very gallant action, for which the navy medal was given to all engaged.

On the 5th of September, Malta surrendered to the English forces under Captain George Martin and Major-General Piggott.

Within the harbour were the 64-gun ships "Athenien" and "Dégo," and the frigate "Carthagenaise," which were also surrendered.

On the 27th of October, the "San Joséf," a Spanish polacca of 14 guns, was cut out from under the guns of a fortress near Malaga by four boats from the 38-gun frigate "Phaeton," Captain Morris.

The boats were led by Lieutenant Francis Beaufort.

On the 17th of November, the boats from a small squadron under Sir Richard Strachan, cut out from Port Navalo, the French 20-gun corvette "Reolaise."

The prize was set on fire and burnt.

The smallest classes of British vessels showed great activity and daring in their encounters with the foe.

All the French coast was watched by English ships of war, and scarcely a fishing boat dared put out from shore for fear of being captured.

Some times, however, the enemy's vessels were obliged to pass from one part of the coast to another, and then our cruisers pounced down upon them like hawks upon doves.

As an instance of this, we mention the fact that the commander of the cutter "Nile," while cruising off the west coast of France, discovered a convoy of fifteen or sixteen vessels (merchantmen) creeping along the shore.

He stood out to sea to encourage them to proceed, and then, having been joined by the "Lurcher" cutter, swooped down upon them.

The frightened merchantmen ran for a point on which a battery had been thrown up; but the "Nile" captured one ship under fire from the shore, and, soon afterwards, five others were taken.

The "Lurcher," in the meantime, had captured three, making, altogether, nine ships taken by these active cruisers, with no other damage than one man slightly wounded on board the "Nile."

On the 10th of December, the 16-gun brig "Admiral Pasley," commanded by Lieutenant Nevin, was captured by two Spanish gunboats, off Ceuta, in a calm.

The Spaniards were armed with guns of such heavy calibre that they cut the English vessel to pieces, firing from a distance far beyond the range of the light guns on board the "Admiral Pasley."

Lieutenant Nevin was afterwards tried for the loss of the vessel, and honourably acquitted.

And now, having described the principal naval engagements of the year 1800, we will proceed to give a brief abstract of the vessels lost by the British, and also by the nations with whom we were at war.

The number of British ships lost was twenty-two, of which two are entered in the official returns as captured by the enemy,* four destroyed in action, and sixteen lost by accident.

During the same year the Spanish lost two ships of war, and the French twelve, *all* of which were captured by the British fleets and cruisers; nine of them were added to our navy.

CHAPTER XXVI.

THE WAR IN 1801—BOMBARDMENT OF COPENHAGEN.

THERE were no signs of peace as yet, and so our navy continued as active as ever.

On the 3rd of January, the boats belonging to the frigate "Melpomene," Captain Hamilton, captured the French brig "Sénégal," of 18 guns, in the Senegal river, Africa. In bringing the brig out of the river she ran on to some quicksands, and was lost.

In this engagement 11 men belonging to the

---

* The ships mentioned as captured were not taken in action, but carried by their mutinous crews into foreign ports.

"Melpomene," including Lieutenant Palmer, were killed, and 18 wounded.

The French corvette "Sans Pareille," of 20 guns, was captured off Sardinia, on the 20th of January, by the 28-gun frigate "Mercury," Captain Rogers. The French ship surrendered without an attempt at resistance.

On the 26th of January, the French 36-gun frigate "Dédaigneuse" was captured by the "Oiseau," "Sirius," and "Amethyst" frigates, off Cape Finisterre.

The French frigate had twenty men killed and wounded. She was added to the English navy, without being re-christened.

On the 29th of January, the 24-gun ship "Bordelais," Captain Thomas Manby, captured the "Curieux," a French brig of 18 long guns, off Barbadoes.

The brig had fifty men killed and wounded, including its captain, who had both legs shot off, and only lived a few hours after. The "Curieux" foundered a few hours after she had surrendered, and five men of the "Bordelais," and most of the French wounded, were lost with it.

When first discovered, the "Curieux" and two other French vessels were chasing the "Bordelais." As soon as Captain Manby discovered them he turned about to meet the enemy, when two of the Frenchmen sailed away, leaving the "Curieux" to her fate.

On the 1st of February, a fleet of seven ships of the line, and several frigates and transports, under Admiral Lord Keith, reached Alexandria, and anchored in Aboukir Bay.

The transports conveyed 16,000 troops, under Sir Ralph Abercromby.

On the 8th, the troops commenced landing, and were opposed by the French; but the landing of all, accompanied by 1,000 seamen, under Sir Sidney Smith, was effected next day, with only a loss of 124 killed and 585 wounded.

Another battle was fought on the 13th, in which the seamen and marines of the fleet were also engaged and suffered some loss.

The fleet and its crew had nothing more to do with the expedition than to bring away the troops sometime after the defeat of the French General Menou and the death of General Abercromby.

On the 13th of February, a French fleet, under M. Gunteaume, captured the English frigate "Success," of 32 guns, Captain Peard.

The 18-pounder 36-gun frigate "Phœbe," Captain Barlow, on the 19th of February, engaged and captured the French 40-gun frigate "Africaine," to the eastward of Gibraltar.

The "Africaine" was from Rochefort, bound to Egypt, and had on board 400 troops, many of whom were killed and wounded.

There were 200 killed and 185 wounded of soldiers and crew.

The "Phœbe" only lost one man killed and 11 wounded.

The prize was added to the English navy under the name of "Amelia."

Denmark and some of the other northern powers complained about their merchant ships in convoy being stopped and searched by English cruisers, and also about the affair of the "Freya," mentioned in the last chapter.

Russia, Denmark, and Sweden formed a confederacy for the purpose of resisting the English, and England resolved to teach them a lesson.

For this purpose, Admiral Sir Hyde Parker was despatched from Yarmouth Roads on the 12th of March.

The fleet consisted of eighteen sail of the line and several frigates and bomb-vessels.

Lord Nelson accompanied the expedition as vice-admiral.

In passing up the Sound, the fleet exchanged a few shots with the towns of Cronenburg and Helsengen, in which about the only damage done to the fleet was by the bursting of a gun on the "Isis," by which accident seven men were killed.

About noon, on the 30th, the fleet anchored near the island of Huën, fifteen miles below Copenhagen, where a council of war was held on board the "London."

After spending twenty-four hours in the boats of the fleet in taking soundings and putting down new buoys in the place of those that had been removed by the Danes, Nelson had not so good an opinion of the defences of Copenhagen as Sir Hyde Parker and some of the other officers, and offered, with ten ships of the line and all the small craft, to destroy the Danish shipping.

Admiral Parker accepted this offer, and allowed Nelson two additional 50-gun ships.

CRESTS OF VESSELS IN THE ROYAL NAVY (A.D. 1870).

On the morning of the 2nd of April, Nelson sailed for the attack.

Owing to the strength of the currents, the "Damascus" and some of the gunboats were unable to join in the action.

Three other vessels, the "Agamemnon," the "Russell," and the "Bellona," in going up the harbour, got aground and were unable to take their stations.

The cannonade commenced about ten o'clock in the morning, and, at the end of three hours, few, if any, of the Danish guns were silenced, and no apparent advantage had been gained on either side.

Admiral Sir Hyde Parker, who was at too great a distance from the scene of action to comprehend the exact state of affairs, and learning that signals of distress were hoisted on two line-of-battle ships, as, in fact, was the case with the "Russell" and "Bellona," which were aground, was induced to hoist a signal for discontinuing the action.

When it was first reported to Nelson that "No. 39" had been thrown out by the commander-in-chief, he took no notice of the communication.

"You know, Foley," said he, turning to the captain, when his attention was again called to the signal, "I have but one eye. I have a right to be blind sometimes."

Putting the glass to his blind eye in that mood of mind which sports with bitterness, he exclaimed—

"Hang the signal! Keep mine for closer battle flying."*

The battle continued, and by two o'clock in the afternoon, the fire of the Danes had nearly ceased along the line, and several of their vessels had struck.

Shots were fired from some of the Danish vessels after they had surrendered, and, to prevent the alternative of giving no quarter, Nelson sent a letter to the Crown Prince of Denmark, advising him to command his officers to surrender, and save bloodshed.

A wafer was handed him for sealing this letter; but he ordered a candle from the cockpit, and sealed it with wax, saying—

"This is no time to appear hurried and informal."

The Danish fleet engaged in this battle consisted of eighteen vessels, armed with 628 guns, 360 of which were 24-pounders, and manned by 4,849 men.

These vessels, many of which were old and dismantled, were anchored in a line about one mile

THE WRECK OF THE "HANNIBAL."

* Southey's "Life of Nelson."

and a half long, and were under the command of Commodore Olfert Fischer.

At the northern end of the line were the two Trekroner batteries, built on piles, one mounting 30 long 24-pounders and 38 long 36-pounders, and both were provided with furnaces for heating shot.

These batteries were guarded by two two-decked block-ships, not included in the eighteen vessels above mentioned.

After the despatch of Nelson's note, the firing was continued by the "Monarch," "Ganges," and "Defiance," at the Crown batteries, from which several of the English fleet had suffered much damage.

The Danish Adjutant-General Lindholm soon after appeared with a flag of truce, and the firing, which had been continued for nearly five hours, suddenly ceased.

The heavy loss sustained by the English in this action is strong evidence of the skill and courage with which the Danes defended their ships. Mr. James estimates the loss of the English at 250 killed and mortally wounded, and 850 recoverably and slightly wounded.

On board the "Monarch," there were 250 killed and wounded. She supported the united fire of the Danish ships "Holstein" and "Zealand," besides being raked by the Crown batteries.

The Danish loss amounted to about 1,800 in killed and wounded, and seventeen vessels sunk, burnt, or captured.

Nelson said that he had "been in above one hundred engagements, but that of Copenhagen was the most terrible of all."*

On the 12th of April, the English fleet left Copenhagen, after taking the guns from the Danish fleet, and burning and destroying all but the "Holstein," of 60 guns, which was the only prize ship taken to England.

On the 6th of May, off Barcelona, the 14-gun brig "Speedy," commanded by Lord Cochrane, captured the Spanish xebec "Gamo," mounting 22 long 12-pounders on the main deck, 8 long 8-pounders, and two heavy carronades on the quarter-deck and forecastle, and manned by a crew of 300 men.

Not liking to stand the fire of so many guns, Captain Cochrane, after the action had continued for forty-five minutes, determined to board. The "Speedy" was laid alongside the enemy, and Captain Cochrane, with only forty men, leaped on to the deck of the "Gamo," attacked 300 men, and took the vessel from them.

The "Gamo" had her commander, Don Francisco de Torres, and 14 men killed, and 41 wounded. The "Speedy" had 4 seamen killed, and 2 officers and 6 seamen wounded. The naval medal was given for this action.

---

* Nelson's "Despatches;" and James' "Naval History," Vol. III.

On the 24th of June, the English 74-gun ship "Swiftsure," Captain Benjamin Hallowell, was captured by a division of the Toulon fleet, under Admiral Ganteaume, and taken into Toulon.

On the 3rd of July, the "Speedy," Captain Lord Cochrane, fell in with the French 80-gun ships "Indomptable" and "Formidable," the 74-gun ship "Desaix," and 38-gun frigate "Muiron," all under command of Rear-Admiral Linois.

They gave pursuit, and after a long and well-conducted chase, the little "Speedy" was overhauled, and compelled to surrender.

Cadiz at that time was blockaded by an English fleet of seven ships and one frigate, under Rear-Admiral Sir James Saumarez, who, learning that Admiral Linois, with the French fleet, had gone to Algesiras, raised the blockade, and sailed in pursuit of him.

The enemy was found on the 7th of July, anchored near Fort San Jago, in Algesiras Roads, where they were attacked.

A severe action then commenced, in which the English vessels "Venerable" and "Spencer," owing to variable winds and calms, were unable to join.

While attempting to cross the hawse of the "Formidable," the English ship "Hannibal," of 74 guns, Captain Ferris, took the ground.

All attempts to get her off were unavailing.

The "Audacious" and "Cæsar" drifted near a battery on an island, and were so severely cut up that soon after, when a light breeze came from the land, they made sail, followed by some of the other vessels, while the "Hannibal" remained aground, and became a total wreck.

Later in the afternoon, Captain Dundas, of the "Calpé," just from Gibraltar, saw the "Hannibal" with the union hoisted downwards, and sent some boats under Lieutenant Sykes to her relief.

The party in the boats were detained prisoners by the French, who had already taken possession of the ship.

The English fleet in this engagement suffered much loss in masts and rigging, and had 121 men killed, 240 wounded, and 14 missing, who are supposed to have fallen over with the masts. The greatest loss was on board the "Hannibal," which did not surrender until 143 men had been killed and wounded. The French loss amounted to 306 killed, and about the same number wounded. Amongst their killed were Captains Moncousu and Lalonde.

Admiral Linois immediately sent to Cadiz for assistance, and a Spanish squadron was without the slightest delay sent to his aid. This fact was learned by Captain Keats, of the "Superb," who remained, after the departure of the English fleet, to watch the port.

He immediately proceeded to Gibraltar, and informed Admiral Saumarez of what he had learnt; and every exertion was made night and day to get the fleet again ready for sea. At daybreak, on the 12th, the fleet again moved out, and in the afternoon the combined fleets of the enemy were met.

Contrary to all expectations of the English, the enemy tried to avoid a battle by flight, and Captain Richard Keats, of the "Superb," 74 guns, who had obtained permission to attack the rear of the enemy, sailed in pursuit, and his vessel being a very fast sailer, it was the first to engage the enemy. On reaching them he ranged alongside the "Real Carlos," a Spanish three-decker, of 112 guns, and commenced firing the larboard guns. At the third broadside, the foretop-mast of the "Real Carlos" was shot away, and the vessel was seen to be on fire.

Seeing that this vessel was pretty certain to be destroyed without any more of his assistance, Captain Keats hauled off, and chased the French ship, "Saint Antoine," of 74 guns, which he overtook, and, after an action of thirty minutes, compelled her to surrender.

While this last engagement was being fought, the Spanish three-decker, "Herminegildo," of 112 guns, taking its consort, the "Real Carlos," for an enemy, bore up to it, and, although it was in flames fore and aft, gave it a broadside.

The two ships got foul of each other, and the "Herminegildo" also took fire.

Both vessels soon after blew up with all on board, and only two officers and about forty men were all who were saved out of nearly 2,000 people.

The English ships, "Cæsar," "Venerable," "Spencer," and "Thames," then arrived, and sailed in pursuit of the French ship, "Formidable," which was overtaken by the "Venerable" and "Thames."

In a running fight, the "Venerable's" foremast went over the side, and a few minutes later, she struck on a reef off San Pedro, about twelve miles from Cadiz.

The rest of the combined fleet soon after entered Cadiz in safety.

The "Superb," "Venerable," and "Thames" frigates were the only English vessels engaged in this affair, and, on the former, fifteen men were wounded and none killed. Aboard the "Venerable," the master, John Williams, fifteen seamen, and two marines, were killed, and about 90 officers, seamen, and marines were wounded.

For this action, Sir James Saumarez was created a Knight of the Bath, and was given a pension of £1,200 per annum.

Captain Richard Goodwin Keats, of the "Superb," who performed the principal work of gaining the victory, received no particular mark of the Government's approbation of his conduct, and was but barely mentioned in Admiral Saumarez's public despatches.

In the month of July, 1801, a squadron of British frigates, employed in watching the enemy's fleet, lay at anchor close in with the harbour of Brest.

The combined fleets of France and Spain were full in their view; still nearer, and quite open to them, was the bay of Cameret, where the French national corvette, "La Chevrette," lay protected by the batteries. In this situation she was considered by the French as no less secure than if she had been in the roads of Brest; while the effect which this seemingly impregnable position had upon the British squadron was to inspire a wish to cut her out.

It was resolved by the commander of the squadron that this attempt should be made.

Accordingly, the boats of the "Doris" and "Beaulieu," manned entirely by volunteers, under the orders of Lieutenant Losack, who had been sent from the admiral's ship to conduct the enterprise, set out on the night of Monday, the 20th of July, to endeavour to bring out the corvette. But a separation of the boats having taken place, no attempt was made that night. Some of the boats having reached the entrance of the bay, lay there on their oars till dawn of day, in expectation of being joined by the rest; and before they got back to the frigates were unfortunately seen, both from the corvette and from the shore.

The enemy now concluded, what they never before imagined, that an attack was meditated. Though they judged it a measure of extreme rashness, they were resolved to omit no possible preparation.

In the morning of the 21st, they got the corvette under way, moved her a mile and a half up the bay, and moored her under the batteries. They put on board of her troops from the shore, so that her number of men now amounted nearly to 400. The arms and ammunition were brought upon deck and the great guns were loaded to the muzzle with grape shot. The batteries were prepared, temporary redoubts were thrown up upon the points; and a gun-vessel, with a couple of 32-pounders, was moored at the entrance of the bay as a guard-boat.

Having taken these precautions, they, in the afternoon, displayed a large French ensign above an English one, as a signal of defiance.

All these manœuvres were well observed from the "Beaulieu," the crew of which ship had shown extraordinary ardour to engage in this enterprise.

Though they now saw that a most desperate resistance was certain, the severe disappointment which they experienced from the fruitless expedition of the former night, filled them with eagerness to make an effectual attempt.

Mr. Maxwell, the first lieutenant, who had not been out on the night before, and who was ordered on an expedition, then in agitation, of carrying fireships into Brest, gladly embraced this opportunity of practising his boat's crew selected on this occasion, preparatory to this grand object, and resolved to head his own shipmates in the attack to be made that night.

This officer, warned by the former failure, resolved to keep his own boats in close order, and should a separation of the other boats happen as before, through any unfortunate accident, to proceed to the attack with the "Beaulieu's" boats alone.

This resolution, so congenial to their wishes, his shipmates heard with much satisfaction, and employed themselves through the day in putting their arms in the best order, particularly in grinding the cutlasses to cut the boarding nettings, and other impediments which they expected to meet with.

When night arrived, six boats, manned with between 80 and 90 officers and men of the "Beaulieu," joined about half-past nine, the boats of the "Doris," "Uranie," and "Robust," the whole being, as before, under the command of Lieutenant Losack. The orders which he then gave were to lie on their oars, or pull easy, as it was much too soon for the attack.

About a quarter of an hour afterwards, Lieutenant Losack, with his own boat, accompanied by some other boats, went in chase of a boat from the shore, supposed to be a look-out boat belonging to the enemy, and, therefore, of consequence to be secured, if possible.

For a considerable time after he parted company, the remainder of the boats continued as he left them, lying-to on their oars, and sometimes pulling easy. Finding he did not return, Mr. Maxwell, reflecting upon the miscarriage of the preceding night, considering that the boats were yet at least six miles from the scene of action, and aware of the time requisite to row that distance against a fresh breeze, judged it expedient, in order that the enterprise might have the best chance of succeeding, to proceed immediately towards the entrance of the bay, a situation evidently more eligible for them to lie-to, should this be necessary, than where they then were.

He therefore, gave way ahead with the boats of the "Beaulieu," and the other boats followed his example.

As they proceeded, they perceived the signals of the enemy, both to and from the shore, and at length they arrived off the entrance of the bay.

It was now half-past twelve.

The moon was sinking beneath the horizon. The wind, which for the first part of the night blew right into the bay, had been dying away, and it was now a perfect calm. Every thing concurred to render this the time at which an attack might be made with probability of success.

The night was too far advanced to admit of any longer delay; and had the attempt been deferred till next night, it must have been made to a great disadvantage, on account of the increasing moon, now in the eleventh day of her age.

However, Mr. Losack, and the boats which accompanied him, were still absent. In consequence of his absence there was much difference of opinion through the remaining boats. Many were undetermined in what manner to act, whether to go on, or return to their ships.

These circumstances were adverted to by Mr. Maxwell, who was now the senior officer.

He saw that there remained but one way of preventing a total failure of the enterprise; and that was to assume the command himself, and immediately proceed to the attack with the boats present. He declared that this was his resolution; he intimated his intention to the boats within hail, and despatched a midshipman to those astern, and seemingly returning with orders to them, in the name of his Majesty's service, to follow the boats of the "Beaulieu" to the attack.

This determination was received with rapture by the volunteers of the "Beaulieu."

About this time, by good fortune, a gentle breeze sprang up from the south, right out of the bay. This breeze, so auspicious to the success of the enterprise, animated them to enthusiasm.

To Mr. Maxwell it dictated a manœuvre singular and daring.

He gave orders, that immediately upon boarding, while the rest were engaged in endeavouring to disarm the enemy's crew on deck, the smartest topmen of the "Beaulieu," whose qualifications he well knew, should fight their way aloft and cut the sails loose with their cutlasses. He also appointed the most trusty hands to cut the cable, one of the best men in the boats for the helm, and hands for the rudder-chains, in case of the tiller-ropes being cut.

Having made this arrangement for setting the ship adrift instantly upon boarding, and thus taking advantage of the favourable breeze, he gave orders for the charge.

The sky being clear, though the moon was set, they soon came in sight of the corvette, and were as soon seen from her.

The instant she hailed, at the distance of four or five cables, she opened a heavy fire of musketry from every part of the ship, accompanied by showers of grape-shot from the great guns.

A heavy fire of musketry at the same time commenced from the shore and batteries; in the face of which the "Beaulieu's" boats, in the most gallant and intrepid manner, rushed on to the attack, most nobly assisted by those of the "Uranie," commanded by Lieutenant Neville, who stood up in his boat, cheering and animating his men with the most undaunted bravery, while the bullets were flying about their heads like hail, and many were dropping down, killed or wounded, before they came alongside. When they reached the vessel, the "Beaulieu's" boats boarded on the starboard bow and quarter; the "Uranie's," one of the "Robust's," and one of the "Doris's" on the larboard bow.

The attempt to board was most obstinately opposed by the French, armed at all points with fire arms, sabres, tomahawks, and pikes, who in their turn even boarded the boats.

Notwithstanding this obstinate resistance, in the course of which the assailants lost all their fire-arms, and had nothing remaining but their swords, the boarding was effected.

The men who had been ordered for that service, proceeded to fight their way aloft. In this attempt several of them were killed, and others desperately wounded; but the rest persevered with unparalleled courage. Many of them, bleeding of their wounds, got upon the yards, upon which they were obliged to scramble out with their cutlasses, upon their hands and knees, the foot ropes having been all strapped up, and surmounting every obstacle, they executed, with inconceivable expedition, the arduous service in which they were engaged.

In less than three minutes after the boats came alongside, in the very heat of the conflict, when almost half of the British sailors were killed or wounded, and the enemy were three to one against them, down came the three top-sails and courses, the ship at the same time casting, the cable being cut outside.

The prompt execution of these operations proved decisive.

The moment the French saw the sails fall, and found themselves, as if by a miracle, under way, and drifting out, they were seized with astonishment and consternation. Some of them jumped overboard, others threw down their arms, and tumbled down the hatchways.

The British sailors now soon got possession of the quarter-deck and forecastle, which in five minutes after boarding, were nearly covered with dead bodies.

The rest of the enemy having retreated below, kept up a heavy fire of musketry from the main-deck and up the hatchways. They also frequently set off large trains of powder, endeavouring to blow up the quarterdeck, and throw the British into confusion.

This obliged the British to divide into two parties. One party guarded the hatchways and gangways, and returned the fire of the enemy with their own arms and ammunition; the other party made sail in order to clear the decks, for which it was necessary for them to throw overboard two or three dozen of the Frenchmen who had fallen in the conflict, among whom were some of their own gallant companions.

In the meantime the breeze was gently drifting the vessel out of the bay, the batteries continuing to direct their fire right upon her, as they had done from the time she got under way.

Scarcely was she clear of the point, from which showers of musketry and grape played upon her, when it again fell calm. This calm left her exposed to the fire of the batteries. Though she was now free from the danger principally apprehended, that of getting on shore, still the two-and-thirty pound shot and shells from all directions were flying about through the ship's side, masts, sails, and rigging.

The state of the boats prevented towing. Some of them were sunk, others were adrift with killed and wounded men, and the rest were engaged in towing out these from under the fire of the batteries. However, a light breeze springing up from the north-east, at length drew her out.

PORTRAIT OF LORD KEITH.

The engagement had now lasted upwards of two hours, though during this time the enemy had kept up a constant fire from the maindeck, and shore, yet the British seamen managed to set every sail in the ship, and had even got top-gallant yards across. The ship being now quite clear of the batteries, and our men having twice threatened that they would give the enemy no quarter if they continued their fire from below, they at last surrendered themselves prisoners of war.

About this time some boats were perceived coming from the direction of Brest, which accordingly were suspected to be enemies.

Mr. Maxwell, therefore, immediately prepared for a new conflict, and had the sides of the ship manned with pikes and arms to defend her. But on nearer approach, these were found to be the boats which had not been present during the action, and with them Mr. Losack, to whom Mr. Maxwell then resigned the command.

The morning's dawn displayed a dreadful scene of carnage, and at the same time, close to the scene of action, the harbour of Brest, with the combined fleets of France and Spain; and, to the enemy, the mortifying sight of one of their ships of war brought out, in their immediate presence, from a position that was deemed impregnable, and sailing down to join the British frigates.

Thus terminated an enterprise, which in this species of warfare may safely be pronounced to be without parallel.

In the late war, many ships of the enemy were, with the greatest gallantry, boarded and cut out by the meritorious British seamen, but the cutting out of the "Chevrette" is distinguished from all similar achievements by several material circumstances.

The enemy were not taken by surprise; they expected an attack, they prepared themselves for it, and they defied it. Not only the vessel, but the batteries on shore which protected her, were in readiness, and on their guard. The British seamen were exposed to a severe fire, both from the ship and from the shore, before they came alongside. They then fought their way up the sides of a vessel full of men, armed with every kind of weapon calculated to resist their attempt.

Having succeeded in boarding, they at once contended with an enemy three times their number, and made themselves masters of the rigging, and got the vessel under way. Exposed to a dreadful fire from the numerous surrounding batteries, and occupied with the conflict within, they brought her, in the night, out of a roadstead narrow and difficult.

All this was done in the presence of the grand fleet of the enemy; it was done by nine boats out of fifteen, which originally set out upon the expedition; it was done under the conduct of an officer, who, in the absence of the person appointed to command, undertook it upon his own responsibility, and whose intrepidity, judgment, and presence of mind, seconded by the wonderful exertions of the officers and men under his command, succeeded in effecting an enterprise which, by those who reflect upon its peculiar circumstances, will ever be regarded with astonishment.

Total of the English killed, 18; wounded, 57; missing, 1.

Total of the French killed:—first captain, 2 lieutenants, 3 midshipmen, 1 lieutenant of the troops, with 85 seamen and troops. Wounded, 1 lieutenant, 4 midshipmen, with 57 seamen and troops.

We think the following anecdotes, descriptive of individual exertions on the memorable occasion above described, will be acceptable to our readers.

Mr. Brown, boatswain of the "Beaulieu," after forcing his way into the "Chevrette's" quarter-gallery, found the door planked up, and so securely barricaded, that all his efforts to force it were ineffectual.

Through the crevices of the planks, he discovered a number of men sitting on the cabin deck, armed with pikes and pistols. With the fire of the latter he was frequently annoyed whilst attempting to burst in.

He next tried the quarter, and, after an obstinate resistance, gained the taffrail.

The officer who commanded the party was at this time fighting his way up a little farther forward.

For an instant, whilst looking round to see where he should make his push, he stood exposed a mark to the enemy's fire, when, waving his cutlass, he cried—

"Make a lane there!"

Then he gallantly dashed among them, and fought his way forward, until he reached his old part, the forecastle, which the men, animated by his example, soon cleared of the enemy.

Here Mr. Brown remained during the rest of the contest, not only repulsing the French in their frequent attempts to retake his post, but attending to the orders from the quarterdeck, and assisting in casting the ship, and making sail with as much coolness as though he had been on board the "Beaulieu."

Henry Wallis, quartermaster of the "Beaulieu," was appointed by the officer who commanded during the attack, to the "Chevrette's" helm.

This gallant seaman fought his way to the wheel, killing one or two of the enemy in his progress. Although severely wounded in the contest, and bleeding, he steadily remained at his station, steering the "Chevrette" out until she was in safety from the fire of the batteries.

On his officer's saying he was afraid his wounds were severe, the brave fellow said it was only a graze, and a prick with a cutlass, and would not prevent him from going again on such another expedition, and wished it were the following night.

He knew there was an arduous and important service about to be performed by the boats of the fleets, and being among the volunteers from the "Beaulieu," concealed the state of his wounds, that he might not be laid aside.

This brave man had served nearly seven years in the ship, and constantly distinguished himself on every service of danger or difficulty that occurred. Was any extraordinary exertion required, Wallis was sure to be foremost. If a man had fallen overboard, he was always, fortunately, in the way, and either in the boat or the water.

During the time he belonged to the ship, nearly a dozen men were indebted to him for their lives, which he had saved by plunging overboard, sometimes even in a gale of wind, at the utmost hazard of his own.

After this sketch of his character, it will be natural to suppose he possessed the confidence of his officer; and his behaviour in this arduous contest justified the high opinion entertained of his courage and perseverance.

Another of these brave fellows, Richard Smith, quartermaster, was desperately wounded while steering one of the boats, before they reached the corvette. After laying stunned for some time, he recovered himself, and was very much distinguished during the whole of the combat on board the "Chevrette."

One of the top-men, who had been appointed to cut loose the sails, was wounded in the body and arm while boarding.

After they gained a footing, the commanding officer observing him going aloft with his arm bleeding fast, desired he would wait while a tourniquet was put on. The brave fellow refused, saying it would be time enough when he had performed his duty.

He persevered, and did not descend until the sails were set. The enemy, among other precautions, having stopped the horses up, he was obliged to crawl out on the yard, and the exertion, while aloft, occasioned his wounds to bleed so profusely, that he fainted the instant he came down.

John Ware, boatswain's mate, lost his left arm by the cut of a sabre while boarding. He fell into the boat, but, having bound up the stump, returned to the charge, and behaved gallantly during the whole of the contest.

On the 27th of July, the 36-gun frigate "Immortalité," Captain Hotham, captured the French 26-gun privateer "Invention."

On the 3rd of August, the frigates "Phœnix," "Pomone," and "Pearl," Captains Halstead, Gower, and Ballard, off the Isle of Elba, captured the French 38-gun frigate "Carrère," after an action of ten minutes.

On the 3rd of August, Lord Nelson, with the fleet under his command, bombarded Boulogne, and sank five gunboats and damaged several others, with but a trifling loss being sustained by the English.

Napoleon's armies having by this time overrun nearly all Europe, he, being relieved by the treaty of Luneville from all apprehensions of a serious continental struggle, turned all his attention to the shores of Great Britain, and made important preparations for invasion on his own side of the Channel. Though not of that magnitude of character which they afterwards assumed, these efforts were of a nature to claim the most serious attention of our Government.

From the mouth of the Scheldt to that of the Garonne, every creek and headland was fortified, so as to afford protection to the small craft which were creeping round the shore from all the harbours of the kingdom, to the general rendezvous of Dunkirk and Boulogne.

The latter harbour was the general point of assembling; gunboats and flat-bottomed praams were collected in great numbers, furnaces heated for red-hot shot, immense batteries constructed, and every preparation made, not only for a vigorous defence, but for the most energetic offensive operations.

The immensity of these preparations was studiously dwelt on in the French papers; nothing was talked of but the approaching descent upon Great Britain; and fame, ever the first to sound the alarm, so magnified their amount, that when a few battalions pitched their tents on the heights of Boulogne, it was universally credited in England that the army of invasion was about to take its station, preparatory to the threatened attempt.

Very many of our countrymen imagined from the determination and courage which Napoleon, throughout all his engagements, evinced, that the attempt to land troops in the English ports might be crowned with success.

These were the thoughts of the timid, which were, of course, considerably augmented by the over sanguine reports the French prints gave of the anticipated attack.

Nothing could possibly exceed the preparations made on the part of Great Britain to withstand the gigantic operations of France.

But, although such was the case, many placed that confidence in Nelson which his superior bravery and knowledge deserved, and felt that, though the note of the Bird of France sounded shrill and loud, the Lion of England was able and could contend against it.

The English fleets at this time in the narrow seas were so powerful, that no attempt at invasion by open force could be made with any chance of success, there being fourteen ships of the line under Admiral Cornwallis, off Brest, and seventeen in the German Ocean, observing the Dutch harbours: but it was impossible to conceal, that the same wind which wafted the French flotilla out of its harbours, might chain the English cruisers to theirs; and, notwithstanding the greatest maritime superiority, we had had many proofs that it was impossible at all times to prevent a vigilant and active enemy from putting to sea during the darkness of autumnal or winter months; and it was easy to foresee, that, even although ultimate defeat might attend a descent, incalculable confusion and distress would inevitably follow it in the first instance.

Influenced by these views, the English Government provided a powerful armament of bombs and light vessels in the Downs, and entrusted the command to Lord Nelson, whose daring and successful exploits at Aboukir and the Nile pointed him out as peculiarly fitted for the enterprise.

Having hoisted his flag in the "Medusa" frigate, he went to reconnoitre Boulogne, the point from which it was supposed the great attempt would be made, and which the French, in fear of an attack themselves, were fortifying with all care.

He approached near enough to sink two of their floating batteries, and to destroy a few gunboats, which were without the pier: what damage was done within could not be ascertained.

"Boulogne," he said, "was not a very pleasant place that morning:—but," he added, "it is not my wish to injure the poor inhabitants; and the town is spared as much as the nature of the service will admit."

Enough was done to show the enemy that they could not with impunity come outside their own ports.

Nelson's eye was fixed upon Flushing.

"To take possession of that place," he said, "would be a week's expedition for four or five thousand troops."

This, however, required a consultation with the Admiralty; and that something might be done meantime, he resolved upon attacking the flotilla in the mouth of Boulogne harbour.

This resolution was made in deference to the opinion of others, and to the public feeling which was so preposterously excited.

He himself scrupled not to assert that the French army would never embark at Boulogne for the invasion of England; and he owned, that this boat-warfare was not congenial to his feelings. Into Helvoet or Flushing he should be happy to lead, if Government turned their thoughts that way.

"While I serve," said he, "I will do it actively, and to the very best of my abilities."

The attack was made by the boats of the squadron in five divisions, under Captains Somerville, Parker, Cotgrave, Jones, and Conn.

The previous essay had taught the French the weak parts of their position, and they omitted no means of strengthening it, and of guarding against the expected attempt.

The boats put off about half an hour before midnight; but, owing to the darkness, and tide and half tide, which must always make night attacks so uncertain on the coasts of the Channel, the divisions separated. One could not arrive at all; another not till daybreak.

The others made their attack gallantly; but the enemy was fully prepared: every vessel was defended by long poles, headed with iron spikes, projecting from their sides; strong nettings were braced up to their lower yards; they were moored by the bottom to the shore; they were strongly manned with soldiers, and protected by land batteries, and the shore was lined with troops.

Many were taken possession of; and, though they could not have been brought out, would have been burnt, had not the French resorted to a mode of offence which they have often used, but which no other people have ever been wicked enough to employ.

The moment the firing ceased on board one of their own vessels, they fired upon it from the shore, perfectly regardless of their own men.

The commander of one of the French divisions acted like a generous enemy. He hailed the boats as they approached, and cried out in English—

"Let me advise you, my brave Englishmen, to keep your distance; you can do nothing here; and it is only uselessly shedding the blood of brave men to make the attempt."

The French official account boasted of the victory.

"The combat," it is said, "took place in sight of both countries; it was the first of the kind, and the historian would have cause to make this remark."

They guessed our loss at four or five hundred. It amounted to one hundred and seventy-two.

In his private letters to the Admiralty, Nelson affirmed that, had our force arrived as he intended, it was not all the chains in France which could have prevented our men from bringing off the whole of the vessels.

There had been no error committed; and never did Englishmen display more courage.

Upon this point Nelson was fully satisfied, but he said he should never bring himself again to allow any attack, wherein he himself was not personally concerned; and that his mind suffered more than if he had had a leg shot off in the affair.

He grieved particularly for Captain Parker, an excellent officer, to whom he was greatly attached, and who had an aged father looking to him for assistance. His thigh was shattered in the action, and the wound proved mortal, after some weeks of suffering and manly resignation.

The total loss to the English in this attempt was 44 killed and 126 wounded.

On the 19th of August the 38-gun frigate "Sibylle," Captain Adam, when off the Island of St. Ann's, discovered a French frigate, which she attacked, and after an action of seventeen minutes, compelled to surrender.

The prize was the frigate "Chiffonne," of 36 guns, which sustained a loss of 23 killed and 30 wounded.

On the 2nd of September, a small squadron, under Captain Halstead, of the "Phœnix," when blockading the port of Porto Ferrajo, saw the French frigates "Success" (formerly British), of 32 guns, and the "Bravoure," 36 guns, and drove them on shore at Vasa.

The "Bravoure" was destroyed, and the "Success" was restored to her place in the English navy.

On the 6th of September the corvette "Victor," Captain Collier, had an engagement with the French 18-gun brig "Flèche" near the anchorage of Mahé, in which the latter vessel was sunk.

CRESTS OF VESSELS IN THE ROYAL NAVY (A.D. 1870).

The "Lark," 18-gun sloop, Captain Johnson, ran the Spanish privateer schooner "Esperanza" under shelter of the Portilla reefs, Island of Cuba, on the 13th of September. Two boats were sent from the "Lark" to cut the Spaniard out, and gallantly succeeded with only a loss of one man killed and 12 wounded. On board the privateer 21 men were killed and six wounded.

On the 14th of September, 690 seamen and marines, under Captain George Long, of the (the 12th October, 1801), a cessation of hostilities was ordered, in accordance with preliminary articles of peace that had previously been signed in London.

A treaty was concluded at Amiens on the 25th of March, 1802.

By this treaty France regained all that had been taken from her in the East and West Indies and Africa. Holland regained her West India possessions except Guiana, which England retained, and the Cape of Good Hope. In the East Indies they

WRECK OF THE "APOLLO."

"Virago," assisted by a party of Tuscans, left the ships "Généreux" and "Dragon," and attacked some French batteries near Porto Ferrajo. After meeting at first with some trifling success in destroying some of the batteries, the party were compelled to retreat with a loss of 15 killed, 33 wounded, and more than 70 missing.

On the 28th of October, the 14-gun brig "Pasley," commanded by Lieutenant Wooldridge, captured the Spanish polacre ship "Virgin del Rosario." The "Pasley" had three men killed and seven wounded; the polacre had 21 killed, including her captain, and 13 wounded. The navy medal was given for this action.

Before the last two events we have mentioned regained Malacca and the islands of Amboyna and Banda, but lost the entire island of Ceylon. Sweden and Denmark had their colonies restored to them, and Spain agreed to relinquish all future claim to the island of Trinidad.

During this long war England had forty-two vessels of war captured by the enemy, five of which were ships of the line, and nine frigates and smaller vessels were destroyed.

During that time there were lost to the navy eighty-two vessels by being wrecked, ten were burnt, and twenty-two were foundered, making a total loss of 165 vessels.

From the commencement of the war, in 1793, to the 28th of October, 1801, the English captured from the French thirty-four ships of the line, and destroyed eleven, besides capturing fifty-nine frigates and destroying sixteen.

From the Dutch were captured eighteen ships of the line and thirty-three frigates.

From the Spaniards were captured five ships of the line and eleven frigates, while five of their ships of the line and four frigates were destroyed.

From the Danes two ships of the line were captured.

In all, England captured 185 vessels, 144 of which were added to her navy.

One of the most unfortunate shipwrecks that had happened for some time occurred on the 20th of March in this year.

The ship "Invincible," 74 guns, was totally lost on the coast of Norfolk. More than 400 lives were lost, including the captain and most of the officers.

The year 1802 was one of peace, and there is but little of interest for that year to be recorded of the navy.

The Board of Admiralty, however, profited from the experiences of the past by condemning the smaller vessels and increasing the power of the larger ones.

On the 6th of January, John Mayfield, and thirteen other seamen, part of the crew of the "Téméraire," were tried by a court-martial, at Portsmouth, for "using mutinous and seditious words, and taking an active and mutinous part in seditious assemblies."

Twelve of them were sentenced to death, and one to receive 200 lashes.

On the 14th, five more of the mutineers of the same ship were tried and found guilty, and on the same day Taylor, Dixon, Riley, and Edmunds were hanged in pursuance of their sentence.

The next day, January 15th, Chesterman, Collins, Hilliard, Fitzgerald and Ward were executed—three on board the "Téméraire," one on the "Formidable," and one on board the "Majestic."

On the 10th of April, 1,000 French prisoners, captured by the navy, were liberated from the depot at Norman Cross, and conveyed to Dunkirk.

CHAPTER XXVII.

THE YEAR 1803—RENEWAL OF THE WAR.

THE peace of Amiens was only a sham, and it is doubtful if any of the parties to it were really in earnest. They were only seeking to gain time.

Buonaparte continued his encroachments on the continent, and made a demand on the English Government to suppress liberty of the press and of speech in the British dominions.

England refused or neglected to deliver up the island of Malta, as she had promised in the articles of the treaty.

This state of affairs could not last many days, and on the 18th of May, 1803, a declaration of war against France was laid before Parliament.

When the English nation found itself once more compelled to go to war, it was very natural that the Government should in the first place look to the state of the navy, and this is how they found it:—

Sea going ships in commission	232
Sea going ships laid up in ordinary	210
Harbour ships in commission	10
Harbour ships in ordinary	156
Vessels building or ordered	55
Grand total	663 ships

To take the command of this vast fleet we had 45 admirals, 36 vice-admirals, 51 rear-admirals, 668 post-captains, 413 commanders, 2,480 lieutenants, and 529 masters; and we may add to these figures 26 superannuated flag-officers, 13 superannuated post-captains, and 49 superannuated commanders.

Turning from the commanders to the commanded, we find that Parliament voted pay for 50,000 sailors and marines during the first two months of the year, when we were actually at peace; 60,000 for the next four, during which period affairs came to a crisis; and 100,000 for the remaining seven *lunar* months.

Nor had the French, Dutch and Spanish dockyards been idle; for in March, 1803, the first of the three nations named above had sixty sail of the line ready for sea or being built.

On the day in which this declaration was promulgated in the Government gazette, the English 36-gun frigate "Doris," Captain Henry Pearson, captured the French 14-gun lugger "Affronteur," which had her captain and eight men killed and fourteen wounded, in a gallant resistance. This was the first hostile encounter between the two nations since the peace of Amiens.

But the British Government did not intend to be content with such small battles as that fought by the "Doris."

A fleet of ten sail of the line and some frigates sailed from Cawsand Bay on the 17th of May, under the command of Admiral Cornwallis, whose flag was hoisted on board the "Dreadnought," 98 guns.

This fleet was to cruise off Brest, and prevent the French ships in that port from joining, or being joined by the vessels prepared in other harbours.

The force under Cornwallis was strong enough for that purpose, but it could not prevent the launch of two 74-gun ships which the French had built in the dockyard at Brest.

However, for many months the English fleet blockaded the French port, and the Admiral Laurent - Jean - François Truguet, would not venture forth, even when a succession of furious south-western gales drove most of the English ships to take refuge in Plymouth and Portsmouth harbours.

The smaller French and Spanish ports of Rochefort, Lorient, Ferrol and Corunna were also carefully watched by squadrons equal in strength to the ships lying in those harbours.

Our Mediterranean fleet consisted of ten sail of the line, commanded by Rear-Admiral Sir R. Bickerton, when war was declared; but as there was every probability that very important events would take place in that inland sea, Lord Nelson was nominated to the chief command.

Nelson hoisted his flag on board the "Victory," and accompanied by the "Amphion" frigate, sailed with the intention of calling on Admiral Cornwallis, off Brest, to know whether the "Victory" was required to strengthen his squadron; intending, if such was the case, to proceed to the Mediterranean in the frigate.

Strong gales, however, had driven Cornwallis from his cruising ground, so after waiting some time, Nelson shifted to the "Amphion," and left the "Victory," with instructions to follow him to the Mediterranean if not required by the commander of the channel fleet.

It was the 8th of July before Nelson found Sir Richard Bickerton, cruising off Toulon. On the 30th the "Victory" joined the fleet, and the vice-admiral once more hoisted his flag on board her.

But no great engagement between the fleets of the two countries took place, so we return to the doings of single vessels and small detachments.

On the 28th of May the French frigate "Franchise," of 36 guns, was captured off Brest, by the "Minotaur," 74 guns, Captain C. M. Mansfield. Of course the small French vessel was unable to offer any resistance to the British ship of the line.

The 18-pounder 36-gun frigate "Immortalité," Captain Owen, and the 18-gun brig "Cruiser" and "Jalouse" chased the French gun vessels "Inabordable" and "Commode" ashore, near Cape Blanc Nez, on the 14th of June, where they were for some time defended by the batteries on shore. After a cannonade between the batteries and the English vessels, the French schooner and a brig were brought off by the boats. Charles Adams, master mate of the "Jalouse," was the only Englishman wounded.

On the 27th of June, the French 10-gun brig "Venteux," moored under some batteries at the Isle of Bas, was attacked by three boats, under the command of Lieutenants Temple and Bowen, of the frigate "Loire," Captain Maitland.

Only two of the boats reached the brig, which was found fully prepared to receive them. The brig was boarded, and captured within ten minutes. The British loss amounted to the boatswain, four seamen, and one marine wounded.

The naval medal was awarded for this action, and Lieutenant Temple was promoted to the rank of commander. The Patriotic Fund also presented swords, of the value of fifty guineas each, to Lieutenants Temple and Bowen.

On the 30th of June, the 74-gun ships "Cumberland" and "Vanguard" captured the French 40-gun frigate "Créole," off Cape Nicholas Mole, in the West Indian island of St. Domingo. The "Créole" foundered on her passage to England.

On the 2nd of July, the English frigate "Minerve," of 38 guns, Captain Brenton, ran ashore, in a fog, near the harbour of Cherbourg. The crew worked for ten hours, while exposed to the fire of heavy batteries, in trying to get the vessel off, but were at last compelled to surrender. The "Minerve" lost 11 men killed and 16 wounded.

On the 11th of July, the 18-gun brig "Racoon," Commander Austin Bissel, captured the French 10-gun brig "Lodi," in an action of thirty minutes. The "Lodi" had 1 man killed and 14 wounded. Thomas Gill, the master, who lost an arm, was the only man wounded on the "Racoon."

On the 25th of July, the French 74-gun ship "Duquesne" was captured by the English 74-gun ships "Vanguard" and "Bellerophon."

In the months of July and August, the 18-gun brig "Racoon," Captain Bissel, acquired some further notoriety for its victories in the West Indies.

On the 17th of August, a French 18-gun brig was driven ashore on the coast of Cuba by the "Racoon," and totally destroyed, though the crew succeeded in getting safely on land.

Captain Bissel continued to cruise off the coast of Cuba, and, on the 13th of October, observed several vessels keeping close in shore, all of which, towards sunset, made for Cumberland Harbour. Captain Bissel dropped anchor in a small bay, thinking that, most likely, the vessels would pass him during the night. At daylight on the 14th, he discovered eight or nine sail, very nearly becalmed, only a few miles to windward.

The "Racoon" immediately weighed anchor, and, with a fine breeze off the land in her favour, proceeded in chase, on which a brig, a schooner, and a cutter hoisted French colours, and fired guns to windward. The brig then attempted to pass between the "Racoon" and the shore, while her consorts endeavoured to join her, by the aid of sweeps. The land breeze, however, took the "Racoon" fairly within range of the brig, which struck, after receiving two broadsides, and proved to be the "Petite Fille," having on board 180 soldiers, of whom 50 were officers of various ranks.

Captain Bissel then looked after the schooner and cutter, which seemed inclined to run down and board him. The "Racoon" prevented this, and, after a contest of an hour, compelled the cutter to surrender—not before she had been converted into something like a wreck. She proved to be the "Amélie," carrying 4 guns, several swivels, and 70 troops in addition to her crew of seamen.

As soon as Captain Bissel had sent a boat's crew to take possession of the cutter, the "Racoon" crowded sail in pursuit of the schooner—the "Jeune Adèle"—carrying six small guns and eighty troops. This vessel, on being fired at, surrendered, without any further resistance.

When the "Racoon" stood in-shore, to rejoin her first prize, Captain Bissel saw that the French troops on board had, during his fight with the schooner and cutter, run the brig on shore among the rocks, after overpowering the prize crew. Fortunately the English seamen composing the prize crew had received no injury, and were able to rejoin the "Racoon."

In this engagement the three French vessels sustained a loss of 40 men killed and wounded, while Mr. Thompson, the master, who received a severe bruise, was the only man wounded on board the "Racoon."

Commander Bissel and Lieutenant James A. Gordon were shortly afterwards promoted, and a sword, valued at one hundred guineas, was presented to Bissel by the Patriotic Fund established at Lloyd's.

On the 14th of August, the East India Company's ship "Lord Nelson," of 26 guns, was captured, when homeward bound from India, by the French 34-gun frigate "Bellone," after having 5 men killed and 31 wounded.

This vessel was recaptured on the 25th, by the English 18-gun brig "Seagull," Commander Henry Burke.

During the month of September, 1803, there was but little done by the navy.

On the 14th of that month, a small squadron, under Captain John Melhuish, bombarded the batteries commanding the town of Dieppe, but with very little effect.

At the same time Admiral Saumarez, in the frigate "Cerberus," with some smaller vessels, bombarded Granville.

On the 27th, some sloops and bomb vessels, under Captain Samuel Jackson, in the 16-gun sloop "Autumn," bombarded Calais for several hours, but did the town little or no damage.

During the month of October there were several gallant deeds performed, which obtained for those who accomplished them, rewards from the Patriotic Fund, but were not of sufficient importance to command any especial notice of the Government.

A sword of fifty guineas value was presented to Lieutenant Hawkins, of the 18-gun brig "Atalante," for destroying three French merchant ships, that had been driven ashore by that brig, under the battery of St. Gildas, at the mouth of the Pennery.

Lieutenant Henderson, of the 18-gun brig "Osprey," received another sword of like value for boarding the French cutter privateer "Ressource," of 4 guns and 43 men, and capturing the vessel with only 17 men.

PORTRAIT OF SIR THOMAS TROUBRIDGE, BART.

Lieutenant Alexander Sheppard was also presented with a sword from the Patriotic Fund for an action fought on the 31st of October in the cutter "Admiral Mitchell," with a French 12-gun brig and an armed sloop.

At the commencement of the war with France the British Ambassador at the Court of Madrid was directed to ascertain how far his Catholic Majesty considered himself bound by the treaty of St. Ildephonso—by which he had agreed to furnish to France a contingent of naval and military force, for the prosecution of any war in which the French Government might at any time be engaged.

This treaty gave France a direct control over the resources of the kingdom of Spain; and was of itself, in the event of hostilities with France, a just cause of an immediate declaration of war by Great Britain against that kingdom.

In the month of July, 1803, the first formal demand of succour was made by France; and in the October following, a convention was signed, by which Spain agreed to pay to France a certain sum monthly, in lieu of the naval and military succour which they had stipulated by treaty to provide: a species of aid the most efficacious and best adapted to the wants and situation of France that could possibly be devised.

However, the British Government thought proper to connive at this for some time, contenting themselves with directing their envoy to protest against the convention as a violation of neutrality, and a just cause of war whenever Great Britain should choose to take it upon that ground.

The subserviency of the Court of Spain to Buonaparte was so complete and notorious, that little hope was entertained that peace could long subsist between Great Britain and that country after hostilities had recommenced with France.

As, however, it was undoubtedly the policy and the plan of Buonaparte to derive all possible assistance from Spain, without having her directly implicated in his quarrel with England, he did not permit her, for some time, to commit any direct and gross acts of hostility: he knew that the greatest benefit he could derive from her was, not men, or even ships, but money; this was necessary to enable him to carry on his Continental warfare, and to follow up his scheme of raising and equipping a navy.

Thus it was that Spain remained for a short time at peace with this country; and represented herself, and wished to be considered and treated by the British Cabinet, as a free and independent nation.

It was soon, however, discovered that her South American treasures were entirely at the disposal of Buonaparte; and that her neutrality was employed for the purpose of replenishing the coffers of our enemy.

Representations and remonstrances were repeatedly made on this head to the Court of Madrid, but in vain; her frigates still came from the New World laden with bullion, which was regularly transmitted to France.

At last, the British Ministry determined effectually to put a stop to these proceedings; and for this purpose Captain Moore, in the "Indefatigable," with three other frigates, was ordered to cruise off Cadiz, to intercept some very richly laden ships which were expected in that port from South America.

On the 5th of October, one of the British squadron made the signal for four sail being in sight, nine leagues from Cape St. Mary; a general chase was immediately commenced, and it was soon ascertained that they were the expected Spanish frigates, making for Cadiz.

The van ship carried a broad pendant, and the ship next her a rear-admiral's flag; as they were not under the least apprehension of being intercepted, or attacked by the British, they did not either attempt to escape nor were they prepared for action.

Captain Moore, having ordered each of his squadron to run up alongside of the four Spanish frigates, hailed them to shorten sail. To this request no answer was given. A shot was then fired by the "Indefatigable" across the rear-admiral, upon which he hove to, and an officer was sent on board to inform him that Captain Moore had peremptory orders to detain his squadron.

The officer, after waiting some time, returned with an unsatisfactory answer, when the "Indefatigable" bore down close upon her opponent, the other British ships doing the same.

The signal for close battle was immediately thrown out; and in less than ten minutes after the engagement commenced, the admiral's second astern blew up alongside the "Amphion," with a dreadful explosion.

On board of this frigate, called "La Mercedes," was embarked a native of Spain, who was returning from America, with the savings of twenty-five years' industry, and with his whole family, consisting of his wife, four daughters—beautiful and amiable women—and five sons grown up to manhood.

Before the action began, the merchant himself and one of his sons went on board the largest ship, from which he witnessed the loss of his whole property and saw his wife, daughters, and four of his sons surrounded with flames, and sinking into the abyss of the ocean.

It would be profanation to attempt by any language to describe the feelings of this man's agonized soul at this dreadful moment; while it would be doing injustice to Captain Moore, not to suppose, from his known character, that it required the strongest sentiments of duty to his country to keep down regret that he had been instrumental in bringing about this sad catastrophe; as soon as the action terminated, he took the unhappy husband and father into his own cabin, and was unceasing in his endeavours to administer all in his power towards the alleviation of his sufferings.

The Spanish admiral's ship continued to hold out for about half an hour after the "Mercedes" had blown up; when, finding that she could not escape, her opponent having got to leeward of her, she struck her colours: her example was immediately followed by another of the squadron; while the fourth, which carried the broad pendant, endeavoured to make her escape.

This, however, she was prevented from effecting, by the "Medusa" and "Lively" giving chase to her: at first she gained on them, but before sunset, Captain Hammond, in the "Lively" (which had outsailed the "Medusa"), having brought her to action, she soon after surrendered.

Notwithstanding every exertion was made by the British sailors to save the crew of the "Mercedes," only forty of them were picked up. This vessel had on board 800,000 dollars, all of which, of course, were lost.

The squadron was coming from Monte Video, and had on board the following goods and effects:—

On account of the king—75 sacks of Vicuna wool, 60 chests of cascarilla, 4,732 bars of tin, 1,735 pigs of copper, 28 planks of wood, and 1,307,634 dollars in silver.

On account of the merchants—32 chests of ratina, 1,852,216 dollars in silver, 1,219,658 gold reduced into dollars, and 150,011 ingots of gold reduced into dollars.

On account of the marine company — 26,975 seal-skins, and 10 pipes of seal-oil.

On board the ship which blew up were—20 sacks of Vicuna wool, 20 chests of cascarilla, 1,139 bars of tin, 961 pigs of copper, and 221,000 dollars in silver.

This statement is taken from the ships' official papers; but it is well known that they never discover nearly the whole of the treasure or merchandise which is brought to Spain from her American colonies; and, indeed, it afterwards turned out that the quantity of specie was much greater than this statement represented it to be.

The following exhibits the force of the Spanish squadron, with the number of men killed and wounded in each ship :—

"La Medée," the flag-ship, 42 guns, 18-pounders, and 300 men, of whom 2 were killed and 10 wounded; "La Fama," 36 guns, 12-pounders, and 280 men, of whom 11 were killed and 50 wounded; "La Clara," 36 guns, 12-pounders, and 300 men, of whom 7 were killed and 20 wounded; "La Mercedes," 36 guns, 12-pounders, and 280 men, of whom only the second captain and 40 seamen were saved.

In the English squadron the loss was very trifling: 2 were killed and 1 wounded on board the "Lively;" and on board the "Amphion," Lieutenant Bennet and 4 seamen were wounded.

The news of this capture excited the strongest sensations in the Governments of Spain and France.

The Ministry of England were charged with piracy and murder, in attacking the vessels of Spain on the high seas, without any previous declaration of war, in contempt of the law of nations. But nothing could be more weak and frivolous than such a charge.

The Spaniards had previously violated their neutrality; and it would have been a dereliction of duty on the part of the British Ministers, a want of regard for the honour of the British Crown, and the interests of the people, to have deferred any longer seeking that reparation by force of arms which was refused by amicable treaty.

It has been observed by a celebrated historian that man has more to fear from the passions of his fellow-creatures than from the convulsions of the elements.

The eruptions of a volcano, or the mischievous effects of an earthquake, form a very inconsiderable proportion to the ordinary calamities of war: a remark which seems justified by experience, and more particularly by the melancholy circumstance which took place in consequence of the explosion of the Spanish frigate before alluded to.

The following incident is a remarkable specimen of the work that may be done by brave men or boys.

On the 7th of November a midshipman of the "Blanche," named Edward Henry A'Court, was sent ashore in a boat, with seven men, to procure sand for the use of the ship.

On their return in the afternoon, they fell in with a French schooner becalmed, and having on board, amongst other passengers, a French colonel and 40 soldiers. A volley of musketry was fired from the schooner into the boat, and one man was mortally, and another severely wounded. The young midshipman immediately gave orders to board the assailant, and, with only five men, he gained the deck and took the vessel.

The French colonel had greatly distinguished himself under Napoleon, at the battle of Arcole, where his skull was fractured.

Upon the metal plate that covered the wound, which extended over a great portion of one side of the head, had been engraven in large letters the word "ARCOLE."

When asked how he could think of surrendering to so small a force as a midshipman and five men, he replied, with a shrug of the shoulders, that " it was all owing to the sea sickness ;" and added that, had he been on shore, the case would have been different.

Strange to say, this gallant action was never mentioned by the commander of the "Blanche" in his despatches, and had not Mr. A'Court possessed influential friends, it is probable that he never would have received the reward due to his meritorious conduct.

However, the affair became known, and the next year he was made a lieutenant.[*]

On the 14th of November the fort of Marine Harbour, Martinique, was captured and the guns spiked, by a detachment of 134 men from the brig "Drake" and the ship "Blenheim," under the orders of William Ferris, of the "Drake." The French privateer schooner "Harmonie" was in the harbour, and fired upon the boats as they approached her, but she was boarded and captured with only a loss of one man killed and five wounded.

On the 2nd of December the French evacuated St. Domingo, and the whole of their naval and military stores were surrendered to the English squadron, under command of Admiral Sir J. T. Duckworth.

During the year 1803 fourteen vessels were lost to the English navy. Three were captured by the enemy, nine were wrecked, and two foundered.

---

[*] Mr. A'Court afterwards became post-captain and Member of Parliament for Heytesbury, in South Wilts.

CHAPTER XXVIII.

THE WAR IN 1804—ALARMS OF INVASION.

AT this time Earl St. Vincent was first lord of the admiralty, and introduced many useful reforms in the service.

Through the activity of the English blockading squadrons and cruisers, French commerce suffered very severely, and a very hostile spirit was engendered in the minds of the French people.

The first consul, Buonaparte, began again to devise schemes for the invasion of England with an army of at least 160,000 men.

To accomplish this it was necessary to provide transport vessels, but, so popular was the idea, that almost every department in the state voted money for a ship of the line; large villages and towns voted frigates, and every commune gave a praam, gun-vessel, or flat-bottomed boat. Vessels were built as far up the Seine as Paris, where a navy yard was established; but the difficulty was to get out to sea and avoid the British cruisers, which watched not only the coast of France, but French possessions all over the world.

On the 3rd of February, 1804, the French 16-gun brig "Curieux," Captain Cordier, was captured by four boats of the English 74-gun ship, "Centaur," Captain Murray Maxwell.

The brig was anchored near the entrance to Fort Royal, Martinique, and the boats from the "Centaur" were led by Lieutenant Robert Reynolds, who was so severely wounded in the action that he did not live to profit by the promotion and honours won by his gallantry on the occasion.

The Indian Ocean, which, in 1803, had been the theatre of operations so disastrous to Great Britain, was, in the following year, destined to be a scene of honour and glory, presenting nothing but trophies to our naval commanders.

In consequence of the former success experienced by the French Admiral Linois, he became remarkably daring and enterprising.

Flushed with victory, he sailed early in the year 1804, directing his attention to the capture of our East India fleets.

His force consisted of the "Marengo," of 84 guns, two frigates, a corvette, and a brig.

The China fleet, which it was the object of Admiral Linois to intercept, consisted of fifteen of the company's ships, twelve country ships, a Portuguese East Indiaman, and a fast-sailing brig; of these, Captain Dance, of the "Earl Camden," as the senior captain, was appointed commodore.

When off the Straits of Malacca, on the 14th of February, four strange sail were seen in the southwest.

Captain Dance, with great judgment, put his ships' heads towards the enemy; four of his best sailers he sent down to reconnoitre; and, having ascertained what they were, called in his look out, and formed the line of battle in close order, under easy sail.

As soon as the French ships could fetch into the wake of ours, they put about, and at sunset were close in the rear of the India fleet, which was in momentary expectation of an attack; but at the close of the day, the French admiral hauled his wind.

Lieutenant Fowler, of the Royal Navy, who was a passenger with Captain Dance, volunteered to go in a fast-sailing vessel to order the country ships to keep on the lee bow of the India fleet; by this judicious arrangement, Captain Dance kept himself between the country ships and the enemy.

Lieutenant Fowler, having executed his order, returned, bringing with him some volunteers from the country ships to serve at the guns (a noble proof of the public spirit of our sailors).

The Indiamen lay-to in line of battle during the night, with the people at their quarters.

At daylight, on the 15th, the enemy were three miles to windward, also lying-to. The British ships hoisted their colours and offered battle; but the enemy, not choosing to come down, at 9 a.m. the India fleet steered its course under easy sail; the enemy then filled and edged towards them.

At 1 p.m. Captain Dance, perceiving that the French admiral intended to attack and cut off his rear, made the signal for his fleet to tack and engage in succession.

The "Royal George" led, and was followed by the "Ganges" and "Earl Camden."

The ships performed this manœuvre with admirable correctness, and stood towards the French under a press of sail.

The latter formed a very close line, and opened their fire on the headmost ships, which was not returned until ours had approached as near as they could get, the French having a great advantage in superior sailing.

The "Royal George" bore the brunt of the action; the "Ganges" and "Camden" came up, and also began to engage; but before any other ships could get up, the French admiral hauled his wind, and stood away to the eastward under all the sail he could set.

Captain Dance made the signal for a general chase, but, after a pursuit of two hours, finding the enemy gained on him, he very properly desisted.

The action was very short; one man only was killed on board the "Royal George," and one wounded; the other ships had none hurt, and received little damage in their hulls or rigging.

To say that Linois was deceived by the warlike appearance of our Indiamen, and the blue swallow-tail flags (*pavillon à queue bleue*) worn by the three largest ships, may save his courage at the expense of his judgment.

"An Indiaman," says the Count de Dumas, "has often been mistaken for a ship of the line."

But when did the Count de Dumas ever hear of seventeen British ships of the line lying-to to await the attack of a French 80-gun ship and two frigates?

The conduct of the company's officers and men on the memorable action off Pulo A'or displayed a fine instance of our national character.

On what occasion has it ever happened that the merchant ships of our enemies have defended themselves, and adhered to each other with so much firmness and decision, against a ship of war?

Our East Indiamen were certainly very fine ships, and had, generally, such an appearance as to be sometimes mistaken for ships of the line; but their complement of men was very inadequate to their size, for fighting, particularly when required to lie alongside a ship of the line.

None of them, we believe, had more than a hundred men, their heaviest metal 18-pounders. The "Marengo" had 700 at least, with a weight of metal on her lower deck, and a scantling which rendered her an overmatch for all the ships of that fleet that could at one time have brought their guns to bear on her.

The two frigates were also very powerful ships; so that the conduct of Captain Dance, in resisting the attack, and keeping his ships in line of battle, instead of ordering them to separate and seek their safety in flight, entitles him to all the praise which can be bestowed on a sea officer.

His Majesty was graciously pleased to confer upon him the honour of knighthood. The Court of Directors also presented him with 2,000 guineas and a piece of plate of the value of 200 guineas.

To Captain Timmins, of the "Royal George," they presented the sum of 1,000 guineas, and a piece of plate of the value of 100 guineas; to Captain Moffat, of the "Ganges," 500 guineas, and a piece of plate of 100 guineas value; to all the other captains, 500 guineas, and a piece of plate of the value of 50 guineas; to Lieutenant Fowler, of the Royal Navy, a piece of plate of 300 guineas value; and the Court of Directors, as well as the public bodies in India, were extremely liberal in pecuniary gratification to every officer and man in the fleet.

Captain Sir Nathaniel Dance had also a pension of £300 per annum settled on him by the East India Company; and this, by a vote of a general meeting of proprietors, was increased to £500 per annum.

Sir Nathaniel Dance was born in London, the 9th June, O.S. 1748, and made his first voyage to the East Indies in 1759.

Before he attained the rank of commander, he had performed eight voyages to the East Indies, one to the West Indies, and one to the Mediterranean.

In August, 1780, he sailed chief mate in the "King George," East Indiaman, on the ninth voyage, which ship was one of the five unfortunately captured off Cape St. Vincent, by the combined fleet of France and Spain, and carried into Cadiz, where he remained six months a prisoner.

In 1787 he made his first voyage as commander on board the "Lord Camden," in which ship he performed four voyages.

In 1803 he sailed for Bombay and China in a new ship, the "Earl Camden," of 1,200 tons burden, carrying 36 18-pounders; and on the 5th February, 1804, left China, on his return to Europe, as commodore of the fleet, which consisted of sixteen regular Indiamen and eleven country ships, the whole valued at ten millions sterling.

It was in prosecuting this service that he fell in with the enemy's squadron, and achieved that victory which filled the world with admiration and surprise.

The nations of the earth had long witnessed the superior energy and skill of British seamen, when exercised on board ships of war; but it was reserved for the present period to crown those efforts with a victory achieved by a fleet of merchantmen, heavily laden, in a manner highly honourable to the national character, and reflecting the greatest credit on every individual engaged, while the abilities of the commodore place his name amongst the most distinguished characters of the British navy.

In addition to the rewards enumerated above, the Bombay Insurance Society voted £5,000, together with a sword of 100 guineas value, to Sir N. Dance, and swords of the same value to Captains Timmins, Moffatt, and Wilson, whose ships shared in the action, as marks of the esteem and admiration with which their minds were impressed, by the skill and gallantry displayed by them on that occasion. They

CRESTS OF VESSELS IN THE ROYAL NAVY (A.D. 1870).

further voted the sum of £100 to be distributed among the men who were wounded in the engagement, or to their families.

In transmitting the above resolutions to Sir N. Dance, the gentlemen appointed thus addressed themselves:—

"In fulfilling so grateful a duty, we might, perhaps, be allowed to dwell with minuteness on the glory which has been achieved for yourself, the fame which results to the country, and the incalculable advantages which have arisen to its vital interests by an exploit so splendid and important; but it is superfluous for us to enter on this extensive field, and we content ourselves merely in offering our tribute of congratulations, proud in the opportunity afforded us of expressing our sentiments on an action which adds lustre to the annals of the empire."

On the recommencement of hostilities in 1803, the West India Islands became objects of especial attention with our government, and the reduction of several of them soon took place.

Martinique, however, had not yet surrendered; and, preparatory to offensive operations, it was considered necessary to obtain possession of, and fortify, the Diamond Rock, whose commanding situation rendered it a post of the highest importance.

Sir Samuel Hood, ever mindful of what would most conduce to the honour of his country, spent much of his time in watching the island of Martinique and Fort-Royal Bay, the chief resort. Six miles to windward of this, and one mile from Cape Diamond, at the entrance of Marin Bay, lies the Diamond Rock, in form very much resembling a round hay stack; on one side overhanging its base, but having deep water all round it.

WRECK OF THE "ROMNEY."

To place a battery on the top of this rock would at first sight appear impracticable.

Its altitude is about 450 feet; a few bushes grow on the top (so they appear to the distant spectator); they consist of the wild fig-tree, whose roots by age have acquired a strength and connection with the interstices of the rock, offering some security to the fastening of a cable.

In January, 1804, a landing was effected.

Having mounted its crumbling sides, rarely, perhaps never before, trodden by man, our enterprising officers and men succeeded in carrying up a line, and ultimately, a stream-cable of the "Centaur," which was firmly moored by the side of the rock; and with one end of this cable clinched round a projecting rock, and the other on board the ship, a communication was established from one to the other.

To the cable a traveller was affixed, similar in principle to that which children put on the string of a kite; to this a twenty-four pounder was attached, and, by means of tackle, conveyed to the top of the rock; another followed, and at last their carriages, shot, powder and tools, with every requisite for the support of a commander, two lieutenants, and 120 men.

The French from the island first beheld the work with contempt, and next with astonishment.

Sir Samuel Hood gave it the name of the Diamond Rock Sloop of War, with the establishment of a vessel of that class.

The occupation of this rock gave the enemy much trouble, and caused them serious loss.

This post, in conjunction with the cruisers, totally intercepted the trade between the south part of the island and Fort Royal; obliging the trade to pass outside the rock, the vessels became more exposed to capture.

In addition to this, the Diamond Rock, as a signal post, was a place of no small advantage.

On the 4th of March, Lieutenant Furber, of the ship "Blenheim," with two boats, containing 50 officers and men, boarded the French schooner "Curieuse," which was moored under a battery at St. Pierre.

The vessel was captured after a hard struggle, but was found moored to the shore by a chain under its bottom, and could not be brought away.

In this action 3 men were killed and 19 wounded.

On the 13th of March, the French 10-gun privateer schooner "Mosambique" was captured at Martinique, by Lieutenant Thomas Forrest and thirty volunteers from the frigate "Emerald," Captain O'Brian. Lieutenant Forrest and his party proceeded to the schooner in a small sloop and ran foul of it, sprang aboard, and drove the crew—double the number of their own party—from the schooner, and brought it away.

On the 17th of March, the French privateer schooner "Renommée," of 12 guns and 87 men, was driven on shore by the 16-gun brig "Penguin," commanded by Captain John Morris, on the bar of Senegal. On the 24th, the schooner was totally destroyed by Lieutenant Charles Williams and a boat's crew.

On the 25th March, the French 36-gun privateer "Egyptienne," was captured by the 14-gun sloop "Hippomenes," Captain Shipley. Two days before, the "Egyptienne" had been much crippled in a fight with the English sloop "Osprey," Commander George Younghusband, in which she had 8 men killed and 19 wounded.

On the 24th of March, the English 13-gun bark "Wolverine," commanded by Henry Gordon, was captured by the French 30-gun privateer "Blonde," when on the way to Newfoundland. There was just time to remove the crew of the "Wolverine," after her surrender, before she sank, which proves that she was defended as long as possible.

When the brave defenders of our country fall in battle, the ardour which impels them to glory, and renders them insensible of their danger, leaves a brilliancy behind which mitigates, in a great degree, our sorrow for their loss; but when they are swallowed up by the casualties of common life, their fate becomes more closely linked with our own, and we feel a deep commiseration for their untimely end.

Such latter was the fate of a great number of the gallant crew of the "Apollo" frigate, of 38 guns, commanded by Captain Dixon, wrecked on the coast of Portugal, together with a great portion of her convoy; the particulars of which distressing event are detailed in the following narrative, communicated shortly after by one of the officers of the "Apollo":—

"On Monday, the 26th of March, the 'Apollo' sailed from the Cove of Cork, in company with his Majesty's ship 'Carysfort' and sixty-nine sail of merchantmen, under convoy for the West Indies.

" On the 27th we were out of sight of land, with a fair wind, blowing a strong gale, and steering about west-south-west. The 28th, 29th, and 30th, weather and course nearly the same. The 31st, the wind came more to the westward, but more moderate. Sunday, the 1st of April, observed in lat. 40 deg. 51 min. north, longitude, per account, 12 deg. 29 min. west.

"At eight o'clock on Sunday evening, the wind shifted to the south-west, blowing fresh; course south-south-east. At ten, up mainsail and set the main-staysail, split by the sheet giving way; called all hands upon deck. At half-past ten, strong breezes and squally; took in the foretopsail and set the foresail. At half-past eleven the maintopsail split; furled it and the mainsail. The ship was now under her foresail, main and mizen storm-staysails; the wind blowing hard, with a heavy sea. About half-past three on Monday morning, the 2nd, the ship struck the ground, to the astonishment of every one on board; and, by the above reckoning, we then conjectured, upon an unknown shoal.

" She continued striking the ground very heavily several times, by which her bottom was materially damaged, and making much water. The chain-pumps were rigged with the utmost dispatch, and the men began to pump: but, in about ten minutes, she beat and drove over the shoal. On endeavouring to steer her, found the rudder carried away: she then got before the wind.

" The pumps were kept going, but, from the quantity of water she shipped, there was every probability of her soon foundering, as she was filling and sinking very fast.

" After running about five minutes, the ship struck the ground again with such tremendous shocks, that we were fearful she would instantly go to pieces, and kept striking and driving further on the sands, the sea making breaches completely over her. We cut away the lanyards of the main and mizen rigging, and the masts fell with a tremendous crash over the larboard side, with the gunwale under water. The violence with which she struck the ground, and the weight of the guns (those on the quarterdeck tearing away the bulwark), soon made the ship a perfect wreck abaft: only four or five guns could be fired, to alarm the convoy and give notice of danger.

"On her striking the second time, most pitiful cries were heard everywhere between decks, many of the men giving themselves up to inevitable death. I was told that I might as well stay below, as there was equal likelihood of perishing if I got upon deck.

"I was determined to go, but first attempted to enter my cabin, and was in danger of having my legs broken by the chests floating about, and the bulkheads were giving way: I therefore desisted, and endeavoured to get upon deck, which I effected, after being several times washed down the gangway by the immense volume of water incessantly pouring down.

"The ship still beating the ground very heavily, made it necessary to cling fast to some part of the wreck, to prevent being washed by the surges, or hurled by the dreadful concussion overboard; the people holding fast by the larboard bulwark of the quarterdeck, and in the main channel; while our good captain stood naked upon the cabin skylight-grating, holding fast by the stump of the mizen-mast, and making use of every soothing expression which could have been suggested to encourage men in such a perilous situation.

"Most of the officers and men were entirely naked, not having had time to slip on their trowsers.

"Our horrible situation every moment became more dreadful, until daylight appearing about half-past four o'clock, discovered to us the land at about two cables' distance; a long sandy beach, extending to Cape Mondego, three leagues to the south of us.

"On daylight clearing up, we could perceive between twenty and thirty sail of the convoy on shore, both to the northward and southward, and several of them perfect wrecks. We were now certain of being on the coast of Portugal, from seeing the above cape, though I am sorry to say no person in the ship had the least idea of being so near the coast. It blowing hard, and a very great swell of the sea (or what is generally termed waves running mountains high), there was little prospect of being saved.

"At eight o'clock, there being every likelihood of the ship going to pieces, and the after part lying the lowest, Captain Dixon ordered every person forward, which it was very difficult to comply with, from the motion of the mainmast working on the larboard gunwale, there being no other way to get forward. Mr. Cook, the boatswain, had his thigh broken in endeavouring to get a boat over the side. Of six fine boats not one was saved, being all stove and washed overboard, with the booms, &c.

"Soon after the people got forward, the ship parted at the gangways. The crew were now obliged to stow themselves in the fore-channels, and from thence to the bowsprit-end, to the number of 220; for out of 240 persons on board when the ship first struck, I suppose twenty to have previously perished between-decks and otherwise.

"Mr. Lawton, the gunner, the first person who attempted to swim on shore, was drowned; afterwards Lieutenant Wilson; Mr. Runcie, surgeon; Mr. M'Cabe, surgeon's mate; Mr. Stanley, master's mate; and several men shared the same fate, by reason of the sea breaking in enormous surges over them, though excellent swimmers.

"About thirty persons had the good fortune to reach the shore upon planks and spars, among whom were Lieutenant Hervey and Mr. Callam, the master's mate.

"Monday night, our situation was truly horrid, the old men and boys dying through hunger and fatigue; also Messrs. Proby and Hayes, midshipmen. Captain Dixon remained all this night upon the bowsprit. Tuesday morning presented us no better prospect of being relieved from the jaws of death, the wind blowing stronger and the sea much more turbulent.

"About noon this day our drooping spirits were somewhat raised by seeing Lieutenant Hervey and Mr. Callam hoisting out a boat from one of the merchant-ships, to come to the assistance of their distressed shipmates.

"They several times attempted to launch it through the serf, but, being a very heavy boat, and the sea on the beach beating so powerfully against them, they could not possibly effect it, though assisted by nearly one hundred of the merchant-sailors and the Portuguese peasants.

"Several men went upon rafts this day, made from pieces of the wreck, but not one of them reached the shore; the wind having shifted, and the current setting out, they were all driven to sea; among whom was our captain, who, about three in the afternoon, went on the jib-boom with three seamen, anxious to save the remainder of the ship's company, and too sanguine of getting on shore, he ventured upon the spar, saying, on jumping into the sea—

"'My lads, I'll save you all.'

"In a few seconds he lost his hold of the spar, which he could not regain; he drifted to sea and perished. Such was also the fate of the three brave volunteers who chose his fortune.

"The loss of our captain, who until now had animated the almost lifeless crew, as well as the noble exertions of Lieutenant Hervey and Mr.

Callam to launch the boat not succeeding, every gleam of hope vanished, and we looked forward for certain death the ensuing night, not only from cold, hunger and fatigue, but from the expectation of the remaining part of the wreck going to pieces every moment.

"Had not the 'Apollo' been a new and well-built ship, that small portion of her could never have resisted the waves, and stuck so well together, particularly as all the after part from the chess-trees was gone, the starboard bow under water, the forecastle-deck nearly perpendicular, the weight of the guns hanging to the larboard-bulwark on the inside, and the bower and spare anchors on the outside, which it was not prudent to cut away, as they afforded resting-places to a considerable number of men, there being only the forechains and cat-head where it was possible to live on, and about which were stowed upwards of 150 men, it being impracticable to stay any longer on the head or upon the bowsprit, by reason of the breakers washing completely over those places.

"The night drawing on, the wind increasing, frequent showers of rain, the sea washing over us, and looking every instant for the forecastle giving way, when we must have all perished together, afforded a spectacle truly deplorable; the bare recollection of which, even now, makes me shudder.

The piercing cries of that dismal night, at every sea coming over us, which happened every two minutes, were pitiful in the extreme; the water running from the head down all over the body, keeping us continually wet.

On this shocking night, the remaining strength of every person was exerted for his individual safety.

From the crowding so closely together in so narrow a compass, and the want of something to moisten their mouths, several poor wretches were suffocated; which frequently reminded me of the Black Hole, with only this difference, that those poor sufferers were confined by strong walls, we by water; the least motion, without clinging fast, would have launched us into eternity.

Some unfortunate wretches drank salt water, some chewed leather; myself and many more chewed lead, from which we conceived we found considerable relief, by reason of its drawing the saliva, which we swallowed.

"In less than an hour after the ship struck the ground, all the provisions were under water, and the ship a wreck, so that it was impossible to procure any part of them.

"After the most painful night that it is possible to conceive, on daylight appearing, we observed Lieutenant Hervey again endeavouring to launch the boat.

"Several attempts were made without success, a number of men belonging to the merchant-ships being bruised and hurt in assisting.

"Alternate hopes and fears now pervaded our wretched minds; fifteen men got safe on shore this morning on pieces of the wreck.

"About three in the afternoon of Wednesday, the 4th, we had the inexpressible happiness of seeing the boat launched through the surf by the indefatigable exertions of the above officers, assisted by the masters of merchant-ships, with a number of Portuguese peasants, who were encouraged by Mr. Whitney, the British consul, from Figuero. All the crew remaining on the wreck were brought safe on shore, praising God for their happy deliverance from a shipwreck which never had its parallel.

"As soon as I stepped out of the boat, I found several persons whose humanity prompted them to offer me sustenance, though improperly, in spirits, which I avoided as much as possible.

"Our weak state may be conceived, when it is considered that we received no nourishment from Sunday to Wednesday afternoon, and continually exposed to the fury of the watery element.

"After eating and drinking a little, I found myself weaker than before, occasioned, I apprehend, from having been so long without either.

"Some men died soon after getting on shore, from imprudently drinking too large a quantity of spirits.

"All the crew were in a very weak and exhausted state, the greater part being badly bruised and wounded.

"About forty sail of merchant-ships were wrecked at the same time on this dreadful beach.

"Some ships sunk with all their crews, and almost every ship lost from two to twelve men each; yet the situation of the remainder was not equal to the frigate's ship's company, as the merchant-ships, drawing less water, were mostly driven close on the shore, and no person remained on board them after the first morning.

"The masters of the merchant-ships had tents upon the beach, and some provisions they had saved from the wrecks, which they very generously distributed, and gave every assistance to the 'Apollo's' ship's company.

"Thus was lost one of the finest frigates in the British navy, with sixty-one of her crew. The number of persons lost in the merchant-ships was also considerable. Dead bodies were every day floating ashore, and pieces of wreck covered the beach upwards of ten miles in extent."

* * * * *

On the 31st of March the boats from the 18-gun brig "Scorpion," Captain Hardinge, and the boats of the sloop "Beaver," Captain Pelly, led by their commanders, cut out the Dutch brig "Atalanta," lying in Vlie Passage at the entrance of the Texel.

This was a very gallant action, and the naval medal has since been given for it.

On the 3rd of April, the cutter "Swift," under Lieutenant Leake, bearing despatches from England to Lord Nelson off Toulon, was captured, after a gallant resistance, by the French xebeck privateer "Experance."

Lieutenant Leake and several of his crew were killed. The despatches were destroyed before the cutter was surrendered.

On the 8th of May, the 18-gun brig "Vincego," commanded by John Westley Wright, was becalmed off the mouth of the river Morbihan in Bretagne, and carried close to some dangerous rocks.

The crew of the "Vincego" exerted all their strength by means of sweeps or oars; but while so engaged, a flotilla of six brigs, six luggers, and five gun-boats, rowed out from the river and commenced a furious attack on the British ship.

Captain Wright's crew consisted only of 51 men and 24 boys; but he fought for two hours against overwhelming odds.

At last the "Vincego" was reduced to a complete wreck, and Captain Wright severely wounded; but not till then was the British flag struck.

The unfortunate captain was recognised as Sir Sidney Smith's friend and companion in escape; and Bonaparte was also informed that some Royalist agents had landed from the "Vincego." These circumstances raised a storm of French indignation against Wright, who was hurried off to his old prison of the Temple at Paris.

Only once afterwards was Captain Wright seen alive; that occasion being the trial of Georges Cadoudal, one of the French Royalist conspirators. Captain Wright was then brought into court as the hundred and thirty-fourth witness in support of the prosecution; but he refused to give any evidence, saying that as a British officer and a prisoner of war, he considered himself amenable to his own government only.

Some time after this, the *Moniteur* (French official journal) announced that Captain Wright had been found dead in his cell, his throat cut from ear to ear. It was, said the *Moniteur*, a very clear case of suicide.

But in England it was suspected that he had been assassinated by Bonaparte's orders; for Captain Wright was always known as a man of very cheerful disposition, and had every prospect of gaining promotion and distinction in the navy.

Great was the indignation against Bonaparte; and thinking people were more strongly convinced that foul play had taken place when a long time afterwards, Savary, the chief of the secret police, in defending the Emperor, disclaimed all participation in the affair, which he called "a dark and mysterious subject," and hinted that Fouché, the minister-general of police, was at the bottom of it.

It does not seem probable that Captain Wright committed suicide, *unless he had been so tortured as to have lost his reason*, or that he dreaded a repetition of the torture.*

The truth about the affair is still buried in mystery.

On the 16th of May, a squadron of frigates and sloops, under command of Sir Sidney Smith, attacked a fleet of prames and gunboats under Rear-Admiral Ver Huel, between Flushing and Ostend. The Dutch fleet mounted 100 guns, and was manned by 5,000 men. Several of the Dutch vessels were driven on shore, but the expedition on the part of the English was pronounced unsuccessful. They lost about 50 men in killed and wounded.

PORTRAIT OF ADMIRAL DUCKWORTH.

On the 12th of July, the French 20-gun ship "Charente," and the 8-gun brig "Joie," were destroyed under Cordouan lighthouse by the 36-gun frigate "Aigle," Captain George Wolfe.

On the 15th of July, the English 14-gun sloop "Lily," Captain William Compton, was captured off Cape Roman, United States, by the French privateer "Dame Ambert," of 16 guns, Captain Lamarque.

This action continued for two hours and a half, and during that time the French made nine attempts to board before they were successful in capturing the "Lily," which had her captain and first lieutenant killed.

On the 19th of July, a small squadron, under Commodore Owen, of the "Immortalité," attacked some French gun-vessels off Boulogne. Three French brigs and a lugger were driven on shore, and several other vessels were much damaged.

On the 31st of July, the French privateer schooner "Hirondelle" was captured near St. Domingo, by three boats from the frigate "Tartar," Captain Maxwell.

The expedition was commanded by Lieutenants Muller and Lockyer, and, although exposed to a heavy fire, the schooner was boarded and captured, with only a loss of 1 man killed and 2 wounded. The "Hirondelle" had 15 men killed and wounded.

On the 26th of August, Commodore Owen, in the "Immortalité," with the assistance of the "Harpy," an 18-gun brig, the 12-gun brig, "Adder," and the cutter "Constitution," attacked

---

* A French author, A. Vieusseux, in his life of Napoleon Bonaparte, says—"Some dark rumours were circulated about Captain Wright having been put to excruciating torture. It is probable that Bonaparte himself did not know at that time all the secrets of his prison houses."

a flotilla of sixty brigs, and upwards of thirty luggers, off Cape Grinez. This French fleet was intended by Napoleon to assist in the invasion of England.

He was in a position where he could see many of the vessels run ashore, and the others dispersed.

In this engagement the cutter "Constitution" was sunk by a shell. The English had 1 seaman killed and 6 wounded.

On the 13th of August, four boats, under the command of Lieutenant Charles Hayman, from the 32-gun frigate "Galatea," attempted to cut out the "General Ernouf," late "Lily," that had been captured from the English.

The boats contained about 90 men, who met with no opposition until they got alongside, when they were assailed by heavy showers of musketry and grape.

In the boat with Lieutenant Hayman were 26 men, more than 20 of whom were either killed or wounded; amongst the latter was the gallant lieutenant, whose wound proved mortal.

The boats were compelled to retreat, after suffering a loss of 65 in killed, wounded and prisoners.

On the 17th of August, the 38-gun frigate "Loire," Captain Maitland, captured the French 30-gun privateer "Blonde," off the French coast.

This vessel was captured after a twenty hours' chase, and a running fight of fifteen minutes, in which the "Loire" had six men wounded.

On the 15th of September, the 50-gun ship "Centurion," Captain Lind, was attacked in Vizagapatam Roads by a part of the French East India squadron, under Admiral Linois, consisting of the 24-gun ship "Marengo," with the frigates "Atalante" and "Semillante."

The "Centurion" maintained an unequal combat with the three vessels for some time, until they retired with only a merchant-vessel for a prize.

The naval medal was granted to those who so gallantly defended their vessel against so much odds.

On the 5th of October, a squadron under Captain Graham Moore, of the 44-gun frigate "Indefatigable," with the frigates "Medusa," "Amphion," and "Lively," met a Spanish squadron from Monte Video, off Cape Santa Maria.

An engagement took place, in which the Spanish ship "Mercedes" took fire and blew up, and the "Fama," "Medea," and "Clara" were compelled to surrender.

The "Mercedes" sank with most of her crew and passengers, only the captain and 40 men being saved.

The "Clara" had 7 killed and 20 wounded; the "Fama" 11 killed and 50 wounded; and the "Medea" 2 killed and 10 wounded.

On board the English vessels only 2 men were killed and 7 wounded.

The prizes captured were of considerable value.

In consequence of this, Spain immediately declared war against England.

The squadron under Commodore Samuel Hood assisted in the capture of Surinam, on the 5th of May, the principal vessel engaged being the "Centaur," Captain Murray Maxwell.

On this vessel Lieutenant Smith, 1 midshipman, the boatswain, and 2 men were killed, and 8 men were wounded.

Goree, on the Coast of Africa, was recaptured on the 4th of March, from the French, by Captain Edward Dixon, of the 36-gun frigate "Inconstant." *

On the 16th of April, it was ascertained that the number of vessels employed in the defence of the country amounted to 1,652.

On the 18th of November, the "Romney," of 50 guns, was wrecked off Texel.

The officers and crew were made prisoners by the Dutch, by whose exertions, at the hazard of their own lives, 300 people were saved.

On the 24th of November, the "Venerable," of 74 guns, was wrecked off Torbay. All the crew except eight were saved.

Adam, Viscount Duncan, who commanded the English fleet at the battle of Camperdown, died on his way to Scotland, on the 4th of August this year. He was born in Scotland on the 1st of July, 1731. At the age of eighteen years he was six feet and four inches high.

The Dutch admiral, De Winter, who commanded the Dutch fleet at Camperdown, was nearly as tall as himself.

After the battle, Duncan said to the Dutch admiral, "I wonder how you and I have escaped the balls in this hot battle."

CHAPTER XXIX.
EVENTS OF 1805.

AT the commencement of the year 1805 the British navy yards were in full work.

Eighty-seven new vessels had been launched during the year 1804, and still the work of construction went on; eighty of the new vessels had been built in private establishments, the government establishments being principally engaged in fitting up, arming, victualing and repairing vessels already afloat.

Many of the new vessels were gun-brigs, drawing very little water, and constructed to carry with ease

---

* Toone's "Chronological Record of the reign of George III.," stated that Goree was captured on the 9th of March.

four 32-pound carronades fitted to throw shells, and two long 18-pounders.

These vessels, though small, were formidable craft for annoying the enemy in his own ports, being able to work much nearer shore than ordinary frigates or ships of the line.

The number of seamen and marines voted for the year 1805 was 120,000, commanded by 50 admirals, 36 vice admirals, 63 rear admirals, 639 post captains, 422 commanders, or sloop captains, 2,472 lieutenants, and 556 masters.

We have already mentioned the Spanish declaration of war against England. On the 4th of January, 1805, three days before the Spanish declaration reached London, a secret treaty between Spain and France was signed at Paris, by which the king of Spain engaged to equip and supply with six months' provisions a fleet of from 25 to 29 sail of the line, and to have them ready by the 30th of March at the latest, to embark 5,000 Spanish and 20,000 French troops.

In another article of the same treaty Napoleon engaged to guarantee to his Catholic Majesty the king of Spain the possession of his European dominions, and the restitution of any colonies that might be taken from him! And yet, in a very short space of time after, we shall see him endeavouring to place his own brother permanently upon the throne of Spain!

This alliance between France and Spain raised the naval forces at Napoleon's disposal to upwards of 70 sail of the line. *On paper* the English had 105 line of battle ships in commission, but only about 80 of these were really fit for service.

However, a strict blockade of the chief French and Spanish ports was maintained.

On the 4th of January, 1805, the 16-gun sloop "Rattler," Captain Mason, cruising off the French coast, found the French 14-gun privateer "Vimereux," lying in shore under a 4-gun battery. This vessel had been very successful in committing depredations upon British commerce, and Lieutenant Dalyell, of the "Rattler," proposed to cut it out.

The expedition to accomplish this feat consisted of 4 officers and 27 men, who were to capture a 14-gun vessel under the protection of a battery and manned by 78 men.

It was a rash and foolish undertaking, in which brave men were led to death by rash and headstrong officers.

Of the thirty-one persons who went in the boats, only six returned unhurt.

For this affair the Patriotic Committee gave Lieutenant Dalyell a sword of the value of fifty guineas and a sum of £100.

The English corvette "Arrow," Captain Vincent, of 31 guns, and the bomb vessel "Acheron," having under convoy a fleet of merchant vessels from Malta to England, were attacked by the French 40-gun frigates "Hortense," and "Incorruptible," on the 3rd of February.

The two war vessels were captured after a chase and fight that lasted nearly two days, but so obstinate was their resistance and so skilful the tactics of their commanders, that 31 of the merchant vessels were saved from capture.

Aboard the "Arrow" 13 were killed and 27 wounded. Immediately after the wounded and prisoners were taken out, after her surrender, she sank.

The 16-gun brig "Curieux," Captain Bettesworth, at the eastward of Barbadoes, captured the French privateer "Dame Ernouf," after a long and animated fight, on the 8th of February.

The "Curieux" had 6 men killed and 5 wounded, including the captain, who was struck by a musket ball on the head.

The French vessel had 30 men killed and 40 wounded.

On the 14th of February, the 36-gun frigate "San Fiorenzo," Captain Lambert, off Vizagapatam in India, pursued the French 32-gun frigate "Psyche," having in her company two prizes.

One prize and the "Psyche" were captured, after a long pursuit and an obstinate battle, in which the "Psyche" lost 3 lieutenants and 54 men killed, and 70 officers and men wounded. On board the "San Fiorenzo" 12 men were killed and 36 wounded. The "Psyche" was added to the English navy. The navy medal was given for this action.

On the 17th of February, the 32-gun frigate "Cleopatra," Captain Sir Robert Laurie, overtook, after a long chase, the French 18-pounder 40-gun frigate "Ville de Milan," Captain Renaud. A long and determined fight took place, while the two ships were running parallel to each other. In overhauling this vessel, Captain Laurie caught a Tartar.

The "Cleopatra" was overmatched in every way, and, after having 22 killed and 36 wounded, was compelled to surrender.

But on the 23rd of February, as the "Ville de Milan," and the "Cleopatra," her prize, were on the way to port, they were encountered by the English 50-gun ship "Leander," Captain Talbot, who gave chase.

During the pursuit, the "Cleopatra," without any resistance, hauled down the French colours and hove to.

Her original English crew then rushed on deck and took possession; while the "Leander" continued the pursuit of the "Ville de Milan," which, after being overhauled, struck without firing a gun.

She was added to the English navy, under the name of the "Milan," and Captain Laurie was appointed her commander, and a sword of the value of 100 guineas was given him from the Patriotic Fund.

On the 20th of March, off the island of Cuba, the "General Ernouf" (late English sloop "Lily") was captured by the 18-gun corvette "Renaud," Captain Coghlan.

After an engagement of thirty-five minutes, the French vessel took fire and blew up. Only 55 men of a crew of 160 were saved by being picked up by the boats of the "Renaud."

On the 5th of April, two boats from the 22-gun ship "Bacchante," Captain Dashwood, were sent into the harbour of Manila, near Havanna, to capture three small French privateers.

The boats were under the command of Lieutenants Oliver and Campbell, and were manned by 35 seamen and marines.

The harbour was protected by a tower mounting three 24-pounders, and garrisoned by a Spanish captain and 30 soldiers.

It was resolved to capture this tower first, which was done with a scaling ladder without the loss of a man.

The privateers had sailed but a few hours before, and the only reward for this daring adventure was two schooners laden with sugar.

On the 15th of April, Captain Woolsey, of the 14-gun brig "Pampillon," while lying at Savanna-le-Mar, sent Lieutenant Prieur, the purser, and 24 men, in a hired shallop, disguised as a drogger, to capture a Spanish felucca privateer that was cruising off the coast.

The privateer, on seeing that the shallop gave chase, came alongside and made fast to it.

The concealed crew then sprang up from below, gave a volley of musketry, and then took the felucca by boarding.

Lieutenant Prieur had but two men wounded, and the Spaniards had seven men killed and eight wounded.

On the 6th of May, four boats belonging to the 32-gun frigate "Unicorn," Captain Hardyman, captured the French privateer cutter "Tape-à-Bord." The "Unicorn's" boats were commanded by Lieutenant Henry S. Wilson.

On the 1st of June, Captain Maitland, of the 38-gun frigate "Loire," sent Lieutenant Yeo with the boats to cut out a privateer that had taken shelter in the Bay of Camarinus, near Cape Finisterre. The privateer was found in company of another, and both moored under a 10-gun battery.

Charles Clinch, the master's mate, in the launch, was told to board the smaller vessel, and Lieutenant Yeo, with the cutters, attacked the other.

Both vessels were captured without loss. The felucca "Esperanza," and three small vessels loaded with wine, were taken out.

On the 4th of June, 1805, Captain Maitland, of the "Loire" frigate, being informed that a French privateer was fitting out at Muros, and being perfectly acquainted with that bay, resolved to attempt her capture or destruction; for which purpose he stood as close in as possible, and, having made every preparation for engaging at anchor, he directed Mr. Yeo, his first lieutenant, with two other officers, and fifty men, to storm the fort which protected the privateer.

The boats in which they were to embark were kept alongside of the frigate till she got well into the bay.

On hauling round a point of land a small battery unexpectedly opened a fire on the ship, which was promptly returned; and as Captain Maitland found that, unless this fire was silenced, the frigate would be much annoyed, he desired Lieutenant Yeo and his men to push on shore and spike the guns.

As they were about to leave the side of the ship, Captain Maitland reminded the boat's crew that it was their sovereign's birthday, which they saluted with three hearty cheers, and pushed off in high spirits for the enterprise.

As the ship drew in, and more fully opened the bay, fresh difficulties presented themselves, for besides the privateer of which Captain Maitland had received information, a very large corvette, called the "Confiance," pierced for twenty-six guns, and a large brig, called "Le Belier," pierced for twenty guns, were seen, apparently ready for sea; but as neither of them began to fire, hopes were entertained that they had not their guns on board.

Captain Maitland, therefore, directed his first and principal attention to a strong fort, which opened a heavy and well-directed fire, every shot taking place in the hull; and as it was evident that the nearer the frigate approached, the more she would be exposed, he anchored in an advantageous position, and began to return the fire, but, owing to the fort being completely embrasured, very little impression could be made upon it.

In the meantime, Lieutenant Yeo, with the men under his command, had made good their landing; as soon as they approached the fort on the point, the enemy abandoned it.

Lieutenant Yeo next directed his attention to such other measures as he thought would best aid the purpose for which he had been sent on shore; he soon observed the strong fort at the entrance of the town, which, as has been noticed, fired with such effect against the "Loire."

CRESTS OF VESSELS IN THE ROYAL NAVY (A.D. 1870).

Notwithstanding the great strength of the fort, both from its position and from the guns which were in it, Lieutenant Yeo was convinced it might be carried by storm; he well knew the bravery of the officers and men that were with him, and that whatever was possible, they would attempt and execute.

He, therefore, ordered them to follow him for the purpose of taking the fort by storm. No sooner was the word given, than he was obeyed with all that energy and bravery which, on such an occasion, Britons always display.

It fortunately happened that the enemy had neglected to secure the gate of the fort, through which the British entered; they were, however, met at the inner gate by the governor with all the troops he could collect, and the crews of the privateers.

Lieutenant Yeo was the first who entered the fort, and, with one blow, he laid the governor dead at his feet, at the same time breaking his own sabre in two.

The enemy had the advantage at first, from the extreme narrowness of the gate; but they were soon dislodged, and compelled to fly to the farthest part of the fort.

Such was their confusion and dismay, that many of them actually leaped from the embrasures, a height of about twenty-five feet, on the rocks below.

The instant the British gained possession of the fort, they laid aside one of their characteristic qualities, bravery, and assumed another, humanity. As soon as the enemy had surrendered, he was to them a fellow creature, to whose assistance and comfort they were anxious to contribute all in their power.

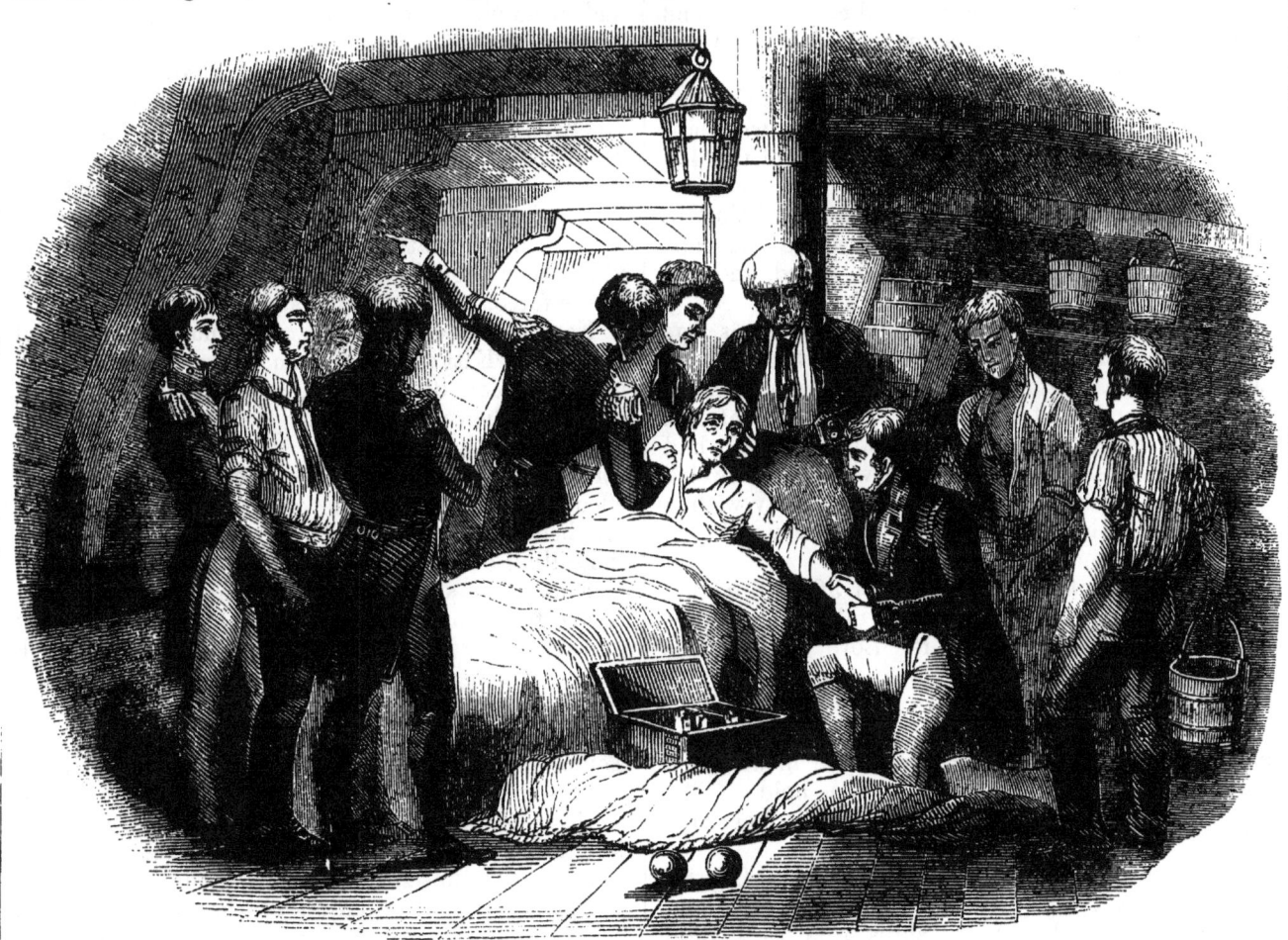

LAST MOMENTS OF LORD NELSON.

Each rivalled the others in relieving the poor wounded prisoners; and their humanity was amply acknowledged and repaid by the gratitude which the unfortunate men's friends expressed when they came to take them away.

Soon after the British flag was displayed on the fort, Captain Maitland took possession of the enemy's vessels already mentioned, and hoisted a flag of truce, informing the inhabitants that, if they would deliver up such of the stores as were on shore, he would do them no damage, which proposal was instantly and cheerfully agreed to.

The captain, in his official despatch, praises in the highest terms the bravery and discipline of such of his men as were on shore.

"Much to the credit of the ship's company," he

says, "the bishop and one of the principal inhabitants of the town came off to express their gratitude for the orderly behaviour of the people, and to make offer of every refreshment the place afforded."

This spirited enterprise was effected at noonday, though the fortress mounted twelve eighteen-pounders, and was garrisoned with more than two hundred and fifty men.

Lieutenant Yeo and six of his men were wounded. For his valour and conduct on this occasion, he was promoted to the rank of master and commander, and finally appointed to the command of the "Confiance," one of the captured vessels.

On the 13th of June, the Spanish privateer schooner "Maria," 14 guns and 60 men, was captured on the Halifax station by the boats of the 40-gun frigate "Cambrian."

Lieutenant George Pigot led the expedition in the launch, and the privateer was boarded and captured with a loss of two seamen killed, and two wounded.

The French privateer "Matilda," of 10 guns, was captured by the "Cambrian," on the 3rd of July, and Lieutenant Pigot, with a crew, was put aboard the prize, and sent to St. Mary's River, after a Spanish privateer and two merchant vessels it had taken as prizes. The three vessels were found twelve miles up the river, captured and taken away with a loss on board the "Matilda" of two seamen killed and fifteen wounded.

On the 19th of July, the English 36-gun frigate "Blanche," Captain Mudge, while taking dispatches from Jamaica to Barbadoes for Lord Nelson, was captured by the French 40-gun frigate "Topaz," Captain Baudin, assisted by two corvettes.

Captain Mudge continued the action until all the masts were crippled, seven guns were dismounted and six feet of water was in the hold. The "Blanche" was set on fire that night by her captors.

A squadron of six sail of the line and two frigates had been long lying in Rochefort, but so closely and constantly blockaded by our ships, that they could not get to sea.

In the beginning of the year 1805, they eluded our vigilance and got out; and about the same time the Toulon fleet, consisting of eleven sail of the line and two frigates, also got out of the harbour.

Lord Nelson had been stationed before Toulon, but it was not part of the plan of this great man to blockade an enemy's port strictly; he rather wished, by keeping at a distance, to entice them to sea; and in the course of the year 1804, he had written rather an indignant letter to the Common Council of London, because they had voted him thanks for having blockaded the ports of the enemy.

The unusual circumstance of two fleets of the enemy having escaped to sea much about the same time, created much alarm in Great Britain; it was impossible to conjecture on what enterprise they were gone, or whither they were bound.

The most common opinion was that Malta was their object; other people supposed that they had gone to Brazil or the West Indies; all, however, were apprehensive that they would do much mischief before they returned to port, or were captured by the British.

The general source of consolation arose from the circumstance that Lord Nelson knew that they were at sea, and that he would use every exertion to ascertain their route, and to come up with them, and, if he did come up with them, not one individual was doubtful of the result.

At length it was ascertained, that, on the 22nd of February, the smaller fleet which had sailed from Rochefort, had made its appearance in the West Indies, and made an attempt on Dominica.

This attempt, however, was only partially successful; the town of Rousseau, indeed, was set on fire during the attack of the French; but on the 27th, they thought it prudent to re-embark their whole force, and to sail towards Guadaloupe.

Early in March, the same armament appeared before St. Kitt's; where the enemy landed, levied a contribution of £18,000, burnt some merchantmen, and then re-embarked.

They also laid the small island of Nevis under contribution, and this was the whole that was effected by this force, as Admiral Cochrane, who had been despatched to the West Indies, as soon as the sailing of the Rochefort squadron was known, alarmed them so, that they thought it prudent to return to Europe. It was fortunate enough to get into Rochefort, though there were several British fleets at sea, and several squadrons were cruising expressly to intercept it.

Although when Admiral Villeneuve sailed from Toulon, Lord Nelson was out of sight of that port, he was speedily informed of the circumstance; and he lost no time in proceeding in that direction which he supposed the enemy had taken.

It struck the British admiral that Malta and Egypt were the destination of the armament, and he accordingly sailed towards Alexandria; but neither there, nor in any part of the Mediterranean, which he crossed in all directions, could he gain any intelligence of Admiral Villeneuve, who, indeed, after having been to sea only a few days, encountered such a violent gale as induced him to return to Toulon.

Lord Nelson, in the meantime, not being able to ascertain where he was, took his station in the Sicilian seas, as the most likely place, either to hear of, or to meet with, the enemy.

On the 30th of March, Admiral Villeneuve again ventured out of Toulon, having employed the intervening time in repairing the damage which his fleet had sustained during its former short cruise; his object now was to reach Carthagena, where he expected to find several Spanish sail of the line ready to join him; but, as they were not in a condition fit for sea or action immediately, he proceeded to Cadiz; here he was joined by one French and six Spanish sail of the line.

His whole fleet now amounted to eighteen sail of the line, in a perfect state of equipment, having on board, besides their full complement of men, 10,000 veteran troops.

With this formidable armament, the French admiral proceeded directly to the West Indies, having forced Sir John Orde, who was before Cadiz with five sail of the line, to retire from that station.

The West Indies were now considered to be in imminent danger, especially as the movements and intentions of Lord Nelson were for some time unknown.

His lordship had waited at Palermo only a sufficient time to take in the necessary supply of provisions, still ignorant of the motions of the French fleet.

About the middle of April, he, at last, learned that it had actually passed the Gut of Gibraltar; he immediately proceeded in the same direction, and, having anchored, early in the month of May, off the Barbary coast, he received certain intelligence that the French fleet had proceeded to the West Indies. The great inferiority of his force to that of the enemy, the distance, the great improbability that he should arrive there before they had done their meditated mischief; none of these circumstances weighed with his active and vigorous mind.

He instantly formed his resolution, and directed his course from the Straits of Gibraltar to the West Indies, having previously received at Tetuan and Lagos Bay such articles of the first importance and necessity as the wants of his fleet demanded.

This was, indeed, a bold and arduous enterprise; Admiral Nelson had with him only ten sail of the line, and most, if not all of these, were foul, having been cruising for more than two years; yet, had he not taken the steps which he did, it is highly probable that all our valuable possessions in the West Indies would have fallen into the hands of the enemy.

So well were the measures of the French planned to distract the attention of the English, that scarcely had the apprehension and alarm created by the sailing of the Toulon fleet reached its height, when the Brest fleet put to sea also. Admiral Gardner blockaded this port with seventeen sail of the line; the enemy came out with twenty-five sail.

The British admiral, however, notwithstanding his very great inferiority, did not decline the contest; but the French contented themselves with a few manœuvres, and then returned to port, leaving the English admiral to continue the blockade, without any subsequent interruption.

On the 11th of May, Lord Nelson left Lagos Bay, in pursuit of Admiral Villeneuve, across the Atlantic; on the 15th of that month he was twenty leagues to the eastward of Madeira; and, on the 4th of June he anchored in Carlisle Bay, in the Island of Barbadoes.

There he was informed that the French admiral had arrived at Martinique, on the 14th of May, but that, from some unknown cause, he had hitherto achieved nothing with his immense force, but the capture of the Diamond Rock, off that island. At Barbadoes, Lord Nelson was joined by Admiral Cochrane, with two sail of the line, and he immediately proceeded against the enemy.

During the pursuit the mind of the gallant Nelson incessantly dwelt on the hope of falling in with the enemy.

He one day observed with great glee—

"There is just a Frenchman apiece for each English ship, leaving me out of the question, to fight the Spaniards; and, when I haul down my colours, I expect every captain of the fleet to do the same, but not till then."

The inactivity of the French has been variously accounted for; the most probable cause was the great sickness among their troops, not fewer than three thousand of whom, it is said, perished at Martinique from the disorders so fatal and common in that climate.

It was also believed that the French and Spaniards, jealous and mistrustful of each other, could not agree in any plan of operations, and that their inactivity was partly owing to that cause.

As soon as it was known in England that Lord Nelson had proceeded to the West Indies, all apprehension subsided, for such was the confidence in him, so firm the belief that where he was, victory was also, that the nation looked upon the great superiority of the enemy as nothing, where Lord Nelson was present.

His lordship was still doubtful with respect to the actual intentions and course of the enemy; but he concluded that Trinidad was as likely an object of attack as any; not only because it was less stronger than many other of the islands, but because it was natural to suppose that the Spanish Admiral Gravina would be anxious to wrest it from us, and to restore it to his own sovereign.

In the short space of twenty-four hours, Lord Nelson had taken in water for the whole fleet, and had also received on board two thousand troops under Sir William Myers.

On the 7th of June he arrived off Trinidad, where he learnt that the enemy had never been, nor could he ascertain their course. He now sailed for Grenada, which he reached on the 9th, where he had the mortification to learn that the fleet of the enemy, amounting to seventeen sail of the line, had that very morning sailed for Martinique, in a northerly direction; this led him to suppose that Antigua was their object, and to it he directed his course; but, on his arrival off this island, he was again disappointed in not meeting with the foe; he ascertained the fact, however, as flattering to him as it was disgraceful to the enemy, that they had, under the impression of terror, which his name inspired, betaken themselves to a precipitate and shameful flight, and were actually on their return to Europe.

Lord Nelson immediately disembarked the troops which he had on board at Antigua; and, having dispatched several fast-sailing vessels to inform the British ministry of the return of the enemy, and to spread the same intelligence in every direction, he sailed in pursuit of his flying foe.

Admiral Villeneuve, with twenty sail of the line, French and Spanish, three large ships armed *en flûte*, five frigates, and three brigs, proceeded, without molestation, till he arrived off Cape Finisterre.

Here he encountered Sir Robert Calder, who was cruising with fifteen sail of the line, two frigates, a cutter, and a lugger.

An action immediately commenced, the following account of which we subjoin, as given in a letter from an officer of one of the English frigates:—

"On the 22nd of July, about 11 a.m., the 'Defiance,' one of the look-out ships, made a signal for a fleet N.W. directly to windward of our fleet, and that they consisted of ships of the line and frigates to the number of thirty.

"About half-past 12 p.m. we could plainly count from our deck from twenty-five to thirty sail lying to. The 'Defiance' getting nearly within gunshot, returned to our fleet, who were then forming in line of battle.

"About 2 p.m. we were considerably within gunshot of the enemy's advanced squadron, when they tacked, and stood to windward of their fleet, then formed in line. We bore up to leeward of their advanced ship, and passed within half gunshot of their whole line, which was formed in a masterly style, and consisted of seventeen sail of the line, and three line-of-battle ships to windward, for the protection of their rear. They had likewise seven large frigates, two brigs, and a very valuable galleon, which one of their frigates had in tow; the frigates were likewise with the three ships of the line, to windward of their sternmost ship.

"Our fleet was at this time six miles to leeward, on the starboard tack, under a press of sail; the enemy at the same time under easy sail.

"A thick fog intervening, prevented the two fleets from seeing each other. Perceiving the galleon in tow by the frigate, and observing that she was the sternmost ship of the enemy's line, we tacked with the intention of endeavouring to cut her off. This sudden manœuvre threw the enemy's frigate into alarm, and she immediately commenced firing signal guns in quick succession, which caused the three line-of-battle ships, stationed to cover their rear, to edge down for her protection.

"Our attempt being thus frustrated we were compelled to edge down to our fleet. The fog at this time cleared a little, and we perceived that our fleet tacked for the enemy, and that the admiral had given the signal to attack their centre.

"As we were edging away, we observed that the van of the enemy had likewise wore for the protection of the galleon, and at three quarters past four their leading ships were in a very critical situation. On passing they hoisted Spanish colours, and we received the whole fire of their three leading ships, upwards of 120 pieces of heavy artillery discharged in one minute on our frigate, while we could only return twenty.

"Thus the action commenced; our leading ship, the 'Hero,' tacked as soon as the enemy opened their fire on us, and commenced a heavy cannonading on them in return. It continued with unremitting fury for three hours and a half, when we saw, on the clearing of the fog at intervals, the French line to windward, and two ships disabled, although we could not distinguish at the time whether they belonged to the enemy or to us.

"At half-past 8 the firing ceased on both sides; the admiral hoisted his distinguishing lights, as did the rest of the squadron, when we could plainly observe our fleet to be in tolerable order, considering the extreme fogginess of the weather, and had apparently suffered but little, although the firing on both sides was extremely heavy.

"We being just to leeward of the admiral, were ordered into the rear to take possession of the two prizes.

"About nine the admiral made the signal to bring-to on the starboard tack, which was complied with by the whole line.

"The two Spanish ships that surrendered had 600 men killed and wounded; their lower masts shot away by the board, so that they were rendered totally unmanageable, and gave us immense trouble in towing them.

"Had the weather been clear, I have no hesitation in saying they would have been completely defeated; but the fog prevented our ships getting near enough, and the French being to windward, were too wise to come nearer to us."

The "Windsor Castle," of 98 guns, was the only English ship which sustained any material injury in the action, and, considering the nature of the conflict in which she was engaged, it is a matter of surprise that she came off so well.

The enemy, haunted with the terrific idea of Lord Nelson, concluded, at first, that it was the squadron under his lordship which they had fallen in with. Under this impression several of the French and Spanish ships at once bore down and attacked the "Windsor Castle," which they mistook for the flagship of the noble admiral himself.

She received the fire of seven ships before she came up with her opponent, and then engaged two French and two Spanish ships of the line, besides a frigate and a brig, for two hours and a half.

The two Frenchmen were driven out of the line, one of the Spaniards dropped astern, and the other struck her colours. Two more French line-of-battle ships coming up on her quarter to rake the "Windsor Castle," the British admiral, in the "Prince of Wales," hastened to her relief, and engaged two of her opponents.

Had it not been for this timely assistance, the consequences would probably have been very serious, notwithstanding the intrepidity of Captain Boyles, and the brave crew of the "Windsor Castle."

One of these brave fellows had his right thigh shot off, and was suffering amputation when he heard that the Spanish ship had struck. He immediately took off his hat, gave three cheers, and exclaimed—
"I shall die happy!"

This action, though by no means decisive, was highly honourable to the British squadron, only the van of which could get into action, the rest of the ships being prevented by the fog from coming up with the enemy.

The loss of the latter, exclusive of the two captured ships, in which, as we have already seen, the slaughter was very great, amounted, by their account, to 55 killed, and 112 wounded.

The British nation were very much chagrined, displeased, and disappointed, when they learnt the issue of this battle.

Sir Robert Calder was severely blamed for not having done more.

DESTRUCTION OF THE "BLANCHE" FRIGATE.

The nation, very naturally, though perhaps not very fairly, conceived what Lord Nelson would have done had he been in the situation of Sir Robert Calder.

They made no allowance for the circumstance (which at any other time would have weighed with them) that Sir Robert had only fifteen sail of the line, while the enemy had twenty sail, besides three large 50-gun ships; nor did they sufficiently advert to the circumstance, that he had actually beaten the enemy, and taken two of their ships.

They merely looked to this, that a battle had been fought between him and the enemy, and that the greater part of the latter had escaped; they also recollected that this enemy had fled before Lord Nelson, though his fleet was so very inferior, and yet had not been beaten by another British admiral.

The disappointment of the public was so great, that it was judged proper to bring Sir Robert Cal-

der to a court-martial, the sentence of which was, that he had not done his utmost to take and destroy every ship of the enemy, which it was his duty to engage; but at the same time they ascribed such conduct to error in judgment, acquitting him completely of any imputation of fear or cowardice, and, therefore, only sentenced him to be severely reprimanded.

After the public mind began to cool, the fate of Sir Robert Calder was thought to be very hard, especially as he had meritoriously served his country for more than forty years.

* * * * *

On the 2nd of August, the 38-gun frigate "Phaëton," Captain John Wood, and the 18-gun sloop "Harrier," Captain Ratsey, made an attack on the French frigate "Semillante," moored under a battery at Jacinta, one of the Phillipine Islands, but, meeting with a spirited resistance, they were repulsed.

On August 6, the 74-gun ship "Blenheim," Captain Bissel, while convoying a fleet from the West Indies homeward bound, was attacked by the French 74-gun ship "Marengo," Rear-Admiral Linois, and the 40-gun frigate "Belle Poule."

The two French vessels were repulsed in a gallant and skilful manner, and not a ship of the convoy was lost.

On the 10th of August, the 18-pounder 36-gun frigate "Phœnix," Captain Baker, came up with the French 18-pounder 40-gun frigate "Didon," Captain Milius.

After much skilful manœuvring, and the exchange of a few broadsides, the two vessels came together, the starboard quarter of the "Phœnix" being on the larboard bow of the "Didon." The French then made frequent attempts to board, but were repelled by the marines.

In the position in which the two ships were, the "Didon" could not be effectively raked by the guns of the "Phœnix," and an extra port hole was cut through the stern windows and quarter gallery. While this gun was being brought to bear upon the enemy the crew of the "Phœnix" were suffering much loss, but the time used in putting the gun in position was not wholly thrown away.

At its first discharge twenty-four men on the deck of the "Didon" were prostrated.

The breeze then freshened, and the two vessels separated, when the action was continued for some time by firing broadsides until the foremast of the "Didon" fell and she surrendered.

On the "Phœnix" 12 men were killed and 28 wounded. The "Didon" lost 27 men killed and 44 wounded.

The "Didon" was a splendid ship of 1,100 tons, and was added to the navy under the same name.

On the 15th of August, the French 16-gun corvette "Faune" was captured by the 20-gun ship "Camilla," Captain Taylor, assisted by the 74-gun ship "Goliath," Captain Barton.

On the 26th of September, the 54-gun ship "Calcutta," Captain Woodriff, having under convoy the "Indus," three whalers, and two ships from St. Helena, encountered Rear-Admiral Allemand with a French squadron, consisting of the 120-gun ship "Majestueux," four other ships, and two frigates. The "Calcutta" was attacked by the "Magnanime" and the "Armide," and was compelled to surrender.

The "Calcutta" had six men killed and six wounded, and was so much disabled in the masts that the French had to keep her in tow for two days. The vessels under convoy escaped.

On the 9th of October, the 36-gun frigate "Princess Charlotte," Captain Tobin, being disguised, was taken by the French 16-gun brig "Naïade," and the 26-gun corvette "Cyane" (late English), for a merchant vessel, and did not learn their mistake until brought to action by the frigate, to which the "Cyane" surrendered, after making a gallant resistance.

The "Naïade" escaped, but was captured a few days afterwards by the 32-gun frigate "Jason," Captain Champain.

During the summer of the year 1805, there were several brief encounters between the blockading squadron, under Commodore Owen, and the Boulogne flotilla.

The service to which Commodore Owen was appointed was very laborious, and but little suited to officers and men anxious to sail in search of honour and valuable prizes, but, nevertheless, it was so effectually performed that Napoleon was disappointed in the hope of invading England with the flotilla.

On the 22nd of August, Vice-Admiral Collingwood commanded the blockade of Cadiz, with eighteen sail of the line.

He was joined by Lord Nelson in his old ship the "Victory," and some other vessels, till the fleet amounted to twenty-seven sail of the line.

Nelson arrived off Cadiz on the 29th of September — his birthday. Fearing that if the enemy knew his force they might be deterred from venturing to sea, he kept out of sight of land, desired Vice-Admiral Collingwood to fire no salute and hoist no colours, and wrote to Gibraltar to request that the force of the fleet might not be inserted there in the Gazette.

On the day of his arrival, Villeneuve received orders to put to sea the first opportunity. Villeneuve, however, hesitated, when he heard that Nelson had resumed the command.

He called a council of war; and their determination was, that it would not be expedient to leave Cadiz, unless they had reason to believe themselves stronger by one-third than the British force.

The station which Nelson had chosen was some fifty or sixty miles to the west of Cadiz, near Cape St. Mary's.

At this distance he hoped to decoy the enemy out, while he guarded against the danger of being caught in a westerly wind near Cadiz, and driven within the Straits.

The blockade of the port was rigorously enforced, in hopes that the combined fleet might be forced to sea by want. The supplies from France were thus effectually cut off.

There was now every indication that the enemy would speedily venture out; officers and men were in the highest spirits at the prospect of giving them a decisive blow—such, indeed, as would put an end to all further contest upon the seas, though at this time Lord Nelson was not without some cause of anxiety.

He was in want of frigates—the eyes of the fleet, as he always called them—to the want of which the enemy before were indebted for their escape, and Buonaparte for his arrival in Egypt.

He had only twenty-three ships—others were on the way, but they might come too late; and though Nelson never doubted of victory, mere victory was not what he looked to. He wanted to annihilate the enemy's fleet.

The Carthagena squadron might effect a junction with this fleet on the one side; and on the other it was to be expected that a similar attempt would be made by the French from Brest; in either case a formidable contingency to be apprehended by the blockading force.

The Rochefort squadron did push out, and had nearly caught the "Agamemnon" and "L'Aimable," in their way to reinforce the British admiral.

Yet Nelson at this time weakened his own fleet. He had the unpleasant task to perform of sending home Sir Robert Calder, whose conduct was to be made the subject of a court-martial, in consequence of the general dissatisfaction which had been felt and expressed at his imperfect victory.

Sir Robert Calder and Sir John Orde, Nelson believed to be the only two enemies whom he had in his profession; and from that sensitive delicacy which distinguished him, this made him the more scrupulously anxious to show every possible mark of respect and kindness to Sir Robert.

He wished to detain him till after the expected action; when the services which he might perform, and the triumphant joy which would be excited, would leave nothing to be apprehended from an inquiry into the previous engagement.

Sir Robert, however, whose situation was very painful, did not choose to delay a trial, from the result of which he confidently expected a complete justification; and Nelson, instead of sending him home in a frigate, insisted on his returning in his own 90-gun ship—ill as such a ship could at that time be spared.

Nothing could be more honourable than the feeling by which Nelson was influenced; but at such a crisis, it ought not to have been indulged.

The order of sailing was to be the order of battle; the fleet in two lines, with an advanced squadron of eight of the fastest sailing two-deckers.

The second in command, having the entire direction of his line, was to break through the enemy, about the twelfth ship from their rear; he would lead through the centre, and the advanced squadron was to cut off three or four ahead of the centre.

This plan was to be adapted to the strength of the enemy, so that they should always be one-fourth superior to those whom they cut off.

Nelson said that—

"The admirals and captains, knowing his precise object to be that of close and decisive action, would supply any deficiency by signals, and act accordingly. In case signals cannot be seen or clearly understood, no captain can do wrong if he places his ship alongside that of an enemy."

One of the last orders of this admirable man was, that the name and family of every officer, seaman, and marine, who might be killed or wounded in action, should be, as soon as possible, returned to him, in order to be transmitted to the chairman of the Patriotic Fund, that the case might be taken into consideration for the benefit of the sufferer or his family.

At daybreak of the 21st, the combined fleets were distinctly seen from the "Victory's" deck, formed in a close line of battle ahead, on the starboard tack, about twelve miles to leeward, and standing to the south.

Our fleet consisted of twenty-seven sail of the line, and four frigates. Their superiority was greater in size and weight of metal than in numbers. They had 4,000 troops on board, and the best riflemen who could be procured—many of them Tyrolese—were dispersed through the ships.

Little did the Tyrolese, and little did the Spaniards, at that day, imagine what horrors the wicked tyrant, whom they served, was preparing for their country.

Soon after daylight Nelson came upon deck.

The 21st of October was a festival in his family, because on that day his uncle, Captain Suckling, in the "Dreadnought," with two other line of battle ships, had beaten off a French squadron of four sail of the line, and three frigates.

Nelson, with that sort of superstition from which few persons are entirely exempt, had more than once expressed his persuasion that this was to be the day of his battle also; and he was well pleased at seeing his prediction about to be verified.

The wind was now from the west, light breezes, with a long heavy swell. Signal was made to bear down upon the enemy in two lines; and the fleet set all sail.

Collingwood, in the "Royal Sovereign," led the lee line of thirteen ships; the "Victory" led the weather line of fourteen.

Having seen that all was as it should be, Nelson retired to his cabin.

The following is a list of ships in the two divisions of the English fleet, given in the order in which they entered into the action:—

Weather Division.—"Victory," 100 guns, Vice-Admiral Lord Nelson (white), Captain Thomas Hardy; "Téméraire," 98 guns, Captain Elias Harvey; "Neptune," 98 guns, Captain Thomas F. Freemantle; "Leviathan," 74 guns, Captain Henry W. Bayntun; "Conqueror," 74 guns, Captain Israel Pillew; "Britannia," 100 guns, Rear-Admiral Earl of Northesk (white), Captain Charles Bullen; "Agamemnon," 64 guns, Captain Sir Edward Berry; "Africa," 64 guns, Captain Henry Digby; "Ajax," 74 guns, Captain John Pilford; "Orion," 74 guns, Captain Edward Codrington; "Minotaur," 74 guns, Captain Charles J. M. Mansfield; "Spartiate," 74 guns, Captain Sir Francis Laforey; "Euryalus," 38 guns, Captain Honourable Henry Blackwood; "Naiad," 38 guns, Captain Thomas Dundas; "Pickle" (schooner), Lieutenant John Lapenotiere.

Lee Division.—"Royal Sovereign," 100 guns, Vice-Admiral Collingwood (blue), Captain Edward Rotheram; "Belleisle," 74 guns, Captain William Hargood; "Mars," 74 guns, Captain George Duff; "Tonnant," 80 guns, Captain Charles Tyler; "Bellerophon," 74 guns, Captain John Cooke; "Colossus," 74 guns, Captain James Morris; "Achille," 74 guns, Captain Richard King; "Dreadnought," 98 guns, Captain John Conn; "Polyphemus," 64 guns, Captain Robert Redmill; "Revenge," 74 guns, Captain Robert Moorsom; "Swiftsure," 74 guns, Captain George Rutherford; "Defiance," 74 guns, Captain Philip Durham; "Thunderer," 74 guns, Captain John Stockham; "Defence," 74 guns, Captain George Hope; "Prince," 98 guns, Captain Richard Grindall; "Phœbe," 36 guns, Captain Thomas Bladen Capel; "Sirius," 36 guns, Captain William Prowse; "Entreprenante" (cutter), Lieutenant John Purver.

The allied French and Spanish fleet consisted of 33 ships; the Spanish vessels being the largest, and having amongst them the "Santa Anna" flag ship of 112 guns, the "Santissima Trinidad," 130 guns, and the "Principe de Asturias," of 112 guns.

Captain Blackwood went on board the "Victory" about six.

He found Nelson in good spirits, but very calm; not in that exhilaration which he had felt upon entering into battle at Aboukir and Copenhagen; he knew that his own life would be particularly aimed at, and seems to have looked for death with almost as sure an expectation as for victory.

His whole attention was fixed upon the enemy. They tacked to the northward, and formed their line on the larboard tack; thus bringing the shoals of Trafalgar and St. Pedro under the lee of the British, and keeping the port of Cadiz open for themselves.

This was judiciously done; and Nelson, aware of all the advantages which it gave them, made signal to prepare to anchor.

Villeneuve was a skilful seaman; worthy of serving a better master, and a better cause. His plan of defence was as well conceived, and as original, as the plan of attack.

He formed the fleet in a double line, every alternate ship being about a cable's length to windward of her second a-head and a-stern.

Nelson, certain of a triumphant issue to the day, asked Blackwood what he should consider as a victory.

That officer answered, that considering the handsome way in which battle was offered by the enemy, their apparent determination for a fair trial of strength, and the situation of the land, he thought it would be a glorious result if fourteen were captured. He replied—

"I shall not be satisfied with less than twenty."

Soon afterwards he asked him if he did not think there was a signal wanting. Captain Blackwood made answer, that he thought the whole fleet seemed very clearly to understand what they were about.

These words were scarcely spoken before that signal was made, which will be remembered as long as the language, or even the memory, of England shall endure—Nelson's last signal—

"ENGLAND EXPECTS EVERY MAN TO DO HIS DUTY!"

It was received throughout the fleet with a shout of answering acclamation, made sublime by the spirit which it breathed, and the feeling which it expressed.

"Now," said Lord Nelson, "I can do no more. We must trust to the great Disposer of all events, and the justice of our cause. I thank God for this great opportunity of doing my duty."

He wore that day, as usual, his admiral's frock coat, bearing on the left breast four stars of the different orders with which he was invested. Ornaments which rendered him so conspicuous a mark for the enemy, were beheld with ominous apprehension by his officers.

They communicated their fears to each other, and the surgeon, Mr. Beatty, spoke to the chaplain, Dr. Scott, and to Mr. Scott, the public secretary, desiring that some person would entreat him to change his dress, or cover the stars; but they knew that such a request would highly displease him.

"In honour I gained them," he had said, when such a thing had been hinted to him formerly, "and in honour I will die with them."

But both Blackwood and his own captain, Hardy, represented to him how advantageous to the fleet it would be for him to keep out of action as long as possible; and he consented at last to let the "Leviathan" and the "Téméraire," which were sailing abreast of the "Victory," be ordered to pass ahead.

Yet even here the last infirmity of this noble mind was indulged, for these ships could not pass ahead if the "Victory" continued to carry all her sail; and so far was Nelson from shortening sail, that it was evident he took pleasure in pressing on, and rendering it impossible for them to obey his orders.

A long swell was setting into the bay of Cadiz; our ships, crowding all sail, moved majestically before it, with light winds from the south-west.

CRESTS OF VESSELS IN THE ROYAL NAVY (A.D. 1870).

The sun shone on the sails of the enemy, and their well-formed line, with their numerous three-deckers, made an appearance which any other assailants would have thought formidable; but the British sailors only admired the beauty and splendour of the spectacle: and, in full confidence of winning what they saw, remarked to each other what a fine sight yonder ships would make at Spithead!

The French admiral, from the "Bucentaure," beheld the new manner in which his enemy was advancing—Nelson and Collingwood each leading his line; and pointing them out to his officers, he is said to have exclaimed, that such conduct could not fail to be successful.

Yet Villeneuve had made his own dispositions with the utmost skill, and the fleets under his command waited for the attack with perfect coolness.

Ten minutes before twelve they opened their fire. Eight or nine of the ships immediately ahead of the "Victory," and across her bows, fired single guns at her, to ascertain whether she was yet within their range.

As soon as Nelson perceived that their shot passed over him, he desired Blackwood, and Captain Prowse, of the "Sirius," to repair to their respective frigates; and, on their way, to tell all the captains of the line-of-battle ships that he depended on their exertions; and that, if by the prescribed mode of attack, they found it impracticable to get into action immediately, they might adopt whatever they thought best, provided it led them quickly and closely alongside an enemy.

As they were standing on the front of the poop, Blackwood took him by the hand, saying he hoped soon to return and find him in possession of twenty prizes. He replied—

THE LOSS OF THE "DORIS" FRIGATE.

"God bless you, Blackwood! I shall never see you again."

Nelson's column was steered about two points more to the north than Collingwood's, in order to cut off the enemy's escape into Cadiz; the lee line, therefore, was first engaged.

"See!" cried Nelson, pointing to the "Royal Sovereign," as she steered right to the centre of the enemy's line, cut through it astern of the "Santa Anna," three-decker, and engaged her at the muzzle of her guns on the starboard side; "see how that noble fellow, Collingwood, carries his ship into action!"

The enemy continued to fire a gun at a time at

the "Victory," till they saw that a shot had passed through her main-top-gallant sail; then they opened their broadsides, aiming chiefly at her rigging, in the hope of disabling her before she could close with them. Nelson, as usual, had hoisted several flags, lest one should be shot away.

The enemy showed no colours till late in the action, when they began to feel the necessity of having them to strike. For this reason the "Santissima Trinidad," Nelson's old acquaintance, as he used to call her, was distinguishable only by her four decks; and to the bow of this opponent he ordered the "Victory" to be steered.

Meantime an incessant raking fire was kept up upon the "Victory." The admiral's secretary was one of the first who fell; he was killed by a cannon-shot while conversing with Hardy.

Captain Adair, of the marines, with the help of a sailor, endeavoured to remove the body from Nelson's sight, who had a great regard for Mr. Scott; but he anxiously asked—

"Is that poor Scott that's gone?" and being informed that it was indeed so, exclaimed: "Poor fellow!"

A few minutes afterwards a shot struck the fore-brace bits on the quarter-deck, and passed between Nelson and Hardy; a splinter from the bit tearing off Hardy's buckle, and bruising his foot.

Both stopped and looked anxiously at each other, each supposing the other to be wounded. Nelson then smiled, and said—

"This is too warm work, Hardy, to last long."

The "Victory" had not yet returned a single gun; 50 of her men had been by this time killed or wounded, and her main-top-mast, with all her studding-sails and her booms shot away.

Nelson declared that in all his battles, he had seen nothing which surpassed the cool courage of his crew on this occasion.

At four minutes after twelve, she opened her fire from both sides of her deck.

It was not possible to break the enemy's line without running on board one of their ships. Hardy informed him of this, and asked him which he would prefer. Nelson replied—

"Take your choice, Hardy; it does not signify much."

The master was ordered to put the helm to port, and the "Victory" ran on board the "Redoubtable," just as her tiller ropes were shot away.

The French ship received her with a broadside; then instantly let down her lower-deck ports, for fear of being boarded through them, and never afterwards fired a great gun during the action.

Captain Harvey, in the "Téméraire," fell on board the "Redoubtable" on the other side.

Another enemy was in like manner on board the "Téméraire;" so that these four ships formed as compact a tier as if they had been moored together, their heads lying all the same way.

The lieutenants of the "Victory," seeing this, depressed their guns of the middle and lower decks, and fired with a diminished charge, lest the shot should pass through, and injure the "Téméraire." And because there was danger that the "Redoubtable" might take fire from the lower deck guns, the muzzles of which touched her side when they were run out, the fireman of each gun stood ready with a bucket of water; which, as soon as the gun was discharged, he dashed into the hole made by the shot.

An incessant fire was kept up from the "Victory" from both sides; her larboard guns playing upon the "Bucentaure" and the huge "Santissima Trinidad."

It had been part of Nelson's prayer, that the British fleet might be distinguished by humanity in the victory which he expected.

Setting an example himself, he twice gave orders to cease firing upon the "Redoubtable," supposing that she had struck, because her great guns were silent; for, as she carried no flag, there was no means of instantly ascertaining the fact.

From this ship, which he had twice spared, he received his death!

A ball, fired from her mizen-top, which, in the then situation of the two vessels, was not more than fifteen yards from that part of the deck where he was standing, struck the epaulette on his left shoulder, about a quarter after one, just in the heat of action.

The bullet must have been fired from aloft, for, striking the epaulette on the left shoulder, it passed into his body.*

Captain Adair, of the marines, Midshipman Pollard, and several others of the "Victory," immediately commenced firing at the mizen-top of the "Redoubtable," and never ceased while there was a man left on it.†

Nelson fell upon his face, on the spot which was covered with his poor secretary's blood.

Hardy, who was a few steps from him, turning round, saw three men raising him up.

"They have done for me at last, Hardy," said he.

"I hope not," cried Hardy.

"Yes!" he replied, "my back-bone is shot through."

Yet even now, not for a moment losing his presence of mind, he observed, as they were carrying him down the ladder, that the tiller ropes, which had been shot away, were not yet replaced, and ordered that new ones should be rove immediately. Then, that he might not be seen by the crew, he

---

* The coat worn by Nelson on receiving the fatal wound was preserved by his adopted daughter, Mrs. Horatio Nelson. The late Sir N. H. Nicolas made this fact known to the late Prince Consort, who ordered the coat to be purchased and presented to Greenwich Hospital, where it is now to be seen in the Painted Hall.

† The man who is supposed to have fired the fatal shot wore a glazed hat and a white coat. He was fired at by two midshipmen and fell with a shot in his mouth.

took out his handkerchief, and covered his face and his stars.

Had he but concealed these badges of honour from the enemy, England, perhaps, would not have had cause to receive with sorrow the news of the battle of Trafalgar.

The cockpit was crowded with wounded and dying men; over whose bodies he was with some difficulty conveyed, and laid upon a pallet in the midshipmen's berth.

It was soon perceived, upon examination, that the wound was mortal.

This, however, was concealed from all except Captain Hardy, the chaplain, and the medical attendants. He himself being certain, from the sensation in his back, and the gush of blood he felt momently within his breast, that no human care could avail him, insisted that the surgeon should leave him, and attend to those to whom he might be useful.

"For," said he, "you can do nothing for me."

All that could be done was to fan him with paper, and frequently to give him lemonade to alleviate his intense thirst.

He was in great pain, and expressed much anxiety for the event of the action, which now began to declare itself.

As often as a ship struck, the crew of the "Victory" hurrahed; and at every hurrah, a visible expression of joy gleamed in the eyes, and marked the countenance of the dying hero.

But he became impatient to see Captain Hardy; and as that officer, though often sent for, could not leave the deck, Nelson feared that some fatal cause prevented him, and repeatedly cried—

"Will no one bring Hardy to me? He must be killed! He is surely dead!"

An hour and ten minutes elapsed from the time when Nelson received his wound, before Hardy could come to him.

They shook hands in silence; Hardy in vain struggling to suppress the feelings of that most painful, and yet sublimest moment.

"Well, Hardy," said Nelson, "how goes the day with us?"

"Very well," replied Hardy; "ten ships have struck, but five of the van have tacked, and show an intention to bear down upon the 'Victory.' I have called two or three of our fresh ships round, and have no doubt of giving them a drubbing."

"I hope," said Nelson, "none of our ships have struck?"

Hardy answered, "There was no fear of that."

Then, and not till then, Nelson spoke of himself.

"I am a dead man, Hardy," said he; "I am going fast; it will be all over with me soon. Come nearer to me. Let Lady Hamilton have my hair, and all other things belonging to me."

Hardy observed that he hoped Mr. Beatty could yet hold out some prospect of life.

"Oh, no!" he replied; "it is impossible. My back is shot through. Beatty will tell you so."

Captain Hardy then, once more, shook hands with him; and, with a heart almost bursting, hastened upon deck.

By this time all feeling below the breast was gone; and Nelson, having made the surgeon ascertain this, said to him—

"You know I am gone. I know it. I feel something rising in my breast,"—putting his hand on his left side—"which tells me so."

And upon Beatty's inquiring whether his pain was very great, he replied—

"So great that I wish I was dead. Yet," said he, in a lower voice, "one would like to live a little longer, too!"

Captain Hardy, some fifty minutes after he had left the cockpit, returned, and again taking the hand of his dying friend and commander, congratulated him on having gained a complete victory.

How many of the enemy were taken he did not know, as it was impossible to perceive them distinctly; but fourteen or fifteen at least.

"That's well," cried Nelson, "but I bargained for twenty." And then in a stronger voice he said —"Anchor, Hardy, anchor."

Hardy, upon this, hinted that Admiral Collingwood would take upon himself the direction of affairs.

"Not while I live, Hardy," said the dying Nelson, ineffectually endeavouring to raise himself from the bed. "Do you anchor."

His previous order for preparing to anchor had shown how clearly he foresaw the necessity of this. Presently, calling Hardy back, he said to him in a low voice—

"Don't throw me overboard," and he desired that he might be buried by his parents, unless it should please the king to order otherwise. Then, reverting to private feelings—"Take care of Lady Hamilton, Hardy; take care of poor Lady Hamilton. Kiss me, Hardy," said he.

Hardy knelt down and kissed his cheek and Nelson said—

"Now I am satisfied. Thank God, I have done my duty."

Hardy stood over him in silence for a moment or two, then knelt again and kissed his forehead.

"Who is that?" said Nelson; and, being informed, he replied "God bless you, Hardy!" And Hardy then left him—for ever.

Nelson now desired to be turned upon his right side, and said—

"I wish I had not left the deck, for I shall soon be gone."

Death was, indeed, rapidly approaching.

His articulation now became difficult, and he was distinctly heard to say—

"Thank God, I have done my duty."

These words he repeatedly pronounced; and they were the last words which he uttered. He expired at thirty minutes after four—three hours and a quarter after he had received his wound.

As soon as Nelson died, Hardy went to the "Royal Sovereign," to inform the vice-admiral of what had happened, and to deliver the command that the fleet should be anchored.

On receiving this message Collingwood replied—

"Anchor the fleet! Why, it is the last thing I should have thought of!"

The fleet was not anchored, and Collingwood was much blamed by many in consequence.

Others have sustained him in the course he took of keeping the vessels under way.

There was some confusion on the "Victory" when it became known that Nelson was mortally wounded.

The French in the "Redoubtable" discovered this, and made preparations for boarding it. They were prevented from doing this by a heavy broadside from the "Fighting Téméraire," Captain Harvey, which struck down nearly 200 men.

While engaged with the "Redoubtable," Harvey saw the "Fougueux," of 74 guns, preparing to lay his ship aboard, on the side opposite the "Redoubtable."

He allowed the vessel to come within one hundred yards, and then poured into it a broadside that reduced it to a wreck. It was then captured by boarding, and with but little resistance.

This vessel, which on entering the action, had a crew of 700 men, had upwards of 400 killed and wounded. The "Redoubtable" was also captured by the crew of the "Téméraire," who boarded it.

The "Redoubtable" was gallantly defended; 300 of her crew had been killed, and 220 wounded before she surrendered.

Nearly as great was the slaughter aboard the "Bucentaure," which surrendered with the French Admiral Villeneuve on board.

The "Santissima Trinidad" had sustained the fire of the "Victory," "Neptune," "Leviathan," and "Conqueror" until it became so disabled that it was taken possession of by a boat's crew from the "Prince."

Before three o'clock ten of the enemy's ships of the line had struck, and several others were much disabled. The fire from them was weakened, and it was evident to all that every man on the English fleet had done his duty.

At the close of the battle the following vessels had surrendered, or were in the possession of the English:—

SPANISH.—"Santissima Trinidad," 130 guns; "Santa Anna," 112 guns; "Neptuno," 80 guns; "Argonauta," 80 guns; "San Augustin," 74 guns; "Monarca," 74 guns; "Bahama," 74 guns; "San Juan Nepomuceno," 74 guns; "San Ildefonso," 74 guns.

FRENCH.—"Bucentaure," 80 guns; "Intrépide," 74 guns; "Redoubtable," 74 guns; "Fougueux," 74 guns; "Algésiras," 74 guns; "Aigle," 74 guns; "Swiftsure," 74 guns; "Berwick," 74 guns; "Achille," 74 guns.

This great victory was won with the loss of 449 men killed, and 1,241 wounded.

Many tales are told of individuals who performed brave deeds on that eventful day. Amongst them is that of Christopher Beaty, a yeoman of the signals on board the "Bellerophon."

Seeing the ensign shot away three times, he mounted the mizen rigging with a Union Jack and stopped the four corners to the shrouds, giving it a wide spread. The French riflemen from the tops of the "Aigle," who had been picking off every man who had for some time appeared on that mast, with a noble feeling that none can but admire, forbore to fire at so brave a man, and allowed him to descend unharmed.

On the following day (the 22nd), the wind blew strong in squalls all day, and the "Bucentaure" was wrecked near Saint Sebastain, and the English crew were saved by the boats of a French frigate.

On the morning of the 23rd, a heavy gale was blowing from the north west.

The "Redoubtable" foundered that morning, and all but 170 of her crew were lost, together with 13 seamen from the "Téméraire," and 5 from the "Swiftsure."

The "Fougueux" prize drifted on shore, having 30 of the crew of the "Téméraire" on board, and was lost with nearly all hands.

The prize crew of the "Algésiras" was overpowered by the French prisoners during the storm —rigged with jury masts and run into Cadiz.

On the same morning, the "Santa Anna" and "Neptuno" were recaptured by five frigates and taken into Cadiz.

On the 24th, the "Indomptable" was wrecked off the town of Rota, and more than 900 men were lost. She had on board the survivors of the "Bucentaure's" crew.

On this day the "Santissima Trinidad" was scuttled and sunk by the "Neptune" and "Prince."

The "Aigle" drifted into Cadiz Bay, and was wrecked on the bar of Port Maria on the 25th.

On the 29th, the "Intrépide" was burnt by the "Britannia," and the "San Augustin" by the "Leviathan" and "Orion."

The "Argonauta" was scuttled and sunk by the "Ajax."

The "Berwick" was wrecked off San Lucar, and 200 of her crew were drowned with her.

It is to this day a disputed point amongst naval men as to whether the fleet would have suffered any more had the dying commands of Nelson been obeyed or not.

The "Defence," "San Ildefonso," "Bahama," and "Swiftsure" anchored on the night of the 26th and rode out the gale in safety, but such might not have been the case had they been anchored two or three days before.

The body of Nelson was brought to England, and for some time was kept lying in state in the Painted Hall of Greenwich Hospital.

On the 6th day of January, 1806, it was buried in St. Paul's Cathedral.

The English people received the news of the battle of Trafalgar with mingled feelings of joy and grief. They had gained the greatest naval victory that had ever been fought. They were relieved from all anxiety about a French invasion. They were independent and secure; but that noble hero by whom so much had been gained was lost to them for ever.

Off Ferrol, on the 4th of November, the English 80-gun ship "Cæsar," Captain Sir Richard Strachan, and the 74-gun ships "Hero," "Namur," "Courageux," "Phœnix," and "Santa Margarita" frigate, after a long pursuit, came up with and engaged the French ships "Duguay Trouin," the "Formidable," "Mont Blanc," and "Scipion," under Admiral Dumanoir, who had escaped from Trafalgar.

After an action of about three hours, the "Formidable" having lost her mizen topmast and her mainmast, and her foretopmast threatening to go over, hauled down her colours.

The "Scipion" soon after followed her example, and was taken possession of by the "Phœnix" and "Révolutionnaire," which had come up and joined in the battle.

The "Duguay Trouin" and "Mont Blanc" tried to escape, but were overhauled by the "Hero" and "Cæsar," and surrendered after an action of twenty minutes.

In capturing these vessels the English had 24 men killed and 111 wounded. The French had 700 killed and wounded. The four captured vessels were added to the English navy.

Off Rochefort, on the 24th of December, the 24-pounder 44-gun frigate "Egyptienne," under command of Lieutenant Philip Crosby Handfield, and the 38-gun frigate "Loire," Captain Maitland, captured the French 38-gun frigate "Libre," Captain Descorches.

DUCKWORTH'S ACTION WITH A FRENCH SQUADRON.

The "Egyptienne" had 1 man killed and 9 wounded. The French frigate had 20 men killed and wounded.

Notwithstanding the loss which Napoleon Bonaparte had sustained by the battle of Trafalgar, and the great probability that whenever his remaining ships ventured to sea they would meet with a similar fate, yet the critical situation of his remaining West India colonies determined him to run all hazards for their support and relief; accordingly, on the 4th of December, 1805, notwithstanding the vigilance of our cruisers, a French fleet, consisting of eleven sail of the line and a number of frigates, made its escape from Brest.

This fleet afterwards divided into two squadrons, and proceeded by different routes towards the West Indies.

One of these squadrons, consisting of six sail of the line and two frigates, soon afterwards fell in with two British transports, with troops, from Gibraltar, and took them.

Having put the soldiers on board the "Volontaire" frigate of 46 guns and 360 men, the French admiral sent her forward to the Cape of Good Hope, not being aware that that settlement had been captured by the British.

On the 4th of March, the "Volontaire" arrived off the Cape, and the "Diadem," of 64 guns, then lying in Table Bay, having observed her at a distance, and, supposing her to be an enemy, immediately hoisted Dutch colours.

The French frigate not suspecting the stratagem, went in and anchored alongside the "Diadem;" on which the latter hauled down the Dutch and hoisted English colours in their place.

The frigate perceived her mistake too late to attempt to escape, and, being unable to contend with such a superior force, surrendered without firing a gun.

Sir Home Popham, on receiving intelligence that a French squadron was in those seas, immediately made every preparation to give the enemy a warm reception, in case they should think proper to attack the Cape.

The English troops, to the number of 217, retaken in the "Volontaire," were immediately landed, and sent to reinforce the garrison.

The squadron at the Cape consisted of the "Diomede," of 50 guns, and two frigates, besides the "Volontaire."

The latter was manned from the other ships, and the whole were moored with springs on their cables, under a battery of 32 guns, from which it was intended to fire red-hot shot if the French squadron should approach to attempt hostilities.

This, it afterwards appeared, was part of the fleet which got out of Brest, on the above-named day, and separated into two squadrons.

One of these took a southern course, while the other proceeded to the West Indies, to which quarter we shall now follow them.

Accounts having been received that the Rochefort squadron, by which the "Calcutta" was taken, had, on their return from Teneriffe, in November, fallen in with and dispersed the convoy bound to the coast of Africa, Vice-Admiral Sir J. T. Duckworth, then off Cadiz, immediately proceeded in quest of them, with his Majesty's ships of the line "Superb," "Spencer," "Donegal," "Canopus," "Powerful," and "Ajax."

He continued to cruise off the Canaries for a given time; on his return to Cadiz, he fell in, on Christmas Day, with a French squadron of six sail of the line.

This was the squadron to which the "Volontaire" belonged, and one of the ships of which was commanded by Jerome Bonaparte, the brother of Napoleon.

"It is impossible," says an officer of the "Superb," "to describe the joy expressed by every one on board the British ships on this occasion; every individual thought himself a king, and expected that day to be one of the happiest Christmases he had ever spent."

But from the very bad sailing of several ships of the fleet, the enemy had the good fortune to escape after a chase of two days.

Uncertain of their destination, Admiral Duckworth took the most effectual means to defeat their views, by immediately detaching the "Powerful," of 74 guns, to the East Indies, with an account of the number and strength of the enemy's squadron, and proceeded himself direct to Barbadoes, following the example of the great and gallant Nelson, when in a similar dilemma.

On his arrival in the West Indies, he took Admiral Cochrane, with the "Northumberland" and "Atlas," under his command, and proceeded off Martinique, in hopes of intercepting them.

But the enemy had pursued a wiser policy.

They had kept well to the northward, and instead of spreading an alarm through the islands, had proceeded by the nearer passage to the Bay of St. Domingo, on the south side of the island of that name, and where the first Rochefort squadron had, the preceding year, succeeded in throwing in reinforcements to the city of St. Domingo, then besieged by Dessalines.

Accounts of their probable destination having been received by a neutral, Sir J. Duckworth, with great promptitude, proceeded to that quarter, and, in the afternoon of the 5th of February, was joined by the "Magicienne" frigate, with a farther corroboration from various vessels spoken, of an enemy's force being in those seas.

Admiral Duckworth continued under easy sail all night, in his approach to the town of St. Domingo, having given orders to Captain Dunn, of the "Acasta," and Captain M'Kenzie, of the "Magicienne," to make sail two hours before daylight to reconnoitre.

At six in the morning of the 6th, the "Acasta" made the signal for two of the enemy's frigates, and, before seven, for nine sail at anchor.

Half an hour afterwards, they were getting under way.

The British squadron approached them fast, in close order, and, before eight o'clock, discovered that the enemy were in a compact line, under all sail, going before the wind for Cape Nisas, to windward of Ocoa Bay, and that they consisted of five sail of the line, two frigates, and a corvette.

The English force consisted of seven sail of the line and four frigates.

Had the enemy remained at anchor, the British fleet would have found it difficult to get at them; but as they bore away, Admiral Duckworth concluded, from the information he had received, that they were endeavouring to form a junction with their remaining force.

He therefore shaped his course in the "Superb," which led the squadron, so as to frustrate any such intention, which was completely effected by a little after nine, and an action became inevitable.

He now made a telegraphic signal to his fleet—
"*This is glorious!*"

Alluding to the enemy's squadron in a situation to be engaged, which was equivalent to victory.

The signal of their gallant leader was hailed with transport by all the British ships, to which he communicated by telegraph, that the principal object of attack would be the French admiral and his seconds.

At three-quarters past nine, he directed the ships to take stations for their mutual support, and engage the enemy as they got up; and a few minutes afterwards, he made the signal for them to engage as closely as possible.

"Just before the action began," says an officer of the "Superb," "Captain Keates suspended to the mizen-stay a portrait of our beloved hero, Nelson. There it remained unhurt, but was completely covered, as was Captain Keates himself, with the blood and brains of poor Brookbank, one of our boatswain's mates. Two or three minutes before the work of death began, officers' hats off on the quarter-deck, our band played '*God save the King*;' then came, '*Off she goes ;*' and next, '*Nelson of the Nile.*' Never was enthusiasm greater than ours, and to it we went with heart and hand."

Soon after ten o'clock, the "Superb," of 74 guns, closed on the bow of the leading ship "L'Alexandre," of 84 guns, and commenced the action.

The enemy had brought that ship, and "L'Imperiale," of 120 guns, together, seemingly with a view to quiet the fire of the English admiral, in the "Superb," before any of the other ships could come up: but in this they were disappointed, for the second broadside from the "Superb" did such execution on board "L'Alexandre," that she became quite unmanageable, and lost her station.

"L'Imperiale" was by this time within pistol-shot of the "Superb," and apparently reserving her fire for the latter; but, in this critical moment, Admiral Cochrane, in the "Northumberland," came up, and notwithstanding the small distance between the "Superb" and "L'Imperiale," he gallantly placed her between them, and received the whole broadside of the largest, and what was esteemed the finest ship in the French navy. Several of the shots passed quite through the "Northumberland" into the "Superb."

In the mean time, the "Superb," having given a very severe dressing to "L'Alexandre," compelled her to sheer off, and went to the assistance of the "Northumberland," which had at one time the fire of three French ships upon her for forty minutes.

The movements of "L'Alexandre" having thrown her among the lee division, Rear-Admiral Louis, in the "Canopus," of 84 guns, availed himself of that circumstance, and the rest of the British ships coming up, the action became general.

Nothing could exceed the coolness and high state of discipline of our brave seamen and marines; for though the enemy kept up an incessant fire upon them, while coming into action, yet not a gun was returned till close aboard, when they opened in a style truly grand and terrific.

The enemy fought with great obstinacy for an hour and a half, when the French admiral, much shattered, and completely beaten, hauled direct for the land, and not being a mile off, at twenty minutes before noon, ran on shore, having nothing but the foremast standing, and that too fell immediately she struck the ground.

The "Superb," being only in seventeen fathoms of water, was obliged to haul off to avoid the same misfortune; but not long afterwards, the "Diomede" pushed on shore, near the admiral, and all her masts went by the board.

About noon, the firing ceased, and when the smoke cleared away, "Le Brave," bearing a commodore's pendant, "L'Alexandre," and "Le Jupiter," were in the possession of the English.

The "Atlas" now approached "L'Imperiale," tried to anchor, but the water was too deep, and she was preparing to give the enemy a double-shotted broadside, when the colours were lowered in token of submission.

As that ship and the "Diomede" could not be got off, they were burned two days after the action, by the command of Admiral Duckworth.

The loss of the conquerors amounted to 74 killed, and 254 wounded; and among the former there was not a single officer. The three French ships which fell into the hands of the English, had 760 killed and wounded.

The loss of the other two could not be correctly ascertained, but certainly was not less than as many more.

"When I contemplate," says the brave Duckworth, in his official account of this victory, "the result of this action, when five sail of the line had surrendered, or were apparently destroyed, in less than two hours, I cannot, though bound to pay every tribute to the noble and gallant efforts of the Hon. Rear-Admiral Cochrane, Rear-Admiral Louis, the captains, officers, seamen, and Royal Marines, under my command, be vain enough to suppose, that without the aiding hand of Providence, such result could have been effected, and with a loss so comparatively small."

The subjoined curious anecdote of the behaviour of a true English game-cock, during this engagement, is related on the authority of an officer who belonged to the "Superb."

"On the poop-deck of that ship was a large wooden fabric, forming an oblong hollow square, and so constructed, that the upper apartments served for marine arms, and the lower for poultry; now it happened, in the very hottest of the action, whilst we were closely engaged with the three-decker ('L'Imperiale'), that a 42-pounder double-headed shot broke through this useful compound structure, destroying no less than 27 stand of arms, as it afterwards appeared, and making terrible havoc among the feathered race; splinters, bayonets, broken muskets, &c. prevailed in all directions. When, lo! from the midst of this 'confusion worse confounded,' up sprang this gallant cock, till then ' unknown to Fame,' and perched on the spanker-boom, crowing exultingly.

"Another shot cutting the boom in two, close at his feet, now drove him from his post. Indignantly retreating a few paces aft on the broken poop, again he fixed his stand; and thence ever and anon was heard his clarion voice to sound amid the 'din of war.' This appears strange, you will say, and yet it is not altogether singular—a circumstance nearly similar, I have heard, took place in the 'Marlborough,' on the memorable first of June, 1794: I say nearly similar, because in that instance the bold bird was *sound* though not *safe;* whereas our little hero was found on examination, to have received many severe contusions, and to have lost an eye, ere he extricated himself from the melancholy ruins of his house, and the sad wreck of his mangled messmates.

"Hardly had the battle ceased, when some of the brave men whose dangers he had thus shared, introduced him to our notice, with an earnest request to save him from the dire hand of our poulterer. Soon we saw him caressed by all, and decorated with rings and ribbons. Never is he to die the death so common to his kind—and this he seems to know; for so perfectly tame is he become, that he will perch and crow on one's arm, feed from the hand, and even admit, without fear, of being fondled like the gentlest lapdog."

After the action, the water being too deep to anchor in the bay of St. Domingo, it was requisite to bring to, with the prizes, to repair damages, put the ships in a manageable state, and shift the prisoners, which took till the afternoon of the 7th; when the admiral detached the Hon. Captain Stopford, in the "Spencer," with the "Donegal" and "Atlas," which latter had lost her bowsprit, with the prizes, to Jamaica.

The "Northumberland," having been fitted with a jury mainmast, Admiral Cochrane returned to his command on the Windward Island station, accompanied by the "Agamemnon;" and Admiral Duckworth himself proceeded to Jamaica, with the "Canopus," "Acasta," and "Magicienne."

The prizes, after being repaired, were sent to England, but "Le Brave" had suffered so severely in the engagement, that she foundered on her passage.

The crew, who had been three days and three nights at the pumps, were all saved except three. In commemoration of this ship, however, her name was given to the "Formidable," captured in November, 1805, by Sir Richard John Strachan.

The thanks of both houses of parliament were voted to the officers and men engaged in this glorious scene.

A pension of £2,000 per annum was voted to Vice-Admiral Sir J. T. Duckworth, and the order of the Bath was conferred on Rear-Admirals Louis and Cochrane. The committee of the Patriotic Fund resolved to present a vase of the value of four hundred pounds, ornamented with emblematical devices and an appropriate inscription, to the former; vases of the value of three hundred pounds each, with appropriate inscriptions, to the two latter.

A sword of the value of one hundred pounds, or a vase of the same value, to each of the captains and commanders; the sum of one hundred pounds to each of the lieutenants of his Majesty's navy, captains of Royal Marines, and other officers, in the second class of his Majesty's proclamation for the distribution of prize-money, who were severely wounded; the sum of twenty pounds to each seaman or marine severely wounded; and the sum of ten pounds to each seaman or marine slightly wounded.

During the year 1805, twenty-six vessels of the navy were lost.

On the 12th of January, the frigate "Doris" was lost near the mouth of the Loire. Captain Campbell, who commanded her, set his vessel on fire to prevent her from falling into the hands of the enemy. The crew were all saved.

On the 21st of December, the transport "Aurora," having on board 250 men of the 26th Regiment, besides her crew, was lost on the Goodwin Sands.

All are supposed to have perished.

Ten vessels under the line were captured by the enemy, the full particulars of which are not given in English Naval History. Eleven vessels were wrecked and five foundered.

CRESTS OF VESSELS IN THE ROYAL NAVY (A.D. 1870).

CHAPTER XXX.

EVENTS OF THE YEAR 1806.

THE British Navy, at the commencement of 1806, consisted of 590 cruisers, or sea-going vessels, 113 harbour vessels, and 130 ships either building or ordered to be built; besides 86 vessels used as receiving ships, hospitals, tenders, despatch boats, &c., &c.

One hundred and twenty thousand seamen and marines were employed to man this immense navy, which consisted altogether of 919 vessels, either actually in existence, or being built as rapidly as possible. The blue jackets continued their dashing exploits, and scarcely an enemy's vessel dared show out of harbour.

On the 2nd of January, the 54-gun ship "Malabar," Captain Robert Hall, and the 18-gun corvette "Wolf," Commander George Mackenzie, captured two large schooner privateers on the south end of Cuba.

They were the "Régulateur" and "Napoleon," the crews of which escaped to the shore, with the exception of a few who were wounded.

On the 6th of January, the boats of the 36-gun frigate "Franchise," Captain Dashwood, under the command of Lieutenant John Fleming, captured, in a harbour near Campeachy, the Spanish brig "Raposa," of 12 guns and 75 men.

Seven of the English crew were wounded, 4 were killed on the "Raposa," and 26 wounded.

On the 9th of January, 1806, the remains of

THE BOATS OF THE "ALEXANDRIA" CUTTING OUT A BRIG AT RIO DE LA PLATA.

Lord Nelson were deposited in St. Paul's Cathedral.

The procession was one of the grandest ever seen in England at the time. One hundred and sixty carriages followed the funeral car.

The funeral services were performed by torchlight.

On the 14th of January, 1806, Admiral Sir J. Borlase Warren sailed from Portsmouth with a squadron of seven sail of the line, two frigates, two brigs, and a cutter. The gallant admiral's flag was now flying on board the "Foudroyant," of 80 guns.

He arrived off Madeira on the 15th of the following month, and continued cruising for some time off the Cape de Verd Islands.

The "London," of 98 guns, commanded by Sir H. Burrard Neale, being a bad sailer, was stationed to the windward of the squadron; and about two o'clock in the morning of the 13th of March, was between two and three miles distant from the other ships, when she observed two strange sail crossing the fleet on a different tack.

The necessary signals were accordingly made, and the admiral directed the squadron to wear likewise on the larboard tack. At daylight he made the signal for a general chase.

By this time the "London" had opened her fire with the largest of the enemy's ships, which proved to be the "Marengo," of 80 guns, commanded by Admiral Linois, and the "Belle Poule," of 40 guns. The enemy endeavoured to escape, but the "London" kept up a running fire upon them till half-past seven, when the "Amazon" frigate, of 36 guns, Captain Parker, being the advanced ship, likewise pursued and engaged the "Belle Poule," which was attempting to bear away.

Sir H. B. Neale having closed with his antagonist, an obstinate conflict ensued.

So well directed was the fire of the "London," that all the officers and men on the quarter-deck of the "Marengo" were either killed or wounded. In the meantime, a running fight ensued between the "Amazon" and "Belle Poule," Captain Parker, the commander of the former, having been obliged to run so far to leeward of the "Marengo," to avoid the fire of her heavy metal, that he was unable to close with his antagonist so soon as he wished.

The action between the frigates continued nearly two hours, within musket-shot, the "Amazon" being unable to approach nearer.

The remainder of the British squadron kept fast approaching.

The "Ramilies," being a prime sailer, first came up with the combatants. Just as she was about to pass the "London," the latter poured in another broadside, which made dreadful havoc among the enemy, above twenty of whom were killed or wounded by that fire alone. Her brave crew then cheered the "Ramilies" as she passed; the latter immediately returned the compliment, and placed herself between the "London" and the "Marengo."

The enemy fired but one shot at her in that situation, which was not returned by her crew, who had orders not to fire till they came within pistol-shot. The French admiral, perceiving that further resistance would be vain, struck his colours, on which the first lieutenant of the "Ramilies" went on board and took possession of his ship.

A few minutes afterwards the "Belle Poule" followed the example of the "Marengo."

In this conflict, the French ships had 65 killed and 80 wounded; among the latter were Admiral Linois, his son, and his first captain, M. Vrignaud. The "London" had 10 killed and 18 wounded; and the "Amazon" 4 killed and 6 wounded.

The only officer killed on board the "London" was Mr. W. Rooke, midshipman, son of Sir Giles Rooke, one of the late judges of the Court of Common Pleas. The "Amazon" lost her first lieutenant, Mr. R. Seymour, and Mr. Prior, second lieutenant of marines.

After the action, Sir J. B. Warren put into Port Praya, in the island of St. Jago, to refit, and after encountering a tremendous storm, in which the "Marengo" lost all her masts, he arrived safe at Spithead with his prizes, on the 14th of May.

The French admiral, Linois, was, on the whole, a most unfortunate, although a very gallant officer. His victory at Algesiras, if such it may be called, in 1801, was more the effect of accident than skill, and in every subsequent attack or engagement, Linois was defeated.

In this last action, he showed much bravery. On his arrival in England (unwilling to trust himself in the presence of Napoleon), he retired on his parole to Bath, where he remained a considerable time; but, having at length made his peace with the emperor, he returned to France.

Before the death of Mr. Pitt, he prepared an expedition for the capture of the Cape of Good Hope from the Dutch.

The naval force of this expedition was under Sir Home Popham, who reached Table Bay on the 4th day of January, 1806.

In a battle which took place with the Hollanders, on the 8th of January, they were completely defeated, leaving on the field about 700 killed and wounded. The killed and wounded of the English amounted to 212.

After this battle Cape Town surrendered, and the colony was annexed to the English dominions.

Leaving Sir David Baird governor of the new colony, Sir Home Popham sailed in April for the conquest of Buenos Ayres, in South America.

On the 8th of March, the boats of the 44-gun frigate "Egyptienne," Captain Paget, were sent to cut out a large privateer in Muros harbour. The boats were led by Lieutenant Philip C. Handfield, and the privateer, which was the "Alcide," of Bordeaux, was captured and taken out of the harbour.

On the 13th of March, an English squadron, under Vice-Admiral Sir John B. Warren, in the "Foudroyant," captured the "Marengo," French 74-gun ship, commanded by Rear-Admiral Linois, and her consort the 40-gun frigate "Belle Poule." In this action, on the English ship "London," of 98 guns, Captain Sir Harry Neale, one officer and nine seamen and marines were killed and twenty were wounded.

The "Marengo" had 63 men killed and 82 wounded.

The naval medal was granted to the "London" and "Amazon" for the capture of the two French vessels.

On the 26th of March, the 36-gun frigate

"Pique," Captain Ross, overtook the French brigs "Phaëton" and "Voltigeur" between St. Domingo and Curaçoa. After the two brigs had been brought to action, and the battle had continued about twenty minutes, the "Phaëton" fell aboard the "Pique," and was immediately boarded by twenty-five seamen and marines, led by John Thompson, the master. As soon as they reached the deck they were met by a heavy fire of musketry, from men who had been concealed. The master and eight men were killed, and eleven of the seamen and marines were wounded. Captain Ross had all thrown aback on the "Pique," and sent a strong party to the relief of the boarders, who soon compelled the French crew to surrender.

The "Voltigeur" was then pursued and captured without resistance. The two vessels were added to the British navy.

On the 28th of March, the 38-gun frigate "Niobe," Captain Loring, captured the French 18-gun corvette "Néarque," in the presence of a French squadron of superior force.

The corvette was carried by a boarding party led by Lieutenant Reynolds.

On the 3rd of April, the 36-gun frigate "Renommée," Captain Livingston, cut the Spanish brig "Vigilante," of 18 guns, and a crew of 109 men, from under Fort Collartes.

She was added to the navy under the name of "Spider."

On the 6th of April, the boats of the 32-gun frigate "Pallas," Captain Lord Cochrane, led by Lieutenant John Haswell, boarded and captured the brig "Tapageuse," lying about twenty miles above Cordovan Shoal.

While waiting for the return of her boats from this expedition, the "Pallas" saw two armed ships and a brig, to which she gave battle and chased the three on shore.

They were the 20-gun corvettes "Garonne" and "Gloire," and the 18-gun brig "Mélicieuse."

On the 17th of April, the 36-gun frigate "Sirius," Captain Prowse, attacked a French flotilla, consisting of brigs and cutters, mounting 97 guns, lying off the mouth of the Tiber.

The "Sirius" attacked the flotilla at sunset, and continued the action about two hours, when the "Bergère," a corvette of 18 guns, surrendered.

The guns in several of the smaller vessels of the enemy were also silenced, but the "Sirius" was too much cut up to take possession of them.

Her loss amounted to nine men killed and twenty wounded.

The King of Naples, by a treaty concluded at Paris on the 21st of September, 1805, engaged to remain neutral in the war between France and the allied powers, and to repel by force every encroachment on his neutrality. Scarcely, however, had six weeks elapsed when a squadron of English and Russian vessels were permitted to land a body of forces in Naples and its vicinity.

This being considered by Buonaparte as an act of perfidy deserving the severest punishment, he issued a proclamation from his head-quarters, at Vienna, on the morning after the signature of the treaty of Presburgh, declaring that the Neapolitan dynasty had ceased to reign; and a French army under Joseph Buonaparte, immediately marched into Naples in three divisions.

On the 12th of February, Capua was invested, and on the 13th that city, with Peschieri, Naples, and other fortresses, was surrendered by capitulation; Gaeta and another alone holding out.

The triumphant entry of Joseph Buonaparte into the capital, to assume the sovereignty, was attended by those acclamations and addresses which can always be procured by power, and the change was received with pretty general satisfaction.

The heir-apparent retired into his dukedom of Calabria, where General Damas, a French emigrant, was endeavouring to organise a levy *en masse*; the province, however, was speedily reduced by General Reignier.

About the middle of April, Sir Sidney Smith had arrived at Palermo, in the "Pompée," of 84 guns, and taken the command of the English squadron destined for the defence of Sicily, consisting of five ships of the line, besides frigates, transports, and gunboats.

With this force under his command, Sir Sidney sailed to the coast of Italy, and began his operations by introducing into Gaeta supplies of stores and ammunition, of which its garrison had been greatly in want.

Having performed this important service, and left at Gaeta a flotilla of gun-boats, under the protection of a frigate, to assist in the defence of the place, he proceeded to the bay of Naples, spreading such alarm along the coast that the French conveyed in haste to Naples part of their battering train from the trenches before Gaeta, in order to protect the capital from insult, and secure it from attack.

It happened, that at the moment when Sir Sidney came in sight of Naples, that city was illuminated on account of Joseph Buonaparte being proclaimed king of the Two Sicilies. It was in the power of the English admiral to have disturbed their festivity; but, as the sufferers from his interference must have been the inhabitants of Naples, and not the French troops or the new king, he wisely and humanely forbore, and made for the Isle of Capri, of which he took possession, after a slight resistance, and placed in it an English garrison.

He then proceeded southward along the coast, giving the greatest annoyance everywhere to the enemy, obstructing by land, and intercepting entirely by sea, their communication along the shore, so as to retard their operations against Gaeta, which was the chief purpose for undertaking this expedition.

On the return of Sir Sidney to Palermo, after the conclusion of this service, he was led, from the active turn and sanguine temper of his mind, to enter with eagerness into the projects of the court, and to second its views on Calabria to the utmost of his power.

Finding him favourably inclined to their schemes, and anxious to distinguish himself by some great exploit, their Sicilian majesties invested the British admiral with the most ample authority in Calabria, and even constituted him their viceroy in that province. But, though active and indefatigable in the duties of his new department, and successful in distributing money, arms, and ammunition among the Calabrians, he soon found, that, unless an English army made its appearance in the country, there was no chance of his producing an insurrection against the French.

It became, therefore, necessary for the court of Palermo, either to abandon the fruit of all its intrigues and machinations, or to prevail on the commander of the English forces in Sicily to invade Calabria with part of his army.

After the evacuation of Naples, Sir James Craig had retired with the English army to Sicily, and established his head-quarters at Messina, as the station best adapted for protecting the island from invasion. There he remained till April, when bad health compelled him to resign his command to Sir John Stuart, who was soon after entrusted by his Sicilian majesty with the defence of the east coast of Sicily from Melazzo to Cape Passaro, and with the command of the Sicilian troops in that district. The army continued in its position at Messina till the end of June, without attempting offensive operations against the enemy.

It was of the utmost importance to England that Sicily should not fall under the dominion of France; and therefore Sir John Stuart, when solicited by the court of Palermo to assist in its schemes on Calabria, hesitated long, and deliberated maturely, before he complied.

But, overcome by the urgent and repeated entreaties of the Sicilian government, encouraged by flattering accounts of the disposition of the Calabrians, and foreseeing that, if success attended the first operations, he should be able at any rate to destroy the stores and ammunition collected in Calabria for the invasion of Sicily, he consented at length to land with part of his army on the continent, and make trial of the loyalty and affection of the people to their former masters.

PORTRAIT OF SIR W. HOSTE.

The enterprise which Sir John Stuart thus reluctantly undertook, he concluded with singular judgment and ability, and brought to a fortunate conclusion, with infinite glory to the British arms, but without any advantages to the court of Palermo, which it had fondly anticipated from the experiment.

A glorious victory gained on the 6th of July by the English, was the signal of a general insurrection in both the Calabrias. The peasants, already prepared to take up arms, rose in every direction against the French, cut off their stragglers, pursued their flying parties, and attacked their posts.

The French, provoked by their defeat, and exasperated by the cruelty of the insurgents, who gave no quarter to such as fell into their hands, retaliated with a savageness and ferocity more disgraceful to their character than the panic terrors which had seized them at Maida.

The villages which declared against them were plundered and burned to the ground, and the inhabitants massacred without distinction of age or sex.

This usage still farther inflamed the Calabrians, whose attacks on their posts were incessant and furious, till, with the assistance of the English, they drove them entirely out of their country. Unable to contend with their numerous and exasperated assailants, the French were compelled at length to evacuate both Calabrias, and to abandon all the cannon, stores, and ammunition which they had collected in these provinces for the invasion of Sicily.

But glorious and successful as this expedition had been, it soon appeared how far it was from having opened to the king of Sicily any prospect of regaining his kingdom of Naples. So sensible was Sir John Stuart of his inability to maintain the ground he had won in Calabria, that from the plain of Maida he announced his intention of returning, without loss of time, to Sicily.

On the 18th of July his head-quarters were at Bagnara, near Reggio; and on the 23rd the fort of Scylla, opposite to Messina, a place of great importance for the secure navigation of the straits, surrendered to one of his officers.

The whole of the British army was now withdrawn from Calabria, except the garrison of Scylla, and a detachment of the 78th regiment, under Colonel M'Leod, which had been sent in the "Amphion" frigate to the coast near Catanzaro, in order to countenance and assist the insurgents in that quarter. This service was effectually performed by Colonel M'Leod and Captain Hoste of the "Amphion."

The French under Regnier were severely harassed in their retreat along the shore from Catanzaro to Cotrone, and the latter place, with all its magazines and stores, fell into the hands of the English.

Sir Sidney Smith was in the mean time actively, if not judiciously, employed along the coast, assisting the insurgents with arms and ammunition, supplying them with provisions, and conveying them from one place to another, in the vessels under his command. By these exertions he contributed materially to extend the insurrection along the coast, and to expel the enemy from the watch-towers and castles which they occupied upon the shore.

These operations were, in some instances, of use, by securing a safer and better anchorage for his ships; but, in others, the blood and treasure which they cost, exceeded the value of his acquisitions.

In one of these adventures, two officers and five seamen were killed and thirty-four seamen wounded, in the attack of an insignificant fort at Point Licosa, which he destroyed when it fell into his hands.

No British troops were stationed anywhere to maintain his conquests, except in the isle of Capri, which was kept as a place of refreshment for the navy; but a number of posts were occupied and garrisoned by the insurgents, such as Amantea, Scalea, and the isle of Dino, on the coast of Upper Calabria, and Maratea, Sapei, Camerota, Palinuro, and other places in the bay of Policastro.

The chief or rather sole use of these posts consisted in the protection which they afforded to the anchorage upon the coast, and facilities thereby given to the British and Neapolitan small craft, of intercepting the coasting communications of the enemy, so as to prevent the supply of his army in Calabria with cannon, which, from the badness of the roads, it was impossible for him to convey by land.

On the 3rd of May, the Spanish schooner "Giganta," lying in the port of Vieja, was cut out by the boats of the 36-gun frigate "Renommée," Captain Livingston, led by Lieutenants Parker, Adams, Nesbit, and Murton.

The schooner was prepared for defence, moored with a chain within a pistol-shot of batteries, and covered by 100 men, drawn up on the beach, besides having a crew of 28 men with boarding nettings triced up, yet she was boarded, and brought off with only seven men wounded.

On the 14th of May, the "Pallas," 32 guns, Captain Lord Cochrane, had a long engagement with the French frigate "Minerva," of 44 guns, off the island of Aix.

After the engagement had continued for some time, Lord Cochrane was compelled to put the helm of his vessel a-weather, and run aboard the enemy to prevent it from escaping.

When this was done, so great was the concussion that the fore-topmast of the "Pallas" came down, the jibboom was carried away, and so much other damage sustained, that as the two vessels separated, the "Minerva" could not be prevented from escaping.

Several events of considerable interest occurred in the Indian seas in the course of the year 1806.

Amongst others was the capture of the Honourable Company's ship, "Warren Hastings," on the 21st of June, in latitude 20 degs. 13 mins. south, longitude about 56 degs. 45 mins. of Greenwich, by "La Piedmontaise," French frigate, of 46 guns, and 385 men. The "Warren Hastings" was not surrendered till after a warm and extremely close action of four hours and a half, in which she had seven men killed and eighteen wounded.

From the uncommon interest which this action excited, in consequence of the atrocious conduct of Moreau, the first-lieutenant of "La Piedmontaise," who afterwards expiated his crimes by a death worthy of his life, it is expedient to give the following detail from Captain Larkin's official account, addressed to the Governor of St. Helena. It is dated from that port, on board the "America," on the 13th September, 1806:—

"At half-past seven A.M., on the 21st June, 1805, we discerned a strange sail to the S.W., standing to the S.E., apparently a long, but a low vessel, under treble-reefed topsails and courses. I continued my course, making as much sail as the wind would permit of my carrying, steering by that time W. by S., with a very strong breeze from N.E. by E., and a large sea on.

"About nine A.M., having gained our quarter, she tacked and stood towards us, letting out the reefs of her topsails. I lost no time in clearing the ship for action, and placing everything in a proper state for defence.

"About half-past nine A.M., she set her topgallant sails, main and fore-topmast-steering sails, though apparently gaining on us before, and at ten A.M. showed a blue ensign and pendant. I did not like her manner of manœuvring, being sensible that an English man-of-war would not have acted as she did; however, I hoisted my colours, and made the private signal.

"At eleven A.M., finding she was gaining upon us fast, I took in all the steering-sails, stay-sails, and hauled the mainsail up, that I might have nothing to draw the attention of my crew from their quarters, save the principal sails for manœuvring, and hauled up a point to the wind. Having made every internal disposition for defending the ship, rose preventer braces, and stopped the topsail-sheets; at half-past eleven I hauled down the private signal, it not having been answered, and placed every soul at their respective stations to await the coming up of the enemy (for it could now no longer remain a matter of doubt), which she was doing very fast.

"At noon she was within a mile and a half of us, when she took in her topmast-steering-sails, staysails, and mainsail, and having neared us to a mile, hauled down the blue ensign, and hoisted French colours; this was what we expected, and were prepared and ready to meet and return her fire.

"About twenty minutes past noon, she opened her fire upon our larboard quarter, with a very heavy round of most exceeding large grape, which we returned, as soon as our guns could bear, pretty warmly; and after about a quarter of an hour's engagement, she filled and went ahead, seemingly astonished at her reception. In this we received some damage in our rigging, which we turned to and repaired as well as we could.

"After she had reached about a mile and a half a-head, she tacked and came down on us again, while we were at the guns to receive her as before. This onset was extremely warm and brisk, and attended with loss on our side of killed and wounded; and so near were the two ships, that I was very apprehensive of our locking yard-arms; again she steered off, and made sail astern.

"Our damage was great; the foremast was shot clear through about one-third from its head; every larboard, and four of the starboard fore-shrouds cut; fore-topsail-tye gone, and mizen-topsail-haulyards, main and main-topsail braces, main-spring-stay, and topmast shot away; our ensign was likewise cut away, but very soon displayed again at the main-topgallant-mast head.

"Scarcely had we time to stopper the shrouds, and reeve preventer braces, before our attention was again called to receive her third attack, she having put about in our wake, and was nearly up. This attack was as warm and as near almost as any, and continued rather longer than the former; but as before she shot a-head, indicating most evidently that she could not lay alongside us, though to all appearance a heavy vessel.

"We now endeavoured to repair our damage as well as time would permit: I furled the top-gallant sails, and hauled the foresail up, for the foremast had received another shot in its aft side, about one third up, which now rendered the state of that mast extremely dangerous, and which obliged me likewise to keep the fore-topsail on the cap, dreading to make sail upon the mast, from the freshness of the breeze and the height of the sea. Hardly had we got the yard-tackles down as preventer-braces, before we were again called upon, by her near approach (she having manœuvred a-head as before) to repel her fourth attack.

"We gave the first gun this time, and the action became, on both sides, extremely warm, and seemingly with increased fury: but, as she had done before, she made astern, having endeavoured to lay alongside four times, without being able to accomplish her end, I had now only the main-topsail untouched, and defying their worst, but otherwise a complete wreck aloft.

"The main-mast shot through, the main piece very badly; mizen-topsail split in two; nearly all the fore-rigging again cut; but, thank God! below we were as firm and as zealous in the cause as at the firing of the first gun, having nothing to lament, saving the very great superiority of the enemy's ship's sailing, which enabled her to take her position to advantage, and attack us in what point she pleased; for as yet we had not the smallest idea of giving her any other superiority.

"We had now to receive the enemy the fifth time, with the main and foremast dangerously wounded, every larboard, and four of the starboard foreshrouds cut, with some of the main ones; not a single brace rove, the yards being kept forward with the force of the wind, with scarcely a running-rope whole, and with two of my upper-deck guns disabled.

"Still so completely wrecked aloft, I looked to the energy remaining below, as the palladium of our safety.

"'Tis true, we had been weakened by five men killed, and about as many wounded; yet so noble, so enthusiastic a spirit pervaded the crew, that I thought little of the loss or damage sustained.

"In this state, and under these circumstances, we received her fifth attack, and on both sides it was more furious than before, and the firing kept up almost incessant.

"Seeing, as I suppose they must have done, that I could do nothing but keep the wind with the sail I had set (only the main-topsail), they backed on my larboard quarter, and kept there, without my being able to prevent her taking so advantageous a position.

"Here she made great havoc and destruction; the mizen-mast, before unhurt, was shot through, about ten feet from the deck, in three places, within six inches of each other, and I perceived that the fate of that mast was very soon to fall, as it suffered greatly; the driver-boom was knocked into splinters; all the coops on the poop were shattered; only one man remaining at the poop carronade; the after quarter-deck-gun, and foremost one, cleared to one man also.

"However, with our every disadvantage, damage, and loss of men (for every man from so comparatively small a number is missed on these occasions, and we had by this time seven men killed, and about ten wounded), I had not the most distant idea of giving up so valuable a ship, while the smallest possible chance remained of defending her.

"But another disaster awaited us, which decided the fate of the day: the mizen-mast fell forward, and blocked up every effective gun on the upper-deck.

"The gun-room was on fire from a shot that had entered by the counter, but which was at length put out by the exertions of my officers and men: my surgeon had lost every instrument by a shot that came into the place where he was amputating and dressing the wounded: the nail of the tiller-rope on the barrel of the wheel drew, and the main and main-topsail-yard came square, by the fall of the mizen-mast.

"Thus circumstanced, I foresaw that we had no alternative but to strike; and, with the consent of my officers, I gave up what remained of the 'Warren Hastings' and her noble crew, which took place about fifty minutes past four P.M. having been engaged nearly yard-arm above two-thirds of the time, from twenty minutes past noon, until ten minutes before five P.M.

"I feel it a duty extremely incumbent on me to mention the firm and steady support I received from the officers with whom I had the honour of defending the ship; nor could more zeal or true courage have been displayed, than what animated the gallant crew under my command. It will be a reflection attended with the most heartfelt satisfaction to me, that every department was filled with its utmost energy.

"The exertions, visible on this occasion, to defend the Honourable Company's property to the point of contention, when defence would have been no longer practicable nor justifiable, will, I trust, be a sufficient recommendation of the merits of the officers and ship's company of the late Honourable Company's ship 'Warren Hastings,' to the Honourable Court of Directors.

"Although the issue of the engagement was unfortunate, still, when the very superior force to which we were opposed, added to other material advantages on the side of the enemy, are taken into consideration, it will, I hope, appear very evident, that they did as much as men could do under similar circumstances.

"The following is a return of the killed, wounded, and stabbed in the action:—

"*Killed.*—Mr. John Edwick, purser; William Miller, ordinary seaman; John Frost, seaman; John White, ordinary seaman; Phatham Laybourne, seaman; William Price, ordinary seaman; John Miles, ordinary seaman.

"*Stabbed after possession was taken.*—Captain Thomas Larkins, commander; Mr. John Wood, second officer; Mr. John Barnes, surgeon; Mr. James Bayton, midshipman; John Bell, boatswain's second-mate.

"*Wounded.*—Mr. James Coxwell, chief officer, slightly; Mr. Edward Davies, third officer; Mr. William Hope, sixth officer; Mr. James Greville, surgeon's mate, broken jaw; John Hoburg, boatswain's first mate, very badly; Frederick Christiana, seaman; David Scot, captain's cook; Joseph Antonio, ordinary seaman; John Mackay, seaman, badly; Charles Williams, ordinary seaman, slightly; Lewis Perraw, seaman; Henry Churchill, baker; George Miller, seaman; John Hoburg, since dead of his wounds.

"However, I am happy to say, that the other wounded, and those who were stabbed, are perfectly well.

"The following is the force of the French frigate 'La Piedmontaise':—

"On her main-deck.—Twenty-eight long French 18-pounders.

"On her upper-deck.—Ten carronades, French thirty-six pounders; four long English nine-pounders, two long brass French eight-pounders, two mortars, capable of throwing grape and canister shot of French thirty-six pounds weight.

"In her tops were fifty men with swivels and rifles, by which it will appear that she is a very heavy frigate, and is quite new, having sailed from St. Maloes in January last, and had only been out from the Isle of France ten days when she fell in with the 'Warren Hastings.' From what I was able to learn, I suppose her to have had about twelve men killed and twenty wounded.

"We arrived at the Mauritius on the 4th of July last, and obtained permission to proceed to England by a neutral vessel, viâ America.

"With my officers and midshipmen, we embarked on board the American ship, 'America,' Captain Isaac Stone, on the 6th of August. Hoping to find some conveyance direct to England, we called into St. Helena, and trust, should you have it in your power to forward us, that you will exert it in our favour, being extremely anxious to lay the unfortunate news before the Honourable the Court of Directors."

The brutal and unprecedented conduct of Lieut. Moreau and his followers, in stabbing the officers of the "Warren Hastings," after her surrender, was publicly stated at St. Helena and in India, by affidavits, from Captain Larkins and his followers; and, if we mistake not, it was given out by Sir Edward Pellew, the commander-in-chief on the India station, in general orders, that should the sanguinary monster be taken, no quarter would be shown to him.

The affidavits alluded to called forth a defence, or rather an attempt at justification, on the part of Moreau, which was replied to by one of the officers of the "Warren Hastings," completely establishing the statements of Captain Larkins.

On the 9th of July, the 74-gun ship "Powerful," Captain Plampin, after a chase and running fight which lasted nearly two hours, captured the French 34-gun privateer "Bellone," Captain Perrond, off Ceylon.

The "Bellone" was added to the English navy as a 28-gun frigate under the same name.

On the night of the 15th of July, twelve boats from the ships of a squadron under the command of Commodore Sir Samuel Hood, attempted to cut out from Verdon Roads, some vessels laden with stores for the French fleet at Brest.

On reaching the harbour, the first thing they attacked was the French 16-gun brig "Cæsar," which was boarded and captured after a gallant defence, in which her captain, M. Fourre, was killed.

Another brig, the "Teazer," slipped her cables

and escaped up the river followed by the store ships. The "Cæsar," although exposed to a heavy fire from the batteries on shore, was worked out; but it was a prize for which too much was given.

Lieutenant Charles Manners, the master's mate, Thomas Helpman, and seven seamen were killed, and thirty-nine men were wounded. A midshipman and nineteen men in one of the boats belonging to the "Revenge," were made prisoners, their boat being disabled by a shot.

On the 18th of July, off Faro Islands, the 38-gun frigate "Blanche," Captain Thomas Lavie, captured the French 18-pounder 40-gun frigate "Guerrière," Captain Hubert.

Only three persons were wounded on the "Blanche," while the loss of the "Guerrière" was twenty killed and thirty wounded.

On the 25th July, the 32-gun frigate "Greyhound," Captain Elphinstone, and the 18-gun brig "Harrier," Captain Ironbridge, while cruising in the Java sea, encountered the Dutch 36-gun frigate "Pallas," the Dutch Company's ships "Batavia" and "Vittoria," and the 14-gun corvette "William."

The "Greyhound" attacked the "Pallas," and the "Harrier" the two vessels of the Company, and all three were soon compelled to surrender. The corvette managed to escape.

The "Greyhound" had one man killed and eight wounded, and the "Harrier" but three men wounded.

The Dutch frigate had eight men killed, and thirty-three wounded; amongst the latter was her captain, who died of his injuries.

On the 27th of July, the 74-gun ship "Mars," Captain Oliver, captured the French frigate "Rhin," which made no resistance.

On the 14th of August, near the Isle of Wight, the 4-gun brig "Phosphorus," commanded by Lieutenant Hughes, was attacked by a 12-gun lugger privateer, manned by 70 men. The brig was only manned by twenty-four men, who several times repulsed the crew of the lugger in its attempt to board. So gallant was the successful defence of the brig, that Lieutenant Hughes was presented by the Patriotic Fund with a sword, value 100 guineas.

On the 22nd of August, the boats of the 32-gun frigate "Alexandria," Captain Edward King, commanded by Lieutenants Lewis and Nagle, boarded and captured a brig and a revenue vessel lying under batteries in the harbour of Rio de la Plata.

The vessels were stripped of their sails, and firmly secured to the shore; and seeing immense difficulty in taking them out, Lieutenant Lewis ordered them to be destroyed. In this action, 6 men belonging to the boats were killed and 13 wounded.

On the 23rd of August, the Spanish 34-gun frigate "Pomona," owing to the strength of the current, failed to enter the harbour of Havanna, and within two miles of Moro Castle. She was seen by the English frigates "Arethusa," Captain Brisbane, and the "Anson," Captain Lydiard, who resolved to capture her. The "Pomona" was anchored within pistol-shot of a castle mounting eleven long 36-pounders. Ten gunboats came out from Havanna, and formed a line for its protection.

The "Anson" sailed in and dropped her anchors abreast the gunboats, while the "Arethusa" took a position for attacking the frigate.

After an action of forty minutes, the gun-boats had been sunk or driven ashore by the "Anson" and the "Pomona" struck to the "Arethusa."

During the battle the castle kept up a fire on the English vessels, until there was an explosion took place within it, and the action ceased.

Aboard the "Anson" not a man was injured; but on the "Arethusa," two seamen were killed, and Captain Brisbane, Lieutenant Higman, and twenty-nine seamen and marines were wounded.

The "Pomona" had her captain and twenty men killed and thirty wounded. She was added to the British navy under the name of "Cuba."

On the 30th of August, the boats of the 20-gun ship "Bacchante," Captain Dacres, led by Lieutenant Norton, captured an armed brig and two armed feluccas in the harbour of Santa Martha.

These vessels were lying under the protection of batteries on shore, but they were brought out without loss of life to the captors.

On the 2nd of September, Captain Rushworth, of the 14-gun schooner "Supérieure," having with him thirty-five of his own crew, eighteen men belonging to the 18-gun ship sloop "Stork," and ten men from the schooner "Flying Fish," proceeded to the harbour of Batabano in Cuba, to destroy some Spanish shipping lying there.

CRESTS OF VESSELS IN THE ROYAL NAVY (A.D. 1870).

Before reaching the town, Captain Rushworth learnt that the alarm had been given, and that his retreat was cut off. He then hastened forward, stormed and captured the battery of the town, which mounted six long 18-pounders. His attention was then turned upon the vessels in the harbour, and he took possession of one felucca, a 12-gun schooner, one French and three Spanish privateers, and six small vessels with cargoes.

All this was accomplished with one man being wounded.

On the 14th of September, the French 74-gun and "Infatigable," were captured, and afterwards added to the English navy.

The English ships, "Monarch" and "Mars," were the principal vessels engaged in this combat, and the former lost one midshipman and three seamen killed and nineteen men wounded.

The French 40-gun frigate, "President," was captured by an English squadron, under Rear-Admiral Sir Thomas Louis, of the "Canopus," on the 27th of September. She was added to the navy under the same name.

On the 11th of October, a small squadron, under

WRECK OF H.M.S. "NAUTILUS."

ship "Impétueux," when in a disabled state, was chased ashore near the mouth of the Chesapeake, by a small squadron under Captain William Hargood, of the 74-gun ship "Belleisle." She was destroyed by the crew of the "Melampus" frigate.

In the month of September, Commodore Sir Samuel Hood, in the 74-gun ship "Centaur," with a squadron of six other ships, while cruising off Rochefort on the 25th, overhauled a French squadron of five frigates and two brigs, under command of Commodore Soliel, from Rochefort, bound to the West Indies.

This fleet was brought to action, and four of the French ships, the "Gloire," "Minerve," "Armide," the command of Captain Burrowes, of the 22-gun ship "Constance," ran on shore, and burnt the French 26-gun vessel "Salamandre," in Erqui Bay. During the engagement, Captain Burrowes was killed by a grape shot from some batteries under which the "Salamandre" had anchored. The fire from the battery then cut the cable of the "Constance," and she drifted aground, where the crew were obliged to leave her with the wounded aboard.

In this affair there were eight men killed on the English squadron, besides the captain and sixteen men wounded.

His Majesty's ship "Athenienne," of 64 guns,

commanded by Captain Raynsford, and manned by a crew of 470 men, sailed from Gibraltar on October 16th, 1806, with a fair wind.

On the fourth day from their leaving they passed Sardinia, and were all in high spirits, fully expecting to arrive at Malta the following day; but, dreadful to relate, at half-past nine o'clock that very night, when going fully nine knots an hour, the "Athenienne" struck on the rocks known by the name of the Skirkes (Esquerques), or Quills. They were completely under water, and at least sixty miles from any shore.

The shock was terrible, and the dreadful consternation into which the crew were thrown, must be left to the imagination to conceive. Every soul was instantly on deck, most of them naked, and in such a state of despair as to be absolutely incapable of making any exertion.

Some went below, and resigned themselves to their fate; while others took possession of the poop, which was highest out of the water, as the lee-side of the quarter was in a very few minutes under water; and some, who had more presence of mind, took to the boats, three of which, containing twenty-seven men, got off from the ship about a quarter of an hour after she struck.

The masts were immediately cut away to lighten the ship, and in order to prevent her falling over on her broadside; but in less than half an hour after, from violent concussion of the rock against her bottom, she filled up to the lower deck-ports, and fell on her beam ends on the larboard side.

Captain Raynsford, who foresaw the total loss of the ship from the first, ordered the boats to be hoisted out, with an idea that they would be useful in towing a raft which was constructing to leeward, and which might have been the means of saving a great many from destruction; but as soon as the jolly-boats were lowered down from their quarters, and clear of the ship, the men—for there were no officers among them—bore up, and were no more seen by their unhappy shipmates, who stayed by the wreck.

The cutter and the barge, on being hoisted out, were stove and swamped; and thirty men, unable to regain the ship, perished. By the fall of the masts several people were killed, and others desperately mangled; and two midshipmen were killed by the spanker-boom crushing them between it and the side.

The termination of the miseries of all seemed fast approaching; and the launch being the only boat that was not either stove or wrecked, was filled with men on the booms; but the water having by this time covered the whole wreck, with the exception of the poop, they had not the mechanical power to move it, nor the necessity of using it, for, to the great joy of every one, she floated off the booms, and escaped the many dangers she had to encounter with the floating pieces of the ship and broken spars.

She afterwards came under the stern, where many, in attempting to swim to her, shared the untimely fate of those who had preceded them.

No entreaties could prevail on Captain Raynsford to quit his ship.

From the first moment of her striking till the time that the launch last quitted her, he conducted himself in the most heroic manner: his presence of mind never forsaking him, and his whole faculties being employed in saving his people.

He and three hundred and forty-six others were supposed to have perished, while only one hundred and twenty-one men and two women were saved.

The "Athenienne" had on board dollars to the amount of ten thousand pounds sterling, and despatches for Malta and Sicily.

The launch left the wreck about an hour and a half after the ship struck, and immediately pulled towards the Island of Maritimo, which they got a sight of at daylight on the morning of October 21, by the assistance of a miserable sail made out of the men's shirts.

At the same time they boarded a Danish brig, that supplied them with a sail, some bread and water, and a little brandy.

They put two officers and twenty men on board of her, who returned towards the wreck, in the hope of saving any who might have been still clinging to it; but the wind blew so fresh, that the Danish vessel failed in this benevolent intention.

It is supposed that the wreck went to pieces soon after the launch quitted her, particularly as the wind continued to increase after the ship first struck, and blew stronger the following day.

Two of the boats which first escaped from the wreck, were in sight when the launch boarded the Dane, and followed them to Maritimo, which they reached about four o'clock in the evening.

They were very humanely treated by the governor, and remained there all night.

The next day they set out for Trepani, in Sicily, where they arrived the same night; and finding a small boat bound to Malta, some of them embarked, and arrived there on the 25th, after encountering all the horrors of a shipwreck, as dreadful, perhaps, in consequence, as was ever experienced.

Among the survivors of this disastrous calamity were Brigadier-General Campbell, Doctor Pym, Lieutenants John and James Little; Mr. Goodwyn, purser; Messrs. M'Lean, Silas Wells, George Thorn, Thomas Manning, John Frances, midshipmen; Richard Byrn and Augustus Cameron, master's mates; Samuel Parker, master, and — Dyer.

Those who escaped during the confusion and necessary hurry for the preservation of their lives, lost all their property which they had brought with them.

On the 18th of October, the 36-gun frigate "Caroline," Captain Rainer, attacked a small Dutch squadron, anchored in Batavia Roads, and succeeded in capturing the 12-pounder 36-gun frigate "Maria Riggersbergen," Captain Juger.

In capturing the vessel the "Caroline" was opposed by three others, but the prize was taken away with but very little loss to the captors, 4 men being killed and 17 wounded. Aboard the "Maria Riggersbergen," 50 men were killed and wounded.

She was added to the English navy, and named the "Java."

On the 26th of October, the "Pit," 12-gun schooner, commanded by Lieutenant Michael Fitton, after a chase of sixty-seven hours, most of the time the crew using the sweeps, ran on shore and captured the French privateer schooner, "Superbe," Captain Dominique Divon, one of the most successful privateers that ever infested the West Indies.

The perseverance and energy displayed by Lieutenant Fitton during this long chase is deserving of the highest praise; but his services, which, on other occasions, were very meritorious, have never been properly recognized by the Admiralty.

Lieutenant Fitton is said to have paid £437 towards the purchase of the schooner "Pit," and the money was never repaid him by the Government.

Through the malice of one admiral he was never promoted to the rank of commander.[*]

On the 20th of November, the 32-gun frigate "Success," Captain Ayscough, ran a Spanish felucca ashore, near Cumberland Harbour.

The felucca was taken by a party in the boats, its crew escaping to the shore.

In this affair Lieutenant Duke was killed, and Lieutenant O'Reilly and 7 men were wounded.

On the 27th of November, a squadron of four sail of the line, under command of Sir Edward Pellew, captured and destroyed a Dutch fleet, comprised of the following vessels:—The 14-gun corvette "William," the brig, "Zee Plaeg," the Dutch Company's 18-gun ship "Patriot," the 36-gun frigate "Phœnix," the brig "Aventurier," and a lightly armed ship.

On the 13th of December, the 16-gun brig "Halcyon," Captain Henry Pearce, captured the Spanish corvette "Neptuno," mounting 14 long 12-pounders, off Cape San Martin.

A sword of the value of one hundred guineas was given to Captain Pearce for this affair by the Committee of the Patriotic Fund.

In the year 1806 the English navy lost twenty-one vessels: four of these were wrecked, eight foundered, and one was burnt.

CHAPTER XXXI.

DOINGS OF THE NAVY IN 1807.

THE year 1807 was marked by one of the most brilliant achievements of the late war. We allude to the conquest of Curaçoa, by the gallant Captain Brisbane.

Before detailing the particulars of that event, however, we will notice another, which also affords striking evidence of the superiority of British prowess. At daybreak, on the morning of the 23rd of August, 1806, Captain Brisbane, of the "Arethusa," having recently resumed his station off the Havanna, with the "Anson," Captain Lydiard, under his orders, discovered a sail, which afterwards proved to be the "Pomona," a Spanish frigate, of 38 guns, from Vera Cruz.

When Captain Brisbane first perceived her, she was within two miles of the Moro Castle, standing for the Havanna, under a press of sail.

He immediately made the signal to Captain Lydiard of his design to lay the enemy on board as soon as he should come up with her; but, aware of his intention, the "Pomona" bore up, having been joined by twelve gunboats from the Havanna, and anchored within pistol-shot of a castle, which mounted sixteen 36-pounders, in three fathom and a half water.

Not deterred by the formidable line of defence which was thus presented, Captain Brisbane, supported by the "Anson" on his larboard bow, anchored the "Arethusa" close alongside the "Pomona," in only one foot more water than she drew. The action immediately became general, and, in thirty-five minutes, the "Pomona" struck her colours; three of the gun-boats having been blown up, six sunk, and three driven on shore on the breakers.

Notwithstanding the severe fire from the castle, the prize was instantly taken possession of. The castle, by firing red-hot shot, set fire to the "Arethusa," but the flames were speedily extinguished, and the castle itself, in which a quantity of specie belonging to the King of Spain had been landed from the "Pomona," soon afterwards fell by a terrific explosion.

In the course of the action, Captain Brisbane was wounded in the knee; but though he suffered excruciating pain, he refused to quit the deck, till victory had decisively proclaimed herself in favour of the British flag.

The total loss of the "Arethusa" upon this occasion amounted to two killed and thirty-two wounded.

Vice-Admiral Dacres, in his official letter to the

---

[*] Allen's "Battles of the British Navy," Vol. II. p. 1

Admiralty, announcing the capture of the "Pomona," justly observed, that "the success attending this bold enterprise, Captain Brisbane was well entitled to, for the promptness and decision with which he anchored in such shoal water, to attack a force of such magnitude."

After Captain Brisbane had secured the "Pomona," and had taken her to Jamaica, he was despatched, by the commander-in-chief, with a squadron of frigates, consisting of the "Arethusa," "Latona," "Anson," and "Fisguard," to reconnoitre the island of Curaçoa, and to ascertain, if possible, whether the inhabitants were disposed towards an alliance with this country.

It was on the 1st of January, 1807, that this little squadron arrived off Curaçoa.

No orders whatever had been given to attack this island; but, having perfectly ascertained the situation of the place, Captain Brisbane formed a plan for carrying it by a *coup de main*; and, imparting his intentions to the respective captains under him, with a zeal for the service, which would have done honour to the character of a Nelson, taking the sole responsibility of the act upon himself, he led his squadron into the harbour, in close order of battle, passing the formidable line of sea batteries by which its entrance was protected, and came to anchor.

It is well deserving of remark, that, previously to this, and unknown to their officers, the men, participating in the spirit of their gallant leader, had ranged themselves for attack; and, when beat to quarters, they were found with the words, "Victory or Death," chalked upon their caps.

As an additional stimulus, Captain Brisbane instantly put on his dress uniform, and proceeded as we have already stated.

"The harbour," as the Captain describes it, in his official letter, "was defended by regular fortifications, of two tier of guns, Fort Amsterdam alone consisting of sixty-six pieces of cannon; the entrance, only fifty yards wide, athwart which was the Dutch frigate, 'Hatslar,' of 36 guns, and 'Surinam,' of 22 guns, with two large schooners of war, one commanded by a Dutch commodore. A chain of forts was on Misleburg's commanding height, and that almost impregnable fortress, Forte Republique, within the distance of grape-shot, enfilading the whole harbour."

The enemy were panic-struck at such unexpected gallantry, and all was confusion.

The pacific notification of Captain Brisbane—that the British squadron was there to protect, not to conquer; to preserve to the inhabitants their lives, liberty, and property—not being attended to, a severe and destructive cannonade commenced; the frigate, sloop, and schooners were carried by boarding, and the lower forts and the citadel and town of Amsterdam were carried by storm.

All this was accomplished in only three-quarters of an hour.

In the progress of this service, Captain Brisbane, the hero of the scene, seemed to "ride upon the whirlwind and direct the storm."

He was the first man who boarded the "Hatslar" frigate, that lay athwart the harbour. He pulled the Dutch colours down with his own hands; and then, followed by about four-and-twenty men, he instantly proceeded to the shore, where he was also the first man at the storming of Fort Amsterdam, the colours of which he likewise struck with his own hands.

The latter achievement will appear the more extraordinary when it is stated that the fort was garrisoned by 275 regular troops.

As soon as he had got possession, Captain Brisbane made his way to the governor, and told him that precisely five minutes were allowed for him to decide upon surrendering.

The governor requested half an hour, alleging that *a shorter time would not save his head in Holland.* Captain Brisbane pulled out his watch, and assented to the time required.

At the expiration of the half-hour, he entered the council-chamber, where the governor and the council were assembled, and inquired whether they had made up their minds to surrender the island and its dependencies to the crown of Britain. The governor immediately presented a paper, containing the following preliminary articles of capitulation, placing the island in the possession of his Majesty; to the whole of which, with one exception, Captain Brisbane agreed:—

"Curacoa, January 1, 1807.

"Preliminary Articles of the Capitulation agreed on by C. Brisbane, Esq., senior officer of His Majesty's ships at Curacoa, and His Excellency P. J. Changuion, governor of that place.

"Art. 1. The Fort Republique shall immediately be surrendered to the British force; the garrison shall march out with the honours of war, lay down their arms, and become prisoners of war. Answer, Granted.

"2. The Dutch garrison of Curacoa shall be prisoners of war, and by His Britannic Majesty sent to Holland, not to serve this war before they be regularly exchanged; and for the due performance of this article the officers pledge their word of honour. Ans. Granted.

"3. The same terms, as in the above article, are granted to the officers and people of the Dutch men-of-war. Ans. Granted.

"4. All civil officers may remain at their respective appointments, if they think proper; and those who choose, shall be sent by His Britannic Majesty to Holland. Ans. Granted.

"5. The burghers, merchants, planters, and other inhabitants, without difference of colour or opinion, shall be respected in their persons and property, provided they take the oath of allegiance to His Britannic Majesty. Ans. Granted, neutral property being respected.

"6. All merchant vessels, with their cargoes, in

the harbour, of whatever nation they belong to, shall be in the possession of their proper owners. Not granted.

"7. A definite capitulation shall be signed upon this basis in Fort Amsterdam. Ans. Granted."

By ten o'clock the British flag was hoisted on Fort Republique; the whole of the island defended by 1,200 militia, besides a considerable number of regular troops, having been reduced, and brought into the quiet possession of the English, by a force not exceeding 800 effective men in less than four hours.

The splendour of this achievement might well excite the astonishment of the commander-in-chief; who, it is said, had calculated that no less than ten sail of the line, and 10,000 land forces, would be necessary for the capture of the island, which had been thus subdued by a mere handful of men.

Vice-Admiral Dacres, in his official despatches announcing the event to government, thus handsomely expressed his approbation of the gallant conduct of the captors:—

"Whilst I contemplate the immense strength of the harbour of Amsterdam, and the superior force contained in its different batteries opposed to the entrance of the frigates, I know not how sufficiently to admire the decision of Captain Brisbane in attempting the harbour, and the determined bravery and conduct displayed by himself, the other three captains, and all the officers and men under his command; and is another strong instance of the cool and determined bravery of British seamen."

Immediately after the capture, Captain Brisbane proceeded to disarm the militia—a most politic measure, considering the very slender state of the British force—and to administer, to the inhabitants of the island, the oath of allegiance to His Britannic Majesty. The Dutch governor having refused to take that oath, Captain Brisbane constituted himself his sucessor, *pro tempore*, and assumed the functions of government accordingly.

On the night of the 2nd of January, Lieutenants Coote and Bligh, with the boats of the frigate "Cerberus," Captain William Selby, boarded and cut out two vessels, anchored under the protection of a battery, near Pearl Rock, Martinique. Besides the troops and batteries on shore, the vessels had the protection of a large privateer, but they were brought off under a heavy fire, in which two men were killed and eight wounded.

On the 5th of January, Captain Lord Cochrane, of the "Impérieuse," sent Lieutenant Mapleton, with the boats, to bring away any vessels that might be in the basin of Arcasson, near Rochefort. The party landed, and, after having stormed and captured Fort Roquette, and laid it in ruins, they took and destroyed several brigs, and other small vessels, that were lying in the harbour.

SIR J. DUCKWORTH IN ACTION; PASSING THE DARDANELLES.

The expedition seemed a very hazardous one, but it was performed without loss.

On the 21st of January, the 32-gun frigate "Galatea," Captain George Sayer, discovered the French 16-gun brig "Lynx," Captain Farganel, and gave chase to it.

During the pursuit, the wind died away, and both vessels being becalmed, the brig commenced using her sweeps in order to escape.

Seeing that she was escaping, the boats aboard the "Galatea," under Lieutenants Walker, Gibson, and Green, and Sarsfield, master's mate, were lowered, and sent to board it.

After a long pull, the boats came within musket-shot of the brig, and then advanced to attack it in two divisions—one on the larboard quarter and the other on the starboard.

A heavy fire of grape and musketry was opened upon them.

In two attacks the assaulting party was repulsed, but a third vigorous assault was successful, and the brig was captured after a few minutes of desperate fighting.

In this enterprise the English lost 9 men killed, including Lieutenant Walker, and had 22 wounded. The "Lynx" had 14 killed and 21 wounded.

On the 27th of January, the brig "Favourite," after a long chase, was recaptured from the French, off the coast of Guyana, by the 32-gun frigate "Jason," Captain Thomas Cochrane.

On the 2nd of February, Monte Video was taken by the English under Sir Samuel Auchmuty. Fifty-seven West Indiamen, and other merchant vessels, were captured by the squadron, besides several gunboats.

In the war then waging between England and France, the Sublime Porte of Turkey gave some immaterial assistance to France, and much of his sympathy.

This displeased the British government, and Lord Collingwood was instructed to send Rear-Admiral Sir Thomas Lewis with three ships of the line, a frigate, and a sloop, to reconnoitre the forts of the Dardanelles and of Constantinople, in case it might be necessary to make an attack.

This was done in such a manner as not to provoke hostilities on the part of the Turks, and the British squadron anchored near Constantinople.

Sir Thomas Louis, having despatches of great importance to send to England, entrusted them to Captain Palmer, of the "Nautilus," and the vessel got under weigh on the 3rd of January, 1807.

A fresh breeze from the N.E. carried her rapidly out of the Hellespont, and soon after she passed the island of Tenedos, off the north end of which two vessels of war were seen.

They hoisted Turkish colours, and, in return, the "Nautilus" displayed

> "The flag that's braved a thousand years,
> The battle and the breeze."

In the course of the day they came in sight of many of the islands abounding in the Greek Archipelago, and in the evening approached the island of Negropont, lying in 38° 30' north lat., and 24° 8' east long., where the navigation became more intricate, from the great number of small islands, and from the narrow entrance between Negropont and the island of Andros.

The wind still continued to blow fresh, and as night was approaching, with the appearance of being dark and squally, the pilot, who was a Greek, wished to lie-to till morning, which was done; and the vessel continued her course at daybreak. They steered for Falconera, in the track so beautifully described by Falconer in his inimitable poem, and made that and the island of Anti Milo in the evening; but they could not see the extensive island of Milo, which is about fifteen miles farther off, on account of the thick and hazy weather which prevailed.

As the pilot had not been beyond the present position of the "Nautilus," and declared his ignorance of the farther bearings, he relinquished his charge, which was resumed by the captain.

Every possible attention was paid to the navigation, and Captain Palmer having seen Falconera so plainly, and being anxious to fulfil his mission as expeditiously as possible, resolved to stand on during the night.

He made himself confident of clearing the Archipelago before morning, and he pricked the course himself, from the chart, which was to be steered by the vessel, and which he pointed out to his coxswain, George Smith, of whose ability he entertained the highest opinion.

He then had his bed prepared, as he had not had his clothes off for the three preceding nights, and scarcely any sleep from the time they left the Dardanelles.

The night that followed was extremely dark, the horizon repeatedly lighted up with vivid flashes, which only inspired the captain with greater confidence, as he thought it would enable them to see much better at intervals, so that, in the event of the ship approaching any land, the danger would be discovered in sufficient time for them to avoid it.

The wind still continued to increase; and, though the ship carried but little sail, she went at the rate of nine miles an hour, being assisted by a lofty following sea; which, with the brilliancy of the lightning, made the night particularly awful.

At half-past two in the morning high land was distinguished, which those who saw it believed to be the island of Cerigotto, and therefore thought all was safe, and that the danger had been left behind.

The ship's course was altered to pass the island, and she continued on her course until half-past four, at the changing of the watch, when the dull monotony of the night was suddenly interrupted by the cry of the man on the look-out, "Breaker's ahead!" and instantly the vessel struck with a tremendous crash.

The shock was so violent that the people were thrown from their beds, and on coming upon deck were obliged to cling to the cordage.

Everything was now thrown into confusion, and all was hurry and alarm.

The crew hastened upon deck, which they had scarcely reached, when the ladders below them gave way, and indeed left many persons struggling in the water, which already rushed into the under part of the ship.

The captain, it appeared, had not gone to bed, and immediately came upon deck when the "Nautilus" struck; when, having examined her situation, he immediately went round, accompanied by his second lieutenant, Mr. Nesbitt, and endeavoured to quiet the apprehensions of the people.

He then returned to his cabin, and burnt all his papers and private signals.

In the meantime, each returning sea lifted up the ship, and then dashed her against the rocks with irresistible force; and in a short time the crew were obliged to resort to the rigging, where they remained for more than an hour, exposed to the fury of the surges, which were incessantly breaking over them.

Dismayed at the distresses they endured, they broke out in the most passionate exclamations;

lamenting for their wives, their children, and their kindred.

The night was so dark, and the weather so hazy, that the rocks could be seen at only a very small distance, and that only two minutes before the ship struck.

The lightning had by this time entirely ceased, and the night was so intensely dark that the people could not see the length of the ship from them; their only hope rested in the falling of the mainmast, which they trusted would reach a small rock which they discovered very near them.

About half-an-hour before daybreak the mainmast gave way, and, providentially, fell towards the rock, whereby they were enabled to gain the land.

The struggles and confusion consequent upon this occurrence may be conceived, but cannot be described.

Several of the crew were drowned.

One man had his arm broken, and several were cruelly lacerated; but Captain Palmer refused to quit his station as long as any individual remained on board; and not until the whole of his people had gained the rock did he make any exertion to save himself.

At that time, in consequence of his remaining by the wreck, he had received considerable personal injury, and must inevitably have perished, had not some of the seamen ventured to his assistance, through a most tremendous sea.

The boats were staved in pieces, though several of the people endeavoured to haul in the jolly boat; but this they could not succeed in accomplishing.

The hull of the vessel being to windward of them, sheltered the shipwrecked crew a long time from the beating of the surf; but, as she broke up, their situation became every moment more perilous, till at last they found that they should be obliged to abandon the small portion of rock which they had reached, and wade to another, which appeared somewhat larger.

By carefully watching the breaking of the seas, the first lieutenant succeeded in reaching the larger rock in safety, and the rest resolved to follow his example; but scarcely was this resolution formed and attempted to be put into execution, than the people encountered a vast quantity of loose spars, which were immediately washed into the channel they had to cross.

Necessity, however, would admit of no alternative but to attempt the passage, when many were severely wounded; and they suffered more in this undertaking than in gaining the first rock from the ship.

The want of shoes was particularly felt, as the sharp rocks tore their feet in a dreadful manner, and many of them had their legs covered with blood.

The appearance of daylight only served to disclose the horrors by which these unfortunate creatures were surrounded.

The sea was covered with the wreck of their ill-fated vessel: many of their unhappy companions were seen floating away on spars and pieces of the wreck; and the dead and dying were mingled together without a possibility of the survivors being able to afford assistance to any that might still be rescued. Two short hours had been productive of all this misery—the ship destroyed, and her crew reduced to a state of wretchedness and despair. Their wild and affrighted looks exhibited the dreadful sensations by which they were agitated; but on being recalled to a sense of their real condition, they had nothing left but resignation to the will of Heaven.

They now discovered that they had been cast away on a coral rock, almost level with the water, about three or four hundred yards long and two hundred broad.

They were at least twelve miles from the nearest islands, which were afterwards found to be those of Cerigotto and Pera, on the north end of Candia. At this time it was reported that several men had escaped in a small boat; and although the fact was true, the uncertainty of her fate induced those on the rock to confide in being relieved by any vessel accidentally passing in sight of a signal of distress they had hoisted on a long pole.

The weather had been extremely cold, so much so, that the day preceding the wreck, the ice had lain on the deck; and to resist its inclemency a fire was kindled by means of a knife and flint, preserved in one of the sailor's pockets, and some damp powder from a small barrel which was washed ashore. They next constructed a small tent with pieces of old canvas, boards, and such things as could be got from the wreck; and were thus enabled to dry the few clothes they had saved.

But notwithstanding this slight alleviation, they passed a long and comfortless night, though partly consoled with the hope that their fire might be seen in the dark, and taken for a signal of distress.

When the ship first struck, a small whale-boat was hanging over the quarter, into which an officer, George Smith, the coxswain, and nine men immediately got, and happily escaped. After rowing three or four leagues against a high sea, and the wind blowing hard, they reached the island of Pera.

This proved to be scarcely a mile in circumference, and containing nothing but a few sheep and goats belonging to the inhabitants of Cerigo, who came in the summer months to fetch away their young. They could find no rain water, except a little in the hole of a rock, and that was barely sufficient, though used most sparingly.

Having observed the fire before mentioned during the night, they conjectured that some of their shipmates might have been saved, for until then they considered their destruction inevitable.

Impressed with this opinion, the coxswain proposed again hazarding themselves in the boat for their relief; and although some feeble objections were raised to it, he continued resolute to his purpose, and persuaded four others to accompany him.

About nine o'clock on the morning of Tuesday, the second day of the shipwreck, those on the rock descried the approach of the little whale-boat; all uttered an exclamation of joy. The surprise of the coxswain and his crew to find so many of their shipmates still surviving, is not to be described. The surf ran so high as to endanger the safety of the boat, and several of the people imprudently endeavoured to get into it.

The coxswain tried to persuade Captain Palmer to come to him, but he steadily refused, saying:

"No, Smith, save your unfortunate shipmates; never mind me."

After some little consultation, he desired him to take the Greek pilot on board, and make the best of his way to Cerigotto, where the pilot said there were some families of fishermen, who would, doubtless, relieve their necessities.

But it appeared as if heaven had decreed the destruction of this unfortunate crew; for soon after the boat departed, the wind began to increase, and dark clouds gathering around, excited the apprehensions of those left behind of a frightful storm. In two hours it commenced with the greatest fury, and the waves rising considerably, soon destroyed their fire.

The rock was nearly covered with water, and the men were compelled to fly to the highest part for refuge, which was the only place that could afford any shelter.

There nearly ninety people passed a night of horror and dismay, and were only prevented from being swept away by the surf, which every moment broke over them, by a small rope fastened round the summit of the rock, and holding on by each other.

The fatigues they had previously undergone, added to what they now endured, proved too overpowering for many, who soon became delirious; their strength was exhausted, and they could hold on no longer.

Their afflictions were still further aggravated by the dread that each succeeding wave would sweep them all into oblivion.

They were but ill prepared to meet the terrible effects of famine; their strength enfeebled, their bodies unsheltered, and in despair of all hope of relief.

Nor were they less alarmed for the fate of the boat.

The storm came on before she could have reached the island, and on her safety their own depended.

The scene which daylight presented was, however, still more deplorable; the survivors beheld the bodies of their departed shipmates, and some still in the agonies of death.

Those surviving, altogether exhausted from the sea breaking over them all night, and the inclemency of the weather—which was such, that many of them, among whom was the carpenter, perished from excessive cold.

They had now to witness an instance of cold-blooded inhumanity, which must leave an eternal stain of infamy on those who merit the reproach.

Soon after daybreak they discovered a vessel with all sail set before the wind, steering directly for the rock.

They made every possible signal of distress which their feeble condition would permit, and were at last gratified at seeing the vessel heave-to, and the boat hoisted out.

Their joy, as may be imagined, was extreme, for nothing short of immediate relief could be anticipated; and they hastily made preparations for rafts to carry them through the surf, in the full confidence that the boat was provided with relief for their necessities.

On her nearer approach, to within pistol-shot, they observed her full of men, dressed as Europeans, who, to their horror and disappointment, gazed at them a few minutes, and then rowed back to their ship.

The galling cruelty of this barbarous proceeding was heightened by observing the strange vessel employed the whole day in taking up the floating remains of that vessel which had so lately borne them.

After this cruel disappointment, and bestowing an anathema which the barbarity of the strangers well deserved, they turned their thoughts during the day towards the return of the boat; but in this, also, they were disappointed, which confirmed their apprehension that she had been lost.

They now began to yield to despondency, and had before them only the gloomy prospect of inevitable destruction.

Thirst became intolerable, and in spite of being warned against it by the instances of its terrible effects, some of them, in desperation, resorted to salt water.

Their miserable companions had soon melancholy experience of its consequences; in a few hours raging madness followed, and exhausted nature could struggle no longer.

Another awful night was to be passed; yet the weather being considerably more moderate, the sufferers had continued hopes that it would be less disastrous than the one preceding; and to preserve themselves from the cold they crowded close together, and covered themselves with the few remaining rags.

But the ravings of those who had drunk salt water were truly horrible; all endeavours to quiet them were ineffectual, and the power of sleep lost its influence.

At midnight they were unexpectedly hailed by the crew of the whale-boat; but the urgent want of those on the rock was water, which they cried out to their shipmates for, though in vain.

Earthern vessels only could have been procured, and these would not bear being conveyed through the surf.

The coxswain then said that they should be taken off by a fishing vessel in the morning, and with this assurance they were obliged to be content.

They now anxiously looked forward to the morning; and for the first time since the wreck, the sun cheered them with his rays.

Whether their disgusting repast afforded them any relief or not is uncertain, for, towards evening, death made fearful havoc among them, and many brave men drooped under their accumulated hardships.

Among these were the captain and first-lieutenant, two meritorious officers; and the sullen silence now preserved by the survivors showed the state of their feelings.

WRECK OF THE "BLANCHE" FRIGATE.

Still the fourth morning came, and no tidings either of the boat or fishing vessel.

The anxiety of the people increased, for inevitable death from famine was staring them in the face. What were they to do for self-preservation?

The misery and hunger which they endured was excessive, and though aware of those means by which mariners in similar circumstances had protracted life, yet they viewed them with disgust.

Still, when they had no alternative, they considered their urgent necessities afforded them some excuse.

Offering a prayer to heaven for forgiveness of the sinful act, they selected a young man who had died the preceding night, and ventured to appease their hunger with human flesh.

During the course of another tedious night, many suggested the possibility of constructing a raft, which could carry the survivors to Cerigotto; and the wind being favourable, might enable them to reach that island.

As this seemed preferable to remaining on the rock to perish by hunger and thirst, they prepared at daylight to put their plan into execution.

A number of the larger spars were lashed together, and sanguine hopes of success were entertained.

The moment of launching the raft at length arrived, but it was only to distress the people with new disappointments; for a few moments sufficed for the destruction of a work on which the strongest of the party had been occupied for hours.

This unexpected failure made several of them still more desperate, and five resolved to trust themselves on a few small spars, slightly lashed together, and on which they had scarcely room to stand.

Bidding adieu to their companions, they launched out into the sea, when they were speedily carried along by the strong currents, and vanished for ever from their sight.

The same afternoon they were again rejoiced by the sight of the whale-boat, and the coxswain told them he had experienced great difficulty in prevailing on the Greek fishermen to venture into the boats, from their dread of the weather. Neither would they permit him to rescue them unless accompanied by themselves.

He regretted the sufferings of his comrades, and his not being able to relieve them; but encouraged them with the hope, if the weather remained fine, that the next day the boats might come.

While the coxswain was speaking, twelve or fourteen men imprudently plunged into the sea, and very nearly reached the boat. Two, indeed, got so far that they were taken in, one was drowned, and the remainder providentially got back to the rock.

Those who had thus escaped, could not but be envied by their comrades, while they reproached the indiscretion of those who, had they reached the boat, would, without doubt, have sunk her, and have thus consigned the whole to irremediable destruction.

Their thoughts were wholly occupied on these passing incidents, contemplating their forlorn condition, and judging this to be the last day of their existence, when suddenly from the lowest ebb of despair they became elated with the most extravagant joy, as the approach of the boats was unexpectedly announced.

Copious draughts of water refreshed their languid bodies; and never before did they know the blessing which the possession of water could afford; it was to them more delicious and valuable than the finest wines.

Anxious preparations were now made to depart from a place which had been fatal to so many unhappy sufferers.

Of one hundred and twenty-two persons who were on board the "Nautilus" when she struck, fifty-eight had perished. It was supposed that eighteen were drowned at the moment of the catastrophe, one in attempting to reach the boat, five were lost on the small raft, and thirty-four died of famine.

About fifty now embarked in four small fishing-vessels, and were landed the same evening at the island of Cerigotto, making altogether sixty-four individuals who were saved, including those who escaped in the whale-boat.

They had passed six days upon the rock, during which time they had not received any subsistence, excepting from the human flesh in which they had participated.

The survivors landed at a small creek in the island of Cerigotto, from whence they had to go a considerable distance before reaching the dwellings of their friends.

Their first care was to send to the island of Pera, for the master's mate and his companions, who had been left behind when the whale-boat came down to the rock.

It was found that they had exhausted all the fresh water, and had lived upon the sheep and goats which they had caught among the rocks, and drank their blood.

All this time they had been in a state of the greatest anxiety for the safety of those who had left them in the boat.

Though the Greeks were unable to aid the seamen in the cure of their wounds, they treated them with great care and hospitality; but medical assistance being important from the pain which the sufferers endured, and having nothing to bind up their wounds but their shirts, which they tore into bandages, they were eager to reach Cerigo.

Cerigo is about twenty-five miles distant, and there they were told an English consul resided. Eleven days, however, elapsed before they could leave Cerigotto, from the difficulty of persuading the Greeks to venture to sea in their frail barks during the tempestuous weather.

The wind at last proving fair, and the sea being smooth, they bade a grateful adieu to the kind families who had sheltered them, and who were so tenderly affected by their distresses, that they shed tears of regret on their departure.

They reached Cerigo in about seven hours, and were received with open arms.

Immediately on their arrival they were met by the English vice-consul, Signor Manuel Caluci, a native of the island, who devoted his house, bed, credit, and whole attention to their service; and the survivors united in declaring their inability to express the obligations under which they were laid by his hospitality.

The governor, commandant, bishop, and principal people all showed them equal kindness, care, and friendship, and exerted themselves to render the time agreeable, insomuch that it was with no little regret these shipwrecked mariners thought of quitting these generous islanders.

After remaining about three weeks, they were informed that a Russian ship of war lay at anchor off the Morea, which was distant about twelve leagues; and immediately sent letters to her commanding officer, narrating their misfortunes, and soliciting a passage to Corfu.

The master of the "Nautilus" determining to make most of the opportunity, took a boat to reach the Russian vessel; but was unfortunately blown upon the rocks during a heavy gale of wind, and very narrowly escaped perishing, while the boat was dashed to pieces.

However, after great difficulty, he got to the ship,

and at length succeeded in procuring the desired passage for himself and his companions to Corfu.

To accommodate them, the Russian commander came down to Cerigo, and anchored at a small port called St. Nicholas, at the eastern extremity of the island.

On February 5, the English embarked on board the Russian ship; but owing to contrary winds, they did not sail before the 15th, when they bade farewell to their generous friends.

They next touched at Zante, a small island abounding in currants and olives; the oil from the latter of which constitutes the chief riches of the people.

After remaining there four days, they sailed for Corfu, where they arrived on the 2nd of March, 1807, nearly two months after the date of the shipwreck.

* * * * *

In the meantime some rumours were set afloat of a design on the part of the Turks to seize the British ships of war. In consequence of this Admiral Lewis rather hastily withdrew.

After this a larger squadron, consisting of eleven vessels, was sent to Constantinople, under Vice-Admiral Sir John Thomas Duckworth.

In passing the Dardanelles, the fleet was exposed to a heavy fire on both sides, and suffered a loss of 6 killed and 51 wounded.

After passing the Castle of Abydos, the fleet encountered a Turkish squadron, consisting of one 64-gun ship, four frigates, four corvettes, and some smaller vessels.

These vessels commenced an action, and leaving them to Sir Sidney Smith with the "Thunderer," "Pompeii," "Standard," "Endymion," and "Active," Admiral Duckworth sailed on to the anchorage beyond.

Before the action between the squadrons had continued long, the Turkish ships were run ashore, and Sir Sidney Smith turned the guns of the fleet upon the battery ashore.

A division of boats under the command of Lieutenant Carrol, then landed and destroyed the fortifications, while another party in boats, led by Lieutenant Cartar, burnt the vessels.

In this affair the squadron commanded by Sir Sidney Smith suffered a loss of 4 killed and 26 wounded.

Admiral Duckworth then anchored a few miles from Constantinople, and commenced negotiating, and for some time nothing was done.

At 9 o'clock p.m., on the 14th of February, 1807, the "Ajax" was at anchor off the Dardanelles, in company with the squadron under Vice-Admiral Sir John Thomas Duckworth, K.B., when, just as Captain Blackwood had gone to bed, the officer of the watch ran into his cabin, and acquainted him that there was a great alarm of fire in the after-part of the ship.

The captain immediately ordered the drummer to beat to quarters, which was effected; and instantly, as he came out of his cabin, he directed the signal, No. 12, to be made, which was accordingly done and repeated, enforced by guns at intervals.

He then called some of the senior officers of the ship, who went down with him to the after-cockpit, and the lower deck, from whence the smoke issued.

He immediately ordered as much water as possible to be thrown down, and the cock to be turned, which he found had been previously done.

When the captain had directed the signal, No. 12, to be made, he also ordered a boat, with Lieutenant Wood, a midshipman, and a boat's crew, to go and inform all the ships near them of the unfortunate situation of the "Ajax."

He had scarcely been three minutes on the lower deck, when he found the impossibility of any officer or man remaining in the cockpit, to endeavour to extinguish the fire, perceiving from the quantity and thickness of the smoke that several men fell down, with buckets in their hands, from suffocation.

To obviate this, Captain Blackwood desired the lower-deck ports to be hauled up to give air; but on finding the harm it produced, he soon directed them to be lowered down, and the after-hatchway to be covered up, in order to gain time, by stopping the vent of the smoke, for the boats to be hoisted, which measure he was induced to adopt, finding that the fire was of that nature, that the ship must soon be in flames.

Owing to there not being any cock leading to the after-magazine, the captain ordered the carpenter with his screw to scuttle the after-part of the ship; but by this time (a period, from the commencement, of not more than ten minutes) the smoke, although endeavoured to be stifled, had gained so much, that though it was bright moonlight, they could only distinguish each other, even on deck, by speaking or feeling; consequently all attempts to hoist the boats out were ineffectual, except in the case of the jolly-boat, which began to take up the men who had jumped overboard.

Immediately as the flames burst up the main-hatchway, which divided the fore from the after-part of the ship, the captain called to everybody to go to the foremost part of the ship, as all hopes were at an end of saving her; he desired every one to save himself as soon as possible.

Captain Blackwood had scarcely reached the forecastle, when he saw all parts, from the centre of the booms-aft, in a raging flame.

When the fire had reached the other part of the forecastle, after exhorting the officers and ship's company (to the amount of 400) who were on the forecastle, and about the bowsprit, to be cool and depend on the boats, and also seeing all hopes of saving the ship were in vain, the captain jumped overboard from the sprit-sail-yard, and, being about half-an-hour in the water, was picked up by one of the boats of the "Canopus," and taken on board that ship much exhausted.

Captain Blackwood acknowledges, that in the execution of the duty which devolved upon him as commander of the vessel, he derived much assistance from all the officers, but particularly from Lieutenants Proctor, Brown, Mitchell, and Sibthorp, and also the master and captain of marines; and with respect to the ship's company, under such circumstances of fire (more rapid than was ever before known), with hammocks below—under the impression of terror which fire at any time creates, but particularly when men are just out of their beds —no people could have behaved with more coolness or perseverance than they did.

In pursuance of the standing orders, Captain Blackwood had received the report from the first lieutenant of his having visited all parts of the ship with the warrant officers and master-at-arms, which he had found clear and safe; he had also received the particular report of the master-at-arms, but not that of the lieutenant of marine guard, who was accustomed to visit all below, and report to him at 9 o'clock, at which hour this unfortunate event took place.

Such is the substance of the captain's account of this unfortunate catastrophe.

We shall now subjoin the observations of a spectator in one of the other vessels.

"The 'Ajax' took fire in the bread room, and in ten minutes she was in a general blaze from stem to stern; the wind blew fresh from the N.E. which prevented the boats of the ships to the leeward from rendering any assistance; but from those to the windward and near her, she was well enough supplied to save upwards of 400 of her people; and those may consider themselves as most providentially preserved, as it had blown a gale all the day, and for two or three days before, and fell moderate towards the evening; a continuance of the gale would probably have rendered all assistance impossible.

"The fire, it appears, had been for some time, comparatively speaking, alight in the bread-room before the alarm was given; for, when the first lieutenant and many others broke open the door of the surgeon's cabin, the after bulk-head was burst down by the accumulated flames and smoke abaft it; and so rapidly made its progress through the cockpit, that it was with difficulty he could regain the ladder, and most of those who accompanied him were suffocated in the attempt.

"On reaching the quarter-deck, he found the fire had out-rid him; and Captain Blackwood agreeing with him that she was past all remedy, they both ran forward to where the majority of the people were assembled, calling on their God for that help they despaired of getting, although many boats were approaching them, so rapidly did the fire work its way forward, and leapt from the sprit-sail-yard, when the "Canopus's" boat fortunately picked them up.

"At this time the boats were assembling under the ship's bows, and saved most who still clung to them; though many, naked, benumbed with cold, and pressed on by others, let go their hold and perished, as did every one who imprudently, on the first alarm, jumped overboard.

"The boats, however, cleared her bows, though many of them were in imminent danger of swamping, from the number of poor creatures who were clinging to the gunwales, and who were obliged to be forced off, and left to perish for the safety of the rest. The ship burnt all night, and drifted on the island of Tenedos, where she blew up at five next morning with a most awful explosion.

"The unhappy sufferers of her ward-room were, Lieutenant Rowe, Lieutenant Sibthorpe, Captain Boyd, of the Royal Marines, Mr. Owen, surgeon, and Mr. Donaldson, master.

"The gunner—unhappy father! had thrown one child overboard, which was saved; but, going down for another, perished in the flames! Of forty-five midshipmen, of every description, twenty-five were lost. Three merchants of Constantinople were on board; two perished, also a Greek pilot. The purser's steward, his mate, and the cooper, were, according to supposition, lost.

"The occasion of the accident cannot, indeed, be exactly ascertained; but that there was a light in the bread-room, when there ought not to have been one, is certain. Several of the people died after they got on board the different ships; the rest were distributed among the squadron."

One woman out of three saved herself, by following her husband, with a child in his arms, down a rope from the jibboom-end.

A court-martial was held on board His Majesty's ship "Canopus," by order of Vice-Admiral Sir J. T. Duckworth, K.B., for inquiring into the cause, and strictly investigating the circumstances by which His Majesty's ship "Ajax" was entirely destroyed, which unanimously acquitted Captain Blackwood, his officers, and crew.

A similar honourable acquittal was also pronounced by the members of a court-martial held off Cadiz, by order of Lord Collingwood.

On the 1st of March, the British fleet—negotiations having failed—commenced what can be called nothing more or less than a retreat. On approaching Castle Abydos, Admiral Duckworth, who was in the "Royal George," ordered the castle to be saluted with blank cartridge. This attempt to pass unharmed was answered by a shower of marble shot and iron shells. The Turks had much improved their defences since the fleet went up, and while passing the fortifications, several vessels were much damaged; 29 men were killed and 138 wounded.

This affair was followed by an expedition to Egypt. It consisted of the 74-gun ship "Tigre," Captain Hollowell, the 38-gun frigate "Apollo," and the brig "Wizard."

These vessels convoyed a fleet of transports,

conveying 5,000 soldiers, under Major-General Frazer.

On the 22nd of March, this fleet took possession of Alexandria, and found in the harbour two Turkish frigates, and a corvette with 16 brass guns.

While the foregoing expedition was being carried on, or off, but little was done elsewhere.

On the 4th of February, the 20-gun ship "Bacchante," Captain Richard Davies, and the "Mediator," Captain Wise, while cruising about the West India Islands, captured the French schooner "Dauphin," and then undertook to destroy the fort at Samana, a resort for privateers.

After a cannonade of four hours, the fort was stormed and taken by a party led by Captain Wise.

Aboard the two vessels two persons were killed and 17 wounded.

On the 1st of March, the boats of the 50-gun ship "Glatton," and the 14-gun brig "Hirondelle," led by Lieutenant Watson, cut out a Turkish vessel lying in the harbour of Sigri. Lieutenant Watson and four men were killed, and nine wounded.

The "Blanche" frigate sailed from Portsmouth, March 3, 1807, under command of Sir T. Lavie. The next morning at two o'clock, they made Portland lights, distant about four leagues. Afterwards they steered a west course, till eight o'clock, then west by south half south.

At this time it began to blow very hard; and, from being under all sail, they reduced to close-reefed fore and main topsails, and got down topgallant yards.

Ushant, by their reckoning, now bore S.S.W. half W. sixteen leagues.

The captain left orders in writing to haul to the northward, the wind being E.N.E. when the ship had run ten leagues, which Sir Thomas Lavie thought a good position to join Admiral Sir James Saumarez in the morning.

At eleven o'clock, Lieutenant Apreece awoke the captain to say that it blew harder; on which he ordered the ship to be brought to the wind on the starboard tack, and the foretopsail to be taken in. The lieutenant had scarcely got out of the cabin before the vessel struck. Everybody was on deck in an instant; sails were clewed up, and the anchors were let go; they rode a little until she parted from her anchors, and was driven upon the rocks.

The night was dreadfully dark and cold, and there was no possibility of discriminating whether the rocks were distant from the land or connected with the shore; happily, however, it proved the latter.

The captain immediately ordered the masts to be cut away, and recommended the officers and men to stay by him and the ship to the last; a few hands got into the quarter-boats, and they were no sooner on the water than they were dashed to pieces; it was about high water, and while the tide flowed the ship lay tolerably easy, until it began to fall, when tremendous breakers covered them.

The captain remained by the wheel, until the vessel divided amid-ship, when he fell over seaward. The crew were all on the side, and hauled him up immediately. It was highly gratifying to his feelings the attention they paid him to the last; and now they caressed him as their father.

H.M.S. "HYDRA" ATTACKING THE FORT OF BEGUO.

In this state they lay about three hours, when the water left the wreck sufficient for them to attempt a landing; and with the exception of a few, they got safe on shore, and assembled under a rock, when three cheers were given to the remains of the unfortunate "Blanche."

At daylight not two pieces of wood were left together, and the masts were shattered into shivers.

The crew, who had saved nothing, made a most shabby appearance.

A cask of rum was the only thing found on the shore, which, after the captain was carried to a cottage, some were so imprudent as to broach, by which about fifteen died.

They landed on a shocking coast, but every attention possible was paid to them. Having been marched about thirty miles, they arrived at Brest, where they were very comfortably lodged and fed in the Navy Hospital. Sir Thomas Lavie was accommodated at the house of the commander-in-chief,

M. Cefforelli, who behaved to him with all the manners of a gentleman.

All the officers were saved :—viz. Sir Thomas Lavie, captain; Robert Basten, first lieutenant; W. Apreece, second ditto; James Alton, third ditto; Roger Taylor, master; J. T. Wilcock, purser; James Brenan, surgeon; James Campbell, lieutenant of marines; T. J. P. Muters, James Ryall, John Rookes, Henry Stanhope, W. J. Williams, Robert Hay, George Gorden, J. T. Secretan, Thomas Gregg, Charles Street, and F. E. S. Vincent.

On the 15th of March, the boats of the 22-gun ship "Comus," Captain Shipley, entered the harbour of Puerta la Haz at Grand Canaria, under the command of Lieutenant Watts. Although opposed to a heavy fire from three batteries on shore, they boarded and brought away six merchant vessels.

In the month of March, a small squadron was blockading two French 74-gun ships in Chesapeake Bay.

From this squadron several men were said to have deserted and joined the American frigate, "Chesapeake," and Vice-Admiral Berkley, at Halifax, despatched the "Leopard," 50-gun ship, with orders to search the "Chesapeake" for the missing men.

On the 22nd of March, the American frigate left Hampton Road and proceeded to sea, when it was overhauled and hailed by Captain Humphreys, who sent Lieutenant Meade aboard to explain his business.

Commodore Barron, of the "Chesapeake," stated that his orders were not to permit the ship's company to be mustered by any officers except their own.

When the boat returned the "Leopard" sailed down within hailing distance of the "Chesapeake," and Captain Humphreys said—

"Commodore Barron, you must be aware of the necessity I am under of complying with the orders of my commander-in-chief."

No satisfactory reply could be obtained from the American vessel, and a shot was fired across its bows.

This was soon after followed by a broadside. At the third broadside of the "Leopard," the American colours were hauled down. The "Chesapeake" was soon after boarded, and four men taken away as deserters.

Aboard of the American vessel 3 men were killed, and 18 wounded.

This outrage on the "Chesapeake," by a vessel of much greater force was, of course, greatly resented by the American people.

The act was disavowed by the English government. Vice-Admiral Berkley was recalled from the North American command, and the "British right of search" was given up, and yet this affair had much to do in leading to the last war with America.

On the 31st of March, the 16-gun brig "Ferreter," Commander Henry Weir, was captured by seven Danish gunboats, and carried into the river Ems.

On the 19th of April, the gun-brig "Richmond," commanded by Lieutenant Heming, discovered a Spanish lugger in a small bay on the coast of Portugal.

In the evening the boats were sent under Sub-Lieutenant George Bush, and the lugger was boarded and captured in the face of a heavy fire, which only wounded three of the victorious party.

This is a navy medal boat action, but there have been more gallant affairs for which the medal has never been given.

The 18-gun sloop "Dauntless," Commander Strachey, in an attempt to deliver a quantity of powder to the Prussian garrison of Dantzic, was captured by the French on the 24th of April.

The "Dauntless" had gone up the river with a fair breeze, which suddenly shifted, and she took the ground near the French batteries, and was compelled to surrender.

On the 14th of May, the boats of the 38-gun frigate "Spartan," Captain Jahleel Brenton, attacked a large polacre ship, which they supposed to be an unarmed merchant vessel.

The frigate had chased it all day, and the boat attack was made in the evening, and led by Lieutenants Weir and Williams, with 70 men.

They attempted to board the vessel on her bow and quarter, but found the vessel defended by a large crew, who had boarding nettings up, and were fully prepared for receiving them.

They were met by a heavy discharge of great guns and musketry, which at the first fire prostrated 63 of the attacking party.

The first and second lieutenant, and 26 men, were either killed or mortally wounded.

There were only seven of the boats' crews that remained uninjured, and those few took back the boats to the frigate.

On the 5th of June, the frigate "Pomone," of 38 guns, Captain Robert Barrie, came across a French convoy under the protection of three armed brigs.

The "Pomone" gave chase, and several of the convoy were driven on shore, and 14 were captured near St. Gilles by the boats under Lieutenant Gabriel.

To prevent the Danish fleet from falling into the hands of the French, and being used against England, the English government demanded that the fleet of Denmark should be delivered over to England, under a promise that it should be restored to the Danes, in as good condition as it had been received, on the conclusion of a general peace.

To this proposal the Danish government at once agreed, but when called upon for its performance, there was so much hesitation that, on the 26th of July, Admiral James Gambier was sent from Yarmouth Roads with 17 sail of the line, 21 frigates, some sloops and bombs, to enforce the fulfilment of the promise.

The Crown Prince of Denmark having decidedly refused to agree to the proposals of the English, preparations were commenced for taking the Danish fleet by force. By the 14th of August the fleet was joined by the 64-gun ship "Agamemnon," Captain Rose, and several other vessels, until the fleet before Copenhagen consisted of twenty-five sail of the line, and forty frigates.

On the night of the 12th of August, one of the Danish vessels, the "Frederickseovan," slipped her cables and sailed for Norway, and the 74-gun ship "Defence," Captain Ekins, and the 22-gun ship "Comus," Captain Heywood, were sent by Admiral Gambier to bring it back.

The "Comus" being the fastest sailer, first came up with the absconding vessel, and ordered its captain to "heave to." This command was refused, and a musket shot was fired from the "Comus," which was returned by a shot from one of the stern guns of the other.

The action now commenced in earnest on both sides, and in forty-five minutes the "Fredericseovan" became so disabled in the rigging that she fell aboard the "Comus." She was then boarded, and, after a trifling resistance, captured and taken back.

She had 12 men killed, and 20 wounded. On the "Comus" only one man was wounded.

On the 23rd of August, while the fleet was waiting for the land force under General Cathcart to construct batteries, the in-shore squadron, consisting of small vessels, was attacked by the batteries, prames, and gunboats of the Danes, and was obliged to retire out of gun shot.

On the 31st of August, a portion of the fleet—the advance squadron—was again exposed to the fire of the Danish batteries, and an armed transport was blown up. The master, James Morgan, and 9 seamen were killed, and 21 were wounded.

All preparations being completed, the bombardment of the city was commenced on the 2nd of September.

For three days and three nights the firing from the English fleet and batteries was continued with but little intermission.

By that time 1,800 houses had been consumed by fire, many streets were levelled to the ground, 1,500 of the inhabitants were killed, and many more were wounded.*

This destruction of life and property was not of those against whom England had declared war, nor had the Danes committed one act of hostility against England.

To prevent the total destruction of the city, General Peymann, to whom the Crown Prince had left the defence of his capital, hoisted a flag of truce on the 5th of August, and the terms demanded by England were agreed to.

During the siege the English lost in the navy and land forces 56 men killed, 175 wounded, and 25 missing.

Many of the killed and wounded amongst the Danes were women and children.

It is said that the Crown Prince sent word to General Peymann from Kiel to burn the fleet, if compelled to surrender the town, and that the messenger bearing this despatch was captured by the English.

Early in October the English fleet sailed for England, taking with them eighteen Danish ships of the line, fifteen frigates, and six brigs, and twenty-five gun boats.

The Danish arsenal was cleared of its naval stores; two of the three ships on the stocks were taken to pieces, and the third was destroyed. Some block ships, which were unfit for a voyage to England, were destroyed. This invasion of neutral rights, that resulted in the capture of the Danish fleet, was received by a general cry of indignation throughout the civilized world.*

The fleet sailed from Copenhagen on the 21st of October, and while sailing down the Sound, the ship "Neptunus," of 80 guns, ran on a sand bank, and had to be destroyed.

The fleet encountered stormy weather on entering the Cattegat, and all the gunboats, except three, had to be destroyed.

On arriving at Yarmouth Roads only four of the line of battle ships taken from the Danes were found fit for active service.

The greatest value of the property seized at Copenhagen consisted in naval stores, and there was not a sufficient quantity of such materials to pay for the expedition fitted out for their capture, although 92 transports, measuring upwards of 20,000 tons, were deeply laden with them.

* * * * *

We must now go back and pick up events as they occurred in the regular order in the chronology of the year.

On the 6th of August, the boats of the 38-gun frigate "Hydra," Captain George Mundy, chased into the harbour of Beguo, near Catalonia, two brigs and one armed polacre ship. They were seen the next morning under the protection of a tower and a battery, and, after about an hour's firing from the "Hydra," 50 seamen and marines were landed, under the command of Lieutenant Edward O'Brien Drury.

They captured the tower while exposed to a heavy fire of grape and musketry, from the vessels and from the shore.

After the batteries were captured, the vessels were attacked and taken. Nearly all of the crews of the three vessels escaped to the shore.

The vessels were warped out of the harbour against a strong breeze. They were the ship

---

* Brenton's Naval History, Vol. II., p. 177.

* Allison's History of Europe, Vol. VIII., p. 256.

"Eugene," of 11 guns; the brig "Caroline," of 12 guns; and the "Rosario," of 4 guns.

The naval medal was granted for this action.

On the 31st of August, the island of Heligoland surrendered to combined English military and naval forces—the latter being under the command of Vice-Admiral Russell.

The single actions of note which took place in the year 1807 were less numerous than in several preceding years; but the contest between the "Windsor Castle" packet, Captain Rogers, going out with the mails for Barbadoes and the Leeward Islands, and a French privateer, on the 1st of October, was of so very gallant and distinguished a nature, as to be particularly entitled to honourable record.

"On the morning of the 1st of October," says the writer of a letter describing the action, "the man at the mast-head called out 'a sail!' We were soon convinced that all hopes of escape by swiftness were vain.

"We therefore had the netting stuffed with hammocks and sails, the arms all prepared, and the hands at quarters, when the enemy began to fire at forty minutes past eleven A.M.; but, as his shot did not reach us, we did not return his fire till about half-past twelve, and so continued till he closed, and grappled us on the starboard quarter, at about a quarter-past one.

"In this situation it became quite calm, and the vessels could not have separated, even had they been inclined.

"As soon as they grappled us, our boarders were prepared with their pikes, but her nettings were so lofty, and so well secured, that they did not attempt to board. Our pikemen, therefore, again flew to their muskets, pistols, and blunderbusses; our captain all the while giving his orders with the most admirable coolness, and encouraging his men by his speeches and example, in such a way, that there was no thought of yielding, although many of our heroes now lay stretched upon the deck in their blood; and then we saw the enemy's deck completely covered with their dead and wounded, and the fire from our great guns doing dreadful execution at every discharge.

"We now began to hear them scream, which so inspired our gallant little crew, that many of the wounded again returned to their quarters. At length, about a quarter-past three, the rascals ran from their quarters; when our captain, with five or six of his brave comrades, rushed on board, killed their captain, tore down their colours, and drove the few remaining on deck below, and the privateer surrendered.

"Our force consisted of a small ship of 180 tons, mounted with six 4-pounders and two sixes, manned with twenty-eight people, officers and boys included, of which there were four of the latter under seventeen years of age.

"The privateer was called 'Le Jeune Richard,' and was the most complete out of Guadaloupe, mounting six long sixes and one long 18-pounder fixed upon a swivel in the centre of her main deck, and traversing upon a circle, so that this enormous piece of ordnance was worked just as easily as a common-sized swivel; and having on board, at the commencement of the fight, eighty-six men, of which number twenty-six were killed, or died in a few hours after the action. It was not till six o'clock that we were disengaged from each other.

"On our side we lost three brave fellows, two of whom were killed on the spot, and the third died on the same evening; another, I fear, is mortally wounded through the breast and shoulder. We had, besides, nine men wounded, and three or four of them badly."

A handsome subscription was immediately raised for the captain of the "Windsor Castle," and numerous acknowledgments of his gallantry poured in from all quarters.

This has universally been acknowledged to have been a very gallant action on the part of the English.

On the night of the 7th of October, the boats of the 22-gun ship "Porcupine," Captain Henry Duncan, under the command of Lieutenant Price, captured in the harbour of Zupaino, the Venetian gunboat "Safo." The gunboat was armed with one long 24-pounder and several swivels, and was manned by 50 men.

On the night of the 25th of October, the boats of the 18-gun sloop "Herald," Captain George Hony, under the command of Lieutenant Walter Foreman, captured the French privateer "César," from under the fortress of Otranto.

All but four of the privateer's crew escaped by a hawser attached to the shore.

Only one of the boarding party, James Wood, the carpenter, was wounded, and one man on the "Herald" was killed by a shot from the castle.

On the 24th of November, the brig "Ann," mounting ten 12-pounders, commanded by Lieutenant James McKenzie, having in charge a prize, the Spanish privateer lugger, the "Vansigo," was attacked by ten Spanish gunboats.

The weather was too calm for Lieutenant McKenzie to escape, and he prepared to receive his enemies.

In less than an hour the "Ann," by her well-directed firing, had dismasted one of the gunboats, and compelled two others to surrender; but as she had but 30 men on board and 40 prisoners to guard, and as he was the bearer of dispatches, Lieutenant McKenzie did not attempt to take possession of the prizes.

The action was maintained by the other gunboats for some time longer, but they finally made off, taking with them the "Vansigo," which had been compelled to surrender.

During the month of November, the "Porcupine," 22-gun ship, Captain Duncan, performed much useful service in the Adriatic by capturing several small vessels of war and others laden with ordnance stores.

In this duty Lieutenant Price was particularly distinguished for his zeal.

On the 3rd of December, the 16-gun brig "Curieux," Captain John Sherif, met the French 24-gun privateer ship "Revanche."

An action commenced, which continued with much spirit for an hour, when the braces, bow-lines and tiller ropes of the "Curieux" were shot away.

Observing this, the captain of the "Revanche" from the brig and sailed off, the "Curieux" being in no condition to pursue it.

The French privateer was manned by a crew of 200 men, while the brig had a crew of but 80, yet Lieutenant Muir was tried by a court-martial, and reprimanded for not having done his utmost to capture the enemy after the death of his captain.

On the 11th of December, the 18-gun brig "Grasshopper," Commander Thomas Searle, had a long running fight, off Cape Palos, with the Spanish brig "San Josef," Lieutenant De Torres. The Spanish brig was armed with ten 24-pounder

TOTAL DESTRUCTION OF THE FRIGATE "ANSON."

put her helm down and ran his vessel aboard the "Curieux."

A long 18-pounder on a traversing carriage was then fired, accompanied by a heavy discharge of musketry, and Captain Sherif and five men were killed, and several wounded. The main boom of the brig was also shot away. Notwithstanding these misfortunes, the French, in an attempt to board, were repulsed.

Lieutenant Thomas Muir, who now had command of the English brig, made an attempt to board the "Revanche;" but, finding that he was only followed by eleven men, he had to relinquish the undertaking.

The French ship soon after became disengaged

carronades, and two long sixes, but her firing from them was very ineffective. She ran ashore under Cape Negreti and struck her colours.

The "Grasshopper" came to an anchor, got her prize afloat, and brought it away, although exposed to a fire while doing so from a body of troops and the Spanish crew, which had escaped to the shore.

During the summer and autumn of this year, Sir Edward Pellew had command of the fleet on the East India station. In August he dispatched the frigates "Caroline" and "Psyche," Captains Rainier and F. B. R. Pellew, to Java, in search of two Dutch vessels that had escaped the year before from Batavia.

While absent on this duty the "Psyche" anchored at Samarang.

On the night of the 31st of August, her boats, commanded by Lieutenant Kerstemann, boarded, captured, and brought out, two vessels, anchored in the road, and which were defended by batteries, an 8-gun brig, and a large armed merchant brig. The two prizes were destroyed. The next morning, September 1st, he chased two ships and a brig, and ran them ashore about nine miles to the westward of Samarang.

The "Psyche" anchored in a position to bring a broadside to bear upon them, and, after a few rounds, the "Resolute," a large armed merchant ship, surrendered. The Dutch national 24-gun ship "Scipio" was the next to strike, and her example was soon followed by the brig which belonged to the Dutch East India Company's service, and mounted 12 guns. The three vessels were taken away, and the "Scipio" was added to the navy under the name of the "Samarang."

On the 5th December, Rear-Admiral Sir Edward Pellew arrived off Point Panka, with a squadron composed of the following vessels:—

"Culloden," 74 guns, Rear-Admiral Pellew, Captain George Bell; "Powerful," 74 guns, Fleetwood B. R. Pellew; "Caroline," 36 guns, Henry Hart; "Fox," 32 guns, Hon. Archibald Cochrane; "Victorie," 18 guns, Commander Thomas Groube; "Samarang," 18 guns, Commander Richard Buck; "Seaflower," 14 guns, Lieutenant William Owen; "Jaseur," 14 guns, Lieutenant Thomas Langhame.

A detachment of troops under the command of Lieutenant-Colonel Lockhart accompanied the expedition.

A demand was first made on the Dutch commodore for the surrender of the war vessels at Griesse, a town a few miles up the river.

The boat that took this demand was detained, and the officer and crew put under arrest, although they went ashore with a flag of truce.

The Dutch commodore refused to give up the ships, and preparations were commenced for taking them by force.

The "Culloden" and "Powerful" were lightened as much as possible, and began ascending the river to Griesse.

On their way they had to pass a battery at Sambelangan, where they received some damage from red-hot shot.

The navigation of the river being very difficult, the ships ran aground several times. On one occasion the "Culloden" was not got off until the guns were taken out and the water started.

This difficulty, however, was overcome, and the squadron at last reached the mouth of the harbour of Griesse. The Dutch inhabitants now repudiated the conduct of the commodore, set the boat's crew at liberty, and were willing to treat for the surrender of the ships.

In this expedition the English were partly defeated by a very simple plan.

The Dutch commodore had the two line of battle ships, a sheer hulk, and a 40-gun merchant ship scuttled.

On the 11th, guns and military stores at Griesse and Sambelangan were also destroyed.

The casualties attending the expedition only amounted to Lieutenant Allen and a few men wounded, and the loss of the fore-yard and some other damage to the "Fox."

On the 21st of December, an expedition under Rear-Admiral Sir Alexander Inglis Cochrane took possession of the Danish island of St. Thomas in the West Indies, and on the 25th, the island of Santa Croix surrendered to the same squadron.

On the 24th of December, a squadron, under Rear-Admiral Sir Samuel Hood, reached Madeira, and on the 26th, took possession of the island without opposition.

In the month of March this year, Sir Home Popham was tried by a court-martial at Portsmouth for withdrawing all the naval force from the Cape of Good Hope, and attacking the Spanish settlements in Rio de la Plata.

He was found guilty and sentenced to be severely reprimanded.

The principal wrecks of naval vessels this year were those of the frigates "Blanche," "Boreas," and "Anson."

The former, commanded by Sir T. Lavie, was wrecked off the coast of France, near Brest, on the 4th of March, and 45 of the crew were drowned.

The latter, commanded by Captain Scott, was wrecked on the Hanway rocks on the 4th of December. Ninety persons were lost, including Captain Scott, his wife, and Lieutenant Hawkes.

His Majesty's frigate "Anson," of 40 guns, Captain Lydiard, sailed from Falmouth on the 24th of December, 1807, to resume her station off Brest.

As it blew very hard from the W.S.W. she was not able to get so far to the westward; however, Captain Lydiard persevered in his endeavours until the 28th.

On the morning of that day they made the Isle of Bas, on the French coast, which they had seen the preceding evening.

There being now every appearance of bad weather, Captain Lydiard determined to return to port, and accordingly shaped a course for the Lizard, the gale still increasing, and it coming on very heavy.

About three p.m., the land was seen about five miles west of the Lizard, but at the time not exactly known, as many opinions were expressed as to what land it was then in sight; the ship was wore to stand off at sea, but had not long been on that tack, before the land was again descried right ahead.

It was now quite certain that the ship was embayed, and every exertion was made to work her off the shore; but finding she lost ground every tack, she was brought to an anchor in twenty-five fathoms, at five p.m., with the best bower-anchor veered away to two cables' length.

By this anchor the ship rode in a most tremendous sea, and as heavy a gale as was ever experienced, until four a.m., of the 29th, when the cable parted.

The small bower-anchor was then let go, and veered away to two cables' length, which held her until eight a.m., when that also parted; and, as the last resource, in order to preserve the lives of as many as possible, the fore-topsail was set, and the ship run on shore, on the sand which forms the bar, between the Loe Pool, about three miles from Helstone, and the sea.

The tide had ebbed about an hour when she struck; on taking the ground, she broached-to with her broadside to the beach, and most happily heeled in to the shore: had she, on the contrary, heeled off, not a soul could have escaped alive.

Now commenced a most heartrending scene to some hundreds of spectators, who had been in anxious suspense, and who exerted themselves to the utmost, at the imminent risk of their lives, to save those of their drowning fellow-men.

Many of those who were most forward in quitting the ship lost their lives, being swept away by the tremendous sea, which entirely went over the wreck.

The mainmast formed a floating raft from the ship to the shore, and the greater part of those who escaped, passed by this medium.

One of the men saved stated that Captain Lydiard was near him on the mainmast; but that he seemed to have lost the use of his faculties with the horror of the scene, and soon disappeared.

At a time when no one appeared on the ship's side, and it was supposed the work of death had ceased, a dissenting minister, hazarding his life through the surf, got on board, over the wreck of the mainmast, to see if any one remained.

Some honest hearts followed him.

They found several persons still below, who could not get up, among whom were two women and two children.

The worthy preacher and his party saved the two women and some of the men, but the children were lost.

About two p.m., the ship went to pieces, when a few more men emerged from the wreck.

One of these was saved.

By three o'clock no appearance of the vessel remained.

To the above account, we subjoin that of Captain Lydiard's steward, who was more immediately about his person, and very correct in his observations:—

"On the 27th of December, cruising off the Black Rocks, and perceiving the approach of a gale, kept a look out for the commodore in the 'Dragon.'

"The next morning (Monday), the gale increasing from the S.W., and not perceiving the 'Dragon' in any direction, at nine o'clock shaped our course for the Lizard, with a view of getting into Falmouth.

"At twelve o'clock, all hands upon deck, the sea running very high; two bow-ports on the starboard side washed away by the violence of the sea, also a port abreast the mainmast, by which means she shipped a great deal of water.

"The captain sent for the master at this time to determine the situation of the ship; and, at half-past twelve o'clock, or thereabout, land was seen about two miles distant; but, from the extreme thickness of the weather, they could not ascertain what part.

"Captain Lydiard ordered the ship to be wore to the S.E., not thinking it safe to stand in any nearer under such circumstances of weather.

"Soon after one o'clock, the master wished him to run in again and make the land, which was supposed to be the Lizard, and that, if we could make it out, we should get into Plymouth.

"Captain Lydiard asked if it could be done without risk; he (the master) said he thought it could.

"The ship was then wore, but the weather still continuing thick, we had a cast of the lead, and, having twenty-seven fathom, we were convinced we must be to the westward of the Lizard, and immediately wore ship again, and made all sail.

"Soon after three o'clock, as the captain was going to dinner, he looked out of the quarter gallery, from whence he saw the breakers close to us, and the land a long distance ahead.

"The ship was wore instantly, and Captain Lydiard's mind made up to come to an anchor; for, had we kept under weigh, the ship must have struck upon the rocks in a few hours.

"The topgallant masts were got upon deck, and she rode very well until four o'clock on Tuesday morning, when the cable parted.

"The other anchor was immediately let go, and the lower yards and topmasts struck.

"At daylight the other cable parted, and we were then so close to the land that we had no alternative but to go on shore, when Captain Lydiard desired the master to run the ship into the best situation for saving the lives of the people; and, fortunately, a fine beach presented itself, upon which the ship was run.

"Shortly after she struck, the mainmast went, but injured no one.

"Captains Lydiard and Sullivan, with the first lieutenant, were resolved to remain with the ship as long as possible. Many people were killed on board.

"The first lieutenant and a number of others were washed overboard.

"It was the captain's great wish to save the lives

of the ship's company, and he was employed in directing them the whole of the time.

"He had placed himself by the wheel, holding by the spokes, where he was exposed to the violence of the sea, which broke tremendously over him; and, from continuing in this situation too long, waiting to see the people out of the ship, he became so weak, that upon attempting to leave the ship himself, and being impeded by a boy who was in the way, and whom he endeavoured to assist, he was washed away and drowned."

This unfortunate officer might truly be said to have sacrificed his life to the high sense of duty, which at all times and on all occasions determined his conduct.

His body being found, was interred with military honours at Falmouth, attended by Admiral Sir Charles Cotton and General Spencer, with all the navy and military officers of the expedition at that port, the captains of the packets, and the mayor and corporation of the town; and was afterwards removed to his family vault in the parish church of Haslemere, Surrey.

The men who survived were conveyed to Helstone, about two miles distant, where they were taken care of by the magistrates, and afterwards sent to Falmouth in charge of the regulating captain of that port.

Among the officers saved were Captain Sullivan, a passenger; Messrs. Hill and Brailey, midshipmen; and Mr. Ross, assistant-surgeon.

During the year 1807, the English navy lost thirty-nine vessels. Nine were captured by their enemies, twenty-one were wrecked, eight foundered, and one was burnt.

CHAPTER XXXII.
1808.

ABOUT this time great improvements were made in the artillery on board the British fleet, greatly increasing the power of each vessel's armament, a thing greatly needed, for there was still plenty of work for our gallant tars, as will be seen in the course of this chapter.

The first encounter of any note took place on the 16th of January, when the 14-gun brig "Linnet," commanded by Lieutenant John Tracy, captured the French lugger "Courier" of 18 guns and 60 men, off Cape Barfleur.

Lieutenant Tracy had to use some stratagem in order to bring the lugger to action.

The "Linnet" was a slow sailer, and by bearing down upon the lugger on first seeing it, it would probably have made off and escaped.

Lieutenant Tracy appeared anxious to escape himself by joining company with some merchant ships and sailing from the enemy.

This scheme succeeded.

The lugger came up with them, and while engaged with one of the merchant vessels, the "Linnet" got within musket shot of it, and fired a broadside that cut away the main-lug halyards.

A running fight then took place for nearly two hours, when the lugger, being in a sinking state, surrendered.

She had her second officer killed and three men wounded.

On the 30th of January, the "Delight," Captain Philip Handfield, while trying to recapture some Sicilian gun-boats, ran aground under the batteries of Reggio.

The vessel was exposed to a deadly fire, under which Captain Handfield and several others were killed.

The "Delight" was burnt by a few of her crew, who escaped to the shore.

On the 7th of February, the 8-gun schooner "Découverte," commanded by Lieutenant Colin Campbell, pursued off St. Domingo two privateers, having in their charge a prize ship. One of the privateers escaped, but the other and the prize-ship were run on shore and destroyed.

On the 8th of February, the boats of the 32-gun frigate "Meleager," led by Lieutenant George Tupman, cut out the French armed felucca "Renard," from St. Jago de Cuba. The French crew escaped to the shore.

The schooner "Découverte," we have just mentioned, after a gallant action, captured the French privateer "Derade," on the 9th of February.

The privateer had a crew of 72 men, seven of whom were killed.

The crew of the schooner only consisted of 37 men and boys, of whom three were dangerously, and one mortally wounded.

On the 13th of February, the cutter and jolly boat of the 20-gun ship "Confiance," were rowing guard off the mouth of the Tagus, a French gun-boat was seen at anchor between two forts.

The boats were under the command of Robert Twist, the master's mate, who determined on trying to capture the gun-boat, which was boarded and carried without loss to the assailants.

The gun-boat had a crew of 50 men, three of whom were killed and nine wounded.

Mr. Twist was promoted, and the medal for a naval boat action was given to those engaged in the affair.

On the 2nd of March, the Danish brig "Admiral Yawl," of 28 guns, was captured off Scarborough by the 18-gun brig "Sappho," Commander George Langford.

The engagement only lasted half an hour, in which there were two men wounded on the "Sappho," and one man killed and another wounded on the "Admiral Yawl," yet the naval medal was granted for the action.

On the 6th of March, the 36-gun frigate "San Fiorenzo," Captain George Nicholas Hardinge, on its return from Pointe de Galle to Bombay, encountered the French 40-gun frigate "Piemontaise," Captain Epron, off Cape Comorin.

The French frigate endeavoured to escape, but was overhawled after a three hours' chase, and brought to action at 200 yards distance.

This engagement did not last long, before the "Piemontaise" again made off, followed by the "San Fiorenzo," which, in the brief action, had three men wounded and some damage done to her rigging.

At daylight the next morning, the French captain seeing that he could not avoid a battle, hoisted his colours, and wore his ship across the bows of the English vessel.

The action again commenced and lasted for about an hour and a half, when the "Piemontaise" ceased firing, bore up, and sailed away.

The "San Fiorenzo" had her main topsail-yard cut in two, the main-royal-mast shot away, and her standing and running rigging so much damaged, that, for some time, she was not able to sail in pursuit.

In this engagement she had eight seamen and marines killed, and fourteen wounded.

After repairing damages, the "San Fiorenzo" again sailed in pursuit of its enemy, which was seen at daylight the next morning about four miles away.

On this occasion the "Piemontaise" did not seem anxious to avoid an action, which was commenced by the two vessels on opposite tacks at the distance of 80 yards.

At the second broadside of the Frenchman, Captain Hardinge was killed by a grape shot, and the command of the "San Fiorenzo" was taken by Lieutenant William Dawson.

ACTION BETWEEN THE "SAN FIORENZO" AND "PIEMONTAISE."

The "Piemontaise," after reaching the beam of the other, wore around, and a severe and close engagement took place, which lasted until the rigging and sails of the French vessel were cut to pieces, and her lower masts and bowsprit badly wounded, when some of her crew waved their hats in token that she had surrendered.

In this last action, the "San Fiorenzo" had the captain and four men killed, and Lieutenant Moysey and seven men wounded, making for the three days' fight, 13 killed and 25 wounded, out of a crew of 186 men and boys at quarters when the first action commenced.

The "Piemontaise" had a crew of 566 men including 200 Lascars and some prisoners, and of this number 48 were killed and 112 wounded.

The "Piemontaise" was the vessel that captured the "Warren Hastings" on the 21st of June, 1806, when Captain Larkins of the captured vessel was so grossly abused by Lieutenant Moreau, of the "Piemontaise," because the two vessels came in collision after the former had surrendered.

It was said that just before the boats of the "San Fiorenzo" reached the "Piemontaise" to take possession of it, Lieutenant Moreau leaped overboard to avoid falling into the hands of the countrymen of one he had so shamefully illtreated.

Two days after her capture, the lower masts of the prize fell over the side, and it had to be towed into Colombo, where the frigate with its prize arrived on the 13th.

The "Piemontaise" was added to the British Navy under the same name, and a sword of 100 guineas value was given by the Patriotic Fund to Lieutenant Dawson.

The navy medal was granted to the survivors of the victory, in 1847—thirty-nine years after the action.

In the spring of the year 1808, an expedition was fitted out, with the view of taking or destroying the Russian fleet in the Baltic, which was supposed to be in reality under the control of the French emperor.

It accordingly sailed from Yarmouth, under the

command of Sir James Saumarez and Sir Richard Keates, on the 10th of May.

The naval force consisted of nine sail of the line, five frigates, six sloops, and thirteen gun-brigs, with upwards of two hundred sail of transports, with troops; eighty of which had horses on board. Several gunboats accompanied the expedition, built upon a new construction, drawing only two feet water, and carrying a long eighteen-pounder and a carronade.

Sir James Saumarez formed a junction with the Swedish fleet in the Baltic; but it was not till August that any proceedings of importance took place.

Sir Samuel Hood, who commanded the " Centaur," addressed a letter to his commander-in-chief, on the 27th of that month; in which he states that the Russian squadron, under the command of Vice-Admiral Honickhoff, after being chased thirty-four hours by his Swedish Majesty's squadron, under Rear-Admiral Nauckhoff, accompanied by the " Centaur" and " Implacable," had been forced to take shelter in the port of Rogerswick, with the loss of one ship of 74 guns.

The Russian squadron appeared off Oro Road on the 23rd.

The arrangement for quitting that anchorage after his Swedish Majesty's ships from Jungfur Sound had joined Rear-Admiral Nauckhoff, were completed on the evening of the 24th.

Early the next morning the whole force put to sea; soon after the Russian fleet was discovered off Hango Udd, wind N.E.; every sail was pressed by his Swedish Majesty's squadron.

From the superior sailing of the " Centaur" and " Implacable," they were soon in advance; at the close of the evening the enemy were not far off in disorder.

On the 26th, about five o'clock, the " Implacable" was able to bring the leeward most line of battle ship to close action; although the enemy's ship fought with the greatest bravery, she was silenced in about twenty minutes, and only the near approach of the enemy's whole fleet could have prevented her then falling into our hands, her colours and pendant being both down.

The Russian Admiral, having sent a frigate to tow the disabled ship, again hauled his wind, and the " Implacable," being ready to make sail, Sir Samuel Hood immediately gave chase, and soon obliged the frigate to cast off her tow, when the Russian Admiral was again under the necessity to support her by several of his line of battle ships bearing down; and Sir S. Hood had every prospect of thus bringing on a general action: to avoid which the Russian Admiral availed himself of a favourable slant of wind, and entered the port of Rogerswick.

The ship engaged by the " Implacable," having fallen to leeward, grounded on a shoal at the entrance of the port; there being then some swell, Sir S. Hood had a hope she must have been destroyed; but the wind moderating towards the evening, she appeared to ride at anchor, and exertions were made to repair her damage.

At sunset, finding the swell abated, and boats sent by the Russian fleet to tow her into port, Sir S. Hood directed Captain Webley to stand in and cut her off.

The boats had made a considerable progress, and the enemy's ship was just entering the port, when the " Centaur" had the good fortune to lay her on board; her bowsprit taking the " Centaur's" fore-rigging, she swept along with her bow grazing the muzzle of her guns, which was the only signal for their discharge, and the enemy's bows were drove in by this raking fire.

When the bowsprit came to the mizen-rigging, Sir S. Hood ordered it to be lashed; this was performed, in a most steady manner, by the exertions of Captain Webley, Lieutenant Lawless, Mr. Strode, the master, and other brave men, under a heavy fire of musketry, by which Lieutenant Lawless was severely wounded.

Nothing could withstand the cool and determined fire of the marines under Captain Bayley and the other officers, as well as the fire from the " Centaur's" stern-chase guns; and in less than half an hour she was obliged to surrender.

Captain Martin now anchored his ship in a position to heave the " Centaur" off, after she and the prize had grounded, which was fortunately effected at the moment two of the enemy's ships were seen under sail, standing towards them, but retreated as they saw the ships extricated from this difficulty.

The prize proved to be the " Sewolod," of 74 guns, Captain Rodneff; she had so much water in her, and being fast on shore, after taking out the prisoners and wounded men, Sir S. Hood was obliged to give orders for her being burnt—which service was completely effected under the direction of Lieutenant Biddulph, of the " Centaur," by seven o'clock in the morning.

In this action we shall see much to imitate and admire.

The chase was to windward; two British seventy-fours led up the Swedish fleet in pursuit of a superior enemy; only the two British ships were able to get into action with the rear of that enemy, from which they cut off and captured one ship of the line; the Swedish fleet by their presence evidently contributing to the defeat.

The " Centaur" had 3 killed and 27 wounded; the " Implacable," 6 killed and 27 wounded.

The force of the Swedes, on that day, under Admiral Nauckhoff, amounted to ten sail of the line.

Of this action and the preliminary movements, the following Russian official account was subsequently published:—

" On the 9th of August, Admiral Honickhoff

set sail from Hangudd with his squadron, composed of nine sail of the line and nine frigates, for Jungfur Sound, for the purpose of reconnoitring the enemy's position, and to form his plan of operations.

"He found the enemy's fleet at anchor in Jungfur Sound, among the cliffs, consisting of eighteen sail, partly line of battle ships and partly frigates.

"Admiral Honickhoff was cruising off Jungfur Sound until the 13th, when his headmost ship made the signal that the enemy's fleet was weighing anchor.

"Admiral Honickhoff immediately detached a corvette to observe the enemy's movements, formed his fleet in order of battle, and beat about to the eastward, in order not to be cut off from his port determined to give battle.

"The same day the enemy's fleet was observed from the mast-head, working towards our squadron, in company with two English sail of the line. Admiral Honickhoff resolved to attack the enemy the following day, and beat about the whole night, in order not to lose the wind.

"At break of day, being off Baltic Port, he discovered to leeward the enemy's fleet, composed of thirteen sail of the line, and five large frigates; among the former were two English ships, one of which was a three-decker, and bore the Admiral's pendant, and the other was a two-decker of the largest size, and among the Swedish was also a three-decker. The enemy's van, headed by two English sail of the line, weared our rear, and at five o'clock in the morning the two English ships attacked successively the sternmost ship of our line, 'Sewolod,' which had somewhat fallen to leeward.

"When Admiral Honickhoff saw the manœuvres of the enemy, he bore down on him with the whole of his squadron. The English, fearful to be cut off from their line, tacked, and were followed by the Swedes.

"Captain Rudnew, commander of the 'Sewolod,' with the utmost gallantry, beat off twice the enemy's attack, but suffered considerably in his rigging. The maintop mast and yard were shattered by the enemy's fire, the foretop gallant mast was split, and the 'Sewolod' was no longer able to maintain her place in the line, of which Captain Rudnew informed the commander-in-chief by signal.

"Admiral Honickhoff, who witnessed the above facts, permitted him to run into Baltic Port, and a frigate convoyed him thither. By this means our line, before a general engagement could be commenced, had lost one ship; and another, the 'Severnga Swesda' (North Star) received on a sudden so much damage in her foretop mast, that she would not carry her foretop sail, and was consequently also disabled duly to maintain her place in the line.

"By this circumstance the enemy gained a great superiority of strength, and Admiral Honickhoff found it accordingly expedient to stand with his squadron off Baltic Port.

"The enemy stood in consequence thereof on the same course, keeping their wind; and the English ships displayed all their skill to cut off our damaged ship, the 'Sewolod,' which was no longer able to keep up with our line.

"In order to frustrate this plan of the enemy, Admiral Honickhoff made signal for the rear to cover the said ship, and afford her all possible assistance; but, owing to her having fallen considerably to the leeward, she was not able, in spite of the utmost exertions made by her own commander, as well as by the captains of the other ships, to round the north point of Baltic Port, and enter that harbour in company with the rest of our ships, but was necessitated to drop anchor on the north side of this island, close in with the shore.

"In the meantime the commander-in-chief entered the above port, brought up in line of battle, and made all necessary arrangements to repulse the enemy; who, however, made no attack, but stood out at sea with his whole fleet.

"Admiral Honickhoff immediately ordered those experienced officers, Captain-Lieutenant Miniskoy and Fuludjew, to put off with all the row-boats of the squadron, to the assistance of the 'Sewolod,' and to endeavour to bring her back to the fleet.

"These two gallant officers used their best efforts for that purpose, but the two English ships of the line coming up, successively attacked the 'Sewolod' and dispersed the row-boats, which Captain-Lieutenant Miniskoy, however, succeeded to rally, and rejoined with them the squadron.

"Captain Rudnew, undismayed by their retreat, continued to make the most vigorous resistance, constantly and closely engaged with one of the two English ships, which suffered severely, and the slaughter was great on both sides; nor would the conflict have been ended, but with the total destruction of the combatants, had not the other English ship also come up with the 'Sewolod' and given his broadside, by which she was completely disabled from continuing the contest any longer.

"It was but then that the English were able to render themselves masters of the 'Sewolod,' or rather her wreck covered with dead bodies; fifty-six of her crew saved themselves by swimming, and the rest were taken prisoners by the English. Rear-Admiral Hood has sent back thirty-seven of them, who were wounded, and states that the loss on board the two English ships has also been very great."

For a considerable time the Russian squadron remained closely blockaded; but as it was, from the position which it had secured, totally out of the reach of the English, all hopes of further capture were deemed useless, and the blockade was relinquished.

On the 13th of March, the 36-gun frigate

"Emerald," attacked a French schooner anchored in the harbour of Vivero, on the coast of Spain.

The schooner was under the protection of two forts, one mounting eight, and the other five 24-pounders.

Captain Maitland of the "Emerald," sent Lieutenant Charles Bertram with a party of seamen and marines to storm one battery, while the frigate was to attack the other.

The Spaniards were easily driven out of the fort by the shore party, and the guns were spiked.

The other fort was silenced by the guns of the frigate, and their attention was then turned to the schooner, which was the "Apopos," of eight 12-pounders, and a crew of 70 men.

Her crew did not remain on their vessel, but posted amongst the neighbouring rocks, they annoyed the English with volleys of musketry.

The schooner had been run on the rocks by its crew, and it was found impossible to get it off.

The prize was set on fire, and the next morning she blew up.

In this undertaking, nine seamen and marines were killed, and thirteen officers and men wounded.

Lieutenant Bertram was promoted to the rank of commander, and the naval medal was afterwards given for the action.

On the 14th of March, the brig "Childers," of fourteen 12-pounders, Commander William H. Dillon, had an engagement in the Baltic with the Danish 18-gun brig "Lougen."

The "Childers" succeeded in escaping into Leith, with a loss of two men killed and nine wounded.

Through some strange whim, the naval medal was given for this action.

On the 22nd of March, the 64-gun ships "Stately" and "Nassau," Captains Parker and Campbell, chased the Danish 74-gun ship "Prindtz," ashore near Greenall, on the coast of Jutland.

After the ship surrendered it was found impossible to get her afloat, and when the prisoners were removed, she was set on fire and destroyed.

In the action the "Stately" had 4 men killed and 27 wounded.

The "Nassau" had one man killed and 16 wounded, and the Danish ship 55 killed and 88 wounded.

On the 4th of April, the 38-gun frigate "Alceste," Captain Murray Maxwell, the 28-gun frigate, "Mercury," Captain James Gordon, and the brig "Grasshopper," Commander Thomas Searle, discovered a Spanish convoy off the coast of Spain, under the protection of twenty gun-boats.

The convoy and gun-boats all sought the protection of some batteries on shore near Cadiz.

A detachment of boats was sent from each vessel to board and bring out some of the convoy.

Although opposed to a tremendous fire from the batteries and gun-boats of the enemy, seven tartans were brought out, two gunboats destroyed and several driven on shore.

This destruction of the enemy's property took place within sight of eleven ships of the line.

The only loss sustained by the English was one man mortally, and two slightly, wounded aboard the "Grasshopper."

On the 23rd of April, the boats of the ship "Daphne," Captain Mason, the sloop "Tartanus," Commander William Russel, and the gun-brig "Forward," Lieutenant Shiels, attacked a Danish convoy laden with provisions for the relief of Norway.

The vessels were moored to the shore, and protected by a fort mounting ten guns. As the boats approached, the Danes abandoned their vessels for the shore, but as soon as they were boarded by the English, from the Danish crews, which were drawn up on the beach and the castle, came a heavy fire of grape and musketry.

This, however, did not prevent the English boat crew from doing their duty, and ten of the Danish convoy were brought out.

On the night of the 23rd of April, Captain Conway Shipley, of the 36-gun frigate "Nymph," assisted by the boats of the 18-gun sloop "Blossom," Captain Pigot, made an attempt to capture the French 20-gun brig "Garotta," lying at Belem Castle, in the Tagus, ready for sea.

The whole force consisted of eight boats, and 150 officers and men.

The boats towed each other to prevent being separated until the order was given to board, when they cast off, and the attack commenced.

Captain Shipley was one of the first men who jumped into the fore-rigging of the brig, and was cutting away the boarding nettings when he was struck in the forehead by a musket-ball, and fell into the sea.

In trying to recover the body of the captain, the gig got foul of the cutter, the crew of which, under Lieutenant Haly, was just boarding the larboard quarter of the brig. The cutter then fell foul of the launch. In this confusion the boats were carried some way down by a strong current, and the enterprise was relinquished.

The body of Captain Shipley was washed on shore and recovered. His loss was much regretted.

On the 23rd of April, the 18-gun brig "Grasshopper," Commander Thomas Searle, and the 14-gun brig "Rapid," Lieutenant Henry Baugh, ran two Spanish vessels and four gun-boats under shelter of a battery near Faro, on the coast of Portugal.

The brigs anchored within a short distance of the battery and gun-boats, and opened fire.

In a little more than two hours two of the gun-boats had been driven on shore, the other two had surrendered, and the Spaniards were driven from their guns in the battery.

The two vessels were then taken out.

They were from South America, and the cargo of each was valued at £30,000.

The "Grasshopper" had one seaman killed and three wounded, and on the "Rapid" three seamen were wounded.

The loss on the captured gunboats was 40 in killed and wounded.

The 18-pounder 36-gun frigate "Unite," Captain Patrick Campbell, captured the Italian 16-gun brig "Roneo," in the Gulf of Venice, on the 2nd of May. The 18-gun brig "Redwing," commanded by

few yards of the breakers, off Cape Antonio, the "Griffon" struck her flag.

Captain William Hoste, of the 18-pounder 32-gun frigate "Amphion," destroyed the frigate "Baleine," lying at anchor in the Bay of Rosas, under the protection of some batteries, on the 12th of May.

The "Amphion" had to work into the Bay, and while doing so, had to return the fire from the "Baleine," Fort Boulton, and a battery of sixteen long 24-pounders, as she sailed on different tacks. Before reaching the "Baleine," that vessel slipped

WRECK OF THE FRIGATE "CRESCENT."

Thomas Ussher, encountered a Spanish convoy off Cape Trafalgar, guarded by seven small armed vessels, on the 7th of May, which carried twenty-two heavy guns, and were manned by 271 men.

When within musket shot of this squadron, the "Redwing" opened fire. Four merchant vessels and several of the armed vessels, in trying to escape, ran on the rocks, and many of the crew were lost in the heavy surf. This occurred on the 7th of May.

On the 11th of May, the 20-gun ship "Bacchante," Captain Samuel Hood Inglefield, captured the French 16-gun brig "Griffon," Captain Gautier, off the coast of Cuba. This was a running fight that lasted for half-an-hour; and when within a

her cables, hoisted her staysails, and ran ashore near the fort.

The "Amphion" soon after anchored near the place the French vessel had left, and opened a sharp fire on the ship and batteries, which was continued until the "Baleine" was seen to be in flames.

Soon after, the "Amphion" cut her cable, and sailed out, having lost but one man killed and five wounded.

On the 19th of May, the 38-gun frigate "Virginie," Captain Edward Brace, captured the Dutch 12-pounder 36-gun frigate "Guelderland," Captain Pool.

The action lasted an hour and a half, when the

Dutch frigate, having her masts and bowsprit carried away, and twenty-five men killed, including her commander, and fifty men wounded, surrendered.

The "Virginie" had only one man killed and two wounded.

The naval medal was given for this action.

On the 24th of May, the hired armed cutter "Swan," of 10 guns, and a crew of forty men and boys, off the island of Bornholm, encountered a Danish 10-gun cutter, which, after an action of twenty minutes, blew up and sank. The "Swan" and its crew received no injury.

The brig "Tickler," Lieutenant Skinner, when in the Great Belt in a calm, on the 4th of June, was attacked by four Danish gunboats. In an action of four hours Lieutenant Skinner and fourteen men were killed, and twenty-two wounded, out of a crew of fifty men. The brig then surrendered.

On the 9th of June, a squadron of small vessels convoying seventy merchant vessels, was attacked off the south end of Saltholm by twenty-five Danish gunboats. One of the English war vessels, the "Turbulent," Lieutenant Wood, was surrounded by the enemy and captured.

The "Thunder" then beat several of the gunboats off, and the Danes retired, taking with them twelve sail of the convoy which they had captured. Lieutenant Wood was tried by a court martial for the loss of the "Turbulent," and honourably acquitted.

The 36-gun frigate "Euryalus," Captain Dundas, and the 18-gun sloop "Cruiser," Captain Mackenzie, while cruising in the Great Belt, on the 11th of June, found several vessels anchored near the shore, and four boats, under the orders of Lieutenant Head, were sent to capture or destroy them.

A gunboat, mounting two long 18-pounders, with a crew of sixty-four men, moored near a 3-gun battery, and protected by a body of troops on the shore, was boarded, captured and taken out, and two large troop-ships were destroyed. Only one man of the party in the boats was wounded, while the Danes had seven men killed and twelve wounded.

Lieutenant Head was presented by the Patriotic Fund with a sword of the value of fifty guineas.

On the 19th of June, the 16-gun brig "Seagull," Commander Robert Cathcart, was captured off the coast of Norway by the Danish 20-gun brig "Longen." The "Seagull" pursued and overhauled the Danish brig, which was the first to commence the action, but before the battle had continued more than twenty minutes, six Danish gunboats, each armed with two long 24-pounders, came from behind some rocks, and in two divisions attacked the "Seagull" on each quarter, while the "Longen," on the larboard bow, raked her with great effect. In less than half-an-hour five of the "Seagull's" guns were dismounted, and she was nearly unrigged.

For some time after, however, she continued combatting her numerous foes until she had five feet of water in the hold, when she struck, having lost eight men killed and twenty wounded.

The "Seagull" went down a short time after she had surrendered, proving that she had been defended as long as either prudence or honour demanded. Lieutenant Hatton, of the "Seagull," although highly praised for his conduct in the action by his commanding officer, was for some unexplained reason neglected by the Admiralty.

On the 26th of June, two boats of the 64-gun ship "Standard," Captain Harvey, captured an Italian gun-vessel, the "Volpe," off the island of Corfu. The boats were under the command of Lieutenant Richard Cull, and the "Volpe" was boarded by Captain Nicolls with the marines.

The captors suffered no loss.

On the 23rd of June, the 22-gun ship "Porcupine," Captain Henry Duncan, drove on shore and destroyed a French vessel near Civita Vecchia.

At daybreak on the 9th July, the "Porcupine" lay becalmed off Monte Circello, on the Italian coast, when two French gunboats were observed stealing alongshore to the westward, convoying a merchant vessel. The boats of the "Porcupine" were immediately ordered out, under the command of Lieutenant Price, assisted by Lieutenant F. Smith, Lieutenant Renwick, of the Marines, Midshipmen B. J. Featherstone, Charles Adam, and J. O'Brien Butler, and sent in pursuit.

The boats of the "Porcupine," after rowing for about eight hours, under a fierce sun, drove the merchant vessel ashore, and forced the gunboats to take shelter under some batteries which defended the small harbour of Dango. But at this moment, three very suspicious vessels coming from the westward, the commander of the "Porcupine" recalled his boats to go in chase of them, but they, being before a fresh breeze, managed to get into harbour among the gunboats.

Next morning Captain Duncan sent the boats of the "Porcupine," under the orders of Lieutenant Price, to capture a 6-gun polacre, which lay further out of the harbour than the others. The polacre had a crew of thirty men who were prepared for an attack, and were assisted by the guns of two batteries, a tower, three gunboats, and by some troops on the shore. Notwithstanding these means of protection the polacre was boarded, and taken out with only eight men, including Lieutenant Price, wounded on the part of the English.

The "Porcupine" drove another polacre ashore on the same coast on the 21st of July. It was destroyed by the boats under the orders of Lieutenant Smith.

On the 8th of August, a part of the crew of the "Porcupine," in the cutter and jolly-boat, commanded by Lieutenant Smith, cut out and captured the "Concepcion," of four guns, lying at the island of Planosa, within thirty yards of a 6-gun battery.

In this action one seaman was killed, Lieutenant Renwick and one seaman mortally, and seven severely wounded.

For his intrepid behaviour while in command of the "Porcupine's" boats, Lieutenant Price was promoted to the rank of commander; and Lieutenant Smith would most probably have been promoted also, but for the misfortune that Captain Duncan's letter to Lord Collingwood on the subject miscarried, and the duplicate sent some time afterwards did not reach its destination at all, his lordship having died.

While these events were taking place, the 38-gun frigate "Seahorse," Captain John Steward, was quite as busy in the Ægean sea as the "Porcupine" in the Adriatic.

In a treaty made with Admiral Collingwood the year before, the Turks had agreed not to send any ships of war into the Ægean. This promise they would probably have kept had not a party of Epirots settled on two small islands at the mouth of the Gulf of Salonica, and with large boats commenced pirating on ships going to Constantinople.

Captain Steward, of the "Seahorse," which had been stationed by Admiral Collingwood near the Dardanelles, to see that the treaty with the Porte was observed, was applied to by the Turkish government for permission to send a force against the pirates on their commerce, but the request was denied.

Knowing that the "Seahorse" was the only English ship cruising in the Archipelago, the Porte resolved to pay no attention to Captain Steward's refusal to his request, and sent two frigates, two corvettes, two mortar-vessels, and some smaller craft against the pirates on Dromo island.

The pirates, it seems, knew of the treaty between the English and Turks, and sent a fast sailing boat to the island of Sira, where the "Seahorse" was lying. The boat reached the "Seahorse" on the 1st of July, and by the 5th, that vessel had beat its way up to the islands, where the Turkish fleet was lying.

One of the Turkish frigates was the "Badere Zaffer," Captain Scandril Kichuc Ali.

She had upon the maindeck 30 brass guns of three different calibres, two of which were 36-pounders, some were 24-pounders, and ten were 18-pounders. On the quarterdeck were two stern chasers and 14 long 12-pounders, and on the forecastle she had two bow chasers and six other guns, making in all 52 guns.

Her crew comprised 543 men.

The other frigate was the "Alis-Fezan," Captain Duragardi-Ali. It mounted twenty-four 12-pounders on the maindeck, and two mortars in the waist, and had a crew of 230 men.

On arriving near the "Badere Zaffer," the "Seahorse" shortened sail, and the Turk was ordered to surrender. This demand was not complied with, and a broadside, with the guns double shotted, was fired into it.

In the sharp engagement that followed, the Turkish commander tried to close with his opponent and board the "Seahorse," but Captain Steward, fearing the superior force of the Turkish vessel in men, avoided a collision, and trusted wholly to his guns.

The "Ali Fezan" came up on the weather-beam of the "Seahorse," and joined in the fight.

The "Seahorse" hauled up, and, when passing astern of the second Turkish vessel, gave it her starboard broadside with such effect, that the vessel soon after hauled her wind and made off, leaving the "Seahorse" to continue the pursuit of the "Badere Zaffer." The action was continued until the Turkish vessel was nearly a wreck, when its commander, Scandril, was made a prisoner by his officers, who surrendered the vessel.

The loss on board the "Seahorse" was 5 men killed and 10 wounded.

On the "Badere Zaffer" 170 men were killed, and 200 wounded, and the ship was so much injured, that it was got into Malta with much difficulty.

On the 3rd of July, the boats of the 18-gun sloop "Wanderer," and of the schooners "Subtle" and "Ballahon," led by Lieutenant George Spearing, made an attack on the French part of the island of St. Martin. The party consisted of 135 men, who landed without much opposition, took the lower fort, and spiked the guns, without much loss.

On ascending the heights to attack the upper batteries, they were met by a storm of bullets that could not be withstood. Lieutenant Spearing and seven others were killed, and thirty wounded.

In trying to reach the boats nearly all the others were made prisoners, and the "Wanderer" then hoisted a flag of truce.

On communicating with the French commander, it was found that the garrison of the upper fort consisted of 900 men.

On the 1st of August, the boats of the 74-gun ship "Kent," Captain Rogers, and of the 16-gun brig "Wizard," Commander Abel Ferris, were sent ashore at the town of Noli, in the Gulf of Genoa, to destroy a convoy anchored there. The boats were led by Lieutenant William Cashman. Two gunboats were captured, with several vessels deeply laden, and some guns on the shore were destroyed.

The 18-gun sloop "Comet," Commander Cuthbert Daly, captured, off the coast of France, the French 16-gun brig "Sylphe," on the 11th day of August. The action was a running fight, which lasted about twenty minutes, in which 5 men were killed and 5 wounded on the "Sylphe."

No one was injured on the "Comet." The prize was added to the English navy, under the name of "Seagull."

On the 16th of August, the French 16-gun brig "Espiegle" was chased and captured by the 38-gun frigate "Sibyl," Captain Upton. It was added to the navy under the name of "Electra."

Upon the same day, the 4-gun schooner "Rook," Lieutenant Lawrence, bearing despatches to England, was captured off Cape St. Nicholas by two French privateers, one of twelve, and the other of ten guns.

The "Rook" made a gallant resistance for one hour and a half, and her commander, Lieutenant Lawrence, was killed. The mate was mortally wounded; when only five men were left uninjured on the deck she was surrendered.

The English 22-gun ship "Laurel," Captain John Woollcombe, off the coast of Mauritius, on the 12th of September, encountered the French 40-gun frigate "Canonière," Commodore Bourayne.

After a very gallant resistance, in which the "Laurel" was much damaged in the rigging, having had her gaff shot away and her mizenmast left tottering, she surrendered.

The "Canonière" had five men killed and nineteen wounded.

Captain Woollcombe was tried by a court-martial for the loss of his ship, but honourably acquitted.

On the 29th of September, the 14-gun brig "Maria," Lieutenant James Bennett, with a crew of 65 men and boys, gave chase to a vessel steering towards Pointe Antigua, Guadaloupe.

Unfortunately for the "Maria," she overhauled the chase, which proved to be the French 22-gun ship "Département des Landes," manned by 160 men and boys, and commanded by Captain Raoule.

No men could have done more in defending themselves and vessel than the officers and crew of the "Maria," but the enemy was too strong for them.

Lieutenant Bennett was killed by three grape shots in his body.

Five others were killed and nine wounded—the brig was foundering, and the English colours were hauled down.

The French saved the brig from sinking by running it on shore.

On the 1st of October, the 18-gun brig "Cruiser," Commander Lieutenant Thomas Wells, fell in with twenty Danish armed cutters and luggers off Gottenburg. The squadron was attacked, and a vessel mounting ten small guns, and manned by 32 men, was captured.

For this action, Lieutenant Wells was promoted to the rank of commander.

Another loss happened to the English navy on the 3rd of October, when the 18-gun brig "Carnation," commanded by Charles Gregory, fell in with the French 16-gun brig "Palinure," Captain Jance.

A sharp action took place, which lasted for more than an hour, when the two vessels, being much crippled in spars and sails, fell foul of each other.

At that time, Captain Gregory and most of his officers were killed, and the "Carnation" was under the command of William Tiplet, the boatswain.

The French then boarded, and were bravely opposed by the boatswain and ten others, but many of the "Carnation's" crew proved themselves rank cowards, and the vessel was taken.

The "Carnation" had a crew of 117 men, out of which number 8 were killed besides the captain and purser, and 27 seamen and marines were wounded. At the time the vessel was carried by the French, there were more than 70 men who should have fought in defending it, but they did not, and the result of the engagement was received with general indignation throughout England.

At the time of the battle, the captain of the "Palinure" was confined to his cot with the yellow fever, and the vessel was commanded by Lieutenant Enseigne de Vaisseau Huguet, who proved himself a brave and skilful officer.

On the 31st of October, the 32-gun frigate "Circe," Captain Hugh Pigot, found the "Palinure" off Martinique. By using her sweeps, the French brig turned around Diamond Rock, and got under the protection of some batteries on Pointe Solomon.

On getting within shot, the "Circe" commenced an action, which ended in fifteen minutes by the surrender of the "Palinure." On the brig 7 men were killed and 8 wounded. The "Circe" had 1 man killed and 1 wounded.

The 64-gun ship "Africa," lying in the roadstead of Malmo, in charge of a convoy, was attacked on the 20th of October, by a fleet of twenty-five large Danish gunboats and seven large launches. The fleet mounted 80 heavy long guns, and was manned by 1,600 men. The "Africa" being becalmed, was unable to change her position easily, and could return but a very ineffectual fire to the enemy, which, stationed on her bows and quarter, kept up an annoying fire with impunity. Night put an end to this attack, which, had it continued an hour longer, must have resulted in the "Africa" being sunk or captured.

Her three lower masts and yards were badly injured. Her boats were destroyed, and her running rigging and sails were much damaged. Nine seamen and marines were killed, and above 50 wounded. The ship was so much disabled that she had to put into port and refit.

On the 8th of October, the 36-gun frigate "Modeste," Captain George Elliot, captured the French 18-gun corvette "Jéna" in the Bay of Bengal. The "Jéna" was overhauled in a chase of nine hours, and captured after a running fight of fifty minutes. She struck without having a man killed or wounded.

On the "Modeste," William Donovan, the master, a very efficient officer, was killed, and one seaman wounded. The "Jéna" was added to the navy, under the name of "Victor."

On the 10th of November, the 18-pounder 36-gun

frigate "Amethyst," Captain Michael Seymour, when off the French coast, met the French 40-gun frigate "Thétis," Captain Jacques Pinsum, leaving Port Larmour. The "Thétis" was from L'Orient, on the way to Martinique, and had on board a number of troops and 1,000 barrels of flour. The unusual fact of a vessel of war being laden with flour, arose from the regulations England had adopted about neutral vessels, preventing them from being employed by the French in the transportation of their stores.

The "Thétis" continued her course, going about nine knots under full sail, while the "Amethyst" pursued, being on her starboard quarter.

As the distance between the two vessels became less, the studding sails and royals of both were taken in, so that in the coming action they should not be encumbered with more canvas than necessary.

Suddenly the "Thétis" rounded to, on the starboard tack, to fire a broadside, with the hope of crippling her opponent.

The "Amethyst" avoided this, and ranged up on the starboard beam to the windward of the "Thétis," when, as the two vessels paid off, there was some sharp and well-directed firing between them.

The battle was continued with much spirit and skill until the mizenmast of the English frigate broke and fell over the quarterdeck, encumbering it and breaking the wheel.

The "Thétis" would have taken advantage of this opportunity for escaping, but, before she was able to do so, her own mizenmast fell, and the battle again commenced.

When the action had continued about one hour and a half, the "Thétis" put her helm up to board the "Amethyst;" and, just as her bow struck, from the latter ship was fired a broadside that swept the forecastle of the "Thétis," which was covered with troops about to board.

The "Thétis" then dropped alongside, and the fluke of the "Amethyst's" best bower anchor entered her foremost maindeck port, and held her.

The action was then maintained for nearly an hour—the "Thétis" being set on fire several times during that time.

At half-past twelve at night, the guns being silenced on the French frigate, she was boarded and taken possession of.

Out of a crew of 436 men, including 106 soldiers, the "Thétis" had her captain and 172 men killed, and 102 wounded. The "Amethyst" had 20 men killed, and 50 wounded.

The "Thétis" was taken into the English service and named the "Brune."

On the 28th of November, Commander William Coombe, of the 16-gun brig "Heureux," determined to cut out some vessels from the harbour of Mahaut, in Guadaloupe.

The party left the brig in three boats, and, after a pull of six hours, reached the harbour.

One division of the party was landed to storm some batteries on the shore, and the other, led by Captain Coombe, proceeded to the vessels. With only 19 men the captain boarded a schooner of two guns and a crew of 39 men, and, after a desperate fight, captured it.

PORTRAIT OF LORD COCHRANE.

Lieutenant Lawrence, with 45 men, took the nearest battery on the shore and spiked the guns. They then boarded a brig, which they captured, and both prize vessels were got under way.

Before they could clear the harbour, the two vessels got aground.

By this time the inhabitants of the town were fully alarmed, and the shore was lined with soldiers armed with field-pieces and muskets.

The men on the prizes became exposed to a heavy fire, and while Captain Coombe was giving the order to abandon the grounded vessels, he was struck by a 24-pound shot and killed.

Lieutenant Lawrence then abandoned the prizes, and the party returned to the "Heureux."

Early in the month of December a small squadron, under the command of Captain Francis Collier, of the 32-gun frigate "Circe," was cruising about the West Indies.

On the 12th, the French 16-gun brig "Cigne," and two armed schooners, were found anchored off Pearl Rock.

Soon after, one of the schooners was seen trying to reach St. Pierre, and Captain Collier resolved to cut it off. The "Circe," with the 18-gun sloop "Stork," and the 16-gun brig "Epervier," and schooner "Express," stood in shore.

The French schooner, to avoid being captured, ran in shore, under the protection of a 4-gun battery, which was flanked by two others, and protected by a party of soldiers.

These batteries were soon silenced by the fire of the squadron, and the soldiers driven from them.

While this work was being done, it was observed that the "Cigne" and the other schooner were landing their cargoes.

The "Circe," "Stork," and "Express" then bore down to save the property which the crews of the English vessels undoubtedly looked upon as their own.

The barge and two cutters of the "Circe," under the command of Lieutenant Crooke, were then sent off, but with orders not to attack the French brig until her guns had been silenced by the fire of the "Circe" and "Stork."

These vessels then stood in, and commenced firing upon the French vessels and batteries.

Soon after they had begun firing, Lieutenant Crooke rashly dashed on to attack the "Cigne."

The boats were repelled with great slaughter.

One boat was captured, another sunk, and the third managed to escape to the "Circe," but out of 68 men who had gone in the expedition, only 12 returned.

As night had now arrived, the "Circe" and "Stork" stood off shore. They were joined the same night by the 18-gun brig "Amaranthe," Captain Edward Brenton.

The next morning, the French brig "Cigne" was seen trying to get into St. Pierre, and Captain Brenton undertook to destroy her with the "Amaranthe."

This work was done without much difficulty.

The brig was run ashore, the crew driven from it, and it was then boarded and destroyed.

The remaining French vessel, the schooner, was then destroyed by the schooner "Express" and the boats of the "Amaranthe."

This important service would have been performed with but little loss, had it not been for the rashness of Lieutenant Crooke, who, however, suffered much for the act, being severely wounded in four places.

In the month of June, 1808, Admiral Collingwood was an impatient spectator of the surrender of a French fleet of five ships of the line and one frigate in Cadiz harbour to the Spaniards under General Morla.

Collingwood had blockaded that fleet in Cadiz Bay for a long time, and he requested the Spanish general to allow him to assist in the capture of the enemy that had caused him so much trouble, but that officer declined.

To avoid danger from the English fleet, and to keep beyond the range of the fire from the castle, the French admiral, Rosilly, warped his vessels into the Canal of Caraca, but the Spaniards built new batteries, and he was compelled to surrender. "Thus," says Alison, "was the last remnant of that proud armament, which was intended to convey the invincible legions of Napoleon to the British shores, finally reft from the arms of France, and that, too, by the forces of the very allies who were then ranged by their side for the subjugation of England, but had since been alienated by his treacherous aggression."

On the 3rd of September, a Russian fleet in the Tagus, under the command of Admiral Sinawin, surrendered to a squadron under the command of Admiral Sir Charles Cotton.

The English were given the possession of the fleet, on condition that it should be returned to the Russian government within six months after the conclusion of peace between Great Britain and Russia.

During the year 1808 nine English vessels of war were captured by enemies, and two were destroyed. Twenty-two ships of war were wrecked in that year. One was the "Crescent" frigate, wrecked off the coast of Jutland. Only 60 out of a crew of 280 were saved.

CHAPTER XXXIII.

1809.

THE British Navy was at this time very strong indeed.

In Steel's Navy List for February, 1809, the total is set down as 1,140 vessels of all kinds, including 59 hired ships, which being deducted, leave the number of 1,081 as government property.

And this immense fleet was officered and manned by 46 admirals, 59 vice-admirals, 71 rear-admirals, 689 post-captains, 543 commanders, 3,036 lieutenants, 491 masters, and 130,000 seamen and marines.

The total amount granted for the sea service was £19,578,467 13s. 9d.

The first naval action of the year occurred on New Year's Day, when the 10-gun brig "Onyx," Commander Charles Gill, captured in the North Sea the Dutch brig "Manly," of 16 guns, commanded by Captain W. Heneyman.

The "Manly" had 5 men killed, 6 wounded, and several of her guns disabled, and her masts and rigging damaged before she surrendered.

On the "Onyx" but three men were wounded.

The "Manly" had lately belonged to the English navy from which it had been captured.

It was restored to its former place, and the naval medal was granted for its recapture.

Next day the 32-gun frigate "Aimable," Captain Lord George Stuart, off Texel, saw and pursued the French corvette "Iris," of 22 guns (24-pounders).

The chase lasted for twenty-four hours, when the "Iris," which was manned by 140 men, and commanded by Captain Macquet, was overhauled and captured.

She had two men killed and eight wounded.

The "Aimable" had but two men slightly wounded.

The prize was added to the English navy, and called the "Rainbow."

On the 5th of January, the 38-gun frigate "Loire," Captain Schomberg, captured the French 20-gun corvette "Hebe," in latitude 39° 24′ north, and longitude 11° 41′ west.

This prize was added to the navy under the name of "Ganymede;" there being already a "Hebe" in the service.

Another deck was put upon her, and she was mounted with thirty-two guns.

At the latter end of December, 1808, a small expedition, consisting of the British 20-gun ship "Confiance," Captain J. L. Yeo, two Portuguese brigs, and some smaller craft, having on board 550 Portuguese soldiers, commanded by Colonel Manoel Marques, appeared off the coast of South America, and gained some successes, which tempted them to still greater enterprises.

Captain Yeo accordingly determined to make a descent upon the Island of Cayenne, a French colony, and on the 6th of January dropped anchor at the mouth of the principal river of the settlement.

At seven o'clock on the morning of the 7th, Captain Yeo landed with 250 men at a point about half way between Fort Diamant and a battery called Dégras de Cannes, the former mounting two long 24-pounders.

Some Portuguese troops were sent to the left to attack Dégras de Cannes, while the seamen and marines of the "Confiance" attacked Fort Diamant.

Both positions were promptly carried, with but a slight loss in wounded to the attacking party, and the remaining Portuguese troops were disembarked.

As soon as this was done, two other batteries were discovered about a mile up the river on different sides.

The Portuguese cutters "Lion" and "Vinganza," were ordered to attack them, but after a short time, Captain Yeo found that the enemy possessed superior artillery, so he determined to land and storm their positions; and although they had to row right up to the muzzles of the guns, the cool bravery of the assailants soon put the enemy to flight.

But as soon as this service had been accomplished, a large body of French troops, under General Victor Hugues, arrived from the town of Cayenne, and attacked the Portuguese troops at Fort Dégras de Cannes.

Captain Yeo, observing this, pushed off with his boats, and after a smart action of three hours' duration, compelled the French to retire to Cayenne.

About the same time, another force threatened Fort Diamant, but finding the English seamen and marines well prepared to receive them, they quickly followed their general's example.

But one strong post still remained to be taken, and that was the French general's private house, before which he had stationed 100 of his bravest troops, with a swivel and a field-piece.

Captain Yeo, not wishing to risk the lives of his sailors and soldiers, sent in a flag of truce, with a summons to surrender.

Then followed an act of treachery such as is seldom heard of.

The French soldiers allowed the boat with the flag of truce to approach within about twenty yards, then fired two volleys and retired.

Captain Yeo thought that possibly this might have been done without the knowledge of the French commander, and again sent his lieutenant with the flag of truce, but this time the field-piece was fired, and soon afterwards the soldiers began with their muskets.

So the English captain determined that as the French would not listen to reason, they should be convinced by force; so he advanced upon the French general's house with a cheer, the British and Portuguese entering at the front as the French rushed out at the back.

Soon after this the French troops laid down their arms.

While these things were going on upon shore, the "Confiance," though three-fourths of her crew and most of her officers were on shore, did good service.

The French 40-gun frigate "Topaze" appeared in the offing with reinforcements for the garrison; but, not at all daunted, Midshipman George Yeo (the captain's brother), though he had only another midshipman, 25 English sailors, and 20 negroes, on board, prepared for action, and by his bold appearance and skilful tactics drove away an enemy carrying twice as many guns and nearly ten times as many men.

On the 22nd of January, the "Topaze," Captain Lahalle, was driven under the protection of a small battery near Pointe Noire, on the island of Guadaloupe, by the 18-gun ship "Hazard," Captain Cameron, the 32-gun frigate "Cleopatra," Captain Pechell, and the 38-gun frigate "Jason," Captain Maude.

In the afternoon, the "Cleopatra," on getting within musket-shot of the French frigate, received a broadside from it.

The "Cleopatra" anchored on the starboard bow of the "Topaze," and returned the fire.

Several rounds were now exchanged until the

outer spring of the "Topaze's" cable was cut, and she backed in shore with her head towards the "Cleopatra," which raked her with great effect.

The "Jason" and "Hazard" then arrived, and, while the former anchored on the starboard quarter of the "Topaze," the latter opened a fire on the battery.

A few minutes later, the French frigate hauled down her colours.

She had 12 men killed, and 14 wounded, out of a complement of 430 soldiers and sailors.

On the "Cleopatra," the only one of the English vessels that suffered any loss, 2 men were killed and 1 wounded.

The "Topaze" was added to the English navy under the name of the "Alcmène."

On the 8th of February, the boats of the 32-gun frigate "Amphion," Captain Hoste, and the 18-gun brig "Redwing," Commander Edward Down, landed on the island of Melita, and destroyed a large amount of government property, and brought away three guns.

The boats were led by Lieutenant Charles Phillot, and were landed under cover of a fire from the two vessels.

The place was defended by more than 400 French troops.

On the 10th February, the French 18-pounder 40-gun frigate "Junon," was captured off the Virgin Islands by the 4-gun brig "Supérieure," the 38-gun frigates "Latona," and "Horatio," Captains Pigot and Scott, being assisted in the latter part of a running fight by the 18-gun corvette "Driver," Captain Claridge.

In this battle the "Horatio" did the principal part of the fighting, and had 7 men killed, and 17 wounded.

Aboard all the English vessels engaged, there were 7 killed and 23 wounded.

The loss of the "Junon," out of a crew of 323 men, amounted to 130 killed and wounded.

The French captain refused to give up his sword to any officer but Captain Scott, of the "Horatio," that being the principal vessel from which this great loss had been sustained.

The "Junon" was added to the English navy, under the same name, and the naval medal was given to the crews of the "Horatio" and brig "Supérieure," from which the "Junon" had first been seen, and by which it had been followed all day.

On the 14th of February, the 38-gun frigate "Belle Poule," Captain Brisbane, chased the French 26-gun store ship "Var," under the protection of the fortress of Velona, on the Island of Corfu.

The next day the "Var" was attacked as she was lying at anchor, and captured without much resistance.

She was added to the British navy, under the name of "Chichester."

On the 24th of February, Martinique was surrendered to an English squadron, consisting of six ships, nine frigates, and twenty-seven sloops, under the command of Rear-Admiral Sir Alexander Inglis Cochrane, in the ship "Neptune," of 98 guns.

This squadron was accompanied by a fleet of transports, having on board 10,000 troops, under the command of Lieutenant-General Beckwith.

In the battle, which resulted in the capture of the island, the troops on shore were assisted by some of the sailors of the fleet, 6 of whom were killed and 19 wounded.

On the 24th of February, an English squadron of four ships, three of 74 guns, and one of 38, all being under the command of Rear-Admiral Robert Stopford (blue), in the 74-gun ship "Cæsar," drove on shore three French 40-gun frigates, the "Italienne," "Calypso," and "Cybele."

The French vessels went ashore under the batteries of the town of Sable d'Olonne, which failed to protect the vessels from being destroyed.

The only vessels of the English squadron that sustained any loss were the "Defiance," Captain Henry Hotham, and the "Donegal," Captain Heywood.

On the former 2 men were killed and 22 wounded; on the latter 1 man was killed and 6 wounded.

On the French frigates 24 were killed, and 51 wounded.

Admiral Stopford then returned to his station, where he was employed in watching the French fleet near Basque Roads.

Here he was joined on the 25th by Captain Beresford, in the 74-gun ship "Theseus," accompanied by four other vessels.

The blockade was continued by Admiral Stopford until the 7th of March, when Admiral Lord Gambier arrived and relieved him of the command.

Lord Gambier, who commanded the Channel fleet, received a despatch from the Admiralty office, on the 19th of March, that the French fleet in Basque Roads was to be destroyed on an improved plan.

Captain Lord Cochrane was to be sent out to join the fleet, and, acting under the orders of Lord Gambier, was to destroy the French vessels with fire-ships.

The English fleet in Basque Roads at that time consisted of the following ships:—

"Caledonia," 120 guns, Admiral Lord Gambier, Captain Sir Harry Neale, Bart.; "Cæsar," 80 guns, Rear-Admiral Hon. Robert Stopford, Captain Charles Richardson; "Gibraltar," 80 guns, Captain Henry L. Bull; "Hero," 74 guns, Captain James N. Newman; "Donegal," 74 guns, Captain Pultney Malcolm; "Resolution," 74 guns, Captain George Burlton; "Theseus," 74 guns, Captain John P. Beresford; "Illustrious," 74 guns, Captain William R. Broughton; "Valiant," 74 guns, Captain John Bligh; "Bellona," 74 guns, Captain Stair Douglas; and the "Revenge," 74 guns, Captain Alexander Robert Ker.

Lord Cochrane joined the fleet, in the "Impérieuse," on the 3rd of April, and preparations for fitting out the fire-ships were immediately commenced under his inspection.

A few days later, the "Ætna" and the fire-ships arrived with a transport laden with Congreve rockets, and also having Mr. Congreve, the inventor, on board.

Besides the ships we have already named, there were now in the English fleet twenty-one frigates and brigs, besides one schooner and three hired armed cutters.

At the distance of 110 yards, in advance of a line of frigates, they had placed a boom, made of the largest cables, and floated by buoys across the channel.

This boom was moored by anchors weighing five tons each, and a line of battle ships was so moored that the broadside of each ship bore upon and supported the boom.

The topmasts of their ships were on deck, and every preparation possible had been taken to protect them from fire.

DESTRUCTION OF A FRENCH VESSEL AT THE ISLAND OF ST. PIERRE.

The French fleet was now commanded by Vice-Admiral Allemand, and was anchored in a very strong position.

It was covered on one side by the Isle d'Aix, which was garrisoned by 2,000 men, and had batteries mounting 30 long 36-pounders, besides some mortars.

On the other side was the Island of Oleron, but a little more than three miles away, and fortified by strong batteries.

When all the preparations of the English fleet were completed, the attack was made on the 11th of April.

The French were well prepared for the peculiar assault which was to be made upon them.

A fleet of seventy-three boats were stationed near the boom for the purpose of boarding and taking away the fire-ships when they arrived.

Only the fire-ships and frigates, and other smaller vessels of the English fleet moved on that eventful night to the attack.

The line-of-battle ships remained anchored in Basque Roads, seven miles from the scene of conflict.

Lord Cochrane directed the leading fire-ship, which contained 1,500 barrels of powder, 400 shells, and a large number of hand grenades.

About half-past eight in the evening of a very dark night, the cables of the fire-ships were cut, and they started for the boom with a strong north-west wind and a tide running more than two miles an hour.

When within three-quarters of a mile of the French line of the Isle of Aix, some of the fire-ships were ignited.

The "Mediator," under Captain Wooldridge, was taken nearer the enemy, and the direction was so well given that it was the first to break the boom and open a passage for the others.

When the boom was broken, the other fire-ships came down, wrapped in flames, making straight for the enemy's fleet.

Many of the fire-ships had been lighted too soon, and blew up too far from the enemy's line to do any damage.

Captain Newcombe, of the "Beagle," and Captain Joyce, of the "Redpole," and Lieutenant Cookesly, of the "Gibraltar," followed the example of Captain Wooldridge, of the "Mediator," and remained on their vessels before firing and leaving, until they would reach the enemy in a burning state.

In coming back in the boats, these officers with their boats' crews were exposed to much danger while pulling against a strong tide and heavy sea, and under the fire of the enemy from the shore.

On seeing the fireships had broken the boom and were coming down upon them, nearly all the French vessels cut their cables, and in the confusion of trying to get as far away as possible, ran ashore.

The next morning at daylight, Lord Cochrane, who had regained his vessel, the "Impérieuse," commenced urging Admiral Gambier by signals to advance.

His first signal to his Admiral who was lying more than seven miles away, was—

"Half the fleet can destroy the enemy. Seven on shore."

At 6h. 40m. he signalled: "Eleven on shore." And at 7h. 40m., "Only two afloat." His signal at 9h. 30m., was: "Enemy preparing to heave off."

In place of immediately making sail, bearing down upon the enemy, and capturing them, Admiral Gambier called a council of war of flag captains; and, not until eleven o'clock, did the fleet get under way.

After proceeding about half the distance to the place where the fleet was so much wanted, Admiral Gambier gave orders for it to anchor under the belief that, until the tide had risen, it would not be safe to venture amongst the shoals in that part of the Basque Roads.

When Lord Cochrane observed that the enemy's ships were again getting afloat, and that three of them, the "Calcutta," "Varsovie," and "Aquilon," were already on the move, he got under way in the "Impérieuse," and dropped down with the tide towards them.

At 1h. 30m. he made the signal: "405," to Admiral Gambier. "The enemy's ships are getting under sail."

Several other signals followed, with the object of inducing Admiral Gambier to send some of the ships to engage the enemy; but the admiral, believing that the enemy's ships could not be got off, and that there was plenty of time to capture them without incurring any risk, no assistance was sent.

Almost driven frantic at the idea of the enemy escaping after nearly having them in his power, Cochrane determined to attack the French with the force then at his command.

He advanced to the attack in the "Impérieuse," and was followed by Captain Bligh with the "Ætna" bomb-ship, and some frigates and lighter vessels.

At two o'clock in the afternoon, he anchored near the Pallas shoals, and, by means of springs, brought the broadside of the "Impérieuse" to bear on the starboard quarter of the French ship "Calcutta," and occasionally threw a shot from the bow and forecastle guns at the "Varsovie" and "Aquilon."

The shots from the brigs "Insolent," "Growler," and "Conflict," which had followed the "Impérieuse," fell far short of the enemy, a fact that was seen aboard the latter vessel, but was not noticed on the vessels where the shots were fired.

On seeing this, Lord Cochrane ordered a few shots to be fired from his vessel at her three consorts, with instructions that care should be taken to have the shots fall short.

This was done, and the officers of the three brigs took the hint and stood further in.

Before the action had been continued an hour, the "Calcutta" struck her flag, and a few minutes later some more vessels coming to the assistance of the "Impérieuse," the "Varsovie" and the "Aquilon" were also compelled to surrender.

A little later, and the enemy's ship "Tonnerre" was set on fire by her crew, who landed on the Isle of Madame.

This ship blew up soon after.

The "Calcutta" was set on fire by an officer of the "Impérieuse," and it also was blown up with a tremendous explosion of a large quantity of powder and ordnance stores with which she was laden.

The enemy's ships "Ocean," "Cussard," "Regular," "Jemappes," "Tourville," and "Indienne" were lying aground near the mouth of the river Charente, and Rear-Admiral Stopford was sent to destroy them with three fire-ships.

The "Cæsar" and "Valiant" that were to accompany the fire-ships both got aground on a shoal, where they had to remain until the next day.

The "Aquilon" and "Varsovie," which were in the possession of the British, were immovable, and were set on fire.

During the night, while they were burning, the French, thinking they were English fire-ships, kept up a brisk fire upon them for several hours.

On the 13th, an attack was made by the brigs and lighter vessels, by the order of Lord Cochrane, on the enemy's vessels ashore, at the entrance of the Charente.

Very little was effected by this attack, the frigates being unable to come up into the action.

Next day the "Impérieuse" was recalled by a signal from Lord Gambier, and Cochrane was superseded in the command of the flotilla by Captain Wolf, of the "Aigle."

Two days after, the enemy's ship "Indienne" was set on fire and destroyed by her own crew.

Violence of the weather now prevented any attempts for the destruction of the remainder of the French fleet for several days.

On the 20th, the English efforts for its destruction were renewed without success.

These efforts were repeated for several days without any effectual result, and on the 29th, the fleet sailed for England.

The loss of life in the English fleet in this prolonged attack on the French vessels was very small, considering the force on land and water against which they were engaged.

Only two vessels sustained any loss in attacking the grounded ships.

The "Impérieuse" had three men killed and eleven wounded. The "Revenge" had two men killed and fifteen wounded.

The captain of the "Aquilon" was killed in a boat by the side of Lord Cochrane by a shot from the burning ship "Tonnerre."

The "Varsovie" had over 100 men killed and wounded.

It is admitted by the French, that had Lord Cochrane the sole command of the English fleet, the destruction of the French vessels would have been complete.

The French officers were panic-stricken by the fire-ships. Some of them threw their powder overboard, and could have made no resistance had there been no time lost in attacking them.

The officers of the lost French vessels were brought to trial for the loss of their ships, and Captain Lafond, of the ship "Calcutta," was condemned and executed, and two others were imprisoned.

The French were but little more dissatisfied with the engagement in Basque Roads than the English.

Nelson had taught the English to expect from their admiral complete and not partial victories, and complaints began to arise against the prudence of Admiral Gambier in not sending the ships to the support of Lord Cochrane.

Admiral Harvey, who distinguished himself as the commander of the "Téméraire," at the battle of Trafalgar, expressed publicly very strong opinions against the conduct of Admiral Gambier; and Lord Cochrane declared that if the thanks of the House of Commons were moved to Lord Gambier he would oppose it in Parliament.

Lord Gambier demanded a court-martial, which was granted, and much evidence was taken from the captains of the vessels in the expedition.

Lord Gambier was honourably acquitted, and Admiral Harvey was then tried by a court-martial for the words he had uttered, and cashiered and dismissed from the service.

He was, however, shortly afterwards restored. His gallantry at Trafalgar had been too great for him to be permanently dismissed from the navy.

It may interest many of our readers to know that Marryat, afterwards author of Peter Simple, &c., was at this time serving on board the "Impérieuse" as a midshipman.

While the English fleet was thus employed in the Basque Roads, other naval events were elsewhere transpiring, to which we must now call the reader's attention.

In the month of March, the frigate "Arethusa," Captain Robert Mends, was busy doing service off the coast of Spain.

On the 15th of that month, her boats, led by Lieutenant Pearson, destroyed the guns on the batteries of Lequito, then in the possession of the French.

The next day, the same party destroyed a number of small vessels and their cargoes in the river Andero.

Four days later, the boats' crews of the same vessel, led by Lieutenant Steele, destroyed the guns at Baigno, while Lieutenant Pearson, on the same day, landed with another party and destroyed the guns at Puissance.

The boats of the 28-gun frigate "Mercury," Captain Henry Duncan, were sent to cut out two gunboats from the Port of Rovigno, on the coast of Istria, on the 1st of April.

The expedition was under the command of Lieutenant Pell, who conducted it in a very gallant manner.

Both gunboats were moored close to two heavy batteries.

One of the boats—the "Leda"—one 24-pounder and six swivels, was prepared with boarding nettings triced up, but she was carried and taken out under the fire of five guns on an island.

In this expedition one man was killed, and Lieut. Pell* and three seamen wounded.

On the 5th of April, the 18-pounder 36-gun frigate "Amethyst," Captain Seymour, gave chase to the French 40-gun frigate "Niemen," Captain Dupotel, bound for the Isle of France. The pursuit was continued that day, and the French vessel lost sight of during the night. The next morning it was again discovered, and the pursuit renewed.

At one o'clock on this day, the "Amethyst" came near enough upon the larboard quarter of the "Niemen" to fire a broadside, when the latter vessel wore.

The "Amethyst" followed, and ranged alongside the other to the windward.

---

* Lieutenant Pell lost a leg on board the "Loire" at the capture of the "Pallas" on the 6th of February, 1800.

After exchanging broadsides, the "Amethyst" moved ahead of the "Niemen," and bore up across her bows, raking her as she did so, and on the same tack took a position on the enemy's starboard bow.

The action was continued in a very skilful manner on both sides for about two hours, when the "Niemen" caught fire, and, being much injured in the masts, was unable to make sail.

The "Niemen" ceased firing, and the "Amethyst" then discontinuing the action, was brought to at the leeward of her opponent.

Soon after, the "Amethyst's" main and mizen masts fell, and nearly at the same moment the main mast of the "Niemen" went by the board.

Early in the evening the "Arethusa," Captain Mends, came up on the "Niemen's" larboard quarter, and after the exchange of a few shots, the French vessel lowered a light, in token that she surrendered.

Aboard the "Amethyst," 8 men were killed and 26 wounded.

Aboard of the "Niemen," 47 men were killed and 73 wounded. She was a new ship, and was added to the English navy under the same name. The naval medal has been granted for this action.

At the beginning of April, Rear-Admiral Sir Alexander Cochrane, with five sail of the line and some smaller vessels, was blocking a small French fleet at Guadaloupe.

A small squadron, under the command of Capt. Philip Beaver, of the "Acastra" frigate, in assisting the main fleet, succeeded on the 14th in getting possession of some rocky islands called the Saintes, whence they opened a fire on three French ships anchored in the roads beneath, and compelled them to move.

These vessels, which were the 74-gun ships "Courageux," "Polonaise," and "D'Hautpolt," on being driven from their anchorage, proceeded to sea, and were discovered by the 18-gun ship sloop "Hazard," Commander Hugh Cameron, of the inshore squadron.

Word was immediately sent to Admiral Cochrane, who made sail with his fleet to meet the enemy.

A running fight took place, when a portion of the English fleet came upon the enemy—a fight which was principally maintained on the part of the English by the 74-gun ship "Pompee," Captain Fahie, and the 18-gun brig "Recruit," Commander Charles Napier.

On the morning of the 16th, the French ships separated, and the "Recruit" and "Pompee" pursued the "D'Hautpolt."

The frigates "Latona" and "Castor," Captains Pigot and Roberts, joined in the pursuit the same day, and the French ship was brought more fairly into action.

The next morning, seeing no chance of escaping from its foes, the French vessel surrendered.

On board the "Pompee" nine men were killed and thirty wounded.

The "Neptune" had one killed and four wounded; the "Castor" one killed and five wounded, and the "Recruit" one man wounded.

Captain Napier was appointed to the command of the prize, which was called the "Abercromby."

On the 23rd of April, a squadron of three vessels, the "Spartan," "Amphion," and "Mercury," Captains Brenton, Hoste, and Duncan, anchored off the town of Pesaro, then occupied by the French.

After some delay in trying to obtain the public property without injury to the inhabitants, the town was bombarded till the French troops were driven out.

Lieutenant Willes, of the "Spartan," then entered the harbour, and thirteen vessels deeply laden were brought out.

Not a life was lost on the part of the English in this enterprise.

On the 2nd of May, the "Spartan" and "Mercury" before mentioned, entered the port of Cesenatio, where several vessels were lying under the protection of two batteries and a castle.

The frigates anchored within grape shot range of the batteries, and opened fire until their guns were silenced.

The boats under Lieutenant Willes were then sent ashore, and the batteries were captured, and the guns turned on the town.

Twelve vessels in the harbour were captured—the castle and magazine blown up—the batteries destroyed, and the guns spiked. No life was lost in this exploit.

A Dutch 6-gun cutter was driven on shore by the 38-gun frigate "Melpomene," Captain Peter Parker, on the 11th of May.

The boats were then sent, under Lieutenants Plumridge and Rennie, and the cutter was boarded and destroyed, while the assailing party were exposed to the firing of a large party on shore.

In this affair Lieutenant Rennie and five men were severely wounded.

On the 15th of May, the 32-gun frigate "Tartar," Captain Baker, ran a Dutch 4-gun sloop on shore near Felixburgh, on the coast of Courland.

The "Tartar's" boats were sent off to destroy the vessel, and were fired upon by the sloop's crew, which had escaped to the shore with their guns, and were joined by some of the neighbouring inhabitants.

The guns of the sloop were turned upon them, and they immediately fled.

When one of the boat's crew entered the cabin of the sloop, he saw the end of a burning candle fixed in an 18-pound cartridge lying on a train that led to the powder magazine.

The candle was nearly burnt down, and the man had just time to extinguish it between his hands. Half a minute more and the explosion of the magazine would have taken place.

On the 17th of May, the 10-gun brig "Goldfinch," Commander F. Skinner, met the French 16-gun corvette "Mouche," and engaged it in a running action. The corvette escaped, leaving the "Goldfinch" much cut up, and with 3 men killed and 3 wounded.

In the month of May, Vice-Admiral Sir James Saumarez, commander of the Baltic fleet, sent a small squadron, consisting of the 64-gun ship "Standard," Captain Hollis; the 38-gun frigate "Owen Glendower," Captain William Selby, and three sloops, to capture the island of Anholt.

On the 18th, a party of seamen and marines, under Captain Selby, landed, and after making a slight resistance, the Danish garrison of 170 men surrendered. In this action, 1 marine was killed and 2 wounded.

On the 23rd of May, the 38-gun frigate "Melpomene," Captain Warren, was attacked by twenty Danish gunboats, while anchored in the Great Belt off Omoe Island. A breeze springing up as the enemy drew near, the cable was cut, and sail made for closing with the boats, which immediately began a retreat. In a running action, from which the boats managed to escape, the "Melpomene" was much damaged in the sails and rigging, and had 5 men killed and 29 wounded.

On the 31st of May, the boats of the 32-gun frigate "Topaze," Captain Griffiths, in an expedition led by Lieutenant Hammond, boarded and brought out nine vessels anchored in the Road of Demata, under the protection of the fortress of Santa Maura.

Amongst the prizes was one vessel, mounting eight guns and six swivels, and a crew of 55 men; one cutter of 4 guns, a felucca of 3 guns, and two gunboats of 1 gun each.

In this action, 1 man was killed and 1 wounded.

On the 14th of June, the 18-gun brig "Scout," Commander William Raitt, met fourteen vessels, under the protection of two gunboats, off Cape Croisette.

The "Scout" gave chase, but was soon brought up by a calm.

The boats under Lieutenant Battersby were then despatched after the fleet, and seven of them were driven into a port nine miles east of the Cape, where they were followed by the boats.

The seven vessels were brought out with only the loss of 1 man killed and 5 wounded.

On the 17th of June, the French frigate "Félicité" was captured, after a three days' chase, by the 38-gun frigate "Latona," Captain Hugh Pigot.

The "Félicité" had escaped from Guadaloupe on the 14th.

On the 24th of June, Rear-Admiral George Martin, in the 80-gun ship "Canopus," Captain Inglis, and the 74-gun ships "Spartiate" and "Warrior," Captains Laforey and Spranger; the 22-gun-ship "Cyane," Captain Staines, and the 18-gun brig "Espoir," Commander Robert Mitford, with a flotilla of gunboats and a fleet of transports, arrived and anchored at the islands of Ischia and Procida. That night, both the "Cyane" and "Espoir," with twelve gunboats,

THE BOATS OF H.M.S. "SPARTAN" AT CESENATIO.

were sent south of the islands to prevent reinforcements from reaching the garrison of the islands.

The next day (the 25th), this fleet had a brief engagement with the French 44-gun frigate "Ceres," the 28-gun frigate "Fama," and some gunboats which attempted to leave Pozzuoli Bay, and were driven back.

This day the two islands surrendered to Admiral Martin.

On the 26th, the "Cyane" and "Espoir," with the English and Sicilian gunboats, captured eighteen French gunboats and destroyed four. In the engagement the Cyane had 3 men killed and 6 wounded.

On the 27th, the French frigates "Ceres," "Fama," and the gunboats weighed and sailed for Naples. The "Cyane" and "Espoir" pursued. In a two hours' chase the "Cyane" came within pistol-shot of the "Ceres," and opened a fire upon her.

A few minutes later the crew of the "Ceres" was reinforced by some men from Naples, and in this part of the chase the "Cyane" was exposed to the fire of some batteries, the corvette, and the gunboats.

Within a mile and a half of the Mole at Naples, the "Cyane" hauled off. Her fore and main masts were badly wounded, her rigging quite destroyed, and the sails cut to pieces.

In this chase 2 men were killed, and Captain Staines, Lieutenants Hall and Ferrier, John Taylor, midshipman, and 15 men were wounded.

The naval medal was granted for this action.

Lieutenant Robert Pilch, with the boats of the 74-gun ship "Bellerophon," captured on the 19th of June three vessels anchored within the islands off Hango Head. The vessels were taken without opposition; but in order to get them out without loss, a battery on shore, garrisoned by 103 men, had to be taken.

The Russians made some resistance, but it was captured, the guns spiked, and the magazine destroyed. The boats with the prizes returned to the ship, having but 5 men wounded.

On the 6th of July, the 20-gun corvette "Bonne Citoyenne," Commander William Mounsey, when on the way from Halifax to Quebec, encountered the French frigate "Furieuse," mounting two long 18-pounders, six long 8-pounders, and twelve carronades, 36-pounders. The action continued for nearly seven hours, when, just as all hands of the "Bonne Citoyenne" were going to board the "Furieuse," she surrendered.

The corvette in this action had her fore and main topmast shot away, and the three lower masts badly wounded, her rigging cut to pieces, and her boats destroyed, yet only 1 man was killed and 5 wounded.

The "Furieuse" had five feet of water in her hold, her three topmasts shot away, her lower mast in a tottering state, and 35 men killed and 35 wounded.

Great Britain being at war with Russia in 1809, and as this power was then carrying on her hostile designs against Swedish Finland, we had a strong fleet in the Baltic, for the purpose of chastising Russia and protecting our ally.

In this sea the Russians had a strong flotilla, which was principally employed in protecting their coasts, and in conveying troops against Finland.

In the month of July, this flotilla took up a position under Percola Point.

The British fleet in the Baltic was under the command of Admiral Saumarez; and as soon as he arrived in the Gulf of Finland, he sent Captain Martin, in the "Implacable," with the "Melpomene," to watch the motions and the operations of the Russians.

As soon as Captain Martin discovered the situation of the enemy's flotilla, he determined to attempt something against it, the result of which is thus recorded in the following extract of a letter from Captain Martin, of the "Implacable," dated July the 9th:—

"The position taken by the Russian flotilla under Percola Point seemed so much like a defiance, that I considered something was necessary to be done in order to impress these strangers with that sense of respect and fear which his majesty's other enemies are accustomed to show to the British flag.

"I therefore determined to gratify the anxious wish of Lieutenant Hawkey, to lead the boats of the "Implacable," "Bellerophon," "Melpomene," and "Prometheus," which were assembled by nine o'clock last night, and proceeded with an irresistible zeal and intrepidity towards the enemy, who had the advantage of local knowledge, to take a position of extraordinary strength within two rocks, serving as a cover to their wings, and from whence they could pour a destructive fire of grape upon our boats, which, notwithstanding, advanced with perfect coolness, and never fired a gun till actually touching the enemy, when they boarded, sword in hand, and carried all before them.

"I believe a more brilliant achievement does not grace the records of our naval history; each officer was impatient to be the leader in the attack, and each man zealous to emulate their noble example, and the most complete success has been the consequence of such determined bravery; of eight gunboats, each mounting a 32 and 24-pounder, and 46 men, six have been brought out, and one sunk; and the whole of the ships and vessels (twelve in number) under their protection, laden with powder and provisions for the Russian army, brought out, and a large armed ship taken and burnt.

"I have deeply to lament the loss of many men killed and wounded, and especially of that most valuable officer, Lieutenant Hawkey, who, after taking one gunboat, was killed by a grape-shot, in the act of boarding the second.

"No praise from my pen can do adequate justice to this lamented young man; as an officer, he was active, correct, and zealous, to the highest degree; the leader in every kind of enterprise, and regardless of danger, he delighted in whatever could tend to promote the glory of his country. His last words were, 'Huzza! push on! England for ever!'

"Mr. Hawkey had been away in the boats, on different services, since last Monday, accompanied by Lieutenant Vernon, whose conduct in this affair has been highly exemplary, and shown him worthy to be the companion of so heroic a man.

"But while I am induced to mention the name of Mr. Vernon, from his constant services with Mr. Hawkey, I feel that every officer, seaman, and marine has a claim to my warmest praises, and will, I trust, obtain your favourable recommendation to the Lords Commissioners of the Admiralty. Lieutenant Charles Allen, of the 'Bellerophon,' was the senior officer after Mr. Hawkey's death.

"I have just been informed that Lieutenant Stirling, of the 'Prometheus,' who was severely wounded, is since dead; his conduct in this affair was very conspicuous, and Captain Forrest speaks highly in praise of the zeal and activity of his services on every occasion.

" I am sure you will readily believe that Captain Forrest did not witness the preparation for this attack without feeling an ardent desire to command it, but I was obliged to resist his pressing importunity, as a matter of justice to Mr. Hawkey."

The loss of the English in this engagement was Lieutenants Hawkey and Stirling, J. B. Mounteney, midshipman, Benjamin Crandon, second master, and 13 men killed and 37 wounded.

The Russians had 63 men killed, and many were drowned in trying to reach the shore. Out of the 127 prisoners taken, 51 were wounded.

The squadron that furnished the boats and men for this enterprise was comprised of the " Implacable," already mentioned; the " Bellerophon," 74 guns, Captain Warren; the 38-gun frigate "Melpomene," Captain Peter Parker, and the 18-gun sloop " Prometheus," Commander Thomas Forrest.

On the 13th of July, a small squadron, under Captain Edward Henry Columbine, consisting of the 32-gun frigate "Solebay," the 18-gun brig "Derwent," and the 12-gun brig "Tigris," with a transport containing 166 troops, captured Senegal, after a trifling resistance, in which only one man was wounded.

On the 14th of July, the boats of the 18-gun brig " Scout," Commander William Raitt, led by Lieutenant Henry R. Battersby, captured a battery at the port of Carri, between Marseilles and the Rhone.

In capturing this place, there was no fighting, and the English did not have a man wounded, and yet the affair was made a naval medal boat action.

On the night of the 28th of July, the boats of the 74-gun ship " Excellent," with the " Acorn," sloop of 18 guns, and the 16-gun brig " Bustard," under the orders of Lieutenant John Harper, were sent into the harbour of Duin, north of Trieste, after a convoy of small merchant vessels chased in there by the " Excellent" that day.

The only fighting on this occasion was by a party of marines, which was landed to disperse a party of the enemy amongst the rocks.

Six armed Italian gunboats and ten laden vessels were taken away.

Commander Katly Robinson, master of the " Bustard," and 7 men were wounded.

An ill-fated expedition to Walcheren sailed from the Downs, under the command of Rear-Admiral Sir Richard John Strachan, on the 28th of July.

The fleet numbered 245 vessels of war, including mortar vessels and hired revenue cutters and other small craft, and was accompanied by 400 transports, with 40,000 troops, under the Earl of Chatham.

This was one of the most powerful fleets fitted out in modern times, containing thirty-seven ships of the line and twenty-three frigates.

It reached the coast of Holland the next day, and, on the 30th, 20,000 men were landed on the island of Walcheren, and took possession of Middlesburgh, its principal town.

For a few days the fleet and land force pushed on with considerable energy, and success seemed certain.

The troops were within less than two days' march of Antwerp, which was wholly unprepared to receive them.

But the Earl of Chatham had not been appointed to the command of the expedition through his abilities.

He had no experience in warfare, and had only been appointed to the command through Court favour. He had no decision or energy.

In place of pushing on to Antwerp, and capturing it before a force could be raised for its defence, he delayed for the purpose of reducing Flushing—a place that could not have been retained by the enemy had Antwerp been taken.

The breeching batteries were opened on the town of Flushing on the 13th of August, and the bombardment was continued for three days, when the town surrendered, with 5,800 prisoners and 200 pieces of cannon.

With the capture of Flushing, a frigate of 1,100 tons fell into the possession of the British, and it afterwards became the " Laurel."

Three ships were also found on the stocks—a 74-gun ship, a frigate, and a brig.

The frigate and brig were destroyed, but the ship was taken to pieces and removed to Woolwich.

The time lost in capturing Flushing, which was of secondary importance, was fatal to the principal objects of the expedition.

The Dutch and French made the most of the time in making preparations, while the greater part of the English army were remaining idly in camp, almost in sight of Antwerp.

The English seemed unwilling to take the advantage of a surprise, and waited until over 40,000 of the enemy's troops had assembled at Antwerp, and put the batteries in a good state of repair.

By the time the French and Dutch were fully prepared for an attack, several thousand of the English troops were in hospital with fever, engendered by the low and swampy locality in which they were camped.

No attack was made upon Antwerp, and, late in the season, the English returned home, having lost over 7,000 men, principally by fever.

On the night of August 14, Commander Nisbet Willoughby, of the 18-gun ship-sloop " Otter," led the boats of his vessel to attack a French brig, lugger, and gun-boat, under the protection of some batteries at Rivière Noire, Isle of France.

The brig and lugger were captured, but the former being secured to the shore by a cable attached to its keel, had to be left behind. The lugger was taken out.

Only 1 man was killed and 1 wounded in this expedition.

On the 26th of August, the boats of the "Amphion," Captain William Hoste, were sent in the night into the port of Cortelazzo, in the Adriatic, after a convoy of small merchant vessels and six Italian gunboats, under the protection of a battery of four 24-pounders.

The battery was captured by a party under Lieutenant Phillott, and its guns were then turned on the enemy's gunboats, which were soon after boarded and captured by a division under Lieutenant Slaughter.

The gunboats were taken off, besides two trabuceulos with heavy cargoes. Five others were burnt. This is a naval medal boat action.

The 10-gun brig "Diana," Lieutenant William Kempthorne, encountered the Dutch brig "Zephyr," of 14 guns, and engaged it on the 11th of September.

After the exchange of a few broadsides, the main topsail sheet of the "Zephyr" was shot away, and she fell on board the "Diana," and struck.

The Dutch vessel had her first lieutenant and 4 men killed and 8 wounded. No one was injured on the "Diana."

On the 21st of September, Commodore Josiah Rowley, of the "Raisonnable," with the assistance of the officers and crew of his squadron, attacked the harbour of St. Paul's, Isle of Bourbon.

The expedition sailed from Fort Duncan, Island of Rodriguez, in the 32-gun frigate "Nereide," and consisted of 604 men and officers selected from the fleet.

A division under Captain Willoughby was landed and captured some batteries, the guns of which were immediately turned on the shipping.

The squadron at that time entered the bay and opened a fire on the French 40-gun frigate "Caroline," and her consorts, which were soon compelled to surrender.

Several of the French officers, rather than surrender their vessel, cut their cables, and drifted ashore, but were all got off without loss.

In this enterprise, the English had 15 men killed, and 58 wounded.

The vessels captured were the "Caroline," the 14-gun brig "Grappler," the "Europe," and "Streatham," two of the Dutch East India Company's ships, and six small vessels.

Before leaving the port, the batteries and magazines of the place were all destroyed.

On the 17th of October, the boats of the 18-gun brig "Pelorus," Commander Thomas Huskisson, and the 18-gun ship sloop "Hazard," Commander Hugh Cameron, were sent to attack a privateer schooner moored under the batteries of Sainte Marie Guadaloupe.

The expedition was led by Lieutenant James Robertson, and although the party was exposed for some time to a heavy fire of grape and musketry, the schooner was boarded and captured.

She was found secured to the shore by a chain cable around her mast, and was set on fire and blown up.

In this affair 6 men were killed and 7 wounded.

On the 26th of October, a squadron of six ships under Rear-Admiral George Martin (Red) in the "Canopus," of 80 guns, Captain Charles Inglis, drove on shore near Frontignan in the Gulf of Lyons, the French 80-gun ship "Robust," and the 74-gun ship "Lion," belonging to the squadron of Admiral Baudin, which had escaped from Toulon. The two ships were set on fire by their own crews and soon after blew up.

The remainder of the French fleet that had escaped from Toulon under Admiral Gantaume consisted of seven merchant vessels, the 16-gun storeship "Lamproie," two armed bomb-ships "Victoire," and "Grandeur," and the xebeck "Normandie." They anchored in the Bay of Rosas under the protection of some large batteries. For the capture or destruction of these vessels, Captain Benjamin Hollowell, of the "Tigre," and a small squadron commanded by Admiral Collingwood, proceeded to attack them.

The expedition reached the Bay of Rosas on the evening of the 31st of October, and anchored about five miles from the town.

The boats of the fleet, under Lieutenant John Tailour, were immediately sent off, and as they drew near the French vessels, the alarm was given, and the seamen gave three loud cheers and dashed on. The "Lamproie" was the first vessel boarded, and was captured after an obstinate resistance, and the "Victoire" and "Normandie" soon shared the same fate.

By daylight the next morning all the French vessels, eleven in number, were either burnt or taken out; and most of this work was performed while the boat crews were exposed to a sharp fire from Castle Rosas and other batteries, and from troops stationed on the shore.

In this engagement the English lost 15 men killed and 55 wounded.

During the month of October several places in the East were captured by the English.

Zante, Cephalonia, surrendered to a naval and military force under Captain John Spranger, of the 74-gun ship "Warrior," and Brigadier-General Oswald.

Cerigo surrendered to Captain Brenton, of the 38-gun frigate "Spartan," and some troops under Major Clarke; and Ithaca to Commander George Crawley, of the "Philomel," and a few troops under Captain Church.

On the 2nd of November, the 18-gun corvette "Victor," Commander Edward Stopford, was captured by the French 40-gun frigate "Bellone." Two of the "Victor's" men were wounded.

During the month of November, an English

squadron of six vessels, under Captain John Wainwright, of the 36-gun frigate "Chiffonne," was sent into the Persian Gulf against the pirates, by whom it was infested.

By this force the town of Ras-al-Khyma was destroyed on the 13th of August, together with about fifty vessels in the port.

The town of Linga was visited the next, and twenty large piratical vessels were destroyed there.

Only four men were wounded on the part of the English.

On the 13th of December, the 18-pounder 38-gun frigate "Junon," Captain John Shortland, and the "Observateur" brig, of 16 guns, Commander F. A. Wetherall, discovered four sail, and bore down towards them.

On coming nearer the vessels, Captain Shortland saw that they were frigates, which answered his

THE SURVIVORS OF THE CREW OF THE "CRESCENT" ON A RAFT.

On the 27th, eleven other pirate vessels were destroyed at the town of Luft.

In the different engagements with these pirates, the English squadron had 5 men killed and 34 wounded.

On the 12th of December, the boats from a small squadron, under the command of Captain George Miller, of the 38-gun frigate "Thetis," were sent under orders of Commander William Elliot, of the brig "Attentive," to cut out the French 16-gun brig anchored under the protection of a fort at Hayes, on the island of Guadaloupe. The fort was captured with little trouble, after which the brig was also taken, brought over, and added to the navy under the name of "Guadaloupe."

private signal by hoisting Spanish colours. The vessels were the French 40-gun frigates "Renommée," Commodore Roquebert, and the "Clorinde," Captain Saint Cricq, and the 40-gun frigates "Loire" and "Seine."

Captain Shortland made the Spanish private signal, and it was correctly answered by the "Renommée."

Deceived by the one he was trying to deceive, Captain Shortland continued approaching, until suddenly the French vessels hauled to the wind on the starboard tack in line of battle.

The "Renommée" now substituted French for Spanish colours, and poured a heavy broadside into the bows of the "Junon."

The latter vessel then ran under the stern of the

other, and gave it a raking broadside. The "Observateur" was then brought to on the larboard tack, and commenced firing at the French frigate at too great a distance to do any execution.

The French frigate "Clorinde" then joined in the battle by coming up on the starboard beam of the "Junon;" and, while those two vessels were engaged, the "Renommée" wore round on the starboard tack, and came down upon the "Junon," striking her upon the larboard beam.

The "Loire" and "Seine" then came up, one at the bow and the other at the stern of the "Junon," and opened fire.

The "Loire" had on board 200 troops, who kept up a destructive fire of musketry.

Captain Shortland was now struck by a grape-shot, which broke one of his legs, and, being otherwise severely wounded by splinters, he was taken below, and the command devolved on Lieutenant Samuel Deecker.

The "Clorinde" now grappled the "Junon," and her crew attempted to board, but were repulsed by a part of the latter's crew, led by Lieutenant John Green, of the Marines, who was killed in the strife.

A few minutes later, and the British frigate was boarded on all sides, and the ensign was hauled down.

The officers and men had done all that men could do in saving their vessel, but the odds were too great against them.

The "Observateur" hauled to the wind, and escaped without loss.

The "Junon" had a crew of 224 men, and of this number 20 men were killed and 40 wounded, including the captain.*

Although but two days' sail from Guadaloupe, the "Junon" was too much damaged to be taken there, and was burnt.

On the 14th of December, the 36-gun frigate "Melampus," Captain Richard Hawkes, after a chase of twenty-eight hours, captured the French 16-gun brig "Béarnais," off Guadaloupe.

The French frigate had one man killed and seven wounded, and two men were wounded on the "Melampus."

The "Béarnais" was added to the English navy, under the name of "Curieux."

On the 17th of December, the 18-gun corvette "Rosamond," Commander Benjamin Walker, captured the French 16-gun corvette "Pampillon," which made but a trifling resistance.

She was the consort of the "Béarnais," mentioned above.

---

* Captain Shortland died of his wounds, on the 21st day of January, 1810, and was buried by the French, at Basse Terre, Guadaloupe, with military honours.

By the 15th of December, several English frigates had assembled, to obtain some revenge for the loss of the "Junon" three days before.

The "Observateur" had conveyed the news of the loss of that vessel to Captain Ballard, of the 38-gun frigate "Blonde," who, with the 38-gun frigate "Thetis," Captain Miller, and the 18-gun sloops "Hazard" and "Cygnet," made sail in search of the French squadron, and the next day they were joined by the 18-gun brigs "Scorpion" and "Ringdove."

On the 17th, the 32-gun frigate "Castor," Captain William Roberts, joined the squadron, with the intelligence that two days before he had been chased by the "Renommée" and consorts.

At daybreak the next morning, the frigates "Loire" and "Seine" were seen sailing from Basse Terre, and all sail was made to cut them off.

The two French frigates being cut off from the harbour they wished to gain, entered the cove of Anse la Burque, where they anchored, head and stern protected by a battery on each side of the cove.

That evening the fleet was joined by the 36-gun frigate "Freija," Captain John Hayes.

The next morning (the 18th), the 74-gun ship "Sceptre," Captain Samuel I. Ballard, arrived from Martinique, and preparations were made for an attack.

The "Blonde" and "Thetis" were sent into the bay to attack the frigates, while the "Sceptre" and "Freija" bombarded the batteries.

The "Loire" and "Seine" frigates were both compelled to surrender, but one which had caught fire blew up, and a portion of the burning wreck falling on the other, it was also burnt.

In the evening the fort was stormed, and the French colours were hauled down by Captain Cameron, of the "Hazard," who was killed an hour after by a grape shot as he was entering a boat to return to his vessel.

The total number killed of the English fleet was nine, and twenty-two were wounded.

The naval medal was given to those engaged in the destruction of the two frigates.

During this year six vessels were captured by the enemy, and one was destroyed.

Eighteen vessels were wrecked, six foundered, and one was burnt, namely the "Unique," Captain Thomas Fellowes, which was destroyed by fire at Basse Terre, in the Island of Guadaloupe, on the 31st of May.

Luckily the greater part of the crew escaped.

During the same year the French lost twenty-two vessels, of which nine were captured, and thirteen destroyed by the English.

Two Russian frigates were captured, and several small Dutch and Danish gun vessels.

CHAPTER XXXIV.
NAVAL DOINGS OF THE YEAR 1810.

THE French coast was so closely blockaded during the year 1810 that the enemy's fleets could not venture out to sea. However, Napoleon still went on building ships, and the British cruisers continued their daring practice of picking up any French vessels that dared venture out from shore.

True, towards the latter end of the summer, some ten sail of the line endeavoured to sail from the Dutch coast; but Rear-Admiral Sir R. J. Strachan, cruising off Flushing, promptly chased them back to port.

The first engagement of any consequence took place on the 10th of January, when the 10-gun brig "Cherokee," Commander Richard Arthur, attacked seven luggers lying near the pier-head of Dieppe.

The "Cherokee" first ran between two of them, and laid on board of one, which was then captured. It was the "Aimable Nelly," of 16 guns and a crew of 60 men; 2 of whom were killed and 8 wounded.

This vessel was taken out while her captors were exposed to a heavy and sharp fire from the other luggers.

A day after this, the 18-gun brig "Scorpion," captured the French 16-gun brig "Orestes," off Guadaloupe, in an action of two hours and a half.

The "Scorpion" had 4 men wounded, and the "Orestes" had 2 men killed. The prize was added to the English navy under the name of "Wellington."

On the 17th of January, the boats of the 36-gun frigate "Freija," Captain John Hayes, were sent under the orders of Lieutenant David Hope, to capture a brig and two other vessels anchored in Baie Mahaut, Guadaloupe.

As the boats entered the harbour they were exposed to the fire of grape shot from two batteries, and also from the fire of the brig, which brought six guns to bear in one broadside.

The brig was boarded and carried, its crew escaping to the shore. The boats' crews then landed and attacked the batteries, both of which were captured, the guns spiked, and the magazines destroyed. A large ship and schooner were then destroyed, and the armed brig was towed out of the harbour.

The Island of Guadaloupe surrendered to an English squadron under the command of Vice-Admiral Sir Alexander Cochrane, and a land force under General Beckwith, on the 6th of February.*

On the 7th of February, a court-martial was held at Portsmouth on Captain Warwick Lake, of the ship "Ulysses," for having, on the 13th of December, 1807, put a seaman named Robert Jeffrey on shore, on a desert island in the West Indies. He was dismissed from the service.

On the 10th of February, the 10-gun schooner "Thistle," Lieutenant Peter Proctor, captured the Dutch corvette "Havik," of ten guns.

The "Thistle," out of a crew of fifty men and boys, had one man killed, her commander, and six men wounded.

The "Havik" had one man killed and eight wounded.

The 22-gun ship "Rainbow," Captain James Wooldridge, and the 18-gun brig "Avon," Commander Henry Frazer, had, on the 13th of February, a running fight with the French 40-gun frigate "Nereide," which cut away their masts and the greater part of their standing and running rigging, and then left them without attempting to capture either.

The "Rainbow" had ten men wounded, the "Avon" two men killed and seven wounded.

On the 13th of February, eight boats of a squadron, under Captain Sir Joseph Sidney Yorke, of the 80-gun ship "Christian VII.," in the Basque Roads, were sent, under the orders of Lieutenant Henry S. Guion, to destroy three French vessels ashore on Point Chantillon.

On the way they were met by nine French gunboats, that came out from the Isle d'Aix to meet them.

The French gunboats were made to retreat, and the three vessels were set on fire and destroyed.

There was little or no fighting in the affair, not a man being wounded on the part of the English, yet the naval medal was given for it—for what reason no one at the present day has the slightest knowledge.

Some brilliant exploits were performed highly honourable to the British arms in the year 1810; none more so than the capture of Amboyna, one of the Malacca islands, and the last of which was

---

* This is the date given by most naval histories for the surrender of Guadaloupe, but "Toone's Chronology of the Reign of George III.," gives the 8th of February as the date of that event.

effected by a small party of seamen and marines, and seventy-six troops.

Captains Tucker, Montague, and Spencer, with the "Dover," "Cornwallis," and "Samarang," proceeded up the harbour on the 9th of February, and made good their landing on the 15th, their whole force amounting to 401 men, under the command of Captain Court, of the Honourable East India Company's Coast Artillery.

The ships began the attack by cannonading the fort and surrounding batteries, which they continued two hours and a half, although exposed to a constant fire of hot shot from the heights on the left of the tower.

In the meantime, the force on shore had stormed the battery of Warmatoo, nothwithstanding the resolute opposition of the enemy, who suffered the loss of two officers and one dangerously wounded.

On the retreat of the enemy, their guns were used against them to some effect.

Captain Court proceeded vigorously in his arduous enterprise along the heights in order to turn the position of the enemy at Batter Gantong, which commanded the town of Amboyna.

After a very fatiguing march, ascending and descending difficult hills, over which there were no roads, and so steep and rugged that the men had to lay hold of the bushes to assist them, both in their ascent and descent, they at last gained an eminence from whence they could command the enemy, who then retired precipitately, and then the battery was entered without further opposition.

Matters having so far succeeded, a summons was sent to the governor on the morning of the 17th.

A capitulation was shortly agreed to, by which, on the 19th, the island was surrendered to the British.

It was agreed that the garrison should be sent to Java at the expense of the British.

The island was defended by about 130 Europeans, and about 1,000 Javanese and Mandarees, exclusive of the Dutch inhabitants, and 2,000 men, the crews of three vessels that were sunk in the harbour.

The total loss of the British in this affair, and at the destruction of a Dutch port at Poolo Combu, in the Celebes, amounted only to five killed and nineteen wounded.

There were also taken seven vessels of war of various descriptions, forty-two government supply vessels, and three neutrals; in all fifty-two.

By Captain Tucker's letter from Amboyna, dated March 1st, it appears that the valuable islands of Saparona, Harouka, and Nassau-Laut, as well as those of Boura and Manippa, likewise surrendered to the British forces; a considerable conquest, considering the small force employed on the occasion.

On the 21st of February, the 38-gun frigate "Horatio," Captain George Scott, captured the French store-ship "Necessité," of 26 guns and a crew of 186 men, commanded by Lieutenant Bonnic.

This vessel was captured after a long chase, and an action of one hour.

On the 11th of April, the 10-gun cutter "Sylvia," Lieutenant A. V. Downy, destroyed, in the Straits of Sunda, a large lugger-rigged prahu, mounting three 18-pounders.

On the 26th of the same month, she captured the Dutch brig "Echo," off the coast of Java.

The "Sylvia" had four men killed, and three wounded, the Dutch brig three killed, and seven wounded.

After the capture of the "Echo," Lieutenant Downy, took possession of two lugger transports, each manned by 60 men and mounting two long 9-pounders.

The naval medal was given for the capture of the "Echo."

On the 12th of April, the late British 22-gun ship "Laurel," then under the name of "Esperance," from the Mauritius, was captured by the 32-gun frigate "Unicorn," Captain Alexander Robert Kerr.

The "Laurel" was restored to the navy.

On the 16th of April, an English squadron of two 74-gun ships, two frigates, and one brig, under the command of Captain George Eyre, of the 74-gun ship "Magnificent," captured the Island of Santa Maura.

The total loss of sailors and troops amounted, on the part of the English, to 24 killed, 127 wounded, and 17 missing.

On the 24th of April, the boats of the 10-gun cutter "Surly" and the gun-brig "Firm," Lieutenants Welch and Little, were sent to the mouth of the Piron to capture the French privateer "Alcide."

The privateer had run ashore to prevent being taken, and was then under the protection of 400 troops.

The boats were led by Sub-Lieutenant Joseph Hodgkin, and the privateer was captured with the loss, on the part of the English, of the second master killed and one man wounded.

On the 30th of April, Captain Nesbit J. Willoughby, of the 36-gun frigate "Nereide," landed with a part of his crew at Jacotel, Isle of France, to capture a large merchant ship anchored there.

Before this could be accomplished, three batteries were stormed, captured, and the guns spiked.

In this work the party from the "Nereide," which only numbered 100 men, were opposed by upwards of 600, yet this number of the enemy were defeated with only a loss on the part of the English of 1 man killed and 5 wounded.

On the 3rd of May, the 38-gun frigate "Spartan," Captain Brenton, while off the port of Naples, encountered a French squadron, consisting of the 40-gun frigate "Ceres," the 28-gun ship "Fama," the 8-gun brig "Sparviere," the "Achille," of 10 guns, and seven gunboats.

The gunboats mounted one long 18-pounder, with crews of 40 men each.

This squadron mounted 95 guns, and, including 400 Swiss mercenaries, was manned by 1,400. To meet this force, the "Spartan" had 46 guns, and 258 men.

Notwithstanding the superiority of the French in men and guns, they were defeated.

The "Ceres" got under the protection of some batteries, the "Fama" was towed by the gunboats to the same refuge, and the brig, "Sparviere" was captured after having 11 men killed.

The loss on the other French vessels was 30 killed and 90 wounded.

On the "Spartan" 11 were killed and 21 wounded.

Captain Brenton was presented by the Patriotic Fund with a sword of the value of 100 guineas.

The boats of the 38-gun frigate "Armide," Captain Hardyman, the 18-gun brig "Cadmus," Commander Thomas Fife, and the gunboats "Monkey" and "Daring," led by Lieutenant Samuel Roberts, entered the harbour of Fosse de l'Oye, in the Isle of Rhé.

On the night of the 3rd of May, seventeen vessels were captured at anchor, but none of them could be brought out, and at daylight the boats had to return to their ships without a single prize they had taken. In this affair Lieutenant Townley and two seamen were killed, and three men wounded.

On the 12th of May, the 18-pounder 36-gun frigate "Tribune," Captain George Reynolds, encountered, off the Naze of Norway, four Danish brigs and several gunboats.

Although the brigs mounted from 18 to 20 guns each, they were put to flight, and, followed by the gunboats, made all sail for the port of Mandal.

The "Tribune" was much disabled, and had 9 killed and 15 wounded.

The boats of the "Amphion" and "Cerberus," under Lieutenant William Slaughter, landed near the town of Grao, in the Gulf of Trieste, on the 29th of June.

The boats' crews were first attacked by a small body of French troops, of whom they captured a sergeant and 38 men.

The party then entered the harbour, and took possession of twenty-five vessels.

Five of these vessels, after great exertions, were taken out by their captors, and eleven were burnt.

In this affair four marines were killed and eight men were wounded, including Lieutenant Brattle.

On the 8th of July, a squadron, under the command of Captain Nesbit Willoughby, captured the Isle of Bourbon.

Most of the fighting done in the capture of this island was by the troops, 22 of whom were killed and 79 wounded.

On the 8th of July, an English squadron, consisting of the frigates "Caroline" and "Piémontaise," Captains Christopher Cole and Charles Foote, and the 18-gun brig "Barracouta," Commander Richard Kenah, with the transport brig "Mandarin," arrived from Madras at Banda island.

This island was fortified with ten sea batteries and two strong castles, all the fortifications mounting together 138 guns.

PORTRAIT OF G. COCKBURN.

Captain Cole, with a force of 140 seamen and marines, landed that night in the midst of a violent storm, and attacked the first battery that came in their way. It was one mounting ten long 18-pounders. The sentinel was killed, and 60 of the Dutch garrison captured without firing a shot.

Castle Belgica was next attacked and taken; Colonel Daring, its commandant, and 10 soldiers of the garrison being killed and 44 officers and men taken prisoners. The rest of the garrison escaped.

The next day the island was surrendered. An immense amount of wealth was captured at Banda, and Captain Cole received the thanks of the Admiralty, the Governor-General of India, and of the Commander-in-Chief.

Four valuable swords were presented to him for this conquest, one being from the crew of his vessel, the "Caroline."

On the 9th of July, three boats from the frigate "Alceste," Captain Murray Maxwell, under the orders of Henry Bell, master, were sent off to attack a convoy of merchant ships protected by a large xebeck. Five of the vessels were driven ashore and three were captured with but little difficulty.

Before the prizes could be brought out, it was necessary that the xebeck should be captured.

Lieutenant Bell led a party in the yawl and barge to accomplish this, but the feat was only performed by much hard fighting.

Out of the 22 men who boarded the xebeck, 16 were either killed or badly wounded.

Lieutenant Bell, before the xebeck was boarded, was severely wounded in the breast by a grape-shot, but succeeded in concealing the injury until the fight was over.

Mr. Addie, a young midshipman, when in the

act of boarding, had his left arm shattered to pieces, but went on and did his duty with the rest, no one knowing that he was wounded till some time after the battle was over.

On the 25th of July, the boats of the 32-gun frigate "Thames," Captain George W. Waldegrave, and the 18-gun brigs "Pilot" and "Weasel," under the command of Henry Prescott, commander of the latter vessel, assisted by Lieutenant Collier, of the "Thames," attacked an enemy's convoy of transports from Naples.

They were laden with stores and provisions for Murat's army at Scylla, and were protected by several gunboats.

The transports were run aground in a place where they were under the protection of two batteries.

Covered by the fire of the brigs, the boats landed, and the enemy's vessels were all burnt, except a few that were brought away.

On the 13th of August, the Isle de la Passe, near the entrance to Bourbon Harbour, Isle of Bourbon, was captured by the boats of the "Sirius," Captain Pym, and the "Iphigenia," Captain Lambert.

The party was despatched in five boats, and consisted of 71 officers and men, under the command of Lieutenant George R. Norman.

The island was captured with a loss to the English of 5 men killed and 12 wounded.

The ship "Sirius," while cruising off Port Louis, on the 21st of August, saw the ship "Windham," which, along with the "Ceylon," had been captured by the French on the 4th of July. Lieutenant Watling was sent with 11 men to board it.

The boats left the "Sirius" in the twilight of early morning, and on drawing near, they were surprised to find that the "Windham" was apparently armed with 30 guns, and near the French batteries.

Through great heedlessness, the party had left the "Sirius" without arms.

Without the slightest hesitation as to what he should do, Lieutenant Watling ordered his men to board the enemy.

Only armed with the boat-stretchers, the 11 men mounted the deck of the "Windham," and captured it, although the vessel mounted 26 guns, was manned by 30 French sailors, and within range of the French batteries.

A few minutes later, the batteries opened fire on the "Windham," and before she could be taken beyond their reach, one French prisoner and three Lascars were wounded.

In the meantime, Captain Willoughby, in the "Nereide," was at Isle de la Passe, surrounded by a superior force that could easily have captured him had they made a vigorous effort.

Word was immediately sent to Captain Pym, of the "Sirius," who came to the assistance of the "Nereide."

On the 23rd, the "Iphigenia" and "Magicienne," Captains Lambert and Curtis, joined company, and the four frigates ran down the channel to the Grand Port, where the heaviest part of the French force was lying.

In sailing down to attack the enemy the "Sirius" grounded on a coral rock when just within range of the French vessel's guns.

The "Magicienne" also grounded when within about 400 yards of her station.

The French squadron consisted of the "Bellone" and "Minerva" frigates, the "Victor" sloop and the "Ceylon" prize.

Between the two squadrons a tremendous cannonading now began, which lasted for about an hour, when the "Ceylon" struck her flag.

A boat was lowered to take possession, but before it was reached, her cables were cut and she was run for the shore.

In the meantime, the "Bellone," with her broadside bearing fair upon the "Nereide," continued pouring upon it a destructive fire.

Captain Willoughby was wounded early in the action by a splinter, that tore one eye out of its socket.

The first and second lieutenants were wounded, the first mortally.

More than half of the crew and soldiers aboard were killed or wounded.

Many of the guns were dismounted. Under these circumstances Captain Willoughby gave orders to cease firing, and for what was left of his crew to remain below, sheltered from the enemy's fire.

A communication was then held with Captain Pym, who urged Captain Willoughby to leave his ship and go to the "Sirius," but this he would not do.

A French boat then came off to learn why the "Nereide" had ceased firing, and its officer was told that she had struck.

It started to go back, but having been damaged by shot-holes, it was unfit for the return voyage, and had to turn back to the "Nereide" to save its crew.

The "Bellone" still continued its merciless fire, and kept it up until nearly two o'clock the next morning.

At daylight on the 24th, she again opened fire on the unfortunate "Nereide," which displayed French colours in the fore rigging, to signify that she had surrendered, but the firing did not cease.

At the mizen topgallant head there was a small union jack flying.

The rigging was all cut away, as well as the halyards by which it had been hoisted.

The flag could not be struck, but the mast was cut away, and the firing then ceased.

The total killed and wounded on board the "Nereide" in this action was 230, leaving just 51 unharmed of the 281 officers and men on board at the time the action commenced.

This heavy loss is partly ascribed to the fact that the vessel was lined with fir wood, which on being struck by a shot, flew over the deck in splinters.

The "Magicienne" had 8 men killed and 20 wounded.

The "Iphigenia" had 5 seamen killed and 13 wounded.

No one was injured on board the "Sirius." On the French ships there were 37 officers and men killed and 112 wounded.

The "Magicienne" could not be moved off, and was set on fire. She blew up with colours flying.

No efforts could get the "Sirius" afloat, and she was set on fire, after most of her stores had been taken out. She blew up on the 25th.

The "Iphigenia" was warped out, and returned to the Isle de la Passe.

On the 27th of August, a French fleet arrived off this place, under the command of Commodore Hammelin, and the next day Captain Lambert surrendered on condition that the officers and crew should be sent to the Cape of Good Hope.

It is said that the three English captains (Pym, Lambert, and Curtis) and their men, on being taken to Port Louis, were treated in a shameful manner and robbed of nearly everything in their possession.

On the 9th of September, seven boats, under orders of Lieutenant Thomas Pettman, left the 98-gun ship "Dreadnought," Captain Collard, off the coast of France, to capture a ship anchored in a creek near Ushant.

As the boats drew near, they were met with a lively fire of musketry from troops on the shore.

Hastening on, they boarded and took the ship, meeting with but little or no resistance from its crew.

Between 500 and 600 soldiers were on a precipice above the vessel, and now opened a fire upon the captors, as they commenced preparations to take the vessel out. Six men were killed, 31 were wounded, and 6 were missing.

On the 10th of September, the 18-pounder 38-gun frigate "Africaine," Captain Robert Corbet, joined Commodore Rowley's squadron at Bourbon. The next day she ran a French schooner into a small creek in the Isle of France.

Two boats were sent, under the orders of Lieutenant George Forder, to bring the schooner out.

The vessel was boarded, but so severe was the fire from a large party of troops on the banks of the creek, that the boat crews were compelled to leave without bringing the schooner away.

In this expedition 2 men were killed and 16 wounded.

Two French frigates and a brig—the 38-gun frigate "Iphigenie" (late "Iphigenia") and "Astree," and the "Entreprenante,"—were seen from Bourbon standing towards St. Denis, on the 12th of September.

Commodore Rowley, in the "Boadicea," with the 18-gun sloop "Otter," and the gun brig "Staunch," went out to meet them.

The "Africaine," at that time, was just returning to Bourbon with the men who were wounded in trying to capture the French schooner the day before. She also sailed in chase of the French vessels.

Darkness prevented a meeting between the two squadrons on that day, but early the next morning the "Africaine" found herself within musket shot of the "Astree."

Fearing that the enemy would enter Port Louis before the "Boadicea" and her consorts could arrive, Captain Corbet determined to engage the enemy at once, and a double-shotted broadside was given to the "Astree."

This was immediately returned; and, at the second broadside from the French frigate, Captain Corbet was mortally wounded.

The French frigate "Iphigenie" soon after bore up, and the "Africaine," under the command of Lieutenant Joseph Tullidge, had to combat with the two.

Soon after, the "Africaine" lost her jibboom and foremast, and then her mizentopmast was shot away.

Lieutenant Tullidge had received four severe wounds, and, although he refused to leave the deck, his wounds must have demanded more of his attention than the ship.

The second lieutenant, George Forder, was shot through the breast with a musket ball, and had been taken below.

The sailing-master, Samuel Parker, had his head taken off by a cannon-ball.

The colours were then hauled down, and, after a few more rounds, which killed several men, including Captain Elliot, of the army, the enemy ceased firing.

On board the "Africaine," 49 men were killed and 114 wounded.

On the French frigates, 10 were killed and 25 wounded.

The French took possession of the "Africaine;" but it was recaptured in the afternoon of the same day by the "Boadicea" and "Otter."

Lieutenant Tullidge, after being tried and honourably acquitted for the surrender of the frigate, was a few months after promoted to the rank of commander.

On the 18th of September, the 18-pounder 32-gun frigate "Ceylon," which had just arrived from Madras to join Commodore Rowley's squadron, was overhauled by the French Commodore Hammelin, in the 40-gun frigate "Venus," with the 16-gun corvette "Victor."

The "Ceylon" tried to reach Bourbon, but was overtaken and compelled to fight.

After losing her fore and maintopmast and gaff, besides being in other ways much crippled, she struck, having 10 men killed and 31 wounded.

In the afternoon of the same day, the "Venus" and "Victor" were seen with their prize by the "Boadicea," which immediately sailed in pursuit, followed by the "Otter" and "Staunch."

The next morning the "Boadicea" ran alongside the "Venus," and after a sharp action of ten minutes, compelled her to strike.

The French frigate had nine men killed, and fifteen wounded.

Two men were wounded on the "Boadicea."

With the capture of the "Venus," the "Ceylon" once more fell into the hands of the English, and Captain Gordon was again appointed to command her.

The "Venus" was added to the navy under the name of "Nereide," the ship that Captain Willoughby had so gallantly defended.

On the 14th of October, the 10-gun brig "Briseis," Commander George Bentham, captured the French 14-gun schooner privateer "Sans Souci," after a chase of eight hours, and an action of one hour.

The "Briseis" had four killed, and eleven wounded.

The privateer had eight men killed, and nineteen wounded.

On the 25th of October, the 10-gun brig "Calliope," Commander John McKerlie, in the North Sea, captured the "Comtesse d'Homburgh" a French privateer schooner of 14 guns.

The "Calliope" had three men wounded.

On the 4th of November, two boats of the 18-gun corvette "Blossom," Commander William Steward, off Cape Sicie, were sent in a calm after a xebeck privateer of 4 guns.

As the boats drew near a fire was opened upon them, which killed Lieutenant Davis and three of the crew, and wounded four more.

Mr. Marshall, midshipman, ordered the men to continue the pursuit, and the privateer was boarded and captured, although defended by 59 men.

Five more men were wounded out of the twenty-six that boarded the xebeck.

The enemy had four men killed, and nine wounded.

The naval medal was given for this as a naval boat action.

On the 8th of November, the boats of the 32-gun frigate "Quebec," Captain Hawtayne, commanded by Lieutenant Richard Yates, captured the French privateer schooner "Jeune Louise."

In this engagement the French Captain Galien Lafont fell in a single combat with Lieutenant Yates.

On the 16th of November, the 14-gun schooner "Phipps," Commander Christopher Bell, chased the lugger privateer "Barbier de Seville," off Calais.

Fearing the lugger would run ashore, the schooner was run foul of her.

A broadside was first poured into the lugger, and it was then boarded and captured.

The prize mounted 16 guns and had a crew of 65 men, 6 of whom were killed and 11 wounded.

She sank soon after her capture, taking down one of the crew of the "Phipps."

The English had been so much annoyed by the French war vessels that had made the Isle of France a rendezvous, that it was determined that place should be captured.

A fleet of one ship of the line, the "Illustrious," of 74 guns, Captain William Broughton, and twelve frigates, amongst which were the "Africaine," "Nereide," "Boadicea," and "Ceylon," and six sloops, with a fleet of transports, containing 10,000 troops under Major-General Abercromby, appeared off the island.

The fleet was under the command of Vice-Admiral Bertie, whose flag was on the "Africaine."

The island was fortified with 209 cannon, and garrisoned by 1,300 regular troops, assisted by 10,000 militia.

It surrendered on the 3rd of December, after an engagement, in which the English had 28 men killed 94 wounded, and 45 missing. With the island were surrendered the 40-gun frigates "Bellone," "Minerve," "Manche," "Anstree," "Nereide," "Iphigenie," the corvette "Victor," and brig "Entreprenante," besides the "Charlton," "Ceylon," and "United Kingdom," that had been captured from the East India Company.

Besides these vessels twenty-four French merchant ships became the prizes of the victors.

The "Bellone" was added to the English navy under the name of "Junon," the "Astree" as the "Pomone," and the "Iphigenie" under her original name of "Iphigenia."

The "Nereide" was no longer seaworthy, and was broken up.

On the 10th of December, the 10-brig "Rosario," Commander Harvey, captured the French lugger "Mamelouck," of 16 guns and 45 men, off Dungeness.

The lugger had seven men wounded, the "Rosario" five.

On the 7th of December, the 10-gun brig "Rinaldo," Commander James Anderson, captured the French lugger "Marauder," of 14 guns and 85 men, near the French coast.

On the night of the 17th of December, the "Rinaldo" encountered four French luggers, two of which ranged up under its stern, each firing a broadside, after which the "Rinaldo" was commanded in an insulting manner to surrender.

The "Rinaldo" tacked, and gave each lugger a broadside.

She then wore around, and gave the largest lugger another broadside, that brought down its masts and sails, when the crew called out for help, and said that they were sinking.

The second lugger, after making an attempt to close with the brig, was compelled to haul off and surrender.

In manning her boats, the "Rinaldo" was carried by a current against the Ower's light vessel, and, in the delay caused by this accident, the large lugger, which proved to be the "Vieille Josephine," of 16 guns, went down, and, out of a crew of 70 men, only three were saved.

While engaged in trying to save more of its crew, the other lugger escaped.

On the 13th of December, 600 seamen and vessels of war. Three were captured, twelve wrecked, and two foundered.

One of the wrecked was the "Cuckoo," 4 guns, wrecked on the coast of Holland near Haerlem.

The crew escaped to shore, but were made prisoners.

In this year was lost to the navy Admiral Cuthbert Collingwood. He was born on the 26th of September, 1750, at Newcastle-on-Tyne.

WRECK OF H.M.S. "CUCKOO."

marines, from the 74-gun ships "Kent," Captain Rogers, and the "Ajax," Captain Otway, the frigate "Cambrian," Captain Fane, and two corvettes, were sent ashore near the Mole of Palamos, on the coast of Spain, to destroy an armed ketch, some xebecks and merchant vessels anchored under the protection of two batteries.

The expedition was led by Captain Fane, and the batteries and some of the vessels were destroyed, with but little loss; but, in returning to the ships, the men unwisely went through the centre of the town, where they were exposed to a sharp fire from French troops posted in the houses.

Thirty-three were killed, 89 wounded, and 87 were taken prisoners.

Amongst the latter was Captain Fane.

In the year 1810, the English navy lost seventeen

Admiral Collingwood was of a meek, mild, and gentle nature, yet no man living had a braver heart.

On first going to sea, he cried like a child, and on being spoken to in a kind, pleasant tone by the first lieutenant, he generously offered that officer a plum-cake, given him by his mother on leaving home.

He was the captain of the "Prince" in the great victory gained over the French by Howe, on the 1st of June, and on writing to his father-in-law after the battle, he says—

"We cruised about like disappointed people looking for what they could not find, *until the morning of little Sarah's birthday*, between eight and nine, when the French fleet of twenty-five sail of the line was discovered to the windward."

Nothing could more beautifully illustrate the man's disposition and character than this.

"If you don't know a man's name," said he to his officers, "call him 'sailor,' and not 'you sir.'"

Of a lazy and incompetent officer he said, "He is living on the navy, not serving in it."

On another occasion he said, "I have no notion of people making the navy a mere convenience for themselves, *as if it were a public establishment for loungers.*"

Collingwood died on the 7th of March, 1810, on board his flag-ship "Ville de Paris," off Minorca.

CHAPTER XXXV.
1811.

HERE was nothing during the early part of this year worthy of record performed by the navy.

There were two or three boat actions of little importance, and two or three wrecks. The frigate "Amythest," of 36-guns, was one of the latter.

She was lost on a reef of rocks near Mount Batten Bay, and the greater part of her crew were drowned.

The crews of some boats who went off to their assistance were also lost.

On the 7th of March, the "Theban" frigate engaged the large French lugger privateer, "La Fortune," and ran it down under her bows.

Only 3 of the lugger's crew of 56 men were saved.

On the 13th of March, an English squadron, under the command of Captain William Hoste, was attacked by a Franco-Venitian squadron, under Commodore Dubourdieu, near the Island of Lissa.

The English force consisted of the following vessels:—

"Amphion," 32 guns, Captain William Hoste; "Active," 38 guns, Captain James Gordon; "Volage," 28 guns, Captain Phipps Hornby; "Cerberus," 32 guns, Captain Henry Whitby.

The enemy's squadron consisted of the French 40-gun ships "Favorite," "Flore," and "Danae," and the 16-gun vessel "Mercurie," and three Venitian vessels, the 32-gun frigates "Bellona" and "Carolina," and the 40-gun ship "Corona."

Besides these were a schooner, xebeck, and some gun-boats.

The actual number of guns on the English fleet was 152, and it was manned by 880 men.

The number of guns on the enemy's fleet was 300, and there were 2,500 men.

Captain Hoste had been for some time anxious to meet the squadron under Commodore Dubourdieu, and would not decline a combat on finding the enemy a little stronger than he expected.

As the enemy's ships were bearing down upon him, Captain Hoste hoisted the flags in telegraphing to the other vessels what is called a "signal," in words "*Remember Nelson.*"

The signal, on being interpreted on the different vessels, was received with loud cheers.

The "Amphion" and "Active" were the first to commence the action by firing upon the "Favorite."

This was about nine o'clock in the morning.

Ten minutes later, the latter vessel was near the weather beam of the "Amphion," with an apparent intention of boarding.

A large crowd of the "Favorite's" crew had assembled on her forecastle, and a howitzer loaded with 750 musket balls was fired at them, producing a great slaughter.

She then hauled to the wind.

The "Danae," "Corona," and "Carolina" then came into action with the "Volage" and "Cerberus."

Since the time the action commenced the vessels had been moving under easy sail, and were soon nearly upon the shore of the island.

In wearing, the "Favorite" struck on a rock and bilged.

"The "Amphion" for some time was engaged with the "Flore" and "Bellona," and perceiving that he was gaining no advantage in his position, Captain Hoste had the vessel edged, and crossing the bows of the "Flore," a broadside was brought to bear upon her for about ten minutes, when she surrendered.

The "Amphion" then turned her whole attention to the "Bellona," and her flag was soon after struck.

The rest of the enemy's ships were now seen trying to make an escape, and a signal was made to give chase.

The "Active" was the only vessel in a condition to obey this order.

She overtook the "Bellona," and, after a sharp action for more than an hour, compelled her to surrender.

As possession had never been taken of the "Flore," owing to the damaged boats and running rigging of the "Amphion," she slowly made sail, stole away, and escaped into Lessina.

The "Carolina," "Danae," and the small vessels of the enemy, also got under protection of the batteries of the same place.

In this action the masts and rigging of the "Amphion" were much damaged, and she had 15 men killed and 45 wounded.

Aboard the fleet there were 45 killed and 145 wounded.

Some of the enemy's ships suffered much loss. On the "Corona" more than 200 men were killed and wounded, and on the "Bellona" 70 were killed and an equal number wounded.

The "Favorite" was set on fire by her crew, and blew up.

The "Corona" was added to the English navy under the name of "Dædalus."

In the preceding year the island of Anholdt was garrisoned by the English for a naval station for Baltic cruisers, and Captain James W. Maurice was placed in command of it.

This proceeding was so much disliked by the Danes that they determined to capture the island. They reached the place on the 26th of March with twelve transports, carrying 1,000 troops and manned by 200 seamen.

The transports were protected by twelve gun-boats, each manned by not less than 60 men, and each mounting two long guns and four brass howitzers.

To repel this force Captain Maurice had 400 men, a few small guns, and an armed schooner.

Fortunately for this small garrison, the 32-gun frigate "Tartar," Captain Joseph Baker, and the 16-gun sloop "Sheldrake," Commander James Stewart, arrived at the harbour on the same day that the Danes appeared off the island.

The Danish troops disembarked on the 27th, about four miles from Fort Yorke.

About 500 crossed the island, and at first they obtained some temporary advantage in the capture of a small battery, but in a general assault they were repulsed, and Major Melstedt, their commander-in-chief, and Lieutenant Holstern, were killed, and Captain Reydez had both legs shot off.

The "Tartar," "Sheldrake," and schooner "Anholdt," all brought their guns to bear upon them, and the Danes soon found that in place of capturing the island they were to be captured themselves.

After trying to obtain better terms they made an unconditional surrender.

The "Tartar" and "Sheldrake" then pursued the gun-boats, two of which were captured, and one was sunk.

In this expedition the Danes had 35 men killed and 21 wounded.

Of the English 2 were killed and 31 wounded.

On the 30th of March, the 38-gun frigate "Pomone," Captain Robert Baine, the 36-gun frigate "Unite," Captain Edward Chamberlayne, and the 18-gun brig "Scout," Commander Alexander Sharpe," attacked two French store ships, the "Giraffe" and "Nourrice," of 26 guns each, lying in the bay of Sagone, Corsica.

These vessels were protected by a 4-gun and mortar battery, a martelle tower, and 200 troops on the heights.

The frigates were towed in by their boats, and about an hour and a half after opening fire, one of the store ships, the "Giraffe," was seen to be burning.

From this the fire spread to the other and to a large merchant ship lying near them.

An hour later and the two vessels blew up, throwing burning timbers into the tower, which was also destroyed.

In this engagement the English vessels had 2 men killed and 25 wounded.

On the 4th of May, the boats of the 38-gun frigates "Belle Poule" and "Alceste," Captains Brisbane and Maxwell, took possession of a small island at the entrance of the harbour of Parenza.

On the 5th, from a battery they erected on this island, they sank a brig lying in the harbour, laden with supplies for the French frigate "Danae."

The object for which they took possession of the island then being accomplished, the party re-embarked, having had three men killed, and four wounded.

Early in May, the French Commodore Roquebert arrived at the Isle of France from Brest, with a squadron consisting of the 40-gun frigates "Renommée," "Clorinde," and "Nereide," each having on board 200 soldiers.

On learning that the place of their destination had fallen into the hands of the English, they sailed for Madagascar.

The next day they were followed by 18-pounder 36-gun frigates "Phœbe" and "Galatea," Captains Hillyar and Losack, the 18-gun brig "Racehorse," Commander James De Rippe, and the 38-gun frigate "Astrea," Captain Schomberg.

This squadron encountered the French on the 20th of May.

In this action the "Clorinde" took up a station under the stern of the "Galatea," and the "Renommée" on her starboard quarter.

In this situation she was exposed to the fire of two powerful opponents for three hours.

During the most of this time, the "Phœbe" and "Astrea" were engaged with the "Nereide."

The French now began to give way and were pursued by the "Astrea," "Phœbe," and "Racehorse," the "Galatea" being too much damaged to take a part in the pursuit.

Her fore and mizen masts were gone, the other masts were much damaged, and she had four feet of water in the hold.

More than sixty of her crew were killed and wounded.

The "Renommée" was captured by the other vessel about ten that night, but the "Clorinde" and

"Nereide" escaped. The loss of life on board the enemy's ships was very severe.

On the "Renommée" 145 were killed and wounded, including Commodore Roquebert, who was killed.

Aboard the "Nereide," 130 were killed and wounded.

The naval medal was given for this action.

On the 8th of May, the 18-gun brig "Scylla," Commander Arthur Atcheson, captured the French 10-gun brig "Canonière," off the Isle of Bas.

Two men on the "Scylla" were killed, and two wounded; and six men killed, including the commander, and eleven wounded on the "Canonière."

The latter had five vessels under convoy, one of which was captured.

On the 16th of May, the 20-gun corvette "Little Belt," Commander Arthur Bingham, when off Sandy Hook, on the way around Cape Hatteras, was overhauled by the United States 44-gun frigate "President," Captain Ludlow, the flagship of Commodore John Rogers.

When the two vessels were within hailing distance, the question was asked "What ship is that?" from both ships, but neither would answer.

A gun was then fired from each ship, and both at the same instant.

Without another word being said an action then commenced, which lasted about half-an-hour, when from an injury to her sails, the "Little Belt" fell off, till her guns could no longer be brought to bear on the other, and she ceased firing.

The firing of the "President" was also stopped.

On the "Little Belt," 11 men were killed and 21 wounded. A boy was wounded on the "President."

The next morning a lieutenant from the "President" came in a boat to the "Little Belt," and after expressing his opinion that it was an "unfortunate affair," returned to his vessel, which then sailed away.

On the 26th of May, the 18-gun brig "Alacrity," Commander Nesbit Palmer, cruising off Elba, saw the French 20-gun brig "Abeille" a few miles to the seaward, and gave chase to it.

Instead of trying to escape, the French brig hove to and prepared for action, as many now believe, greatly to the disgust of several officers of the "Alacrity."

"The "Abeille," being a fast sailer and well handled, managed to keep on the quarter of the "Alacrity," and continued pouring upon her a sharp and vigorous fire.

The "Alacrity" soon became nearly unmanageable. Some of her officers were killed, others wounded, and a few were driven by fear from the deck.

The first lieutenant, Thomas G. Rees, was killed early in the engagement. Had this not been the case, the action might have terminated differently.

The second lieutenant was absent with a dozen men in a prize. David Laing, the master's mate, and a young midshipman named Warren, were mortally wounded.

Captain Palmer received a slight wound between a thumb and forefinger, and, after going below to have the wound dressed, did not return to his duty. There was much blame attributed to him for this, and there would have been much more had not the captain died a month after of lockjaw.

James Flaxman, the boatswain, although severely wounded, was the only officer who remained on deck doing his duty. His efforts, however, could not save the vessel, and the colours were hauled down.

On board the "Alacrity," 5 men were killed and 12 wounded.

During the following two months there was very little to record of the doings of the navy; although of a few unimportant events that occurred most naval historians have managed to fill a few pages.

The boats of the 18-gun brig "Pilot," under the orders of Lieutenant Alexander Campbell, on the 26th of May, after destroying one vessel, brought off three more from the town of Strongali, in the Gulf of Taranto.

In the year 1811, H.M.S. "Guadaloupe," of 16 guns, commanded by Captain Tetley, was cruising under the high land of the coast of Catalonia, on her way to join the fleet under the command of Sir Edward Pellew, off Toulon.

A pleasant breeze blew right into the gulf, and they were gaily proceeding under top-gallant and royals, when the look-out man at the masthead vociferated—

"Three sail in-shore, ahead!"

The first lieutenant was instantly aloft with his spy-glass, and reported, a square and two fore-and-aft rigged vessels.

All hands were instantly on deck, and all heads busy in anticipating prize money. All sail was soon made, and studding sails set, with a view to cut them off from making port.

As, however, the "Guadaloupe" neared her expected prize, and their hulls became visible, they soon discovered they had mistaken the character of their prey.

One of them proved to be a large brig-corvette, carrying a commodore's pendant, in company with an armed sloop and xebeck. They had now gone too far to recede, even if they had been so inclined, as the wind was dead against their getting out, except by tack, and the gallant captain determined to give the enemy battle at all hazards.

They still continued their course, gradually shortening sail and making all secure as they approached.

The enemy also advanced to meet them, so that in a short time they could make out each other's force, and saw at once that they had fearful odds to encounter.

Fortunately, before they met, the wind veered, so as to bring them in opposite tacks, two or three points free.

They met each other under topsails; but previous to coming within shot range, Captain Tetley called all hands aft, and addressing the crew in the most cool and collected manner, pointed out to them their situation, and stating it to be his determination to bring them into action, it was for them to fight their way out, as the enemy being so superior in force, and they on a lee-shore, and almost within range of the batteries, they must either beat or be beaten.

Inspired by the gallant address of their commander, the crew gave three hearty cheers, and every soul on board, with the exception of the captain, stripped for the fight.

The yards and every other spar which might endanger their safety, by being wounded, were hung with iron chains; the guns, which were mounted on long slides, were loaded with round and grape up to the muzzle, and then screwed up to point blank mark, determined that their first broadside should tell home amongst the enemy's men, who appeared to be very numerous.

In this state they were fast nearing each other; even a whisper was not heard on board the little bark, and every man was at his station.

On reaching within pistol shot, they hoisted their colours, and the enemy did the same; but as they had determined to waste neither powder nor shot, they were resolved to run alongside and receive the enemy's fire first.

As soon, therefore, as their bows were opposed, the gallant captain gave the command—

"Men, secure yourselves."

In an instant every man fell flat on the deck, and the next moment the enemy poured in his broadside from eleven guns of the same calibre as their own, accompanied by a rattling volley from their small arms.

In a moment every man was on his feet, unhurt; and the captain of each gun having the lanyard of his gunlock in his hand, a deadly broadside was poured into the enemy's quarter and stern, together with a volley from the marines and small-arm men.

They then immediately sheered up on the larboard side, and before he could return the first fire, they slapped another broadside into him.

After the first broadside, they heard a most dreadful crash on board the enemy, and the second only served to increase the confusion.

After this, they continued fighting at close quarters for nearly an hour and a half, till at length the crews of both ships became so exhausted that it was quite the turn of a straw which would have the best of it.

Once more, however, the wearied but gallant crew of the "Guadaloupe" rallied, and cheered with such hearty goodwill, that Johnny Crapaud, daunted with the sound, turned tail on the victorious British, and not being cut up as they were in sails and running rigging, made all sail and ran into port, which was close under their lee—so close that the shot from the batteries actually passed them during the latter part of the action.

PORTRAIT OF LORD EXMOUTH.

The "Guadaloupe" was so dreadfully mauled in her standing and running rigging that they could not work the vessel, nor set a single sail in pursuit of their flying foe; and it was fortunate for them that they had smooth water, or their masts might have been endangered; she therefore escaped, much to their regret.

Had the action commenced a little farther off shore, there is no doubt they would have secured the prize.

Independent of the corvette alongside, they had also her two consorts, the sloop and xebeck, upon them during the early part of the action; and had it not been for a providential circumstance, they might have suffered severely from the raking position which the xebeck took under her stern, and, into which she kept continually firing from her great guns, not daring to come near enough for her small arms to take effect.

Fortunately for the English, they had, during their cruise, erected shot-lockers at the stern sheets, and boxed them off on each side of the rudder, for the purpose of trimming her by the stern, whereby the stern-posts were blocked up, in consequence of which, the shot from the xebeck took no effect upon her decks, but lodged in the lockers, where, coming in contact with their 32's, they were stopped short, or otherwise split.

For some time they were unable to get a gun to bear upon the xebeck, till at length the third officer, assisted by one of the midshipmen, and the remaining crew of the gun being but two, succeeded in sluing the aftermost quarterdeck gun, so as to bring it to bear upon the decks of the little wasp which had so long annoyed them; and having loaded it with canister shot almost to the muzzle, it was fired with such deadly aim, that the staggering xebeck fled without returning to the contest; and the armed sloop was so alarmed at the execution of their single gun, that she did not dare to venture within reach, but left them to manage as they could with the commodore.

After they had been engaged some time, the yard-braces, and other running rigging of the "Guadaloupe" being shot away, and the wind almost lulled into a calm, the enemy fell on board of them with his bowsprit directly over their stern, and, at the moment they could not alter the position of the vessel for want of headsail to pay her off; but, observing that the crew of their opponent was forsaking their guns, and rushing forward to the bows with the intention of boarding them, the captain immediately called out for boarders, and all that could, instantly rushed to the point of attack to repel the enemy.

At this moment, by a fortunate shift of wind, the vessel's head paid round, which brought their disengaged broadsides to bear upon the enemy, and clearing them of her bowsprit, prevented the necessity of their waging battle on their own decks.

This proved a fortunate circumstance; for the enemy having left the guns and rushing forward to board, the broadside made fearful execution among them, and completely sickened them from any wish to prolong the contest; but having made good their retreat, the crew of the "Guadaloupe" were piped from quarters and supplied with refreshments; after which they turned to repair damages, in order to get out of the reach of danger.

Having secured their standing rigging, spliced and rove new running rigging, cleared the decks as well as they could, and made ready in case of meeting a fresh opponent, they made sail, gained an offing, and bore away for the fleet off Toulon.

On examining their loss in men, it was found not so heavy as might have been expected, considering the force opposed and the length of time they were engaged; one man was killed and twelve wounded, of whom one died in the hospital.

His wound was the result of cowardice, for during the hottest part of the fight he became so appalled, that he took refuge under the lee of the long boat amidships, and lay under her bottom, stretched at length, in full idea of security.

While thus skulking, a 2-pound grape shot passed between the booms through the bottom of the boat, and carried away with it part of the poor fellow's face, whilst another spent ball lodged in the fleshy part of his back, near the shoulder blade bone.

The first lieutenant received a singular wound in his breast.

At the commencement of the action he commanded the fore deck guns; while there, a musket ball from the enemy struck, it is supposed, one of the backstays, or some other hard substance, whereby it got flattened and spent, and then obliquely entered his breast, taking in with it three folds of his black silk neckerchief which hung down loose.

Fortunately for him the silk prevented its entering far, so that the ball was extracted without difficulty, and without doing him any material injury.

The remaining portion of the crew who were wounded speedily recovered.

They soon joined the fleet off Toulon, where they astonished their brethren by the picture they cut, the riddled state of their mainsail sufficiently attesting the severity of the fire they had been under, while the hull had suffered so much, that the vessel was dismantled, her stern frame partially renewed, many shot between wind and water, and upwards of a hundred others taken out of the sides, and new spars to replace the wounded ones; while a respite of a few weeks made both vessel and crew all ataunt again.

The comparative force of the vessels engaged was as follows:—

English Force.—The "Guadaloupe," sixteen 32-pound carronades, complement on board 104 men and boys. Loss: one killed, twelve wounded, one of whom died afterwards.

French Force.—"Tactique," twenty-two 32-pounders, manned by 200 men, picked out of the other vessels in port for the express purpose of carrying the "Guadaloupe" by boarding. Loss: ten killed, forty wounded; but subsequent accounts stated their loss to have been more.

The xebeck was armed with 8 guns, having a crew of 80 men.

Her loss could not be ascertained, but there is no doubt she must have suffered severely from the discharge of grape which was poured upon her decks.

As to the armed sloop, they counted her nothing, having scarcely seen her since the action began.

They were also under the fire of the batteries on shore, during a great part of the action, a shot from whence actually carried away their main royal mast.

They learned, some time afterwards, that these three vessels had actually been sent out with express orders to carry them off hand by boarding; but poor fellows, they got grievously disappointed.

This action took place on the 27th of June.

On the 4th of July, a brig was captured in the harbour of Port Hercules, on the Italian coast, by the boats of the "Unitie," Captain Chamberlayne, and under the orders of Lieutenant Crabb.

On the 11th of July, several merchant vessels were captured and brought out of Porto del Infreschi, by the 32-gun frigate "Thames," Captain Charles Napier, and the "Cephalus," Commander Clifford.

On the 27th of July, ten vessels were burnt, and several brought from the town of Ragosniza, in the Adriatic, by the boats of the "Active," Captain Gordon.

The boats were under the orders of Lieutenant William Henderson.

These and a few other little affairs were all that occurred until the capture of Java and its dependencies, on the 18th day of December, by a fleet under the command of Rear-Admiral Robert Stopford.

This fleet consisted of four ships of the line—the "Scipion," of 74 guns, Captain Johnson, being the admiral's flagship, thirteen frigates, seven sloops, and a number of transports carrying 800 troops, under the command of Major-General Wetheral and Colonel Gillespie.

In the engagement, that resulted in the surrender of the island of Java, 141 sailors and soldiers were killed and 788 wounded.

The frigates "Sir Francis Drake" and "Phaëton," Captains Harris and Pellew, and the sloop "Dasher," Commander Kelly, were then sent to the island of Madura, where they landed on the 30th of August.

A fort, manned by nearly 400 Madura pikemen, was first captured, and a summons was then sent under a flag of truce to the governor of the island to surrender.

His answer was, that unless the English quitted the fort in ten minutes, and left the island immediately, they should be shown no quarter, but be all put to death.

The attack on the Dutch was immediately commenced by two divisions, led by Captains Harris and Pellew, and, after a sharp action of about five minutes, the Dutch fled and the island was captured with a loss of 3 killed and 28 wounded.

On the 2nd of August, the boats of the frigate "Quebec," of 32 guns, Captain Hawtayne, and the 16-gun brig "Raven," Commander George Lennock, and two gun brigs were sent, manned by 117 men under the orders of Lieutenant Blyth, to cut out some Danish gunboats in the river Jahde, island of Nordeney.

One of the gunboats was boarded and carried in gallant style by Lieutenant Blyth, and, just as they were going to turn the guns on the other gunboats, the powder which was on deck exploded, and killed and wounded 19 men.

The gunboats were all captured and taken away, two men being killed and nine wounded, besides those injured by the explosion, of whom six died.

Lieutenant Blyth, who was severely wounded and blown overboard by the explosion, was promoted, and the naval medal was given for the action.

On the 2nd of September, the gun brig "Manly," Commander Lieutenant Simmonds, was captured off the coast of Norway by the Danish 18-gun brigs "Loland," "Alsen," and "Sampsoe."

On the 7th of September, the 28-gun frigate "Barbadoes," Captain Rushworth, and the 16-gun brig "Goshawk," Commander Lilburn, attacked seven gunboats off the French coast, and drove them into Calvados.

The next day the 36-gun frigate "Hotspur," Captain Percy, stood in and attacked them.

One gun brig was sunk and two were driven ashore.

In this engagement the "Hotspur" sustained considerable damage, and had 3 killed and 22 wounded.

On the 21st of September, the 38-gun frigate "Naiad" and the 10-gun brigs "Rinaldo" and "Redpole," and the 18-gun brig "Castilian," had an engagement with some French prames and gunboats off the coast of France, near Boulogne.

The French prame "Ville de Lyon" was captured after making a gallant resistance, in which she had between 30 and 40 men killed and wounded.

The "Naiad" had 2 men killed and 15 wounded. Four others were killed and wounded on the other vessels.

In the annals of the British navy, there are many instances of captured ships being retaken by the resolution and bravery of the prisoners.

The following deserves to be recorded, as affording an example of truly British conduct, in a boy of about thirteen years of age.

The "Fame," a merchant vessel, belonging to Carron in the Firth of Forth, on her voyage from London to Arbroath, was captured on the 25th of October, 1811, at one o'clock in the afternoon, off Shields.

The vessel which took her was the French privateer "Grand Fury," of sixteen guns, four only of which were mounted, and 75 men: six Frenchmen were put on board the "Fame," and all her own crew taken out except an old man and a boy.

The Frenchmen were directed to carry her to a port in France; but on the day after she was captured, a strong gale came on from the southeast, which drove her out of her course to the northward. The wind soon after shifted to the north-east, and blew with increasing violence.

The vessel was now nearly unmanageable, and drove into the mouth of the Firth of Forth.

Neither the Frenchmen nor the old man were acquainted with the navigation of this Forth, and, indeed, scarcely knew where they were; nor would the boy have ascertained the situation of the ship (as the compass was rendered useless for the want of candles, which had been either all expended or thrown overboard, and the vessel was driving before the wind without any attempt to steer her) had it not been for the light on the small island of Inch Keith.

As soon as the boy descried this, he knew that the vessel was in the Firth of Forth, and he was permitted by the Frenchmen to take the command and direction of her.

He steered directly up the Forth, and as he passed the "Rebecca," which was lying at anchor in St. Margaret's Hope, he hailed her, that he had six French prisoners on board, and demanded assistance, in order to get them secured.

At first they thought he was not in earnest, but

on his repeating his statement and demand, a boat was sent off from the "Rebecca."

The moment that it reached the "Fame," the boy seized the Frenchmen's pistols, which he claimed as his right by conquest, and would not give them up to the "Rebecca's" crew.

The prisoners acknowledged that the boy was an excellent steersman, and that he alone was the means of saving their lives, as well as the vessel and cargo.

On the 2nd of November, the frigates "Thames," Captain Charles Napier, and the "Impérieuse," Captain Duncan, entered the harbour of Palinuro, on the coast of Calabria.

A force was landed that captured a fort, threw its guns into the sea, and blew up the fortification. Six gunboats and twenty-two small merchant vessels, laden with oil and other goods, were captured and brought off.

In this adventure, on the part of the English 4 men were killed and 11 wounded.

On the 10th of November, the 16-gun brig "Skylark," Commander James Boxer, and the 12-gun brig "Locust," Lieutenant John Gedge, chased twelve French gunboats off Calais.

One was driven ashore, and one carrying four 24-pounders, and manned by 60 men, was captured. The naval medal has been given for the action.

On the 27th of November, the 74-gun ship "Eagle," Captain Rowley, captured a French frigate in the Atlantic. There was but little injury done the vessels or crews of either side.

On the 29th of November, the French 40-gun frigate "Pomone," one of a small squadron of vessels, under Commodore Montfort, was captured off the island of Augusta by the English frigates "Alceste" and "Active," Captains Maxwell and Gordon.

On the two frigates 15 men were killed and 45 wounded. On the "Pomone" there were 50 killed and wounded.

CHAPTER XXXVI.

EVENTS OF 1812.

HE war still raged furiously on the continent, and British ships still scoured the seas, though, as the enemy had no large fleets, the only encounters that took place were between small squadrons and single ships.

The first event of any importance in the naval chronology of the year took place on the 2nd day of February, 1812, when the 12-pounder 32-gun frigate "Southampton," Captain James Yeo, encountered the "Amethyste," of 44 guns, a vessel in the service of the government of Hayti, and commanded by a man named Gaspard.

Doubting the legality of this man's commission, Captain Yeo required him to go to Jamaica, and be examined by the admiral at Port Royal.

Gaspard denied the right of the English war vessels to act as the police of the sea, and refused to go.

Captain Yeo then commenced enforcing his wishes.

An action began which lasted about half an hour, when the "Amethyste," having lost her main and mizen mast, and being otherwise much injured, surrendered.

In the few minutes the action had lasted, 105 men had been killed on the Haytian frigate, and 120 wounded.

The "Southampton" had one killed and ten wounded.

The "Amethyste" was taken to Jamaica, but afterwards restored.

His Majesty's ship "Amelia," Captain Irby, cruising off the coast of Africa, was about to leave Sierra Leone river at the end of January.

Captain Irby being informed by Lieutenant Pascoe, of the "Daring" gun brig, that he had been compelled to run his brig on shore and blow her up, being chased by a French frigate, which, with two other ships, he left at anchor off the De Loss islands, he despatched Lieutenant Pascoe to reconnoitre.

He returned with intelligence that the French force consisted of two frigates of the largest class, "L'Arethuse" and "Le Rebes," along with a Portuguese vessel which they had captured. Captain Irby consequently resolved to cruise off these islands, in order to fall in with any other British ships of war that might be coming that way, and to protect the trade to Sierra Leone.

On the 6th of February, one of the frigates stood out to sea, and on the 7th, the other stood towards the "Amelia," which had lain off the island of Tamara during the night.

In the hope of drawing her from her consort, Captain Irby continued standing out to sea until sunset, when, not seeing the other frigate from the masthead, he shortened sail, wore, and stood towards her.

At forty-five minutes past seven, P.M., the two ships commenced a brisk cannonade within pistol-shot, and the action was continued determinedly till twenty minutes past eleven, when the frigate hoisted sail and bore away, leaving the "Amelia" in a very crippled condition, her sails and rigging being cut to pieces, and her masts injured.

The "Amelia" had twice fallen on board the enemy in the attempt to thwart his hawse, when he made attempts to board, but was repulsed with loss.

Captain Irby, in his despatch, says—

"The superior force of the enemy, the consi-

On the 13th of February, the 38-gun frigate "Apollo," Captain Taylor, captured the French 20-gun store-ship "Merinos," off Cape Corse. The French vessel had 6 men killed and 20 wounded.

On the 22nd of February, the 74-gun ship "Victorious," Captain Talbot, and the 18-gun brig "Weasel," Commander John Andrew, encountered the French 74-gun ship "Rivoli," Commodore Barre, and the brigs "Jena" and "Mercure."

WRECK OF H.M. SLOOP "WOOLWICH."

derable quantity of gold-dust we have on board, as well as the certainty of the other frigate coming up, would not have prevented me from a renewal of the action, if it had not been totally impracticable."

The slaughter on board the "Amelia" was too evident a proof of this, which, with the disabled condition of the ship, demonstrates how effectively the guns of the enemy were served.

The return of the killed, and of those who afterwards died of their wounds, was 51, and of the wounded, 95. Among the killed were three lieutenants, and Lieutenant Pascoe, late of the "Daring." Captain Irby was also wounded severely, In this state he proceeded homewards, and on the 22nd of March arrived at Spithead.

A long chase then ensued, and the "Weasel" was the first to come up with the enemy.

She exchanged a few broadsides with the "Jena" and "Mercure," when the latter blew up and the "Jena" again made off.

Only three of the crew of the "Mercure" were saved.

When the "Victorious" overhauled the "Rivoli," the two vessels stood towards the Gulf of Trieste, and with courses up and royals set, commenced a furious action, which lasted for three hours, when the "Weasel," which had been recalled, came up to the assistance of its consort, and the "Rivoli" soon after struck.

The "Victorious" was much damaged in her

masts and rigging, her hull shattered and her boats destroyed.

She had 27 killed and 99 wounded.

The "Rivoli" had 400 killed and wounded out of a crew of 810 men.

She was added to the English navy under the same name.

In March, 1812, the Sicilian flotilla, under the command of Captain Hall, assisted by a portion of the 75th regiment, performed a daring and successful exploit on the coast of Calabria, which was reported by Sir Edward Pellew, the admiral in the Mediterranean.

In a letter to Lord William Bentinck, Captain Hall states that the enemy, having thrown up new works, Pietra Nera, on the coast of Calabria, confided so much in their strength, that a convoy of fifty armed vessels assembled for the purpose of transporting timber and other government property to Naples.

Captain Hall, on receiving this information, proceeded on the night of the 14th, with two divisions of the flotilla, and four companies of the 75th regiment, commanded by Major Stewart.

Arriving at daylight, 150 of the soldiers, and an auxiliary force of seamen, were landed under the command of Lieutenant Le Hunt.

Major Stewart promptly led them to occupy a height defended by a whole battalion and two troops of cavalry, with two pieces of artillery.

The daring attack was obstinately resisted, until the commander of the enemy's forces, and most of his officers were either killed or became prisoners, the height, the scene of conflict, being thickly covered with their dead.

The flotilla, under the direction of Captain Imbert, during this deadly conflict, briskly cannonaded the batteries, which held out resolutely, until Lieutenant Le Hunt advanced with his seamen and gallantly carried them by storm.

The brave assailants now became possessed of everything, and launched the most valuable vessels and timber, and finished the enterprise by setting fire to the remainder.

The enemy suffered the loss of 150 killed and 163 wounded.

The two guns were also taken possession of.

The brave leader, Major Stewart, was unfortunately killed by a musket, while he was in the act of pushing off from shore, after the embarkation of the military.

His loss was severely felt, and much regretted.

Considering the desperate struggle they had been engaged in, their loss was trifling compared with that of the enemy, who, although they fought desperately, were compelled to yield to the superior bravery and skill of their gallant assailants!

Such were the brilliant services of the Sicilian flotilla; services which command the admiration of the soldier; of him who thinks upon the soldier's fate, and of him who cherishes the feats of arms.

On the 27th of March, the 10-gun brig "Rosario," Commander Booty Harvey, and the 16-gun brig "Griffon," Commander George Trollope, had an engagement with a division of the Boulogne flotilla, of which two brigs were captured and three were run on shore.

One midshipman was killed, and four seamen wounded on the "Rosario."

On the 4th of April, the boats of the "Maidstone" frigate, Captain Burdett, captured the French privateer "Martinet," off Cape de Gatt; Lieutenant Arthur McMeekan conducted the expedition, and was promoted for the manner in which it was conducted.

Lieutenant Alexander Dobbs, with the boats of the 74-gun ship "Leviathan," Captain Patrick Campbell, boarded and captured a French privateer brig of 14 guns and 80 men, off the Port of Agaye, on the 29th of April.

The brig being aground could not be brought out, but four vessels were captured and taken away as prizes. Two men were killed and four wounded of the party belonging to the boats.

On the 29th of April, several row-boats were captured in a small harbour on the coast of Malaga by the boats of a squadron under Captain Thomas Ussher, in the 20-gun ship "Hyacinth."

The row-boats, under a chief named Barbastro, for a long time had been committing great depredations on commerce, and Captain Ussher determined to destroy them.

The boats of the "Hyacinth," the 16-gun sloop "Goshawk," the gun brig "Resolute," and No. 16 gunboat, led by Captain Ussher, first captured a battery on the Mole head.

The gunboat and some of the other boats, under Commander Lilburne, then captured the row-boats. So far all had gone well; but this good fortune was not to last.

A castle with guns commanding the harbour, opened a fire on the boats, and some French troops attacked the battery on the Mole head, just as Captain Ussher and his men had spiked the guns and were about to leave.

A sharp fire of musketry was also opened from the Mole wall, and Commander Lilburne was killed.

The prizes were all abandoned but two—Barbastro's vessel and the "Napoleon"—which were taken away.

In this expedition there were 15 killed and 53 wounded.

On the 9th of May, sixteen laden French vessels were brought out from under the batteries of the town of Languelia, by a party in the boats of the 74-gun ships "Leviathan" and "America," Captains Rowley and Campbell, and the 18-gun brig "Eclair," Commander John Bellamy.

A party of 250 marines were landed, under the orders of Captain Henry Rea, and captured two batteries, while the boats of the squadron took possession of the prizes.

In landing, the yawl of the "America" was capsized, and ten marines and one seaman were drowned.

The loss in the enterprise was 16 killed and drowned, and 20 wounded.

The 32-gun frigate "Thames," Captain Charles Napier, with the 18-gun brig "Pilot," Commander John Nicolas, captured the Port of Sapri, defended by a strong battery and a tower, on the 14th of May.

The fortifications were blown up, and twenty-eight vessels were captured.

The gallant action which we are next about to record was performed off the coast of France by Captain Hotham, of the "Northumberland."

Having discovered two French frigates and a brig steering under a press of sail for Port L'Orient, he endeavoured to cut them off. After several skilful manœuvres, he succeeded in getting near them, just as they were about to enter the harbour. Steering parallel to them, at the distance of about two cables' length, he opened his fire, which was returned, not only by the fire of the enemy's ships, but also from three batteries, and for twenty-one minutes was very destructive to the sails and rigging of the "Northumberland."

His next object was to prevent the enemy from passing on the outside of a dry rock, and compelling them to pass between the "Northumberland" and it; this they were afraid to do, and in endeavouring to pass on the inside of the rocks they all grounded.

The "Northumberland" was now anchored in six and a half fathoms water, with her broadside on the enemy, at point blank range; and they had all fallen on their broadsides, and the mainmasts of one frigate and the brig were gone.

In this situation, Captain Hotham kept up a constant fire upon them for more than an hour; by this time they were dreadfully shattered, and one of them completely in flames.

At five minutes before eight in the evening, this frigate blew up with a dreadful explosion; and at ten o'clock the other frigate was discovered to be on fire; and as the brig was in such a state as to be completely unfit for service, even if she could be got off, Captain Hotham weighed anchor and got to sea.

The gallant captain gives the following circumstantial and interesting account of this action, in a letter addressed to Rear-Admiral Sir H. Neale, dated "Northumberland," off the Penmarks, May 24, 1812—

"On Friday, the 22nd instant, at a quarter after ten A.M., the N.W. point of the Isle Groa (Grouais), bearing from the 'Northumberland' N. by compass, ten miles distant, and the wind very light from the W. by N., they were discovered in the N.W. crowding all possible sail before it for L'Orient.

"My first endeavour was to cut them off to windward of the island, and a signal was made to the 'Growler' (seven miles off in the S.W.) to chase; but finding I could not effect it, the 'Northumberland' was pushed by great exertion, round the S.E. end of Groa, and by hauling to the wind as close as I could to the leeward of it, I had the satisfaction of fetching to windward of the harbour's mouth before the enemy's ships reached it.

"Their commander, seeing himself thus cut off, made a signal to his consorts, and hauled to the wind on the larboard tack, to windward of Point Taleet, and they appeared to speak to each other.

"I continued beating to windward, between Groa and the continent, to close with them, exposed to the batteries on both sides, when I stood within their reach, which was unavoidable. The wind had by this time freshened considerably, and was about W.N.W.

"At forty-nine minutes after two P.M. the enemy (in force as above described) bore up in close line ahead, and under every sail that could be set, favoured by the fresh wind, made a bold and determined attempt to run between me and the shore, under cover of the numerous batteries with which it is lined in that part.

"I placed the 'Northumberland' to meet them, as close as I could to the Point de Pierre Laye, with her head to the shore, and the maintopsail shivering, and made dispositions for laying one of them alongside; but they hauled so very close round the point, following the direction of the coast to the eastward of it, that in my ignorance of the depth of water so near the shore, I did not think it practicable, consistent with the safety of his Majesty's ship (drawing near twenty-five feet), to prosecute that plan.

"I, therefore, bore up, and steered parallel to them, at the distance of about two cables' length, and opened the broadside on them, which was returned by a very animated and well-directed fire of round, grape, and other descriptions of shot, supported by three batteries, for the space of twenty-one minutes, and was very destructive to our sails and rigging.

"My object during that time was to prevent their hauling outside the dry rock named Le Graul; but in steering sufficiently close to it to leave them no room to pass between me and it, and at the same time to avoid running on it myself, the utmost difficulty and anxiety were produced by the cloud of smoke which drifted ahead of the ship, and totally obscured it.

"However, by the care and attention of Mr. Hugh Stewart, the master, the ship was carried within the distance of her own length, on the south-west side, in quarter-less seven fathoms, and the enemy were in consequence obliged, as their only alternative, to attempt passing within it, where there was not water enough, and they all grounded, under every sail, on the rocks between it and the shore.

"The sails and rigging of the 'Northumberland' were so much damaged that I was obliged to leave the enemy to the effects of the falling tide, it being only one quarter ebb, while I repaired the rigging and shifted the foretopsail, which was rendered entirely useless, working to windward during that time under what sail I could set, to prevent falling to leeward, in which interval, at five o'clock, the 'Growler' joined, and fired on the enemy occasionally.

"At twenty-eight minutes after five, I anchored the 'Northumberland' in six and a half fathoms' water, Point de Pierre Laye bearing N.W. half N., the citadel of Port Louise E. three-quarters N., and the rock named Le Graul N. half E., two cables' length distant, with her broadside bearing on the enemy's two frigates and brig at point-blank range, all of them having fallen over on their sides next the shore as the tide left them, and exposed their copper to us, and the mainmasts of one frigate and the brig were gone; and from thirty-four minutes after five till forty-nine minutes past six (which was near the time of low water), a deliberate and careful fire was kept up on them, at which time, believing that I had fully effected the object of my endeavours, the crews having quitted their vessels, all their bottoms being pierced by very many of our shot, so low down as to ensure their filling on the rising tide, and the leading frigate being completely in flames, communicated to the hull from a fire which broke out in her foretop, I got under sail.

"Three batteries fired at the ship during the whole time she was at anchor, although the position was so far well chosen that she was out of the range of two of them; the other (to which the enemy's vessels were nearest) reached her, and did as much execution in the hull as all the fire she had been exposed to before.

"I directed the commander of the 'Growler' to stand in and fire, to prevent the enemy from returning to their vessels after I had ceased.

"At five minutes before eight, the frigate on fire blew up with an awful explosion, leaving no remains of her visible.

"At the close of day, I anchored for the night, out of the reach of the batteries on both sides, Point Taleet bearing N. N. W. half W. the point of Groa S. S. W. half W. the enemy's vessels N. by E.

"At ten the other frigate appeared to be on fire also (some smoke having been seen on board her from the time the firing ceased), and at half-past eleven the flames burst forth from her ports and every part with unextinguishable fury; which unlooked-for event leaving me nothing more to attempt in the morning, the brig being quite on her beam-ends, and very much damaged by our shot in every part of her bottom, even very near her keel, I weighed anchor at midnight, with a very light air from the northward, with the 'Growler' in company, profiting by the brightness of the moon to get to sea; but it was so near calm that I made very little progress, and, therefore, saw the frigate burning from head to stern all night, and explode at thirty-five minutes after two in the morning of yesterday, leaving a portion of her after-part still burning, till it was entirely consumed; and in the course of the day I had the satisfaction to see, from off the N. W. point of Groa, a third fire and explosion in the same spot, which could have been no other than the brig.

"During the time of firing on the enemy's vessels, a seaman, who states himself to be a native of Portugal, captured in the ship 'Harmony,' of Lisbon, by the frigates, on the 22nd of February, swam from one of them to the 'Northumberland,' by whom I am informed, that their names were 'L'Arianne,' and 'L'Andromache,' of 44 guns and 450 men each, and the 'Mameluke' brig, of 18 guns and 150 men; that they sailed from the Loire in the month of January—had been cruising in various parts of the Atlantic, and had destroyed thirty-six vessels of different nations (Americans, Spaniards, Portuguese, and English), taking the most valuable parts of their cargoes on board the frigates (and they appeared very deep for ships so long at sea), and one vessel they sent as a cartel to England, with about 200 prisoners.

"I am happy to have now the gratifying duty to discharge, of bearing testimony to the creditable conduct of every officer and man I had the honour to command on the occasion above related, whose zealous exertions in supporting the honour of his Majesty's naval power, and in humbling that of the enemy, were conspicuously displayed, without regard to the peculiar intricacy of the situation, or the risks and difficulties which appeared to interpose; and I hope the circumstances of his station may permit me to make particular report of the services of the senior lieutenant, John Banks, without prejudice to, or neglect of, the other meritorious and deserving officers, who were all equally inspired with intrepidity, and possessed with confidence and coolness, which rendered that qualification the more valuable.

"But as the safety of his majesty's ships, and the success of the operations which resulted, in a navigation so narrow and difficult, with almost every description of danger to avoid, is attributable, next to Providence, to the ability with which she was steered and conducted under the direction of Mr. Stewart (the master) and the pilot, I should be wanting in my duty if I were to omit to represent to you that nothing could exceed the firmness, good judgment and skill of those officers, whose experience on the coast was extremely beneficial to the service, and Mr. Stewart's counsels were of the greatest assistance to me.

"Lieutenant J. Weeks, commanding the 'Growler' gun-brig, made every effort that vessel was capable of to render assistance, and showed a perfect readiness to execute the few directions I had occasion to give him.

"I should rejoice, sir, if I were able to close this

narrative without adding a report of loss and injury sustained, but neither you nor any other authority to whom you may communicate it, will expect that a ship should have been so long at different periods under the fire of the enemy's various batteries and vessels without some loss; but I am thankful it is not greater than is expressed in the report I have the honour to enclose; and I am glad to say, that the officer wounded (namely, Lieutenant William Fletcher) will soon be recovered.

"The damage the ship has sustained is little in the hull, but more in the masts, yards, and rigging.

"A line-of-battle ship, with sails bent and topgallant-yards across, lay in the harbour of L'Orient, a spectator of the operations of the day, at the entrance of it, but the wind did not serve till night for her coming to the support of her friends.

"Every assistance, however, was afforded them of boats, men, &c., from the port, directed, as I apprehend, by the admiral in person."

The report above referred to, enumerates 5 killed and 28 wounded; which, considering the nature and extent of the service performed, is trifling, and, no doubt, mainly attributable to the admirable skill and bravery displayed in this important action.

PORTRAIT OF ADMIRAL CODRINGTON.

On the 4th of June, the boats of the 32-gun frigate "Medusa," Captain Bouverie, captured the French store-ship "Dorade," of 14 guns, lying in the harbour of Arcasson.

The boats were led by Lieutenant Josiah Thompson, who, with his men, met with a gallant resistance from the crew of the store-ship, 23 of whom were killed or wounded.

Five of the "Medusa's" men were wounded. In bringing out the prize, she grounded on a sandbank, and was set on fire and left.

Six days afterwards, the 18-gun brig "Swallow," Commander Edward Sibey, had an engagement with the French 16-gun brig "Renard," off the island of St. Marguerite.

The "Renard" and a consort, the schooner "Goéland," were compelled to seek the protection of some batteries on the shore, with a loss on board the "Renard" of 14 killed and 28 wounded. The "Swallow" had 6 killed and 17 wounded.

* * * * * * *

About Midsummer in this year war was declared by the United States against Great Britain, owing to long and aggravated disputes about the right of search and our blockade of continental ports, which was, of course, very injurious to American trade.

This would have been an act of excessive temerity on the part of the United States, as their naval force then consisted of only seven or eight frigates and a moderate number of smaller vessels, while the British fleet amounted to nearly a thousand sail of all sorts (large and small), except for the fact that we were still engaged in the protracted and desperate war with France under Napoleon.

The naval strife with America was remarkable, taking, for some time, an exactly opposite result to that which might have been expected.

In various single combats between ships of nominally the same force, the British flag, which had successively triumphed over the armadas of Spain, France, Holland and Denmark, was hauled down before that of her Transatlantic foe.

The exultation of the Yankees knew no bounds, and it became their standing boast that "the British whipped the world, and the Americans whipped the British."

In England the surprise and chagrin were no less than the exultation of their adversaries.

But upon due inquiry, consolation was found in the causes of the disasters.

It proved that they were chiefly owing to an overwhelming superiority in force of the enemy, joined to their extraordinary pains in equipment, manning and armament, while, sooth to say, the English, after a long course of unbroken victory, had become rather careless, and in their discipline relaxed.

On the 19th of August, the British frigate "Guerrière" (captured from the French), was taken after a severe action by the American frigate "Constitution."

But why? Because the British ship was only of 1,090 tons, with a complement reduced to 264 in all, whereas the Yankee ship was 1,530 tons, with 468 men altogether, and a proportionate superiority in guns, having 24-pounders on her main deck against the English 18-pounders.

On the 25th October, the English frigate "Macedonian," rated at 38 guns and carrying 48, was captured by the frigate "United States," rated at 44 guns and carrying 54, heavier than those of the "Macedonian;" the former having 292 men, and the latter 478.

The action lasted about two hours, and the loss of the English in killed and wounded was 104 men. In size the "United States" was exactly the same as the "Constitution;" the "Macedonian," 1,080 tons.

Again, on the 29th December, the "Constitution," American frigate, once more fell in with a British frigate, the "Java," of 38 guns (carrying 46), with 377 men, and, after a desperate action of between two and three hours, off the coast of Brazil, the "Java" struck, with a loss of 122 men in killed and wounded. The "Java" measured 1,070 tons only.

In each of these three actions the British ship continued the battle against her overpowering adversary until she had lost almost all her spars, and become ungovernable, as well as suffered severely in her crew and hull.

The stubborn defence of these ships against such superior force was, in fact, nearly as glorious as victory.

The American public did not know, or affected not to know, the immense disparity in force between the contending ships, and only boasted that their frigates had captured John Bull's frigates; but their naval men, however partial to their own country, knew better the real secret.

Among their other contrivances was the practice of stationing in the "tops" of their ships, expert riflemen or sharpshooters, whose part it was to fire down on the deck of their opponent and pick off his officers and men.

Nelson, according to Southey, was too chivalrous and heroic to adopt this plan—"He had a strong dislike to the practice, not merely because it endangers setting fire to the sails, but also because it is a murderous sort of warfare, by which individuals may suffer, and a commander be now and then picked off, but which never can decide the fate of a general engagement."*

The Yankees, however, with their calculating temperament, considered that it might be very useful indeed between single ships.

They also adopted some peculiar sorts of bar and star shot for their cannon, with the intention of more quickly stripping and tearing their opponent's sails and rigging, and thereby rendering them unmanageable.

All is fair in love and war, and we do not know that we have any right to complain of these "dodges," or to ridicule them—on the contrary, the fact of the Americans designing, building, arming, and equipping such superior ships is a proof of brains at least, and we may call it cunning or wisdom, as we please. But we do say their victories were rather inglorious, against such inferior force.

Several English 18-gun brig-sloops, during the years 1812—1814, were successively taken by different American ship-sloops—the former being two-masted vessels, with 110 to 120 men; the latter three-masted vessels, with 140 to 170 men, and 20 to 22 guns.

The smallness of the American navy enabled them to man each ship very fully and completely with picked seamen; while, after twenty years of war, many of the British ships were short of complement, and their crews scraped together with the offscourings of the country, undersized men, and felons released from the jails.

Upon these repeated reverses, the dormant vigilance of the British Admiralty and naval officers was awakened. A better class of ship was selected and sent over to contend with the Americans, and some of an improved size were built to meet them on more equal terms.

On the 6th of July, a squadron consisting of the 64-gun ship "Dictator," Captain James Stewart, the 18-gun brig "Calypso," and the 14-gun brig "Podargus," and gun brig "Flamer," attacked the Danish 24-pounder 40-gun frigate "Nayaden," and the 18-gun brigs "Lealand," "Samsoe," and "Kiel," near Mardoe, on the coast of Norway.

The "Calypso" and "Dictator" did all the fighting with the frigate and brigs, while the "Podargus" and "Flamer," the latter being aground, were engaged with some gunboats.

The Danish vessels were compelled to surrender, the frigate being so much cut up that she was not worth taking away.

The next day, while the English squadron was going down the narrow passage from the harbour to the sea, they were attacked by a fleet of gunboats.

The two prize brigs got aground and were abandoned.

Aboard of the English squadron 9 men were killed and 35 wounded.

The loss of the Danes is said to have been about 300 killed and wounded.

On the 16th of July, the "Eole," of Dunkerque, a privateer lugger of 6 guns, was captured off Heligoland by the boats of the 18-gun corvette "Osprey," and 10-gun brigs "Britomart" and "Leveret."

The boats were under the orders of Lieutenant William Dixon, who, with eleven men, was wounded in the engagement, and two men were killed.

On the 21st of July, the 10-gun schooner "Sealark," Lieutenant Thomas Warrand, captured the French lugger privateer "Ville de Caen," of 16 guns, off Start Point.

The "Sealark" ran on board the lugger, and a sharp engagement followed that lasted more than an hour, when the lugger was boarded and carried.

The "Sealark" had 7 men killed and 22 wounded. The lugger had her commander and 14 men killed and 16 wounded.

Four boats and 80 men of the 38-gun frigate "Horatio," Captain Lord George Stewart, captured

---

* Had Nelson, indeed, filled his tops with small-arm men, it would most likely have saved his own life, by killing or distracting the attention of the enemy's sharpshooters.

an armed cutter and schooner, and a 400-ton ship up a river of Norway on the 2nd of August.

The three vessels made an obstinate resistance, and were boarded and captured with a loss on the part of the English of 9 men killed and 16 wounded.

On the night of the 12th of August, a boat with 7 men, under the command of Michael Dwyer, master's mate, of the 20-gun ship "Minstrel," Captain John Peyton, was rowing guard off the Island of Alicant. They were watching three French privateer schooners, and seeing that they did not escape from port without notice of the same being given to the "Minstrel" and her consort, the 18-gun brig "Philomel," lying off the harbour, the position of the privateers in the harbour being thought too strong to be attacked by the two English vessels.

Mr. Dwyer, having learnt that there were only 30 troops in the battery on shore, and 20 in the castle, resolved to land and capture the battery with his boat's crew of 7 men.

The party landed about three miles from the town, and marched to the battery.

Instead of 30 men, it was garrisoned by 80 Genoese; but it was captured by 8 Englishmen, the troops flying from the place, after making but a slight resistance.

Not long after they had gained possession of the battery, it was attacked by 200 French soldiers.

Not until Mr. Dwyer had received seventeen bayonet wounds and a shot through his shoulder, and every man but one was severely wounded, did the French gain possession.

The French were so pleased with the wonderful courage displayed by these few English sailors, that Captain Foubert invited Captain Peyton of the "Minstrel" to dinner, and released Mr. Dwyer and the rest of the wounded prisoners.

Lieutenant O'Brien, with the boats of the frigate "Bacchante," Captain William Hoste, entered the harbour of Port Lema, near Rovigno, on the 31st of August, and captured three armed vessels, carrying seven long guns, and manned by 72 men, and seven vessels laden with timber.

On the 8th of September, the 10-gun schooner "Laura," Lieutenant Hunter, was captured off the coast of Delaware by the French 18-gun privateer brig "Diligente."

Lieutenant Hunter received five wounds before he became incapable of further duty, and fifteen men of his small crew being killed or wounded, the schooner was boarded and carried.

The "Diligente" had nine men killed and ten wounded.

On the 18th of December, the French 40-gun frigate "Gloire," Captain Rousin, was chased and overhauled by the English 18-gun corvette "Albacore," Commander Henry T. Davis.

On coming up with the frigate, the corvette opened fire upon it, when the former hauled up to rake the latter, and Captain Davis saw that he was mistaken in the force of the vessel he had pursued and caught.

He immediately tacked, and managed to escape with the loss of Lieutenant Harman killed, and six men wounded.

CHAPTER XXXVII

1813.

IN the year 1812, the French, Danish, and Dutch navies lost five ships of the line and frigates, besides some sloops and smaller vessels. The British in the same period lost twenty-six vessels.

For the naval service of the year 1813, Parliament granted a trifle over £20,000,000 sterling; the number of seamen and marines allowed for being 140,000.

On the 6th of January, 1813, the boats of the 38-gun frigate "Bacchante," Captain William Hoste, and the 18-gun brig "Weasel," Commander James Black, pursued two divisions of gunboats off Otranto, in the Adriatic. Lieutenant O'Brian, in the "Bacchante's" barge, overtook and captured one gunboat, mounting two guns, and manned by 36 men. Two other boats, on their way to the shore, were then pursued and captured. The boats of the "Weasel," at the same time, captured two other gunboats. The boats of the "Bacchante" were under the orders of Lieutenant Thomas Whaley.

The same day the boats of the "Havannah," Captain George Cadogan, attacked and captured a French gunboat, having a crew of 35 men and protected by troops with muskets ashore.

The boats were under the orders of Lieutenant William Hambly.

Besides the gunboat three merchant vessels were brought off.

One man, Edward Percival, the master's mate, was killed, and two seamen of the boats' crews were wounded.

The Island of Augusta, in the Adriatic, surrendered, on the 29th day of January, to the English 38-gun frigate "Apollo," Captain Taylor, the "Experience" privateer, four gunboats and 250 troops.

On the 6th of February, the 38-gun frigate "Amelia," Captain Frederick Irby, had a long and severe engagement off the coast of Africa with the French 40-gun frigate "Arethuse," Commodore Bouvet.

This action continued for nearly four hours without any great advantage being obtained by either, when the two separated, and did not meet again.

The loss on board the "Amelia," out of a crew of 350 men and boys (of whom there were 30), was 51 killed and mortally wounded, and 90 severely and slightly wounded.

The "Arethuse," with a crew of 375 men, had 31 killed and 74 wounded.

On the 8th of February, the United States 6-gun schooner "Lottery" was attacked and captured in the Chesapeake river by nine boats of a squadron of four frigates, under the command of Captain George Burdett.

The boats were under the orders of Lieutenant Kelly Nazer.

The crew of the schooner only consisted of 28 men, of whom all but 9 were killed or wounded.

Amongst the killed was John Southcomb, her commander.

On the 24th of February, the 18-gun brig "Peacock," Commander William Peake, gave chase off Cape Caroband to the American 20-gun corvette "Hornet," Captain James Lawrence.

When the two vessels were near each other they passed on opposite tacks and exchanged broadsides. Soon after, the "Hornet" bore up and ran the "Peacock" on board on her starboard quarter.

From this position she kept up a fire that finished the battle in less than fifteen minutes.

The "Peacock's" hull and masts were cut to pieces, six feet of water was in her hold, her commander and four seamen were killed, and her master, one midshipman, the carpenter and thirty men were wounded.

The "Hornet" was but slightly damaged in her spars, and had one man killed and two slightly wounded.

The Island of Ponza, on the coast of Naples, surrendered to an English force consisting of the 32-gun frigate "Thames," Captain Charles Napier, and the 36-gun frigate "Furieuse," Captain William Mounsey, having on board a battalion of troops, under Lieutenant-Colonel Coffin, on the 26th of February.

On the 18th of March, a party with the boats of the "Undaunted," Captain Thomas Ussher, boarded and captured a tartan under the battery Cami, near Marseilles.

The boats' crews were under the command of Lieutenant Aaron Tozer.

The battery was destroyed and the tartan taken out with the loss of two men killed and one wounded.

On the 20th of March, the "Captain," a 74-gun ship often mentioned in this work, took fire at Plymouth. To prevent her getting amongst other ships when her cables were burnt she was sunk by discharging heavy guns at her hulk.

On the 31st of March, an expedition commanded by Lieutenant Shaw, of the "Volontaire," Captain Waldegrave, landed at Sourin, between Toulon and Marseilles.

The boats and their crews belonged to the "Volontaire" and the "Undaunted," above mentioned, and the "Redwing" brig of 18 guns.

Two batteries garrisoned by 40 troops were captured and the guns thrown into the sea. While this work was being done, eleven vessels of a French convoy were captured and several more destroyed by some of the boats conducted by Lieutenant Syer.

On the 3rd of April, an English squadron, under the orders of Admiral Sir John B. Warren and Rear-Admiral George Cockburn, chased four armed schooners into the Rappahannock, a river running into Chesapeake Bay.

The squadron consisted of the 74-gun ships "San Domingo" and "Marlborough," the "Maidstone" and "Statira" frigates, and the brig "Fantome." The boats of this squadron were sent to capture the schooners. The "Marlborough's" boats, under command of Lieutenants James Scott and George Urmston, were in advance, and performed the principal part of the work before the others arrived.

The four schooners were captured, with a loss to the English of 2 killed and 11 wounded. The Americans had 6 men killed and 10 wounded.

As usual, during the year 1813, the English lost more vessels by the fury of the elements than by the fire of the enemy's guns.

Many distressing wrecks took place, and in one case, the wreck of the ship "Woolwich," all the crew perished, though a boat put off from shore to the rescue.

On the 22nd of April, the 18-gun brig "Weasel," Commander James Black, had a sharp action with ten gunboats in charge of a convoy in the Bay of Boscalina.

In about three hours, three of the gunboats surrendered, two were driven on shore, and one was sunk.

In the evening, the boats were sent to destroy the gunboats ashore.

This work was performed, and eight sail of the convoy were also destroyed.

On the 28th of April, the boats of the "Marlborough," "Maidstone," "Dragon," "Statira," "Dolphin," "Highflyer," and "Racer," landed at French Town, on the Chesapeake river. The "Fantome," "Mohawk," and three tenders, accompanied the boats, as well as 150 marines, besides the usual boat crews. A 6-gun battery, deserted by a few militia, was captured, and some public property destroyed.

One division of the boats destroyed a store of flour up the Susquehannah. No lives appear to have been lost in this enterprise on either side, yet the officers were promoted for the service, and the men were all entitled to the naval medal.

On the 2nd of May, the boats from the "Repulse," "Redwing," "Undaunted," "Volontaire," and other vessels of the English squadron on the coast of France, were sent ashore, under the orders of Captain Michael Ennis, to destroy some batteries at Morgion, between Toulon and Marseilles.

Six laden vessels were seized and taken out, and the batteries and gun carriages destroyed. In this affair two men were killed, and Lieutenant Shaw and three others wounded.

Captain P. B. V. Broke, the gallant commander of the "Shannon," had been appointed to watch the American ship "Chesapeake" as she lay in Boston Harbour, and about the middle of May, 1813, she appeared to be nearly ready for sea, and engrossed all the attention of our intrepid hero.

For various reasons his anxiety was naturally great.

The "Chesapeake" seemed to present the last chance, that season, of avenging the insulted honour of the British flag—of confounding the insolent pretensions of an enemy whose triumphs had originated solely in superiority of force—of making the Americans feel that, upon equal terms, they were unable successfully to contend against the prowess of their parent stock.

"Before this time," says a young officer in a letter to his friends in England, "the British navy never had a fair chance—never one.

"We have always had to cope with a mightier force, and though 'tis like high treason for a British officer to make such an assertion, the best tacticians and the possessors of the best resolutions, had the striped flag of the United States waving above their heads.

"This is breathing no word of disparagement to the English fleet at large; but the navy has latterly been so neglected by the government, that when brought into competition with one in first-rate condition and order, the issue of such a contest would not, to any reasoning mind, admit even of a doubt—much less when we consider that the infamous, unfair system existing in our navy, which

FOUNDERING OF THE SHIP "VORTIGERN."

gave a man not a glimmer of a hope of ever changing the forecastle for the quarter-deck.

"The Americans saw the evil, and reversed the circumstances, and the consequence has been that they have robbed our fleet of many a brave man, and of many a good ship too."

Serious apprehensions were entertained lest the last frigate might escape from her antagonists, as others, favoured by the weather, had lately done.

Had the "Chesapeake" once passed beyond the blockading squadron, she would inevitably have effected considerable mischief amongst the British trade where least expected; and she might probably have fallen in with English ships of war, which, being of inferior force, or weakened by the manning of prizes, would have been much less capable of supporting the national fame than the "Shannon" and the "Tenedos," which had been particularly appointed to watch, and were thoroughly prepared to meet, her.

Under these considerations, Captain Broke regarded it as an important duty to obtain, by any honourable means, a meeting with the enemy.

He had previously sent several verbal invitations to Commodore Rogers to meet the "Shannon" and "Tenedos," his two frigates, with the "President" and "Congress."

The contest would have been very unequal; but Captain Broke trusted that his gallant second, Captain Parker, would vanquish the "Congress" in time to assist him against the "President," should there be occasion for such aid.

The badness of the weather, however, prevented the continuance of a close blockade, and afforded Rogers the opportunity of escape.

It is probable, too, that, independently of his having other objects in view, the American commander, when out, might not have deemed it prudent to seek a meeting with the British frigates, without an assurance on their part that they would not receive assistance from other ships.

This consideration induced Captain Broke to draw up and combine, in a written form, the substance of the different proposals which he had already sent in to the captain of the "Chesapeake."

In this letter, which was expressed in the following terms, Captain Broke endeavoured to answer every objection that could possibly be made to his wishes.

"*H. B. M.'s ship 'Shannon,' off Boston,*
"*June*, 1813.

"SIR,—As the 'Chesapeake' appears now ready for sea, I request you will do me the favour to meet the 'Shannon' with her, ship to ship, to try the fortune of our respective flags.

"To an officer of your character, it requires some apology for proceeding to further particulars. Be assured, sir, that it is not from any doubt I can entertain of your wishing to close with my proposals, but merely to provide an answer to any objection which might be made, and very reasonably, upon the chance of our receiving unfair support.

"After the diligent attention we had paid to Commodore Rogers, the pains I took to detach all force but the 'Shannon' and 'Tenedos' to such a distance that they could not possibly join in any action fought in sight of the Capes; and the various verbal messages which had been sent into Boston to that effect, we were much disappointed to find the commodore had eluded us, by sailing the first chance, after the prevailing easterly winds had obliged us to keep an offing from the coast.

"He, perhaps, wished for some stronger assurance of a fair meeting.

"I am, therefore, induced to address you more particularly, and to assure you that what I write I pledge my honour to perform to the utmost of my power.

"The 'Shannon' mounts twenty-four guns upon a broadside, and one light boat gun, eighteen pounders on her main deck, and thirty-two pound carronades on her quarter-deck and forecastle, and is manned with a complement of 300 men and boys (a large proportion of the latter), besides 30 seamen, boys, and passengers, who were taken out of recaptured vessels lately.

"I am thus minute, because a report prevailed in some of the Boston papers that we had 150 men, additional, lent us from 'La Hogue,' which really was never the case.

"'La Hogue' is now at Halifax for provisions, and I will send all other ships beyond the power of interfering with us, and meet you wherever it is most agreeable to you, within the limits of the undermentioned rendezvous, viz:—

"From 6 to 10 leagues east of Cape Cod Lighthouse, from 8 to 10 leagues east of Cape Ann Light, on Cashe's Ledge, in lat. 43, north, at any bearing and distance you please to fix off the South Breakers of Nantucket, or the Shoal in St. George's bank.

"If you will favour me with any plan of signals or telegraph, I will warn you (if sailing under this promise) should any of my friends be too nigh or anywhere in sight, until I can detach them out of my way, or I would sail with you under a flag of truce to any place you think safest from our cruisers, hauling it down when fair to begin hostilities.

"You must, sir, be aware that my proposals are highly advantageous to you, as you cannot proceed to sea singly in the 'Chesapeake' without imminent risk of being crushed by the superior force of the numerous British squadrons which are now abroad, where all your efforts, in case of a rencontre, would, however gallant, be perfectly hopeless. I entreat you, sir, not to imagine that I am urged by mere personal vanity to the wish of meeting the 'Chesapeake;' or that I depend only upon your personal ambition for your acceding to this invitation: we have both nobler motives.

"You will feel it as a compliment if I say that the result of our meeting may be the most grateful service I can render to my country, and I doubt not that you, equally confident of success, will feel convinced that it is only by repeated triumphs in *even combat* that your little navy can now hope to console *your* country for the loss of that trade it cannot protect. Favour me with a speedy reply. We are short of provisions and water, and cannot stay long here.

"I have the honour to be, sir, your obedient humble servant,

(Signed) "P. B. V. BROKE,

"Captain of H. B. M.'s Ship 'Shannon.'"

"N.B.—For the general service of watching your coast, it is requisite for me to keep another ship in company to support me with her guns and boats when employed near the land, and particularly to aid each other if either ship in chase should get on shore.

"You must be aware that I cannot, consistently with my duty, waive so great an advantage for this *general* service, by detaching my consort, without an assurance on your part of meeting me directly; and that you will neither seek or admit aid from any other of your armed vessels, if I detach mine expressly for the sake of meeting you.

"Should any special order restrain you from thus answering a formal challenge, you may yet oblige me by keeping my proposal a secret, and appointing any place you may like to meet us (within three hundred miles of Boston) in a given number of days after you sail; as, unless you agree to an interview, I may be busied on other service, and perhaps be at a distance from Boston when you go to sea.— Choose your terms—but let us meet.

"*To the Commander of the U. S. Frigate 'Chesapeake.'*"

ENDORSEMENT ON THE ENVELOPE.

"We have thirteen American prisoners on board, which I will give you for as many British sailors, if you will send them out; otherwise, being privateers' men, they must be detained."

Some rough weather occurring, it was not found practicable to send the letter in till the morning of the 1st of June.

In the interim, however, the proposed measures had been taken to secure fair play to the enemy.

Captain Capel having left Captain Broke in charge of the blockade, whilst he went into port for water, the "Chesapeake" had no line-of-battle ships to fear; and Captain Broke detached all the remaining ships to such a distance, as precluded the possibility of their affording him any assistance in the anticipated action.

On the 1st of June, observing that the "Chesapeake" lay a long time with her sails loose, and wasting the morning, though she had a fair wind to come out, it was apprehended that she might not sail that day.

Captain Broke therefore sent in his challenge, to quicken her movements.

The "Chesapeake," however, stood out of the harbour before the boats reached the shore; and Captain Broke having no assurance that she would not receive aid from other armed craft in Boston in case of being crippled in action, stood across the bay, till about five leagues from the land, directly opposite to Boston Lighthouse.

There he lay-to, to wait for her, in such a position that the action might be seen from the heights over the town.

"To meet the foe she lies prepared;
  Her guns run out, her decks all cleared,
    Preventer-braces rove;
  Stopper'd is every topsail sheet,
  Slung all her yards, her hammocks neat
  Afresh are stow'd, her shot complete;
    And in her tops above,
  And ranged along her gangways, stand
  Of musketeers a numerous band,
  That boast with quick unerring aim,
  The rage of fiercest foes to tame."

The approaching action excited the liveliest interest, and the most confident anticipation of victory amongst the people of Boston.

A number of pleasure-boats, it is said, came out with the "Chesapeake," to see the "Shannon" compelled to strike; and a grand dinner was actually preparing on shore, for the "Chesapeake's" officers, against their return with the prize.

The "Shannon" was lying-to, under topsails, topgallant sails, jib, and spanker, with just steerage-way, awaiting the approach of the "Chesapeake," and leaving it in her power to commence the engagement as she pleased, either at a distance or close, either on the starboard or larboard side.

She came down in a very gallant style, on the "Shannon's" weather and starboard quarter, till within half pistol-shot.

The "Shannon's" men having orders to fire as they could get their guns to bear, commenced by firing first their after-guns on the maindeck, and then their aftermost carronade on the quarterdeck, just as the "Chesapeake's" bows were upon their quarter.

These two guns were distinctly heard before the "Chesapeake" returned her fire, which then became furious on both sides.

But the superiority of the "Shannon's" fire was so great, that at her second broadside nearly all the men were swept from the upper deck of the "Chesapeake."

About this time the ships came in contact, and the "Chesapeake" having shot rather ahead, was caught by one of the "Shannon's" anchors, and lay obliquely athwart her starboard bow, exposed to a most tremendous fire from the "Shannon's" afterguns, which, battering her lee-quarter, and entering her portholes, from thence towards the mainmast, strewed her maindeck with killed and wounded.

A small open cask of musket cartridges, in an open chest abaft the mizenmast of the "Chesapeake," now caught fire and blew up, and when the smoke it occasioned had blown away, Captain Broke saw the favourable moment, and instantly, with a few men, not exceeding 20, boarded her about the mizen rigging, from the starboard bow.

Not a man was left standing on the "Chesapeake's" quarterdeck when she was boarded, but about 20 made a slight resistance, on her gangway, who were instantly driven before the foremast, and there being obliged to stand, fought desperately, but were quickly overpowered.

A few endeavoured to get down the fore-hatchway, but in their eagerness prevented each other; some jumped over, and one or two of them escaped by getting in again at the maindeck ports.

Captain Broke and his first boarding party were almost immediately followed by between 30 and 40 marines, who secured possession of the "Chesapeake's" quarterdeck, dislodged the men from the main and fore-tops, that were firing down on the boarders, and kept down all who attempted to come up from the maindeck.

Being thus completely captured, Mr. Watt, the first lieutenant, ran aft, and seizing the British colours from a sailor who brought them from the "Shannon," bent them, and was in the act of hoisting them above the American, when he was struck on the forehead by a grape-shot, and killed in the very moment of victory.

He was shot by one of the "Shannon's" maindeck guns, the commanding officers of which did not know that the contest was already decided.

At the commencement of the brief contest which took place on board the "Chesapeake," Captain Broke had the misfortune to be wounded.

He was in the act of charging a party of the enemy, who had rallied on their forecastle.

He first parried a blow from the butt-end of a firelock, which had been raised to strike him.

At the same instant, as it were, another of the Americans made a charge at him, with a bayonet; but that, also, he successfully turned aside.

The colours of the "Chesapeake" were down, when Captain Broke received a severe wound with a sabre, from one of three men whom he was earnestly calling upon his brave followers to spare.

The man was instantly dispatched; and one of the "Chesapeake's" midshipmen, who, having been in the foretop, slid down a rope, and alighted close to Captain Broke, at the moment, would probably have experienced a similar fate, but for his humane interference.

The capture having been completed, Captain Broke, in a state of exhaustion and insensibility from exertion and loss of blood, was taken on board of his own ship, which, with her prize, afterwards proceeded to Halifax.

The loss on board the "Shannon," out of 330 men, was 3 officers and 23 men killed; Captain Broke, 2 officers, and 58 men wounded; 87 total.

On mustering the crew of the "Chesapeake," the following day, they found that out of 440 men, the second lieutenant, master, marine officers, some midshipmen, and 90 seamen and marines were killed; Captain Lawrence mortally wounded, and the first and second lieutenants, some midshipmen, and 110 men also wounded; making a total of killed and wounded between the two ships of nearly 300 men, or 20 men for every minute the ships were in action.

The "Chesapeake" was a fine frigate, and mounted 49 guns, eighteens on her main deck, two-and-thirties on her quarterdeck and forecastle. Both ships came out of action in the most beautiful order, their rigging appearing as perfect as if they had only been exchanging a salute.

Each fought from their tops, with guns and small arms.

The "Shannon" had a four-pounder mounted in one of her tops, from which she fired 50 canister shot at each discharge.

These, by spreading greatly, did much execution. It was from some of the "Shannon's" top-men that Captain Lawrence, the commander of the "Chesapeake," received his mortal wound.

He had been carried below before the boarding commenced.

The "Shannon," suffered most on the fore part of the maindeck and forecastle, and her greatest loss of men was on those parts.

The "Chesapeake" was terribly battered on her larboard bow and quarter; amidships there were not many marks of shot, which must have entered her portholes, as the whole of her maindeck was strewn with dead and wounded.

"The enemy," says Captain Broke, "came into action with a complement of 440 men; the 'Shannon' having picked up some recaptured seamen, had 330."

Thus it appears to have been the result of mere *accident* that the 'Shannon' was *only one hundred and ten men short of the number of her opponent!*— In this instance, American vanity, raised to the most inordinate height by their former successes in three very unequal contests, was mortified in the extreme, and stung almost to madness, by this unequivocal proof of their inferiority to us in fair and equal combat; hence we account for the ridiculous and extravagant falsehood of their statements, the baseness of their calumny, and the inveteracy of their malice.

"According to them, the fire of the 'Chesapeake' was more 'vivid and effectual,' until the 'Shannon' threw on board of her, 'an immense body of combustibles and inflammable matter, like an infernal machine of a new and horrible construction, which enveloped the 'Chesapeake' in a volume of flame to her very tops; and that to the effects of this all-destroying explosion, the 'Shannon' was entirely indebted for her victory."

The only circumstance that could have given rise to this wonderful tale of mysterious horror, was the cask of musket cartridges which caught fire, and blew up abaft the "Chesapeake's" mizenmast, which had been placed there by themselves, to supply their marines.

These cartridges not being confined, exploded with so little violence, that scarcely any of the effects were to be traced on her quarterdeck; the only appearance of a singe that was to be found, was a small portion of the spanker-boom, and that so slight as to be scarcely visible.

Their assertion that the superiority of the "Chesapeake's" fire was proved by the fact of "its having carried away the jib-boom, and fore and mizen royal-masts of the enemy," is totally false. Neither of the ships lost a single spar.

The damage sustained by both was in their hulls; and that of the "Shannon" was trifling indeed, compared with that of the "Chesapeake."

There was found on the "Chesapeake's" decks more shot than could have been fired away had the battle lasted several hours, among which were (besides grape, canister, and double-headed shot) bars of wrought iron connected by links, so as to form an extended length of five feet, and others with four bars of more than a foot each, all connected at one end by a ring, which expanded in four points as they flew.

The "Shannon" had only round shot, grape and canister; but many of the "Chesapeake's" canisters were afterwards opened, and all were found to contain in the centre angular and jagged pieces of iron of various shapes and sizes; and all their musket cartridges had three, and some four buckshot loose in the powder; the evident design of which must have been, not merely to disable and to destroy (for round balls are equally effectual for these purposes), but to increase the torment and retard the cure of the wounds they inflicted.

They had also a large cask of unslacked lime, with the head open, standing on the forecastle, and a bag of the same on the foretop; and their intention was (if they had had time) to throw it by handfuls into the eyes of our men when they attempted to board.

It happened that, on the evening of the day on which the account of the action between the "Shannon" and the "Chesapeake" arrived, Mr. Croker had occasion to advert to some statements of Lord Cochrane, in the House of Commons, on a former night, respecting the capture of the "Macedonian."

By reading the sentence of the court-martial which had been holden on the officers of that ship, he vindicated the gallantry of her commander, the discipline and bravery of her crew, and their signal display of coolness and courage to the last; and then, as a new instance of the bravery and skill of those officers and seamen which, he observed, the noble lord had been so much in the habit of depreciating, he detailed, in a style of lively, brilliant, and enthusiastic eloquence, the unexcelled, the almost unparalleled conduct of Captain Broke.

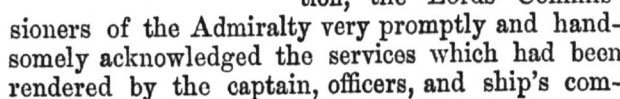

PORTRAIT OF ADMIRAL SIR M. SEYMOUR.

The statement was new to the house; and the effect which it produced was almost equal to that of electricity.

Towards the close of his speech, Mr. Croker remarked, that the British sailors not only boarded from every deck, but even those who were aloft sprang upon the enemy's yards, and stormed their tops.

Lieutenant Falkiner, he added, had described the action as the most beautiful and gallant scene that he had ever witnessed. After the arrival of the dispatches relating to the action, the Lords Commissioners of the Admiralty very promptly and handsomely acknowledged the services which had been rendered by the captain, officers, and ship's company of the "Shannon."

They complimented Captain Broke in the most flattering manner upon his gallant achievement, and informed him that they had awarded him the honour of a medal; adding, that they had immediately promoted the two surviving lieutenants (Wallis and Falkiner) to the rank of commander, and Messrs. Etough and Smith to that of lieutenant; and that they should be happy to attend to the reward or promotion of such petty officers or seamen as Captain Broke might particularly recommend for their conduct in the engagement.

On the 25th of September following, his Royal Highness the Prince Regent was pleased to confer upon Captain Broke the dignity of a baronet of the kingdom of Great Britain and Ireland, as an *especial* mark of royal favour.

On the 12th of June, the American schooner "Surveyor" was captured in York River by the boats of the 32-gun frigate "Narcissus," Captain John Lumley. The boats were under the command of Lieutenant John Cririe.

The schooner only had a crew of sixteen men, who defended their vessel in so gallant a manner, that their commander's sword was returned to him with many compliments. The English had three men killed and six wounded.

The boats of the "Bacchante," Captain Hoste, under the command of Silas T. Hood, captured seven gunboats and two batteries at the town of Lela Nova, on the coast of Albruzza, on the 12th of June. Three men were killed and six wounded of the boats' crew.

On the 23rd of June, the French privateer "Fortune" was captured on the coast of Catalonia by the boats of the 32-gun frigate "Castor," Captain Charles Dilks. The loss in the boats was four killed and nine wounded.

On the 11th of July, the American schooners "Scorpion" and "Asp" were captured at the entrance of the Yeocomico river by the boats of the 18-gun brigs "Contest" and "Mohawk." The boats were led by Lieutenants Roger Curry and William Hutchinson.

The British had two men killed and six wounded. The American lieutenant was killed, and nine of a crew of 25 were wounded.

On the 5th of August, the English 14-gun schooner "Dominica," Lieutenant George Barrette, met the Franco-American privateer schooner "Decatur," of 7 guns, one being a long 18-pounder on a pivot carriage.

For some time the "Decatur" used the long gun, then closed, and ran her jib boom through the "Dominica's" mainsail.

The crew of the "Decatur" then boarded; the English were overpowered by numbers, and the commander and 17 others killed, and 47 wounded, being only one less than the whole number of the crew.

On board the "Decatur," 4 were killed and 15 wounded.

On the 14th of August, the United States 20-gun brig "Argus," Captain William Allen, was captured off the coast of Ireland by the English 18-gun brig "Pelican," Commander John Maples. On board the "Argus" 6 were killed, and Captain Allen and 17 others were wounded.

On the "Pelican," the master's mate, Mr. Young, and 1 seaman were killed and 5 wounded.

The advantage in the armament of the vessels was in favour of the "Pelican," as she carried 32-pounders and the "Argus" 18-pounders.

On the 5th of September, the English 14-gun brig "Boxer," Captain Samuel Blyth, discovered and overtook the American 16-gun brig "Enterprise," Lieutenant William Burrows, off the coast of Maine.

Captain Blyth, of the "Boxer," was killed at the first broadside.

The "Boxer" was a bad sailer, and the American brig was able to take and keep favourable positions for raking her.

Lieutenant McCleery, who had the command after Captain Blyth was killed, seeing that all efforts to escape from or conquer the other was hopeless, ordered the colours to be struck.

On board the "Boxer," 3 men were killed besides the commander, and 17 wounded.

One man was killed on the "Enterprise" and 11 wounded.

On the 9th of September, the schooner "Alphea," of 8 guns, Lieutenant Thomas Jones, pursued and overtook the French 14-gun privateer schooner "Renard."

In the battle that ensued, the "Alpha" blew up, and not one of the crew were saved.

The "Renard" had five men killed and 31 wounded.

On the 10th of September, the English squadron on Lake Erie, under Commodore Robert Barclay, met the American squadron under Commodore Perry.

The English flotilla consisted of the following vessels.

The ship "Detroit," Commodore Barclay; the ship "Queen Charlotte," Commander Robert Finnis; the schooner "Chippaway," master's mate, John Campbell; the brig "Hunter," Lieutenant Bignell; the schooner "Lady Prevost," and sloop "Little Belt."

This fleet mounted 68 guns and was manned by 370 men.

The American fleet mounted 64 guns, but they were much heavier than the English, and their vessels were manned by 600 men. Commodore Perry advanced to the attack with a signal flying, consisting of the words of the dying Lawrence of the "Chesapeake"—"Don't give up the ship."

The action was commenced between the "Detroit" and the "Lawrence," Commodore Perry's vessel.

The "Queen Charlotte" then engaged the "Niagara," which was supported by two schooners.

The "Lawrence," after an action of about two hours became so disabled that Commodore Perry deserted her for another vessel, and her colours were hauled down.

Captain Finnis, of the "Queen Charlotte" was killed, and Lieutenant Stokes being severely wounded, there was not another officer aboard capable of commanding the ship, and its flag was struck.

The "Detroit" on being attacked by the "Niagara," to which the American commodore had repaired, was compelled to surrender.

The "Hunter" and "Lady Prevost" surrendered immediately after, and the "Chippaway" and "Little Belt," while trying to escape, were overtaken and captured.

The loss on board the English squadron was 41 killed and 93 wounded. On the American squadron 27 were killed and 96 wounded.

Commodore Barclay, his officers and crew, were acquitted of all blame by the court-martial that tried them for the loss of the vessels. Their failure was principally attributed to the want of more men and heavier guns.

On the 13th day of October, the 12-gun schooner "Telegraph," Lieutenant Timothy Scriven, attacked the French 16-gun brig "Flibuster" near the entrance of Bayonne River.

The action was decided by the appearance of the English brigs "Challenger" and "Constant," when the French set fire to their vessel and went ashore.

On the 14th of October, the 36-gun frigate "Furieuse" saw in the port of Marinello a convoy of nineteen vessels under the protection of some gunboats, a castle and a tower.

A party was landed under Lieutenant Walter Croker, which stormed the fort. The frigate attacked the battery and soon destroyed it. Sixteen of the vessels were captured, two of which were sunk, and the other fourteen, laden with cargoes, were taken out.

Two men belonging to the frigate were killed and ten wounded.

On the 21st of October, the Batavian 40gun-frigate "Wesser," Captain C. Laar, surrendered to the 74-gun ship "Rippon," Captain Cole. The "Wesser" had been harassed for two days by the 18-gun brigs "Scylla" and "Royalist," which were unable to capture, and unwilling to leave it. The "Scylla" had two men wounded and the "Royalist" had two men killed and nine wounded.

On the 23rd, the "Wesser's" consort, the 40-gun frigate "Trave," Captain Van Muren, was found in a crippled state and captured by the 36-gun frigate "Andromache," Captain George Tobin. This vessel, as well as the "Wesser," was added to the English navy.

On the 9th of October, the "Thunder" bomb, Commander Watkin O. Pell, captured in the Channel the French 16-gun lugger privateer "Neptune," of Dunkerque. The "Neptune's" helm was put up for the purpose of boarding the "Thunder." As the two vessels came together, a party from the latter boarded the privateer, and captured it after a slight resistance.

The "Neptune" had 4 men killed and 10 wounded. The "Thunder" had but 2 men wounded.

The naval medal was given for the action.

On the 1st of November, the 16-gun "Snap" captured the French privateer lugger "Lion," mounting 16 guns, and manned by 69 men. In the action, 4 of the privateer's men were killed, and 6 wounded.

On the 26th of November, the boats of the 74-gun ship "Swiftsure," Captain Edward S. Dickson, captured the French privateer schooner "Charlemagne," of 8 guns and 93 men.

The boats of the "Swiftsure" were under the orders of Lieutenant William Smith. Five of the boats' crews were killed and 15 wounded.

CHAPTER XXXVIII.
1814.

AT the beginning of this year the number of ships in the English navy was 1,032, including those in ordinary, &c. Of these there were in commission 116 sail of the line, 20 vessels with from 50 to 44 guns, 157 frigates, 110 sloops, 7 fire ships, 199 brigs, 40 cutters, and 50 schooners, making the total number in commission 768.

We now proceed to record what they did towards paying for the expense of maintaining them.

On the 5th of January, the fortress of Cattaro, in the Adriatic, surrendered to Captain William Hoste, of the 38-gun frigate "Bacchante," which had for a consort the 18-gun brig "Saracen," Commander John Harper. The attack upon the fortress had been continued for ten days, before it surrendered, and during that time the two vessels had only one man killed and one wounded.

On the same day, the French 40-gun frigate "Ceres," Captain Le Baron de Bourgainville, was captured off the Cape de Verde Islands by the 18-pounder 38-gun frigates "Niger" and "Tagus," Captains Peter Rainier and Philip Pipon.

She was added to the English navy under the name of "Seine."

This was a remarkable battle, it lasting for several hours and only one man being killed.

On the 16th of January, the 74-gun ship "Venerable," Captain James Worth, the 22-gun ship "Cyane," Captain Thomas Forrest, and brig "Jason" (a prize), Lieutenant Moffat, while off the Canary Isles, gave chase to the French 40-gun frigates "Iphigénie" and "Alcmène," Captains Emeric and Villeneuve.

The "Venerable" commenced the action with the "Alcmène," which put her helm up and ran on board the "Venerable." In place of coming to the assistance of her consort, according to arrangement, the "Iphigénie" hauled sharp up and made off.

The "Alcmène" was then boarded by a party led by Captain Worth, and the French colours hauled down. She had 30 men killed, and 50 wounded, including her captain amongst the latter.

The "Iphigénie" was pursued by the "Cyane" and "Jason" for three days, when, on the approach of the "Venerable," she surrendered.

Both vessels were added to the English navy under the names of "Gloire" and "Dunira."

On the 23rd of January, the 18-pounder 36-gun frigates "Creole" and "Astrea," Captains George Mackenzie and John Everleigh, pursued the French 40-gun frigates "Etoile" and "Sultane," Captains Phillibert and Thuars.

When the four vessels met, a very sharp conflict took place between them, in which the English vessels were so much cut up, that they might easily have been captured, had the French officers known their real condition. They did not, and the "Creole" was allowed to escape, and the French frigates bore away without capturing the "Astrea," as they might easily have done.

The "Creole" had 10 men killed and 26 wounded. Aboard the "Astrea," Captain Everleigh and 8 men were killed, and 37 wounded.

The 56-gun frigate "Majestic," Captain John Hayes, gave chase to the French 40-gun frigates "Atalante" and "Terpsichore," and a Spanish 20-gun ship and a merchant vessel, their prizes, on the 3rd of February. A running fight of two hours followed, when the "Terpsichore" surrendered, with a loss of 3 killed and 6 wounded. The other vessels escaped.

On the 13th of February, Vice-Admiral Sir Edward Pellew, of the "Caledonia," his flag ship, Captain Lord Percy,* and the 98-gun ship "Boyne," Captain George Burlton, chased three French sail of the line and three frigates into Toulon, where they were obliged to relinquish the pursuit from the reception they met with from the batteries of the harbour.

Two men were killed and 40 wounded on board the "Boyne." On the French vessels 81 were killed and wounded.

On the 25th of February, the 38-gun frigate "Eurotas," Captain John Phillimore, gave chase to the French 40-gun frigate "Clorinde," Captain Legarde. After a furious engagement for about fifty minutes, both vessels became dismasted, and the "Clorinde" got beyond the reach of the "Eurotas'" guns. Captain Phillimore, who was wounded early in the engagement, then consented to go below, and Lieutenant Robert Smith proceeded to rig jurymasts for the purpose of once more coming up with the enemy.

The "Eurotas" was now joined by the 36-gun frigate "Dryad," Captain Edward Galway, who closed with the "Clorinde," when she surrendered.

On board the "Eurotas," 21 were killed and 39 wounded.

On the French frigate 30 were killed and 40 wounded.

She was added to the English navy under the name of "Aurora."

On the 7th of March, the United States privateer "Mars" was driven on shore and destroyed by the boats of the English frigates "Belvidera" and "Endymion," and the sloop "Rattler."

The boats were led by Lieutenant John Sykes, first officer of the "Belvidera."

The "Mars" carried 15 guns, and was manned by 70 men.

On the 12th of March, the 18-gun brig "Primrose," Commander Charles Phillott, discovered the king's packet brig "Marlborough," John Bull, commander, bound to Lisbon.

The latter vessel took the "Primrose" for an American, and sailed from her, at the same time making the private signal, which was not seen from the vessel in pursuit.

After dark, the night signal was made aboard the packet, but it was not understood on the "Primrose."

The "Marlborough" was overtaken and hailed, but her only answer was a broadside.

A sharp action then ensued, in which the packet was much damaged in her masts and rigging, and had three feet of water in her hold, 2 passengers killed, and 10 men wounded, before Captain Phillott discovered that she was an English vessel.

The loss on the "Primrose" was 1 seaman killed and 13 wounded.

Had Captain John Bull, of the packet, been willing to treat an enemy with civility, and answered Captain Phillott's hail with words instead of a broadside, this unfortunate affair would not have happened.

On the 26th of March, the French frigates "Etoile" and "Sultane," which, on the 23rd of January, were engaged with the "Creole" and "Astrea," were discovered by the 38-gun frigate "Hebrus," Captain Palmer, and the 16-gun brig "Sparrow," Commander Francis Loch.

An engagement began, in which the "Hebrus" and "Sparrow" were joined by the 74-gun ship "Hannibal," Captain Sir Michael Seymour.

The two French frigates separated, the "Etoile" being pursued by the "Hebrus" and the "Sparrow," and the "Sultane" by the "Hannibal."

The "Etoile" was captured by the "Hebrus," near Pointe Jobourg.

The latter vessel had 13 killed and 25 wounded. On the "Etoile," 40 were killed and 73 wounded. For her capture Captain Palmer was presented with a gold medal, and the naval medal was given to all.

The "Hannibal" overtook the "Sultane" in the afternoon of the same day, and she surrendered after receiving one broadside.

Both frigates were added to the British navy. The "Sultane's" name was not changed, and the "Etoile" became the "Topaze."

During the months of February and March, the United States 32-gun frigate "Essex," Captain David Porter, and the 20-gun ship "Essex Junior," were blockaded in the Port of Valparaiso, Chili, by the English 36-gun frigate "Phœbe," Captain

---

* Since Duke of Northumberland.

James Hillyar, and the 24-gun ship "Cherub," Captain Thomas Tucker.

The "Essex" and her consort proceeded to sea in a storm on the 28th of March, met the "Phœbe" and "Cherub," and were compelled to fight.

Yonge says, in his "Naval History of Great Britain," that there were 100 English sailors on the "Essex," and when they saw that she would be compelled to surrender, they jumped overboard;

"Hague," with the frigates "Endymion" and "Maidstone," and 14-gun brig "Borer," under the command of Richard Coote, commander of the latter vessel, were sent up the Connecticut river.

The party consisted of 136 men, who, on the following day, after a skirmish with the Americans, destroyed twenty-seven vessels and a quantity of naval stores; 2 men of the party were killed and 2 wounded.

WRECK OF THE SHIP "COMUS," OFF NEWFOUNDLAND.

40 succeeded in reaching the shore; 31 were known to have been drowned, and 16 were picked up.

Aboard the "Essex," 24 were killed and 45 wounded.

On the two English vessels 4 men were killed and 10 wounded.

The boats of the 24-gun ship "Porcupine," Captain John Coode, were sent, on the 2nd of April, under the orders of Lieutenant Dunlop, after a French flotilla near the river Gironde.

The party in the boats had first to disperse some troops on the shore. It then brought off a brig, six gunboats, a schooner, and a barge, with a loss of 2 men missing and 14 wounded.

On the 7th of April, the boats of a squadron under Captain Thomas Capel, of the 74-gun ship

The others received the medal for a naval boat action, which they might have deserved had circumstances made the expedition a little more difficult.

On the 20th of April, the 36-gun frigate "Orpheus," Captain Hugh Pigot, and the 12-gun schooner "Shelburne," Lieutenant David Hope, captured the United States 18-gun corvette "Frolic," Commander Joseph Bainbridge. She was added to the navy as a 22-gun ship, and called the "Florida."

On the 29th of April, the 18-gun brig "Epervier," Commander Richard Wales, three days from Havana, encountered the United States 18-gun brig "Peacock," Captain Lewis Warrington. At the first broadside of the "Peacock," three of the

"Epervier's" guns were dismounted, and in a few minutes she was completely unrigged, and her sails cut to pieces by the continuous shower of langridge, bar and star shot that was poured upon her from the "Peacock."

After the "Epervier's" main-boom had been cut away, falling on the wheel and rendering the vessel unmanageable, and her maintop mast shot away, the "Peacock" began firing at her hulk, and disabled every gun but one on her larboard side.

There was but one plan left, and that was to board the enemy, but this could not be done, as a large number of the crew—a majority of them—expressed a determined unwillingness to do so. The foremast of the "Epervier" was expected to fall every moment, and she had five feet of water in the hold.

Eight men were killed, and her first lieutenant, John Hacket, and fourteen men, were wounded. Under these circumstances Captain Wales ordered the colours to be struck.

The "Peacock" was but slightly injured, and only two of her crew were wounded.

Captain Wales and his officers were honourably acquitted by a court-martial for the loss of the vessel, which had a wretched crew, many of whom were disaffected, and apparently quite willing that the enemy should win the day.

Paris capitulated to the allied armies on the 31st of March, and on the 5th of April, Bonaparte renounced all claim to the throne of France, and Louis XVIII. was recalled. On the 28th of April, Napoleon sailed for Elba in the English 38-gun frigate "Undaunted," Captain Thomas Ussher, and England and France were at peace.

The war with America, however, continued, and on the 6th of May, Sir James Yeo, in the "Prince Regent," of 58 guns, with the "Princess Charlotte," of 42 guns, the "Montreal," "Niagara," "Charwell," "Star," and "Magnet," with 1,100 troops, under Lieutenant-General Drummond, made an attack on Oswego, on Lake Ontario. This force met with a slight opposition from about 600 American militia, 6 of whom were killed, 38 wounded, and 60 were taken prisoners. Three small vessels, a large quantity of naval stores, and 2,400 barrels of provisions were taken. The barracks and all public buildings were destroyed.

One hundred and fifty seamen and marines were despatched by Sir James Yeo, under the orders of Commanders Popham and Spilsbury, to Sacket's Harbour, an American town on Lake Ontario, on the 30th of May. They were attacked by 150 American riflemen and some Indians, and were made prisoners. Mr. Hoare, master's mate, and 18 men were killed, and 50 were dangerously wounded.

On the 28th of June, the 18-gun brig "Reindeer," Commander William Manners, gave chase to the United States 18-gun corvette "Wasp," Captain Johnson Blakely.

When the "Reindeer" reached within musket-shot of the "Wasp," on her starboard and weather quarter, she opened fire. A spirited cannonade followed, which lasted until the "Reindeer" became unmanageable, and fell foul of her enemy in a position that exposed her to a raking fire.

To stop the slaughter of his men, Captain Manners made an attempt to board. He was already severely wounded in two places, but was the first to attempt boarding the enemy, calling on his men to follow.

At that instant, two musket balls passed through his head, and he dropped upon the deck dead. Soon after, the American crew boarded, and the "Reindeer" was captured.

On board the "Reindeer," 25 men were killed, and 42 wounded.

On the "Wasp," 11 were killed, and 15 wounded. The brig was so much injured that she was destroyed by her captors. James, in his "Naval History," says:—

"This may be pronounced one of the best-fought sloop actions of the war. The British crew had long served together, and Captain Manners was the idol and delight of his men. They were called the 'pride of Plymouth.'"

The crew of the "Reindeer" numbered 118, that of the "Wasp," 173.

On the 12th of July, the 4-gun cutter "Landrail," Lieutenant Robert Lancaster, was captured in the Channel after a two hours' engagement, by the United States privateer schooner "Syren," of a much superior force.

On the 30th August, while the 38-gun frigate "Menelaus" was lying in Chesapeake Bay, a party landed under the orders of Sir Peter Parker, its captain, and attacked a band of American volunteers.

The Americans were driven from their camp and very indiscreetly pursued.

They seemed to prefer a running fight, and of the 104 men who landed, Sir Peter Parker, a midshipman, and 12 men were killed, and 27 wounded.

The remainder of the party escaped to their ship, taking with them the body of their captain.

The 18-gun brig "Avon," Commander James Arbuthnot, met the American 18-gun corvette "Wasp," which had just left the port of L'Orient, where she had refitted after her late conquest of the "Reindeer."

On the 1st of September, an action began, which, in a few minutes, rendered the "Avon" in an ungovernable state.

The aftermost guns on the engaged side were covered with the mainsail and other wreck—the mainmast was over the board, and the brig was incapable of making any resistance.

The "Avon" then surrendered, and just as a boat was being lowered from the "Wasp," to take possession, the English 18-gun brig "Castilian," Captain David Braimer, came up, and the "Wasp" immediately made sail.

The "Castilian" pursued, but was recalled by signals of distress from the "Avon," which was sinking.

Captain Braimer sent all his boats to bring away the "Avon's" crew, and just as the last boat load left, she went down.

On board the "Avon," the first lieutenant, John Pendergast, and 9 men were killed, and 32 wounded, including the commander.

The "Wasp" had two men killed and two wounded.

The "Wasp," of which the Americans may well feel much pride, never reached America, but is supposed to have foundered off Madeira about three weeks after her battle with the "Avon."

On the 3rd of September, an expedition from an English squadron, under Rear-Admiral Edward Griffith, of the 74-gun ship "Dragon," was sent to destroy the United States 36-gun frigate "Adams," Captain Morris, in the Penobscot River.

The expedition was led by Lieutenant George Pedlar of the "Dragon," assisted by George I. Percival of the "Tenedos," and Francis Ormond of the "Endymion."

The "Adams" was lying at the town of Hamden, protected by a large body of militia, that ran away on the approach of the English.

On seeing himself so shamefully deserted, Captain Morris set fire to the "Adams" and two other vessels, all of which were burnt.

The expedition then went to Bangor, where one ship, a brig, three schooners, and a sloop were also destroyed.

Only 1 seaman was killed, and 9 wounded in performing this important service, which was of much loss to the enemy.

On the 10th of September, the English squadron on Lake Champlain, under Commodore Downie, sailed for Platsburg, to assist Sir George Prevost in his attack with a land force on that place.

The English squadron consisted of the "Confiance," "Linnet," "Chubb," "Finch," and ten gunboats, mounting in all 84 guns, and manned by 714 men.

The American squadron, under Commodore Thomas Macdonough, lying at Platsburg, to oppose the British, was comprised of the following vessels:—

The "Saratoga," "Eagle," "Ticonderoga," "Preble," and ten gunboats, mounting in all 86 guns, and manned by 981 men.

In the beginning of the action Commodore Downie, who engaged the "Saratoga," with the "Confiance," was killed.

The most of the gunboats deserted, and the "Finch" ran on some rocks and struck her flag.

In a short time the whole squadron was knocked to pieces, and captured, except the gunboats that deserted. On board the English squadron 57 men were killed, and 92 wounded; and on the American 52 were killed, and 58 wounded.

Many attribute this defeat of the English squadron to Sir George Prevost, who did not give the co-operation of the land force at the proper time.

We must now turn back for a few weeks to notice the proceedings of the squadron under Rear-Admiral Cockburn at the mouth of the Potomac River.

On the 17th of August, a squadron under Rear-Admiral Pulteney Malcolm, in the 74-gun ship "Royal Oak," with three frigates, three sloops, two bomb vessels, and eight transports, with a body of troops under Major-General Ross, joined Rear-Admiral Cockburn, who had arrived at the Potomac some time before.

Admiral Cockburn proposed to General Ross that they should attack the city of Washington. This was agreed to, and 4,000 troops were started up a river for the city.

On the way to Washington the troops met with but very little opposition, neither did the flotilla that reached Alexandra, eight miles from the capital.

On the 24th of August, the battle of Bladensburg was fought.

Considering their numbers, the Americans made but little resistance. Only 64 of the English troops were killed and 185 wounded.

The troops with the naval brigade marched on and took the American capital that day. All the public buildings, one frigate, and a large quantity of naval stores were destroyed; 206 cannon were taken, and 30,000 stand of arms. The navy yard was burnt by the Americans themselves.

The squadron under Captain Gordon, consisting of the frigates "Seahorse" and "Euryalus," and three bombships that went up to Alexandra, were equally successful.

Twenty-one sail of prizes were taken away, and many more were destroyed. This was accomplished with only the loss of 7 men killed and 35 wounded.

The full particulars of the proceedings of the English troops and naval brigades in Virginia at that time occupy many pages of some naval histories; but, under the belief that the history of the time and place belongs more to a military than naval history, we have done nothing more than state a part of what took place.

On the morning of the 13th of September, an English squadron, consisting of four mortar ships and a rocket ship, commenced the bombardment of Fort McHenry at Baltimore.

The firing was continued all day, apparently without any success.

According to the American account, the English were repulsed with loss at Baltimore, and compelled to haul off.

There may be some truth in this, for historians are generally so prejudiced that we can only judge of the incidents they describe by results, and it is certain that the English gave up the assault on Baltimore.

The English 20-gun ship "Hermes," Captain Henry W. Percy, with the 20-gun ship "Carron," and the 18-gun brigs "Sophia" and "Childers," anchored off Fort Bowyer, commanding the passage to Mobile in Florida, on the 13th of September.

This fort mounted 28 guns, 32 and 24-pounders. The "Carron" and "Childers" anchored too far away to receive much injury from the fort, and consequently did it no damage.

The "Hermes" became crippled, and was swept aground by a current. She had to be abandoned, and was set on fire.

The squadron then withdrew. The Americans say it was repulsed.

On board the "Hermes," 17 men were killed and 23 wounded—five of them mortally. On the "Sophia," 6 were killed and 16 wounded.

On the 26th of September, the boats of the 74-gun ship "Plantagenet," Captain Robert Loyd, the 38-gun frigate "Rota," and the 18-gun brig "Carnation," were sent to capture the American privateer schooner "General Armstrong," anchored in Fayal Roads. The privateer was mounted with seven guns, and manned by 90 men.

Seven boats, manned by 180 men, under command of Lieutenant William Matterface, of the "Rota," were sent against it.

After a long pull, the boats arrived within hail, and were met by a fire of cannon and musketry, that sank two of the boats, and killed and wounded most of the men in them.

The other boats immediately returned to the squadron.

In this repulse Lieutenants Matterface and Norman, of the "Rota," 1 midshipman, and 31 men were killed and 86 wounded.

No loss was sustained by the privateer. The next morning the "Carnation" stood in to attack the American vessel, which was burnt by its crew to prevent it being captured.

The "Carnation" should have been sent against it at first, for the privateer, with its seven guns, could have stood no chance with a brig of 18.

On the 9th of October, the boats of the 40-gun frigate "Endymion," Captain Henry Hope, were sent, under the orders of Lieutenant Abel Hawkins, to capture the United States privateer 18-gun brig "Neufchatel," lying off Nantucket.

The boats' crews made a gallant attack, but were beaten off with heavy loss. Twenty-eight men were killed, including Lieutenant Hawkins, and 37 were wounded.

Before the boats could leave the brig, the American crew became the assailants, and captured the launch, making prisoners of those of its crew who were not killed.

On the 14th of December, an expedition in boats was made by the crews of the squadron under Vice-Admiral Sir Alexander Cochrane, against some American gunboats at Malheureux Island Passage in Lake Borgne, Florida.

The gunboats were captured, but at considerable loss.

Of the English boat crews, 20 men were killed, and 74 wounded. On the gunboats, 6 were killed, and 35 wounded.

The expedition was conducted by Captain Lockyer, of the frigate "Seahorse." He was wounded in the action, and promoted for his gallantry on the occasion.

The American government being determined upon an expedition to the East Indies the latter part of the year 1814, a squadron, consisting of the "President," "Peacock," and "Hornet," along with the "Macedonian" and "Tom Bowline" brigs, laden with stores for their use, was ordered to proceed to the Bay of Bengal.

On the night of the 18th of November, the "Hornet," which had been left at New London as a guard-ship, succeeded in eluding the blockading force, and reached New York.

The British squadron, which, about this time, cruised off the port of New York, was commanded by Captain John Hayes, of the "Majestic," of 56 guns, who had under his orders the 40-gun frigate "Endymion," Captain Henry Hope, and the 38-gun frigate "Pomone," Captain John Richard Lumley.

Between the time of her quitting Halifax and her junction with Captain Hayes, the "Endymion" had experienced a serious misfortune.

On the 9th of October, when off the shoals of Nantucket, she fell in with the American privateer brig "Prince de Neufchatel," of 18 guns.

It being calm, Captain Hope detached his boats, under the orders of Lieutenant Abel Hawkins, of the "Endymion," to capture the privateer.

The boats were repulsed, after sustaining the loss of Lieutenant Hawkins, 1 midshipman, and 26 seamen and marines killed: the second lieutenant, 1 master's mate, and 35 seamen and marines wounded: besides which, the launch was captured and the crew made prisoners.

On the 31st, the "Endymion" fell in with the 56-gun ship "Saturn," Captain James Nash, bound to Halifax; and sending on board, along with her surgeon and his servant, 28 wounded officers and men, received from the "Saturn," to replace the severe loss she had sustained, 1 lieutenant, 4 midshipmen, and 33 seamen and marines.

On the 13th of January, 1815, Captain Hayes was joined by the "Tenedos" frigate, of 38 guns, Captain Hyde Parker.

Although at this time close off the Hook, and in sight of the American squadron at anchor near Staten Island, the British ships were the same evening blown off the coast by a violent snow-storm.

On the next day, the 14th, the weather became more moderate; but the wind blowing fresh from the W.N.W., the squadron could not get in with the Hook.

Having no doubt that Commodore Decatur would take advantage, as well of the favourable state of the wind as of the absence of the British squadron, Captain Hayes, in preference to closing the land to the southward, stood away, to the northward and eastward, with the view of taking a station in the supposed track of the American squadron on its way out; and singular enough, at the very instant of arriving at the point, about an hour before daylight, on the 15th, Sandy Hook bearing W.N.W., distant fifteen leagues, the principal object of search to all the British captains made her appearance very near them.

Considering the chance of escape greater, by taking a separate departure with the ships of his squadron, Commodore Decatur, in the afternoon of the 14th, weighed and put to sea with the "President" and "Macedonian" brig, having left directions with Captain Warrington to join him at the Island of Tristan d'Acunha, with the "Peacock," "Hornet," and "Tom Bowline."

At half-past eight P.M., owing partly to a mistake in the pilots, and partly to the ship's increased draught of water, from the quantity of stores on board of her, the "President" struck on the bar, and did not get off for an hour and a half.

Having, besides some trifling damage to her rudder, shifted her ballast and got herself out of trim, the "President" would have put back, but the strong westerly wind prevented her.

Accompanied by the brig, the American frigate now shaped her course along the shore of Long Island for fifty miles, then steered south-east by south, until, at five A.M., on the 15th, she encountered the "Majestic" and her companions.

Three of the ships appearing right ahead, the "President" hauled up, and passed about two miles to the northward of them; and at daylight, Commodore Decatur found himself, as he states, chased by four ships—the "Majestic," about five miles astern, the "Endymion," a little further in the same direction, the "Pomone" six or eight miles on his larboard, and the "Tenedos" barely in sight on his starboard quarter.

The "Tenedos," indeed, having parted from her squadron the preceding evening, was taken for a second enemy's ship, and Captain Hayes ordered the "Pomone" by signal, to bear away in chase of her.

Consequently, the "President," at first was pursued by the "Majestic" and "Endymion" only.

These and the American frigate were soon under all sail, steering about east by north, with the wind now at north-west by north.

At half-past six A.M., the "Majestic" fired three shots at the "President," but, owing to the distance, without effect; nor, for the same reason, probably, were they returned.

Towards noon, the wind decreased, and the "Endymion," in consequence, began to leave the "Majestic," and gain upon the "President."

The American frigate commenced lightening herself by starting her water, cutting away her anchors, throwing overboard provisions, spare spars, boats, and every article of the sort that could be got at; she also kept her sails constantly wet from the royals down.

The "President" opened a fire upon her stern guns, which the "Endymion" returned with her bow-chasers.

A shot from the "President" came through the head of the larboard fore-lower-studding sail, the foot of the mainsail, and the stern of the barge on the booms, and perforating the quarterdeck, lodged on the maindeck, without doing any other damage.

Owing to the advance of the "Endymion" in her starboard and lee-quarters, the "President" luffed occasionally, to bring her stern guns to bear, and was evidently much galled, whereas, the greater part of her shot passed over the "Endymion."

The "Endymion," having, for the last twenty minutes, maintained a position within half point-blank shot on her quarter, the "President" brailed up her spanker, and bore away south, to bring her antagonist on her beam, and endeavoured to effect her escape to leeward.

Putting her helm hard a-weather, the "Endymion" met the manœuvre, and the two frigates came into close action in a parallel line of sailing.

The "President" now commenced with musketry from her tops, and the "Endymion" returned the fire with her marines, hauling up occasionally to close with her antagonist, without losing the bearing of her broadside.

The two ships were now not more than half musket-shot apart; the "Endymion," with her rigging and sails considerably cut, and the "President," with the principal part of her damage in the hull, as betrayed by the slackened state of her fire.

The "President" hauled up, apparently to avoid her opponent's fire.

Profiting by this, the "Endymion" poured in two raking broadsides; then hauled up also, and again placed herself on the "President's" starboard quarter.

The "President" shot away the "Endymion's" boat from her larboard quarter, also her lower and main-top-gallant studding sails.

For a short time the "President" did not return a shot to the vigorous fire still maintained by the "Endymion."

Re-commencing, then, the "President" shot away the "Endymion's" main-topmast studding-sail and mainbrace, and at length hauled suddenly to the wind, as if to try the strength of their antagonist's masts.

Having no fear for these, the "Endymion" trimmed sails, and, hauling up, bestowed another raking fire; to which the "President," now evidently much shattered, replied with a discharge from the stern gun.

In ten minutes the American frigate kept more away, firing only at intervals; and at 7h. 58m., p.m. ceased altogether, and showed, or appeared to show, a light.

Conceiving that the "President" had struck, the "Endymion" also ceased firing and began to bend new sails, her present ones having been cut into ribands by the "President's" bar and chain-shot; one of which had torn away twelve or fourteen cloths of her foresail, stripping it almost from the yard.

While the "Endymion" was thus compelled to drop astern, the "President" continued her coast to the eastward, under a crowd of canvas, much relieved, no doubt, by the absence of the former; but about half past 11 p.m., the "Pomone" came up, and gained a position upon the "President's" larboard quarter, and, luffing up, fired her starboard broadside, but did little or no damage.

The "President" immediately shortened sail and luffed up also, as if to pour a broadside into the "Pomone."

Instead of that, however, the American frigate hailed that she had surrendered, and hoisted a light in her mizen rigging.

Not hearing the hail, and mistaking the object of the light, the "Pomone" fired a second broadside, acknowledged to have been as ineffectual as the first.

On this the "President" luffed up still sharper, as if to lay the "Pomone" on board, and instantly hauled down her light again hailing that she had surrendered.

At this time the "Tenedos" who had been hailed by the "Endymion" and informed that the only two boats her misfortune with the "Neufchatel" had left her were destroyed, ranged up on the "President's" starboard side, and hailing was answered, that the American frigate "President" had surrendered.

Captain Parker immediately sent a boat and took possession; as did, nearly at the same moment, Captain Lumley, of the "Pomone."

Having repaired her running rigging, bent new courses, main-topsail, jib, fore-topmast-staysail, and spanker, and trimmed them to the wind, the "Endymion" went again in chase, as fresh as when she began the action, and was not very far astern of the "Tenedos" when the "President" struck.

The principal damages sustained by the "Endymion" have already been detailed.

Her fore-topmast was struck badly, but none of her other masts in any serious degree.

If the high firing of the "President" displayed its effects in the disordered rigging and sails of the "Endymion," the low firing of the "Endymion" was equally conspicuous in the shattered hull and lower masts of the "President."

The starboard side of the ship was riddled from end to end, particularly near the quarter.

Almost every port-sail and port-timber, both on the main and the quarter deck, exhibited marks of shot.

Three shots had entered the buttock, one of which had passed into the after-magazine.

Several shots had entered between wind and water, and some under water, which had cut the knees and timbers much.

A great many shots had also passed through the ship, between the main and quarter decks and in the waist; but, as a proof of the slight effect of the "Pomone's" fire, one shot only had entered in the larboard side which passed through at the tenth port, and carried away the upper sill, clamp and diagonal knees.

With so many shot-holes in her hull the "President" might well have six feet water in the hold.

Five or six of her guns were completely disabled.

The "Endymion" had 11 killed and 14 wounded; the "President," 35 killed and 70 wounded.

The "President" was the largest frigate at the time in the world, and of superior force to the "Endymion."

On the 25th the two ships arrived at Bermuda.

On the 8th of March, after having undergone a partial repair, the "President," accompanied by the "Endymion," sailed from Bermuda for England, and on the 28th both ships arrived at Spithead.

The "President," of course, was added to the British navy; but her serious damages in the action, coupled with the length of time she had been in the service, prevented her from being of any great utility.

CHAPTER XXXIX.
1815.

OST people thought at the commencement of this year that peace was at length to return, for Napoleon had abdicated, and had been sent to the island of Elba to exercise there a mimic sovereignty. But, on the first of March, 1815, he landed once more on French soil, and soon a mighty army rushed to his standard.

Upon this Lord Exmouth (the title had been conferred on Sir Edward Pellew) was sent with a fleet to the Mediterranean, and all the British fleet was once more actively employed.

The war with America still continued.

On the 20th of February the 22-gun ship "Cyane," and the 20-gun corvette "Levant," Captains Falcon and Douglas, fell in with the American frigate "Constitution," Captain Charles Stewart. After a long chase the "Constitution" overtook the two, which kept near each other in their flight, and commenced using her heavy guns, which immediately dismounted five guns of the "Cyane."

The "Levant" soon had to bear up to refit, and, in her absence, the "Cyane" was compelled to strike—her masts and yards being quite useless.

Two hours after the "Levant" returned to the assistance of her consort, and again opened fire on the enemy.

On learning that the "Cyane" had surrendered, she bore up to escape, but, in doing so, she received a raking fire that took away the wheel, and she then surrendered.

On board the two English ships 8 were killed and 37 wounded.

On the "Constitution" 6 were killed and 18 wounded.

A court-martial at Halifax in the following June honourably acquitted Captains Falcon and Douglas of any blame for the loss of their vessels. The "Constitution" had a crew of 472—or 170 more than the crews of the other two, and her guns were much heavier.

On the 26th of February the 13-gun schooner "St. Lawrence," Lieutenant Henry Gordon, was captured by the United States 14-gun brig "Chasseur." This, for two small vessels, was a very gallant action.

The "St Lawrence" had 6 killed and 18 wounded out of a crew of fifty men, and the "Chasseur," with a crew of 115 men, had five killed and eight wounded.

The 18-gun "Penguin," Commander James Dickinson, saw, on the 23rd of March, the United States 20-gun corvette "Hornet" off Tristan d'Acunha—made up to it, and fired a gun.

The "Hornet" replied to this by a broadside. In a few minutes the effect of star and bar-shot from the "Hornet" was seen on the sails and rigging of the "Penguin," while at the same time, the round and grape shot was doing its merciless work on her deck.

Seeing that the fire of the enemy was much superior to his own, Commander Dickinson resolved to board.

But just as he was about to put this determination to a trial, he fell, mortally wounded.

Lieutenant James McDonald then took command, and ran the "Penguin" aboard the "Hornet," when the former's foremast fell aft along the larboard side, preventing the guns being used on the side next the enemy.

The brig was now too unmanageable to be brought around, and seeing that further resistance was useless, the brig was surrendered.

Besides the commander, the boatswain and 4 men were killed, 4 mortally wounded, and 27 severely wounded on the "Penguin."

On the "Hornet" 2 were killed, and 11 wounded.

Like other similar victories gained by the Americans in this war, the one over the "Penguin" was wholly owing to superiority of force, to their ships being armed with better guns, and with larger and more efficient crews.

Having but a few vessels, the Americans could easily man them with picked men, when many captains in the English service were obliged to take anything they could get.

Out of the 122 of the "Penguin's" only 12 of them had ever been in action before.

A majority of American vessels were built, armed, equipped, and manned in a more intelligent manner than the English.

The Americans depended more on skill and ingenuity than the English, and less on bull-dog courage and obstinacy.

The battle between the "Hornet" and "Penguin" was fought after the conclusion of peace between England and the United States, which was ratified by President Madison at Washington, on the 18th of February. It is stated that three days before the action, Captain Biddle, of the "Hornet," was told by the captain of a neutral vessel that articles of peace had been signed.

On the 28th of April, the "Hornet," when in company with her consort, the 22-gun corvette "Peacock," was pursued by the English 72-gun ship "Cornwallis," Rear-Admiral Sir George Burlton. In the chase, the "Peacock" and

"Hornet" separated, and the "Cornwallis" pursued the latter. In the pursuit, a man was lost overboard from the ship, and the time lost in picking him up enabled the "Hornet" to escape.

So hard was the corvette pressed in the chase, that her guns, muskets, shot, and nearly everything heavy and moveable, were thrown over to increase her speed, and she managed to escape.

On the 30th of April, the 74-gun ship "Rivoli," Captain Edward Dickson, after a running fight, and then a sharp action of 15 minutes, captured the French 40-gun frigate "Melpomene," Captain Collet.

The French had 6 men killed and 28 wounded. On the ship one man was mortally, and 6 slightly wounded.

On the 17th of June, the 18-gun brig "Pilot," Commander John Nicolas, had an engagement off Cape Corse with the French 28-gun ship "Legere," Captain Toufet.

The action lasted nearly two hours, when the French ship hauled to the wind and escaped.

On the "Pilot," two men were killed and twelve wounded.

The loss on the "Legere" is said to have been 22 men killed and 79 wounded.

On the 30th of May, the "Arniston," a transport ship, was wrecked near Cape Lagulas, and only 6 persons were saved out of 350 aboard. 351 bodies were thrown on shore and buried near the beach.

On the 30th of June, the American 22-gun corvette "Peacock," Captain Warrington, arrived at Anjier, in the Straits of Sunda.

In this port was lying, at the time, the East India Company's 14-gun brig, "Nautilus," Commander Charles Boyce.

Three respectable people—one the master attendant at Anjier, went off to the "Peacock" in a boat and informed its commander that peace had for some time been established, but they were not believed.

In spite of this, the Captain of the "Peacock" demanded the surrender of the "Nautilus."

Lieutenant Boyce resisted the demand to strike his colours, and an action commenced which ended in the surrender of the brig.

The "Nautilus" had 6 men killed; Mr. Mayston, the chief officer, was mortally wounded, Lieutenant Boyce lost a leg, and 7 others were wounded.

Of course everyone knows that on Sunday, June 18th, 1815, was fought the great Battle of Waterloo, which for ever crushed the power of the great Bonaparte, Emperor of the French. With the battle itself we have nothing to do, but the British navy had much to do with the future of the ex-emperor.

Napoleon had found that the French people were weary of his rule, which was one of incessant bloodshed. He also knew that if he fell into the hands of either Russian, Austrian, or Prussian troops, his life would not be safe, so he resolved to throw himself on British generosity.

Accordingly, he sent a flag of truce from the town of Rochefort to H.M.S. "Bellerophon," which, with some frigates, blockaded the port. The captain of the vessel informed the envoys that, *as a private individual*, Bonaparte would be well treated in England, if he thought proper to go there, but he could not answer for the ultimate intentions of the British government—with which reply they (the envoys) departed.

On the 14th of July, when the state of affairs looked still more serious, the envoys (M. M. Savary and La Cases) paid a second visit to the ship, carrying with them an autograph letter from Napoleon to the Prince Regent of England, in which he said:—

"I come like Themistocles to seat myself on the hearths of the British people."

A more absurd simile was never penned, and Captain Maitland, of the "Bellerophon," could only repeat his former words, namely, that he was willing to convey Napoleon to England, *without, however, entering into any promise as to the reception he might meet with there, as he was in total ignorance of the intentions of the British government as to his future disposal.*

The fallen emperor and his suite went on board the "Bellerophon" on the 15th of July, and on the 24th the vessel anchored off Torbay.

On the 26th they were ordered to Plymouth, sound means having been taken to prevent communication with the shore.

Afterwards he was transferred to the "Northumberland," and conveyed to the Island of St. Helena, where he died on the 6th of May, 1821.

So ended the long, long war, which had been waged chiefly on his account, and the world was once more at peace.

CHAPTER XL.

PARTICULARS OF SHIPS.

THIS would obviously be an incomplete history of the Navy without descriptive particulars of the vessels composing it at different periods.

In the early part of this work we have given drawings and descriptions of the ships in use at the commencement of English history, and it is now time to refer to those in the reigns of the Georges. What principally arrests the attention of the student is the constant and steady growth of size in vessels—the ancient British coracle, or boat, was succeeded by the galley, or the small sailing craft of the Saxons or Danes; then by the decked ships of the early middle ages; then by the lofty and awkward galleons and three-deckers of the days of the Tudors and the Stuarts, and at length by the enlarged and improved vessels of George the Third. During his reign the development of size was continuous and remarkable.

In 1765, the celebrated ship "Victory," of 100 guns, was launched. She was a three-decker of 2,165 tons, and the largest up to that time built in England, being 186 feet long in lower deck, 52 feet broad, and 21 feet 6 inches deep in hold.

WRECK OF THE "PANDORA."

Other three-deckers, built soon after that time, and rated of 98 or 90 guns, were about 200 tons less in size; but upon the breaking out of the French revolutionary war (after the peace from 1783 to 1792), we find an increase of scale in most classes of ships; the "Queen Charlotte" and "Royal George," of 100 guns each, were nearly 2,300 tons.

In 1804, the "Hibernia," of 2,500 tons, was launched, and in 1808, the noted "Caledonia," of over 2,600 tons.

This last vessel was considered almost perfection. At the present time, it is lying off Greenwich, re-christened "Dreadnought," and used as a marine hospital.

A similar increase attended the two-decked ships. About the date 1760 or 1770, the usual size of a 74 was 168 feet long, 47 wide, and 19 to 20 deep in hold, making a little over 1,600 tons; but an augmentation was soon given, to 1,700 tons in some instances; and at the commencement of the 19th century, the usual scale for new ships of this force was 1,750 tons; others were still larger.

The first "frigate," strictly so called, was according to James, the "Southampton," of 32 guns, launched 1757, and which remained afloat until about 1813.

According to other authorities the "Constant Warwick," designed by Pett, was the first frigate, and of about 300 tons, built in 1646.

The "Southampton" was 124 or 125 feet long, 35 wide, and 12 feet deep in the hold, admeasuring 670 tons.

She carried 26 12-pounders on her main deck, 4 6-pounders on her quarter-deck and 2 6-pounders on her forecastle, and about 220 men.

When the "carronade," a short, light gun with a wide bore, was invented about 1779, it was gradually introduced as an addition to the armament of ships, and a few were given to each, but without altering their rating, so that in 1812 the "Southampton" actually carried 40 guns in all, besides a boat gun, having 12 of these carronades on her upper batteries and 2 of the 6-pounders being withdrawn, while she was still called a 32-gun frigate.

Some few thirty-twos were built, at intervals, of 700 tons, but in 1794 several were launched of nearly 800 tons, and eventually a small number of 900 tons.

Of brigs there were probably very few about the year 1760 much above 200 tons; but they soon reached 250, and about the close of that century a new class of 18-gun brigs was established of the size of 380 tons, and proved very useful.

A three-decker, it should be explained, is, or rather was, a vessel having three complete ranges of guns, one over another, extending from bows to stern, and in addition there were always guns on the deck open to the sky, of which the fore part is called the forecastle, and the afterpart the quarter-deck; over the sternmost part of the quarter-deck is a short, light deck again, called the poop, and upon that were often mounted four or six carronades.

The two-decker would have two complete ranges of guns under cover, besides the spar-deck guns, and those on the poop. Thus a 74-gun ship often carried in all 80 or 82 guns.

Frigates were vessels with only one complete range of guns besides those on the spar-deck, and they seldom had any poop.

Corvettes, or ship-sloops, had only one range of guns, and that without the supplementary guns on spar-deck; in fact, they generally had no spar-deck, but sometimes merely a small "top-gallant forecastle" forward, and a poop aft.

The word "sloop" was applied very vaguely sometimes to corvettes, rigged as ships, i.e. with three masts; sometimes to armed brigs and schooners, and sometimes to small vessels with only one mast, similar to cutters.

A brig has two masts, and on which the sails stand across the breadth of the vessel. A schooner has also two masts, but with the principal sails standing fore and aft, or in the direction of the vessel's length.

The dimensions of English ships in the last century were for the most part insufficient, the space between decks very confined. The best line-of-battle ships had only 6 feet from the plank of one deck (floor) to the beam overhead, frigates had generally less, and corvettes and brigs less again.

In the "Southampton" frigate just referred to, the distance horizontally between the main deck guns (centre to centre) could not have been more than 9 feet 3 inches; but in larger frigates, it was eventually made 10 feet or more, and in line-of-battle ships never much less than 11 feet.

Foreign nations, as the French and Spaniards, built finer ships, and more scientific in design, but our sailors excelled theirs in skill of management, whether at peace or war.

Thus, in 1780, when we were building 38-gun frigates of 940 tons, the French built them of 1,060. The Americans, towards the close of the century, laid down vessels of 1,530 tons, which were then the largest frigates in the world. Till the year 1813, we had scarcely more than one frigate actually built in this country to carry guns heavier than long 18-pounders, although two or three 64's had been "cut down" into frigates with 24-pound guns, and two or three French ships with 24-pounders had been captured. The French 84-gun ships on two decks measured 2,250 tons, when our 98-gun ships on three decks measured 1,970 tons.

Subsequently we shall have occasion to notice the constructive development of the Navy from the time of George III. up to that of Victoria.

A line-of-battle ship, i.e. either a three-decker or two-decker, used to take from three to six years in building, and was roughly estimated to cost about £1,000 per gun. At a later period (1832), a large 50-gun frigate, "Vernon," was built in only six months.

An idea of the size of the spars may be given by stating that formerly the height of the mainmast, from step to truck, was something about equal to the length of the vessel, and the stretch of the main yard was generally about double the greatest width of the ship. The main yard of a 74, being 96 feet long, would weigh 4¼ tons.

In number of crew, British ships were generally less fully manned than those of any other nation. Our 74's usually had 590 men, when the French had 650 or more; our 38-gun frigates had 284 to 300 men, when the French had 300 to 350; and so on in proportion with other classes of ships.

CHAPTER XLI.

THE BOMBARDMENT OF ALGIERS, AND BATTLE OF NAVARINO, 1816—1827.

IN consequence of numerous piracies committed by the Algerines, a fleet of ten ships, five brigs, and four bomb vessels, sailed from Plymouth Sound for Algiers, on the 28th of July, 1816, under the command of Admiral Lord Exmouth, better known to the reader as Sir Edward Pellew.

In the Bay of Gibraltar, this fleet was joined by a Dutch squadron of six vessels, under Vice-Admiral Van de Cappellen, who was anxious to take a part in the work of punishing the Algerines for their numerous offences against the commerce of Europe.

Apparently the Algerines thought the business of piracy well worth protecting and preserving, for Algiers was fortified by more than 1,000 guns, most of them of large size.

At 2.30 p.m., some of the Algerine batteries commenced firing on the ships, which had just arrived and hove to in the bay.

The flagship of Lord Exmouth was the "Queen Charlotte," of 100 guns, Captain William Brisbane. This vessel was one of the first to answer the enemy's fire, by a broadside at the mole, which was soon demolished, as well as some batteries over the town gate leading to it.

During the battle, the flagship of Rear-Admiral Milne, the "Impregnable," Captain Edward Brace, was exposed for some time to the fire of the lighthouse batteries, and to an eastern battery of two tiers.

So destructive was the fire sustained by this ship, that in a short time, 150 men were killed and wounded aboard of it, and Captain Milne sent a message to Lord Exmouth for another vessel to divert some of the fire from him.

During this time, the "Leander," Captain Edward Chetham, was attacking the Algerine boats and row galleys with great success, and Lieutenant Peter Richards, of the "Queen Charlotte," was sent with the barge to destroy a frigate lying near the mole.

The frigate was set on fire, and the barge returned with only a loss of 2 men killed.

A rocket boat, in the command of Aaron S. Symes, followed the barge without orders, and on its return, was exposed to a heavy fire from some batteries, and 1 man was killed and 9 wounded.

The vessels in the harbour were set on fire by the mortar and rocket boats, and the flames from them soon spread to the arsenal and store-houses on the mole.

The city was also on fire in several places from shells thrown by the bomb vessels.

A sloop containing 143 barrels of powder was then run on shore, close to a battery, under the orders of Lieutenant Richard Fleming, and set on fire.

The vessel exploded about nine o'clock. The bombardment was continued until about ten o'clock that night.

The "Queen Charlotte" then cut her cables and stood out with a signal for others to follow. In going out, the "Leander" was near being lost.

Being much damaged aloft, she was nearly uncontrollable, and drifted near the mole and the burning ships.

With much difficulty and loss of life, she was towed off by the "Severn."

The scene in the Bay of Algiers that night has been described as one exceeding grand.

The burning ships illumined the atmosphere, while a heavy thunderstorm, with bright flashes of lightning, added to the grandeur of the scene.

On board the British fleet during the day 128 men were killed, and 690 wounded.

On the Dutch fleet, which performed a very praiseworthy part during the battle, 13 men were killed, and 52 wounded.

The next morning Lieutenant Burgess was sent with a flag of truce, and met by an officer of the port.

It was agreed between them that hostilities should cease.

The damage done to the Algerines consisted of four frigates, five corvettes, and twenty-five gunboats destroyed, the mole and arsenal blown up, and an immense quantity of naval and military stores and storehouses destroyed.

On the 29th, the terms of a treaty were agreed upon between Captain Brisbane and the Dey.

Christian slavery was to be abolished for ever; and 1,200 Christian slaves were restored to freedom; 382,500 dollars, which had been paid by Sicily and Naples for the redemption of slaves since the beginning of the year, were to be paid back; 30,000 dollars were to be paid to the British consul as compensation for the loss of his property, and a public apology was to be made for his imprisonment.

The work to be accomplished by this expedition was a great one, for the defences of Algiers were supposed by many to be impregnable, and the loss of life sustained by its assailants shows that it was defended by brave people, skilful in the art of war.

* * * * *

On the 4th day of April, a protocol was signed at St. Petersburg, guaranteeing protection to the inhabitants of the Morea from ill-treatment by the Turks, under Ibrahim Pacha.

The following summer a squadron of English ships under Vice-Admiral Sir Edward Codrington, a division of French ships under Rear-Admiral De Rigny, and a Russian squadron under Rear-Admiral Count Heiden, met in the Mediterranean to enforce obedience to it.

A conference took place between the naval commanders and Ibrahim, on the 25th of September, 1827, in which the Pacha promised to suspend hostilities against the Greeks until he received instructions from Constantinople, and that his fleet should not leave the harbour until then.

Trusting to this promise, most of the ships of the three squadrons were withdrawn from before Navarino harbour, in which the Turkish fleet was lying.

The English admiral sailed for Zante, but, scarcely had he arrived there, before the "Dartmouth," which had been left behind, arrived with the news that the Turkish fleet were putting out to sea.

Admiral Codrington immediately returned, and, although having with him at the time but one frigate and two corvettes, he succeeded in inducing the Turkish fleet to return to Navarino.

By the 15th of October, the three squadrons were again anchored off Navarino, blockading the Turkish vessels.

All further attempts to communicate with Ibrahim were unsuccessful, and it was then resolved to enter the harbour and compel him to listen to reason.

On the 19th of October, orders were issued to each commander, and directions given them for their observance the next day.

To these instructions Admiral Codrington added the following advice of Nelson:—

"If a general engagement should take place, no captain can be better placed than when his vessel is alongside one of the enemy."

The English fleet consisted of seven ships, one corvette, three brigs and a cutter—the "Asia" of 80 guns, Captain Edward Curzon, being the admiral's flagship.

The French had five ships and two corvettes, and the Russians eight ships.

In standing into the harbour the British and French ships formed the weather or starboard column and the Russians the lee.

Moored in the form of a crescent the Turkish and Egyptian fleet awaited their approach.

This fleet consisted of one ship of 84 guns, two of 74; two of 60; two of 50; fifteen 48-gun frigates; twenty-six large corvettes; eleven brigs, and five fire ships—in all more than one hundred vessels, mounting nearly 2,000 guns.

This force was supported by several strong batteries and forts commanding the harbour.

The action was commenced by the Turks, who fired upon a boat from the "Dartmouth," and killed Lieutenant Fitzroy and several of its crew.

Early in the action two of the enemy's vessels, an Egyptian and a Turkish ship, were nearly knocked to pieces by the fire of the "Asia," and fell off to the leeward but little better than wrecks.

The allied fleets suffered much from the forts and batteries, but this did not prevent a single vessel from doing its duty in the destruction of the enemy's vessels.

In this long engagement, which lasted from two o'clock in the afternoon until night, there was not a vessel in the fleet, but what was managed to the perfect approbation of the admirals.

The result of the action shows the admirable co-operation of all, a result that cannot be better described than in the words of Admiral Codrington, who stated in his official letter referring to the enemy's fleet, that—

"Out of eighty-one men-of-war, only one frigate and fifteen smaller vessels are in a state ever to be again put to sea."

In the destruction of this fleet, the English had 272 killed and wounded, the French 187, and the Russians 198.

It is admitted by English officers that, "had the French or Russians not taken their full share in the day's proceedings, the British must have been annihilated."

* * * * * *

Admiral Samuel Hood, whose name has often been mentioned in this work, died on the 27th of January, this year, in the 96th year of his age.

He was at the time Governor of Greenwich Hospital.

There is one vessel and its captain often mentioned in these pages, of whom the reader may like to learn something more.

On the 8th of February, 1816, the "Alceste," Captain Murray Maxwell, sailed from Portsmouth for China, having on board Lord Amherst, the English embassador to that court.

On the 18th of February, 1817, the "Alceste," that had stood so many battles with her French foes, while returning with Lord Amherst from China, was wrecked on some rocks near Sunda, and soon after sunk. No lives were lost.

Edward Pellew, Viscount Exmouth, was born at Dover on the 19th of April, 1757, and was a descendant of a well-known and respectable Cornish family.

While a boy at school a house was on fire which contained a quantity of gunpowder.

No one would volunteer to remove the powder. It was the work of a man, but there were none present who would do it. It was removed by young Pellew—a boy.

He early evinced a desire for a seaman's life, and was placed by his friends aboard the "Juno" as a midshipman.

Pellew first found an opportunity of distinguishing himself in America at the time of the revolt of the Colonies.

When Pellew became a commander he often displayed more activity, courage, and skill than any of the men under his command, and never required of officers or men a dangerous duty he was unwilling to assist in performing.

Several times he saved the lives of men who had fallen overboard.

Some of the crew of his vessel were once amusing themselves by swimming, and Captain Pellew, who was observing them, heard a boy say—

"I'll have a good swim, too, by-and-bye."

"The sooner the better," said Pellew, and he pushed the boy overboard.

He immediately discovered that the boy could not swim, and jumped over and saved him, although dressed to dine with his admiral.

He was so bad a horseman that he once rode a donkey in reviewing a body of marines.

While doing so, he was attended by a negro boy named Neddy, who had learnt the vulgar appellation of the animal, and said to his master—

"Here be three Neddys now, massa."

PORTRAIT OF SIR THOMAS BRISBANE.

Lord Exmouth was appointed to the chief command at Plymouth on the death of Admiral Duckworth in 1817.

He retired in 1821, and died at his house in Teignmouth on the 6th day of February, 1833, in the 76th year of his age.

A few days before his death, he appeared to think himself much better than he had been for some time, and said—

"I have been going to the leeward, but now I think I am working to the windward again."

He was buried at Christow, and the pall used at the funeral was the flag under which he fought at Algiers.

CHAPTER XLII.

THE FIRST CHINESE WAR.

N defiance of all Chinese law, large quantities of opium, which was formerly one of the chief articles of merchandise in India, were sent to China.

When it became known that the East India merchants might require some assistance in compelling the Chinese to buy their drug, the English government were quite willing to give it, and two frigates, the "Volage" and "Hyacinth," were placed on the China station.

In 1837, Captain Elliot represented to Lord Palmerston that English seamen were openly engaged in violating Chinese laws, by smuggling opium into China, but he declined to interfere.

Besides the dispute between the Chinese authorities and English merchants about the introduction of opium into China, there were other difficulties.

In an affray in the month of August, 1839, at Macao, between some English sailors and Chinese a Chinaman was killed. Commissioner Lin demanded that the homicide should be delivered to him for punishment, which demand was refused by Captain Elliot, the superintendent of the opium trade.

It was probably owing to this affair that Admiral Kwan, with a Chinese fleet of twenty-nine vessels, demanded an Englishman of Captain Smith, of the "Volage," on the 3rd of November, 1839. An engagement with this fleet had been expected for several days, and Captain Smith, after hearing this demand, did not wait any longer for an attack, but commenced one himself.

The ships then ran down the Chinese line, with the wind on the starboard beam, and firing broadsides at the junks as they passed. The lateral direction of the wind enabled the vessels to perform the same thing from the other end of the line, which they did by running up again, with their larboard guns bearing on the Chinese.

One war junk was blown up, three were sunk, and several were severely damaged, when Admiral Kwan ordered a retreat. This affair may be called the first battle of the opium war.

The next year a small fleet arrived in China to settle all difficulties immediately. Sir J. Bremer, the commander, on arriving at Canton River, established a blockade, and then sailed with a part of the fleet for the island of Chusan.

This island was captured on Sunday, the 5th of July, 1840.

Several months were now lost in vain attempts to make treaties; the Chinese promising everything merely for the purpose of gaining time.

On the 7th of January, 1841, all efforts at making a treaty having failed, Commodore Bremer commenced an attack on the Bogue forts, two of which were captured that day, and further proceedings were stopped by the Chinese by another offer to negotiate, which caused another delay.

Having learned that they were being humbugged again, the British commanders again proceeded to business.

The island of Hong Kong was taken in her Majesty's name and the English flag hoisted upon it, and a squadron, composed of the "Wellesley," "Calliope," "Samarang," "Alligator," and two others, attacked the batteries of Wangtong, while the "Blenheim," "Melville," and "Queen" attacked the fort at Anunghoy.

In a few hours a long chain of forts and batteries which the Chinese thought impregnable, were all captured, and many Chinamen, including their celebrated Admiral Kwan, was killed.

In the engagement, the English only had 5 men slightly wounded.

On the 27th, the "Calliope," "Madagascar," and "Nemesis," sailed up the Canton River to Whampoa Reach, and drove the Chinamen from some fortifications and a fleet of junks, killing about 300 of them.

After this, there was a suspension of hostilities for about six weeks, during which there was some trading done.

Articles of a treaty had been signed by the commissioners on both sides, and were sent to the Chinese emperor for his approval.

Much to the disappointment of all, the imperial cabinet rejected the treaty, and said that the war must continue.

"They are," said the celestial monarch, speaking of the English, "like dogs and sheep in their disposition. It is difficult for Heaven and earth to bear any longer with the English; and both gods and men are indignant at their conduct."

On the 24th of May, 1841, the English forces made an attack on Canton.

A large number of boats were towed up to the city by the steamers "Atalanta" and "Nemesis," while the 49th Regiment, the 18th Royal Irish, the 37th Madras Native Infantry, and Bengal Volunteers, were to act on the land.

On the morning of the 26th, the Chinese hoisted a white flag on the walls, and Canton was in the possession of the English, with only a loss on their side of 15 killed and 112 wounded.

After the capture of Canton, Sir Henry Pottinger, the new plenipotentiary, sailed with the fleet for Amoy, where they anchored on the 25th of August. The attack on Amoy was commenced the next day by the "Sesostris," which passed the batteries, throwing into them shot and shell.

She was followed by other vessels as they took up a position in a line of the forts.

A tremendous and continuous fire was maintained for about two hours, when the Royal Irish were landed under the command of Sir Hugh Gough.

The Chinese did not wait for their near approach, but fled, and Amoy was won without the loss of a life to the captors.

As the soldiers landed, a Chinese mandarin, the second in command, ran into the sea and drowned himself. Another officer, high in command, was seen to cut his own throat as the English drew near him.

From Amoy the fleet sailed for Ting-hae, which was attacked on the 1st of October by the ships and a land force.

The Chinese defended this place with more than their usual courage, and in consequence their loss was more severe.

It was captured with only a loss to the English of 2 men killed, and 24 wounded.

The troops were then re-embarked, and the fleet sailed for Ching-hae, near Ningpo.

This place was captured on the 10th of October. Ningpo was taken without the slightest opposition on the 12th.

But little was done by the fleet after this until the following May, when, on the 18th of that month, 1842, the "Cornwallis," "Blonde," and "Modeste" assisted in capturing the city of Chapoo.

They anchored abreast the batteries and silenced its guns, while the troops were engaged in landing.

A part of the fleet next sailed for the Yang-tze Kiang River.

At the junction of that river with the Woosung, some batteries were captured, in which were found 253 guns, some of them brass, and upwards of eleven feet long.

In capturing this place, the "Blonde" and "Sesostris" received some injury, and on the fleet 2 men were killed, and 25 wounded.

The fleet then sailed for Chin-keang-foo, which was attacked on the morning of the 21st July, 1842.

Most of the troops defending this city were Tartars, and they made a very gallant resistance, but their courage was of little avail against shells.

The heat of the sun was so overpowering this day, that many of the troops landed fell dead from its effects.

On entering the city, it was found that many of the Tartars had committed suicide, after killing their wives and children.

In every garden, the wells were found full of women and children, murdered by their husbands and fathers, as is supposed, to prevent them from falling into the hands of the hated English.

In August following, the fleet sailed up the river to Nankeen, off which it anchored on the 9th.

Just as every preparation was made for an attack, Sir W. Parker, of the fleet, and Sir Hugh Gough, the commander of the troops, received news from Sir Henry Pottinger, the plenipotentiary, to suspend operations, as a treaty had been agreed upon.

This inglorious war then ended.

It was a war not suited to old English tars. It was a war in which their skill and valour were invested for no worthy objects. There was no honour to be gained by it.

CHAPTER XLIII.

OPERATIONS ON THE COAST OF SYRIA, 1840.

HE Pacha of Egypt, Mehemet Ali, rebelled against the authority of the Sublime Porte in the year 1839, and kept possession of the Turkish fleet lying in Alexandria.

What this event had to do with England and other nations of Europe, history does not explain in a satisfactory manner, and probably never will, but the most of them thought it necessary to interfere in the quarrel.

It was supposed that France favoured the cause of the Egyptian Pacha, with a view to obtaining a footing in the East, and this was sufficient cause for England, Russia, Prussia, and Austria to join in a league to support the Porte.

In September, 1840, the following English ships assembled in the Mediterranean, under the command of Admiral Sir Robert Stopford:— "Princess Charlotte," 104 guns, Admiral Sir Robert Stopford, Captain Arthur Fanshaw; the "Powerful," 84 guns, Commodore Charles Napier; the "Bellerophon," 80 guns, Captain Charles J. Austin; the "Revenge," 76 guns, Captain W. Walgrave; the "Asia," 84 guns, Captain William Fisher; the "Implacable," 74 guns, Captain Edward Harvey; the "Ganges," 84 guns, Captain Barrington Reynolds; the "Rodney," 92 guns, Captain Robert Maunsell; the "Thunderer," 84 guns, Captain Maurice Berkeley; the "Vanguard," 80 guns, Captain Sir David Dunn; the "Edinburgh," 72 guns, Captain W. W. Henderson; the "Hastings," 72 guns, Captain John Lawrence; the "Benbow," 72 guns, Captain Houston Steward; and the "Cambridge," 78 guns, Captain Edward Barnard.

Besides these ships of the line, there were five frigates, two corvettes, five steam vessels, four brigs, and some smaller vessels.

On the 9th of September, this fleet was joined by three ships of war, under the command of Rear-Admiral Bundiera, and five Turkish ships, commanded by an English admiral—Sir Baldwin Walker.

That night a party of marines and Turkish troops were landed on the cape near Beyrout.

On the 12th of September, the town of Gebail was bombarded.

When the firing from two or three of the smaller vessels had been continued for nearly two hours, during which the "Cyclops" had thrown several shells into the town, a party of marines and mountaineers were landed under the command of Captain Austin.

With much difficulty the party crossed stone dykes and cactus fences, until near the castle, when they were received by a heavy fire of musketry from loopholes near the ground.

Not thinking it advisable to stand and be shot at by an unseen enemy, the party retreated to the boats with 5 men killed and 18 wounded.

The next day the Castle Gebail was abandoned by the Arnaut troops, who were in want of provisions, and it was taken possession of by the mountaineers.

Had the place been properly defended by 500 good men, the Mediterranean fleet could not have captured it.

The walls were built of blocks of stone 20 feet long and 12 feet broad.

On the 15th of September, the "Carysfort" and "Cyclops" opened fire on the town of Bartroun, which was soon after taken by a party under Lieutenant Thompson in the boats of those two vessels, and of the "Hastings."

On the 25th of September, a party under Lieutenant Charlewood, of the Benbow, in the boats of that vessel and the "Carysfort" and "Zebra," attempted to destroy some stores at Tortosa, but were obliged to relinquish the undertaking with the loss of 5 killed and 17 wounded.

On the 24th, the Egyptian troops were driven from Tyre by the bombardment of the "Castor" and "Pique," and the town was taken possession of by the English.

On the 27th of September, a squadron consisting of the "Thunderer," the Austrian frigate "Guenviera," the 18-gun brig "Wasp," and a Turkish corvette, with the two steam frigates "Cyclops" and "Gorgon," attacked the town of Sidon.

This expedition was commanded by Commodore Charles Napier.

The capture of this place was accomplished with but a trifling loss to the allies, there being only 4 killed and 2 wounded.

In the assault on the town, the brave Hassan Bey, the leader of the Egyptian troops, was killed.

On the 9th October, more than 2,000 Egyptians were defeated and captured near Beyrout.

The people along the Syrian coast, encouraged by the aid they were receiving, and being still loyal to the Porte, took possession of Tripoli, Tortosa, Latakia, and other places, until there remained but St. Jean D'Acre in possession of the troops of Mehemet Ali on the coast.

To capture this place the greater part of the allied fleet sailed from Beyrout, on the 31st of October, having on board 3,000 Turkish troops.

Soon after 2 p.m. the attack commenced.

Commodore Napier's division opened a fire on the western line of batteries, which was the strongest part of the town, and the other vessels anchored to the eastward.

A tremendous fire was kept up for about two hours, when the principal magazine of the fortress blew up, a fortunate incident for the allies, which is supposed to have been caused by a shell from one of the steam vessels.

The signal to cease firing was then hoisted, and the ships continued at anchor that night without being molested.

In the morning a strange sight was before them. St. Jean D'Acre was torn to pieces.

The guns of the fortress, and the stones that once composed it were scattered over the site of the town.

Two regiments, that were formed on the ramparts at the time of the explosion, were completely annihilated.

Every living creature within an area of 6,000 yards was killed, and the loss of life is supposed to have been nearly 2,000 persons.

The loss on board the English ships was 12 killed and 32 wounded; on the Austrian ships 2 killed and 6 wounded, and on the Turkish ships 4 killed and 3 wounded.

CHAPTER XLIV.

VOYAGES OF DISCOVERY.

IT is not alone in deeds of war that the English navy should fill a broad space of the pages of history. Great and noble deeds have been performed by its officers and crews without the shedding of blood—great deeds that have required quite as much skill, courage and perseverance as are met in encountering the horrors of war.

Amongst the first of English officers of the navy who have been sent abroad on peaceful expeditions, was Commodore Byron, who sailed on the 3rd of July, 1764, in the "Dolphin," accompanied by the "Tamar."

This expedition was simply for a voyage of discovery. Byron discovered some small islands, obtained more complete information of the Falkland Islands, and took possession of them in the name of George the Third, King of Great Britain.

After the return of Byron, Captain Samuel Wallis was appointed to the command of His Majesty's ship "Dolphin," and sailed on another voyage of discovery, accompanied by the "Swallow" sloop and the "Prince Frederick" store-ship, on the 22nd of August, 1766.

Wallis is said to have first visited Taheite.

In 1768, at the instigation of Mr. Joseph Banks, a naturalist, another expedition sailed for the Pacific. It only consisted of one vessel, the "Endeavour," which was commanded by Lieutenant James Cook.

James Cook was born in 1728, and was the son of a day labourer.

He early went to sea, and slowly worked his way into notice, and was of much assistance at the capture of Quebec, in acting as pilot and guide.

The "Endeavour" sailed on the 26th of August, 1768.

The discoveries and explorations of Cook have been an immense source of wealth to England, and it is undoubtedly owing to them that Australia and New Zealand are now flourishing and important colonies of England.

On the 12th of July, 1776, Captain Cook sailed on this third voyage, from which he never returned.

STORM IN THE BLACK SEA, 1854.

While lying at Karakahue Bay, on the island of Hawaii, Sandwich Islands, a boat belonging to the "Discovery," one of Cook's vessels, was stolen.

Cook went ashore, and endeavoured to get the king aboard his ship, with the intention of keeping him there until the boat should be returned.

It is said that Cook persisted in this, after being told that the boat had been destroyed for the purpose of obtaining the nails.

The king was stopped on his way to the shore by several of his subjects, who were unwilling to see him go aboard the vessel.

At that critical moment, when the difficulty of maintaining peace was so great, two natives, who were crossing the bay in a canoe, were wantonly fired at by some men in a boat, and one of them was killed.

This act made further forbearance on the part of the natives a vice they could not be guilty of Some one exclaimed, in the native language, "It is war!" and an attack was immediately commenced on Cook and his boat's crew, which resulted in the captain and four or five of the crew being killed.

There is a difference in the account given by the natives of Hawaii as to the manner in which they were treated by the white people, and the one generally received amongst English people.

It is said by them that their temples and gods were desecrated by the crews of Cook's vessels, that they received no remuneration for the tons of food they were required to furnish, and that Cook punished the innocent with the guilty, and paid no attention to any of their complaints about the actions of the crew.

Soon after the return of Cook's third expedition, Lieutenant Bligh was sent in the "Bounty" to the Pacific to procure bread fruit trees for the purpose of introducing them into the West India Islands.

After a visit to Taheiti, the crew of the "Bounty" mutinied, and the commander and several others were put into an open boat far out at sea, and left to do the best they could.

The mutinous crew then sailed back for Taheiti, and after suffering incredible hardships, Captain Bligh reached England.

On the 10th of August, 1790, Captain Edwards was commissioned to take the command of the "Pandora," of 24 guns, and 160 men, and capture the mutineers of the "Bounty."

Edwards anchored in Matava Bay on the 23rd of March, 1791.

On the first communication with the natives, Edwards learnt that Christian, the chief of the mutineers, with nine of his companions, had slipped the "Bounty's" cables, and gone off to sea, leaving their companions on the island.

Four of the mutineers on the island voluntarily surrendered, and Lieutenants Corner and Haywood were sent with 26 men to the north side of the island to capture the others.

With the assistance of the natives, the mutineers were pursued to the heights in the interior, surrounded, captured, and marched down to the ship with their hands tied behind them.

After leaving Taheiti, the "Pandora" was wrecked on a coral reef, and 35 of the crew and 4 of the prisoners were drowned.

The officers succeeded in reaching England, after suffering many hardships.

The valuable discoveries of Captain Cook excited the desire for more, and a dispute with Spain respecting Nootka Sound being settled, it was thought necessary to send an officer to Nootka, to receive from the Spaniards a formal restitution of the territories they had seized, to survey the coast, and to obtain every possible information of the state of the country.

For this purpose a ship was commissioned and named the "Discovery," to which Captain Vancouver was appointed.

It mounted ten 4-pounders, and ten swivels, and was manned by 130 men, including officers. It sailed on the 11th of March, 1791. On the 29th of the following December Vancouver reached Taheiti, having discovered several small islands on the way.

Here he met with the "Chatham," Lieutenant Broughton, that had started as a consort with the "Discovery" on the voyage.

Broughton had also discovered several islands, and taken possession of them in the name of his Majesty. One of them was Chatham Island.

Vancouver then proceeded north to Nootka, where he obtained much valuable information of the country in that part of the world, and visited and partly surveyed the coast of the large island that now goes by his name.

He left the "Discovery" anchored in the Shannon on the 12th of September, 1795, and proceeded to London, having been absent four years, eight months, and twenty-nine days.

Sir John Franklin, one of the unfortunate of the naval officers sent by the British government on voyages of discovery, was born at Spilsby, Lincolnshire, 1786.

He early manifested a love for a sailor's life, and, when a boy, walked twelve miles on a holiday to see the ocean.

When fourteen years of age he went to sea as a midshipman, and was at the battle of Copenhagen.

His last voyage in the service of his country was with the "Erebus" and "Terror," to the north, in search of a passage from the Atlantic to the Pacific, for which he sailed from England on the 23rd day of May, 1845, and never returned.

Relics of the expedition which have been found give evidence that Franklin reached a space comprised between the 97th and 100th meridian of longitude.

If he reached that point he discovered a North-West Passage—the object of his search.

CHAPTER XLV.

THE RUSSIAN WAR, 1854.

WAR being declared by France and England against Russia, a fleet was despatched under Admiral Dundas to the Black Sea.

In this war, the first shot fired by the British navy was on the 22nd of April, 1854, at Odessa.

It was a premature commencement of operations by that force, in revenge on the Russians for firing upon a flag of truce.

Baron Osten-Sacken, the Russian commander at Odessa, in a letter to Admiral Dundas, dated the 14th of April, positively denied the assertion made by Captain Loring, that the Russians had fired at a flag of truce. This statement, however, was disbelieved, and about seven o'clock on the morning of the day above mentioned the attack was commenced by the allied fleet, numbering nine ships, five of which were English.

When within about 2,000 yards of the batteries on shore, the steamers moved around in a circle, about half a mile in diameter, each taking its turn in discharging a heavy broadside as it came nearest and opposite the town.

This plan of attack was continued with little result until about 1 o'clock p.m., when the batteries of the Imperial Mole, the principal object of the attack, blew up.

The guns of the steamers were then turned upon ships within the Mole, and the firing was continued until they were all destroyed by being burnt or sunk.

This cannonade lasted about ten hours, and during that time the English had 1 man killed and 9 wounded. The French had 2 men killed by an accident to one of their own guns, and not by the enemy.

In this attack the allies endeavoured to spare private property as much as possible, but the destruction of the lower part of the town was unavoidable.

The shops, factories and warehouses were set on fire by the rocket boats, and the flames spread to that part of the town most densely inhabited.

It is supposed that more than 40,000 people were made houseless by the result of those few hours' bombardment.

The Emperor Nicholas immediately issued a decree that "the military stores, batteries, and all other works of defence destroyed by a division of the combined squadron shall be reconstructed at the expense of the city of Odessa."

In this attack, besides the destruction of the batteries, one Austrian and eight Russian ships were burnt.

While stationed in the Black Sea the fleet suffered very severely from a hurricane which blew with great fury for some hours. But the damage done to the Royal Navy was nothing compared with the havoc done to the lighter transports and store ships.

A naval squadron, under the command of Vice-Admiral Sir Charles Napier, sailed from the Downs for the Baltic Sea on the 13th of March, 1854. This fleet was comprised of eight screw line of battle ships, four screw frigates, and four paddle steamers.

Before reaching its destination, this fleet was reinforced by the "Neptune" of 120 guns, under Rear-Admiral Corry, and several other vessels.

On reaching the Gulf of Finland, Admiral Napier established a blockade of all the ports along the coast, effectually depriving Russian vessels of the use of the Baltic.

In the month of May, Admiral Plumridge, with a part of the fleet, sailed for the Gulf of Bothnia, where he destroyed forty-six merchant vessels, 50,000 barrels of pitch and tar, and an immense amount of naval stores.

Two of his vessels, the "Odin" and "Vulture," were sent to Gamla-Kaleby to seize any vessels or naval stores that might be found there.

The ships were unable to reach the port, the water being too shallow, and four boats, well armed and manned, were sent in.

On coming near the shore, the boats hoisted a flag of truce, and the officer demanded the surrender of the town.

The Russians invited an attack, and the flag of truce was hauled down.

A boat from the "Odin" then went forward to reconnoitre, and was fired upon by the Russians from an ambuscade, and several men in the boat were killed.

The fire was returned by the boats, and in the action that followed, the "Vulture's" paddle-box boat became so much injured, and her crew so much cut up, that she drifted on shore, and was captured.

The other boats were compelled to retreat, after suffering a loss of 54 officers and men killed, wounded, and missing.

In the month of May, Captain Hall, in the "Hecla," was sent with Captain Yelverton, of the "Arrogant," to reconnoitre Hango Bay.

Before returning, they sailed up a narrow river to the town of Eckness, where they destroyed some heavy batteries, and captured a large merchant ship, with a valuable cargo, which they returned with to Hango Roads.

Soon after this, the "Dragon," "Hecla," and "Magicienne" bombarded the fort of Gustavus Vasa, in Hango Roads.

On the 8th of August, a party of French and English troops were landed from an allied fleet near Bomarsund, and began to erect batteries.

On the 13th, the French commenced the attack on a detached tower at the west of the other fortifications, which they captured after a sharp action the next morning.

The next day (August 15), two batteries, manned by seamen from the English portion of the fleet, which was under the command of Admiral Plumridge, opened fire on Fort Nottich, near the principal fortifications of the place.

At the same time, the bombardment of the principal fort was commenced by the fleet, five vessels firing heavy shot and shell at a long range.

The place surrendered the next day at noon.

The loss of the English during the attack and capture of Bomarsund was one officer, Lieutenant Wrottesly, and 1 private killed, and 7 wounded.

There were captured and taken 2,235 prisoners, and more than 200 guns.

Before the fleet sailed, the forts were completely destroyed by being blown up with mines.

During the summer the "Miranda" and "Brisk," screw steamers of 15 guns, and the "Eurydice" sailing vessel of 26 guns, were sent to the White Sea to blockade Archangel.

Leaving the "Eurydice" to blockade this place, the two steamers made an attempt to capture Solovetskoi, but were unsuccessful, and on the 23rd of July, they anchored off the town of Novitska.

This place they bombarded, stormed the batteries, and burnt the buildings.

Later in the summer they destroyed much of the town of Shaley Island, while a town called Kola was completely reduced to ruins.

The names of the commanders of the "Miranda" and "Brisk" are not given in the Annual Register for 1854, whence this account is taken.

In the summer of this year Admiral Price, with three English vessels, the "President," 50 guns, "Pique," 40 guns, and "Virago," 6 guns, accompanied by a French squadron of three vessels, under Admiral Des Pointe, visited the Russian settlements on the Pacific. On the 28th of August, they arrived off the town of Petropaulowski, the principal sea port of the Russian province of Kamschatka.

The next day Admiral Price died on board the "President" of a wound caused by a pistol-bullet, fired by his own hand.

He was succeeded in the command of the English squadron by Sir F. Nicolson.

The allied forces in their attack on the town of Petropaulowski were defeated and compelled to leave it with a loss on the part of the English of 1 officer killed, and 9 wounded, and 29 men killed and 147 wounded. The French met with about an equal loss.

CHAPTER XLVI.

THE WAR IN 1855.

N 1855, another admiral was chosen in the place of Admiral Sir Charles Napier for an expedition to the Baltic Sea.

This year Rear-Admiral Dundas was appointed to the command of the Baltic fleet, but not the Admiral Dundas who commanded the Black Sea fleet the year before.

By the middle of July, there had assembled in the Baltic eighty-five English vessels of war, carrying 2,098 guns, and sixteen French vessels, mounting 408 guns, under the command of Rear-Admiral Penaud.

In all, including gunboats and mortar-boats, etc., there were 101 vessels, mounting 2,506 guns.

History gives no record of another force so strong having been sent forth which accomplished so little.

On the 5th of June, Captain Fanshawe, of the "Cossack," sent a cutter into Hango with a flag of truce, to land three prisoners that had been captured in some Russian merchant vessels.

Besides these three prisoners were four other persons, that had been taken by the "Magicienne," and were to be released.

The boat was commanded by Lieutenant Geneste, and as it did not return by the time it was expected, another boat was despatched with a flag of truce to look after it.

The boat which had been first sent was found, and in it the dead bodies of four of its crew.

It was subsequently ascertained that when the party landed with the flag of truce, they were fired upon by a party of soldiers, who gave the first evidence of their presence by a volley, that killed and wounded 11 men.

This affair is called by the English people a massacre.

The Russians say that they saw no flag, that if there was such a thing carried by the boat's crew, it was not conspicuously displayed, that the officer of the boat should have waited until the flag had been recognised, and until he had obtained permission to land according to the established rules for such occasions, and that had the boat pushed off after landing the prisoners, the people in it would not have been molested.

On the 9th of August, the allied fleet commenced the bombardment of Sweaborg.

The firing was kept up with but little intermission until about four o'clock on the morning of the 11th, and during the time it continued it is estimated that 1,000 tons of shot and shell were thrown into the forts by the English alone.

The assailants, finding that they were only injuring themselves more than the enemy, abandoned the siege.

The Baltic fleet did not attempt anything more this year worthy of record.

A small flying squadron remained to continue the blockade, and the rest of the fleet returned to their homes, where its officers heard many murmurings of discontent at the little they had accomplished.

In the month of May, Captain Lyons was sent with a squadron into the Sea of Azof.

At Berdiansk, he destroyed many vessels, loaded with corn.

At Arabat and Genitchi, more damage of a similar kind was done to the enemy, and it is estimated that the amount of stores destroyed at Kertch and the Sea of Azof amounted to four months' rations for 100,000 men.

The squadron under Lyons then left Genitchi for the mouth of the River Don.

At the town of Taganrog, a few miles up this river, the government stores were destroyed, which ended the feats of this squadron for the season.

The bombardment of forts and villages, and the destruction of small accumulations of government stores, and other work of the fleet sent to the Russian War, did not materially affect the enemy, but it pleased the people at home, who were always anxious to hear something from its fleets.

CHAPTER XLVII.

THE SECOND CHINESE WAR.

1856—1860.

THE events of which we are now about to speak will be remembered by many of our readers.

On the 8th of October, 1856, the "Arrow," a small vessel with an English colonial register, manned by Chinamen, but owned by a British subject, while lying in the Canton River, near the Dutch Folly Fort, off Canton, was boarded by the Chinese authorities, and the crew taken away prisoners on the charge of piracy.

The English flag is said to have been flying on the "Arrow" at the time, and Mr. Parkes, the English consul at Canton, demanded that the men taken from the lorcha "Arrow" should be returned to it, and that the crime of which they had been accused should be investigated according to articles of treaty between the two nations.

This demand was refused.

This dispute led to Sir John Bowring, the English plenipotentiary, applying to Sir Michael Seymour, the commander-in-chief of the British fleet on the China station.

On the 23rd of October, Admiral Seymour, on board the "Coromandel," and with a fleet of gunboats, took several forts that defended the approach to Canton, and burnt some buildings.

On the 25th, he took the Dutch Folly, a 50-gun fort, on a little island opposite Canton.

As Commissioner Yeh still continued obstinate, a fire was opened on some of the government buildings of the city, amongst which was Commissioner Yeh's residence.

Yeh now offered a reward of thirty dollars for the head of every Englishman, which the English answered by breaching the walls of the city, and taking possession of his house.

Another attempt at a parley followed and failed, and on the 3rd of November, the bombardment of the city was resumed.

On the 5th, a large number of war-junks were destroyed, and the French Folly Fort was taken possession of.

On the 13th, Admiral Seymour attacked and took the Bogue Forts, which mounted more than 400 guns, with only a loss of 1 boy killed and 4 men wounded.

In the latter part of May, 1857, Commodore Elliot, with a small fleet of gunboats, went up the Escape Creek from the Canton River, and destroyed a large number of war-junks.

About the same time, Admiral Seymour left his flagship, the "Calcutta," and, in company with Commodore Keppel, went in the "Coromandel," with four gunboats, up the Canton River as far as Macao Fort.

The next morning, a fleet of seventy-two junks was attacked and destroyed by Seymour, while Keppel, in a channel to the right of Hyacinth Island, was equally busy.

Earl Elgin, who had been selected as the ambassador to the Emperor of China, arrived at Hong-Kong in July, 1857; but as part of the force destined to prepare the Chinese for receiving him had to be despatched to India on account of the mutiny, the Chinese difficulty had to wait for a settlement.

By the following December, when the English were again ready to resume operations in China, they were joined by the French, who had also found a wrong to be settled.

On Monday, the 28th of December, the bombardment of Canton was commenced. East, or Linn Fort was first captured, then Magazine Hill.

Gough Fort, at the north, was then attacked, captured, and blown up.

On the morning of the 5th of January, 1858, the troops entered the city, and did not leave it until the governor, the Chinese general, and Commissioner Yeh, were captured. A long delay followed, in which there were no means of communicating with the Chinese Government at Pekin.

To expedite matters, Lord Elgin resolved to proceed with an armed force to the capital, and on the 19th of May, the fleet arrived at the mouth of the River Peiho, which they found to be strongly fortified on each bank.

The English and French at last determined to force their way up the river, but the attempt was not made until the 24th of June, the intervening time being lost in abortive diplomacy.

Admiral Hope, who had the command of the squadron for this work, gave orders for the booms across the river to be forced, and the "Opossum," which made the first attempt, broke through the first barrier, and was followed by the "Plover" and two gunboats.

As they drew near the second barrier, a heavy fire from the forts and some guns that had been concealed from view, was opened upon them.

The "Plover" became so disabled that Admiral Hope was obliged to shift his flag to the "Cormorant," which, with other vessels, had come up.

Soon after, the "Kestrel" sank in the river, and the "Lee" had to be run ashore to prevent her doing the same.

An hour later, and the fire from the Chinese batteries had nearly ceased, and a detachment of sappers and miners, a brigade of marines, and a division of English and French seamen were landed. As the boats touched the shore the fire from the forts and batteries was reopened with deadly effect.

The men sprang out of the boats into the mud, and struggled forward.

The officers could have known nothing of the difficulties the storming party would have to encounter, or the attempt at the time would not have been made.

Before the walls could be reached three deep ditches had to be crossed, and the work of reaching the ditches—struggling in deep mud, exposed to a murderous fire—was a feat not easily accomplished.

A few officers and about 50 men of the 1,000 landed, succeeded in crossing the ditches, but the ladders were broken by the round shot or lost in the mud.

The order was given to retire, and many were shot down while waiting to get into the boats, some of which had been destroyed by shots from the forts.

In this affair the English had 64 officers and men killed and 252 wounded, besides 25 killed and 93 wounded on the gunboats.

The "Plover" and "Lee" that were ashore, could not be got off, and fell into the hands of the enemy.

The "Cormorant" was sunk by the Chinese guns at her anchors.

After this affair the squadron sailed for Shanghai.

During the year 1858, some of the smaller vessels in the service were made useful in clearing the China Sea of pirates.

On the 4th of August, Lieutenant Wildman, in the gunboat "Staunch," attacked four large pirate junks near Wanchow.

In an attempt to board one of them, the men were met by a shower of stink-pots, that compelled them to draw back.

One of the men who had leaped on to the pirates' deck ahead of his comrades, was cut to pieces and thrown over.

The gunboat now sheered off and renewed the fire from her howitzers, until a second attempt to board proved successful.

On the 22nd of August, Commander Creswell, of the gun vessel "Surprise," and two boats from the "Cambrian," attacked a large fleet of pirate junks anchored in a bay of the Leman Islands.

The pirates made preparations for defence, and opened a brisk fire upon the boats.

The shells thrown from the "Surprise," however, were certainly a surprise to them.

Two of the largest junks were blown up, and the battle ended by nineteen of the junks being burnt, and seven taken possession of.

One of the junks mounted 28 guns, and the whole fleet carried about 230 guns.

Another more extensive expedition against the pirates, was commanded by Captain Vansittart, who had under his command the "Magicienne," "Plover," "Inflexible," and "Algerine."

This expedition sailed along the coast from Hong Kong, as far west as Mamee, and took or destroyed twenty-six fighting junks, and seventy-four smaller vessels, in all mounting 236 guns.

Early in August, 1860, an English and French force again assembled near the mouth of the Peiho. They were now properly prepared to compel the Chinese government to make a real instead of a sham treaty and to obtain some satisfaction for the defeat of the year before.

On the 14th, the batteries at Tanghu were captured by the land force that had been sent ashore, and 45 guns were found within them.

The troops were then marched on to attack the Taku forts, which, after a brief siege, were also captured.

In the succeeding events that resulted in the capture of Pekin, and the looting of the emperor's palace, the naval power had but little to do.

Admiral Hope with his squadron entered the river Peiho and proceeded as far as Tien-tsin; but there was no work for him to do.

* * * * *

We will not conclude this work without a brief notice of one of England's greatest naval heroes, who departed this life within the memory of our youngest readers.

The Earl of Dundonald, or Lord Cochrane, the name by which he will always be remembered with most respect by Englishmen, was born on the 14th of December, 1775, at Annsfield, Lanarkshire.

At the age of seventeen, he joined the "Hind," of 28 guns, at Sheerness, as midshipman.

There has never been a commander in the British navy who has on so many occasions distinguished himself for bravery that amounted to a reckless disregard for life as Lord Cochrane.

In a cutting-out expedition where a few men in a boat were expected to conquer four or five times their number, Lord Cochrane was ever most happy.

It was the frequent exhibition of this fiery nature that made his name respected throughout the world, and which led to his receiving an invitation to command the navy of Chili, when treated by his countrymen as a felon.

Like every other brave man, Lord Cochrane had enemies.

Some of them were created by the heroism he displayed in the defeat of the French at Basque Roads, where he, by force of genius, obtained some fame that others had not the energy to seize.

Soon after midnight on Sunday, February 20th, 1814, a man, calling himself Colonel Du Bourg, who afterwards proved to be Captain De Berenger, was admitted to the "Ship Inn," Dover.

He was dressed in a military great coat of grey colour, and a uniform embroidered with gold lace.

On his breast was a star, and a silver medal was worn around his neck.

He was in the uniform of a staff officer, and said that he had just arrived from Paris with glorious news. His news was—

"Buonaparte pursued and killed by the Cossacks. Allied sovereigns in Paris. Immediate peace."

This news was communicated to the port admiral, who had command of the telegraph, and it was sent everywhere.

The man who brought it took a chaise and four, and started for London.

When near the metropolis, he took a hackney coach at Marsh Gate, Lambeth, and was driven to Lord Cochrane's house in Green Street.

The funds went up, and Lord Cochrane sold out all he possessed to the amount of £139,000, and made £2,000 by the operation.

The news that caused this rise in the funds was false, and Lord Cochrane and some others were prosecuted and brought to trial.

He was sentenced to pay a fine of £1,000—to one year's imprisonment—and to stand in the pillory at Westminster, the place he represented, for one hour.

The latter part of this sentence the government were compelled to remit.

Sir Francis Burdett declared that he should stand in the pillory by the side of his friend, and to calm the excited state of the public mind, the government did not enforce the fulfilment of the full sentence.

The money to pay the fine was raised in one day by small subscriptions, and was paid with a £1,000 note.

This note, it is stated, is now to be seen at the Bank of England. Its number is 8,202, the date June 26, 1815.

On the back of the note the following words are written—

"My health having suffered by long and close confinement, and my oppressors being resolved to deprive me of my property or life, I submit to robbery to protect myself from murder, in the hope that I shall live to bring the delinquents to justice. "COCHRANE.

"King's Bench Prison, July 3rd, 1815."

Cochrane was now dismissed from the navy, in which he had fought so bravely; the title of Knight of the Bath was taken from him, and the king-at-arms kicked his banner out of the chapel, according to ancient custom.

A motion was brought forward in the House of Commons to have him expelled from it, and the hero broke his prison, scaled a high wall, and took a part in the debate as to whether he should be expelled or not.

He left prison a disgraced man in the country for which he had done so much.

Nearly heartbroken by the degradation to which he had been driven, he sailed for South America, followed by his wife, a true-hearted English woman, and two children.

While in Peru, at the capture of the Spanish treasure ship "Antonio," he was joined by his boy, who had escaped from his mother and got aboard his father's ship.

Just before the action commenced, Cochrane locked the boy in the after-cabin, but, like the son of his father, the boy crawled through the quarter-gallery window, and made his appearance on the deck in a midshipman's uniform made for him by the sailors.

He remained on deck even after being covered with the blood of a marine, whose head was shot off while standing by his side.

The cutting out of the "Esmeralda" from under the guns of the fortress of Callao was, perhaps, the most brilliant achievement during the whole course of the war in South America. The intrepidity which distinguished the character of Lord Cochrane was on this occasion most conspicuous, and that promptitude in providing for emergencies for which he was so much admired was displayed in a manner worthy of his high reputation.

The Spanish authorities were not without suspicions of some meditated attack from our resolute and enterprising countryman, and under this impression, they had communicated with the British frigate the "Hyperion," and the "Macedonian," a ship belonging to the United States, both at the time lying in the harbour. With the commanders of these vessels it was arranged that, in the event of a night attack being made, they should exhibit lights, in order that the garrison might know them to be neutral, and avoid firing upon them.

Whether his lordship was aware of this understanding we cannot tell, but his foresight rendered the expedient of little importance. Independent of the "Esmeralda" being protected by the guns of the fort, she had the support of a corvette, two brigs of war, several armed merchantmen, and between twenty and thirty gunboats.

While the Royalists were thus taking their measures for securing themselves against the operations they naturally expected would be directed against them, Lord Cochrane, with silent celerity, was preparing for carrying the object of his visit into effect, and for this purpose, he had secretly caused a number of empty puncheons to be ballasted in such a manner that they would float perpendicularly in the water. Each of these was placed in a boat, in charge of two men.

It was near eleven o'clock at night, on the 6th of November, when 180 seamen and 100 marines, in two divisions, under the command of Captains Guise and Crosbie, and led by Lord Cochrane in person, left the squadron, and approached the anchor ground of the "Esmeralda" in two launches.

So silent had been their advance towards the object of attack, that they were within hail before their motions were observed by a sentry in one of the gunboats astern of the enemy.

"Silence or death," was the brief reply of the admiral of the patriots, and the next moment Lord Cochrane's foot was on the deck of the Esmeralda.

The resistance for some time was maintained with much spirit by the Spaniards, but before one o'clock on the morning of the 6th, the fire from their small arms was silenced, and the ship in possession of the admiral.

The prize was now towed out from the harbour, under a heavy discharge from the guns of the fort. The "Hyperion" and the "Macedonian" displayed their lights, when the puncheons already mentioned were instantly unshipped, each carrying a similar signal to that of the neutrals.

By this dexterous manœuvre, the fire from the garrison was distracted, and rendered in a great measure ineffectual, as it oftener fell in the direction of the neutrals, or among the lights of the floating puncheons, than in the wake of the enemy, the Spaniards being quite at a loss to distinguish the lights of their friends from the decoy ones sent adrift by their assailants, who were now making their way in comparative security to their squadron.

Amidst the whole of the daring exploits which distinguished the naval career of his lordship, we believe the action we have related will stand unrivalled for cool intrepidity, skilful leading, and provident calculation.

The loss of the Spaniards amounted to 150 men, some of whom, particularly Captain Coy, were killed by the guns of the fort.

The "Esmeralda" had just completed her stores, and was ready for sea, having three months' provisions on board, besides stores for two years.

The loss on the part of the Chili squadron amounted to about 50 killed and wounded. Among the latter was the admiral, who was struck on the thigh by a musket-ball in the early part of the action.

Lieutenant Grenfell, an able officer, who has since obtained by his merits distinguished rank in the Brazilian service, was also severely hurt on the occasion.

The garrison of Callao were so enraged at the daring nature and success of the attack, that on the following day they attacked and murdered an officer and boat's crew belonging to the American frigate, the "Macedonian," excusing themselves for this atrocity by the pitiful assertion, that "Cochrane, devil as he was, would not have succeeded if the Americans had not assisted him."

No one or two countries could give sufficient employment to such an old sea lion as Cochrane.

From Peru he went to Brazil, and from there to Greece, ever fighting in the cause of liberty.

Years passed, and Cochrane returned to his native land, where he was reinstated in his command in the navy, and afterwards made rear-admiral. His father, too, being dead, he succeeded to the title, Earl of Dundonald, and afterwards rose to the highest naval command.

He died in the year 1859.

* * * * * *

Little more remains to be said. Of late years we have enjoyed peace—consequently our navy has had no opportunity of distinguishing itself.

The character of the navy itself has, in the meantime, been greatly changed.

About eleven years ago, public attention was called to the fact that the French were busily engaged in the construction of a ship of war, which was to be coated with plates of iron armour, and so rendered impregnable to cannon shot.

The plan had often been discussed; the practice was now watched eagerly, and it soon became very evident that Great Britain would be compelled to have ironclad ships.

During the war between the Northern and Southern States of America, ironclad vessels were subjected to very severe trial.

English and French ship builders and naval officers watched everything that took place, and armour-plated vessels became more common.

It was evident that the wooden walls of Old England were to be replaced by ramparts of more solid and durable material.

Since that time, we have gone on adding to the thickness of our armour plating, and then increasing the penetrating power of our guns, till we have now the strongest ships and the most powerful artillery in the world, manned, we may say, by the bravest of brave men.

Yet the iron monsters of the deep are found to have their bad qualities as well as their good.

One of them—the ill-fated "Captain"—went to the bottom, in weather that a Newfoundland fishing-smack would have thought nothing of; and more recently we were within a hair's breadth of losing the "Agincourt." But these things teach us the faults to be avoided in future.

At the commencement of the year 1871, we had forty-eight armour-plated vessels afloat, and ten more in course of construction, some of which will be complete and launched before these words are published.

To man the fleet, we have 61,000 officers, seamen, boys, and marines, as well as a kind of maritime militia, known as the Naval Reserve.

The following is a list of the iron-clad ships in the British Navy at the commencement of the year 1871:—

	GUNS.
Achilles	26
Active	8
Agincourt	28
Audacious	14
Bellerophon	14
Black Prince	28
Caledonia	30
Defence	16
Enterprise	4
Erebus	16
Favourite	10
Hector	18
Hercules	14
Hotspur	2
Inconstant	16
Invincible	14
Iron Duke	14
Lord Clyde	24
Lord Warden	18
Minotaur	34
Monarch (turret-ship)	7
Northumberland	28
Ocean	24
Pallas	6
Penelope	11
Prince Albert (turret-ship)	4
Prince Consort	24
Repulse	12
Research	4
Resistance	16
Royal Alfred	18
Royal Oak	24
Royal Sovereign (turret-ship)	5
Scorpion (turret-ship)	4
Sultan	12
Swiftsure	14
Terror	16
Thunder	14
Thunderbolt	16
Valiant	18
Vanguard	14
Viper	2
Vixen	2
Volage	8
Warrior	32
Waterwitch	2
Wivern (turret-ship)	4
Zealous	20

At the same time the following iron-clad vessels were being constructed:—

	GUNS.
Cyclops (turret-ship)	4
Devastation (turret-ship)	—
Fury (turret-ship)	4
Glatton (turret-ship)	2
Gorgon (turret-ship)	—
Hecate (turret-ship)	4
Hydra (turret-ship)	4
Rupert (iron-clad ram)	—
Thunderer (turret-ship)	—
Triumph	14

A Naval History of Great Britain would be incomplete without a few words respecting Greenwich Hospital. This noble building occupies the site of the old palace, which was such a favourite residence of King Henry VIII. and Queen Elizabeth.

Greenwich Palace was in a very dilapidated condition at the period of the restoration, and was pulled down; the north-western wing of the present building being erected by the celebrated artist, Inigo Jones.

Queen Mary, the wife of King William III., is said to have suggested the plan of founding an asylum for disabled seamen of the Royal Navy, and the unfinished palace of Greenwich was considered suitable for the purpose, and was accordingly enlarged and adapted to the purpose.

Sir Christopher Wren, who was as generous as clever, volunteered to superintend the building without receiving any pecuniary reward; and the foundation stone was laid with great ceremony on the 3rd of June, 1696.

The works were hastened on, and in two years the exterior of the building was finished, though the building was not opened for the reception of its inmates till 1705, or nine years after its commencement.

Since that time, the buildings have been greatly improved and enlarged, and many noble lands have been given to endow it.

Its funds are obtained from parliamentary grants, from the forfeited estates of the Earl of Derwentwater, who espoused the cause of the Pretender, and from bequests of benevolent individuals, amounting in all, to over £150,000 per annum.

The estimate of the sum required to defray all demands of the year ending March 31st, 1870, amounted to £133,966, of which sum £79,507 was for pensions to seamen.

But the pensioners are no longer maintained in the grand palace; *home* is considered the best place for them, and, accordingly, they are sent to end their days with their relatives and friends.

In connection with Greenwich Hospital is a school for the instruction of the children of officers, petty officers, and seamen.

These boys are admitted into the navy at the age of ten or eleven years, are clothed, disciplined and educated till they reach the age of fifteen, when they are sent to sea, or provided for in some other way.

Greenwich Hospital is under the control of a governor who ranks as admiral, and a captain-superintendent.

In the school is a chaplain and principal, assisted in his duties by fourteen masters.

All honour then to Greenwich Hospital, though no longer the home of the Greenwich pensioner.

* * * * *

The history of the British Navy is now told, imperfectly perhaps, but with a most anxious desire to do full justice to the gallant men, who for ages past have guarded our coast. We have seen British ships and British seamen in every part of the ocean; and in every instance they have displayed the same invincible gallantry—have always been the same hardy, intrepid, and devoted servants of their country.

Well may Britain be proud of the glorious British Navy.

FINIS.

NAUTICAL TALES;

OR ADVENTURES BY SEA AND LAND.

"FOR A MOMENT HE STOOD IRRESOLUTE; AND THEN ALLOWED THE STRANGER TO APPROACH."

No. 1.—THE HOLY BRACELETS:

A TALE OF THE DAYS OF KING ALFRED.

CHAPTER I.

WHAT FERTILISED THE SOIL OF ENGLAND.

THE battle was over. The fight was done.

After an obstinate engagement the Anglo-Saxons had been utterly defeated by the ruthless and savage Danes—defeated with great slaughter.

The combat had been long, fierce, and sanguinary. In those days, when men fought hand-to-hand with sword and shield, and from a short distance with spear and bow and arrow, the battles were very terrible. Men fell dead and dying, gashed with numerous and hideous wounds, while hundreds perished from a want of proper knowledge of chirurgery.

The field was strewed with the combatants of both parties.

The awful fight had taken place at no great distance from the sea, and in sight of the ships of the Danish pirates, who were the same pests to England in those days as the Romans, Scots, and Saxons had, in days of yore, been to the aboriginal inhabitants.

The Britons had been defeated, but, though yielding before superior numbers, retreated slowly in the direction of an extensive wood. Their brows were sullen, and their eyes gleamed with intense fury. To be beaten was to be shamed; and yet fortune so willed it.

Foremost in the fight, retreating even more slowly than the others, was a young man armed only with sword and buckler. His costume was simple in form, though rich in quality, and his head was surmounted by a kind of helmet. Not a word escaped his lips as he now warded off the blows of the powerful men who were opposed to him, and then attacked them in return.

GRATIS SUPPLEMENT TO No. 1 OF BRETT'S NAVAL HISTORY.]

Around him were several fair men like himself, but of more stalwart frame, who wielded heavy hammers instead of swords, and strove as much as possible to protect the one who appeared to be their chief.

The skirts of the wood were now reached, and profiting by the coming darkness, or stricken by a panic, the Anglo-Saxons broke their line and fled in extreme confusion. The Danes, not knowing the wood, or fearful of an ambush in the dark, halted, with a firm determination to follow up their victory in the morning.

And where, all this time, was the brave youth with the golden hair?

Turning to check the flight of his immediate friends, the young man had fallen to the ground and lay slightly stunned in some bushes over which he had tripped.

Rising, after some few minutes, he looked sadly around. Alone, of all that brilliant army, he remained in the front of the victorious foe, returning to their camp to celebrate victory in deep goblets of their national drink.

He stood, with his sword-point touching the earth, with his handsome face gazing after the foe, and his eyes sad and thoughtful. After a moment he turned away, and walked beneath the shelter of the wood, intending to seek refuge, doubtless, in some of its most secret and unknown fastnesses.

The night, however, was dark in the extreme, and, after in vain trying to find his way, the young man clambered into a tree, where, after some hours spent in deep thought, he fell into a restless and uneasy slumber.

From this he was awakened by a clang of arms close at hand; and, peering down from the branches, he saw that the Danish pirates were scouring the forest in search of their enemies, whom they hoped to plunder of their valuables as well as of their young men and women.

England in those days was covered by forests, which, if not so immense and primeval as those of the American continent, were, at all events, in many instances as dense, so that men were able to lie hidden in large numbers for months without being found out. No true Saxon was ever known to act as a guide to the Danes, so that their task was a hard one.

All that day, however, they persevered. The wood was full of scouting parties, and the young man had to lie still. Towards evening the baffled pirates came, returning to their ships, while one party, headed by a tall and handsome man of about thirty, with a sinister expression, clad in complete but rude armour, halted beneath the very tree occupied by the fugitive.

He was a very powerful man, and appeared bursting with vexation at the futility of his search. After giving vent to his anger in language far more forcible than polite, he strode away to the Danish camp, around which the pirates had thrown up a rude embankment of earth.

Becoming assured, after a short time, that immediate danger was at an end, the young man slid from the tree, and, weak and faint, turned to go further into the wood.

As he made a first step, he halted. Somebody was close to him. He stood irresolute a moment, and then allowed the stranger to advance.

It was a youth of less than sixteen, armed with bow and arrows, as well as a long, slight-pointed lance.

"A friend, I see," he said, bowing gracefully.

"Yes; one who has passed a day and a night in yonder tree," replied the young man, with a dry smile, "without food or water. This part of the coast was strange to me, until this battle led me hither. Boy, if you could take me to where there is water and an oatmeal cake, I shall feel grateful."

"Follow me, sir soldier," said the youth. "I have been on the track of that tall pirate all day. He and I are old acquaintances. I would,"—tapping his lance—"become more intimate with him."

"How so, my brave youth?" continued the other, following in his wake with a smile.

"Six months ago—the last time the sea-robbers came here—he sacked my father's house, stole all our goods, and would have carried off my dear cousin Rowena, had not a brave band of youths fallen suddenly on him, and saved her from his clutches."

"You are, then——" observed the other, quietly.

"Edgar, the son of Earl Ethered," said the boy, a little haughtily. "And, as you have spoken first, pray allow me to ask who you may be?"

"By the holy rood, yesterday, my brave boy, I was even Alfred, King of England," was the quiet reply. "What I am now, Heaven only knows; for the present, a poor fugitive in search of meal and water."

The youth doffed his cap respectfully, and then proceeded to conduct him towards deeper wilds, anxious, like every boy or man in the land, to preserve the young prince who had already shown such startling evidences of noble character, courage, and goodness.

For the present, Alfred's army was hopelessly dissolved, and that portion of fair England at the mercy of the pirates.

All this he heard with a dark frown, vowing, by God's mercy, that such a state of things should not last long, even if he perished in the struggle and gave his blood to fertilize the soil of England.

CHAPTER II.

THE ISLAND HOME.

FAR in the depths of the pathless forest, then haunted by fierce, wild animals, was a piece of water of limited extent, surrounded to the very edge with large and stalwart trees, the growth of centuries. The water was apparently wholly abandoned to water fowl and the beasts of the field, so solemn was the stillness that reigned around.

Birds twittered and sang on lofty boughs, the wood gave forth occasionally odd sounds, but nowhere was there any sign of man.

Presently, however, some bushes were displaced, and two creatures of the loftier species appeared.

These were Alfred and his young guide, Edgar, who had led him thus far from his persevering and ruthless foes.

Edgar stepped upon a small landing place, stooped beneath a bush that overhung the water, and drew out something like a canoe, made, however, from withes and skins, into which he preceded the prince. Both were wearied and footsore, having travelled nearly all night, with no other sustenance than water, acorns, and berries.

As soon as both were seated, the boy gave the boat a push from the shore, after which he impelled it rapidly across the still, open space of water. In five minutes he was hailed from the opposite bank, and, giving a satisfactory reply, was allowed to land.

Alfred had requested that his incognito should be observed, though he well knew that it exposed him to some strange rebuffs and vicissitudes. He was to be announced to all save the earl as a British warrior who had escaped one of the last from the field of battle.

As it happened, the earl and one serving man alone stood on the strand to receive them. The former started with surprise; but, noticing his son's look of caution, refrained from speech, leading his unexpected guest into the interior of what was truly his island home.

A small hill had been fortified by means of a stout stockade, round which a natural stream had been carried by artificial means. Within this were erected numerous huts of various dimensions, enough to shelter some fifty armed men, many of their wives and children, and the earl's whole family.

The comforts and elegancies of life were well known to our ancestors in those days, even to silk embroidered hangings, carved furniture, decorated and inlaid with gold, silver, and precious stones, while dress was both fanciful and luxurious. Plate of gold and silver was not uncommon, while their harps were of elegant and elaborate make.

But the stern earl had buried all his treasures—a too free display of which on the part of the Britons excited the cupidity of the Danes—and lived here in the primitive simplicity of a forest chief. Except his soldiers, he had but one attendant, while Rowena, in place of tiring maid, had a swine-herd to do her service.

He himself led the way to a hut, only distinguished by its size from the others, and, opening the door, bade his sovereign welcome.

No one was present save himself, his son, and the king.

"My friend," said Alfred, kindly, "whatever may happen in time to come, thank this gallant boy for it. He saved my life, and I shall never forget. But enough of that; let us be seated, good earl. My soul is on fire, nor can I rest until something be done to drive forth these insolent invaders, who are no more pleasant to you, fair Rowena, than to us."

Rowena merely blushed, curtsied, and moved on one side with Edgar.

A long conversation now ensued between the king and the earl. Both were equally anxious to drive the insolent invaders into the sea; but the Danish pirates were so numerous, so audacious, and hitherto so united, that the task was difficult, almost hopeless.

"My good earl," said Alfred, at last, "while the footstep of a foreigner treads the soil of my native country in enmity, England is not England, and I am no king. It must be done."

And, after a few more words, the wearied and exhausted prince shared a frugal meal with the fugitive earl, after which, he snatched a few hours' sleep. When he awoke, he found that messengers had started in all directions to warn those of his followers who were true to him, to meet him that day week, then to venture England's future in one great battle.

The king was delighted at the energy and devotion of his friend, but at once declared that a week's idleness was out of the question.

He and Edgar would scout daily, examining the enemy's camp, as nearly as possible, and thus obtain a knowledge of their future designs, as well as present force. Edgar, young stripling as he was, was only too glad to obey the orders of his monarch, while Rowena, flattered at the preference, put no obstacle in the way.

Attired as simple men-at-arms, and carrying each the terrific hammer of the Saxons, with dagger, and with each a bow and arrow, the young monarch and his bold attendant were ferried over to the forest. Edgar, whose father's castle was not many miles distant, in the hands of some of the pirate hordes, knew every inch of the forest, and easily led Alfred along its pathless wilds as readily as if there had been marked roads.

The king marvelled at his sagacity—how, like a wellbred hound, he turned neither to the right nor the left, and by midnight led him to a wooded eminence whence he could make out the fires of the enemy's camp, extending on each side for above a mile.

The king seated himself, and, with sorrowful eye, scanned the mighty host.

"We must examine them at dawn of day," he said, after a long pause. "We must lie here for an hour or two."

"Not here, sire," replied the youth, respectfully, and led King Alfred down a slope into a dark and lonesome valley, where suddenly they saw a light and heard voices.

Edgar halted; but the king, anxiously believing he was on the track of the enemy, bade him lead on.

Edgar obeyed, taking, however, the most minute precautions not to betray his presence by any incautious act.

In this way the two soon stood within sight of some dozen armed men, six of whom were Danes, and six Britons.

Two stood apart, men of tall stature; one the king and Edgar recognised as Hastings the pirate, the other as a rude, gigantic, and powerful Englishmen, roughly armed, with a singularly hard countenance.

"Your hand upon it, Edwolf," said the mighty Dane, speaking so as to be understood with great difficulty. "To-morrow you will lead us, by ways known to yourself, where I may capture the fair Rowena."

"My hand upon it," replied the other, in a hoarse voice; "at two hours after dawn be here. Remember the silver and gold——"

"Shall be thine," growled Hastings, and hurried away with his men.

Edgar clutched his bow, and might have acted incautiously but for the king.

"Leave them to me," said Alfred, stepping forward right into the midst of the startled and amazed group of Anglo-Saxons.

"What want you? Who are you?"

"Your king, Edwolf the Saxon, whom you would betray to the pirate Dane," replied the youthful monarch, more reproachfully than harshly; "is it well, my friends?"

"We are outlaws—we know no king," said the leader, sullenly, while the others looked perseveringly on the ground; "we have been injured by Earl Ethered."

"He shall do you justice when the fight is over," continued the king, firmly; "in the meantime ye are no outlaws. I enrol you in my body-guard. Come."

Alfred smiled as all rushed forward, including their ferocious-looking leader, and bent the knee to the monarch they had never seen, but in their hearts revered so much.

"Come, Edgar; said I not they were friends?" cried the king, patting the huge outlaw on the shoulder. "You must give us shelter for the night."

And they did, disputing only who should watch over him during his dreamless sleep.

CHAPTER III.

THE VOW OF THE HOLY BRACELETS.

FIRE, famine, and slaughter marked the track of the Danish pirates wherever they went, on more than one occasion followed by a plague which fell both upon human creatures and beasts. No wonder, then, that king and people were anxious to get rid of them.

After the first panic of the defeat was over, the emissaries sent out by the earl found a ready response from all classes, and on the eve of the appointed day the forest became alive with men. They came in droves, they came in hundreds, in scores, in half dozens, but all brought brave hearts and valiant souls to the conflict.

The scouts announced that the Danes, who held Castle Ethered on the left and Castle Elbald on the right, were preparing for another great foray into the interior of the country, leaving only a portion of their troops to guard their huge fleet of ships.

The left wing was commanded by Hastings, the right by Guthrum, the former having sworn a mighty oath that he would slay every man, woman, and child that came into his hand until he found the peerless Rowena.

The young king swore no oath, but he made a vow that, for their insolence and cruelty, the Danes should be severely punished.

Apprised by their scouts, the Danes kept a good lookout. They, however, only expected a partial attack, and, therefore, on that memorable morn when the British hordes came forth from the forest their surprise was unbounded, the more that on the slopes behind they could clearly make out the women-harpers prepared beforehand to chaunt victory.

Some among the Danes as usual would have made a hollow treaty, and retreated with their plunder to their own country; but the haughty chiefs, confident in their superior valour, in their gigantic strength, in their discipline, in their fortified camp, determined to fight.

The Raven flag was hoisted—that flag they believed enchanted, because woven by the three daughters of one father in a single afternoon—and the rude earthen entrenchments manned by all their forces.

King Alfred, surrounded by his best chiefs, and followed by dozens of rough outlaws like Edwolf, resolved to die for him, led the centre of his troops. By his side was Edgar.

The very best and bravest officers in England led the different columns.

As soon as they were near enough, the signal was given, and arrows fell on all sides like hail. In this the English had the advantage, their archers being unequalled in the world; and still as volley succeeded volley, on rushed the men, until at last bows and arrows were cast on one side, and with such a cry as might have astonished a modern Highland regiment, the Britons rushed to the assault.

The ditch of the camp was merely a trench from which the earthwork had been thrown up, no Dane believing the English audacious enough to attack them. It was crossed, therefore, in a moment, and now began such a mêlée as can only occur between men equally brave, stubborn, and determined.

Battle-axe and hammer, sword and mace, dagger and knife, were all at work. Now the Danes yield, and then the Raven's wings were seen to droop; now the stout Britons are hurled back in the ditch, and the Raven clapped his wings—so cried the soothsayers.

Backward and forward swept the tide of battle, now ebbing, now flowing for our gallant countrymen. Soon they fought on piles of friends and foes, and wherever the fight was hottest, keenest, and fiercest, there was King Alfred and the brave young Edgar.

Nothing could resist their impetuosity, supported as they were by the élite of the army. And now Hastings, finding his men began to cast longing eyes at the ships, knew that he must do or die. Rallying round him the fiercest and most desperate of his crew, and waving his ponderous battle-axe, which few other men could lift, he dashed at the king.

Now Alfred, brave and accomplished, and highly gifted as a soldier, had not the physical force of his gigantic adversary, who made directly for him, fully aware that with his death the contest would cease. He was fiercely and resolutely supported by his followers. Desperate, fearful was the conflict. Alfred knew his object, and tried to force his way to meet him for some time in vain.

At last the two stood opposite one another, armed one with a stout sword, the other with his huge and awful axe. It rose in the air, and the king darting onwards to strike him, the weighty, death-dealing weapon must have struck him, when, with a wild and savage cry, Edwolf darted forward to the rescue, and received the blow full on the shoulder.

"Oh! king, have I done well?" he cried, and fell bleeding, dying in their midst.

Alfred had no time to thank his faithful follower, but, with a dark frown, rushed at Hastings, who fell, and with him the Raven flag.

On all hands, on every part of the line, the English were victorious.

When all had surrendered, Alfred as usual showed himself as generous as he was brave. The first impulse of the British chiefs was to destroy all the ships and make slaves of the men. Not so the young prince. A very large proportion, after defeat not caring to go home, he commanded to go away to the east and settle under Guthrum—which they did, turning Christians and becoming in good time as good, honest Englishmen as any of the Saxons.

Those under Hastings, however, offered to make a treaty on condition that their arms and ships were restored to them; and, to make the treaty binding, they agreed to swear upon the Holy Bracelets they wore—and which they have buried with them when they die—never to molest England again, and in all things to be true and faithful friends.

Alfred, who knew the tremendous character of this oath in the eyes of the Danish people, and being so heart-honest himself, not only accepted their solemn asseverations, but gave a feast in the Castle of Ethered to Hastings before his departure. His own three ships were then restored to him, with which he sailed away.

The others Alfred retained, intending to destroy some, and of others to make the nucleus of a British fleet.

And so the false Dane departed; and next morning the two maidens who slept in an outer chamber to guard Rowena were found dead in their room, while the lovely cousin of the brave Edgar was absent, as were also two old Danish serving-women, who hitherto had always been trusted.

Alfred was more moved, perhaps, than ever he was in his life, and acted with an amount of vigour which astonished even his admirers.

With the defeat of the horde of Danish pirates, the isolation of some, and the departure of others, all immediate danger had ceased.

The prince, therefore, only paused to select a council of regency, to give directions to his most devoted leaders, and then, selecting the best of the ships captured from the Danes, equipped it well, and started in pursuit.

(*To be continued.*)

NAUTICAL TALES;

OR, ADVENTURES BY SEA AND LAND.

"EDGAR UNDERSTOOD, AND LEANED OVER THE RAMPARTS."

THE HOLY BRACELETS:
A TALE OF THE DAYS OF KING ALFRED.

CHAPTER IV.
THE PURSUIT.

Though England was far from being a maritime power, and ships were rareties, it was a matter of no difficulty to find amid its sturdy fishermen and coasters a bold and hardy crew.

When, therefore, it was known who was to command them, both soldiers and sailors were found in abundance.

The name of Alfred had long since become synonymous with all that was brave and good.

Victory seemed to have folded him to her breast as one of her chosen sons, and they looked forward consequently to certain and inevitable glory.

The great difficulty was to find a pilot. Few Englishmen knew exactly where Denmark was situated, except the general direction.

Those were days when the compass was unknown, and men navigated by the sun, moon, and stars.

At length, however, one of the Danes who had submitted to the power of England consented to guide them.

The vessel selected by the king was a one-masted boat, with one large sail, and a row of oars and large sweeps on each side. It was inconveniently crowded with men and provisions.

None, however, hesitated, and soon, amid the loud cheers and earnest prayers of the multitudes who watched them from the sea-shore, the good ship "Alfred," as it had been christened, started on its way.

The king had little better accommodation than his fellows, and sat behind the steersman, gazing anxiously forward, as if hoping already to catch a glimpse of the treacherous pirate. Besides the actual purpose of his journey, the king was glad to see a little more of the world. Twice had he visited Rome and once Paris, but never had he made a voyage on the ocean. It proved pleasant enough at first, but soon they found that the North Seas exhibited a different character to bays, the mouth of the Thames, and such-like places to which they were accustomed.

Storms, adverse winds, with all the accidents incidental to inexperienced navigators, retarded their progress, and soon a terrible dearth of provisions and water caused the men to murmur deeply.

There was, however, no remedy but to go on, the Dane assuring them that they could not be more than a day's sail from the point of Denmark on which the castle of the pirate Hastings was situated.

But for the king, who sternly bade them refrain, the Dane might have suffered injury; as it was, he solemnly vowed to do his best, and, before nightfall, declared that he could make out in the far-off distance an outline of the much-sought-for castle.

The pilot, who professed to be a bitter enemy of Hastings, now suggested that they should hasten forward in the dark, conceal themselves in one of the many fjords or creeks, in which the coast abounded, and there decide on their future course of action.

The prince acquiesced, and all that night soldiers and sailors rowed in turns, until, very shortly before daybreak, they were close upon a rocky shore, where, but for their pilot, they must inevitably have been cast away.

Soon, however, they were moored stem and stern under the lee of a mighty basaltic rock, and the whole crew disembarked.

The guide informed them that the castle of the pirate Hastings was a mile distant, to be reached only through an arid and stony valley. It was, further, well situated, and defended by a fierce and lawless band of the most wild and savage race among the Danes.

But neither Alfred, Edgar, nor any of the English hesitated. They were inflamed to the highest pitch of fury at the foul treachery of Hastings, increased not a little by hunger.

After, therefore, taking their last mouthful of oatmeal, with a drink of spring water, the gallant little troop, soldiers and sailors, all save three ship-keepers, sallied forth on their adventurous journey.

The Danish guide, who had sworn fealty to his new sovereign, walked between young Edgar and the king. The latter, too generous readily to believe in treachery, would have shown more confidence, but some of the more experienced soldiers insisted on every precaution being used.

In this way they reached to a point within sight of the castle, a heavy mass of stone and wood, surrounded by a deep and wide ditch, within which were drawn the vessels of the renowned pirate, four-and-twenty in number.

From the keep floated the Raven flag, before which hitherto all had bowed.

The castle was well built, with lofty towers and battlements, and was defended by at least twenty times their own number.

To attack it openly was simply madness. What, then, was to be done?

King Alfred turned to the Dane, and eyed him keenly.

"You have become an Englishman, have sworn fealty to me, now is the time to show your truth," he said.

"Mighty king, not for love of you or yours have I followed the pirate Hastings; he robbed me of a daughter as he has this youth of a cousin. Could I slay him I would."

"We can trust you, then?"

"On the faith of a true man," he said, with stern ferocity.

"What, then, would you do?"

"I was a serf of Hastings; at no great distance live my father and mother, old people, who will gladly shelter and aid me. Let this brave youth accompany me. I will procure him a disguise. With that we will enter the castle, which I know well."

"Go on, good Dane."

"When night comes you can go on board yonder three-masted ship—it is the admiral's: you will find food in abundance. No watch is kept; in fact, the seamen are dispersed to their homes, while within, all thought will be of revelling. You see yonder tower over the masts of the great ship?"

"Certainly."

"When the time for attack is come, a flame shall rise on yonder battlement—act quickly."

Edgar had made no remark, but listened attentively. When he found the king assented, he merely drew his short cloak around him and waited for the Dane to start.

His way was back, round a swamp at the rear of the castle, behind which was a small village, on the edge of which was the hut inhabited by the parents of Goten the Dane. They were very aged, and saw their son with gloomy satisfaction. Into his motives they never inquired, and when he dressed Edgar in a rude peasant garb, and took milk and cheese as an offering to the castle, merely smiled.

The loss of their beautiful grand-daughter, dead some months, had rendered them callous.

Leading the way to the land entrance of the fortress, the Danish peasant with his attendant boy easily obtained admittance, handed his offerings to the major-domo, and was invited in consequence to share the festivities of the hour. About an hour before, the fair Rowena, dishevelled and in tears, had gone through a form of marriage. Weeping and partially insensible she had retired with her waiting woman, while Hastings, as usual, took his seat at a banquet with his captains, which was to be prolonged far into the night.

Edgar shook with passion. He could not speak, only knowing the language imperfectly, but when he and Goten were alone, he asked what there was to be done.

"At sunset the bride and all the ladies will come to the evening banquet."

"I will be there," replied Edgar, clutching his short sword, which he wore under his goat-skin tunic.

How that day passed he never knew. He was in a frenzy of rage and fear.

When, however, night came, Goten took advantage of the bustle in the castle to clamber up the outer stone stairs, which led to the battlements. These were level with the principal yard of the great ship, which lay close to the walls.

Edgar peered over and saw that the deck was crowded with men, whom he at once recognised as his friends. He at once pointed out to Goten that the beacon-light, which might have been dangerous, was now unnecessary if their friends could but clamber up to the wall.

All this while the brave and enduring Saxons remained perfectly still.

Goten reflected a moment, and then pointed to the spar which all but touched the ramparts.

Edgar understood, and, leaning over, caught its extremity in his hand, and swung over until he hung by his two hands. Then he crawled along the yard, and, descending the rigging, rejoined his companions.

It took the sailors and fishermen a very short time, working in silence, to make a ladder of rope. Long before it was finished Edgar was again on the ramparts with a stout cord, with which to haul up the means of entering the castle.

As soon as it was ready, he and Goten pulled it up, made it fast, and then, like ghostly shadows of the night, the English warriors ascended and took their places on the ramparts of a fortress containing an overwhelming number of enemies.

The first to ascend was Alfred the king.

CHAPTER V.
THE BANQUET AND THE SURPRISE.

WITHIN the castle walls, in a large hall—a mixture of barbaric grandeur and rudeness—sat the pirate Hastings and his horde. Feasting was the order of the day.

The politic Dane had not united himself to Rowena by a pagan marriage—of no validity in her sight—without an object. The beautiful girl had some claim to the throne, and in default of legal heirs to Alfred was by many believed to have a right.

At all events, whatever was the real state of the case, Hastings fully intended, on the strength of this enforced alliance, to collect a large army and navy, and assail England, with the additional prestige of being a rival claimant for the throne.

Though he knew the idea to be utterly absurd in itself, it would induce many to follow him, while, also, it might influence some of the Saxons to yield gracefully to superior forces.

"Divide in order to govern" is an axiom known since kingdoms have existed.

Hastings was one of those bold, unscrupulous men, without heart or honour, who live but for ambition and pleasure. Human life to him was dross, woman's delicacy and purity a mere myth for boys to believe in.

His own friends and followers were never safe from his ungovernable fury.

Imagine, then, a gentle, lovely English maiden in his clutches. The dove and the falcon is not strong enough a comparison. Rowena trembled, and yet, though she had been held while the pagan rite of marriage had been gone through, she was determined to die rather than recognise it as a nuptial union.

She was summoned to the evening banquet by four Saxon women, so long slaves of the Dane as to have half forgot their own misery, but who acutely felt the wretched position of their fair countrywoman.

They were, however, powerless to give assistance, and could only beg her to come to the feast without compelling them to employ force.

The forced bride rose pale, calm, and serene. A terrible light beamed in her eye, as within her bosom she placed a small, pointed, shining dagger. Self-immolation was contrary to her religion, but surely there could be no crime in slaying the false enemy of her country, the savage ravisher who had stolen her from home and kindred.

Yes, it should be done, at the banquet, in the bridal-chamber, anywhere, even though she were torn to pieces by wild horses the next minute.

They had decked her out with perfect regal splendour, and, as she entered the banquet hall, every man rose, and hailed her as their queen.

Rowena coldly bowed, and seated herself on a double throne beside the half-intoxicated Hastings, who took her left hand; her right clutched the murderous dagger.

"Fair Rowena, queen of my heart, why so stern? You are now my wife."

"A Christian girl can be no pagan's wife," she replied, coldly.

"Girl," said Hastings, gravely, but with a dark and ominous frown, "you are my wife; but, as I wish our union to be as binding as possible, you shall be wedded by your own priests as soon as we land in England. I swear it, by my Holy Bracelets!"

Rowena eyed him with a look of scorn.

"Miserable pirate and robber!" she cried; "pillager of the homes of my people, think you that my priests would aid you in cementing more strongly such an union as this? Never! Heaven will yet protect me!"

Hastings laughed loudly.

He was of too coarse a nature to understand the modesty of an English maiden shrinking from the gaze of a number of men on such an occasion as this, knowing, as they did, that she was a captive and a forced bride.

"My pretty wife," he said, as he forced her to a seat by his side, "you will soon forget your haughty airs and forgive me, and even love me for making you what you are. Right royally shall you queen it ere long over your own native land when the mad man who has attempted to stem my victorious course is dead and his forces dispersed. Drink," he shouted, wildly, as he rose and held a sparkling goblet on high, "drink, my friends and warriors, to Rowena, future Queen of England!"

A loud clamour at once arose.

Goblets chinked, huzzas rent the air, and then, inflamed with wine and gratified vanity, Hastings once more resumed his seat, little dreaming what eyes were bent upon him with all the malignity of resolute vengeance.

To explain this we must return for a time to Alfred and his followers.

It was as much as Goten could do to restrain the impetuous ardour of the Saxon king, who, confident in the courage of his men, and their devotion to his cause, desired at once to burst in upon the banqueters.

"Have patience," whispered Goten, "they will soon be so full of drink that they will be an easy conquest. I will creep down towards the banquet hall and watch, unseen, their movements. I will give you notice at once when the favourable moment arrives."

"But, Rowena; there is danger to her meanwhile," interrupted Edgar.

Goten smiled grimly.

"Nay," he cried. "If danger threatens her, I will myself rush in and destroy the tyrant at my life's cost."

So saying he glided away.

The sentinels on the tower, never dreaming of danger, had joined the revellers below, for high and low in the castle that night had freedom to do as they listed.

There was no difficulty therefore in Goten's path.

He glided down the stairs, keeping in the shadow if any attendant approached, and was soon concealed behind the heavy drapery that shaded the door of the banquetting hall.

Here he had a full view of the scene, and saw the interview between Rowena and Hastings.

"Curses light upon his dark brow!" he muttered, as he saw his evil glance light upon the Saxon maiden. "This night my child, thou shalt be avenged."

He saw that intoxication was already beginning its work, and judged it time to go.

As he turned to do so, he met a pair of eyes, gleaming on with a baleful look of recognition.

"Ah, Goten! traitor! What do you here?" he cried. "Help!"

But he said no more.

The goatherd's knife quivered in his chest, and the body fell heavily beneath the drapery.

"Now, then, is the time," muttered Goten, and hurried up once more to the battlements, where his eager friends were awaiting his return.

He had not many moments disappeared when Hastings rose.

"Friends," he said, " the banquet is now ended; one more brimming goblet to my fair bride, and then I leave you. Your health, my peerless wife!"

"Never yours!" shouted a loud voice, as Edgar leaped through an open doorway, and rushed, sword in hand, towards the pirate chief, followed by Alfred, the warriors, and the gallant crew.

The Danes, although taken by surprise, were yet not cowed. The surprise was a terrible and inexplicable one, but the reward of victory would now indeed be great.

Fortunate for them was it that they had not abandoned their swords.

In the first confusion, Edgar had reached Rowena, whom he caught round the waist, and dragged away, aiming a futile blow at the pirate's head. With a savage roar, as of a wild beast brought to bay, Hastings drew his sword, and would infallibly have slain both Edgar and Rowena but for a stout, rough personage who now appeared upon the scene.

Goten, the goatherd, dashed at Hastings with a heavy sword, which he had snatched from the armoury.

"Die, tyrant!" he said, wielding the ponderous weapon, which Hastings avoided, felling the goatherd to the earth with a blow of his fist.

As he did so, several of the torches were upset, some of the hangings caught fire, and a dense smoke arose in the banquet hall.

The cries were for Denmark on one side, for England on the other; but the Saxons soon found that retreat was absolutely necessary if they would escape with life.

Goten lay dead or dying on the ground, while Hastings, furious at the daring interruption to his banquet, was bent at least on winning the guerdon of victory.

He saw before him Edgar, Rowena, and Alfred, King of England.

These would indeed be prizes, and with a loud and ringing cry, he led his captains, recovered from their panic, to the attack.

At this moment, some ten or twelve men, women, and youths, English in every feature, came rushing hastily armed.

They were slaves who had made a bold dash for freedom, and who, in addition to being an armed reinforcement, were able to supply the place of Goten the guide.

Alfred had passed the word to his friends to retreat slowly, and they did so, fighting as they went. It was not a bit too early, for the men-at-arms, roused by the terrible clangour, were rushing to the support of their daring captains, and the Anglo-Saxons would have been overwhelmed.

Some of the slaves led the way to a narrow passage, down which, at a given signal, the whole party made a dart, leaving only some four to bring up the rear.

These were Alfred, and three of his most stalwart captains, armed with heavy hammers. Fuming with rage, foaming at the mouth with passion, uttering more oaths in a minute than history could record in an hour, Hastings pressed on.

His blows were ever directed at the hateful English king; but whether it was the activity of the young prince, his ready wit and science, or the devotion of his followers, none reached him.

Suddenly, however, while making a more than usually furious charge, Alfred met him, struck down his sword, and hit him so terrible a blow on the head as to throw him backwards insensible into the arms of his foremost captain.

Alfred did not hurry himself, but slowly retreating soon found that all the rest had escaped by a postern gate and were awaiting him on board some of the pirate vessels. No time was lost. Hurrying ashore, the gallant English band of heroes, who had contrived each to collect a bundle of food of some kind, began their retreat.

Edgar and Rowena were side by side, hand in hand, determined to die rather than fall into the hands of one who would have no pity or mercy. Fortunately they had taken notice of the way by which Goten had led them, and were therefore in full retreat before the Danes were ready to pursue.

The blazing castle occupied the Danes for awhile, as they were fearful of the sparks reaching the shipping, which, above all things, they valued.

This reprieve gave the English time to reach their ship, and to put off from the narrow fjord. The men in charge had taken in water, so that all was ready; though how to escape the many vessels which would soon be in pursuit, was a mystery.

King Alfred assumed the command of the ship, steering by the north star, and was fortunately a long way off before the pirates were in pursuit. Hastings, who had been heavily stunned, could give no orders for some time; but, when he did recover, they were fierce and sanguinary.

Every ship, every cockle-boat, every fishing-craft was to follow as it was got ready, and rendezvous in the Thames, whence they would ravage, plunder, and conquer England. To a certain extent he kept his word; for, for three whole years, the great pirate chief continued to plague and worry England. The war continued all that time, the Danes receiving reinforcements and provisions every day.

But Alfred had taken a lesson from these buccaneers, and, assisted by his youthful admiral, Edgar, he built large ships, with which he drove some of the pirates into the sea, while his brave soldiers fought the others valiantly on shore.

At length the inimical Danes were vanquished, and peace restored to England. Alfred and his admiral— soon the husband of Rowena— never rested until they had a force of one hundred ships to protect the tight little island; and this desperate incident in the life of Alfred the King and Edgar the Admiral may be said to be the origin of that British fleet which has since done such wonders in every corner of the globe.

The Supplement GIVEN AWAY with No. 3 of BRETT'S NAVAL HISTORY will contain the commencement of a New Story—"THE PRINCE OF THE SEAS."

NAUTICAL TALES;
OR, ADVENTURES BY SEA AND LAND.

"THE DYING CHIEF PAUSED."

THE PRINCE OF THE SEAS:
A Tale of the Norman Invasion.

CHAPTER I.
THE LONELY TOWER.

It was on a broken portion of the cliff—with above its beetling, dark-shadowed brow—that one night, in England's early history, a boy stood watching the mighty river below.

It was high water, and the moon threw its silvery radiance over the gently heaving sea, and imparted a spectral aspect to the chalky fragments which, at a little distance, lifted their heads from the waters like advanced sentries from the shore.

Above, perched like an eyrie on a mighty rock, was a tower of powerful construction. Though the time was so little apart from that when Roman rule prevailed in England, people already raised the question as to its origin.

At all events there it was, a monument of architectural strength if not of beauty.

The boy had come forth simply because he was sad, and occupation was necessary.

There was revelry indoors—revelry which he, at his age, could not indulge in.

He craved for action, and for some reason or other he

was detained a prisoner in that solitary building, to which he had been sent to learn the profession of a sailor nominally, in reality of a pirate.*

Arthur the Lonely only knew that for two years he had left his home in some distant land, and had been brought to this lonely tower to become the attendant page for a time of one of those worthies, who, on the strength of a stronghold, however slight, made themselves independent of all law and control.

And yet, though many a time and oft the chief under whose orders he acted had gone forth in his long, swift galley, he had as yet never accompanied him.

His utmost knowledge of the sea was floating about with arbalet and snares in a coracle, of which he was completely the master. On the present occasion, his design was to creep down the side of the almost precipitous rock, there to rob the sea mews and curlews of their eggs or callow brood.

The rock below the platform on which he stood was rugged in the stream, and almost inaccessible to any but a cliff climber. But Arthur the Lonely had dared its perils many a time and oft, and did not hesitate one moment even in that black darkness.

Treading a well-known way, clinging to projections of the rock, clutching at sprouting weeds and shrubs, the boy was half-way down, and near where a cavernous opening yawned, when a singular sound fell upon his ears.

Casting his eyes upon the river below he saw that a vessel was making for a small sheltered cove or creek to the southward of the tower. Her clumsy construction, her wicker-work sides covered with leather, her mast of unbarked pine, and her sail of painted matting, which remained hoisted, despite the want of wind, proclaimed her one of the lower class of pirates who did their work at night, and to whom pillage of the most ignoble kind was always welcome.

The sea-kings, the nobles and princes who followed the profession of corsairs, were very different to these crawling miscreants who murdered man, woman and child, who stole cattle wholesale, and gorged themselves in blood and ale at every opportunity.

The more distinguished pirates were educated to exist with the most excited and most pleasurable vitality in the tempests of war; and no failure deterred them, because having no home but their ships or a conquered country, no profession but piracy, no provisions but their spoils, they had no chances of enjoyment or even existence but from the battle.

Alfred the Lonely watched the vessel with a keen eye. Their object appeared to him to surprise the tower. Well, what then? During his two years' residence in the place, he had been little more than a prisoner, kindly but rudely treated—unable in any way to account for the strict confinement in which he was placed.

But he had partaken of the hospitality of Rereward the Saxon, and he would not let him be surprised like a sleeping swineherd.

With these thoughts in his head he at once began the difficult and dangerous ascent of the cliff.

On ordinary occasions he was wont to descend to the strand, and regain the tower by another route; but on the present occasion he resolved to dare the more perilous road.

Looking upward, the sough and moaning of wind and sea at his feet, Arthur the Lonely moved slowly along the surface of the rock.

It was almost perpendicular, with nothing to assist him but roots and projecting stones on which to rest his feet. Fortunately he was young, light, and agile, and finally reached the rocky terrace under the tower, out of breath and exhausted.

Two minutes' rest sufficed him. He could no longer see the enemy, but he could hear them and even others collecting in the creek below.

How to re-enter the tower! In defiance of all rules and regulations, he had come forth at midnight, and any discovery under, no matter what circumstances, was sure to entail disgrace and punishment.

The small window of the room he occupied was twelve feet from the ground, and he had descended from its narrow aperture by means of a leather strap borrowed from one of the men's belts.

But the strap was withdrawn.

Alfred the Lonely clasped his hand, and had in his own mind determined at any risk to arouse the keeper of the gate, when the strap was thrown out, while a pretty, girlish face, with a profusion of curls, appeared at the aperture.

"Out again," she said, with a merry and pleasant laugh.

"Hist! Hilda. Silence. There is danger in the wind—say nothing," he replied, and, aided by the leathern thong, was soon beside her in the rude chamber. "Your father——"

"Is in the banquet hall."

Without a word, Alfred the Lonely hastened to where the owner of the tower was carousing with his chief men and some visitors. He entered hurriedly where they sat over their ale and mead, and at once stood behind the chair of Elstane the Cruel, as he was commonly called.

"Well, boy, what is it?" he asked.

"The tower is about to be attacked by the coast pirates," replied Alfred, coldly.

"Ha! and how is it none warn me but you?" cried the savage chief.

"Because none have seen them as yet."

"You have done well, boy. Come with me," said the chief, rising, and making some trifling excuse to his guests, he hurried to a small terrace overlooking the waters below.

Alfred, without a word, pointed to the bay to the southward, and to the creek which led inland.

Five of these wild corsairs were making their way slowly up the little winding river, which ceased to be navigable two miles in the interior.

"Boy," said the chief, speaking more kindly to him than yet he had ever done, "you have done well. You are your father's true son."

"My father!" cried Alfred the Lonely.

"Well, well, of that another time. Now, I would scourge these northern wolves who dare beard a lion in his den. Wilt out with me, boy?"

"And glad," said the boy, delighted at the tempting prospect.

The chief descended to the armoury, allowed the boy to arm himself with sword and buckler, and then, bidding the warder keep a good look-out, sallied forth to follow in the track of the pirates.

---

* This is historical. Hastings, the great rival of the Saxons, was selected by Ragnor Lodbrog to initiate his son, Biorn, in the habit of piracy, which showed that he possessed the virtues of a viking—intrepidity, activity, and ferocity. Snorre gives a similar instance in Olaf Helga's history. This prince first began piracy at the age of twelve, under the influence of Ran, his father-in-law.

CHAPTER II.

THE PIRATE HAUNT.

Elstane the Cruel knew every inch of ground. Near his tower a large wood or weald stretched for some miles, after which several populous villages and fortified homesteads were known to exist. In all probability these pilfering marauders, who actually navigated the coast with huge rafts behind them, on which they placed prisoners and bits of salted beef and pork indiscriminately, had come on one of their usual plundering expeditions.

The care they took to conceal their presence, indicated this sufficiently.

Elstane, with the boy close behind him, entered the wood, amid which grew some of the magnificent trees of Druidical times, and soon came to where the pirates had entrenched themselves.

They had selected a pool near the very head of the stream to draw up their vessels, and did not appear to think any other fortification desirable.

Elstane, standing under the shelter of a large oak, scrutinised the robbers. Several of them were collected together in a group. As the Saxon chief gazed on them his brow lowered.

"These are no common pirates," he said. "Boy, we must go round to the front; we may there learn something."

And the chief stalked slowly through the forest, until he stood above the pool in which the half dozen pirate vessels lay.

The spring which supplied the stream rose in a copse at no great distance, where the bubbling waters made a small pond. From this two rivulets diverged, one to the westward, the other to the northward.

"These marauding villains must be punished. I would not leave one to return to his home, if I had my will," said the chief, speaking to himself.

"If their ships were destroyed, 'twould aid much, I ween," observed the boy.

"Yes; but how?"

Alfred the Lonely smiled, and pointed to the tiny rivulet which supplied the northern water. He then explained that, in sport, he had often dammed it up thus, when the tide was out, leaving the pool below completely without water.

The chief smiled grimly as he watched the boy stoop, collect handfuls of clay, and commence his work. In half an hour the task was concluded, and water ceased to flow towards the foot of the tower.*

Elstane then turned away in the direction of the castle, and, eagerly snatching at the boy's idea, while the pirates lay in complete security, got out some twenty men, and had, at low water, a strong dam erected, to keep out the tide from the narrow opening of the river.

Then he awaited the result.

At dawn a loud tumult in the piratical camp announced that they were astir. All in the tower were ready to receive them, while a trusty old harper had been sent about to rouse the common people to an attack on their ships.

Even Elstane the Cruel was surprised when he found that the enemy were far stronger than he expected. As he had suspected over night, their leaders were very different men from what might have been expected from the vessels in which they had come. Rough as was the general horde, there were many richly-armed adherents of the Norman race already working their way to supremacy in England.

Their armour, their accoutrements, and weapons indicated that they were of no mean lineage.

They marched with every weapon of modern invention, and when a summons to the tower to surrender remained unanswered, a general discharge of bolts and arrows followed. The tower, as a matter of course, was surrounded by a moat, while the heavy drawbridge was pulled up.

Arthur looked from the one terrace of the tower in amaze. Much as he had heard of deeds of blood and warfare, this was his first view of the reality. He was determined, however, boy as he was, to do his best.

To his great surprise, Elstane armed him with the utmost care, giving him a helmet and visor quite proof against any ordinary arrow.

"They are seven hundred against forty," said the old pirate, grimly, "and, as you have destroyed their ships, will fight to the death to be revenged. And now, boy, know two things—the game yonder feluccas fly at is yourself. Death will be far preferable to capture. Keep close to me, and in the hour of peril I will prove your faithful friend."

Alfred the Lonely listened with astonishment and awe, but asked no questions.

The hour of the fight had come.

The assailants were provided with ladders, with battering rams, with every means of forcing to an entrance to the tower. From circumstances in connection with his wild profession, the tower was well victualled, but could scarcely be expected to hold out against such superior forces.

It was quite clear to Elstane that those in command were persons used to the art of war. A huge ladder, quite high enough to reach the summit of the lower tower, was carried by a hundred men, who advanced under the galling support of twice as many archers and slingers.

Not a soldier could appear on the ramparts but he was riddled with arrows or stunned by heavy flights of stones.

And still the ladder came on, not ten minutes elapsing before it was applied to the wall.

Now began a fearful combat. The assailants, many of them regular Norman soldiers, were better protected and better armed than the pirates, while the lower sort, though less well provided, were bold in the extreme. The very weight of numbers was in their favour.

Elstane the Cruel, however, made a desperate defence. After exhausting their ammunition in the shape of arrows, the men took to their heavy clubs, and dealt death and destruction on every side. As fast as the well-clad Normans and the rugged Danes of the North of England crowded up to the top of the ladder, they were either hurled back, bleeding and wounded, into the moat, or met their fate upon the battlements. Elstane had well chosen his men. They were stern, dogged, and valorous unto the point of death.

But numbers and discipline soon began to prevail. At least ten of the defenders lay dead or dying on the ramparts.

Still Elstane fought in desperate silence, and beside him, bold, unyielding, and indomitable, was the boy, Arthur.

His arm was a bright battle-axe, with which he dealt blows which astonished those who only judged him by his slim appearance.

As yet, thanks to the pirate chief, he had been un-

---

* Historical. Happened at the mouth of the Lea River.

wounded, though one of the Norman leaders steadily aimed at him through the whole combat.

Upon this man fell the full weight of the pirates' blows, which enraged him to such an extent, that at last, with a wild cry, he rallied his men, and the ramparts were carried.

Two minutes later there was a cry for quarter, and the tower was captured.

"Where is Elstane—where is the boy?" asked the leader of the assailants.

No one knew. In another moment the victors were spread over the castle searching for the fugitives. In vain.

CHAPTER III.

THE SECRET OF THE TOWER.

WHEN Elstane saw that all was lost he clutched Arthur by the arm and plunged down a narrow stone flight of steps to the courtyard below. From this place he gained the banqueting-room, where the women were collected awaiting the result of the final combat.

Hilda was among them, and stood out in bold relief, both from her beauty and resolution.

Elstane said not one word, but signing to Hilda to accompany them, the three followed the rude flight which led to the tower vaults.

These reached, the chief barricaded the door by means of a wooden bar and iron chain, and fell almost insensible to the ground.

"Boy," he said, clasping the other's hand, "I am wounded unto death, and have only a few minutes left to speak."

"Father!" cried Hilda.

"Silence, my child. You are the daughter of one to whom death has been familiar since he can first remember existence. Do not disgrace your origin. I ask but time to speak to Arthur."

Hilda bowed her beautiful head in her hands and wept in silence.

"Boy," began the pirate chief, "know you why you have been guarded so carefully, and why your precious person has never before been exposed to the risks of warfare?"

"I have no thought why, though the life of inaction has been hateful."

"I cannot explain all. It is sufficient for you to know that you are England's hope. Your father is Harold, King of England—now sought to be overthrown by the accursed Normans. My mind misgives me that sorrow has come to your father, and that your existence has been betrayed to the foe, else why this attack?"

The dying chief paused.

"I the son of my king, the brave Harold!"

"Yes, boy. He and Norman William have ever been enemies; and when a prisoner, your father vowed to give you up as a hostage to him. Repenting this promise, he employed me to steal you away and guard you as the apple of his eye. Have I not done so?"

"You have."

"Hark, they come. You and Hilda—poor girl, what will become of her?"

"Leave that to me," said the young prince.

"Thanks, thanks—away—the—the—well——"

And the wild corsair, whose gaping wound had been bleeding profusely, spoke no more.

Arthur understood. In those days, when every man's hand was against every other man's, all such retreats were compelled, above all things, to be well provided with water.

A narrow well in the solid rock had been cut so that if beleaguered for days and weeks they were still able to hold out.

Arthur lost no time. Snatching up Hilda, who was half crazy with grief, he rushed to the well mouth. It was not more than three feet across, with a stout roller, from which depended the cord and bucket.

"Hilda, dear Hilda," he said, "for my sake, be quick."

Mechanically she obeyed. Putting her feet in the bucket, and holding to the rope with her hands, the sturdy youth slowly lowered her into the gloomy depths below.

As soon as he knew the bucket to be level almost with the water, he fastened the handle, and prepared to descend himself. At this moment a heavy concussion against the door warned him that the foe had discovered their retreat. A shower of stones, or, rather, rocks, would soon dislocate that door.

Hand over hand he descended, to find Hilda seated in the mouth of the cave well, where the water overflowed towards the sea.

"Not a moment is to be lost!" said Arthur, and, ere the words were well spoken, the fall of a heavy stone showed that their way of escape was suspected.

Hand in hand the young couple, thrown so strangely on the wide world, descended a narrow path, and, without hesitation, plunged into the wood beyond.

That a search would be made the boy well knew, and he had resolved to fight to the last gasp rather than be taken.

Brave as a lion, the discovery of his parentage could scarcely add to his loftiness of soul; and yet the fact of a girl being cast upon his protection raised him singularly in his own eyes.

The wood was dense and intricate, and well known to Arthur, who led Hilda to where an army might have searched for them in vain.

It was well, however, that he did exercise this caution, for, ere an hour passed, the shady alleys of the forest were being searched in all directions by the infuriated Normans and their followers, who were all the more exasperated that, during the attack on the tower, the lower class of Saxons, inhabitants of the woods, had found the vessels high and dry, and burned them as one system of vengeance.

Night, however, came without their being discovered in the retreat selected by the boy.

To Arthur every nook and cranny of the old wood was known.

He had too often hunted the wolf and the wild boar not to have discovered secure hiding-places, and to one of these he took Hilda.

It was more like a fox hole than any thing else, and to enter it he was obliged to crawl on his hands and knees.

The inside once gained, however, it widened into a cavern, and the two sat on the rough ground to await events.

"How came you to discover this place?" asked the trembling girl.

"I killed its original owner," replied the youth, in a quiet tone.

And then, noticing the other's look of horror, he added—

"Reassure yourself, it was only a she wolf. I had slain one of her young, and, made furious by rage, she came at me open-mouthed. I wounded her with an arrow, but, this rendering her only the more savage, she leaped at my throat, and was only prevented from lacerating my flesh by a smart blow with my battle-axe."

NAUTICAL TALES;
OR ADVENTURES BY SEA AND LAND.

"A LOVELY FACE LOOKED DOWN UPON HIM."

THE PRINCE OF THE SEAS:
A Tale of the Norman Invasion.

"But," cried the girl, listening with open mouth, "may not others find their way here?"

"I am here to defend you," he said, clutching his little weapon, which, however, in his hands, had more than once proved a formidable one. "Hist!"

The entrance to the cavern was under the roots of a couple of large trees, and lay in deep darkness; the inside was faintly lit up by some narrow fissures in the grass-grown soil above.

The young Arthur had heard footsteps, heavy ones, as of mailed warriors. He signed to Hilda not to speak, and then crawled to the entrance.

He at once made out a tall, grim warrior with six powerful men at his heels.

"The imp must have taken shelter here," he said. "By Heavens! I will burn the whole forest but I will have him. The girl, too, has escaped. On, on! there must be some means of finding him. A thousand marks of gold, besides rank and land. It is, indeed, worth the expedition."

And all the while they poked about with their lances.

After awhile, pointing to a tree, the chief left one man as sentry.

This man was rudely armed and dressed, but was of powerful frame. Leaning against a tree, he began his duty as sentry, by yawning and closing his eyes.

Arthur peered a little forward to catch a glimpse of the retreating foe. As he did so, he slightly stumbled.

He was half kneeling, with bow and arrow in his hands.

The man opened his eyes, and rapidly raising his hands to his mouth was about to utter a cry that would have awakened the wildest echoes of the forest, when, with the rapidity of the true marksman, Arthur fired without apparently taking aim, and hit the man in the neck. The arrow went right through, and the soldier fell an inert lumbering mass on the ground.

Not a minute, however, was to be lost, and taking Hilda by the hand, Arthur led her away through the darkening shadows of the forest to another hole; this time in the side of a rock, whence he had often watched his quarry and destroyed his game. Except one wild and startling shout, which proclaimed the discovery of the body, no more was heard of the pursuers.

As soon as it was quite dark, he led the silent girl to the great river's edge, made her seat herself in a small boat, and, seizing the paddle, pushed out upon the gloomy waters.

It was a dirty and stormy night, with eight miles of stormy sea, rather than of river, to cross. Many a time and oft had Arthur done so alone, and screamed with delight as he was tossed upon the waves.

But now he had charge of one younger than himself, while thoughts of the future assailed his soul. Keeping his eye on the opposite coast, with an occasional glance at the lofty and desolate tower in the distance, the boy managed his boat with consummate skill. It was an arduous task, and one which occupied several hours; but at last, wearied and exhausted, he reached the shelter of some lofty cliffs, and, landing, drew the boat upon the strand.

Rest was now all that was needful to both, and, after some few words of comfort, Arthur, having found a small, sheltered hollow for Hilda, reversed his own boat, and slept soundly.

It was late next day when he awoke and looked around.

He was alone. Running to where he had on the previous evening secreted Hilda, he found that she had disappeared.

He called, he ran up and down, and hunted everywhere; he clambered up the cliffs, and gazed around. In vain; for no trace of human life was to be seen.

Far off in the distance he saw something flutter like a bird's wing—it might have been a sail—but, whatever it was, it disappeared, and was swallowed up in the great void of ocean.

Arthur came down to the shore utterly desolate and alone. He was bitterly disappointed, for in his heart of hearts he loved little Hilda, and now he was alone.

His mind, however, was soon made up. His father was King of England, menaced with rapine and conquest by the Normans. His place, as a son, was beside that father, and find him out he would if he searched ever so long.

Ideas of geography the youth had none; but he knew that the army of England was to be found somewhere to the southward and westward, and this direction he determined to take.

For two weary days and nights he wandered in the direction he had selected, guided by the sun and by such slight indications as could be afforded him by peasants, swineherds, and the toilers of the soil.

In this way he at length reached an arm of the sea about a mile across, which he must either go round or make a raft to ferry himself over. He decided on the latter course; and, it being night, clambered into a tree on the edge of the water, and slept.

A little after dawn he awoke, and was about to descend from the tree, when loud, ringing voices attracted his attention. Gazing downward, he saw a long, swift, and powerful boat drawn up near the shore, while its crew were engaged in preparing the morning meal.

By their voices, he knew them to be native English, while they appeared a party of bold rovers of the seas by their arms and armour. They were all young men, of stalwart and handsome mien.

Without hesitation, he leaped from his tree, and advanced to where a personage, more richly dressed than the others, leaned upon his sword in deep thought.

As Arthur approached, it could scarcely have been said that he saw him. When, however, the youth stood before him, he raised his head.

"What seek you?" he said, scrutinising the tall, slight youth keenly.

"To join the king's army, and fight the insolent foreigner," replied Arthur.

"The king's army," the other continued, mournfully, "is dispersed, and Harold sleeps in a bloody grave on the mournful field of Hastings."

"My father dead!" cried Arthur, involuntarily.

"Heavens!" exclaimed the tall, handsome chief, "you call Harold father?"

"My name is Arthur; my knowledge of my name and rank is not many hours old."

The other, proffering him a seat beside him on the sward, heard his whole story, and, when he had finished, respectfully addressed him.

"Your existence, prince, must be kept a profound secret. Who knows what may happen? For the moment, the Normans are triumphant everywhere. To oppose them on land is useless. But the seas are open —what say you? With this swift galley we can prey upon our foes, worry them, destroy their ships, and, perhaps, who knows, rally our disheartened countrymen to revolt. When that day comes, I, for one, will hail you my king."

"I love the life of a sailor," cried Arthur.

"Then shall you, noble boy, be our chief—Prince of the Seas," cried the Englishman.

CHAPTER IV.

THE CRUISE OF THE "BLACK ROVER."

FROM that hour the Normans had an inveterate and ubiquitous foe. Built upon the admirable models introduced by King Alfred, the swift and well-trimmed galley known as the "Black Rover," outstripped every vessel in the royal navy.

Whether she chased a fat trader, or fled before overwhelming forces, she was uniformly successful.

Having the conquered people for friends and allies, the corsair knew when to time his attacks.

Castle after castle was stormed and pillaged by the connivance of native serving-men.

Lying by day in some secure and sheltered creek or bay, the "Rover" would come out at night, and bear down like a hawk on the vessels which communicated between England and Normandy. So terrible were its depredations, that the Conqueror offered large rewards for its apprehension, and severely punished those who were unfortunate enough to suffer defeat.

So terrible became the vessel, always well-manned and well-appointed, that a sharp look-out was kept night and day on all ships that had to venture on that dangerous coast.

But in the dark, in the storm, in the calm, the "Black Rover" would creep up, board the craft, whatever its size, and kill all who resisted.

The terror of its name was carried even inland to the centre of the country; and Norman William knew that he was not rightful king as long as he could not end the career of the Prince of the Seas.

He little suspected that its daring young chief was the son of Harold, whose existence was a continual menace to him.

At length, however, it began to be bruited abroad that a rightful heir to the throne of England was in existence; no lazy Athelstane, but a bright youth, worthy to compete with that Alfred whose reign was doomed to be looked back to age after age as the one bright spot in English history.

The king upon the throne heard of the king who threatened his existence, and at last, somehow or other, the secret was made known that Arthur was the youth, and at once decreed the annihilation of the celebrated cruiser.

But though snares were laid, and even treachery resorted to, the "Black Rover," kept the seas, and defied alike open attack and trickery.

So beloved was he that many a time and oft people sacrificed their lives to save him.

And all the while, by sea and by land, Arthur the Lonely sought for Hilda, who had so mysteriously disappeared.

He was in stature a man, though not sixteen years of age, very powerful, and very handsome. Maidens smiled upon him, but in vain. Hitherto the image of his girlish love remained indelible, and he turned away with a sigh from the allurements of the most beautiful.

One favourite resort of the "Black Rover" was a deep, narrow creek, opposite the lone tower where he had passed such eventful years. A good look-out warned them of the approach of the foe, while they lay snug, and without any fear in their secret retreat.

The Normans had not penetrated to this district, which, nominally under the sway of the Norman king, was entirely devoted to the old state of things.

Here many of the families of the outlaw resided, and they were able to live in peace upon occasion.

The necessity for such a refuge existed more and more every day.

The Norman king, furious at the impunity with which the corsair ravaged his coasts, bearded his navy, and pillaged his stores and money on the high seas, was preparing to encompass him round.

Two of the finest cruisers in his service were ordered to keep perpetual watch over the "Black Rover," while large rewards were offered secretly among the peasantry for their betrayal.

But neither Prince Arthur nor his lieutenant, Henga, believed in these reports.

After an unusually fortunate cruise, they returned to their secret haunt, concealed the swift galley in its usual place, and went on shore.

Surrounded by woods, and many winding water courses, was a large house, an ancient Roman villa, turned into a Saxon residence. The owner of it was a widow lady, whose Saxon husband had been killed at the battle of Hastings.

She was rich in land and flocks, but not in children.

Her girls had died young, her sons had perished with their breasts to the foe.

She was very lonely, and yet so noble and generous was her heart, that all she possessed was at the service of those who still held out against the insolent foe who now trod English hearts under his mailed heel.

The officers and crew of the "Black Rover" were, of course, made specially welcome, and upon this occasion the lady held a high festival in their honour, to which all the men of the corsair, with their affianced wives, were invited.

Every man had either a wife or a chosen bride save Arthur, who looked on the gaieties with something of contempt.

His heart was far away.

He was dreaming of the past and of the future—of the past, in the form of Hilda; of the future, in the hope of successful insurrection against the proud conquerors of England's soil.

The day he landed from the cruiser he wandered alone. He saw the hill, he saw the lonely tower, and clambered up the rocks to overlook the river where he had lost the girl of his heart.

Suddenly he turned, and as he did so nearly lost his foothold, as he gazed upon a lovely face looking down upon him. She opened her eyes widely, and there was a kind of recognition, and then she fled.

That evening Arthur the Lonely was unusually anxious as he looked around the room where the mistress received her visitors.

Suddenly Elfrida, the aged but still handsome widow, approached him with a smile.

"You are alone unmated," she said, kindly. "Will you not accept a companion at my hands?"

Arthur turned to thank her, when his eyes became distended with surprise.

Before him, older, more lovely than ever, stood the blushing form of Hilda, the daughter of Elstane the Cruel.

The lady smiled.

"Was I right?" she asked.

"Yes," replied Hilda, with roseate blushes mantling on her cheek; "it is my friend, my brother."

Arthur could not speak for some minutes for astonishment and emotion.

During the night the two had passed on the banks of the Thames, Hilda had become alarmed at some noise, and, rising in the dark, had proceeded to look for Arthur. Turning the wrong way, and still pursued by the fear of some savage animal, she had clambered up a cliff, and taken her way into the interior of the country.

After wandering about for many hours, some poor

people had found her, and, knowing the kindness and goodness of Elfrida, had taken her thither, where, ever since, she had found a home.

Little did she ever suspect that the renowned cruiser, the corsair who defied the whole power of Norman William, and kept the kingdom in an uproar, was her old friend and brother—Arthur the Lonely.

Just as this explanation was over, and Arthur was expressing his delight at their reunion, the lady of the house was summoned by a domestic. She left them for a few minutes, and then hurriedly returned, followed by a soldier of high rank, in full armour.

His helmet visor was raised, and, with a savage cry, the lieutenant of the "Black Rover" recognised a man of high rank at the Court of the usurper—a born Englishman.

"Death to the Earl of Wessex!" he cried.

"Hold, rash man!" exclaimed the earl, in a voice of thunder; "you are betrayed. This house is surrounded by an overwhelming force, and, at the first signal, your vessel will be destroyed. I have come forward as a friend."

"A friend!" replied the other, while an angry murmur went round the room.

"Yes; I have two Norman colleagues who demand your capture and death. In honour to me, they have allowed me one quarter of an hour to save you. That time I avail myself of, and offer you life and liberty on two conditions."

"Name them?"

"That you cease to molest our shores," answered the stalwart earl. "Any further resistance to the new order of things, is useless. I know it. You can only damage individuals; your cause is hopeless. Speak quickly. In return for life, will you give me this promise?"

A sailor entered, and whispered to the prince and lieutenant. They were surrounded by an overwhelming force, and resistance was in vain.

"We promise," said the lieutenant, after a word with Arthur the Lonely. "Your second condition?"

"That you leave England for ever, taking with you your families. There are many pleasant places where you can settle and be happy. Decide quickly; my time is nearly over."

Every one, officers and crew, looked for his wife, or promised wife. They were already by their sides.

Arthur folded his arms, and was about to approach the renegade earl.

"Silence! Speak and you die," whispered his lieutenant. "The word you would utter would seal the fate of all."

The youth, burning with indignation, turned to Hilda, "Am I to go alone?" he said.

"No," she murmured, with a sad glance at her foster-mother.

"Go," said the noble lady, "and when you have chosen your time, let me know. I will join you."

Arthur clutched the half reluctant girl by the hand, and led her away. A postern gate was opened, and a path gained which led to the secreted galley.

As usual, it was well provisioned, and ready for sea. Though so strangely crowded, the half-laughing pirates contrived to make room for their unexpected companions, and at dawn of day the strangely-freighted vessel took its departure, sailing after some time to the northward.

For several days their course was undecided, but at last a great tempest settled the question.

They were blown out of their course, utterly ignorant of in what direction, for several days, at the end of which they found themselves close to some land.

The storm abating, they entered a pleasant harbour. The country, through not so agreeable as England, was well enough, and suited to hardy mariners. They resolved to settle, and at once set to work to build houses.

Before a month a town had arisen, and some of the few inhabitants coming forward, they found they had fallen upon the Orkneys.

This finally decided them. They were all sailors; they loved the deep; and though land was very useful to supply food, and as a residence for women and children, the ocean would still be their home.

The good Elfrida was sent for, and she came, with stores of cattle, and brought also a priest to consecrate the marriage of her friend. Arthur, who was declared king of the region, married Hilda, and for many years lived, not to see his higher ambitious hopes realised, but to be happy, honoured, and respected as

PRINCE OF THE SEAS.

N.B.—*The Title of the Story for the next Supplement will be "The Wreck on the Caskets."*

NAUTICAL TALES;

OR, ADVENTURES BY SEA AND LAND.

"'COME HITHER. I WANT YOU,' SAID THE KING."

THE WRECK ON THE CASKETS.

CHAPTER I.

THE KING AND THE PRINCE.

"Come hither, William, I want you," cried Henry Beauclerk, as he drew aside the tapestry that lined the walls of the stately presence chamber of Harfleur Castle, and touched the arm of his son, as, with a party of young nobles, he at that moment passed down the hall.

"Want me, your highness?" replied the bold and handsome prince, at once detaching himself from his youthful friends, and stepping to his father's side.

"Yes; come this way, I shall not detain you a moment," and Henry and his son passed slowly down the long hall, in earnest conversation, as the knot of young nobles, bowing profoundly to the king, retired to the opposite end of the hall.

"Has anything disturbed your highness? You look anxious and full of care; what ails you, father?"

"I ail nothing, my son, nothing; and yet, though all has gone well, a shadow like that of death sits ghost-like on my heart."

"Father!" exclaimed the young prince, in more surprise than fear at this admission of his parent—an admission so opposed to the whole tenor of his life, "what is it?"

"Come this way, I will not keep you long," replied

King Henry, as he halted and raised a fold of the arras, under which both he and the prince instantly passed from sight.

Entering a low arched door, and pushing aside the inner tapestry, Henry led the way into a small but lofty chamber, built in the heart of the castle wall.

Two grated loop-holes, high up above the tapestry, afforded a gloomy kind of light to this well of a royal closet.

Sinking into a chair, the king pointed to a seat for his son, and at once began the conversation.

"You know, William, that if the wind should shift, the fleet will weigh anchor to-night."

"Yes; I heard those weatherwise prophets, the sailors, wrangling about the matter down at the harbour," he replied, listlessly.

"And what said they?"

"Your highness's pilot, a churl of a Saxon, and all those in charge of the Cinque Port fleet, swore the wind would chop round with the flood tide, and wagered a stoop of Metheglin round, your highness would be half over the channel ere midnight."

"So think I, and would, therefore, have you and your young company ready to follow me directly. Indeed, I wish you to keep in close company with the royal argosy."

"Have no fear of that, father. 'La Blanche Neuf' is a first-rate sailer, and when the time arrives will keep in easy hail of the 'Royal Tiger' all the way to Southampton; but that will not be to-day."

"Why do you think so?"

"Because after the pilots had tired themselves with throwing up bits of straw and withered grass to see which way set the wind, my captain, old Fitz-Stephen, swore there would be no wind to-night."

"He is wrong, I am sure; but time will show."

"All the pilots from Piccardy and Bretange of course took part with Fitz-Stephen, who is himself a Breton, and they are gone to carouse at the 'Dolphin' till the wind shall be propitious."

"Whether right or wrong I shall be on board at an hour's notice, and shall expect you to follow me instantly, as it is of the utmost consequence that we should enter London together as soon after landing as possible," observed Henry, calmly, as his son and legitimate heir looked up with some surprise as if expecting the king to proceed and explain his meaning.

"I do not see the necessity for such haste, your highness; besides, I am engaged to play a challenge at bowls with young Ralph de Warrener, Stephen Bigod, and some others, in the pleasurance at Southampton."

"Enough for you to know, William, that it is of the utmost importance, both to yourself and the security of my crown, that we should meet the Parliament as quickly after our return as our good horses can bear us to Westminster," replied Henry, more seriously.

"Why so, having so lately met the estates of both realms?" inquired the prince, unwilling to lose his return match at bowls.

For a moment the king surveyed his son with a displeased and troubled look on his still handsome and dignified countenance; then, suddenly assuming an expression more of sadness than of anger, he replied—

"You know enough of the history of your family to understand what has taken place since your grandfather conquered this kingdom of England."

"I know that you are sovereign of England and Duke of Normandy in right of——"

"Usurpation and foul injustice, my son; in right of the strong hand and stronger will," rejoined Henry, in a subdued tone.

"Usurpation, father!" exclaimed the young prince, amazed by his father's words.

"Your tutor, I perceive, has, not to shame your father in your eyes, kindly kept my sins from your knowledge, William; but now it has become my painful duty to open up to you the whole craft and villany of my life."

"Tell me nothing, father, but that I am your son, and, after you, the rightful lord of England!" cried the prince, with passionate vehemence.

Henry started as if stung as his beloved son enunciated the last words; but after a moment, with an effort, he resumed, letting his hand fall kindly on that of the prince.

"William of Normandy left three sons to share his large possessions—William the Red, Robert, whom men called Curthose, and others Unfortunate, and Henry, myself, to whom, from my studious turn of mind, the monks gave the name of Beauclerk."

"But my Uncle Rufus was killed in the forest by Tyrrel," interposed the prince, quickly.

"He was, and died without heirs."

"Then you, of course, became the lawful king?"

"You forget; I had another brother."

"Yes, I remember, Curthose; but he had been dead for many years."

For a moment the king shaded his eyes with his hand, then said, calmly—

"Your Uncle Robert still lives."

"Lives! your elder brother still lives!" exclaimed the prince, full of interest and astonishment. "I always heard he returned in safety from the Holy Land; but lives! Oh, father, where?"

"In Wales."

"Oh, tell me all! Poor Uncle Robert; he who was so stout a soldier of the Cross. I will go to him, and hear all about the Infidel and the Holy Sepulchre. Tell me more of my Uncle Robert, father."

"Peace, boy, peace; you know not what you ask," replied the king, hoarsely.

"Is there some fearful story connected with his name, oh, my father?"

"Boy, boy, you will drive me mad. When I invaded Normandy, and took your uncle prisoner, it was to save the duchy from the schemes of Louis, the French king."

"Then you brought your brother Robert with you to England?"

"I did. Now, William, let one answer end this subject. For twenty years Robert, Duke of Normandy, has lain a sightless captive in the dungeons of Cardiff Castle."

"Holy Mother! oh, my father!" and the prince hid his face in his hands, while the king, with a look of agony and remorse, watched his son's reproachful grief.

"Robert's fate, with his incapacity for government, give me small concern," continued the king. "He was but a source of ceaseless trouble. It is his son I fear."

"His son! Oh, my father, have I then a cousin?" cried Prince William, springing to his feet. "A cousin who is——"

"Your lawful sovereign."

The prince dropped into his chair as if shot, and again hid his face in his hands.

"Who is he?" murmured the youth, faintly.

"Prince William; he whose league with France, Burgundy, and Orleans have given me such grievous trouble."

"Let me hear all, father; all."

"You now know why, to make your seat on the throne firmer than mine had been, that six months back I summoned the peers of England, and made them take the oath of allegiance to you as my successor."

"You mean on my eighteenth birthday?"

"Yes. The same ceremony was repeated, two days ago, at Rouen, when all the barons of our Norman possessions assembled to do homage to their future king, William the Third that shall be."

"And my cousin, Prince William?"

"To break up the powerful league formed against me in the present, and you in the future, I have won over the Pope to discredit your cousin's claims, and bind himself to your exclusive interest."

"That was a master stroke of policy."

"But not equal to the next, William."

"What was that, your highness?"

"Fulke, Count of Anjou, was the very soul of the league against me."

"What, the father of my dear Isabel?" asked the prince, with a flushed cheek.

"The same; his power and influence were so great, that even Louis was kept firm by his resolution."

"How did you overcome the prejudice of so rank an enemy?"

"By playing on his ambition."

"His ambition. How?"

"The Duke of Burgundy had affianced his daughter to your cousin, to become his wife *whenever* he should be king of England."

"Ah! he king!" and the youth's eyes sparkled with unwonted energy.

"On hearing this, I demanded Fulke's daughter, and sole heir of the rich province of Anjou, in marriage for you."

"And the count accepted your offer?"

"With the greatest joy; he will bring her over in state to England in two months, when you will be formally married. I shall, at the same time, create you Duke of Normandy, and soon after you will take up your residence here as a sovereign prince till, on my death, you unite both realms as king of England."

"And will the count be faithful?"

"I would stake my crown on his fidelity. But now you know all particulars necessary, go, and bid farewell to your affianced bride, and hold yourself ready to embark the moment the wind shifts."

"I suppose Marie and Richard are to accompany me in 'La Blanche Neuf?'"

"Of course. I trust your brother and sister entirely to your care."

"You know that is a duty of love, father," replied the prince, rising.

"And that it may last to the end of your lives is my daily prayer to Heaven. But now, farewell; remember, I shall expect the 'Blanche Neuf' to be close in my wake."

"I will aboard, your highness, the moment I hear your signal."

"Then, farewell, my dear son; my pilot augurs a swift and prosperous passage."

"I hope so, too, for dear Marie's sake; but adieu! adieu!"

And waving his hand gaily to the king, Prince William drew aside the tapestry of the royal closet and re-entered the spacious hall of the keep.

Henry gazed with sad but loving eyes on the noble carriage and well-knit, manly figure of the handsome youth who had just left him, and the swinging arras through which he had passed had long sunk into repose before the anxious father could withdraw his eyes from the spot where he had last seen all he had toiled for so long, all he loved and truly valued in life.

CHAPTER II.
PRINCE WILLIAM AND HIS BRIDE.

"HAST seen aught of my sister, Warrener?" Prince William asked of one of his youthful friends, as he re-entered the great hall, and after looking round, made up to a group of his gay companions.

"I saw the Princess Marie here but now, in company with the lovely Isabel of Anjou," replied Ralph de Warrener, looking round the almost deserted hall.

"Where can they have disappeared so suddenly?"

"Nay, methinks you will find them on the battlements of the keep, for I heard your brother Richard urge their visit to the ramparts ere their departure," suggested young Hubert, another of the prince's favourites.

"That boy is ever full of some mischief; why take the girls to such a dizzy height as that?" replied William.

"To show them the king's fleet at anchor, and to try a new cross-bow upon any truant rook or pigeon he may scare from its nest in the battlements," replied Philip Fitzhugh, a young Breton noble.

"I'll go seek them on the leads; meanwhile, you, my lords and gentlemen, make all needful preparation for the voyage, and be ready at the first signal to go on board."

"Our necessaries are all embarked already, and we but await the order to follow you, and ship ourselves," cried young Vavasour, gaily. "But, why insist upon an accepted fact?"

"For my part, I am weary of this dull Harfleur," added another.

"And so am I; soul-weary of it; I would his grace had tarried at Rouen two days longer."

"There were tennis-courts and bowling-greens, and things to live for at Rouen; but here—bah! all is grim-faced stone and iron-visaged war."

"If my affianced bride, the beautiful Isabel, were sailing with us, I would as gladly bid farewell to these grim towers as you, my lords," replied Prince William; "but, as it is the king's pleasure that the 'Blanche Neuf' should follow the 'Tiger,' go; and, while you look to the wind, I'll find the lady Isabel and the princess."

And, waving his hand in adieu to his companions, Prince William passed under the arras, and quitted the hall.

Five minutes later, after a weary ascent of the narrow turnpike or newel stairs, lighted here and there by narrow stone slits, or loop-holes, the prince suddenly emerged on the large, square esplanade forming the roof of the lofty donjon or keep.

At the farther end, and seated between the machicolations on the smooth embrasures, was a group of some half dozen ladies, with their eyes steadily bent to seaward, while the rough winter wind was blowing out their long veils like the streamers of a ship.

At the ladies' feet, winding up the spring of a small Genoese cross-bow, knelt a clear, open-faced, handsome lad of fourteen, his bright eyes flashing as they followed the gyrations of a flock of pigeons his presence had frightened from their nests.

"Keep still, Isabel, and I'll have that fellow with the black crest," observed the boy prince, as, after fitting his bolt, he raised the bow and took aim.

At that moment his brother's gold spurs struck the last step of the newel stairs, when the lady, who had paid no heed to the boy's remark, suddenly looked round, and, instantly rising, hurried forward to meet her future husband.

"There, now, William, that's too bad; you always spoil my sport. By the Conqueror's beard, if I haven't shot a poor pigeon, and missed the fellow I meant to hit," and the boy pointed petulantly to a bird, that was seen rapidly falling into the base court. "I won't lose my game, for all that, though it's only a stupid hen. Hie! you there, De Warrener, you let that bird alone," shouted the boy, springing into one of the embrasures, and fearlessly gazing down from the giddy height.

Having attracted the attention of the young noble below, the lad sprang back on the roof or level rampart, and, calling to his sister, who had hid her face in her veil, he said—

"Come away, Marie; and you, girls. I am tired of this place. I shall go and get old Fitz-Stephens to give me a row in his little cutter; this is so dull. What are you covering your face for?" the boy demanded, pulling the veil roughly from her hands.

"Oh, Richard, you so frightened me when I saw you looking over the ramparts, and the wind blowing so strong; the thought makes me shudder still," replied his meek-eyed and gentle sister, as she threw her arm round the boy's neck, and looked with loving tenderness in his large, fearless eyes.

Richard gazed at her for a moment with a puzzled expression of countenance; then, throwing off her arm, he answered contemptuously—

"Afraid! Well, you women are a set of cowards."

"Shall we go to the oratory, ladies, and sing an 'Ave,' before we go on board the 'Blanche Neuf?'" the gentle princess inquired of the four ladies who attended her.

"That will do admirably. You can all sing Aves and Credos, and tell your beads in the chapel, while I and old Fitz have a sail round the harbour," Richard interposed: then added, impatiently, "Come away, and don't waste time here; and for William and Isabel, can you not see they don't want us? What a frightened sluggard you are, Marie! Come away."

And, taking his sister's hand, the boy began to drag her quickly towards the narrow and precipitous stairs

"Richard," cried Prince William, springing up from the side of his betrothed, and confronting the youth on his way to the stairs, "see that you conduct your sister and these ladies in safety, and without alarm or hurry, to the chamber of the princess, for, if I find you at any of your boyish tricks, you will have to answer for it to me."

"I was only impatient to get my bird," replied Richard, conscious he had gone as far as his brother's good nature would warrant.

"Go, then; but be near at hand when the standard shows the king has left the castle."

Affectionately kissing his gentle sister, Prince William handed her and her ladies down the first few steps, and then, with a courteous smile, raised his plumed bonnet, and hastened back to his beautiful Isabel.

Insensible to the November cold, or the gloom of the fast closing day, the young lovers, enclosed in each other's arms, Isabel's graceful form half hid in the prince's cloak and capuchin, sat and talked, utterly regardless of time or tide.

"Two months hence, mine own dear Isabel, your father will bring you to England, and then, dearest, you will be mine, and we shall part no more," and, as he spoke, he pressed her closer to his heart.

"I would you were not going so soon; the wild aspect of the heavens frightens me, and my heart is full of ungovernable fears," replied Isabel, creeping nearer to her lover's side, with a vague presentiment that they should meet no more.

"Nay, this is idle timidity, Isabel. What should you fear?"

"I fear the rocks, the tempests, and the thousand dangers of the seas."

"Our ships are yare and stout, our crews are sturdy Bretons, or hardy English, who make the sea their cradle; have, then, no fear; with a steady wind, twenty hours will—what ails thee, Isabel?"

The prince spoke with sudden alarm, as Isabel, throwing off the hood, stood grasping the battlement, and gazing with absorbed attention on the half-distinct and hazy scene below.

"See you or hear you aught? Speak, my beloved! What is it?"

"Do you not hear that bell? And, hark! there is a trumpet," she exclaimed, breathlessly. "And, see, the wind has veered to the north; the ships are crowding sail; the king's on board; I see the standard in the storm; and—oh, God! oh, Holy Mother!—you must go!"

The prince had risen at the same moment as Isabel, and noted with considerable surprise the angry and stormy nature of the sea and sky, and saw what had hitherto escaped his notice, that the wind had suddenly settled into a strong gale from the nor'-east.

The jangle of church or convent bells, with the far-off blast of a bugle, was heard faintly over the howling wind and the thunder of the surf on the shore.

Fully satisfied with these sights and sounds, the prince followed Isabel's gaze, and, for a moment, let his eyes contemplate the scene that lay so far beneath him.

Through the ragged rents in the hearse-like rack of clouds, the last rays of the wintry sun peered like a fiery eye on the world of strife and gloom.

Far out to sea white-crested waves were rising in ceaseless motion, while ships of all size and shape were, like curlews, spreading their white wings to the rough breeze.

The wide estuary and bay, so late a void and watery desert, was now alive with tall, careening ships.

It was, however, upon the harbour itself that the prince's eyes were chiefly centred.

Here, like pigmies, were seen crowds of men in confused heaps, as they escorted the great dignitary of the day, King Henry, to his ship.

Even as he gazed, the very words of Isabel became enacted beneath his eyes.

The heavy standard fell over the ship's stern, a dozen long streamers fluttered from the mast-head to the water like countless lengths of ribbon.

At the same moment the one huge sail fell from its boom, and its two corners being sheeted home to the deck, the ungainly machine began to move slowly from her moorings.

As the "Royal Tiger," with bellying canvas, moved from her berth, the three rampant lions emblazoned on the square sail, loomed out large and monstrous in the night air.

The next moment a row of trumpeters in scarlet tabards, came to the stern rail, and blew so loud a flourish that even at the altitude of the keep it sounded shrill and harsh.

Another instant and the round, unsightly basket at the mast-head blazed up like a vast cresset, flinging its flood of fiery light, like a dread beacon, far and near.

Nautical Tales;
OR ADVENTURES BY SEA AND LAND.

"THE KING LAY SENSELESS ON THE FLOOR, STRUCK DOWN BY THE FATAL NEWS."

THE WRECK ON THE CASKETS.

"The king's at sea, I shall be late. Come, my dearest Isabel, our last moment of adieu and love is come."

And catching the fair girl in his arms, Prince William hurried with his light burthen to the stairs.

With Isabel's kisses yet on his cheek and lips, the young prince reached the base court alone.

"The Princess Marie, with her ladies, has gone aboard with all your grace's lords and nobles," observed one of Prince William's attendants, as his squires and knights gathered round.

"And my brother Richard, what has become of him?"

"The young prince, unable to have a sail, went on board an hour since to see a brace of Norway kestrels, that Rudolph the falconer has brought for his pleasure," replied one of William's esquires.

"Let us hasten to the harbour, then, or surely Fitz-Stephen will rate us soundly for our delay."

"Nay, your grace, it is we who have to dance attendance on the drunken Breton, not he on us."

"What mean you? Fitz-Stephen not only knew the king's mind, but had, moreover, my father's orders that the 'Blanch Neuf' should be within hailing distance of the 'Tiger.'"

"True; and see, your grace, the king's beacon is already miles at sea."

And the esquire pointed to the fast disappearing light at the mast-head of the king's ship.

"But wherefore this delay; the harbour seems empty, and every ship has her white wings outspread against the leaden sky?"

"The captain of the 'Blanche Neuf' is nowhere to be found."

"Why, I saw him myself at noon at the 'White Dolphin,' with a score of boon friends discussing the weather."

"He left there hours since, and all search for him is fruitless, while one half the crew are either drunk or mutinous."

"The iron collar and the lash will bring them to their senses; and, by holy mother, they shall have it, too; but—hark! what is that?"

And, attracted by the shrill notes of a trumpet, the prince looked over the wall, and beheld in the street below a mounted pursuivant galloping fiercely up the town, and at every court and corner blowing a loud alarm.

"Sir Hugh Lambert has sent a herald to root out this boozing pilot, your grace."

"Let us on board then at once, as Fitz-Stephen may return to his ship at any moment."

And surrounded by his attendant knights, squires, and grooms, Prince William hastened from the castle, and proceeded down the dark and narrow streets to the harbour.

CHAPTER III.

THE "BLANCHE NEUF."

THE royal ship, or galley, specially set apart for the conveyance of the heir apparent of England, though not one of the largest, was reported to be one of the best and swiftest sailers in Henry's navy.

Her lofty stern rose, with a graceful curve inward, thirty feet from the water, and terminated in a carved figure, representing the head of a war-horse; her bow sharp, for the better cleaving of the sea, was adorned with a carved pillar some ten feet high.

The use of this pillar was two-fold; it served as a hold for the anchor, and to secure the stays of the mast.

Abaft the mast, for she carried only one, was erected a richly-decorated house, with doors, windows, and containing a few small apartments; these, and the building itself, constituted the sole cabin accommodation of the vessel.

From the mast to the bows the "Blanche Neuf" was undecked and open, the space being fitted up with three tiers or *banks* of benches for the sixty rowers, whose sturdy arms propelled the vessel in contrary winds or calms.

A long, strong oar, like a baker's peel, and working on a pivot at one side of the ship's stern, served the purpose of a helm, and was usually under the control of the pilot.

A forked pennon fluttered from the mast-head, and on a strong boom or spar beneath was brailed up the ship's mainsail, her only canvas.

A row of oval shields, with the cognizance of the owner emblazoned on each, were suspended outside of the bulwarks, showing that the "Blanche Neuf" carried a certain number of knights, or men-at-arms.

Such was the appearance of this famous galley, as Prince William and his attendants reached the quay at which she still lay moored.

The hiss and roar of the sea, as the flood tide came in dashing surges with the blustering wind, fast rising to a gale, combined with the shouts of men and the oaths and discord that reigned on board, made up a perfect hell of noise and confusion.

"Peace, thou blaspheming hound, or, by my father's beard, I'll fit those hoary limbs with lasting fetters!" exclaimed the prince, as he sprang on deck, and grasped the upraised arm of Fitz-Stephen, as, foaming with rage, he staggered after some of his drunken sailors, wielding a knotted rope with savage fury. "Silence, profane! Hast thou forgotten in thy swinish orgies, that my sister, the Princess Marie, and her ladies are in yonder house? Away, thou drunken fool!"

And contemptuously flinging the old man from him, he turned to his chief and most trusted officer, saying,

"Sir Hugh Lambert, bring up a score of men-at-arms, and cleave to the chine the first man who disputes his duty, or neglects an order. To your posts, and your blood be on your own heads."

And he waved the astonished and subdued sailors to their several duties.

Roused by the tramp of the heavy armed men, whom Sir Hugh began to place as sentries along the deck, the stunned and half-sobered captain rose from under the gunwale, where he had fallen.

"I hope your grace will forgive——" began Fitz-Stephen, respectfully, approaching the prince with uncovered head.

"Attend to your ship, and say no more," replied the prince, half turning away.

"I never thought of the fleet sailing with a sou'-westerly wind, and, therefore, never hurried, as I wanted a wind from the south'ard."

"And yet every ship of the fleet but yours is at sea, and with a flowing sheet."

"What do those Cinque Port pilots, and ignorant English know of navigation? By St. Anthony, the whole lot of them don't know so much of a real gale as a Breton fisherman. Bah! they are curs!"

"And yet the 'Tiger' is already hull down, and the king's beacon almost out of sight," replied the prince, pointing to a faint speck on the far horizon, where the blazing basket of fire at the mast-head gleamed against the scowling sky like the dying light of a glowworm.

"I see her, your grace; but a Breton captain needs no star to guide him to his port. I'd steer the 'Blanche Neuf,' bless her sweet keel," and he struck his heavy fist on the ship's bulwarks with a force that might have stunned an ox. "I'd take her through the gates of purgatory with my eyes shut. Never you fear, prince, I'll lay you alongside the 'Tiger,' with her five pilots, in less than two hours."

"You know the king's orders, and I hope you will be able to fulfil them by the morning."

"Think it is done already, prince; we shall be over the bar in ten minutes. Gilbert!"

And, calling to his first mate, or lieutenant, Fitz-Stephen went forward.

"Have you seen my sister and her ladies, Sir Hugh, since they came on board?" asked Prince William, as he leant against the larboard bulwarks to secure his jewelled bonnet from the fury of the wind.

"I have, your grace, and I believe they have some time since retired to rest."

"I will not disturb her then. Poor Marie, she dreads the sea, and we shall have a rough night. Holy Mother, grant that she may sleep it through. Is Richard looked to?"

"Asleep long ago, with the jesses of a kestrel fastened to either wrist, a new purchase of the falconer for the royal boy."

"I hope the accommodation for the young lords of England and Normandy is somewhat better than on our trip from Portsmouth; it was little better then than that of swine. Have you looked to it?"

"I have; and had the deck below us completely swept, and then littered with fresh straw. They were so delighted with the change that I don't think one of them was awake five minutes afterwards."

"I will but bid my sister good night, and join you presently. The wind is raw and chill; bring seats and a flagon of Burgundy, for I shall not to bed to-night," Prince William replied, as he left his faithful friend and monitor, and opening one of the doors of the house, disappeared in the cabin.

While Sir Hugh was ordering a servant to procure seats and wine, Fitz-Stephen had contrived to reach the end of the half-deck, where, in the void beyond, sat the sixty rowers, as mute as statues, each man with his oar across his knees.

"Give me your schedule, Gilbert. Are all on board? Hold the light straight, you lurching fool," hiccoughed the captain, as he opened the paper his mate placed in his hand and tried to steady himself under the light of the ship's lantern that Gilbert held up for his convenience.

"Sir Hugh Lambert—Ralph de Warrener—Lion—Lion—"

"Lionel," corrected Gilbert, looking over his captain's shoulder.

"Yes; I see—keep the light steady—Lionel Vavasour—and—and—" replied Fitz-Stephen, trying to read the list of his passengers' names.

"Oh, it's all right, I dare say. What stupid figures you do make! What's the total? a thousand and——"

"A hundred and forty-six, all the sons of our best nobles, and eighty men-at-arms," replied the mate.

"And they are all stowed safe under hatches?"

"All; an hour ago."

"Then that'll do; here, take care of the schedule. Where's that pig-sticking butcher of Rouen I hired to look after the rowers?"

"Black Jack, come aft here to the captain," cried the mate, addressing the lines of rowers who sat like motionless blocks in the gloom of the forecastle.

"Here I am," exclaimed a tall, powerful, black-bearded man, armed with a long, flexible ash pole to correct the lagging or indolent rowers, as he sprang on the half-deck.

"Are your men all right and in their banks?" demanded Fitz-Stephen of the butcher, or ganger, of the rowers.

"All; and I'll keep them to their work, or they shall have a taste of supple Kate," and the butcher, as he spoke, made his long wand whistle so loud and near the captain's ear, that Fitz-Stephen sprang back with a muttered oath.

"All hands on deck! haul in the cable, and let fly the mainsail!"

In an instant twenty men bounded up at the captain's shrill call, and while some threw off the bight of the hawser and stowed away the slack, others, cat-like, mounted the stays, and getting outside the boom, dropped the mainsail.

While some of the crew were hauling home the corners of the main sheet, and fastening ropes to the rings in the deck, and the ship's bow fell from off the wooden pier, the captain, followed by Gilbert, hurried aft, and together they seized the long oar by which the "Blanche Neuf" was steered.

As the two men threw their weight on the strong lever, and the ship headed out of the estuary, the sail, with a report like thunder, suddenly bellied out, and every line and thread of halyard and canvas drawing, the "Blanche" sprang forward like a goaded courser.

"Ease her; ease her, Gilbert! By Holy Mother she's going like a mad thing!" gasped the captain, almost choked by the rush of wind that encountered them, as the galley reaching the bay encountered the whole force of wind and sea.

But, as if rather maddened than curbed by the howling gale, the "Blanche" bounded from wave to wave like a screaming curlew, with creaking mast and groaning timbers, at times half burying her bulk in the yeasty trough of the sea.

"If she jibs and kicks in this way, captain, we shall never keep her in, and when she gets into the open she'll take her head like a startled horse," observed the mate, throwing all his weight on the oar, in the effort to bring the ship's head to the north.

"You are about right there, Gilbert; and may I have a double penance at Lent if I don't think the cursed jade has got the bit in her teeth already. Here, you!" cried Fitz-Stephen, hailing a sailor. "Pass the word for the butcher to come aft; his crew are not likely to be wanted while this wind holds, and I've a use for him."

"Want me, captain?" asked Black Jack, as a few moments later he contrived to reach the stern—no easy matter, through all the pitching and rolling of the labouring ship.

"Yes; and put some of your strength to this pole, for it's almost more than Gilbert and I can manage."

The captain had not pressed the butcher into his new duty a moment too soon, for the ship, having just cleared the bay, encountered the sudden rush of the down-channel gale.

The "Blanche Neuf" staggered, sank, rose, and sank again, half drowned in the force and fury of the overwhelming waters, while the three men strained their hearts nearly out to keep the ship's head to the north.

The gale that, in the Gulf of Normandy, had seemed but a breezy discord, became out in the channel an appalling tempest, in which the royal galley was flung from sea to sea, like a useless waif.

"What a Stygian darkness wraps the land we have left, Lambert, while all before looks like thunder streaked with lightning," observed the prince to his companion, as they grasped the back-stays of the mast for a support.

"It is a gloomy night, indeed," replied Sir Hugh, glancing at the low, flying scud, that, like a moving pall, swept over the dark sky.

"I like this elemental war, Lambert; like it much. Are those flecks of white in the far distance the wings of birds or the gleam of a ship's sail?" the prince suddenly asked, turning his head to address the captain.

"Holy Mother! is your grace there?" replied the captain, astonished to hear the voice of the prince on deck at such an hour, and in such a season. "Go to your berth, prince, I pray you; 'tis a rough and troublous night, and we shall have fouler weather yet, I take it, ere we again see the light of day."

"Nay, by your leave I shall keep on deck; and when I feel tired, my cloak and yonder corner will make a couch good enough for a soldier," Prince William rejoined, pointing to the bulwarks.

"As your grace wills. But touching those flecks of light, I take them to be the rear ships of the fleet," Fitz-Stephen added, perfectly sobered by the threatening aspect of the heavens and the heavy responsibility of his position.

"I cannot see my father's beacon; and yet, by this rate of sailing, we must be almost flying after the 'Tiger's' heels."

"Light-a-foot as she always is, I never knew the 'Blanche' tear through the water at such a rate; she springs under us like a bird."

"And the 'Tiger——?'"

"Aye, aye, prince, we'll look after her. Here, you Lietchstein, go aloft, and look sharp out for the king's beacon."

"In what quarter?" asked the man addressed, swaying himself by a loose halyard.

"Right a-head, sheer over the ship's prow."

As rapidly as the pitching of the vessel would allow the sailor to perform this dangerous duty, he climbed up the weather braces, and twining his arms round the top of the mast, stood on the mainsail boom, and gazed out on the stormy night.

After a long and steady scrutiny of the distant horizon, the sailor descended and approached his captain.

"Can you see the 'Tiger's' light?"

"I see a light, and only one, but that is far to windward."

"Ahead, you mean; straight ahead," replied the captain sharply.

"The only light is down there on our larboard bow," Lietchstein retorted, doggedly.

"It can't be, Gilbert; either we mistook the bearings of the Cape, or the king has run for shelter."

"Hardly that, with such a wind, captain," said the mate, decisively. "Here, you take my place at the rudder, Lietchstein, and I'll take a look aloft."

"And while you are deciding that point, Fitz-Stephen, I'll lie down and sleep," remarked the prince, folding himself in his cloak, and contentedly stretching himself in the lee scuppers.

CHAPTER IV.

THE SHIPWRECK.

So loud and ungovernable had the storm now become, and so heavily began the "Blanche Neuf" to labour in the cross sea, that, with all his expedition, it was full twenty minutes before the mate returned to his post.

"Well, Gilbert, is he right?"

"Yes, captain; the light's down here on our larboard bow, rather smaller than I should have expected to find the 'Tiger's' beacon, but plain enough."

"And what to the nor' and nor'-east; have you searched well?"

"Black as night all round, except here and there a rent in the grey scud, showing an inky sky beneath; it's the only gleam of light on earth or heaven."

"It must be so. I was sure that Romney boat, the 'Tiger,' could never breast such a sea as this. The king has run for Plymouth."

"That the king has run for Plymouth, or one of the Cornish ports, is like enough; but I think the 'Tiger's' a yare craft, and fit to face out this gale."

"Our duty is, of course, to follow; and I shan't be sorry to be quit of this dead strain, that opens every seam like the jar of a door."

"Where is the prince?"

"Fast asleep, yonder, in the cold and wet; the lad will make a rare soldier; the young cub, too, grips like a lion," Fitz-Stephen muttered in a whisper, as he pointed to the sleeping and unconscious prince.

"What's to be done, captain?"

"Where lies Cape La Hogue?"

"Far down here, on our weather quarter."

"Then take in a reef in the mainsail, and bring the ship's head to the west, straight down channel."

A few minutes served to effect this manœuvre, and then the "Blanche Neuf" darted forward, like a wild horse suddenly freed from all restraint.

Not as heretofore, cresting each wave, and pouring from her gaping timbers floods of brine, but bursting through the seas like an arrow, every surge breaking over her bows, and half drowning the shivering rowers.

"Keep her head a bit more to the north, Gilbert. Holy St. Francis! at what a rate she goes!"

Half an hour might have elapsed from the time the "Blanche's" course had been altered, and the captain and crew had almost become reconciled to the fearful speed at which she cleft her way through the water.

At last the sight so anxiously looked for became suddenly visible from the deck of the prince's galley.

At the moment the captain sighted what he thought to be the royal beacon, a faint opening in the sky showed to the mate's astonished gaze the constellation of the Great Bear.

The mate gave one rapid glance at the then only known guide of the mariner, and, with a face from which all vestige of colour had fled, fixed his eyes on the distant light.

"Holy Mother forgive us!" exclaimed Gilbert, grasping his captain's arm. "See, yonder is Charles's Wain," and he pointed to the dimly seen constellation. "And there is the Island of Aurigny."

"Alderney!" gasped Fitz-Stephen, in terror.

"Aye, that fatal spot, right under our bows."

"And that hideous noise is——?"

"The *Ras de Catte*—the race of Alderney."

"Oh, God!" and the stunned and horrified captain hid his head on his mate's shoulder.

"Here, you, the butcher, away to your post; rouse up your men, and see that every rower works his best; for on the next ten minutes depend the lives of all and the welfare of England. Quick, to your duty!"

At the mate's voice, Black Jack resigned his post at the rudder, and, seizing his rod of office, instantly rushed forward, and, by blows and curses, soon roused his wet and shivering crew.

At the same instant, by the united influence of the helm and sail, the "Blanche's" head was laid to the north, and, the sweeps being got out, every nerve was strained to work her from off the dead set of the *Ras de Catte*.

For a space that seemed like an age, the mate and captain watched the immovable ship, as, with broadside on to the current, she was being swept to destruction, while the Ras, like a thousand mill races, was bearing her to ruin.

"She moves! she moves! Pull for your lives!" cried Gilbert, almost frantic with anxiety and dread.

Two granite rocks, like gigantic steeples, rose towering up, hardly a cable's length from the ship's bows, while the furious waves, lashed into froth, wrapped them to their pinnacles in foamy shrouds.

"Haul her closer to the wind, and use your larboard sweeps with a will. Now, all together, strong and steady!" shouted Fitz-Stephen, as he watched the first motion of the "Blanche" to cross the race.

"She's caught the breeze, captain, and is drawing off. A few steady strokes now, my men, and we are safe."

As the mate spoke, the "Blanche," under the united force of wind and oars, began slowly to heave ahead, but passing as she did so so near the rocks that the spray fell on her deck like a thunderstorm.

Sharp, and loud, and distinct, above the war and turmoil of the elements, rose the crash of broken oars, as sweep after sweep snapped short in the hands of the rowers.

But by desperate exertion, and the aid of Providence, the immediate danger was avoided, and the "Blanche" shot uninjured past the "Monk's Chair."

(*To be concluded next week.*)

NAUTICAL TALES;
OR, ADVENTURES BY SEA AND LAND.

"HE STOOD WITH ONE ARM THROWN ROUND HER."—(See "*The Last of the Buccaneers*.")

THE WRECK ON THE CASKETS.

CONCLUSION.

With a long-drawn breath of relief, the captain passed his hand across his brow as this one danger was overcome.

His mind, however, was still deeply troubled, for he well knew that not half the perils of the night were past.

"I begin to think, Gilbert, that yonder light is no human beacon after all," whispered the captain, as the eastern end of the Island of Alderney was seen like a shadow on their beam.

"Why so?"

"Because it's now down where I know no ship could live in such a night as this among——"

"What?"

"The Caskets!"

A sudden exclamation from the forecastle, and the crashing of a number of oars, told the two officers of some sudden misfortune.

Before Gilbert could well realise the fact that they were within a hundred fathoms of that archipelago of fatal rocks, the Caskets, the ship, in a moment, encountered all the force of the storm.

So overwhelming was the rush of wind and tide, that nearly every sweep was shivered in the rowers' hands, the rudder was broken short off by the deck, and the mainsail, torn from its cleets, was fluttering in rags round its swaying boom.

"Launch the long-boat; get out——"

The rest of Fitz-Stephen's order was lost in the noise and terror of the next instant.

Before the words could well escape him, the "Blanche Neuf" had been drawn into a vortex, and after a few rapid gyrations in the water, hurled with deadly force broadside on the rocks that, like giant teeth, stood up sharp and ghastly from the sea.

The shock was so sudden and unexpected, that every one was flung from his position, some into the sea, others on the deck, stunned and bleeding.

The torn and splintered timbers let the water in like a flood, while the mast, displaced from its step, fell like

[GRATIS SUPPLEMENT TO NO. 7 OF BRETT'S NAVAL HISTORY.]

thunder across the deck, and crushing the upper portion of the house beneath its weight.

The destruction was wide-spread, and the despair general.

One half of the rowers were already drowned at their banks by the inrush of the sea, while, from the hold and after-deck, men-at-arms, knights, and barons, driven like rats from their holes, streamed on deck from the encroaching water.

All was terror and confusion; rolled violently against a broken spar, the prince was rudely roused to consciousness from his heavy sleep.

Possessing many of the best qualities of his father, unquestioned courage, and an almost intuitive perception of coming danger, Prince William saw their awful situation in a moment.

"Where are your boats, captain? Have you all ready for the ladies?" he cried, as, in his attempt to reach Fitz-Stephen and Sir Hugh Lambert, the ship was again violently dashed on the rock, and the prince flung to the deck.

From that shock all order ceased, and the few remaining minutes were of the keenest horror.

At a sign from Sir Hugh, a dozen stout men-at-arms suddenly seized the prince, and, despite his desperate struggles, bore him to the long-boat that, at the ship's side, alternately rose above the bulwarks, and then sank to a depth lost in the darkness.

"Unhand me, serfs! Where is the princess? where are her women? Lambert, draw off these men, or by Heaven I'll use my poniard!"

And the youth laid his hand on the jewelled hilt of his dagger.

"Leave her to me, prince, I have a boat for her special use, and will save her at the hazard of my life."

And as the soldiers forced the prince into the overloaded boat, Sir Hugh hurried forward to the opposite quarter of the ship, where he had left the only other craft the "Blanche" carried under the guard of two of his most trusted men.

Long as these things have taken to describe, they occurred in such rapid succession, that hardly two minutes had passed from the galley's striking when the awful climax of the drama occurred.

Sir Hugh Lambert had just reached the half-demolished house, and was calling on the princess to come forth, when the "Blanche Neuf" parted amidships, and the whole stern sunk in deep water.

Sir Hugh, with all the youthful nobles, were sucked into the flood, and for an instant the cock-boat with its two soldiers, was seen on the brink of the gulf, and the next moment was dragged into the yawning abyss.

The fore part of the ship, with the wreck of the cabin swarming with struggling forms, was left rocking in the tempest like a cradle impaled on the point of a rock.

Within a few hundred yards of this fearful picture, one moment flung up as if to meet the sky, the next sinking beneath the beam of sight, the over-crowded long-boat was seen struggling with the tempest.

Clear and shrill over the war of nature and the fierce oaths of men was heard one wild shriek of despairing women.

The moon burst, as if by magic, from her surrounding pall of darkness, and one lovely form was seen flinging its white arms for aid.

"It is my sister's voice," cried Prince William, shaking off those who, in kindness, held his arms, and springing up; "put back and save her; back, I say."

"The boat will hold no more."

"Peace, slave! It shall hold her if I find a grave here myself. Back, I say, back!' and, drawing his sword, he compelled the unwilling crew to return to the wreck. "Marie, Marie! my beloved Marie, throw yourself into my arms. Quick! and fear not," exclaimed the prince, as a few moments later the boat rose to a level with the rocking wreck.

Scarcely had the words escaped him, when a score of miserable wretches sprang from the forecastle into the long-boat, which, instantly swerving round, foundered, while the bows, freed from this counterpoise, lurched over, and sank.

One faint shriek rang out for a moment on the wild night, and then all was solitude and silence, except the voice of the raging storm.

The mast, with one struggling atom of humanity clinging with death clutches to its frail support, was the last survivor of that lately crowded ship.

The drowning mariner, after many vain efforts, at last flung his benumbed limbs across the mast, and rode the boom like the vampire of the storm.

"Who's there?" exclaimed a choking voice from the deep, as a strong swimmer writhed himself round the mast, and sat, haggard, weak, and panting, near the rescued man.

"Blessed St. Anthony! Captain, are you alive? Methought all—all were gone, and no one left to share the watch of this awful night with the butcher of Rouen."

"I have fought desperately for life with the stubborn wave for one purpose, and one only. Life has no longer joy for me," replied Fitz-Stephen, wiping the brine from his eyes.

"For what purpose, captain?"

"To see some trace of the long-boat; but I cannot find her. Oh! say you have seen her. Say the word!"

"The long-boat? Why she foundered half-an-hour ago, swamped by the crew of the forecastle, when the prince returned to save his sister," replied the butcher.

"And the prince himself?" eagerly demanded the captain.

"Went down with her, and never rose again."

"Dead! Drowned! Then I have nothing more to do with life," and, before the butcher could understand what his captain meditated, Fitz-Stephen plunged headlong in the coming wave, and disappeared for ever.

For days King Henry sat pale and anxious in the royal closet of Southampton Castle, expecting each hour to hear tidings of his son.

Every ship of the fleet, save the "Blanche Neuf," had come to port: she only of all his ships was missing; of all his company his cherished son, the source of all his pride and ambition, was alone absent.

In his belief that they had put into some port for safety, couriers travelled night and day from Dover to Penzance, but still no tidings could be gained of the missing galley.

On the evening of the fourth day a tall, gaunt, black-bearded man was ushered into the presence of the king.

From this man, the butcher of Rouen, the sole survivor of nearly three hundred souls on board the "Blanche Neuf," the king heard all the particulars of the shipwreck, of the prince's efforts to save his sister, of his loss, and of Fitz-Stephen's death.

The king heard the sad recital to the last detail, and then, with a long gasp of suffering, sank insensible at the narrator's feet.

From that hour to the day of his death, a period of eleven years, Henry Beauclerk was never known again to smile, or was the faintest tinge of colour ever again seen to animate the pale visage of the heart-broken sovereign.

THE LAST OF THE BUCCANEERS;
OR, THE FLIRT AND THE VIXEN.

CHAPTER 1.

THE NET SPREAD—THE SPANIARDS' RETURN—A RUNAWAY MULE AND A LOST HEART.

"Have you seen the coffers safely aboard, Pedro?" inquired Don Guzman, the late Governor of Cuba, addressing one of his European servants, as he entered the saloon where his master was seated.

"I have, your excellency, and seen to the stowing of everything myself," replied the man, respectfully, but at the same time with that familiarity of tone that speaks of long servitude and faithful attachment.

"Then everything is on board, Pedro?"

"All but a few trifles for the Donna Caterina's cabin," added the servitor, glancing to the end of the saloon, where, on a pile of richly embroidered cushions, lay the delicate form of a lovely girl of eighteen.

Two mulattoes about her own age, whose long, silken hair hung below their waists, and only by the deeper tone of their skin, a shade less beautiful than the exquisite form they cooled, sat on the carpet at the head and feet of the young donna.

Each attendant was armed with a large fan, made of the most gorgeous feathers of tropical birds, and with their untiring work cooled the air, and kept off the small gilded flies from the face and book of the indolent beauty.

"And what do you regard as trifles, Pedro?" asked Don Guzman, looking up from his writing with a quiet smile.

"Well, your excellency, I should be sorry if the donna knew what I call trifles, but, as my arrangement of our dear donna's cabin struck her gentlewomen with horror I left the Signora Eustacia, and the two French maids—"

"Arranging it after their own ideas of taste, elegance and comfort, eh?"

"Exactly, your excellency, and when they had got rid of my contaminations, and after rating me soundly for daring to think that a Castilian lady could ever want an easy chair to lounge in, I was sent on shore to find work more congenial to my depraved tastes."

"Never mind what they say, Pedro; but tell me, did you ask the captain when he expects the 'Santissima Maria' to sail?"

"I did, your excellency, and he hopes to be in the straits by the morning; and, for my part, I rejoice at the news."

"What, Pedro, are you weary of this lovely country? I should have thought after fifteen years' residence, Cuba would have become as dear to you as Leon or Castile."

"I am a Spaniard, like your excellency; and, to a true Iberian, no spot on earth is equal to the peninsula, where he first knew life," Pedro replied, drawing himself up with dignity. "But it is not the country, your excellency; Cuba is all very well to walk on, but the ignorant natives are getting troublesome."

"Indeed! how can their ignorance affect you, Pedro?"

"Why, your excellency, they get so inquisitive; and the idle sailors who hang about shore to ply their boats are worse than any."

"How so?"

"They ask so many questions. During the last week I have had to employ several of them to take your excellency's effects on board the 'Santissima Maria,' and I have been half choked with stupid questions."

"But you need not have answered them."

"True, your excellency; but I was provoked into making replies."

"Indeed, Pedro; how were you provoked? I should like to hear how a staid, sober man like you could be provoked into a rejoinder," replied Don Guzman, laying down his pen, and laughing at Pedro's perplexed countenance.

"Why, you see, your excellency, these big sailors speak and act just like a parcel of babies, and it makes a man feel quite savage to hear them jabber for half an hour, and all for nothing."

"Upon what subject?"

"That's the aggravating part of it, for it's really nothing after all; but I'll try and give your excellency an idea of their foolish nonsense. To-day, for instance—"

"Why particularly to-day?"

"Oh! one day's just the same as another, for that matter; and then, I remember this last trip better than what took place yesterday."

"Go on, and let me judge of your forbearance, Pedro."

"This morning, when I escorted your excellency's coffers to the beach, the four men who have generally rowed me and the luggage to the 'Santissima Maria,' great, hulking, brigand looking, but harmless, honest fellows—"

"Well, I suppose they were waiting for you, as usual, to hire them?"

"Exactly so, your excellency; and, when I pointed to the mule-cart, they darted to it, and like a parcel of boys began to dance round it, muttering to themselves, in a villanous *Lingua Franca*."

"To what purpose?"

"Nay, your excellency, I could not make out; all I could understand was, that one swore, as I thought, by his eyes and legs—though that was not likely—and said something about the 'rhino come at last.'"

"Well, go on."

"Blessed Saint Lawrence, how strong they are, and how they did work! Two of them made no more of one of those heavy coffers than I should of your excellency's valise; and, in less than ten minutes, they had placed the six chests in the boat."

"I see nothing in all this to excite your displeasure, Pedro," observed the don, calmly.

"Not yet, your excellency; but no sooner do we get away from shore, than one of the black-bearded children stops rowing, and, laying his immense fist on one of the coffers, says to his comrades, 'I'll bet you a plug o' bacca' that them boxes are filled with—'"

"Filled with what? Go on," replied his master, as Pedro dropped his voice, and looked with an alarmed expression at the listless donna.

"Their words nearly made my hair stand on end with horror. But then, your excellency, these sailors are such children, that they have no idea of Spanish propriety, and don't know what they say," Pedro added, apologetically.

"And what did they say the boxes were filled with?"

"Why, that which made them so heavy was the donna's farthingales and petticoats, and other women's gimcracks," replied the man, in a deprecatory whisper.

"Insolent varlets! and did you undeceive them?"

"No, your excellency, that was only the beginning of the conversation; another wagered a glass of grog it was the young woman's shoes and stockings. This sort of thing, your excellency, was getting so indelicate, that I could bear it no longer, when—"

"Well, what next?"

"They all drew in their oars, and left the boat pitching in the heavy surf while they disputed among themselves, betting from an inch of pig-tail up to a doubloon that each knew what the coffers contained."

"Eventually, however, they *did* guess the truth?"

"Not a bit of it, your excellency, and we should have been rocking there till now if I had not interfered."

"In what manner?"

"After guessing that the chests were filled with your old cocked hats, one of them, more cunning than the rest, swore that it was nothing but maravedis which you were taking home, to buy candles with for a church."

"Farthings, indeed! the profane scoundrels."

"I couldn't stand that, your excellency, so I told them, that, if they did not hold their tongues, and row me to the galleon, I'd hail the guard-boat, and give them in charge."

"That brought them to their senses I hope?"

"Yes, after a time; the fact is, they had worked themselves into such a state of excitement, that, till they were satisfied, one way or another, so as to decide who had lost or won, they didn't seem to have the power to row."

"So you had to be referee and judge?"

"'You are all wrong, every one of you,' I cried, growing angry at their stupidity. 'How do we know that,' shouted one of the sailors, 'unless you tell us what is in them?'"

"What answer could you make to that," Pedro? observed the ex-govenor, quietly.

"I think I was equal to the occasion, your excellency," replied Pedro, with a dash of pride. 'And will you take your oars and be satisfied with the truth?' I said, as they suddenly became quiet.

"'Yes, yes, we will believe the senor,' they shouted, dropping their oars into the water."

"'Then those coffers, which you ignorantly called boxes, contain the private fortune of his excellency, Don Guzman, and are filled with ingots, or bars, of gold and silver.'"

"Well, Pedro, that silenced and astonished them, I suppose?"

"Not near so much as your excellency would think; indeed, I very much suspect they didn't believe me."

"Perhaps it was as well they should not."

"However, they set to work manfully, and were so handy and obliging, that they wouldn't let the sailors on board help them, but stowed the coffers themselves in the strong-room, under the chief cabin."

"You left all safe, I hope, Pedro?"

"As safe, your excellency, as when the treasure left the palace. I locked the door, put your seal over the padlocks, and placed two sentries to keep guard, and here are the keys."

As Pedro concluded his account, he placed the keys of the strong-room before the ex-governor.

"What time did the captain say he would send the barge for myself and the Donna Caterina?"

"About vespers, your—"

"Did you speak to me, papa?" said the donna, closing her book, and looking round languidly.

"No, Caterina; but you had better get ready, we must be on board in two hours;" then turning to his confidential servant, added, "Pedro, you can leave us now."

"I wish we were safe in Cadiz, papa," said the beautiful girl, as she rose and crossed the saloon to her father's chair, and made a sign for her attendants to retire.

"Why so, my darling?" the father replied, looking up fondly in her lovely face.

"I cannot tell, but I have a foreboding, an unaccountable dread of this voyage. Oh, for the dear plains of Andalusia and our own silvery Quadalquiver," she exclaimed, folding her small white hands.

"Can you remember Seville then, Caterina?"

"Remember it! Ah, yes, how well! it is only ten years ago since I joined you here, and I was eight years old then."

"True, my love, true; but why should the thoughts of this voyage alarm you, you have been used to the sea?"

"Oh, I do not dread the sea or tempests; I fear enemies, and those horrid wretches, pirates and freebooters," she replied, in unfeigned alarm.

"Now, Caterina, you distress yourself quite needlessly. Spain, just now, is at peace with all the world, and the age for buccaneering went out with Queen Anne and the Fourteenth Louis."

"But those horrid heretics, the English, still practice piracy."

"Make your mind easy on that matter, my child; that sort of business does not pay, and the English are now too fond of making bargains to run such a risk."

"How so, papa?"

"Simply because a pirate is like a two-edged sword, and is as likely to cut a friend as a foe."

"Then you don't believe that there are such cruel wretches in existence as pirates?"

"I certainly do not believe the English either practice or encourage it. The only rover I ever heard of for years, was a Frenchman, who once infested the West India Islands."

"A French pirate! Oh, that is so different; the French, you know, are all catholics, and then they are naturally so polite, not like those uncouth heretics."

"I expect the nature of a pirate is much the same, from whatever country he may come; but you need not even fear a visit from the French marquis."

"A marquis, papa! how romantic! Is he very handsome?"

"Well, it was reported that he was the scion of an illustrious family, and I believe the scoundrel was considered good-looking; and, by St. Iago, the villain was young enough."

"Oh, papa, what names to call a French nobleman!" exclaimed Caterina, her notions of romantic adventure horrified by the use of such coarse terms to a young and dashing hero.

"What do you mean?" demanded the ex-governor, looking at his daughter.

Caterina, thinking that perhaps she had said too much, was silent for a minute, then she said—

"You called him a villain."

"And very good names too for a cut-throat; but, thanks to the Dutch, I believe society got rid of the scoundrel three or four years ago."

"Got rid of him, poor unfortunate victim! how?"

NAUTICAL TALES;

OR, ADVENTURES BY SEA AND LAND.

THE LAST OF THE BUCCANEERS;

OR, THE FLIRT AND THE VIXEN.

CONTINUED.

"By hanging him to his own yard-arm, and by sinking his ship."

"Alas! what a lamentable fate for a nobleman, I could weep for his untimely end."

A Spanish abjurgation, which, translated into vulgar English, would have sounded very much like—

"Confound him, and his end too," half escaped the don's lips, but he smothered the unfinished sentence, and, turning to his daughter, merely added, with an affectionate smile,

"As we have very little time to spare, go, Caterina darling, and get ready for the barge."

And, fondly kissing her, the father and daughter parted, to prepare for the homeward voyage.

* * * * *

"What are you looking for, Pedro?" asked Don Guzman, as, at the head of a procession of mules, with his daughter and servants, he halted at the top of the incline that led to the beach.

"I was looking for my four watermen; I promised to give them a doubloon to drink your excellency's health and a prosperous voyage. But, I can't see anything of them. It's very strange, for they take to rum as babies do to milk."

"Papa, who is that handsome young officer who has just taken off his hat?" cried Caterina, indicating with her eyes a group of naval officers and young reefers, who stood on the right of the fair speaker.

"Is he like what you have heard of the poor marquis?"

"St. Iago! what marquis? That fellow? Oh, that! why he's a heretic to be sure, and English sailor, that's all, Why, Caterina, santissima Maria!—what the devil's the matter with your mule? Holy Mother!—curse—hang the brute, he's off!"

Part of this speech was addressed in petulant remonstrance to his daughter, as his eye fell on a young and handsome English lieutenant, who, with a few brother officers, was courteously greeting the departing ex-governor and his fair daughter.

The latter, and more irritable portion of his apostrophe, was addressed to Caterina's mule, that at first seemed to be seized with an unaccountable passion for dancing on his hind legs.

Having performed this feat entirely to his own satisfaction, and completely dispersing his companions, with the duenna and the donna's maids, the brute took it into his head to bolt.

And this he did in so violent and alarming a manner as fully to justify Don Guzman's oath and final ejaculation.

Taking the bit in his mouth, and nearly hiding his head between his legs, the mule, with fiery eyes and invisible ears, charged the crowd on his right, and at a furious gallop made for the precipice that for seventy feet rose sheer from the rocky strand.

"By the Lord he's off, and there they go like ninepins!" shouted an English middy, nearly convulsed with laughter as he watched the grimaces of the floundering crowd, as they helped one another to regain their feet.

"Who'd have thought to find so much pluck in a donkey?"

"You are an ass not to know a mule from a donkey," replied a brother reefer.

"None of your slack chaff, Master Pelham, or—— Why, where the devil's Chester off to?" the young middy asked, suddenly missing his lieutenant.

"Following his inclinations, I suppose," replied Pelham, glancing after the terrified quadruped; "but it's too hot and too fatiguing a race for me."

"What do you mean? Pursuing the mule?"

"No, you muff, following the lady."

"By Jove, he'll be over the cliff; run—call after him, Pelham, your legs are longer than mine. Quick!"

"Bother you and your long legs; do you think I am going to exhaust myself on such a day as this? I shall be in time enough for the death, never fear."

"Oh, I can't stand it; he'll be killed. Chester! Chester! ahoy!"

And the youth set off at full speed after his young lieutenant.

When the Donna Caterina's mule first started for what may be called a race of death, he had thrown the rest of the cavalcade into such confusion that no one was in a condition to follow.

Don Guzman's age and anxiety rendered him totally incapable to assist his daughter, could he even have released his feet from his restive mule.

Pedro was at the water's edge, adjusting the cushions of the barge; and of the crowd who saw the donna's predicament, no one had the courage or the thought to stop or intercept the runaway mule.

"Santa Maria! Holy St. Francis! Blessed St. Dominick! Stop him! stop him! Yah! Mother of Heaven, the accursed brute will be over the cliff!"

The above exclamations came from the crowd of spectators, who, finding their lungs more obedient than their legs, shouted in chorus, adding by every cry additional speed and terror to the frightened animal.

So rapidly had the whole incident passed, that Chester's hat, which he had raised in respect to the ex-governor and his daughter, was still in his hand when the mule rushed by him.

Regardless of the unequal race, or the steep incline of the grassy mountain, the young lieutenant bounded after the mule, straining every nerve to overtake and get before the terrified animal.

Finding it impossible to head the maddened brute, Chester threw open his arms, and implored the frightened girl, who still courageously kept her seat, to fling herself off.

But the heretic's language was Greek to the terrified Caterina.

There was, however, no mistaking the look of agony

with which he flung his hat over the precipice not a dozen yards from where he stood.

Nor could she mistake the imploring cry with which he flung his arms open for the last time to receive her.

The disappearing hat of the lieutenant first aroused Caterina to the awful nearness of her danger. The truth fell on her with crushing intensity.

Uttering one faint agonising cry, she flung herself from the mule, and fell insensible into the arms and around the neck of Chester.

Scarcely was he conscious that he held the lovely donna in his embrace, when the mule sprang from the precipice, and was instantly lost to sight.

A shout of joy told Don Guzman of the safety of his child before he had the courage to raise his head from the shoulder of the man on whom he leant for support.

He saw that Caterina was safe in the arms of the strange Englishman, and motioned to his servants to lead him to the barge.

Scarcely had the old man—years older by those few moments of agony—taken his seat, when the young lieutenant placed his foot on the gunwale of the state galley.

Pausing a moment to remove the maiden's unconfined hair from his eyes and mouth, before he resigned her to the outstretched arms of her women, he bent down to take one last look of that still and placid face.

As he gazed on her death-like countenance, Caterina opened her eyes and met that deep and anxious look, that seemed to search her to the soul.

For an instant she encountered the glance with soft and glistening orbs, and then those envious clouds, the snowy lids, seemed in a moment to shut out the sun and light from the young sailor's heart.

Resigning her to her women, Chester felt his hand firmly grasped, as Don Guzman, almost unable to speak, drew him down to whisper—

"We shall meet again, young man, when I shall be better able to thank you than I can do now. The Holy Mother bless you! and the Lord have you in his keeping. Farewell!"

And nervously pressing his hand to his lips, the don gave a sign, and the barge grated over the shelly beach.

As the boat rocked in the deep water, Caterina lifted her head from her father's shoulder, and catching the wistful glance of Chester, muttered some soft Spanish word of thanks and farewell.

Then, as if she felt she had not done enough, she waved her hand, and as the crew dipped their oars, she half rose from her seat, and cast her handkerchief towards the shore.

Swift as a hawk pounces on his prey, the lieutenant sprang breast deep into the sea, and caught the dainty fabric ere the brine could soil its perfumed texture.

CHAPTER II.

THE FATE OF THE "SANTISSIMA MARIA."

On the fourth morning after the events of our last chapter, the Spanish galleon, the "Santissima Maria," with the year's revenue of the Island of Cuba, and the private fortune and family of its late governor, had worked clear of the rocks and shoals of the Antilles.

The last of the farthest group of barren keys and verdant isles, had faded in the western horizon, and the broad blue Atlantic stretched like a heaving plain of azure on every side.

Two objects alone broke the magnificent monotony of this matchless scene of sky and water.

The one was the slow sailing and cumbersome galleon, which, with every inch of canvas set, was gently forging ahead, as she not ungracefully rose and fell on the long heaving billows.

The other object formed a marked contrast to the first.

This was a tall, graceful, square-rigged, clipper-looking frigate, that with topsails and courses, cleft the sea with the velocity of a shark pursuing its prey.

The loose cordage and clumsy sails of the "Santissima Maria," set off to tenfold advantage the tapering spars and taut lines of the frigate, whose shrouds, like threads of gossamer, cut the blue sky with their sharp tracery.

From the nearness of the two vessels it was evident that the graceful frigate on the galleon's beam meant to overtake, or, at least, speak the Spaniard.

If such an idea had entered the mind of the captain of the "Santissima Maria," he certainly took no heed of the stranger's wish, implied or understood, but, wrapped in his sense of national dignity, kept the even tenor of his way.

A stream of fire, and a puff of white smoke, leaped like a flash of lightning from the deck of the frigate.

Before the boom of the heavy gun had struck the ear of a soul on board the galleon, a shot crossed her forfoot, and, with a heavy plash, dropped into the sea, a dozen fathoms from her bows.

There was a language in that shot which the Spanish captain could not possibly misunderstand, though it took several minutes before his tardy crew could reply to it.

Slowly, at length, however, the towers and sword of Castile and Arragon rose over the ship's canvas, and the golden field of Spain spread its folds on the breeze.

That this was not the object of the stranger's salute, was instantly made evident by the firing of a second shot.

Instead, however, of aiming across the Spaniard's bows, the second missive was sent with such true effect, that it struck the foremast about ten feet from the deck.

The next instant, with a fearful crash, the mast, with all its spars and top hamper, fell in thundering disorder over the ship's side.

Before the foremast had touched the water, a second crash forward, and a louder one aloft, with the falling of blocks, sails and spars, told of the shivered bowsprit and the ruined maintop, that hung a perfect wreck against the strained mizen.

The ruin and confusion was complete, and long before the enraged captain of the galleon could obey the frigate's behest, and take in sail, the impatient officer of that vessel poured in a broadside from his deck guns.

It took a few moments for the astonished Spaniard to recover his horror at the audacity of the man who could dare to make a target of his Catholic Majesty's flag.

But when that sacred emblem was seen draggling on the blood-stained deck, the captain's rage knew no bounds. He shouted to his men to fire.

The next instant, three of the six guns he carried, more for show than use, were discharged against the bulwarks of the audacious stranger, whose only cognizance was a strip of red bunting.

Whether the stranger was annoyed by the return of his fire, or enraged by the mischief effected by the grape shot, with which the pop-guns were charged, it was impossible to say.

But half-a-dozen boats instantly shot from under the frigate's stern, and while her lower ports were thrown open, twenty formidable muzzles peered ominously from the ribs of her shapely side.

The fighting seemed to have ceased as suddenly as it had begun, only the graceful and treacherous stranger, like a half-sleeping tiger, lay indolently rising and falling on the breathing deep, just showing, as an admonition, the fangs of his starboard battery.

For the next quarter of an hour, the boats, crowded with men, were passing to and fro, in rapid succession, from galleon to frigate.

The crew worked like a hive of labouring ants, with such silence and despatch, that when the enterprise was finished, the officer in charge of this duty made a sign to his superior as he walked the poop.

The individual in question, habited in a blue blouse, secured round the loins by a red sash, watched till all the boats were swinging at their davits and the gangway on the gun deck had been removed.

Satisfied on these points, the officer raised his cloth cap, and, on the instant, the whole starboard broadside was discharged, as with the precision of one gun, into the galleon.

A succession of shrieks from the saloon below the frigate's poop, told of the presence and the alarm of women, as their terrible battery poured out its noisy note of death and destruction.

The man in the blue shirt spread his arms on the taffrail, and looked indolently towards the "Santissima Maria."

This vessel, so lately an example of Spanish pride and dignity, now with all her standing rigging gone, or hanging in tattered shreds, lay like a sheer hulk on the blue water.

So at least she had looked the instant before the frigate's broadside struck her bulging ribs.

When the mysterious-looking officer first observed her after the receipt of his starboard battery, the galleon, with her port quarters torn up in frightful rents, from keel to bulwarks, lay like a log on her beam ends.

It was only for a moment, however, that she remained in that perilous position; righting almost in an instant, she rolled heavily to port, and then, with a seeming shudder, settled on an even keel.

The death-warrant of the crew and the hull of the "Santissima Maria" had been signed, and it was but a matter of seconds when the *coup de grace* would be given.

With a cold, unchangeable smile, the stranger watched the rapid sinking of the Spaniard, as her deck became almost level with the ocean.

Distant as the two vessels were from each other, the calm insensible watcher could just discover a sudden commotion among the doomed crew, as the water rushed through the scuppers, and the men looked despairingly at the davits, from which their boats had been forcibly taken.

The old Spanish hull oscillated two or three times, as though violently rocked by some Titan of the deep; and then, as if all strife was over, she quietly settled down.

The waves of the Atlantic rolled over the last inch of the proud flag of Spain, and the "Santissima Maria" vanished for ever from human sight.

The commander of the light and graceful frigate rose quickly to his feet, and, approaching the poop-rail, exclaimed, in a loud, clear voice, but speaking in French—

"Swab the decks and rig the plank."

Like the trumpet to the war-horse, that voice was heard in all parts of the ship, and obeyed with instant alacrity.

A few bodies that had lain about the deck were flung into the sea, and while men with mops and buckets of water were restoring the original whiteness to the main deck, others were lashing up loose cannon, and erecting an apparatus between the fore and main mast.

So rapidly were the captain's orders executed, that when he paused from his short walk across the poop, some fifty of the crew were gathered in the waist of the ship, and about a dozen men with pinioned arms stood in a row before them.

Foremost among the latter was our former acquaintance, Pedro; the rest were made up of Don Guzman's servants and a few of the galleon's crew.

"Have the men been offered terms, Jaques? Do they know the conditions?" asked he of the blue blouse, descending the poop, and surveying the pinioned men.

"Yes; they have been told, but refuse," replied the first lieutenant, a low-browed, scowling-looking villain.

"We have no time to lose; proceed to work," rejoined the captain, carelessly, as he returned to the poop.

"Though I lost my wager about the petticoats and maravedis, old boy, I owe you a good turn, Pedro, and will let no one make a fool of you but myself. Come, don't be a fool, but take the oath," muttered a bearded fellow at the man's side, as he opened his knife to cut his bonds.

Pedro turned suddenly at the well-remembered voice, and recognised in the speaker and his immediate companions the four watermen who had so completely pumped him in their trips to the "Santissima Maria."

"What's the fool staring at?" cried the lieutenant. "Quick! the plank or the oath!"

"Never! I am a Spaniard! Death before dishonour!" exclaimed Pedro, shaking off the kindly-meant touch of the bearded sailor; and, mounting the steps, walked firmly to the end of the plank that projected some six feet from the bulwarks.

On reaching the extremity of the board, he raised his face to the sky, and muttering, "Holy Mother intercede for me!" sprang into the water and instantly disappeared.

Two more mounted the steps, and, as if emulous for death, bounded off the fatal plank, and, like Pedro, sunk in an instant.

"The oath! we'll take the oath!" exclaimed the remaining prisoners, who thereupon were at once unbound and led below.

"Clear the decks, open the stern ports, and ease her off half a point."

As the captain spoke, he entered his cabin under the poop; and the ship, so lately the scene of confusion and death, pursued her course, as if no such deed of murder had been perpetrated.

CHAPTER III.

THE "FLIRT" AND THE "VIXEN."

"I am as much in the dark on this matter as you are yourself, Caterina," observed Don Guzman, as he walked up and down the elegant cabin of the strange vessel, in reply to some remark of his pale and terrified daughter.

"You do not think, then, that we have fallen into the hands of some remorseless pirate," Caterina asked, timidly, as she crouched into a corner of the sofa, where, with her women, she had taken refuge.

For an instant the face of Don Guzman assumed a paler shade than natural; but it was only for a moment, for, with a flushed brow and a petulant exclamation, he suddenly stopped, and replied hastily—

"How foolishly you talk, Caterina; this is only some international affair, for which his country will have to make ample atonement."

"What country, papa?"

"We shall very soon know that, depend upon it.

That is say—look here, Caterina; there are my private coffers, and the government revenue, placed with us in this cabin."

And he pointed to a number of chests placed in one corner of the saloon.

"Besides," he added complacently, "I am allowed to wear my sword, and you see the shutters have been removed from the cabin windows."

At this junction the door was opened, and a valet, entering, exclaimed, in French—

"The captain, M. Moncerf."

The individual designated by that name immediately entered the cabin; and, in the most courteous and affable manner, bowed, and introduced himself to father and daughter.

The blouse and red sash had been thrown aside, and from head to heel, with hat in hand, he now appeared in the complete costume of a French naval commander.

Inviting Don Guzman and Caterina on deck while the servants arranged the disordered cabin, the captain obligingly led the way to seats on the poop.

"Holy Virgin! what has become of the 'Santissima Maria?'" ejaculated Caterina, after a rapid inspection of the surrounding sea.

"Ah, why will the lovely Donna Caterina distress her gentle nature by thoughts of traitors?" observed Moncerf, with one of his most obsequious bows.

Though in age little turned of forty, and dressed with the utmost care and elegance, Moncerf's once handsome face, had, from dissipation or passion, acquired so hard and sinister an expression, that the donna turned almost in fear from the bold gaze with which he greeted her.

"Traitors, Captain Moncerf?" asked the don, equally astonished with his daughter. "And prey what has become of the galleon?"

"Nay, Don Guzman, as a soldier, you will understand when I say she has suffered the fortune of war; her fate might possible have been mine."

"Am I to understand, captain, that, in obedience to your orders, this duty has been imposed upon you?"

"Unquestionably, as your excellency has said."

"Then, I presume, we are now under the French flag?"

"Can your excellency doubt it?"

"And the name of your vessel, captain, is——"

"'The Flirt.'"

"'Tis a strange name for a French frigate. And what may be your armament?"

"We are pierced for forty guns, but can mount more," replied the captain, carelessly, as he turned to his first lieutenant. "Well, Jaques, what is the glass for? Was my surmise correct?"

"It was," was the short and sullen reply.

"So, the bull-dog is bent on showing his teeth," replied the captain, with a low laugh, as he took the ship's glass, and swept the southern horizon.

"Has your excellency any idea of the character of that sail yonder, on our starboard quarter?" he continued, with a pleased smile, pointing, as he spoke, to a ship under full sail, some three or four leagues distant.

"No, captain, I confess my ignorance of all such matters; I only understand she is coming on very fast."

"Yes, she is coming on, as we sailors say, hand over hand, and she is bringing the wind with her, too. Mon Dieu! the old tub sails well."

"You do not think her so fine a vessel as your own?"

"Mon Dieu! no. Has your excellency eyes? The 'Flirt' is a very gem of a ship. That hulk, bah!"

"If I mistake not, she is flying the English colours; your country is at war with Britain?" the don asked, inquiringly.

"Yes; we generally have a quarrel on, we love each other so dearly."

"Then you mean to fight him?"

"No, your excellency, I shall not fight him."

"What! you will——?"

"I shall sink him."

"She is a war-ship, and I should think much of your own size and strength," replied the don, inspecting the coming ship through the telescope.

"She is called the 'Vixen,' mounts twenty-six guns, and carries a crew of two hundred and sixty men."

"I see you are short handed, for I observe your crew is very small, therefore it is policy to avoid an action."

"Your excellency is mistaken, I shall not avoid the 'Vixen,' but yet I shall sink her."

And Moncerf concentrated a fearful amount of deadly hatred in his voice as he repeated the words, "sink her."

"You are as good as a gazette, captain; knowing her guns and crew, perhaps you are familiar with her commander's name?"

"Oh, yes, his name is Watson—Commodore Watson."

"What, he who, when in charge of the 'Brunswick,' cleared the coast of that buccaneering French rascal, whom the Dutch say they hung at his own mast-head some four years ago?"

Had the don's attention not been engaged watching the "Vixen" he must have seen the dark and deadly scowl on the captain's face, as he answered indifferently—

"The same."

"Then you have met this Englishman before?"

"Yes; we had a passing acquaintance before I left this station for the China seas."

"But you must have met since then?"

"About three months ago I heard there was a divinity at the Havannah, whom not to see and love was to have no eyes, no soul, no being," exclaimed Moncerf, with passionate fervour.

"But being a Frenchman, and possessed of those properties, you saw and were enamoured?"

"Your excellency shall hear. I had just seen the enchanting beauty in the theatre, and was hastening to offer her the eternal homage of my hand and heart."

"A declaration of love in a theatre, captain?"

"Why not? I was sure of being accepted. My destined bride was before me, when that Englishman, the captain of yonder corvette, met me in the lobby. He had just arrived at the Havannah with his leaky old tub for repairs."

"Then you met each other in the box lobby of the theatre?"

"Precisely. The recognition was mutual and decisive. We retired to arrange preliminaries for a future meeting, and, will you believe it, donna?" the captain continued, smiling and bowing to Caterina.

"Believe what, Captain Moncerf?"

"That that untoward rencontre debarred me of the happiness of flinging myself at your feet."

"Were you in the theatre on the night of my visit?" she asked, with a tone more of surprise than interest.

"And am I to understand that this is a purposed meeting for a duello between the 'Flirt' and the 'Vixen?'" asked Don Guzman, by no means relishing the tone of insolent gallantry assumed by the French commander towards his daughter.

NAUTICAL TALES;
OR, ADVENTURES BY SEA AND LAND.

THE BUCCANEERS IN ACTION.

THE LAST OF THE BUCCANEERS;
OR, THE FLIRT AND THE VIXEN.

CONCLUSION.

"It is a long time after the provocation to seek redress—three months; but then these English are so droll," and he smiled complacently.

"My sovereign being at peace with England, I shall be compelled to stand neuter in this action. Still, I wish your crew was stronger."

And his excellency glanced at the knots of sailors who had collected in the bows and waist of the ship, and seemed to eye the coming corvette with uneasy and anxious glances.

Moncerf, with a smile at Don Guzman's doubts, gave a sign to Jaques, who, by a like means, passed the signal forward.

The sudden sound of a drum beating the rappel was heard instantly traversing the lower decks of the "Flirt," and, a moment after, a perfect swarm of human beings poured up on deck, and crowded into every foot of the stately ship.

From stern to stern guns were cast loose, tompions withdrawn, and, with linstock, ramrod, and sponge, every gunner was at his post.

While this sudden and startling scene was taking place on deck, a perfect hive of men had flung themselves on the several shrouds, and, like a confused multitude of busy pigmies, were seen hurrying up the ratlines.

At the first sight of the black, scowling villains, who streamed up from every hatchway and companion, fore and aft, Caterina had grasped her father's hand, and, with a convulsive clutch, gazed with an alarmed look in the don's face.

Before her lips could frame a word of alarm, however, every man on deck had sunk beside his gun, under the shelter of the high bulwarks, or had shrank from sight behind the netting of the tops and cross-trees; while from spindle to deck—except a few hands to shorten sail, and an officer or two—not a man was visible of the many hundreds on board.

"It is a singular fact, Don Guzman, that a heretic does that which neither his Catholic nor his Christian majesty allows."

"In what respect, captain?"

"Why, the heretical English allow a *padre*—or chaplain, as they term him—to nearly every vessel in the service; while our august masters think one confessor to a thousand men is quite enough."

"Then there is a chaplain on board the 'Vixen?'"

"Exactly so; and that I may secure his good offices, is the reason why I shall send a boat to invite him aboard the 'Flirt.'"

"For what purpose?"

"Ah! if the donna only knew my heart," replied the captain, bowing and smiling to Caterina, "she would know what a slave I am to the most lovely of her sex, and that, to calm a lady's prejudices, I would travel half a world."

"What prejudices, may I ask?"

"Ah! adorable Caterina! you put me to my shrift. There are many forms and ceremonies of life to which the mind of a gentle lady would think the hand of a padre indispensable; such as——"

"Such, captain, as——"

"Marriage, for instance."

Donna Caterina instantly rose, and pointing to the fast-approaching corvette, took her father's arm and moved towards the companion.

"As that blundering heretic may take it into his head to bark without any warning, and as you, Don Guzman, can have no interest in our strife, I must beg you to retire with the donna to a place of safety," Moncerf observed, as the "Vixen" forged within a few cables' length of the "Flirt's" starboard quarter.

With a flushed face and a highly irritated manner Don Guzman led his daughter to the companion.

At that moment the boom of an unshotted gun pealed on the air, and both father and daughter turned involuntarily to look around.

As they did so the towering sails of the "Vixen" seemed almost to overhang the deck of the "Flirt," though, in fact, the two vessels were yet some distance apart.

It was, however, neither the nearness of the antagonist ship nor her cloud of canvas that for an instant spellbound Don Guzman and his daughter.

At the main-truck of the "Flirt," and almost above their heads, spread out that hope-despairing cognizance of the buccaneer.

A black flag, with the skull and cross-bones in white!

"Holy Mother, protect my child!" muttered the ex-governor, as he led the terrified girl to a cabin beneath the water-line, dimly lighted by two ship lanterns.

All remained still and silent on the deck of the "Flirt," as, with St. George's cross at the main, and a commodore's pennon at the fore, the "Vixen" surged majestically up.

With a smile of triumph, Moncerf noted her crowded decks, and observed her open ports, with the lighted linstocks gleaming like fire-flies in the gloomy 'tween-decks of the corvette.

Expecting the "Vixen" to wear ship, and begin the action with her port batteries, Moncerf had kept his crew in close quarters, till he saw the helm of his antagonist put about.

Then, at a signal, in an instant, every man sprang to his gun, and every port was opened for action.

The "Vixen," however, instead of shortening sail, to the astonishment of the Frenchman, carried on, and was crossing the "Flirt's" stern before the order to fire could be executed.

Carrying all the wind with her, the "Vixen" escaped every gun of that fearful battery, and was within a biscuit's cast of her enemy's stern rail when her two mid-ship pivots were fired in passing.

Loaded, one with grape and the other with chain shot, the effect of that discharge on the pirate's crowded main-deck was fearful.

Jaques, Moncerf's first lieutenant, was killed at his captain's side, while the small shot, spreading like hail, carried wounds and death from poop to waist.

It was not, however, the fate of his lieutenant, or the havoc among his crew, that caused Moncerf to stamp so passionately on the deck, and draw his sword with such energy.

It was the effect of the chain shot which, after striking down Jaques, buried itself in the mizen.

So deep had the iron entered the wood, that, at the first touch of the rudder, the tall mast fell with a rending crash over the "Flirt's" port bulwarks, hurling a swarm of small-arm men into the sea, and disabling all the poop and after guns of that side.

Almost at the same instant the "Vixen" rounded on the "Flirt's" port, and poured in the whole of her starboard battery, the pirates replying with all the guns they could bring into action.

In the meantime, a most murderous discharge of firelocks, blunderbusses, and pistols was being exchanged between the men in the tops and rigging of either vessel.

Captain Watson, determined to cripple his foe and prevent all chance of his escape, had placed a small howitzer in his maintop, with special directions to cut up the enemy's spars and sails.

Satisfied with the mischief already done, and what was still being effected by his crew aloft, Captain Watson, without stopping to give another broadside, forged his ship ahead, and boldly crossed the "Flirt's" fore-foot, repeating in the bows of the pirate the fire of his pivots, which had already been so destructive over the poop.

A few more turns of the wheel laid the corvette yard-arm to yard-arm, on the pirate's starboard beam.

The fight, which had hitherto consisted chiefly of a few nautical manœuvres on the part of the English commander, now became a close and deadly battle, carried on upon the one side with all the desperation of men fighting for their lives, and on the other by men determined to die or conquer.

For fifteen minutes the pirates fought their guns with all the energy and determination of invincible courage, and though their decks were covered with dead, and their guns unmanageable with the heaps of slain, they still fought bravely on.

The corvette, in the meantime, had suffered a severe but not an equal loss, the crowded state of the pirate's decks exposing him to a frightful carnage.

It was in her rigging, however, that the "Flirt" had suffered her most fatal injury.

All her sails and standing gear hung in ribbons, and the "Vixen" lying to windward, cut off all chance of escape.

During a momentary pause, while the pirate's crew rolled their dead into the sea, and cleared their guns for further action, the "Flirt's" foremast fell by the board just as Lieutenant Chester, with some twenty or thirty blue jackets, dropped on her deck.

While the two vessels had been closely engaged pouring in their destructive broadsides and doing their utmost to sink or ruin each other, there had been no possibility of boarding on either side.

Shocked by the numbers of the casualties he saw on board his own vessel, Lieutenant Chester, after having in vain attempted to leap from the "Vixen" to the "Flirt," suddenly conceived the idea of dropping on her deck.

At the moment the enemy's foremast went by the board, Chester sprang into the ratlines, and was scarcely a minute gaining the maintop.

Here, addressing the men in charge of the gun that had just effected such service, he called on them to follow him.

Swinging himself to the next spar, Chester, waving his cutlass, ran along the narrow and giddy mainyard with the facility of a cat.

In less than a minute thirty men, Indian fashion, were hurrying along the unsteady spar, eager to back their favourite lieutenant.

The enthusiastic youth, grasping his cutlass between his teeth, seized a loose halyard, and the next instant was on the deck of the "Flirt," in the midst of a crowd of ferocious enemies.

"Thank you, Pelham. You've given that fellow his grog at all events," exclaimed Chester, as the young midshipman we have already mentioned, parrying a blow at Chester's head, shot the pirate dead with his pistol.

It was not to be supposed that the buccaneers would tamely submit to have their vessel taken by storm, or would resign an inch of deck while a man was left to dispute possession.

A body of combatants consequently gathered round Chester and his party, and a hand-to-hand encounter of a deadly and ferocious nature instantly ensued.

Captain Watson, having watched Chester's courageous manœuvre, poured in another broadside from his lower guns, and then running his ship close alongside the "Flirt," headed his boarders as he hurried forward to the bows.

A minute later he had cleared the pirate's taffrail, and had made good his possession of the poop.

The deck of the "Flirt" now became a perfect hell of confusion.

Oaths, shouts and execration rising from the midst of the rattle of musketry, the clash of pike and cutlass, the yells of blasphemy and the groans of the dying.

Moncerf, who saw his best hopes ruined by the superior tactics of his enemy, did all in his power by edging off his ship, and keeping the "Vixen" at a distance, to make his broadsides tell on the corvette.

Now on the poop, the next moment in the bows, the gun-deck or the waist, wherever danger threatened or duty called, Moncerf like a dauntless leader, was at every post.

Narrowly escaping the death that hurried a score of his crew into eternity, by the fall of the foremast, the buccaneer chief was just in time to cross swords with Chester, as he touched the deck of the "Flirt."

A rush of blue jackets, however, soon separated the two leaders, and Moncerf, after stretching two of the English at his feet, hastened to the quarter-deck, exclaiming to his second officer—

"Tell off a score of men to launch and rig the long-boat; see to arms, water, and provisions, and when all is ready, stow away the treasure. Quick!"

"At the port-bows or the gangway?" inquired the sub-lieutenant.

"No; bring her to the stern windows."

Seeing his men giving way before Chester, he rushed back, and, with voice and action, led them again to the fight, and the next instant disappeared from the sight of his crew.

It was at this moment, with a loud shout, that Captain Watson and his boarders took possession of the buccaneer's poop.

As these rushed forward, Chester for the second time drove back his enemies, and the next minute, with a ringing cheer, the two parties united.

While captain Watson was sweeping the deck, and driving the pirates down the hatchways, Chester and Pelham were hauling down the black flag, and hoisting St. George's Cross at the peak of the captured "Flirt."

"Trail that gun aft, and give those villains on the gun-deck a taste of grape; they have been twice summoned to surrender."

With extraordinary dispatch the captain's order was obeyed, and, as the pirates still fired up the hatches, the muzzle of a gun was depressed over the combings of the main-hatchway, and fired on the desperate crew below.

With the thunder of that report all sound of strife and battle ceased, as in a moment.

"I have drowned the magazine, your honour; and the men have thrown down their arms," observed a quarter-master, coming up to the captain.

"Look to the lights, and have the prisoners handcuffed. What now?"

"I think there are women on board, your honour; for I heard a terrible screaming on the after part of the orlop deck," replied the officer to his captain's question.

"Women? Go, Chester, and see what it means."

The young lieutenant, with Pelham, the quartermaster, and a few sailors, made an instant rush for the companion, and were quickly lost to sight.

Chester was passing the cabin door to reach the orlop deck, when the voice of Moncerf was heard exclaiming—

"Quick! bring the boat under the stern window. Now, donna, your hand. Stand back, old man; back, or by heaven I'll lay you at my feet."

"Back, thou infamous cutthroat, detested pirate. Come on, now, Santa Maria," replied Don Guzman, throwing himself before his daughter.

Moncerf gave a loud laugh, and the next instant was heard the clash of swords, followed by the piercing shriek of Caterina, as she cried—

"Save my father! Oh! Holy Mother, my father!"

Chester heard no more, but, springing back, dashed open the door and confronted the buccaneer.

Don Guzman, disarmed and beaten down, was on his knee in the centre of the cabin, while his daughter covered his defenceless person with her body.

With his face dark with rage and disappointment, Moncerf grasped one of Caterina's arms, while he held the point of his sword within an inch of the old man's throat.

"Move but a finger, and you are dead. The boat, there, quick! Come, Caterina."

And the buccaneer attempted to drag her from her father's breast.

"Infamous villain, let go the lady!" cried Chester, springing forward, and dashing up Moncerf's sword.

With a cry of joy and confidence, Caterina wrested herself from the grasp of the pirate, and threw herself in the arms of the young lieutenant, while Pelham placed himself before the old man.

The passion of Moncerf at finding himself robbed of his lovely prize was perfectly furious, and putting all his strength in one thrust, he made a deadly lunge at Chester's heart.

The lieutenant had scarcely time to save himself and Caterina by a dexterous parry, when Pelham's hanger was driven through the pirate's chest under his sword arm.

"A thousand curses!" gasped Moncerf, as he half turned on his heel, and with an abortive stroke at the midshipman's head, fell lifeless at the feet of the rescued Caterina.

Two hours later, all evidences of slaughter having been removed from either vessel, the corvette and her prize were proceeding under easy sail for Europe.

By the time the "Vixen" reached Cadiz, both Don Guzman and Caterina had found time to thank the lieutenant for his acts of timely service, and a few months later the donna rewarded her handsome preserver with her hand and the devotion of her love.

THE END.

SAVING OF THE MAGAZINE AT JERSEY.

On Monday, the 4th of June, 1804, being the anniversary of the birth-day of our sovereign, all the forts of this island fired a royal salute, by order of his Excellency the Commander-in-Chief; the guns of the New Fort on the Mount of the town were also fired; after which a corporal of the invalid company of artillery having received the matches, deposited the same in the powder-magazine at the top of the mount, which is bomb proof, and in which were 209 barrels of gunpowder, bombshells ready filled, chests full of all kinds of cartridges, and a large quantity of other combustibles.

The magazine was then locked, and the keys carried out of the fort.

About six o'clock in the evening, at which time the officer on guard is usually at dinner with the other officers of his regiment, the soldiers perceived smoke issuing from an air-hole at one end of the magazine, upon which they immediately began to leave the fort; Mr. Lys, the officer of the signals, then being at his post in the watch-tower, on the top of the Mount, observing the confusion among the soldiers, and hearing some of them call out "Fire!" immediately went down, and before they had all left the fort, plainly perceived the smoke issuing from the two air-holes at each end of the magazine.

At this instant he met Thomas and Edward Touzel, brothers, carpenters in his employ, coming to assist in lowering down the ensign staff, which they had put up in the morning for the purpose of celebrating the day.

Mr. Lys directly sent Thomas Touzel to his Excellency the Commander-in-Chief, to acquaint him with the dangerous situation of the magazine, and to Captain Salmon of the artillery for the keys.

Thomas Touzel, before he went away, endeavoured by every means in his power to prevail on his brother Edward to leave the place, representing to him the imminent danger he was exposed to if he remained; but Edward Touzel answered, that "as he must die one day or other, he was ready to sacrifice his life at that moment in endeavouring to save the magazine and town from destruction;" and observing a soldier going away, called to him to stop and help him to break open the door, which, however, the soldier refused; he then asked another soldier, William Penteney, belonging to the light company of the 31st regiment, who immediately acquiesced, saying—

"He was ready to die with him."

Having shook hands together, Edward Touzel snatched up a bar of wood, and broke the barrier of the pallisade which surrounds the magazine, and with a hatchet which he accidently found in his way, knocked off the padlock of the inner barrier, by which means he got access to the door, knocked off both the padlocks, and entered the magazine.

He then called to Mr. Lys, who stood on the outside, "that the magazine was on fire, and they should all inevitably be blown up!" Adding, "Never mind, we must try to save it, huzza! God save the king."

So saying, he instantly seized the bundles of linstocks with their matches on fire, and the handles almost entirely burnt, and threw them out to Mr. Lys and William Penteney.

Mr. Lys found a cask of water near the magazine, but having no bucket, he and William Penteney, with their hats and a small pitcher, conveyed water to Edward Touzel, who remained within, but whom they could hardly see for smoke.

Edward Touzel quenched the fire with the water they brought him, and as soon as he had extinguished all that appeared, called to Mr. Lys that he was almost suffocated, and requested some refreshment.

His hands and face were very much scorched.

By this time many persons had come to their assistance, and Mr. Lys having procured a glass of spirits and water for Edward Touzel, he drank it, and soon after began to revive.

Thus, thanks be to God, and next to Him to the intrepid courage of Edward Touzel in particular, and to Mr. Lys and William Penteney, the fire was got under.

Captain Leith of the 31st, and Mr. Murphy of the same regiment, the officer on guard, together with several other officers, on being informed of the danger, immediately repaired to the spot with such soldiers as they could collect; and Captain Leith who commanded, as well as the other officers, used extraordinary exertions in emptying the magazine, so that no spark of fire might remain concealed; when, by a miracle of Divine Providence, which seemed to have interfered to preserve the town of St. Helier and its inhabitants from the dreadful calamity which threatened them, they discovered two more boxes of ammunition on fire, in which were several powder-horns filled, several port-fires and tubes with a cartridge full of powder, near that part of the box which was burning, the flannel of which was actually singed; and an open barrel of gunpowder near it, to which the fire would inevitably have been communicated.

A rammer of a gun was almost consumed, and several of the rafters of the magazine on fire.

This action was communicated to the committee of the Patriotic Fund in London, who immediately resolved that the sum of five hundred pounds be presented to Lieutenant Philip Lys, having a wife and eight children; the sum of three hundred pounds to Edward Touzel; and that an annuity of twenty pounds for life be settled on William Penteney.

NAUTICAL TALES;

OR, ADVENTURES BY SEA AND LAND.

THE CRUISE OF THE TIGER;
OR, THE ADVENTURES OF SIR THOMAS CAVENDISH.

It was on a bright spring day, in the first week of April, 1581, that Queen Elizabeth, having dined at Deptford, on board the ship in which Drake circumnavigated the world, threw herself back in her chair to listen to the recitals of daring and adventure performed by the new-made knight, as, on a stool, removed to a respectful distance, the narrator gave his sovereign the general heads and incidents of his expedition.

The Earl of Leicester, with his son-in-law, the handsome young Essex, Sir Walter Raleigh, and many other nobles and royal favourites, stood on either side of the regal seat, while her ladies and a group of less important personages filled up the space behind.

Leaning on the back of the Queen's chair, however, was a youth who demands our special notice.

His rich but plain dress, with the cap and feather he held in his hand, showed that he had no claim to the title of either courtier or nobleman, while his lithe graceful figure, and his familiar nearness to the sovereign, showed that he held some post about the Queen's person, probably that of page in waiting.

The handsome youth listened with eyes, ears, and every faculty of his soul, to the wonderful accounts of peril, riches, and adventure, as they fell from the lips of the weather-beaten narrator.

"How now, master Cavendish?" exclaimed Elizabeth, sharply, as, at the conclusion of Drake's narrative, she rose and turned abruptly on the astonished youth.

"Fore heaven! hast thou a mind to be our tirewoman, that thou standest between us and our maidens?" she continued, as several of her ladies rising from a bench behind the royal chair advanced towards their mistress.

"Pardon me, your grace," replied the confused youth, kneeling as he spoke; "but I was so wrapt in Sir Francis's wonderful recital, that I dared, for a time, even to forget my sovereign."

"'Twas a marvellous tale I grant," replied Elizabeth, pacified by the homage and candour of the youth. "And such young bloods as thou, might win our favor, and do worse than give the haughty Don a few more such homely lessons."

"Sir Francis," she added, addressing Drake, as she moved from under the rich awning that had been spread on deck for her reception, "we thank you for your good cheer, and will, ere long, find you still more noble occupation in our own service."

Gathering her ladies round her, she continued in the most gracious manner:

"Fare you well, gentlemen. Forget not, Sir Francis, to visit us at Greenwich; we would advise with thee on matters touching our fair new ships at Woolwich."

Extending her hand to be kissed by the kneeling Sir Francis, Elizabeth and her obsequious courtiers quitted the ship, which was then the pride and wonder of the nation; and, with her ladies, entered the clumsy waggon, at that time called a coach, when the procession set out for the palace at Greenwich.

If young Thomas Cavendish had been entranced by the recital of the bold and wondrous achievements of Drake in the Pacific or Southern Ocean, the few words of the Queen had fired his imagination to such a degree that from that hour, one thought, and one only, took absolute possession of his mind.

That thought was how to win the Queen's favour, and earn wealth, honour and fame, in some degree worthy of mention, beside the achievements of the honored Sir Francis Drake.

For the next four years, this idea, shaped into a rude scheme of adventure, formed the ruling principle of the young man's life.

Had he been a tried navigator, Elizabeth might have assisted him with ships or money; or, had he possessed a reputation or title, some of the rich merchants of London would have come forward with capital to further any bold or promising adventure.

But, as an unknown and friendless speculator, he found himself without a friend to advise or encourage him.

A few years prior to the above circumstance, the father of young Cavendish, a wealthy landed proprietor of Devonshire, had died, leaving to his only son Thomas a large fortune in ready money, and a landed estate of great value.

By the influence of his friends, young Cavendish seems to have been introduced at Court, where his youth, good looks, and social qualities, soon made him a favorite, not only with the Queen, but among his compeers and courtly companions.

As he grew to man's estate, he was seized with a passion for the universal extravagance of the period, a taste for splendid dress, rich furniture and external display, which Elizabeth, with all her prudence, rather encouraged than censured in her courtiers.

By such means as these, and the other prevalent vices of the time, Cavendish had by the period when he reached his twenty-third year, totally dissipated the ample fortune left to him by his father.

When, therefore, Elizabeth hinted at a way in which he might obtain fame and her royal favour, he was literally without means; and, beyond the slight stipend he derived from the Privy purse as a hanger on of the court, he possessed nothing.

His friends could not, or would not, further his romantic passion, and the rich merchants who could fit out expeditions for a Hawkins, a Frobisher, or a Raleigh, turned a contemptuous ear to the appeals of the untried enthusiast.

At last, young Cavendish resolved to sacrifice all future prospects in the furtherance of his one cherished idea, and determined either to become a rich and illustrious man or to die a beggar.

To effect this, he mortgaged or sold his estate, and, with the money it realised, began the preparations for his daring adventure, upon his own resources.

Most of the youths of Cornwall and Devonshire, in that age, seem to have been born with a passionate love for the sea; young Cavendish formed no exception to this general rule, and to this strong love of the sea he appears to have added a thorough knowledge of navigation, with all the qualities of a good sailor.

Having once possessed himself of sufficient means to start an enterprise, it took but a short time to fill in the details.

Ships and provisions were purchased, and volunteers flocked from all quarters; the great difficulty of the young commander being to select the best men out of the numbers who presented themselves.

This expedition consisted of a squadron of three small vessels. The largest, the "Tiger," was only a hundred and twenty tons burthen, while the "Hawk," the next in size, was but sixty tons, and the "Lapwing," the third, was only registered at forty tons.

This squadron was manned by a hundred and twenty three, officers and men, all told, and on the morning of July 21st, 1586, Thomas Cavendish, going on board the "Tiger," set sail from Plymouth Sound, and stood down channel before a favorable breeze.

So inflamed were the passions, and so brilliant the fancies, of every individual, with the hope of reaping incalculable wealth from this enterprise, that, from the commander to the meanest ship boy, nothing was seen or heard but rejoicing and gladness at the prospect before them.

The dangers, privations, and weariness of the long voyage they had to brave, with the smallness of the ships in which they were about to risk their lives and fortunes, were all for the time forgot in the hope of adventure, and the wild thirst for riches.

After a few slight inconveniencies, Cavendish reached the latitude of the Canaries; and running down the western coast of Africa, put into Sierra Leone, where, staying a week to wood and water and refresh his crew, he again put to sea at the beginning of October.

Crossing the Atlantic, he steered for the mouth of the Gulf of Mexico, hoping to be able to capture one of the rich galleons bound to Spain, either from the islands or the continent.

But after waiting for several days and failing to make a prize, Cavendish directed his course due south, and running down the South American coast, crossed the equator and continued his route, till in latitude 10 deg. south, he stood in for the Brazilian shore, and, attacking the town of St. Lucia, compelled the inhabitants to ransom their lives and houses with a round sum of money and a considerable number of live cattle.

The success of this undertaking was, in many ways, beneficial to the young commander; the cattle supplied his ships with an abundance of fresh provisions, and the want of which the crews already began to experience.

The ransom, too, paid by the Spaniards for their town, though by no means large, was sufficient to keep his men in good humour, many of them having shown great discontent at their want of success, while cruising in the Gulf of Mexico.

But that which proved of most importance to Thomas Cavendish, was the able and spirited manner in which he had led the attack on St. Lucia, in face of the armed inhabitants, and the way in which he captured their town, without the loss of a man on his own side.

Up to this time, not one of his crew knew of what mettle their leader was made; but in this affair he gave such proof of bravery and judgment, that his men instantly formed a high opinion of his genius and capabilities.

Taking advantage of the good understanding among his crew, Cavendish again put to sea, and, holding still a southerly course, took every advantage of a nor'-easterly wind to reach the great point of his voyage, while the season was still favorable for his passage of the Straits of Magellan.

The great aim and ambition of Cavendish had been, from the first, to reach the Pacific ocean, and repeat on the coasts of Peru and Mexico, or New Spain, some of those achievements which had given such *eclât* to the narrative of Drake.

As yet, he had confided this secret intention only to his lieutenant, Richard Winter, a son of the celebrated captain of that name; and Winter, though fully agreeing to all his friend's plans, saw more clearly than his leader all the risks and positive dangers of such a course.

"What greater risk can we incur in threading these narrow waters of Magellan, than we hourly brave here on the Atlantic?" inquired Cavendish, as he and the lieutenant sat on the raised stern of the "Tiger," in close conversation on their future proceedings.

"I see many and grave ones," replied his chief officer.

"Tell me them freely; you know, Winter, I have implicit confidence in your judgment."

"First, I do not believe, with the exception of myself, there is a man in our squadron who has ever seen the Horn, as they call the Southern Cape; or the Straits of Magellan."

"So much the better; they will the more readily follow where we lead. But go on."

"The Straits are beset with dangerous shoals, rocks, and whirlpools; while the winds either blow in a hurricane, or, after baffling the mariner for days, fall to a dead calm."

"All these dangers Drake surmounted; and, by God's help, so will we!" exclaimed the enthusiastic Cavendish.

"I have no fear on that head; what the Spaniard or Portuguese can do, 'twere foul wrong to think an Englishman could not achieve."

"What other fear hast thou?"

"The discontent, if not mutiny, of the men, when they see the rocky jaws through which they must needs pass."

"By heaven, I'll shoot the first craven who dares to show a sign of fear!" cried Cavendish, laying his hand on the stock of one of his pistols.

"You will not find me far from your side, if it must come to that; but I would rather navigate the Straits with a crew of merry dogs than sulky men," added Winter, confidently.

"Where lies thy meaning, for I see thou hast one?" asked Cavendish.

"I'll put it level before thee," replied the lieutenant, bluntly.

"Speak on."

"The men believe we are running thus far south to attack the Spaniards in their rich possessions on the Plate river."

"And so I would, but, by the delay, we should lose the season for the passage of the Straits, and be thrown back for the best part of a year."

"I know it; but if we pass the Rio Plata, the crews will grow mutinous, or insist on returning to the Gulf."

"I will signal the 'Hawk' and 'Lapwing,' and tell the men at once what glorious fortune awaits us in the Pacific," exclaimed Cavendish, rising quickly.

"Sail ho!" cried a youth from the mast-head.

"A moment; tarry, captain," replied Winter, laying his hand on Cavendish's arm; as he cried in reply to the sailor.

"Aye, aye! Where away?"

"Here on our starboard bow. Land ho!" exclaimed

the same speaker from aloft. "Land low down on the west."

"It is Cape Maria; I thought we must be well up with it," added Winter, addressing Cavendish.

Then in a confidential whisper he added:

"If that sail is one of the Don's treasure ships, bound for San Sebastiano to wait the fleet, and we can take her, the men would face ten thousand devils without a murmur."

"Then, by heaven! she shall be ours. Signal, 'Enemy in sight, and a prize!'" cried Cavendish, addressing the master, as Winter mounted the rigging to examine the distant sail.

The sailing master had scarcely complied with his captain's order, and reported the two vessels as having answered the signals, when the lieutenant returned on deck.

"What do you make of her, Master Winter?" asked the young leader, eagerly, as his friend hurried aft to where he stood. "What is she?"

"A full rigged carrack, with good fat ribs."

"Then, I'll bet a doubloon to a tester, they'll be worth our picking," put in Enoch the master, rubbing his hands, and grinning with evident delight.

"What's her burthen, think'st thou?"

"Such a craft might stow four, nay, perchance, five hundred tons," replied the lieutenant.

"Fore heaven! a famous prize, and a right royal ship!" responded Cavendish, enthusiastically. "What sayest thou, showed she no flag?"

"Not an inch! her pilot's as cunning as a fox. She's lying to under bare poles."

"How's that; did not the look-out cry 'Sail ho?'"

"Aye, true; and, when we first saw her, she was staggering under every inch of canvas she could spread."

"But now, you say, she's under bare poles?"

"Aye, there's the cunning of the old Spanish fox; the moment he spied us, as he did about the same time that we sighted him, he struck his sails and hauled down his flag, in the hope that his bare spars and white masts would not be seen against the sea and sky."

"I'll bet five pistoles to a Queen Bess penny, that old fox has been in the trap before, and left his brush, or a paw behind him," exclaimed Enoch, slapping his thigh with a report like a pistol.

"By the chart, and our reckoning, Winter, we should be about four leagues from the shore?" said Cavendish, more as a question put to his lieutenant than as a certified fact of his own knowledge.

"Somewhere there about, captain; and that clever old pilot has been hugging the shore as long as possible, and was just putting farther out to sea when we saw him."

"Why should he do so?"

"Because the coast here-away is studded with lagunes and sunken rocks, and the shore they say shelves fearfully."

"If that be the case, then, fore heaven! I'll out-manœuvre the sly dog, cunning as he is." And, springing to the port-gangway, he shouted—

"Lapwing, ahoy!"

As Cavendish hailed, the two vessels, at the moment, in obedience to his signal, were bearing down under all sail, and tearing through the water as if they meant to board or sink the "Tiger."

"'Lapwing,' ahoy!" the leader repeated, as the light craft come bounding within a biscuit cast of the commodore.

"Stand in shore; take soundings as you go, and keep the prize from running on the beach."

A hoarse but indistinct reply came from the cutter, as, like a well managed steed at full speed, the light craft swung round, and hauling in her courses, dashed in a perfect mist of spray and foam past the fore foot of the "Tiger."

Scarcely had the "Lapwing" flashed by the commodore's bows, to execute her missions, when the "Hawk" with all her sails aback, ranged up within speaking distance of the young commander.

"Now, captain, quick please, or that cursed little pink will have all the fun to herself!" exclaimed a husky voice from a seal-skin cap, as the speaker, a weather-beaten old man, stood on the gangway of the "Hawk," holding on by a back-stay.

"Don't be jealous of an old messmate, Carew; Drayton won't have all the fun, as you call it," replied Cavendish, laughing at the old sailor's disappointment.

"You lay the 'Hawk' athwart the Spaniard's hawser, and, if he tries to work north, give him a dose of your supper pills. I'll look after him to windward."

With a grim smile of satisfaction that brought to light a ghastly slash in his cheek, Carew sprang back on the deck of his ship, and, giving his orders, the "Hawk," slowly forged ahead.

"The carrack has set her sails, and is wearing round to the south," shouted the youth from the look-out.

"I thought as much, by Jove!" cried the captain, as he sprang into the mizen shrouds and looked towards the Spanish ship, which, from the altered course of the "Tiger," was now plainly visible to the eager crew.

"The Don has understood our manœuvre, and is trying to run back to port; but I'll have him, if I die in the attempt."

"See how cleverly the 'Lapwing' is working in shore of him, while old Carew is bringing the 'Hawk' down in his wake. Now, Drayton, give him a shot, and make him sheer off the land."

"Hurrah!" shouted Cavendish, as the lieutenant finished speaking, and pointed in the direction of the carrack.

"There! Drayton is speaking already."

At that moment the boom of a gun was heard over the water, and the little "Lapwing" was half hid in smoke.

"See, captain, the carrack has had a slap right in her bows, and is standing out with all sail set, to escape from our little wasp."

"Aye, aye, I see! We'll cross his hawse before another hour's over our heads, or my name's not Cavendish. All hands, aloft!" shouted the captain, now thoroughly roused.

"Set royals and studding sails, and throw out a reef from the spanker!"

With a cheer, the men threw themselves into the rigging, and, like a troop of monkeys, lay out, or ran along the yards, perfectly indifferent to the rolling and pitching of the ship beneath them.

The additional canvas made the "Tiger" heel to leaward, till half her deck was washed by the seas through which she tore, half hid in surge and foam.

"Well done, Carew!" cried the captain, as, some half hour later, the "Hawk" sent a round shot through the carrack's stern windows.

"Ease her off half a point, master, and take in a reef in her topsails; we have her now. Why is the 'Lapwing' backing out, and what's that signal at her peak?" asked Cavendish suddenly of his lieutenant.

"Heave the lead!" shouted Winter to the boatswain before answering his captain.

"Quick there, heave! The water shoals, and the passage is full of rocks," the lieutenant added, turning to his leader.

"Too shallow for the 'Lapwing's draught! yes, by heaven! and see, Winter, the Spaniard knows his ground, and is furling sail. He thinks we cannot touch him."

"Confound the fool! He means to show fight too. Look there, captain, he has unmasked his brazen teeth."

"All the better; they are only deck guns, and bark worse than they bite."

The captain of the Spanish ship, driven off the deep water channel in shore by the "Lapwing," and finding it impossible to regain his port, had availed himself of his knowledge of the coast to run for a deep pool, where the reefs on either side protected his ship as in a dock; the passage by which he had entered being too dangerous to be attempted, by either the "Hawk" or "Tiger."

"Curse that fellow's coolness! there goes his anchor."

"Never mind, Winter, we must cut him out, that's all. Signal crew to cease firing, and save his powder; his guns cannot reach the enemy, ours may. Master at arms!"

"Here I am, commodore!" replied one of the crew, advancing.

"Try the range of your bow guns on the carrack. Now, Winter, order out three of the boats, and tell Drayton and Carew to send one each. There's smooth water yonder, by which we may enter this ugly looking dock."

While Enoch, the master, and Winter were lowering the boats and arming the men, the master gunner had brought one of his pieces to bear on the Spaniard; and the next moment the shattered bulwarks of the carrack were seen flying in all directions.

Evidently enraged at this conduct, the captain of the Spanish ship hoisted the Castilian flag and discharged his whole broadside at the "Tiger," the shot, however, of his small brass guns fell into the sea some fathoms short of their destination.

Without replying to this useless broadside, Cavendish waited till the two boats from his consorts were under his counter, when, giving the word, the men streamed down the ship's side and quickly filled the "Tiger's" boats.

Surprised that the English had not repeated their fire, the Spaniards quietly reloaded their carronades and waited to see when the enemy, who they believed to have been fairly baffled, would sheer off and leave them to resume their voyage in peace.

The sudden appearance of a line of boats startled though it did not discourage the Spaniards, who believed themslves perfectly secure. As the boats neared the reef, the enemy fired his carronades, but this time their shots pased over the heads of those in the boats.

Cavendish, who led the way in the "Tiger's" launch, made for what appeared an opening in the reef, and, dashing into the still water beyond, steered direct for the carrack's bows, followed by his other boats.

The remaining two, under the command of Carew and Drayton, found a channel lower down, and at the same moment made for the carrack's stern.

The Spaniards, amazed at the audacity in attempting to board a vessel so securely placed, were unprepared for the rush of boarders, who, in a moment, stormed their deck, both at stem and stern.

Drawing their swords and pistols, however, they gathered round their captain at the foot of the main-mast, and, for ten minutes, kept up a hot and determined resistance.

Nothing, however, could stand against the furious English onslaught, and their circle was soon broken; and, as the Spanish flag was hauled down, and the thrust of a cutlass brought the captain on his knee, the Spaniards broke into groups and fled.

"Hold hard, messmate!" cried Enoch, parrying a blow at the prostrate captain. "I said the old fox had lost a paw, or he wouldn't have been so cunning; don't you see the poor beggar has expended his larboard fin?"

As the rough sailing master spoke, he grasped the Spanish captain, who was expecting the finishing stroke, by his collar, and setting him on his feet added, while he refused the sword offered him:

"No, no, give that to our commodore; and if your fellows don't want to sup with old Nick, tell 'um to hold hard."

Though the captain did not understand a word of Enoch's speech, he comprehended his gestures, and, seeing the folly of further resistance, called to the Spaniards, who were still hopelessly prolonging the fight, to surrender.

In obedience to this order the crew threw down their arms, and the next minute the ship was in the hands of Cavendish and his band.

To make a hasty burial of the dead, and clear the deck of the wounded, was a business of short duration, and, in less than an hour from the boarding of the carrack, all the boats from the three ships, with those of the "Mother of God," the name of the prize, were alongside and being loaded with the captured cargo.

Fifty chests of specie and gold in ingots, were sent on board the "Tiger," while ten cases of quicksilver, being too heavy to remove, were left in the hold of the carrack.

Cavendish next divided his prisoners equally among his own vessels, and, putting an English crew aboard the prize, left the Spanish captain to act as pilot to his own ship.

When these operations had been effected, the anchor was weighed, and the carrack brought safely out of her natural dock.

The crews were so delighted with the success of this undertaking, that, on the first mention of their commander's intention of entering the Pacific, they, with one voice, seconded his proposal with loud shouts of approval.

Sail was instantly set, and, with the prize in the centre, the squadron held southward with a flowing sheet; and when night closed in, all evidence of the American coast was lost in mist and distance.

From this time the crews became daily sensible of the altered state of the temperature, till, when in latitude 50 deg. south, they began to suffer all the rigours of an Arctic winter.

The hope, however, of still greater plunder to be gained in the Peruvian waters, made the men bear up against the hardships of their voyage, and early in January, 1587, six months after leaving England, the "Tiger" and her consorts at last entered the Straits of Magellan.

If the hardships endured by the men for the last month had been great, they now became almost insupportable; blinding snow storms, and hurricanes of wind, rain and hail, were incessant.

The cold was almost beyond endurance, while their sails, one moment limp and soaked with rain, were the next converted into sheets of immoveable ice by the intense frost.

To all these hardships was added the constant dread of shipwreck from the shoals, rocks, and floes of ice that perpetually encountered them.

NAUTICAL TALES;

OR, ADVENTURES BY SEA AND LAND.

THE CRUISE OF THE TIGER;
OR, THE ADVENTURES OF SIR THOMAS CAVENDISH.

CONCLUDED.

To keep up his men's spirits under such dangers that demanded their vigilance night and day, Cavendish went from ship to ship (when the weather permitted) and encouraged the crews with brilliant accounts of the glorious climate and the untold plunder that awaited them at the other end of the straits.

After suffering five weeks of incessant hardship, toil, and fatigue, the crews of the squadron at last saw the Pacific before them, and, spreading their wet sails to a southerly breeze, ran northward, with every hour increasing their hopes and gladness.

Towards the end of March, Cavendish stood in towards the coast of Chili, and sighting a small town and fort in latitude 42 deg. south, made signal for his other ships to join company.

The Spaniards, both in the town and fort, seemed for a time perfectly unconscious of danger, and taking the squadron as part of the expected fleet from Spain, never thought of their guns, till the "Tiger," hoisting her colours, turned her broadside on the fort.

In the river behind the fort lay three ships, a large carrack and two caravels, all loaded with flax and hides, part of the fleet destined for the Philippine Islands.

Leaving Winter and Carew to bombard the fort, Cavendish, in the boats, resolved to attack the town, and cut out the prizes.

This was a work both of great trouble and labour, for the current of the river was so strong that after vainly trying to stem it, under a galling fire from the banks, he was obliged to land, and advanced to the town on foot.

In this hasty march over a morass he was not only harassed by the Spaniards on his flank, but by random shots from the "Tiger" and "Hawk," who occasionally overshot their range.

On reaching the town, the inabitants fled to the woods, when Cavendish at once took possession of the ships, the few men left on board making but a feeble resistance.

Casting loose the hawsers that secured the prizes to shore, he allowed them to drop down with the current to the mouth of the river.

Springing on board the carrack, and seizing the tiller to keep her off the bank, Cavendish for the first time became aware of a small pink or pleasure yacht, of about ten tons burthen, that was lashed to the carrack's port-quarter.

Attracted by the extreme beauty and lightness of the craft, which seemed built of a different wood to that in use for ordinary ships, Cavendish ordered two of his men to let themselves down on the pink's deck, and see with what she was loaded.

The fort had already struck to the united attack of the "Tiger" and "Hawk," and the caravels had crossed the mouth of the river, and, under easy sail, were being worked out to sea.

The greater size of the carrack, and her strong lashings to the shore, made her removal a task of greater time and difficulty; but, when once she was cast off, her momentum down the river was so great that all Cavendish's skill was required to keep her from fouling the bank on either side.

The commodore was consequently unable to watch the execution of the order he had given in respect to the pink; and had, for the moment, forgotten all about her, till roused by a sudden splash in the water and the shouting of his men for help.

Turning hastily round he beheld, to his astonishment, the two men struggling in the middle of the channel, and, the pink, with her painter cut, darting down the river like an arrow, with her two immense lateen sails spread to the breeze.

Enraged at this act of what he deemed treachery, Cavendish threw ropes to his men, and, ordering sail to be set, followed at full speed the light-footed craft.

Before he could reach the bar of the river, however, the pink had dashed through the squadron unchallenged, and was out in the offing, and with sails and sweeps stretching away like a sea-bird.

Fortunately, the "Lapwing" was close at hand, and Cavendish, springing on board, sent an order to Winter and Carew to look after the prizes and wait his return with the pink.

Crowding all sail on the schooner, he stood after the runaway, till the hull of the "Lapwing," under her press of canvas, darted like a bolt from a catapult.

The sea had risen with the wind, and the long heavy swell of the Pacific rendered the sweeps on board the pink utterly useless; but, to compensate for their loss, the crew had hoisted a jib, in the hope of maintaining the favourable distance already gained.

Short as the time had been between the shipping of the oars and the setting of their jib, it had enabled the "Lapwing" to lessen her distance so far as to warrant Cavendish in bringing his long-bow chaser to bear on the flying pink.

"Wait for the next swell, Drayton, and take a steady aim at his main-mast," cried the commodore, as the captain of the "Lapwing" began to sight his long seven-pounder.

"All clear there from the recoil!" shouted Drayton, as he placed the linstock on the breach of the bow-chaser.

There was a flash, a roar, and a volume of smoke, that for a few moments completely enveloped the forward part of the schooner.

When the smoke cleared away, the "Lapwing" was found to have shot ahead of the pink, which, with her main-mast splintered and trailing astern, was seen, broadside on, labouring in the trough of the sea.

Putting his helm hard up, and taking in part of his sails, Cavendish was enabled, by the time the crew of the pink had cleared the wreck, to lay the "Lapwing" alongside of the disabled fugitive.

At this moment the crew of the schooner became aware that the deck of the pink was thronged with men, and at least a score of bearded Spaniards, armed with pistol and cutlass, were standing ready to dispute possession of their ship.

A hard-faced man, dressed like a grandee, with plumed hat, cloak, and doublet, stood among the crew, waving his long toledo, and pointing derisively to the English.

All these particulars the eye of the young commodore took in at a glance, and commanding Drayton to stay and look to the safety of the "Lapwing," he swung himself by a halyard on to the deck of the pink, followed by more than half of the schooner's men.

From that moment a scene of indescribable horror and confusion ensued; blow answered blow, and life was given for life. The Spaniards fought as if possessed by fiends, and sold their lives with a prolonged and deadly vengeance.

Though wounded and bleeding, Cavendish made repeated attempts to reach the Spanish leader, and had twice followed him round the narrow and half submerged deck; but on each occasion of their swords crossing, the crew of the pink rushed in and separated them.

A few men, and these badly wounded, only now remained to dispute possession. Leaving these to his crew, Cavendish again looked round for the Spanish leader, when, at that moment, the report of a pistol below the deck, and the death shriek of a woman, caused him to turn suddenly in the direction of the sound.

"Women on board, by heaven!" cried Cavendish, as, followed by Enoch, he bounded down the companion ladder and entered the cabin of the pink.

Had there been time Cavendish would have paused to gaze in wonder on the size and elegance of the saloon in which he stood; and might have marvelled at the Persian carpets and Venetian mirrors that covered the floor and gilded panels of the apartment.

Every sense, however, was absorbed in the living tableau before him. The Spaniard he had been seeking stood in the centre of the saloon, holding a lighted linstock in one hand and a pistol in the other.

Facing this harsh-looking, imperious Spaniard stood a tall, beautiful girl of eighteen, her dark eyes and exquisitely cut features turned contemptuously on the haughty man who confronted her.

A bleeding and lifeless woman lay weltering on the rich carpet on one side of the don, while a kneeling girl on the other clutched with frantic grasp the lady's satin robe, as with her other hand she put aside the Spaniard's pistol from her temple.

"Consent, lady! consent, and save me! Oh, look at Isadora, and save me!" cried the kneeling girl, in accents of the wildest terror, glancing with a shudder at the dead body of her companion.

"Swear to pass as my wife, and be silent on what has passed, to these accursed English, and your life is safe. Refuse, and, by the blessed St. Iago, the girl dies; and with this light I will send the ship and all on board to eternity! Swear!" hoarsely growled the Spaniard, again levelling the pistol at the girl's head.

"Save me, Donna Silvia! save me!"

"Swear, girl, swear!" repeated the Spaniard. "Hark to that noise on deck. Another moment, and it will be too late. Swear!"

"Never, villain! never!" replied Donna Silvia, disdainfully.

"Then death and eternity for all!" added the Spaniard.

And stepping back, he hurled the flaming linstock through one of the mirrors into the magazine byond.

All this had occurred so rapidly that before the Spaniard could draw the trigger, the pistol was dashed from his hand by Cavendish, and Donna Silvia firmly grasped in his arms.

With a loud, insulting laugh, the ruffian pointed to the broken mirror, and, folding his arms on his chest, cried contemptuously—

"Fool! heretic! pirate! thief! you are too late! The train is fired!"

"Secure the girl, Enoch, and follow me. Die, execrable dog, die!" Cavendish exclaimed, as the hilt of his sword rang on the Spaniard's ribs, and the hidalgo fell dead at his feet.

With all his youth and agility, Cavendish had scarcely reached the deck, when a terrible explosion blew out the stern and bows of the pink, which instantly sank by the head, throwing the stern high up in the air.

"Look to yourselves; all hands aboard. Quick! for your lives!" shouted the commodore, as twining his arm in a halyard he drew himself and Donna Silvia on board the "Lapwing," followed by Enoch, with the insensible maid, and some half-dozen of his crew.

"Ease her off, Drayton. Quick! or we shall be too late; the fire is running aft," exclaimed Cavendish, excitedly, as Drayton ported his helm, and the schooner fell off from the now blazing pink.

An instant later, and a second and more terrific explosion scattered the rest of the burning craft to atoms. The air was darkened with smoke and splinters, and the sea far and near covered with ruins.

And of the late beautiful yacht, with her deck covered with the dead, dying, and still contending foes, not an evidence was left.

A shattered spar or a smouldering sail, as they were swept by on the rolling sea, were all that the Spaniard's vengeance had left of the late dainty pink, while the "Lapwing," beating to windward, was trying to rejoin her consorts in the offing.

The concussion caused by the explosion of the pink made the schooner tremble to her very keel, while the falling fragments of the wreck filled the donna's mind with feelings of the wildest terror.

Closing her eyes, the beautiful Silvia tightened her hold of the strong man who held her in his arms, and for the time he was bearing her to the cabin of the "Lapwing" she seemed lost in emotion and fear.

Taking advantage of the apparent insensibility of his lovely captive, Cavendish pressed a passionate kiss on the soft, full lips of the seemingly unconscious donna.

While stealing away, however, he encountered a pair of such large and lustrous eyes, which, though closed, had by no means been insensible, that, like a culprit detected in a dishonest act, he returned, and throwing himself at the lady's feet besought her forgiveness for his unworthy conduct.

What Donna Silvia might have said, or in what terms reproved his audacity, or whether maddened by a smile that was just dimpling her lovely mouth, he might not have repeated the offence, it is impossible to say, for at that moment they were interrupted.

"Here's the young woman, your honour, and as she's opening her ports and dead lights I take it she's a-heaving to," exclaimed the sailing master, as he entered the cabin, and deposited his recovering burthen on the padded locker by the side of her mistress.

Cavendish sprang instantly to his feet, thinking at the moment what an ill-mannered ugly brute Enoch was, and feeling in his heart that he would like to make him still more hideous by a good thrashing.

The old sea-dog, however, was quite unconscious that anything was particularly wrong with his storm-beaten figure-head, and so far from thinking himself an intruder began to take so much interest in the recovery of the young handmaiden as to be quite ignorant of his commander's knitted brows and impatient gestures.

"Now, Enoch, we must on deck; the schooner is pitching as if she had slipped stays."

And Cavendish abruptly cut short some soothing and tender remark the master was growling into the girl's ear, and the meaning of which she could only surmise from his well meaning but rough attentions.

"Aye, aye, your honour, all right; she is a-kicking like furies," replied Enoch, rising and hurrying on deck.

Cavendish only remained a moment to assure the donna that she should have a more endurable cabin when they reached the "Tiger," and, taking a distant but courteous farewell, followed his trusty officer to the deck.

Two hours later the "Lapwing" ran abreast of the commodore's ship, and the best cabin of the "Tiger" having been hastily fitted up for her reception, the Donna Silvia was conducted on board.

Delighted and charmed as Cavendish was by his beautiful captive, and many as were the happy moments he found time to pass in her society, the duties imposed upon him by the greed and rapacity of his crews compelled him to make all softer feelings subservient to the great aim of the expedition.

The squadron was consequently soon again at sea, and before the end of the week had captured and destroyed two more prizes.

Standing again towards the land, he stormed and took the towns of Paita and Acapulco.

Loading his ships with an immense amount of plunder obtained from the sack of the latter settlement, he sailed slowly northward along the coast.

In this manner, landing repeatedly to destroy Spanish settlements, and compelling the inhabitants to ransom their lives and property, he ravaged nearly the whole of the Chilian and Peruvian sea board.

In these perpetual descents he added vast sums to his already immense treasure, and spread universal terror among the unprepared Spaniards.

In vain the inhabitants of the plundered towns sent out despatch-boats to apprise expected ships from Europe of the presence of the enemy. Cavendish, ever on the watch, always intercepted or destroyed them.

Having heard from his prisoners that war had been declared between Spain and England, and of the dreadful vengeance Philip meant to take on Queen Elizabeth and her people with his wonderful fleet, Cavendish threw aside all reserve and burnt and pillaged wherever he came.

Avoiding such places as Lima and Panama—strongly garrisoned and powerfully defended cities, and against which his small force would have been utterly useless—Cavendish again stood from the coast, and made a prize of every vessel which he encountered.

For several months he had heard from his prisoners and at the different settlements he had sacked, of the great annual galleon, expected from Europe, loaded with specie and all the rich merchandise of the old world.

This vessel, the "Santa Anna," a ship of between seven and eight hundred tons burthen, was soon expected at Lima and all the towns down the eastern coast; her arrival with news and goods from Europe being held as a perfect jubilee at every town at which she touched.

To capture this rich prize was the great hope and aim of Cavendish's ambition. On the success of this undertaking he looked for distinction and honour both from his queen and country.

After performing a few daring exploits along the coast of New Spain, or Eastern Mexico, the commodore heard that the rich prize from Cadiz was at the Philippines, and might be expected in those waters within a week or ten days.

Determined at whatever risk to attempt her capture, Cavendish suddenly stood off the coast, and setting all sail bore up for California.

Finding a small but well sheltered haven close to Cape St. Lucas, the extreme southern point of California, he there artfully hid his ships, while he lay in wait for the Spanish galleon.

From the tree-tops and the crevices of the rocks his eager crew by day and night kept a steady look-out for the anxiously expected prize.

For prize she would be, every man of his crew already felt certain, and indeed began to speculate on their share of the wished-for plunder.

The small band with whom Cavendish had sailed from England had, by sickness, death, and the casualties of his many actions afloat and ashore, been by this time greatly reduced.

On the third day after the squadron had lain in ambush, the expected prize hove in sight, and all was instant bustle on board the different ships.

It was not till now, when he mustered his men, that Cavendish became aware of the serious ravages of war and sickness on his small, but to the last, courageous band.

As was expected, the galleon made for Cape Lucia, and getting close to the promontory dropped her anchor under the lee of the bluff.

It was now, from his place of hiding among the rocks, that Cavendish was for the first time enabled to judge of the size and importance of the coveted prize.

The "Santa Anna" was a full-rigged galleon, or merchantman—for that time, of immense proportions—and fitted out with every modern improvement of the age.

She carried eight long brass guns on her main deck, and had large and securely guarded tops to each mast, in each of which half a score of small-arm men might have been securely lodged.

It was not her size or armament, however, that caused Cavendish a moment's uneasiness; it was the sight of her crew that induced that deep frown that gathered on his face, and that savage biting of his nether lip, as though he would transfix it with his teeth.

The galleon was literally swarming with men, and a finer set of foes and seamen the eyes of the young commander had never lighted on.

An involuntary sigh broke from Cavendish, as he contemplated the enemy, and thought of his own handful of men.

Fortune, however, was destined to favor him this day even beyond his most sanguine expectations.

About sundown six of the "Santa Anna's" boats were lowered, and these being filled with casks and manned by a large number of the crew, were sent on shore for water.

From the tent and provisions taken it was evident the watering party were not to return to the ship till the morning, when the "Santa Anna" would at once stretch across to the Gulf of Panama.

With an anxious heart Cavendish watched the boats make for the watering place, saw the men roll their casks into the adjacent wood, and removing their tent and provisions leave the boats moored on the strand.

As the last man disappeared from the beach the commodore descended to the cove where his ships were docked, and at once joined his men, who were all ashore and anxiously awaiting his return.

Taking his officers into his confidence, they waited for the darkness that usually precedes the rising of the moon, when, in three boats, under the command of Carew, Drayton and Winter, Cavendish cautiously led the way out of the haven in the "Tiger's" longboat, and while he and two others pulled with muffled oars for the lights in the galleon, Carew crept to the watering place, and having cleverly secured the unprotected boats pulled out to take his share in the fray.

So cautiously had Cavendish conducted his boats, that their crews had scaled the bows of the "Santa Anna," and were in possession of the forecastle, before the Spaniards could realize the fact of an enemy's being on board.

The hurrah of the English as they dropped on the Spaniards' deck, with the terrified shouts of the overpowered watch ran through the ship like wildfire, while from every companion and hatchway the roused crew streamed up on all sides.

If they had at first been taken by surprise, they atoned for their mistake by their subsequent activity and courage.

For a moment the two parties looked defiantly at one another; the Spaniards regarding their handful of foes with contempt, while the English surveyed with a grim smile the enemy they meant to annihilate.

The next instant, with a yell of defiance, the antagonists closed in a deadly encounter, and amid the shout and fury of battle were heard the oaths and imprecations of the dying and the wounded.

Cavendish, seeing the fearful odds to which his men were opposed, had endeavoured to seize the two forward guns, hoping to turn them on the enemy.

But the Spaniards, seeing the object of the English, threw themselves in such numbers on the crews of the "Tiger" and "Hawk," that, for a time, Cavendish and his party were driven back, and followed to the very bows of the "Santa Anna."

At this critical moment, and when the Spaniards were about to secure the guns, Carew with half-a-dozen fresh hands mounted the gunwale, and springing among the enemy drove them back in turn, and eventually secured the guns.

Like a returning wave the united English renewed the charge, and soon possessed themselves of all the deck, from the mainmast forward.

The whole afterpart of the ship was still literally crowded with Spaniards, who, having organised themselves into companies and being well armed with musketoons, kept up a galling and destructive fire on the English, who had only pistols to reply with.

To counteract the withering effect of their musketry, Cavendish turned the pieces of artillery he had just secured on the compact front of the enemy.

The Spaniards, who knew the guns were unloaded, sprang forward on the English, and the close and deadly contest was resumed.

While Cavendish, Winter, and Carew were thus engaged in maintaining their doubtful ground on the slippery deck, Drayton and Enoch were endeavouring to charge by means of some loose powder and a bag of nails one of the useless guns.

"Back, lads, back!" shouted the captain of the "Lapwing," as he and Enoch trailed the gun forward.

A lane was instantly made in the line of fighting English, and before the crowded Spaniards could comprehend the threatened danger, the piece was fired point blank on the massed foe.

The effect of that discharge was awful in the extreme; the charge, scattering in its passage, mowed the Spaniards down like grass, and strewed the quarterdeck with heaps of writhing wretches.

Without allowing the enemy time to recover from this appalling disaster, Cavendish flung himself and crew on those antagonists still capable of disputing the possession of the ship.

Though fearfully thinned by repeated assaults, and the loss of the water party, who, as helpless spectators, heard the din of battle from the shore, the crew of the galleon still far outnumbered the English, fighting with a determination that would sooner die than yield.

Twice had Cavendish, though covered with wounds, forced the enemy to the stern-rails of the "Santa Anna," sweeping the deck fore and aft; and twice had the Spaniards, closing up, driven back their invaders.

Clearing his eyes from blood and smoke, Cavendish was urging his men to a last effort, when a ringing shout was heard from the after-hatch, and the next moment a troop of English sailors sprang upon deck, and, tearing the arms from the dying foe, fell with a shout of triumph on the rear of the enemy.

Between thirty and forty English sailors whom the crew of the "Santa Anna" had captured on the voyage out, and whom they had confined on the orlop deck in bilboes, hearing the fighting on board and the voices of their countrymen, by desperate efforts freed themselves of their irons, and, bursting upon deck, were just in time to turn the scale of victory.

Never was aid more unexpected, and, at the same time, more needed and welcome.

Bringing out his squadron from their hiding place, Cavendish, the next day, began to remove the costly cargo of the "Santa Anna" on board his other ships.

The value of the prize far exceeded his most sanguine expectations. Chests of rare spices and drugs and bales of costly merchandize were to be counted by the score, while, in addition to jewels, plate and rich furniture, there were chests of specie, containing the immense sum of 122,000 Spanish dollars.

Having secured the entire contents of the great "Santa Anna," and revictualled his ships from her abundant stores, he carried his prisoners ashore to join their comrades.

Leaving them enough food to carry them to Panama, he took possession of their boats, and telling the captain to build a raft to take him to his empty ship, set sail three days after the battle for England.

Stopping a few days at St. Helena for wood and water he set sail for home, and arrived safely off Plymouth on the 9th of September, 1588.

Though the country was at the time in a state of general rejoicing at the recent defeat of the Spanish Armada, people flocked from all quarters to witness the wonderful display made by Cavendish and his ships, and when, a few days later, he sailed up the Thames, the banks of the river were lined with crowds to witness his triumphant progress.

Cavendish himself, in a costly dress, stood on the poop, with his fair captive, the lovely Silvia, now his promised bride, standing in her jewelled robes at his side.

So immense was his own share of the plunder, that Sir Thomas Cavendish purchased estates that were considered in those days equal to an English earldom.

Thus ended the first piratical expedition undertaken by Sir Thomas Cavendish against the Spaniards in South America on both their seaboards.

THE END.

NAUTICAL TALES;

OR, ADVENTURES BY SEA AND LAND.

BUCCANEERS AT WAR.

THE "VIPER" AND THE "FOX."

CHAPTER I.

THE FOX ASLEEP.

It was a hot, sultry afternoon in the July of 1674, and the soft scenery, and tranquil water around, and forming the Bay of Weymouth, never looked more dreamy and peaceful.

It was a sight that might have excited the admiration of the most enthusiastic lover of natural beauty.

The rows of white houses, built in a crescent round the bay, contrasted pleasingly with their green palings and trim gardens, with the wide sweep of yellow sand, and the distant strip of shelly beach.

A heavy merchantman on her way up channel, lay at anchor just inside the horns of the bay; one or two luggers, a collier-sloop, a few hoys, and a sprinkling of fishing boats, all moored, and most of them with their sails spread out to dry, dotted the surface of the bay.

"When do you expect the 'Viper' round from the Lizard, Gilbert?" asked a young man of about five-and-twenty, dressed in the civilian garb of the period, of his companion, as he descended the wooded slopes on the eastern side of the bay.

"She ought to have been here this morning, Ralph," replied his friend, a young man who, though probably only of his own age, possessed such dull and heavy features, that he might well have passed for thirty.

The costume of Gilbert Coverdale, the owner and commander of the expected "Viper," was of infinitely superior material to that of his companion, and, though there was much of the rakish gallantry of the court in the style of his hat and ornamented rapier, the whole was sobered by a dash of the sailor's habit.

"What, in the name of all the fiends, keeps the brig so long after time?" Coverdale exclaimed suddenly, as the two stopped at an opening in the trees, which commanded all the bay for miles around.

"Here's the evening tide almost flood, and not a sail as big as a crow's wing on the west," he added petulantly.

"What makes you in such a hurry, Gilbert? I thought you were to be married before you put to sea."

"Of course I am."

"Then, what folly to be out of humour by the non-arrival of the 'Viper;' she'll creep up with the night breeze, depend upon it, and you'll find her snugly moored in shore by the morning."

"Yes, and in the darkness, that sly, suspicious-looking schooner will have sneaked away before I can overhaul her."

"Not she; she has been there a week, and made no sign of moving," replied his friend.

"I know it, curse her! and for a week that craft has been a constant source of irritation and annoyance to me."

"But why?"

"Because I cannot make her out. Do you know, Ralph, I have an instinctive hatred for that low, crafty-looking schooner."

"A hatred for a ship! nonsense, Gilbert, you are talking absurdly."

"I tell you I feel a hatred against that craft, such as I feel towards my one mortal enemy." And Coverdale spoke with such suppressed energy and vindictive passion, that Ralph had to look searchingly into his face to be assured that he heard correctly.

"Indeed! a somewhat absurd feeling, I should say, to entertain against a mass of mere wood and canvas. And pray, who is the living object of such violent animosity?" inquired Ralph Seyton, as he paused in front for a reply.

"Why, the man who has been my curse and bane from boyhood upward. He, who at school, robbed me of distinction and mastery; who, through every subsequent year, has crossed and blighted me; my evil genius, Basil Spencer."

"Why, I thought you had been parted for years? Spencer is in the Chinese seas."

"Aye, and there I hope some hurricane or typhoon will sweep him and his hopes to eternal perdition."

"Well, you are a good hater, Coverdale, I must say. If I bore an enemy such a grudge, I'd rather have my quarrel out in blows, and end it that way."

"Perchance I may, Seyton; it is one of my most ardent hopes; grant heaven, that we may meet, ship to ship, and hand to hand!"

"But what has brought young Spencer into your thoughts to-night?"

"That cursed schooner, lying there so low, so rakish, so sly and treacherous. The hateful thing's an enigma, and reminds me of Spencer."

"Except a solitary form, at times seen in the bows, she might be a sea-waif, or spectre bark," observed Seyton, scanning the long, low craft, as she lay almost motionless in the bay.

"Had the brig arrived as I expected, I'd have anchored near enough to see who and what she is. I'd have found out the mystery of that foul tub."

"Now, there your spleen and prejudice make you not only unjust but untruthful. Your seaman's judgment must tell you that the schooner as a craft is faultless."

"I have no patience to hear you praise her," replied Coverdale, petulantly. "Why, you are as infatuated as Ethel."

"How so?" and Seyton laughed lightly.

"Why, this morning, Ethel said to me quite enthusiastically, 'Look, Gilbert, look, what beautiful lines that schooner has got!'"

"And what did you say?"

"Say? Why, laughed at the idea of her talking about the beautiful lines of a ship. It was perfectly ridiculous."

"Why so?"

"Why, my good fellow, she knows nothing whatever about a ship, and could not tell the difference between a back-stay and a jib-boom."

"All the fitter for your instruction, then. She'll be your wife to-morrow morning, and, when the 'Viper' comes to take you on your wedding trip, you will have a splendid opportunity of teaching her."

"And, if she's as quick at learning sea terms as other nonsense, she'll make an apt pupil; she's as clever as she is cunning."

"Look there, Gilbert, look!" cried Ralph, suddenly grasping his friend's arm, and pointing to the bay.

"Look at what?" and Gilbert's eyes naturally directed themselves to the west, where he expected to sight his tardy brig.

"I see nothing."

"Here, man; here, to the east. See how silently and ghostlike she is stealing away."

It took Gilbert full a minute to bring his eyes to the point to which Ralph's hand was directing. The next moment he gave a start, and ejaculated—

"By Heaven! the schooner's under weigh!"

"Yes; and without showing a hand, or the creak of a block, she has set her fore-sail and jib. There's something mysterious in all this, Gilbert."

"It is something more, it is positively suspicious, Ralph. She has caught the little breeze there was, too, and is stalking away without leaving a ripple to mark her wake."

As Coverdale spoke he and Ralph stepped clear from the wood, and stood on a bank in front of the trees, while, shading their eyes from the glare of the setting sun, they gazed on the fast receding schooner.

When the unknown craft had nearly doubled her distance from the shore, she set her topsails and royals, and sheeting home her mainsail, was laid directly in the sun's eye, as she ran down channel.

"She's off, by Jove! and got all the wind with her!" muttered Coverdale, half aloud. "I'd give something to know who and what she's got on board."

"He'll have long legs who overhauls that craft, Gilbert."

"I'd try it, though, if I had the 'Viper' here! What's that she's running up to the main-truck? You have your pocket-glass, Ralph, look."

"Some bit of bunting or other," replied Seyton, watching a small flag that had just reached the mast-head. "Stay, there's something on it."

"Her name, I suppose?"

"No, there are no letters. It's something long and black."

"What does it look like?"

"Something like a—yes—like a dog, with a long tail. No, by George! I have it now, the sun falls on it. It is a Black Fox."

"Let me see!"

After gazing intently for some minutes, Coverdale returned the glass to his friend.

"You are right. I thought there was something sly and cunning in that craft, and her name answers my suspicion; but I will be better acquainted with that Fox before I die, or I am no true Coverdale."

After watching the mysterious schooner till she had fairly vanished in the golden mist of the setting sun, the two young men slowly descended to the beach, and skirting the town of Weymouth, approached the park gates of Crawley Hall.

This was the residence of Squire Coverdale, uncle to one of the young men we have just introduced, and the father of the beautiful Ethel, who, the next morning, was to become the happy bride of her cousin Captain Gilbert Coverdale.

Within half-an-hour of the two friends reaching the hospitable mansion of Squire Coverdale, the alarm bell of the Hall was heard far and near, calling up all the retainers of the house, and startling the inhabitants of the town by its ominous peal.

Men scoured the park, while mounted grooms dashed into the adjacent woods, or madly tore along the roads in search of the lovely Ethel and her maid.

The lady and her faithful abigail had strolled out some time before sunset to meet and return with the bridegroom, who had gone with Ralph to a village about two miles from the Hall.

From that moment, however, they seemed to have disappeared from all observation, and it was not till the arrival of Gilbert Coverdale at the Hall that the Squire had any doubt or misgiving as to his daughter's safety.

During the whole night the unavailing search was continued, and only with the morning was any clue found to the missing fair one.

A cow-boy had seen two ladies with mantles and hoods, meet a gentleman near one of the wooded recesses of the bay, and while a black man opened a path through the bushes, the others followed laughing, to the beach.

Attracted by the gaiety of the party, and the unusual appearance of strangers in such a place, the boy followed, and was just in time to see the gentleman hand the ladies into a boat, manned with sailors, that shot out from the foliage of the bank.

Dropping their oars silently into the water, the boat glided from the shore, and almost before the boy could credit his eyes, had reached the strange schooner in the bay, on board of which boatmen and ladies instantly disappeared.

Sent early to bed, he had heard nothing of the missing bride till the morning, and then recorded what he had seen.

"By heaven, my instincts were right! I felt the presence of that hated devil."

"Of whom do you speak?" demanded the angry Squire.

"Of that fiend, Basil Spencer, who has once more, but for the last time, crossed my path. I will have an awful day of reckoning!" and Gilbert Coverdale clenched his hands, and looked malignant vengeance.

"Spencer! impossible! she has seen no one, and Basil has not been near the Hall for months," the squire replied indignantly.

"I tell you," cried the jilted bridegroom, passionately stamping on the floor, "he is the captain of that cursed craft, and has lain, like the 'Fox' he is, under our very windows for the last week, till ——"

The sentence was cut short by the quick, deep boom of two heavy guns, that shook all the windows, and made everyone start by the abruptness of the report.

"Vengeance!" exclaimed Gilbert Coverdale exultantly, as, springing on one of the window seats, he dashed open the casement, and, pointing to a fine brig that was rounding into the bay, he continued with a bitter laugh——

"See at last—at last, the 'Viper.' Now for pursuit and vengeance!"

CHAPTER II.

THE FOX FOLLOWS HIS INSTINCTS, AND THE VIPER PROVES THAT HE IS NOT BLIND.

ABOUT a year subsequent to the events narrated in the first chapter, the long, low, rakish-looking craft, schooner-rigged, with a black Fox on her bunting, was lying, her sails all aback, in the Indian Ocean.

During those twelve months, the schooner had well

supported her character to the name she bore, as far as craft, daring, and stealing generally were concerned.

In those few months, every maritime state in Europe had had occasion to acknowledge with humiliation and grief, that there were water as well as land Foxes.

And that this rascal, with the sleek lines and the black brush, was the incarnation, as far as pluck and audacity went, of all the foxes, red, white or black, in the world.

In one respect, however, the salt water Fox seemed to have changed his nature; he no longer hungered after farmyards, or licked his lips over tender goslings, and imaginary pullets.

Our Fox preferred ships to hen roosts, and throve marvellously on the cargoes of fat argosies.

The Black Fox, on the whole, was not a bad animal of his sort, and never destroyed in wantonness; all his pretty cubs, as the captain facetiously called his ruffian crew, were well bred, and perfect gentlemen in their manners; always took off their hats to a woman, bade their victims good-bye with a kindly smile, and never cut a throat or knocked a man on the head except in self-defence.

It is true these amiable traits of character were unappreciated, if not quite thrown away, on those who fell into their hands.

Those persons, smarting under the sense of lost doubloons, diamond crosses, and a few hundred bars of gold and silver, maligned the "Fox's" crew shamefully.

Indeed, they were reported to have sworn to their sweethearts and padres that a more villanous set of scoundrels never issued from that nest of heretics and robbers—detested Albion.

We mean to show in this chapter how unjust all foreigners' opinion of England and Englishmen really is, and how prejudiced a Frenchman or a Spaniard becomes when you empty his purse for him.

It was a lovely morning, the faintest ripple just curled the placid bosom of the Indian Ocean, occasioned by a light breeze from the north-east.

The "Fox," as I have said, sat almost motionless on the burnished flood, with her sails all aback.

So, in fact, were the sails of two other vessels that lay within a cable's length of her bows.

One was a large unwieldy looking carrack, with bulging sides, like a fat alderman; this was the "San Joseph," a Portuguese trader, bound from the Tagus to the rich settlement of Goa, on the Coromandel.

Her cargo consisted chiefly of monks, friars and priests, silver candlesticks, gold chalices, and such costly ornaments, all meant for the new cathedral at Goa.

On the whole, the dead cargo of the "San Joseph" was regarded by the "Fox" as a valuable one.

The other craft was a trim, dapper, well-rigged brigantine, the "Stag," a Frenchman, built for speed and tonnage too.

The captain and owner had just completed a rapid and prosperous voyage to Pondicherry, and was returning in great glee with the product of his voyage, in two chests of specie, to *la belle France*.

All three vessels chanced to near each other about eight in the morning; the Frenchman, in his hurry to reach Bordeaux, was waving kind good-byes to the Englishman, while the more cumbrous Portuguese, after asking his longitude, was equally anxious to make the Indian coast before dark.

A couple of shots, right and left, from the bows of the "Fox," brought both vessels to their senses in an instant.

Sails were furled or put aback, and the "Stag" and the "San Joseph" became almost motionless.

Such an immediate obedience to nautical language in two large and well manned ships was not to be attributed to the size of the "Fox" or the weight of her carronades.

It was, in fact, to be attributed to the sudden influx of her crew, who, springing up from every quarter, seemed literally to swarm over her deck and rigging.

An order to send the captain and three chief officers on board the "Fox" with the ships' papers, was quickly complied with.

Treating the captains and their boats' crews as hostages, but showing them every courtesy, Basil Spencer, the commander of the "Fox," to save his men from unnecessary fatigue, ordered the crew of the Frenchman to unload the Portuguese ship.

And, for fear this should create any national jealousy, he made the lazy Portuguese unload the lively Frenchman.

Having satisfied himself that the two crews had removed all the important part of the treasure, and seen it safely stowed in the strong-room of the "Fox," Captain Spencer closed his hatches, and ordered round his captives' boats.

"I am extremely sorry to have been under the necessity of interrupting your breakfast this morning, gentlemen," he observed, courteously, as he led his hostages to the gangway.

"And I would have solicited the pleasure of your company to dinner, but, honestly, I do not like the look of the weather," and he glanced round the horizon as he spoke.

"Monsieur is too good!" replied the French captain, with a shrug of the shoulders, and an ironical smile.

"No, upon my life I am sincere; I know something of these seas, and think every commander should be on board his own ship when danger threatens," replied Spencer, in frank good humour.

"I see nothing, Senhor Capitano, to justify storm," observed the Portuguese, with a contemptuous look at the serene sky.

"Monsieur Reynard is a clever dog," observed the Frenchman, as the bunting was lowered and stowed away, and caught sight of the full-length effigy of the Fox, "but his legs may not always save him," he added, slyly.

"Then Monsieur, he must look to his teeth," rejoined Spencer, laughing.

"His teeth will not last for ever, and he may some day lose his tail—brush, you English call it."

"Monsieur is unnecessarily alarmed; with such a promising pack of cubs as these, I think my brush is tolerably safe;" and Spencer laughed merrily, as he pointed to his bearded crew.

"Sacré!" muttered the Frenchman, as he stepped into his boat, and continued to grind between his teeth a string of Gallic oaths; while Spencer, bareheaded, was bidding both captains farewell at the gangway.

"Make all snug, Mr. Dermot, and send the men below, they will have work enough before the day is over; and keep a sharp look out," cried Captain Spencer, addressing his chief officer, as he turned from the gangway.

"Brail up, and stand to the southward, Mr. Dermot; if those fools choose to run their heads into the lion's mouth, why, let them do it," he added, as he reached that part of the ship which might have been regarded as the quarter-deck.

As rapidly as a score of willing hands could effect the change, the sails of the schooner were brought round the halyards, made taut, the helm put hard-a-port, and the "Fox" was going through the water at five knots an hour.

"Has your mistress completed her toilet yet, Dinah?" Spencer asked suddenly, as with his hand on the companion rail, he was abruptly encountered by a good-looking, merry-faced Creole girl.

"Yes, sar, she send me to know what keep massa so long."

"I'll tell her that myself. You'll find Dick somewhere forward," he replied with a slight laugh, as he took the girl's place on the companion.

"Dick, sar! what massa mean?—dis chile, sar, ab——"

What else the blushing and confused girl might have said, was rendered unnecessary by the rapid disappearance of the captain.

With the evident intention of completing her vindication when the skipper returned on deck, Dinah placed herself in readiness, and, leaning over the starboard quarter, began contemplating the wash of the tide.

"Why, Ethel, I declare you look more beautiful than ever; that dress becomes you so well," exclaimed Spencer, entering his wife's luxurious cabin.

"Oh Basil, are you not tired of complimenting me yet? I should have thought your stock of flattery would have been exhausted by this time," replied the beautiful girl, advancing to meet her husband.

"If truth is flattery, Ethel, I never wish to tire of speaking it to you; but I have something to show you."

"Something pretty, Basil?"

"Almost as pretty as yourself."

"Oh, I know," she cried joyously, as Basil put his hand in one of his capacious pockets—"it is one of the King's little pet dogs."

"My wise little Ethel is wrong for once in her life. See, is there anything like a King Charles in this?"

"O! oh! what a beautiful thing!" and Ethel fairly held her breath in admiration, as she contemplated a diamond cross, with a delicate gold chain, every alternate link being gemmed with ruby and emerald.

"Yes, it's a pretty toy of its sort, and I thought how nicely it would become your snowy neck."

"Oh, no, no, no, I couldn't!" and she held up her hands almost in fear of some threatened danger.

"Nonsense! why it has been on my mind these six months. I thought it would become you so beautifully."

"Don't look so disappointed, Basil, I could not wear what, perhaps, has been taken from some poor girl, the gift of her mother."

"Upon my life, you are wrong, and you do me wrong too: you know I don't take from poor girls, or rich ones either."

"Then, where did you get it?"

"I got it out of the sacerdotal pocket of the Bishop of Goa, the state passenger on board the 'San Joseph.'"

"What, just now?"

"Yes; his Eminence forgot to send it with the rest of the church service, so I had politely to remind him of the fact, and where his sacristan had deposited it for greater safety."

"And he sent it?"

"Oh, certainly, my information was too accurate to be disputed, and I have no doubt he fully believes that all we heretics have direct communication with the arch fiend."

"Poor man; perhaps he meant it as a present for a niece or a sister."

"Nothing of the kind, Ethel. This was specially made to adorn the plastered and painted effigy of the Madonna in the new cathedral at Goa."

"Is this possible?"

"Quite true; and I thought it a sin to dress up a hideous doll with such a work of art, while a beautiful creature like you, love, had no fitting cross to wear. So I resolved, before it left the artist's hands, that this costly gem should be my wife's."

"Sail ho!" exclaimed the voice of Dermot, speaking down the companion.

Basil Spencer flung the chain over the neck of his no longer resisting wife, and having pressed it down with a kiss, he bounded back on deck.

"Where away, Mr. Dermot?" he asked, after a rapid glance round the deck to see if all his orders had been obeyed.

"On our weather bow, captain; but she lifts so fast you can see her already from the deck."

"What do you make of her?"

"I could only see her royals from the main top, but she's square rigged and a spanker, I should say, by the rate at which she lifts."

"Aye, aye, she has caught the first of the gale, and is bringing it down with her."

"Yes, we shall have it, and so will our friends there to windward. Poor devils, how they are running their noses into it," and the mate laughed, as he pointed to the two plundered ships, now nearly hull down in the distance.

"I'm going aloft to look at this strange sail. In the meantime, make all snug above and aloft."

Springing into the main rigging, Spencer mounted to the top, and, taking out his glass, stood for nearly half-an-hour watching every motion of the approaching vessel.

After a long and patient scrutiny of every spar and sail, Spencer swept the horizon with his glass, looked intently at the sky, and the thread-like clouds gathering here and there over the blue, and then slowly descended to the deck.

"Take another look at her, Dermot," observed the captain, preventing all questions by putting his glass in the mate's hand, and walking aft.

Looking down on the compass in the binnacle, and then glancing up to the vane on the mast head, Spencer folded his arms, and walked the deck for full ten minutes in perfect silence.

"I have seen that brig before, captain," remarked Dermot, as he took his place by his commander.

"I suppose so."

"He wants to speak us very hard."

"I see he does; he makes signals enough."

"And he means mischief, too."

"That's but natural, Dermot," and Basil smiled quietly.

"His metal's heavier than ours, but our plucky cubs are more than a match for his thick-headed crew."

"I am not thinking of that, Dermot," and Spencer spoke half sadly.

"Don't you mean to fight him, then?"

"Oh, yes, he shall have his revenge, but it won't be to-day. Down with your royals and topsails. Quick! It's coming up, by George."

This order was given so suddenly that twenty men sprang into the shrouds, and after a brief noise and flapping, the folds of canvas were soon securely trailed to their spars and lowered.

"Curse the fellow, how he pesters," continued Spencer, stamping impatiently, as the approaching brig hoisted another signal, and fired a gun.

NAUTICAL TALES;

OR, ADVENTURES BY SEA AND LAND.

BUCCANEERS AT WAR.

THE "VIPER" AND THE "FOX."

CONCLUDED.

The report, however, was unheard in the sudden rise of the wind, and the hiss of the foaming waters.

"What shall I do, captain?"

"Oh, show him the brush, and keep it flying," replied Spencer, holding on by a weather brace, as the "Fox" was already burying her bows in the heavy seas.

In less than two minutes the schooner's ensign was hauled firmly to the trucks, and made fast.

The smoke of two impotent guns was seen to leap from the brig's side, as she rose on the crest of a wave, as if in answer to the expected cognizance.

The next moment, a broad white flag, with a black adder in the act of striking, fluttered at the brig's main-top.

"Ease her away a point and a half, Mr. Dermot, and keep the helm hard up. In with the main and fore sails; quick, lads! quick!"

Scarcely had the willing hands stripped the schooner of her canvas, and the vessel been brought round to the point the captain had ordered, when the expected tempest broke in all its fury.

The "Viper," which was scarcely a league to windward, was in an instant lost in a fog of intense darkness, through which the thunder roared, and the lightning played in sheets of lurid flame.

On the very margin of this rushing darkness, rode the "Fox," under bare poles, her hatches battened down, and every sea sweeping her deck from stem to stern, as she sank into the watery abyss, or rose, staggering on the crest of a billow.

CHAPTER III.

THE DUEL, AND WHAT BECAME OF THE "FOX" AND THE "VIPER."

"He has fairly brought us to bay at last, captain," Mr. Dermot observed to Spencer, as the two walked the deck of the "Fox," about noon, some six weeks subsequent to the storm.

"Yes, he has, Dermot, but ever since he came out of that typhoon, we have given him many a long run and crafty double among these lagoons and islands of the Persian Gulf."

"I'll engage he's had more excitement in that way than he bargained for," laughed the chief mate.

"And that he has driven the brig through narrower channels than he ever before dreamed of risking the 'Viper' in, rejoined the captain.

"She has proved herself a first-rate craft, and with the 'Fox' and her, I'd face any danger," added Dermot, enthusiastically.

"And now, having tried each other's capabilities, we must, like the gladiators of old, enter the arena, and fight for the mastery."

"And we must be quick, too, for see, the 'Viper's' opening her jaws, and darting out her fangs," cried the mate, pointing to the brig, that, lying abreast of the "Fox," and just within range, was opening her ports, and running out her guns.

"Is all the spoil landed, and every man's share told off?"

"That was done before sunrise, and everything arranged in case of accidents, as you wished it."

"And the jolly-boat?"

"Behind the sedges, there," and he pointed to the low shore, "ready to start forward in a moment, if necessary for the ——"

"That will do, Dermot; I'll just say a few words to Mistress Spencer, and will be with you by the time you have beat to quarters."

Leaving the deck, Captain Spencer descended to the cabin set aside for his wife and her women, but now, all its costly mirrors and gay fittings removed, looking the abode of misery and discomfort.

When Basil returned on deck, he found all the men at their quarters, the gunners with their lighted linstocks, and the others swarming the tops, the booms and rigging.

A loud cheer of welcome greeted Spencer from his men, as he returned armed amongst them.

A slight puff of wind off shore, had imperceptibly carried the schooner nearer her antagonist, and quite within range.

Waving his morion above his head, as an answer to the greeting of his crew, Basil sprang on a carronade amidships, and, drawing his sword, gave the loud and distinct order to—

"Fire!"

Captain Coverdale, who had watched with intense eagerness every sign and motion on board the "Fox," at the same moment sprang on the gangway rail, and grasping a brace for support, gave his men the welcome order for action.

Such was the violence of this first exchange of broadsides, that each vessel rolled over nearly on her beam-ends, and back again as low as her ports, from the recoil.

The next instant the men in the tops and rigging of either vessel, poured in their volley of small arms, the guns were run out, and the round shot kept up their thunder from the deck below.

The battle had now begun, and was being contested with deadly hate and determination.

Both commanders hurried from point to point of their several vessels, exposing themselves to the hottest danger, and displaying all the cool judgment of experienced seamen.

The superior weight of the "Viper's" metal had already shown itself in the fearful breaches made in the "Fox's" sides and bulwarks. Still the crew worked their guns with a despatch that gave them the advantage of four broadsides to three.

The loss on both sides was great, and the deck of the "Fox" was strewn with the dead and dying.

"How are our spars, Mr. Dermot?" asked Spencer of his mate.

"All sound as yet, I think, captain," was the prompt reply, glancing at the tall, graceful masts.

"Set the four courses, then; this catspaw from the shore will carry us athwart her bows, when we can rake her with our swivel."

Dermot's answer was drowned in the roar of the next broadside, and the crash of rending timber, while the space on which the mate had just stood was in a moment heaped with mangled bodies.

"Luff! luff!" cried Spencer to the men at the helm, as amid all the turmoil of the fight, a dauntless band had set the jib, foresail and foretop-sails, and the "Fox" began to walk away from the "Viper."

"Starboard! aim at his masts, Dermot. Hard astarboard! hard up! there she is—perdition!——"

The "Fox," catching the fitful breeze that came off shore, had shot in splendid style from the side of her antagonist, and was just in the act of crossing the "Viper's" bows, when, with one fearful crash, down came foretop, jib, mainmast and foremast, to within ten feet of the deck.

The swivel which Dermot was firing sent its scattering shot into the falling rigging, killing its own men, and scarcely harming the enemy.

The wreck and havoc was complete; and for a moment the battle ceased, while each party surveyed the ruin.

Part of the wreck had fallen into the sea, and was dragging astarboard, but by far the larger portion had fallen on the "Viper's" bows, carrying away her foretop and jib-boom, and flinging more than a score of the "Fox's" crew, stunned and bleeding, on the enemy's deck.

In that instant of suspense, the voice of Spencer was heard clear and distinct through both vessels.

"Clear away the wreck, and up with the 'Fox!'"

The latter part of the order was the first executed, and the ensign, dragged from the water, was nailed to the stump of the mainmast.

Before, however, the most important part of the duty could be performed, and the two ships separated, Coverdale led a strong body of boarders across the wreck, and with a triumphant shout, sprang on board the "Fox."

His triumph, however, was of short duration, for Spencer, seeing the threatening danger, rushed forward with all the men he could collect, and met his foe hand to hand in the waist of the schooner.

Short time was given for parley or recognition; the flashing eye, and the swift descending blow, was the sole greeting on either side.

While this obstinate, but unequal struggle for the mastery of the deck was taking place forward, such guns as were yet serviceable, were being worked with energy by a band of the "Fox's" crew abaft.

Twice Spencer and his party drove Coverdale's boarders into the bows, and twice had the "Viper's" men hurled their antagonists back as far as the mainmast.

The overwhelming numbers of the enemy, however, were too great to be resisted long, and after forcing them back some distance, Spencer was compelled to circle his few remaining men round the broken foremast, and thus keep their antagonists at bay.

At this moment, a shout from Dermot, who, though wounded, had been toiling at the wreck, told Spencer that the schooner was free, when, breaking up his ring, he charged Coverdale with such force that he drove his party again into the bows.

In effecting the difficult task of clearing the wreck, the bows of the "Fox" veered round, and the tide bearing her on, she went drifting down with her starboard, or uninjured side, towards the "Viper."

Coverdale's quick eye saw the danger that threatened him, and as the two vessels were parting, he sprang into the bows of his own ship.

Making a rapid clearance of his deck, Spencer trailed all his guns starboard, and, the next moment, the cannonading became more deafening than ever.

Again the bulwarks were shattered to pieces, the deck torn under their feet, and all the mystery of the schooner's midships revealed to daylight.

Nor had the "Viper" suffered less severely; two-thirds of her starboard side were one yawning breach down to the water's edge, while, of her standing gear, the mainmast alone remained bare and tottering.

"Quartermaster," cried Spencer, addressing the man at the helm, "lay her athwart the 'Viper's' quarter."

"Aye, aye, sir, if possible, but she doesn't answer well," replied the man, porting his helm.

"All right! See, she is paying round! All hands ready for boarding," continued the commander, as followed by some score of wounded but still resolute men, he moved forward to be in readiness for the spring, when the two vessels again joined.

"Six feet water in the hold, and fast settling by the head," whispered Dermot in the ear of his captain.

"Signal for the boat then, and remember your oath, Dermot," replied Spencer, calmly.

"And you, captain?"

"My place is aboard the 'Viper.' Quick, Dermot, and tell her——"

The rest of the sentence was drowned in the last exchange of broadsides, making both vessels tremble to their keels, and roll like drunkards on the water.

"Tell her what?" asked Dermot, anxiously.

"To be brave, and—farewell. Forward, lads, to glory!"

As he spoke the bows of the "Fox" struck the "Viper" abaft the gangway, when her mainmast fell with a splitting crash, and falling to port, swept the deck of many of her best hands.

At the same moment Spencer and his boarders sprang on the "Viper's" deck, when a scene of wild turmoil and deadly struggle ensued, rendered for the time almost unearthly by the volumes of smoke and flame that rose from the "Viper's" hatches.

The "Fox's" last shot had reached her vitals, and the brig was a raging volcano.

"Fire! fire! The magazine has caught!" shouted the distracted crew, as they leaped in desperation on board the sinking "Fox."

Spencer saw the danger, and calling off his boarders, sprang back, but only to find the bows of his schooner beneath the water, and her deck covered with the enemy.

"No quarter! no mercy! Death to all!" shouted Coverdale, throwing himself before Spencer, to prevent his reaching the quarter-deck.

"Basil! Basil!" shrieked Ethel, bursting from Dermot's grasp, and rushing forward.

"Back on your life, back!" exclaimed Spencer, beating down Coverdale's guard, and bounding to her side.

"Ten thousand dollars to him who saves the woman!" shouted Coverdale, following aft with his crew.

"Off, villains, she is my wife!" exclaimed Spencer, as covered with wounds, he parried wildly the blows aimed at his head.

"Ten thousand dollars!" cried Coverdale, making a lunge at Spencer with his rapier, and pointing a pistol at his head.

Swift as thought Basil turned aside the thrust, and

sent his sword through the breast of his adversary. With the last efforts of life, Coverdale drew the trigger of his pistol, and the raised arm of his rival fell by his side, as his body dropped at the feet of his distracted wife.

A deafening roar, a blinding flood of light, and a shock like that of an earthquake shook sea, earth and air, and the "Viper," one instant a mass of fire and flame, had vanished into millions of atoms.

A boat, with three women, and filled with wounded and dying men, was seen pulling madly for the shore.

The "Fox" oscillated for a minute from side to side, then, with a downward plunge, sank with her dead and wounded beneath the Persian Sea, a few smouldering spars of the "Viper" alone remaining to mark the grave of both.

In a lovely cottage, far up on the banks of the Thames, there lived a one-armed man in the prime of life, with a beautiful wife, but of himself or his history nothing was known, save that he was passing rich, was commonly known as the Captain, and his villa gates were surmounted by the effigy of a Fox.

CAPTAIN KIDD.

CHAPTER I.

KIDD'S START IN LIFE, AND HOW HE QUELLS A MUTINY.

It was on a lovely morning in the month of May, 1695, when the "Adventure," a large galley of thirty-six guns, and eighty men, left Plymouth Sound, under the command of Captain Kidd, bound for the West Indies.

The high seas were so infested at that time by pirates and buccaneers, that commerce was completely paralysed by the audacity with which those miscreants prosecuted their infamous and murdering expeditions.

But, though the trade of England languished, and half of her merchants were bankrupts in consequence of these sea-robbers, nothing effectual was done to chastise or stop them.

King William drained the country of every ship and man he could obtain, to carry out his insane war with France; and it was left to the merchants themselves to fit out small ships, to punish these common enemies of mankind.

Most of the vessels, which, at great expense and anxiety, had been fitted out to protect their homeward bound ships, had, after a month or two's service, hoisted the black flag, and begun to pillage and murder on their own responsibility.

So insolent and intolerable had these pirates become in the West Indies, about the year 1694, that the Governor of Jamaica recommended the merchants of London to fit out a ship well manned and armed for the purpose of exterminating the miscreants from the Caribbean Sea.

At the same time, he sent over a man of known integrity and honour, who had done his country good service in former wars, an officer for whose character the Governor became responsible.

This man was Captain Robert Kidd. Under his auspices, the "Adventure" was fitted out with every possible requisite for the purpose for which she was designed.

A special commission was obtained from the king, empowering Kidd to take and destroy pirates, wherever he found them, and investing him with supreme authority.

In addition to this, a second commission, under the royal signet, was granted to him, authorising Kidd to make war on any of his Majesty's enemies, especially on the French, whose ships or towns he might destroy or burn as he pleased.

It is of this celebrated individual, and of his career, that we now propose to treat.

A fine, fresh breeze, soon carried the "Adventure" clear of the Channel, and then Kidd shaped his course for New York. On his run across the Atlantic, however, he sighted, pursued, and took a French vessel, called a Banker, which proved a capture of some value.

Soon after, he entered New York harbour with his prize; here he engaged extra hands, and increased his crew to a hundred and sixty strong able men; at the same time, he entered into a fresh agreement with his crew.

By this agreement, forty shares of every prize were to be allotted to the captain and owners, while, in addition to his wages, every seaman was to have one share of the plunder.

The crew, delighted with this arrangement, were ready to follow their new captain anywhere, and do anything he ordered.

Having sold his prize and shared the money, Kidd set sail for Madeira, and the Cape de Verde Islands.

Here he regularly refitted, took in wood and water, bought extra guns, and laid in an abundant stock of fresh provisions, wine, and ammunition.

Instead, however, of returning to the West Indies to exterminate some of the buccaneers, he ran down south, doubled the Cape of Good Hope, and bore up for Madagascar.

Stopping here only long enough to take in wood and water, Kidd bore up for the Red Sea, intending to lie in wait for the Mocha fleet.

Scarcely had he got his ship in hiding under shelter of one of the islands in the Straits of Babel Mandel, when, a fleet of seventeen Moorish ships, convoyed by English and Dutch men-of-war, hove in sight.

Nothing daunted by the frigates, Kidd put to sea at night, and, getting among the merchantmen, poured a broadside into one of the largest, and attempted to carry her off.

The convoy, however, were too quick for him, and, bearing down on the "Adventure," compelled Kidd to relinquish his capture and sheer off.

Smarting with rage at his disappointment, Kidd, on the following day, fell in with a Moorish craft, laden with bale goods and spice; this vessel being unarmed, was soon made an easy capture.

As Kidd believed the Moors had secreted their gold under the cargo, and the crew denied the fact, he ordered the prisoners to be strung up by their arms, and beaten with cutlasses, in the hope to make them reveal their treasure.

Finding this scheme of no avail, he ordered his men to pitch the cargo overboard, expecting to find the money in the hold.

Enraged at discovering from the confession of a Lascar, that the Moors had hidden their gold in the bales he had thrown overboard, and, that there was literally nothing left worth taking, Kidd ordered his men to make marks of the crew with their pistols.

This inhuman conduct was only cut short by a breeze springing up, which compelled Kidd to return to his ship, when he shaped his course for the Coast of Malabar.

Here he fell in with several Portuguese boats, and small craft, and in a few weeks, made a considerable booty.

On his way back to the Red Sea, he chased and took a Portuguese ship, bound for Goa, with a mixed cargo of rice, silks, wax, and other merchandise; these, with a hundred sacks of corn, he removed on board the "Adventure."

Kidd was about taking the prize as a consort, and had just told off a crew, under the second mate, to take charge of her, when a Portuguese man-of-war was seen bearing down upon him.

The Governor of Goa having heard of Kidd's piracies on the Malabar coast, and of his cruel treatment of the captive Moors, had sent this frigate to protect Portuguese ships, and punish the buccaneer for his audacity.

Determined not to be intimidated by a government ship, with a few more men and guns than himself, Kidd, much to the astonishment of the enemy, threw off the empty prize and beat to quarters.

Ranging up to his antagonist he poured in a tremendous broadside of heavy guns and small arms, that perfectly astonished the Portuguese, not only by the rapidity of the attack, but by the execution that resulted from it.

Staggered, but not disheartened, the enemy returned the compliment with despatch and energy, and the two ships, in five minutes, were enveloped in a perfect fog of blinding smoke.

Had the antagonists been fighting for their national honour, they could not have displayed more dogged courage and determination.

After a close action of nearly twenty minutes, a breeze sprang up, which, clearing off the smoke, filled the sails of each vessel, and the combat became a running fight.

Having the weathergage, the galley hung on her enemy's quarter with the tenacity of a bloodhound, hulling her ever and anon, with her heaviest shot.

For three hours this exchange of running broadsides continued with unabated spirit.

In the meantime, the prize having exchanged signals with the man-of-war, set all her canvas, and was following chase in the wake of her countryman.

At this point, Kidd reflected that whatever honour he might obtain by fighting a well-manned and well-armed frigate, would hardly compensate for his loss in the way of profit.

Though much of his rigging had been damaged, his spars were as yet uninjured; his heaviest misfortune consisted in the loss of one of his quarter boats, three shots in his hull, and fifteen men dead and wounded.

Resolved to stop this unprofitable action, Kidd suddenly put the "Adventure" about; and, determined that the empty prize should be of no use to the frigate, he bore down on her.

Pouring the whole weight of his broadside into the hapless merchantman, he shattered her bulwarks to the water's edge, making her rock like a cradle and swallow tons of brine at every oscillation.

Crowding all sail, the "Adventure" stood north, leaving the frigate, with her sails aback, lowering her boats for the assistance of the sinking merchantman.

About sunset they came up with a heavy galleon, trading between Aden and Bombay. Both vessels for a time kept at a respectful distance, eyeing each other with distrust and caution.

At length Kidd hoisted the English colours, when the galleon showed the Dutch flag. On this the two vessels neared each other, when the usual civilities took place; and as they were both steering the same course, they agreed to keep company through the night.

In the morning, however, the Dutchman had forged more than a league ahead, and, with every sail set, was fast increasing her distance; on this Kidd put the "Adventure" round and stood due west.

"Slipped through our fingers like greased lightning; and such a haul as that; worth ten lacs, if she was worth a copper," muttered a surly-looking officer, who came aft to direct the steering.

"What the devil are you grumbling at, quartermaster?" asked Kidd, stopping in his short walk across the deck to confront the speaker. "And what are all the hands doing idling there forward?" he continued, as, with a deep frown, he observed the crew lounging on the forecastle.

"I am not grumbling," replied the man, still more sullenly; "and as for the men—why, I reckon they have something to say."

"And you have come to say it, I suppose. Here, aft all of you!" cried Kidd to the quartermaster, and then calling to the men to approach.

"Now, what have the crew got to say?" he continued, as the men assembled abaft the mainmast.

"They say," rejoined the quartermaster, speaking more insolently now he was backed by the men, "that the galley is foul, and cranky, and full of leaks, and not seaworthy—that the Dutchman would have made a splendid ship for our purpose."

"Quite new, tight as a tub, and a first-rate boat on a wind," interposed some dozen of the men, in noisy chorus.

"And, as a prize, she would have been worth a thousand dollars to every man on board."

"And I didn't take her?" added Kidd, as the man ceased.

"No, you didn't; and that's where it is—she might have been so easy took; and we all look on it as a shame."

"Who's commander here, you or I? Do you think you mutinous hound, that while I am captain I will be dictated to by you or the crew?"

"You may swagger; but you are only a thief, like the rest of us. I say, and so do the men, that we have been cheated out——"

Before the words were finished a bullet from Kidd's pistol had stretched the quartermaster dead at his feet.

The half-uttered shout of rage and vengeance that burst from the hundred and fifty bearded ruffians on deck was drowned in the loud, clear voice of Kidd, as he cried—

"Beat to quarters!"

And before the first ruff of the drum had ceased every man was at his gun, the boarders drawn up on the port and starboard bows, and the small-arms men ready to spring into the fore and main chains.

Such was the force of habit and discipline that the whole manœuvre had not taken three minutes to execute, and a silence like death, broken only by the wash of the tide on the ship's run, reigned on the deck of the galley.

NAUTICAL TALES;

OR, ADVENTURES BY SEA AND LAND.

CAPTAIN KIDD.

CONCLUDED.

Kidd stood with folded arms against the binnacle, calmly surveying the scene, and not till every man had taken his allotted place did he relax a muscle.

When all was hushed, and the lately rebellious crew was once more under control, he drew a pair of double-barrelled pistols from his belt.

Methodically looking at the priming, and cocking each barrel, he slowly advanced, a pistol in either hand, through the midst of his crew.

"Is there any man here who questions my authority? Is there any one willing to keep the quartermaster company to Davy Jones?" he demanded, in a loud ringing voice, in his way from stem to stern, darting a keen glance from side to side, and halting every few paces to look in his men's eyes, and repeat his question. "Is there any man who dares dispute my will? If so let him stand forth and take his billet," and turning round that all might hear his words, he slightly raised his right-hand pistol.

Kidd waited for full a minute in the centre of the ship, as if for some expression in the form of a reply, but every man stood motionless and silent, like a statue of stone.

"Bo'swain, fling that carrion into the sea! Pipe down the hands, and swab up the deck," he continued, pointing to the dead body, as he calmly put up his pistols and slowly descended the companion to his cabin.

CHAPTER II.

KIDD MAKES AN EXCHANGE WHICH HE DOES NOT REGARD AS A ROBBERY.

The next day Kidd sighted a large Moorish ship, which, by her size and depth in the water, promised to be a goodly prize.

Kidd hoisted French colours, and fired a gun, to order her to lie to. The Moor, however, took no notice of this command, and having the wind in his favour, set more sail and stood for the mouth of the Persian Gulf.

The "Adventure" had now become so foul and leaky, that though every stitch of canvas was set which the spars would carry, it was evening before Kidd could overhaul the coveted prize.

Determined not to be baulked in her capture, the galley was run within half a cable's length of the Moor, and a destructive broadside poured in.

The effect of this discharge among her crowded decks was terrible; and the next minute the "Queda"—the name of the merchantman—lay a passive captive alongside of the galley.

This proved to be by far the richest prize that Kidd had yet taken, and his crew were consequently in the highest state of delight.

In a few days the "Queda" was carried into a port higher up the Gulf; and her rich cargo disposed of to the native merchants.

When the proceeds of the ship and cargo were put together, it yielded a share of nearly three hundred pounds a man; while Kidd's forty shares for himself and owners, all of which he appropriated to himself, amounted to nearly ten thousand pounds.

Kidd now made for Madagascar, intending there to careen and repair the "Adventure," and make her serviceable till he could purchase a new ship.

As he approached the north-east point of the island, the look-out sighted a ship lying snugly at anchor, in a sequestered cove or small bay.

Kidd was soon at the masthead himself; and by the aid of a good glass, made out the stranger to be a splendid new three-master, with the French ensign flying at her peak.

"What do you make of her, captain?" asked the first mate, as Kidd descended to the deck in high glee.

"Oh, she's a lovely creature, all a-taut and trim, like a girl going to church; with a figure-head like a mermaid, and lines as fine and taper as a fishing-rod!" replied Kidd, rubbing his hands.

"One of them New England spankers they boast about."

"Not a bit of it; there's no John Bull utility in her, she's French all over."

"French!"

"Aye, and isn't ashamed of her colours."

"What do you mean to do, captain, if I may ask?"

"Take her, Mason—take her."

"And her crew?"

"Well, they will want some place to put their heads in, poor devils, or at least as many of them as are left. I think I will make them a present of the 'Adventure';" and the captain laughed facetiously.

"Poor devils, indeed, then," and the chief mate laughed in company. "Why, we can hardly keep her afloat now."

"Idleness is the mother of mischief, Mason; and they can employ their spare time in making the old tub seaworthy;" and again Captain Kidd, who was in a merry mood, laughed gaily.

"Boatswain!" he added, quickly, turning to that functionary, "chop away some of those ratlines and shrouds, and make her look as forlorn as possible."

"As if she had come out of action, captain?"

"Exactly so; and get up the lilies, and run the bunting half-mast high. This breeze and the tide, will carry us into the cove before evening."

He then turned to one of a knot of his most trusty men.

"Master Gunner, you can palaver French like a native, can't you?"

"Yes, captain, I'm equal to their outlandish lingo, while my two mates are born Mounseers," replied the officer addressed.

"That's all right, come aft here, and I'll tell you the little game I want you to play."

About two hours later the galley, with her sails and rigging all tattered and torn, with the French flag hanging half-mast high, to denote her distressed condition, partly sailed and partly drifted within a quarter of a mile of the strange ship.

As soon as she got fairly abeam of the Frenchman, some half dozen lame and sickly men were observed to let go the anchor, and then while two or three were languidly working a chain pump, the rest contrived to lower a boat.

Then four men, with bloody bandages on their heads, crawled slowly over the ship's side, and getting into the boat, began to pull feebly towards the Frenchman.

In the meantime some thirty or forty of the French crew had been intently watching these proceedings, and were particularly struck by the laboured manner in which the approaching boat was being rowed.

The gunner's mate having hailed the stranger in French, the gangway was opened, and a whip being thrown into the boat, the master gunner and his two mates pulled their weary limbs upon deck.

The fourth man, and the strongest of the crew, though seemingly the most exhausted, folded his arms on the gunwale, and appeared too weak to move.

Seeing the sickly state of the three men, the mate, who had charge of the "St. Louis," offered his visitors seats, before hearing the tale they had come to record.

The story was a sad one.

The "Fleur de Lis" was on her return from the Malabar coast with a rich cargo, when she was pursued, and, after a desperate resistance, captured by an English pirate by the name of Kidd.

Out of a crew of twenty-five men, they had lost fifteen in the useless struggle, while every one of the survivors was either badly wounded, or suffering from scurvy.

Captain Dupon, their humane commander, was too feeble to get over the ship's side, or he would have come himself.

"And the pirate—this dog of an Englishman—what did he do? Where is he now?" asked the sympathizing French mate.

"After taking out our cargo, and all our provisions, except a little water and salt pork, he left us with two shots in our hull, and just as you see us now," replied the chief gunner.

"He then bore away for Malabar, and we, that is, as many as could work, hoisted a little sail, to keep her before the wind; and, as we couldn't stop the leaks, we have been working night and day at the pumps, just to keep her afloat," continued the gunner's mate, taking up the conversation.

"*Mon Dieu!* and what can I do for you, my poor countryman?" cried the humane French mate, after venting a few energetic curses on the detested English.

After delivering the rest of their dear captain's message, and accepting a glass of *eau de vie* each, the three men, after an affectionate embrace, got into their boat, and pulled slowly back to the "Adventure."

Captain Dupon, *alias* Kidd, having watched the progress and return of the boat, retired to his cabin to receive his ambassadors, and hear their story.

"You have played your parts admirably, as far as I could see; I only hope you haven't overdone it," observed Kidd, as the four from the boat and a group of his best men stood around him.

"Not a bit, captain," replied the master gunner. "Bless you, they are as green as babbies, and would swallow a best bower and cable, if you only greased it enough."

"Well, who is she?—what's her tonnage?—how many hands does she carry? and what's she doing here?"

"Well, captain," began the gunner's mate, "she's called the 'St. Louis;' is six hundred tons' burthen; has a cargo of broad cloth and calicoes, and is here to trade with the natives. Her captain and twenty of her crew—her complement is fifty—are gone up the country to see the king of this part of the island."

"They have been gone two days, and are not expected back for two more," put in the chief gunner.

"And what about the succour we require?" demanded Kidd.

"The mate will send a boat's crew in about an hour, to cobble up the leak for the night; and to-morrow he'll show us where we can careen the 'Fleur de Lis,' as we have called her, when she can be regularly overhauled."

"They little know the work they have cut out for themselves, if they mean regularly to overhaul the 'Adventure.'" And Kidd, who had never been in better spirits, laughed boisterously.

About an hour later the cutter of the "St. Louis," manned by ten light, active men, ran alongside the galley, and were soon on her deck.

Captain Dupon, as they imagined him to be, advanced, leaning on his two faithful gunners, to welcome them, though being too faint to speak, one of his supporters expressed his thanks.

Under the guidance of Mason, the chief mate, disguised as a Spaniard, the Frenchmen were led below; here they were instantly gagged, and, being unarmed, were easily overpowered and secured.

The sound of mallets and heavy hammers soon satisfied those on board the "St. Louis" that their countrymen were actively engaged in their work of charity.

In the meantime the Frenchmen's boat had been cautiously brought to the lee of the galley, where, with those of the "Adventure," she was quickly filled by the pirates.

As it grew late, the "St. Louis" signalled for her boat to return, and hung a lantern over her port gangway, as a guide in the dark.

A thick fog hung over the surface of the water, completely hiding the hull of either vessel, though the masts and spars were still visible to each other.

This was the time that Kidd and the best part of his crew, with muffled oars, pulled away from the galley.

As the "St. Louis'" cutter approached, the three master gunners who were in her began singing a French song, while the other four boats cautiously pulled to the starboard side.

"Here they come, at last," said the French mate, lowering the lantern into the boat, which one of the men instantly extinguished by plunging it into the water.

By the momentary glimpse the mate obtained of the cutter's crew, he saw they were all dressed like the men who had left, and he had consequently no misgiving as they mounted the ship's side.

Scarcely had the gunner's party reached the deck of the "St. Louis," when Kidd and his company, who had silently boarded on the starboard side, rushed forward, and the astonished crew of the Frenchman were hemmed in, front and rear.

So sudden was the attack, and so overwhelming the number of their assailants, that the men of the "St. Louis" were overpowered and bound almost without resistance; certainly without a casualty or the infliction of a wound.

Collecting their prisoners under a guard in the bows, Kidd and his delighted followers passed the night in inspecting their prize, examining her stores, tasting her provisions, and making themselves happy with the wine and liquors they found in her hold.

With the first peep of day the anchor was atrip, and in half an hour the "St. Louis" was alongside the "Adventure," when the captive Frenchman, under the wholesome fear of a circle of bayonets, were found working most desperately at the pumps, the water having during the night very considerably augmented.

Captain Kidd, who, when in a good humour, was particularly careful of his crew, accepted the services of the Frenchmen to remove all the treasure and valuables of the galley aboard the prize.

He next had all the guns, small arms and ammunition carried from the armoury and magazine of the "Adventure," and safely deposited in the hold of the "St. Louis."

In fact, he so completely lightened the galley by removing everything of any value, that one pump was found sufficient to keep the water under.

Though the poor Frenchmen worked with a reluctant will, and the pirates lent a cheerful hand to the heavy task, it was late in the afternoon before Captain Kidd had removed all his property on board his splendid new ship.

When everything was arranged, and the liberated Frenchmen were drawn up on the quarter-deck of the galley, Captain Kidd, and his interpreter, the master gunner, sprang on the gangway of the "St. Louis," the hawser was thrown loose, and as the wind filled her sails she glided slowly to sea.

"Give my compliments to your captain, when he returns," cried the gunner, speaking for Kidd, and addressing the disconsolate mate, "and say how sorry I am I was prevented enjoying the pleasure of his society."

"Sacré!" hissed the mate between his closed teeth.

"Adieu, my children!" continued the gunner, with imperturbable gravity, "and as you know the best situation for careening your ship, our kind captain would advise you not to lose time in performing so necessary a business——"

"Peste!"

"For he bids me say, in confidence, her bottom is so rotten, he doesn't think she can hold together a day longer. Adieu! adieu!"

At this point the "St Louis" had forged some fathoms ahead, when both Kidd and the master gunner took off their hats in mock solemnity, and made the wretched Frenchmen a profound bow.

Scarcely had the two vessels passed out of speaking distance when all was activity and bustle on board the "St. Louis," which soon proved herself to be a first-rate sailor—flying from her late anchorage like a bird.

For the next three weeks a succession of good fortune attended Kidd. Hardly a day passed without the capture of some rich ship, either outward or homeward bound.

These, however, were by no means all bloodless adventures, as some of the Dutch and English Indiamen that fell into his hands were not taken without a considerable loss of life on both sides.

At length, loaded with wealth, his crew became clamorous for a run on shore, and an opportunity of spending some of their amassed treasure.

To satisfy his men, Kidd doubled the Cape, and proposed crossing the Atlantic to New York, and there allowing them a month's holiday.

With this intention he ran up the African coast, and when in the latitude of Madeira, fell in with one of the Spanish Plate fleet. A large galleon of 800 tons, having been disabled in a storm, had fallen astern of her companions and their convoy.

On this crippled and luckless ship Kidd fell, with his customary audacity and boldness, and actually carried and rifled her in sight of her consorts, who, not hearing any firing, were ignorant of her peril.

So great was the wealth—in ingots of gold, bars of silver, and precious stones—that, in a few hours, was carried on board the pirate, that every man was said to have netted a thousand pounds by the day's work.

As for Kidd, his proportion in jewels alone was believed to be equal to one-half of his crew's share.

Kidd was on the point of leaving the state cabin of the Spaniard, when he understood that the bland old gentleman with the shaven crown, who occupied it, was the Archbishop of India, returning to Europe after a visit of inspection.

Requesting a private interview with the holy father respecting his spiritual health, Captain Kidd, highly edified by the bishop's conversation, took his leave in about half-an-hour.

From the gravity of Kidd's manner it was inferred that he had had some serious conversation with his Eminence; and so, indeed, he had, though the nature of it did not transpire.

When in the privacy of his cabin, Kidd drew from his breast the gold head of a crosier, richly set in jewels, and two rubies and an amethyst of great size that had once formed conspicuous features in the episcopal hat or mitre of the Right Reverend the Bishop of All the Indies.

CHAPTER III.

KIDD BURIES HIS TREASURE; AND HOW HE HIDES THE SECRET.

For the next two years Kidd, in the "St. Louis," confined his depredations to the Caribbean Sea and the Gulf of Mexico, distributing his favors equally between French, Spaniards and English.

In these piratical cruises it was supposed that he had amassed so incalculable an amount of treasure, that the report of it became a common talk among his own crew.

These ruffians, though by no means cavilling at their own share of the spoil, began to grumble at the *forty* shares the captain always reserved for himself, a proportion which they thought most unjust, since Kidd had long given up the story about the owners and their dues.

For the last six months one of the finest frigates in the British navy, the "Rasper," of forty-six guns, had been sent out from England on purpose to capture and destroy this, the most daring, successful, and cruel of all the buccaneers of that time.

Kidd had been fully apprised of this fact, and for some weeks had been dodging the "Rasper" from island to island, and was running from Cuba in a north-west direction for the continent, somewhere on the coast of Florida.

One day, when in sight of the land, Kidd invited three of his most trusted men to dine with him in his cabin, and after dinner, when the grog was passing freely, he observed—

"Do you know, lads, why I am running in shore now?"

"Can't tell, unless to bamboozle the 'Rasper,'" replied Miles, his coxswain.

"No, lads, I'll tell you; I must trust somebody, and I have long marked you out as the men I can depend upon."

"I hope so, captain," responded the other two.

"Well, I am going to bury my box of treasure, in case this cursed frigate should overhaul us, so that there shall be a nest-egg for a rainy day, boys; for what's mine is the crew's."

"Bravo, bravo, captain!" exclaimed the two men.

"It must be a precious big nest-egg, I'm thinking," cried Miles, with a drunken laugh, "for I'm blest if you haven't taken care to feather your nest."

"Shame! shame! you deserve a clout on the head," cried the other two.

"And who'll give it me?" asked Miles, with a drunken swagger.

"Peace! till I have finished," continued Kidd, with an ominous glint in his eye. "I have selected the place where I mean to hide the treasure; the hole is already dug, and I want you three to bury it."

"And how's it to be got ashore without the crew knowing it?"

"Lower it from the stern window when it's dark."

"And what are we to have for our trouble, and for keeping our jaws shut," demanded Miles.

"Two hundred guineas apiece," replied Kidd, laying three small canvas bags on the table.

"Not half enough; I won't do it under five."

"Then take that, you discontented hound!" and Kidd levelled a pistol, and fired in the coxswain's face.

The man instantly fell forward across the table, while the other two started to their feet.

"Sit still, lads, we are well quit of such a mercenary dog; when I trust you with my secret it is for the good of all. Here, boys, take your money, and divide Miles's share between you."

This liberality of the captain soon pacified the men; and, having slipped the coxswain through a port hole into the sea they all resumed their grog.

In the evening the "St. Louis" was brought to anchor behind one of the many wooded islands that stud the north-east coast of Florida.

The night was very dark; and about eight bells, all being quiet, Kidd and the two sailors lowered from the cabin-window an immense iron-bound chest.

A boat came under the stern to receive the coffer.

Removing all traces of their tackle, Kidd and his two men dropped into the boat, and then pulled to shore.

Rowing about three miles up a sluggish river, they at last came to a belt of firm ground.

Making fast their boat at this place, they landed; and lighting their torches, the negro led the way to a spot where, for the last week, he had been secretly digging the trench, which was to receive Kidd's treasure.

"My eyes and limbs, Captain, ain't it deep!" cried one of the men, looking down the huge square hole.

"Deep and safe, Jack, that's all; the ground's light. But now make haste, lads."

Returning to the boat, by means of the block and tackle, the coffer was landed, and drawn on rollers to the brink of the trench. Fixing their pulley to a branch of the overhanging tree, the immense chest was finally lowered into the dark pit.

"Now, Jack, you must reeve this coil into one of the handles, and here, Jem, you must do the same with the other, so as to have something to haul at when we want the box up. Look sharp, lads, before the moon's up!"

The men sprang down while the negro held one of of the torches, so as to light them.

Putting his hands in his pockets as he bent over to give directions, Kidd suddenly levelled two pistols at the heads of the stooping sailors, and instantly fired.

The men fell over the chest without a groan, the flambeau dropped from the negro's hand, and Sambo fell on his knees before his cruel master.

It was late before the two men had finished their task, and still later when the boat was again under the stern of the St. Louis; and when Kidd drew himself up into his cabin, and turned the boat adrift, he was alone.

At daylight, the "St. Louis" worked her way out to sea, and stood up the coast with a southerly breeze.

"Sail on the starboard bow; square-rigged too, and by the living jingo! the cursed 'Rasper' herself!" cried the chief mate.

"Curse him!" muttered Kidd, as he surveyed the dreaded frigate, as she bore down upon them.

"I suppose we must fight, Mason?"

"Or strike; the thief means to drive us on shore."

"Pipe the hands to dinner, then, and let the men have a bellyful to fight on."

By the time the men had finished their hasty dinner, a shot from the "Rasper" crossed the pirate's fore foot.

Up went the skull and cross-bones at the forepeak, while the black flag floated broadly out from the main.

"Keep her away a point and a half and let her pass," shouted Kidd, as his men stood at their guns.

"Starboard, hard-a-starboard! Ha-ha-ha! Fire!"

By this double and quickly-executed manœuvre, the "Rasper" shot ahead of the pirate, and thus placed herself between him and the shore.

Before the frigate could well wear ship, the "St. Louis," following her close, poured in her broadside, creating for a moment tremendous havoc and confusion.

The "Rasper," however, was commanded by a skilful seaman, and had a brave crew, and in another minute the broadside was returned with stinging effect.

Working slowly round as on a vast pivot, the two ships, nearly of a size, went circling round, pouring in their deadly cannonade.

Kidd soon saw that his only chance with such an adversary was to fight at close quarters.

At the moment, however, of his attempting to run the "St. Louis" aboard the frigate, a round shot carried away his jib and jibboom, and brought down his foretop, rendering her unmanageable.

Prevented by this misfortune from working to windward, she slowly dropped to leeward, when the "Rasper," following up her advantage, drove her so far in shore as to be within sound of the breakers.

"All ready, forward!" shouted Kidd through his trumpet, as another of the frigate's broadsides sent a perfect tempest of splinters and shot past him.

"Let go the anchor! He shall have it now!"

Scarcely had the clamour of the rushing cable ceased, or the pirate's head come up with a jerk, as the anchor gripped the bottom, when the "Rasper" bore down, and lay gunwale to gunwale with the doomed ship.

Then began a contest such as naval warfare seldom sees; the pirates fighting for their lives, disputing every inch, like incarnate fiends.

For an hour this scene of ruin and carnage continued, till the main and mizen of the pirate, coming with a crash to the deck, laid more than half of her crew dead or helpless.

A rush of boarders from the frigate overpowered the few remaining combatants. Mason, the mate, was cut down by the lieutenant of the "Rasper," and Kidd was disarmed, overpowered, and bound before he could utter his battle cry, "Crossbones, to the rescue!"

In ten minutes more, all opposition over, the St. Louis was burning to the water's edge; and, three months later, Captain Kidd and eight men, the sole survivors of his crew, were tried and condemned at Newgate, hanged at Execution Dock, and their nine bodies suspended in chains along the banks of the Thames.

Thus perished Captain Robert Kidd, one of the vilest and most successful of the miscreant buccaneers, and with him perished all record and clue to that vast treasure buried in the swamps of Florida.

NAUTICAL TALES;

OR, ADVENTURES BY SEA AND LAND.

MORGAN, THE BUCCANEER.

CHAPTER I.

Morgan certainly stands at the head of the Buccaneers who pillaged the Spanish possessions so unmercifully in the seventeenth century.

What is a buccaneer? asks the reader.

Well, that you will learn, if you have patience to read further; for Morgan is the best type of the class I could offer you. But if you wish for some immediate definition, turn to your dictionary, where you will learn that buccaneer is " a cant word for the privateers or pirates of America."

To this I would add that a buccaneer is neither one nor the other, but a little of both. Thus they carried on after the fashion of privateers, but without having letters of marque, or the authority of their sovereign to wage war against his enemies upon their own particular account; and moreover (and it is very difficult to mark the distinction between buccaneers and pirates in view of this), they pillaged the nations with whom their country was not at war.

Having settled the question of what is a buccaneer, I proceed to sketch out the career of the notorious Morgan.

He was born in Wales, of parents in humble circumstances, but withal not needy. The plodding toil of husbandry had no charm for his restless spirit, and he early quitted his father's roof to take to the sea.

One of his first voyages was to Barbadoes, which, as my young readers are aware, is in the West Indies. Here he sojourned a considerable time, when the glowing accounts of travellers and adventurers of Jamaica filled him with a desire to visit that island.

Barely had he reached there, when he embarked on board a vessel of doubtful character for a cruise, in the course of which, mainly under his direction, a valuable prize was taken, which greatly influenced his after career.

During his succeeding voyages he made himself a marked man amongst his comrades. His address in the art of war, his particular skill in the use of offensive weapons, earnt him the admiration of all around him.

He was the best shot of the ship's company. He handled sword, pike, or pistol with equal dexterity; and, added to this, he was every inch a sailor.

Boldest amongst the bold, Morgan addressed himself to the most desperate tasks with a coolness and intrepidity which astonished all beholders; and it is no exaggeration to affirm that in all his career he was never taken by surprise.

Such qualities as these naturally brought to command amongst the adventurous spirits with whom his lot was cast.

He undertook everything with such a cool assurance that he invariably succeeded, and his fame spread like wildfire.

A cunning rogue too, was Morgan, and handled the dice-box with the same skill as a ship. Gambling was the prevailing vice of the age amongst these restless spirits, who dissipated in play their illgotten gains.

The consequence of this was that Morgan, by his undaunted bearing, earnt the lion's share of the plunder in their piratical cruises, and by his skill with the dice-box he cleared out the pockets of his comrades, who suffered themselves to be swindled by the cunning Welshman out of the money and valuables that they had spilt their blood in winning.

Having thus accumulated a goodly store he invested it in the purchase of a vessel, or rather in the part purchase, for he had partners in the speculation, who gave him not only the command, but also great advantages in the sharing of the plunder.

After this, the first chance of distinction that he gained was with Manswelt, a veteran sea-rover, who had resolved to make a descent upon dry land, when a favourable opportunity presented itself.

With this purpose he formed a fleet of fifteen vessels, furnished with six hundred men, all specially chosen for the business.

These six hundred men were, with scarce a single exception, the greatest scoundrels you can well conceive. One and all had been engaged in some lawless traffic. Most of them had been a cruise or so on buccaneering expeditions; a greater portion too had spent many of their dark nights in defrauding the excise—running cargoes of spirits, wines, tobacco, lace, and other items, which in the legitimate course of trade, should return heavy customs' duties to swell the royal coffers. Many had dabbled in the ebony trade—in other words, the slave traffic; and, finally, not a few had cruised on yet blacker excursions than all these—when the very flag they carried was of inky hue, decorated with the deathly emblems of skull and cross-bones.

They were not particular to a shade in these good old times, you see.

The fact is, that when you make one step upon the downward path, the rest of the descent is performed with amazing rapidity.

They began by smuggling—for strangely enough there is a very common sentiment on this head shared by nearly every sailor—aye, and landsmen too, for the matter of that—that it is justifiable to defraud the customs.

People, whose honesty in every other transaction of life is beyond question, scruple not to smuggle anything; and yet if one examines the question plainly put, there can be no great diversity of opinion about it.

But this dissertation is leading me away from the subject of Morgan and his buccaneers.

To resume.

The little fleet sailed off to attack the Island of St. Catherine.

The Spanish garrison of the island was numerous, well-armed, and protected by strong forts and batteries; and they made a vigorous resistance.

But it was all in vain.

Their fiery courage went off all at once like a rocket, and the buccaneers adding a dogged resolution to their bravery, conquered with but comparatively small loss.

Their principal object in this capture was to secure a guide to lead them to a richer prize—the town of Nata, which they had determined to pillage.

This town is situated in the south sea, upon the other side of the Isthmus of Panama, and they counted upon securing a fitting guide at St. Catherine's Isle, which was a convict establishment.

Their plans were well laid, for they secured the services of a Mulatto, who was a native of Nata, and who promised to conduct them.

But once the conquest of St. Catherine's Isle achieved they did not care to abandon it, but leaving one of their captains as governor of the island, with a small garrison, they started upon their grand expedition.

They took their Spanish prisoners on board, and landed them at night within a few miles of Porto-Bello, and then running up they surprised the Spanish watch at the mouth of the river, and so made sure of an easy conquest. But an Indian having discovered them, run off in hot haste to the governor, or president of Panama, who for once acting with prompt energy, mustered a tolerable force to oppose the landing of the buccaneers.

Indeed, so formidable was the appearance of the force that Manswelt decided that prudence was the better part of valour, and he retreated, rather disappointed at their non-success.

Amongst the Spanish prisoners was a traitor, who, to curry favour with his captors, started a plan as audacious in sound as it was facile in execution, when they came to look into it closer.

This was to sack the town of Cartage, or as it is better known to us, Carthagena.

At the period of which I write, Carthagena was a rich and flourishing town, and comparatively without defence, for it was never thought that the desperadoes would travel so far from the usual scene of their exploits.

They pursued the same tactics as usual, landed a boat's crew at dark at the mouth of the river nearest the town, and so surprised and overpowered the river-watch before an alarm could be given. Then they ran their fleet up the river, and landed a large body of their men, and marched with all haste towards Carthagena.

At first all went as merry as marriage bells.

They found houses on their way well stored with provisions; and so they regaled with very little thought of the morrow.

But after the first two days they entered upon a wilder country, with never a house to be seen, but instead, a mountainous and rocky district, where provisions ran low, and their courage drooped in proportion.

Murmurs were heard increasing in seriousness every hour.

The buccaneers were composed of British and French, and the two nations quarrelled continually.

Now and again they came across a straggling Indian, whom they mercilessly slaughtered for the few provisions they generally carried.

At length a bag of flour having been captured in this unceremonious manner by an Englishman, he refused to give any share of it to his French comrades, and a quarrel and scramble ensued, which would have become general had not Morgan put it down with an iron hand.

The consequence of all this was, that after several days' march, matters assumed a grave aspect, and Manswelt took counsel with Morgan, and resolved to retreat and abandon the enterprise.

Having re-embarked, they returned to St. Catherine's Isle, where they found that their officer in command of the garrison, left by their own party, had taken steps that looked like making the island a permanent resting-place.

Adjoining St. Catherine's was another and smaller island, with which they easily communicated by means of a bridge. In this island they had already planted very extensively, and they estimated roughly that this would always furnish a garrison of the larger island with provisions.

From here Morgan and Manswelt sailed to Jamaica, where they demanded of the governor a commission, or legal authority for their piratical raid, and assistance of men and arms.

But the governor declined, upon the ground that his Britannic Majesty was at peace with the King of Spain.

He next tried the same tactics with one of the French islands, but the governor gave the same reason for refusing as the governor of Jamaica had done.

Then Manswelt resolved to go to New England, and obtain both a commission and people to re-stock the island of St. Catherine with British blood.

But Manswelt fell sick, and died on the way.

The entire and absolute command of the whole fleet then devolved upon Morgan, who was not long in showing the metal he was made of.

But to conclude with the isle of St. Catherine.

This island was of the very highest importance to the Spaniards, who feared that the Buccaneers would be able to so fortify themselves in it, that presently nothing would be able to drive them forth.

This spot they looked upon as the key to the whole of the West Indies, and therefore they resolved upon desperate measures, before the evil grew too great to be remedied.

They equipped four vessels with six hundred men, under the command of Don Josef Sancho Ximenes, Major-General of the garrison of Porto Bello.

Before, however, they could come to hostilities, Don Juan Perez de Gusman found the means of making them overtures, which Saint Simon (the officer left in command by Morgan) made no difficulty in accepting, seeing how very inferior was his force to that of the Spaniards.

The negotiation concluded, the Spaniards were allowed to take possession of their island without striking a blow.

The Spanish despatches of the time written to tickle the king's eye, gave the wildest account of this expedition, the writers not merely contenting themselves with announcing a glorious victory in general terms, but also going into minute details of the tactics employed—the desperate, albeit useless resistance of the English. Yea, there were even particulars of personal acts of bravery; all of which did infinite credit to the writers' invention, amused the Dons—and hurt nobody.

But here comes the curious part of the story.

The governor of Jamaica, who was a slow thinker, began to fancy that St. Catherine's would indeed be useful to them, and so he tardily fitted out a small vessel with men and women to people the island; arms and ammunition, and a commission for Saint Simon.

Now the Spaniards showed that what they wanted in courage they made up in cunning, and as soon as they saw the vessel approaching, they hoisted the English colours on their forts, and the vessel with all it contained fell into the trap!

CHAPTER II.

Morgan inaugurated his sole command of the fleet by a daring project.

He assembled his officers, and laid before them a scheme for surprising an inland town, which was the seat of one of the chief Spanish industries of those parts—namely, the leather traffic.

This town was supposed to contain a deal of treasure, chiefly in silver, and the robbers were full of eagerness for the rich spoil.

Morgan then weighed anchor, and carried his fleet over to Port St. Maria. He cruised from here to the small islands adjoining and back, so as to avert suspicion from his real design.

His great precaution was to keep out of sight of the Spanish hunters, who were always roaming about the coast in search of game. But his whole attention being turned in this direction led him to neglect other precautions, and a Spaniard who had been a long time prisoner with the Buccaneers, and picked up a smattering of English, contrived to escape overboard at nightfall, and swim ashore.

By this time they had begun to look upon these English rovers as veritable bogies, and the governor set himself about his defence with marvellous alacrity.

He assembled all his able-bodied men, and armed them. He sent messengers off to all the neighbouring towns for assistance, and very soon found himself with eight hundred armed men under his orders.

A large detachment was told off to fell trees, and these were strewn about the way to impede the enemy's advance.

He likewise organised several plans of some intelligence to catch the Buccaneers in ambuscade.

And then he drew up all his force in battle array in a large open prairie.

When Morgan discovered the almost impassable state of the country he guessed at once that his plans had been discovered.

However, he was not a man easily discouraged.

Putting a bold front upon the matter, he made for the woods, and so avoided the timber strewn ground, and leading his men without let or hindrance through, brought them up in front of the governor's little army drawn up in the Savannah in battle array.

As soon as the English appeared on the ground the governor ordered his cavalry to deploy, and soon Morgan's host was surrounded.

Now instead of being in the least dismayed by this formidable host, Morgan prepared to deliver them battle with the coolness of a veteran general.

Their colours were unfurled, and the drums beat.

"Reserve your fire, my men!" cried Morgan, "let them get within easy range."

The men obeyed, albeit with signs of impatience, and the cavalry was almost upon them when, at a preconcerted signal, they fired a withering volley into their masses.

Many a saddle was emptied; yet the Spaniards stood their ground bravely.

Still the determined attitude of the Buccaneers kept them at a respectable distance, threatening and inactive, while Morgan's men re-loaded, and peppered them.

At length a sharp volley staggered the Spaniards, and Morgan, promptly acting upon this, ordered his men to advance.

Their audacity frightened the Spaniards, who galloped off the ground, hotly pursued by the British adventurers, until reaching the town, they rallied a little, and began to reform.

But now Morgan, being in the town, threatened to burn it, unless they yielded at once; and upon their submission, they were all driven into the great church, while the robbers sacked and pillaged.

Yet their diligence was not very well rewarded. The piles of silver treasure—the stores of precious metal, of which they had dreamed, were not forthcoming; for upon the first alarm the whole had been carefully concealed, or carried off.

The whole of the monks had made good their escape too, and this greatly enraged the triumphant robbers; for the church, always possessed of a worldly weakness for wealth, was at this epoch of blind superstition a very mine of gold and precious metals.

In vain did the robbers endeavour to force the townsfolk to confess where their treasures were hidden.

They tortured many old men; for Morgan and his fellows were execrable wretches; but failed to learn anything whatever.

The pillage lasted for a fortnight, at the expiration of which period Morgan made a formidable demand for ransom to save the town from being burnt to the ground.

This was to be paid by the richest of the townsfolk according to their promise, but as the money had to be fetched from some distance, the ever active Morgan had five hundred head of cattle driven off to the coast, slaughtered, and partly salted to revictual his fleet.

Now, while they were thus engaged upon the coast, some of Morgan's men out, scouring the country for stray poultry, general plunder, and game, fell in with a negro slave, bearing a letter from the governor of Saint Jago to the inhabitants of Princes Port, in which he urged them to temporise with Morgan and the heretic robbers, promising shortly to come to the rescue with an overwhelming force.

Morgan accepted the hint, and pressed the Spaniards for the ransom, but seeing that they only paid in promises, he got everything advanced for re-embarking; for, although they were not wanting in courage, they did not choose to fight for fighting's sake.

They did not, as a rule, risk their skins, unless there was something more than mere vengeance to be obtained.

They shortly afterwards sailed for one of the small islands, where they landed, and reckoned up their plunder.

It amounted to between fifty and sixty thousand crowns, partly in coined money, and partly in ingots and metal. This was independent of the rich prizes of cattle and sundry articles of value, and of the bales of silks, brocades, and valuable stuffs of all kinds; the total value of which was almost incalculable.

But such stuffs are of course of value only where there is a market for them, whereas silver and gold are current all over the civilised globe, so that Morgan did not care to return with so little to Jamaica.

Many of his French adherents who owned vessels, quitted him in spite of all his efforts to conciliate them, and returned alone to Jamaica.

But Morgan, ever fertile in plots, had soon another expedition planned.

This one excelled in audacity the last enterprise, and promised, if successful, to give them the richest prize that they had yet taken.

He designed, in fact, a descent upon Porto Bello, a small town upon the north coast of the Isthmus of Panama.

Porto Bello attracted Morgan's cupidity, because it was here that the King of Spain's galleons came to load the silver and divers precious metals that were sent over from the mines of Peru to Panama, and which were brought over to that port on mules.

Although a small town, the rich nature of the traffic conducted at the port elevated it into the very first importance.

Cargoes of exceeding value were discharged there.

A writer of the period, who quaintly enough decries the odious courses of Morgan, while he admits that he served under that redoubtable pirate in most of his excursions, gives us some very curious details upon this town, which the small space at my command here does not allow me to repeat in detail.

Suffice it to say, that when the Spanish galleons arrived, Porto Bello was in a constant state of movement.

It was like a perpetual fair.

The dealers from all the neighbouring villages and towns flocked in shoals to the port, and lodgings and shops were at a very high premium.

The most meagre apology for a bed let at an exorbitant rate.

Nothing was thought of four or five hundred crowns for six weeks' rent of a single room or shop.

The only wonder is, that as Porto Bello offered such tempting advantages to speculators, and as speculators were never wanting in any age—that the place was left in the undisturbed possession of comparatively few for so long a time.

But, from all accounts, there were serious drawbacks. Fevers of all kinds were prevalent at certain seasons, and epidemics were frequent; indeed, it was for this reason that no vessel could venture to remain longer than six weeks in the port.

As Morgan was sailing off, he fell in with an English adventurer, commanding a vessel considerably larger than any of the Buccaneer's fleet, and on Morgan making known his desperate intention to him, he volunteered to join the expedition.

This raised Morgan's force to nine vessels, and four hundred and seventy men.

Now very few facts will show of what mettle Morgan was. The bay on which Porto Bello is situated was guarded by two almost impregnable forts, garrisoned by three to four hundred soldiers. Besides these, there were always four hundred men under arms. This forms a total of 700 to 800 men. Add to this that they were strongly guarded by artificial and natural defences, and it will be easily understood how the dauntless bearing of this redoubtable Welshman shed a lustre upon his name, that not even his odious acts could entirely destroy.

Prudent in council as he was bold in the field, Morgan placed the piloting of the fleet in the hands of an Englishman, who had lived a long time at Porto Bello.

This man led them to Port Naos, which is distant about twenty miles from Porto Bello, where they arrived at nightfall, and from here they navigated along the coast, favoured by a gentle breeze, until they came to a port about halfway between Porto Bello and Naos, and which the Spaniards called El Puerto del Ponton.

"Lower the boats!" cried Morgan.

The command was promptly obeyed, and they pulled rapidly to shore, landing at a spot called El Estera de Longalemo.

In the dead of the night they got ready their arms, and, led by the Englishman, the surprise party advanced rapidly towards the town.

They had marched in this way some considerable distance, when their leader, who was a little ahead, was seen to raise his arm, and wave a warning to them!

Then he dropped upon the ground suddenly, and in a moment they perceived him crawling along upon his hands and knees!

Suddenly he bounded up and fell upon a man who was in the act of raising a musket to his shoulder.

A brief struggle ensued, and the man was thrown to the ground!

CHAPTER III.

THE capture of this sentinel was effected without the slightest noise, and the man was a prisoner before he knew where he was.

They found the man very much alarmed, and, in consequence, easily moulded to their will: for the atrocities of the Buccaneers were such (and they had naturally been exaggerated) as to fill everybody with fright, as soon as Morgan and his worthies appeared.

This prisoner was brought before Captain Morgan and examined.

From this it transpired that the garrison was in good condition, that there were very few civilians called upon to serve in the defence with the soldiers; and that the Buccaneers could assuredly pillage the town, in spite of the fortresses.

"Tie him up," said Morgan; "fasten his hands behind his back."

This was done.

"Now," pursued Morgan, "lead us on; but beware how you trifle with us!"

The man protested by all the saints in the calendar that he would be true to them. But Morgan naturally felt that too much reliance was not to be placed on a man who changed his allegiance so readily.

However, he cut short his vows of fidelity, and bade him lead on.

"You have to consult your own interests," he said. "If you lead us well, we shall pay you well, and take you off with us afterwards, so that you have nothing to apprehend from the Spaniards—if you attempt to play us false, we shall hang you up to the first tree."

They marched on, the prisoner leading the way, until they came upon a redoubt, garrisoned by a troop to which the captured sentinel himself belonged.

Morgan sent this man forward, therefore, to hold a parley, bidding him tell them that they should not be harmed if they would render themselves prisoners without making any resistance; but if, on the contrary, they would not hear reason, he would put them to the sword to a man.

The Spaniards only replied by blazing away.

Muskets, pistols, and small ordnance made a great clatter, but did no great harm, beyond alarming the town.

This enraged Morgan, who made a furious assault on the castle, and, finding a large store of powder there, he blew up the whole of the garrison.

(*To be continued.*)

NAUTICAL TALES;

OR, ADVENTURES BY SEA AND LAND.

MORGAN, THE BUCCANEER.

CONCLUDED.

This was intended by the captain of this gallant, but brutal expedition, to strike terror into the town beyond; but owing to the imperfect light of morning scarcely dawning, and numbers being at rest at this early hour, it partly failed in its effect.

The pirates marched on to the assault of the town, and so promptly were their measures taken, that, in spite of the noise and warnings of their approach, many of the inhabitants were yet in bed. Then there ensued a scramble that beggars all attempts at description.

The Spaniards sprang from their beds to conceal their treasures, and many jewels and precious stones were cast into wells and cisterns, buried in the earth, or under the flooring of the dwelling-houses.

One party of the pirates told off previously for that duty, rushed off for the convents and religious houses, and made all nuns and monks prisoners; and this was looked upon as a master-stroke of Morgan's.

The governor, who was a brave fellow, made frantic efforts to rally the citizens into defending themselves; but, panic-stricken, they fled before their assailants in every direction.

Seeing this, the governor fought his way to one of the few forts that remained in their possession, and from this point of vantage, he kept up an incessant fire at Morgan's host.

But even bravery alone could not avail them against discipline and trained skill in the use of arms.

While the Spaniards fired at random, one shot in twenty taking effect, Morgan had told off a body of picked marksmen from his force, and posted them in advantageous positions, with precise orders about firing.

They had to aim at the mouths of the enemy's guns; and so surely did they direct their fire that nearly every shot took effect.

The combat had lasted from the break of day until noon; yet Morgan could not bring the defenders of this fortress to submit, and with this force still opposing him, the day was far from being won.

The sole aim and end of the expedition was plunder, and the richest portion of the treasures had been carried to the fortress. This Morgan knew, and he was resolved at all hazards to reduce it.

Accordingly, at noon, he sent a flag of truce, with a message to the effect that no quarter would be given, unless instant submission were made.

The answer was returned immediately in these terms.

"We ask no quarter—we expect none—we shall neither give nor take quarter."

Exasperated at their obstinacy, Morgan made preparations for an assault.

He had a number of ladders constructed wide enough to allow three or four men to mount abreast.

This done, he gave orders for the nuns and monks to place them against the walls, thinking, by so doing, to perplex the garrison.

But in this he was mistaken.

They blazed away as hard as ever, and hurled over pots of combustibles, such as sulphur, gunpowder, seething pitch and tar, killing or wounding horribly as many of their own countrymen as of the enemy.

The command was given to assault, and the Buccaneers advanced in force, scaling the ladders, while Morgan's marksmen picked off the unfortunate Spaniards as they ventured to appear upon the ramparts.

Now came the tug of war.

They fought their way to the walls right valiantly; but this gained, a desperate struggle ensued, in which many of the assailants and some of the Spaniards were hurled over to the ground.

But the pirates had the stouter hearts. They hurled in a shower of hand grenades (with which each man of the storming party was armed), and then with sabre and pistol they fell upon them.

The carnage was fearful.

Seeing that it was now utterly hopeless to contend, the Spaniards should have retreated, or demanded quarter; but their officers made frantic efforts, and insisted upon them fighting to the last.

Obstinately every foot of ground was contested. The ground, the walls, and ramparts were covered with bodies of the slain or wounded, and the blood ran like water.

At length, however, one by one the Spaniards were cut down or made prisoners, and the governor still stood, sword in hand, bleeding from a score of wounds, and encumbered by the piles of slain around him, defying the foe to the last.

The pirates—great scoundrels though they were—could not be insensible to his bravery, and they called upon him to surrender, now that resistance was in vain.

But to no purpose.

"Never!" he replied, waving his reeking sword. "Never! Come on!"

His wife and daughter, upon their knees, implored him to give in that his life might be spared.

But to them, likewise, he turned a deaf ear.

"Better to die as a brave soldier," returned the hero, "than be hanged as a coward!"

The words were barely uttered when a pistol bullet brought him down.

The victory was now complete.

They placed the men and women prisoners apart, and the wounded they shut up in another place alone, leaving them to get well as best they could, for they had no medical assistance to give them.

This done they fell to their carouse, as they called it, eating and drinking everything they could lay hands upon.

Maddened with liquor, they gave themselves up to all kinds of debauchery, and speedily reduced themselves to such a hopeless condition that fifty courageous men might easily have retaken the city, and killed the Buccaneers to a man.

Next day they held a council, and examined several of

their prisoners, with a view to make them confess where the chief part of the riches of the town were concealed; but they either could not or would not divulge these matters, and many were put to the torture in consequence.

I do not care to dwell upon the sickening details of these atrocities. Suffice it to say that several of the hapless prisoners died upon the rack, and others succumbed very shortly from the effects of the tortures.

These villanous deeds make one forget the gallant bearing of the adventurers; the brilliancy of their exploits and their skill and courage throughout.

Nothing could so utterly have tarnished the lustre of their name; but for this, the admiration of their undaunted courage made many forget or look over the fact that, after all, they were but a band of freebooters, of pirates and robbers.

CHAPTER IV.

They had now been at Porto Bello a fortnight, during which time they lost numbers of their men, as many by reason of the unhealthy climate as from the reckless debaucheries which characterised their career.

Meanwhile the President of Panama, having gained tidings of the capture and pillage of Porto Bello, set vigorously to work to raise troops wherewith to fall upon the Buccaneers. His purpose was to effect this with no less secrecy than despatch, so as to come down upon the pirates and surprise them.

But this he would not have done in any case.

Morgan obtained early intelligence of the Moor, but the truth is that he utterly despised the Spaniards, and he knew that, at a push, he could always retreat to his vessels with all his men.

However, as the time drew on, he deemed it prudent to embark, which they were about to do when a scout ran up to Morgan with the startling intelligence that the Spaniards from Panama were upon them in great force.

The Buccaneers betrayed great consternation at this, but Morgan, to reassure them, went on with his preparations with the coolest deliberation.

He had some of the chief prisoners brought before him, and commanded them to pay the ransom of the town in a sum of 200,000 crowns, in default of which ransom he would assuredly burn the town, and blow up the forts.

While this negociation was proceeding the Spanish reinforcements approached.

Now, on their way, they had to pass through a narrow defile which could be guarded by a small body against a very superior force, so hither Morgan despatched a hundred men.

The Spaniards came on quite unsuspectingly until they were well into the pass, when suddenly a withering fire was opened upon them from each side, and beyond.

The Spaniards, confused, fired a few random shots, and tried to retreat, but much loss was sustained before they could get clear of this ugly trap, on account of the crowding of the place.

The commander of the troops held a parley with the Buccaneers, and made known to them that he was about to march against them with 2,000 men. No quarter would be given, he said, unless they retired at once.

To this Morgan made answer that he would not leave without the ransom, unless he was at the very last extremity. To this he audaciously added that, unless the ransom were not very speedily forthcoming, he would blow up or burn the town under the President's eyes.

Morgan's boldness and assurance alarmed them, and the President recommended them to temporize with him while messengers were dispatched to Carthagena for a fleet to come and surprise the hardy robbers.

But the Spaniards did not get over the ground fast enough to accomplish this project. Morgan, in vulgar parlance, "put on the screw," and frightened them so, that the townsfolk begged the President to come to terms with him at once.

"These Englishmen are devils!" they said. "They fought us against odds, and against every advantage, for our forts could have held out against ten times the number of the garrison, and our officers rushed on to certain death in very rage and disappointment."

The President, therefore, on mature deliberation, gave his permission for them to treat as best they could with Captain Morgan.

It was therefore agreed that in the space of four days they should raise 100,000 crowns as ransom for the town, forts and prisoners.

The President, whose name was Don Juan Perez de Gusman, was an officer of great note in the Spanish service, and had earned a great name in Flanders; and he was amazed at the manner in which these daring adventurers had taken such a town with no better arms than muskets, stout hearts and iron muscles; for, according to all precedent, he would have deemed it impossible to reduce such a formidable place without the aid of cannon, and a regular siege, according to established usage.

He sent Captain Morgan some presents, and a flattering request to see the arms that he had used to accomplish such deeds of valour.

Morgan returned some polite message, with a musket.

This was an improvement upon any of the muskets of the day, and, till then, unknown to Don Juan Perez de Gusman. He was much gratified with the sight of it, and with Morgan's civility.

He sent back the messenger to Morgan, with an emerald ring of great value, and a message to this effect:—

"I thank your great captain for his courtesy, and beg his acceptance of this ring as a mark of my admiration of his valour. It is to be regretted that such brave people should not be employed in the service of some great prince in a just and honourable war."

Morgan returned his thanks to Don Juan, and told his messenger to add:—

"I have sent his excellency one of our new guns to examine, and he has been pleased to express his admiration of it. Tell his excellency that, before long, we shall endeavour to increase his good opinion, by showing him our address for using the weapon on the town of Panama."

Very soon after this the ransom was brought down in ingots and bars of silver.

This settled, they spiked the cannon of the forts, and embarked for Cuba, where they made the division of the spoil.

They found, when they came to reckon it up, that they had in gold and silver, both in ingots and in coined money, and jewels, which were not estimated at a quarter their value, not less than 260,000 crowns.

This was the modest estimate they made of their treasure, although the amount of rich cloths, silks, various stuffs in bales, and sundry articles of merchandise was beyond estimation.

It was their custom to look upon the richest spoil as comparatively valueless, unless it was in gold, silver, or precious stones.

The division of the plunder being made, they sailed for Jamaica, where they were received with open arms—more especially by the tavern-keepers, into whose pockets the hard-earned gains eventually dropped.

And riot and debauch became the order of the day, until their money was squandered away.

CHAPTER V.

I have not the space here to recount in detail all the exploits of this extraordinary character; nor would they perhaps interest the general reader, for the recital would inevitably become monotonous, seeing that his whole career is but a repetition of such scenes as I have already described.

Morgan was unlike his comrades in one important particular.

Instead of squandering his portion of the spoils, he deposited them in places of safety, and before long be became a man of money.

By this time he began to have had enough of his adventurous course of life, and it is more than possible that he would have retired into private life henceforth, but for the clamorous demands of his former comrades, who, now falling into destitution and debt, besought him earnestly to lead them to some fresh enterprises.

Morgan was by no means insensible to the flattering proof of their devotion and confidence in him; and in spite of all his former resolves, he consented to lead them forth to fresh scenes of adventure.

Of these I shall but describe one.

This was his attempt upon the city of Panama, which has filled the world with wonder and admiration of his daring and skill ever since that remarkable epoch.

On the 18th of August, 1670, he set out from the castle of Chagre with twelve hundred men, five boats laden with artillery, and thirty-two canoes.

The first day they sailed about fifteen miles, and reached a spot called De los Bracos, where a party of the men went ashore to sleep and stretch their limbs, which were cramped from long crowding in the narrow limits of the boats.

A party of foragers scoured the woods, but returned empty-handed, for the Spaniards had fled, carrying all their provisions with them, on the approach of the much-dreaded Buccaneers.

This was a dire misfortune, for many of their number were worn out with fatigue and hunger, and yet had to content themselves with no better nourishment than a pipe of tobacco.

Upon the second day they came to a place called Cruz de Juan Gallego.

Here they were compelled to quit their boats and canoes, for the river was almost dried up from want of rain, and even the shallow parts were blocked up with fallen trees.

The journey now became both long and tedious, by reason of the bad road and the absence of anything like food.

As they went on, the Spaniards fled before them, carrying off every scrap of eatables, and, but for their indomitable courage, they must have succumbed.

Towards noon of the fifth day they came upon a place called Barbacoa, where, after a diligent search, they had the great good fortune to light upon two sacks of meal and wheat, two great jars of wine and some plantains.

These came in most opportunely, and probably saved the lives of many of their party.

Morgan had these provisions judiciously distributed to such of his men who were the most exhausted.

And the march was resumed for a time with redoubled vigour. But forty-eight hours passed without a repetition of such good fortune, and the whole party was reduced to a truly pitiable plight.

They ate up some leather bags, and washed the unsavoury meal down with copious draughts of clear water, of which, fortunately, there was plenty at hand.

They ate the long grass, the leaves and twigs of trees, to assuage their hunger.

Another day passed, and they came upon a plantation, and a barn full of maize!

Then great was their rejoicing. Such feasting; but it presently died away, and then they began to break out into murmurs against their redoubtable leader.

Matters were becoming grave, when one of the men discovered a chimney smoking in the distance!

They gave shouts of joy, and pushed on vigorously, and presently they were gratified at seeing the town, though as yet very far distant.

Upon the eighth day Morgan told off an advanced guard of two hundred men who went on to reconnoitre, and give warning of any possible ambuscade.

After ten hours' march they came to a place called Quebrada Obscura.

Here, all upon a sudden, a flight of three or four thousand arrows caused them no little alarm, for they could not perceive whence they came.

A skirmish ensued here rather in favour of the Indians, who fought with great bravery until their chief fell wounded, when they fled, having killed eight of Morgan's men, and wounded ten more.

An hour later they fell in with a party of twenty Spaniards, whom they tried hard to capture; but their speed and knowledge of the country enabled them to make good their escape.

A party of scouts had been sent up a high mountain to reconnoitre, and presently, to the infinite joy of their comrades, they announced that they could perceive the South Sea at no great distance; and, still better, they could see in the valley at their feet a quantity of cattle.

The pirates lost no time in possessing themselves of these, and a general slaughter took place. Beeves, cows, calves, horses were slain—cut, or rather chopped into huge hunks, and thrown upon their wood fires to be devoured, charred, and burning.

It looked more like a cannibal feast than a meal of civilised Europeans.

The next signal for general joy was the announcement that they were within sight of the steeples of Panama. They danced, shouted, yelled, and threw up their hats as though they had already captured the city.

Towards evening, a body of horsemen, fifty strong, rode out from the town to ascertain the cause of such a noise and tumult. They rode up almost within musket shot, and blew a great deal upon a trumpet; for the Dons were always famous for their observances of the "pomp of glorious war."

They shouted defiance and menaces, calling them dogs. "*Perros! Nos Veremos!*"

With which they rode off, with the exception of seven or eight horsemen, who remained hovering about the camp to watch the motions of the Buccaneers.

The sight could not have been very gratifying, for having posted their sentinels about the camp, they fell to eating the remnants of their beef and horseflesh kept from the last feast; and then they lay on their backs, and slept.

Later on two hundred horsemen rode back, and posted parties here and there, so as to block the Buccaneers in upon every side.

But the adventurers showed no symptoms of alarm, unless such a feeling could be gathered from the most discordant chorus of snoring that ever saluted mortal ears.

Next day they were stirring betimes, and soon upon the march.

But they little thought of the warm reception in store for them.

Having reached the summit of a hill, they found themselves overlooking a champaign country, with the city beyond.

At their feet the Spanish forces were drawn up in battle array; and a single glance showed them to be so numerous, that the Buccaneers began to wish themselves out of the business.

The governor of Panama showed considerable military knowledge, by the manner in which his force was disposed.

It consisted of two squadrons, four regiments of foot, besides cavalry. In addition to this, they introduced a curious element of warfare into the contest—as novel and alarming in aspect as it proved useless in practice.

This was a great number of wild bulls, which were driven by a strong party of Indians and negroes.

As Morgan surveyed this formidable host, he had a momentary heart-sinking.

Yet they were fairly in a trap; there was no choice; nothing remained to them but to do, or die.

Morgan gave a sweeping glance over the field, and promptly set his force in motion.

And from the onset did this remarkable man show his good generalship.

He ordered on a body of two hundred men, who were expert marksmen, with the guns, towards a part of the field which was soft and marshy, hoping to lure the enemy's cavalry into challenging them.

Nor was he disappointed in this hope.

Their shouts of "*Viva el Rey!*" rent the air, and they spurred their horses boldly on to charge them, but once in the marshy ground, their horses sank so deeply, that they could make no headway.

Seeing this, Morgan promptly shouted his command—

"Down, and give them a volley, lads!"

The men obeyed, and poured in their shot so sharply that the Spanish column turned completely round.

But they stuck bravely to their work, and supported by a strong body of infantry, charged on, and strove might and main to throw the Buccaneers into disorder.

Morgan hurried forward a troop to intercept the infantry, and drove them off, so that the cavalry began to get roughly handled, and retreated.

Then the Indians and negroes were called upon to play their part in the fray.

They goaded the wild bulls on, and set them charging upon the Buccaneers, but the noise and din of the battle frightened them so that they nearly all took flight, and what few succeeded in breaking through the lines tore the English colours to pieces, when they were all shot dead.

The horsemen were now killed or dispersed to a man, and the infantry, taking fright, fired a harmless volley, and threw away their arms, so as not to be impeded in their flight.

The slaughter was enormous here, considering the numbers engaged, for over six hundred Spaniards were killed on the plain, besides wounded, and numbers of prisoners; and the loss of the Buccaneers was likewise very great.

But fired with pride and joy at their victory, they marched on to the town.

And now the most desperate part of their task had to be performed, for the Spaniards had posted forts in every direction to harass the enemy, and so well did they ply their cannon with small shot and pieces of iron, that numbers of the Buccaneers fell almost at every step.

Yet with stout hearts and indomitable wills, they pushed on, driving all before them, until they were masters of Panama!

The taking of Panama was the most wonderful exploit connected with Morgan's career. He led up a body of half-famished men against a strong city guarded by troops, which outnumbered his even after the carnage; his men were mowed down by their cannon, with which the Spaniards were well provided; and they had a powerful body of cavalry to boot.

Yet in the face of every difficulty they fought their way to the city, sacked and burnt it!

The burning was Morgan's express work, nor was this the only thing which has rendered his name odious to posterity.

The cruelties practised upon the hapless prisoners who fell in their hands are beyond description.

Neither age nor sex was any protection.

They covered themselves with glory in their valiant conquest of the city—even remembering its object—but they tarnished most fatally the lustre of their acts by showing that after all they were but robbers and assassins!

The plunder they made in this capture is beyond estimation, and Morgan was a made man for life.

This was the last notable action of Morgan's career.

After this he retired to Jamaica, to enjoy the riches he had plundered the Spaniards of. Here his endless wealth found him favour with all men.

He lived in princely luxuriance for a long while; the odious acts connected with his name were forgotten, and they heaped civic dignities and endless honours upon him.

For a considerable time matters went on in this way, but then came a reverse.

The governor of Jamaica was recalled, a successor was named in his stead, and Morgan was summoned to England to answer his misdeeds to the country upon the bitter complaints of his most Catholic Majesty the King of Spain, the governor at the same time being summoned to answer for the countenance which he had given to Morgan and the Buccaneers.

NAUTICAL TALES;

OR, ADVENTURES BY SEA AND LAND:

CAPTAIN AVERY,
THE PIRATE-PRINCE OF MADAGASCAR.

CHAPTER I.

Having given you an idea of a Buccaneer in my sketch of Morgan's career, I purpose taking a glimpse at the Pirate proper.

For this purpose I have selected a notorious character, as a fair type of this class of freebooter—Captain Avery.

As I shall only give a very brief outline, and record but simple facts, without any colouring of my own, I warn such of my young readers as have read of Captain Avery's exploits already, and have learnt to regard him as a marvel and a hero of romance, according to the conventional type, that my short narrative is destined to lift the veil of fiction which has tinged the pirate's character with so rosy a hue, and show him as he really was, a desperate scoundrel, whose career was one long tissue of falsehood and baseness; who betrayed his so-called friends with as little remorse as his enemies, and who cut a very poor figure indeed.

An attempt has been made by certain writers of fiction to make of Avery, as of Morgan, a very great character; daring, rash, and perhaps of loose principle, but yet, withal, full of manly impulses, and of a chivalrous nature.

Rubbish!

Avery was as great a rascal as Morgan, or greater, but lacked Morgan's wit and daring.

Morgan had the tact to invest himself with a sort of privateering character, although he carried no letters of marque, and so could not have been strung up as a pirate by the first power which should chance to lay hands on him; and, moreover, he conceived and executed enterprises worthy of a great commander.

But there was no mistake about Avery.

A pirate he was, and a very paltry fellow to boot; for what little he did to make a noise in the world was but a repetition of the stalest of stale tricks.

Pirates have existed as long as ships have sailed.

History tells us how Julius Cæsar was made prisoner by pirates near the Isle of Pharmacusa.

It was then the custom to tie their captives back to back and drop them into the sea. More modern pirates have made their prisoners "walk the plank," but it shows that the rogues have not refined their cruelties.

These pirates would have served Julius Cæsar as they did their regular prisoners, had not his purple robe and the richness of his train given them a notion that more was to be got by his ransom than his murder.

They therefore offered him his liberty if he would procure a ransom of twenty talents—a sum which they thought to be exorbitant.

Cæsar smilingly offered them fifteen, and they were overjoyed no less than surprised.

They gave him permission to send some of his servants to fetch the money, and although he was forced to pass about a fortnight in bondage, with only three servants remaining out of his retinue, he betrayed so little fear or embarrassment with them that he positively obtained a sort of ascendancy over them.

On going to sleep, he ordered them to be silent, threatening to hang them if they disturbed his rest.

He gambled with them, and recited them verses and dialogues, treating them as asses, and to other names as little complimentary when their intelligence was not capable of seizing the merits of his compositions.

He diverted his captors in this fashion until his domestics returned with the ransom.

As soon as he regained his liberty, Cæsar armed and equipped a fleet of vessels at his own cost, and sailed at once against the pirates, whom he surprised at anchor near the islands where he had been made their prisoner.

Having secured all his former captors, and a few more into the bargain, he seized all the treasure he could find in their vessels to indemnify him for the cost of the expedition, and carried them off to a place of security and appealed to Junius, the then governor of Asia.

Junius, however, seeing no profit to be made over judging the prisoners, observed that he would see at his leisure what was to be done.

This did not satisfy Cæsar, who returning, hanged the prisoners as he had jocularly threatened them while he was their captive.

But I am running away from Captain Avery all this while.

Few adventurers have enjoyed so great a reputation upon so very meagre a foundation as Avery.

Upon one of his exploits was built up a story, which was a most absurd and extravagant romance, based, it is true, upon fact.

In Europe he got to be talked of as a person of consequence. He was spoken of as the founder of a new monarchy.

It was said that he had accumulated immense riches, and married the daughter of the Grand Mogul, whom he had taken prisoner in an Indian vessel.

Nay, they gave out that he had got children by this marriage, and so established the succession to his new kingdom.

It was averred that he had built forts and established magazines, and armed and equipped a powerful fleet, manned by sailors of all nations, whose courage was equal to their experience.

The legend added, that he gave commissions to the captains he appointed to the command of his vessels, and orders to the governors of his forts in his own name; and that, in a word, he was regarded as their prince.

How far true and how far false these histories, the following brief outline of this sea-robber's life will show.

CHAPTER II.

Avery was born near Plymouth, and he was brought up by his parents to the sea.

From this port he made several voyages in merchantmen as mate.

Before the Peace of Ryswick, and during the alliance of Spain with England and Holland, the French, at Martinique, carried on a contraband trade with the Spaniards in Peru.

The laws of Spain then forbade any people, whether friends or foes, to trade with their Indian possessions; and menaced them with seizure should they venture to set foot upon their territory.

The native Spaniards wished to monopolize the trade with their colonies, and to enforce their laws upon this head, they kept a certain number of vessels as coast-guards, cruising about in those waters.

These coast-guards had orders to seize any ships venturing within ten or twelve miles of their coasts.

But so few and poorly armed were these vessels that they dare not venture to tackle such ships as the French employed in this illicit traffic.

The Spanish Government, therefore, employed several foreign vessels upon this service, and some Bristol merchants equipped two ships, mounted with thirty guns, and a hundred and twenty men each, besides all munitions of war and thorough victualling.

They were to have sailed to a Spanish port, to receive orders, and to take on board some Spanish gentlemen, who went as passengers to New Spain.

Avery was appointed first mate in one of these vessels, the "Duke," commanded by Captain Gibson.

Now Avery had no sooner engaged on board this ship, than his ambition took a daring and treacherous form.

He was an insinuating character—flattering, persuasive, and possessed of what sailors call the gift of the gab—and having sounded the crew, he made all easy to seduce them from their allegiance.

Everything favoured his nefarious schemes.

Firstly, Captain Gibson, who was every inch a sailor, was spoilt by a fatal passion for drink, and Avery took advantage of a fit of drunkenness of his officer to openly avow his schemes to the more favourably inclined of the crew.

He designed to seize the vessel, and, having assumed the command, to steer her against those very Spanish-Indian coasts which they were there to protect.

"We can make ourselves rich for life," he said. "One job will do it, and it is all over, instead of cruising about all your lives for sailor's pay."

This argument caught them, and all was ready for the execution of the scheme, which was to be carried out upon the following night.

He made it executable so promptly, in order to leave the men as little time as possible for reflection and possible backsliding.

Unfortunately, however, for the conspirators, Captain Gibson, instead of remaining on shore that night to get drunk, fuddled himself on board, and went to bed about nine o'clock.

This, however, did not change their plans; for, as such of the men who were not in the plot had also turned in, the deck was left in the hands of Avery and his accomplices.

At ten o'clock, the hour fixed upon by agreement, sixteen men in the scheme rowed over from their consort, the "Duchess," previously signalling them according to a prior understanding.

They set to work at once to guarantee themselves against interruption from below, by fastening down the hatchways and barricading the cabins.

Then they gently, noiselessly as possible, weighed anchor, and stood out to sea.

This was the most desperate stroke that Avery ever committed, for there were several vessels anchored about, and amongst them a Dutch frigate, carrying forty guns, whose skipper was offered a great sum of money if he would pursue the "Duke," but he refused, and Avery sailed off triumphant.

Presently Captain Gibson, who had been aroused by the rocking of the vessel, or the confusion going on above, called out, and Avery, with two of his men, entered the cabin.

"What's the matter?" demanded Captain Gibson, in a half drowsy voice, which showed some spice of alarm withal.

"Nothing," replied Avery.

"But," said the captain, "the ship must have slipped her anchor. I am certain she is free."

Then, as Avery made no reply, he added—

"What sort of weather is it?"

"Why," said Avery, "the fact is, that we are out at sea, with a fresh wind, and the weather is as fine as you could desire."

"At sea!" reiterated Captain Gibson, aghast. "What do you mean by that?"

"Fear nothing," replied Avery, with great coolness, "only tumble out and dress yourself—be lively. I am chosen captain in your place, so this is my cabin—get out. I am going to Madagascar to make my own fortune, as well as that of all these brave companions who link their fortunes to mine. Be one of us if you like. We are ready to receive you amongst us, and, perhaps with time and good conduct, you may rise to be lieutenant. If you don't like the notion, I will give you a small boat to get back to land as best you may."

Captain Gibson, who was at first greatly alarmed, grew reassured at this, and agreed to leave at once.

Avery then assembled the crew, and told them what had occurred, and gave those who wished to leave him permission to return in the boat with Captain Gibson.

Six men, in all, availed themselves of this, and they trusted themselves thus to the mercy of the waves at a considerable distance from shore.

It is to be hoped that this rough lesson, which sufficed to sober the captain completely, had a beneficial effect upon his after life.

It certainly ought to. But drunkenness is a fatal evil, and is generally difficult to eradicate from any nature in which it has taken root.

However, history gives us no further tidings of Captain Gibson.

Our present business is with Avery alone.

The pirates pursued their way to Madagascar without taking a single prize, or falling in with any adventure worthy of note.

Arrived at the north-east of that island, they fell in with two small vessels, which had been deserted by their crews on the appearance of the "Duke" in sight.

The fact is, that the crews of these vessels were also pirates—being deserters from the West Indies, and seeing the "Duke," they took her to be a frigate sent in pursuit of them.

Her size frightened them, and feeling how powerless they were to oppose such a force, they fled to the woods, and did what they could to defend themselves.

Avery, however, guessed shrewdly at the state of the case, and he sent on a few men to make overtures to them, saying, that if they chose to join him, they would make up such a force as would ensure their mutual safety.

They were a long time in being brought to reason, for they felt sure that it was but a trap set for them.

Posted in the woods, in a strong position, with advanced sentinels, they would only allow one or two of the strangers to approach at a time.

Avery, seeing this, set their minds perfectly at rest upon this score, by landing a small body of his men unarmed.

The alliance was thus effected to their mutual satisfaction, for the two small vessels were so insignificant, that they never could have taken any prize worth considering; whereas Avery deemed the two small vessels a valuable auxiliary to his force.

Having thus augmented his force, Avery cruised along the coast of Arabia; they fell in with a vessel at the mouth of a large and important river, which they took for a Dutch ship from the West Indies.

The "Duke" sent a signal shot after her, upon which, to their surprise, she run up the pavilion of the Great Mogul at her masthead.

The "Duke" hereupon gave her a broadside, which fell ridiculously short, and the Great Mogul's vessel was put about to fight them.

Very little manœuvring ensued.

The two small vessels managed to get alongside, and their men swarmed up her sides, upon which she struck her flag.

This was about all the engagement of which so much was made in glorifying the robber Avery.

As it turned out, there was on board of the vessel a daughter of the Great Mogul, who, with a number of persons of quality of her land, was about making a pilgrimage to Mecca, in accordance with Mahometan custom.

Each person carried an offering for the tomb of Mahomet, of great value—that of the princess being all but priceless.

The Oriental custom was to travel in the greatest magnificence, and the consequence was that a prize of enormous value fell into the pirates' hands.

Each member of the suite of her highness had a train of slaves and other domestics, and besides the incalculable store of jewels, plate, gold and silver, and divers descriptions of treasure, they carried a fabulous sum of money to defray the incidental expenses of the journey.

The pirates, having stripped the vessel of every object of any value they could lay hands upon, returned to their own ships, and purposed steering for Madagascar, with a view of erecting forts and entrenching themselves in security, so as to protect the fruits of their lawless achievement.

But, as I shall show, Avery's treachery rendered all these projects useless.

As they sailed towards their destination, Captain Avery sent word to each of the commanders of the smaller vessels, begging them to come on board the "Duke" to hold a council with him.

This they agreed to.

Once there, Avery's oily tongue stood him in good stead.

He proceeded, in a roundabout way, to explain to them the danger of having so much valuable treasure on board such small vessels, which could offer so little protection to it in case of danger.

This sounded so reasonable that, when Avery suggested the advisability of carrying all the treasure on board the "Duke," they fell in with his views at once, and actually carried their treasures into the clutches of the cunning rogue, Avery.

Here the coffers containing them were, by the captain's own express desire (treacherous rascal!), sealed down.

For the next twenty-four hours they sailed in company.

But Avery had other plans in view, and he made these known to his own crew.

"We have now on board," he said, "enough to make us happy for the rest of our lives—that is, for ourselves alone—but shared with our allies, it will so reduce each man's share that it will become insignificant."

They fell in with his views at once, and upon the second night they profited by the thick fog which hung over the water to make off upon a different course.

The consequence was that when daylight appeared the crews of the smaller vessels were amazed and filled with consternation to find that the "Duke" had disappeared—vanished, melted, as it were, into thin air.

As soon as they were out of sight of their late comrades, whom they had so vilely abused, they began to consult upon their prospects.

Captain Avery advised them to proceed at once to America, where, being unknown, they could easily find the means of selling their plunder under assumed names.

They made for Providence Island, where they remained a considerable time.

But, in the end, they began to reflect that the size and mounting of their vessel might cause them to be looked upon with suspicion in New England, where they intended proceeding.

To avoid this, Avery suggested selling the vessel, under the pretence that it was a ship which belonged to certain large landed proprietors, who, having failed in their scheme, gave orders for it to be sold for their account.

With the proceeds of this barter they purchased a small vessel, in which they cruised along the coast, some of the men landing in certain parts with such share of the plunder as Avery pleased to allot them.

Amongst the plunder was a large quantity of diamonds of rare value, which Avery had managed to smuggle away in the confusion, as though he did not understand their value.

Arrived in Boston, several of his crew established themselves upon their portion of the booty. But Avery judged shrewdly that the disposal of his diamonds was well nigh impossible in such a town, and at the same time would probably expose him to suspicions of piracy.

He changed his plans again, therefore, and proposed to several of his companions, who remained with him, to sail for Ireland, which plan they all agreed to adopt.

Once in Ireland, they separated, eighteen of them remaining in Dublin, where they were pardoned their misdeeds by the king.

And now Avery found himself more embarrassed than ever about the sale of his diamonds.

He lived in continual fear and dread of discovery, and so never once dared to essay the disposal of his booty.

In Bristol, however, he met with some old acquaintances, in whom he could confide.

He went from here to Devonshire, and discovering his trouble to an old friend at Bideford, who counselled him to place the diamonds in the hands of certain Bristol merchants, who would dispose of them at their full value, providing he made them a fair recompense.

The affair was thus negociated, and the strictest secrecy was enjoined by Avery, and promised by the merchants.

They gave him a trifling sum to pay his debts, and to pay for his immediate wants, and left him, promising a remittance in full when they had disposed of the diamonds and plate.

A long delay occurred, and the little money he had received was all spent, and Avery again found himself very hard pressed indeed.

At length, by dint of importuning them continually, he succeeded in obtaining another trifle, but a sum utterly insignificant, and which only kept him from starvation for a time.

About this time Avery's doings were the talk of everyone.

They found their way into print, and when he had barely a rag to his back, or a crust to eat, he came across his exploits, printed in a pamphlet, and garnished up with fables that sounded like the Arabian Nights.

Captain Avery was called the Splendid Adventurer and the Buccaneer Crœsus, for such was the respect paid to wealth in our kingdom in those dark ages, that they could not call a man a downright pirate, who had made such a stupendous fortune as Avery was represented to have done.

Here, for the first time, did Captain Avery discover (according to the pamphlet in question) that he had married the daughter of the Great Mogul, and established himself at Madagascar, where he was treated as a prince.

He had a court, an army, vessels of war, and was possessed of fabulous wealth.

According to the ingenious author of the pamphlet, who did not quote his authorities, by the way, the magnificence of Prince Avery's court surpassed anything conceivable by the mere hangers-on of European palaces.

This was bitter irony to the wretched Avery, who was actually starving at the time!

It tortured him, for the fable he read gave him hints of what he might have done had he possessed the wit. Not that ever he dreamt it possible to realize the idea of the hero of this romance.

But he might have kept his ill-gotten fortune had he steered clear of England.

At length, in despair, he went to Bristol, and boldly tackled the merchants who had received his treasure.

Thus pushed into a corner, the mask fell from their face, and they showed Avery in so many words the realization of his worst fears.

"Now, really, my good man," they said, "you have troubled us enough with your wishes—we can't be annoyed in this way—leave us in peace."

"Give me back my property," said Avery, hoarsely.

At this they affected surprise, and said they knew not what he meant.

Few words were exchanged, for, upon Avery's persisting, they said—

"If you continue to annoy us, nay, if we hear any further of this matter, we shall be compelled to have you given up to the authorities. You may have seen how they treat pirates—Prince Averys or paupers—on Monday."

On Monday two men had been hanged for piracy at Plymouth, and Avery was but too glad to sneak away in silence.

The wretched dupe had not received more than the thousandth part of the value of his treasure in all, and now he was cowed by these two tricksters.

Had he possessed either courage or the wit, it would have been very different with him.

With a little courage he would have played the desperado, and forced the knaves to disgorge with a pistol at their heads.

A little wit would have told him how idle was their threat to hand him over to the authorities, seeing that they would thus have compromised themselves, and that in England the receiver of stolen goods is treated with no less severity than the thief!

But the miserable wretch crept out and stole away, and got on board a merchantman, to work his way round to Plymouth, whence he walked to Bideford.

At Bideford he fell ill. The bitter chagrin and disappointment aggravated his complaint, and the want of proper necessaries did the rest.

In a few days he died in utter destitution and was buried as a pauper!

———

The fable of Avery's career, of which I have already spoken, was still a theme of universal conversation, and so generally was it believed in, that at the very moment that the wretched man was dying of starvation in Bideford, his magnificence was actually being discussed in our Houses of Parliament, and a debate going on as to the advisability of sending out a fleet to put a stop to such a redoubtable force, before it harmed our trading vessels to any serious extent!

NAUTICAL TALES;

OR, ADVENTURES BY SEA AND LAND.

THE PIRATE KINGS OF MADAGASCAR.

CHAPTER I.

In the brief outline of Captain Avery's career, which I gave in my last, it will be remembered I left some of the characters at a most critical moment.

The adventures of the notorious and much lauded scamp, Avery, had to be concluded, and this led me to neglect certain particulars which form a sort of branch history of the persons engaged in his (Avery's) next notable exploit.

You will, doubtless, remember, that in the capture of the treasure-ship, which contained the daughter of the Great Mogul, Captain Avery was materially aided by two small vessels, whose commanders and crews put the most implicit faith in their traitorous ally.

A thorough recapitulation of the circumstances is surely unnecessary to those of my readers who have followed out the story of Avery; suffice it to remind you, that, gulled by the frankness which Avery so well knew how to assume, they, the luckless wights, were induced to convey all their portion of the spoil on board Avery's ship.

Then Avery took advantage of their confidence to steal away in the night, change his ship's course, and when daylight came again he was out of sight.

The wretched dupes could not be brought to believe that they had been deliberately robbed by their accomplice, or, rather, they chose to defer their belief in what was, alas, but too apparent, and, filled with vague misgivings, they held on their course.

But the time soon came when the most sceptical were forced to perceive, and to admit, that they were egregiously duped.

Arrived at the spot fixed by general consent and understanding as their rendezvous, there were, of course, no signs of Avery.

Then they were forced reluctantly to see the ugly truth, and to admit that they were in no trifling dilemma.

They could not see their way clear to any further exploits by sea, for they had no means of victualling their ships.

True, there was no lack of provisions of all kinds there. Poultry and game were in abundance; of fish there was a plenty; of cattle all that could be wished for.

But all this was unavailing, for they lacked one commodity most precious to the sailor, that we, landsmen, are accustomed to look upon with indifference, no doubt from the ridiculously low price of it in our country.

In a word, the expedition was stopped for—salt!

Thus, a sea voyage was an impossibility, so they accepted the only alternative with the best possible grace, and set about establishing themselves in that country.

With this resolve, they carried all that was of use or value from the two ships, and built their camp, their sails being soon converted into capital tents.

They possessed many articles which, added to the advantages owned by the land—the plenty of game and provisions of all kinds—promised to make their stay there tolerably agreeable, as far as creature comforts go.

But, more than all this, they possessed a very considerable quantity of fire-arms and powder and ball.

Now, on the second day after their landing, they were surprised by the appearance of some white men, upon whom they were within an ace of firing, for they were in mortal dread of the black natives of the island.

These men were portion of the crew of a vessel which, in concert with another ship, had received a commission to sail to the river Gambia, in Africa, with orders to attack the store and property of the French at Goorie, upon the coast.

A few days after they had set sail, however, they were overtaken by a violent tempest, in which one of the vessels got badly used. So, after losing its great mast, and sustaining great damage to its rigging, the captain cruised about awhile, signalling for his consort, which had disappeared in the hurricane; but they had to turn back, and make for their starting-place, to refit and repair damages.

The second vessel, which was commanded by one Captain Thew, was more fortunate.

Instead of continuing his voyage, however, Captain Thew altered his ship's course, and sailed for the Cape of Good Hope.

Having doubled the Cape, they made sail for the straits of Babelmandeb, which, as all my young readers are aware, is the entrance from the south of the Red Sea.

Here they fell in with a vessel coming from India, and bound for Arabia, with immense treasure. This the intrepid Captain Thew scented, and he conceived the bold plan of overpowering the vessel.

Now, there was a very strong crew on board the treasure-ship, and, besides the crew, not less than three hundred soldiers, who were to be transported to an adjacent port.

Yet Thew gave chase and overhauled her, boarding her in spite of the crew and troops.

Some of the prisoners they made informed them that there were five more vessels expected shortly, all more or less richly laden; and Captain Thew, grown hungry for riches at this first essay, was for cruising about, and falling upon them as they came up.

But a strong party of the crew, headed by the quarter-master, opposed this so violently, that he was forced to yield a reluctant consent to go away and divide the spoil in a place of safety.

Now came the extraordinary portion of the story.

The plunder was of such immense value, that, upon the division being made, it was found that there would be rather over *three thousand pounds sterling* per man—a sum that reads like a fable, when we consider what must have been the minimum strength of a crew that could perform such a feat as that which I have just described.

Therefore, with the sole view of protecting their illgotten gains, they abandoned piracy, and steered for Madagascar. But Captain Thew could not so readily forego his ambitious projects, and shortly after he quitted the main body, and, with a chosen few, made for Rhode Island, from whence he contrived to make his peace with government.

CHAPTER II.

At the time that Avery's former allies settled in Madagascar with Captain Thew's late associates, the country was in a perpetual state of turmoil.

The natives, who, I need scarcely tell my readers, were negroes, had a number of petty princes constantly at war with each other.

They were brave enough, but they had certain habits in their system of war which did not at all harmonise with more civilised ideas of making war.

For instance, they made slaves of all their prisoners, and these slaves they were at liberty to sell or slay as best they pleased.

The pirates, thus "retired from business," soon found that their alliance was courted by all parties; for, a few skirmishes in which they took part, just to keep their hands in, as it were, the negroes observed that the victory was always with the side upon which the white men fought!

The reason of this was very simple indeed.

The negroes had no fire-arms, and did not even know how to use those terrible weapons of modern warfare.

So great did their fear become of their guns, that presently, when a battle was about to take place, the sight of one or two white men in one of the ranks was sufficient to make the opposing force to fly without striking a single blow!

Now, this signal advantage served not alone to render the name of the pirates redoubtable, but also to make them very powerful.

The white men soon won a number of slaves of both sexes, and of these they disposed according to the custom of the country in which they had gone to reside.

The men they employed as slaves to till their ground—to sow their rice and other grain. They made them hunt and fish for them, and, in short, do all the labour that there was to be done.

Besides these profitable acquisitions they had numbers of the natives who paid them tribute money for the privilege of living under their protection, and so to guard them from the enmity of their neighbours.

They selected the most comely women for their wives, and abandoned their European prejudices in favour of polygamy, taking as many wives as they could support.

By degrees the pirates withdrew from each other, to live apart each with his wives and slaves, forming a kind of court, and they, themselves, living like so many petty princes. The results of this may readily be anticipated.

Jealousies presently arose amongst them, and disputes were frequent.

From angry words, naturally they were not long in coming to blows; and then they marched against each other in force, until civil war grew to be the order of the day, and several of their number were killed.

But before this state of things had lasted very long, an accident obliged the survivors to cling together for their common security.

The white men, like all men suddenly come to power, behaved like the greatest tyrants.

They took a savage delight in committing revolting cruelties.

The slightest fault of their dependants was punished with unnecessary severity; and the negroes, goaded to desperation by these atrocities, formed a conspiracy to exterminate them in a single night.

So well were their plans laid, and so secretly all their measures advanced, that it would assuredly have succeeded, but for a happy chance.

A negress, who owed them certain obligations, walked a distance of over twenty miles in the space of three hours to put them upon the alert—going from house to house—for they lived far apart, as I have already said.

Thus you see, considering the overwhelming masses that the negroes could have brought to this massacre, their purpose would have easily been effected but for the timely warning of the good-natured negress.

The white men lost no time in assembling, so that, when the surprise party marched down upon them, they were not a little disconcerted at finding them ready armed for their reception; and they retired without offering to strike a blow.

This unpleasant adventure they accepted as a warning, and they took several notable measures for their own protection.

They did their best to stir up dissensions amongst the negroes, practised upon their feelings of jealousy and desire for revenge, and so kept them in a continual state of broil amongst themselves.

When any of them had committed an outrage which brought down a large force of their countrymen, the protection of the white men guaranteed them from harm, for the pirates were so powerful and so dreaded that the boldest of the natives would not dare a contest with them.

These adventures had by this time increased and multiplied in a very remarkable degree.

Each had a prodigious family of children in the course of a few years, and that is why they were obliged to separate, and split into tribes like the Israelites of yore.

Besides their children they had each a vast number of slaves and dependants, so that each of them possessed the power and authority which are the distinctive marks of sovereignty. Yet flattering as this may have been to their pride, their positions were not divested of great anxieties.

Like all tyrants, they slept more upon thorns than roses.

They were in constant dread of an attack from the natives, and they fortified themselves in houses, more resembling citadels than the habitations of private persons.

They chose spots covered with timber, and situated near some river. They built up ramparts round their houses so high that there was no danger of an assault from the negroes, who had no ladders.

They dug deep ditches all round for further protection.

Besides this they had cut a passage through the wood, which was like the maze at Hampton Court. The paths were so narrow that they could only go through them in single file, and they were moreover well lined with thorns and spikes, which would have made short work of any unfortunate who had ventured upon a night adventure to surprise the citadel.

CHAPTER III.

Such was the condition of the pirates, when, after having been upon the island twenty-five years, Captain Woode Rogers, commanding the "Delight," with forty pieces of cannon, put in at their harbour, where no vessel had anchored for at least eight years.

The pirates, seeing such a large vessel appear in sight,

were filled with consternation, for they felt sure that it was sent to capture them.

Foolish men!

They felt themselves of such vast importance there that they could but think the whole world must be occupied by their doings. They little thought that their very existence had been forgotten, and that in all probability there was not an individual in Britain who could have recollected so much as their names.

At first they ran and concealed themselves in the labyrinths of which I have spoken, and dared not venture forth; but by degrees they gained courage, and went up on the hills to take observations.

Then presently they saw the ship land several men unarmed, as though for the purpose of some peaceful traffic, and, gaining courage, they emerged from their hiding places, and went forward to meet the sailors.

After a five-and-twenty years residence upon the island you will easily understand that little remained of their original garments.

Some few shreds and patches of cloth were all that remained in evidence of them having once covered their nakedness with fabrics of civilised manufacture. But now they presented more the aspect of so many Robinson Crusoes very much run to seed.

The effect of such a string of scare-crows was very ludicrous, and the English sailors were not a little tickled at their appearance.

They, however, soon remedied the defects in their apparel, for it transpired that Captain Rogers had come there with the avowed intention of purchasing slaves.

The pirates had plenty of such merchandise to dispose of in return for clothes, arms, ammunition, and spirits.

The "Delight" remained there some time, and the pirates used to go on board very frequently, and were seen on many occasions to examine the ship with unusual interest.

Their curiosity knew no limits.

Presently, however, there came an explanation of their singular behaviour.

Captain Rogers observed that whenever a boat's crew went ashore they were an unnecessary time gone, and this aroused his suspicions.

So he waited his opportunity, and, taking one of the men apart, taxed him so sharply with something underhand that the fellow confessed all at once.

The kings of Madagascar, as they got to be called, had not forgotten their piratical instincts in spite of their twenty-five years' residence in that country, and they cast longing eyes upon a vessel of forty guns, which they fondly thought would enable them to renew the exploits of their youth if they could only surprise it.

To this end they sounded the men by degrees, and succeeded in gaining over several with plausible speech and promises of huge shares of plunder.

Captain Rogers was not to be frightened by this plot, but, by one prudent measure, he succeeded in upsetting all their majesties' plans.

He ordered his boats off to fetch the slaves as usual, but only allowed one man, who was in command, to land for the purpose of negociating with the pirates.

The latter, in despair at this move, sailed round and round the "Delight" in their canoes, but did no great things, for they found the ship so well guarded at every point that it would have been sheer folly to attempt a surprise.

The slave purchases having been effected, Captain Rogers weighed anchor, laughing in his sleeve at the Kings of Madagascar.

This is all that has ever been known of these remarkable men

The "Delight" left them all their sovereignty, but fewer subjects, since they had exchanged the chief part of them for powder and ball.

The "Delight" found only eleven of them remaining out of the considerable number that had originally landed there and early in the eighteenth century there were some of them still living in the same state of savage royalty.

It is indeed very probable that some of their descendants are still to be found upon the island, but it is not likely that they would care to boast of their ancestry, for, independently of their piracy, they were all black sheep. He, of whom most particulars are known, was a Thames waterman, who had to fly the country for murder.

In my next I purpose giving you some particulars of the career of a most extraordinary character; one Mary Read —*a female pirate and adventurer*.

I have only to observe, as the details I have dressed into the form of a narrative appear to be fiction of the most extravagant description, that my chief authority is the account of the trial of a number of persons for piracy, amongst whom this Mary Read appeared, together with another woman named Ann Bonney, both these women being disguised as men.

Those who feel any particular interest in verifying my statements may easily consult the same authorities as myself.

THE EXTRAORDINARY ADVENTURES OF
MARY READ, THE FEMALE PIRATE.

CHAPTER I.

THE biography of this marvellous creature would furnish enough stirring incident to make a sensation novel, and half-a-dozen naval dramas into the bargain.

Mary Read was made prisoner and brought to trial at about the same time as Captain Rackham and other notorious pirates; and in the examination came out the whole story.

Her history contains many important details, which, however, I am compelled, for certain reasons, to omit. Yet there remains ample, I am sure, to secure the reader's interest.

The sceptical reader may say, how is it that so little is remembered about this female pirate, if she did such wonderful things, and became so notorious?

The reason is simple.

The trial of this batch of pirates took place at Jamaica.

No doubt that it was talked of a great deal about that time in England, but in the island of Jamaica the traditions are preserved to the present day. Moreover, there are the criminal records of the State to testify to the truth of the whole.

Mary Read was born in England.

Her mother, when very young, married a sailor, who left on a cruise and never re-appeared.

He had been away some months when a child was born—a boy—which Mrs. Read had great trouble with, for it was a puny and sickly infant, that struggled on feebly for a time and died.

The Widow Read was very young and comely, and she soon was sought in marriage by a man of as little constancy as her first husband, who quitted her as the latter had done.

Soon she had a second child born to her; this time it was a girl, and a robust infant, that it was clear would be easily reared.

To conceal her misfortune, she went to live in another part of the country, and struggled on bravely to earn her living.

But it was hard work, small pay, and often bread was all they could get for weeks together; sometimes even this was running short.

Still she kept up until the wolf was actually at the door, and then, at a sore strait, the poor woman resolved to go to seek the assistance of her mother-in-law—that is, the mother of her first husband.

Here a difficulty arose.

The child!

Her mother did not know much of the child which had been the result of the poor woman's marriage with her son: but this much she did know—it was a boy!

Sore was her need, and in her trouble she resolved to dress her little girl in boy's clothes.

This was the foundation of the marvellous incidents which marked the career of this child later in life—for this child is no other than the heroine of this short biography—Mary Read, the Female Pirate.

It was a hazardous trick to play, especially with an old woman; yet she resolved to risk it, and so well did little Mary appear in male garments, that the deception was never discovered.

Indeed, arrived at the old woman's house, she took such a fancy to her supposed grandson, that she wished to adopt him!

But to this the mother, a little frightened, was, of course, opposed.

Her mother-in-law, however, would not be said nay.

"Why refuse to leave me the boy?" said her mother-in-law. "He will be well cared for, clothed, fed, and sent to school. And you will find it very hard to give him bare bread to eat."

"True, mother," was the reply; "quite true, and yet——"

"And yet you had better leave him with me," said the old woman, decidedly.

"No, no!"

"Why not?"

"Because I never could suffer to be separated from my dear son," replied her daughter-in-law. "He is my only consolation in my widowhood."

With this she gained her point, and the mother-in-law consented to allow her a small sum weekly to aid in the support of the *boy!*

This continued for a considerable time until Mary Read attained the age of thirteen years, when the grandmother dying left them in a sad strait.

Then it was that Mary's mother told her the story of her secret—why she, a girl, was dressed as a boy.

Mary had grown very tall and stout, and looked a fine, sturdy lad; and she possessed all the boldness of the sex she personated all her life.

She sought for a situation, and, before long, succeeded in obtaining the place of footman in a lady's household.

CHAPTER II.

Now, although Mary Read was, at this time, only between thirteen and fourteen years of age, she looked a good deal more; and, as girls generally do, she made a very good-looking boy indeed.

Her good looks were the cause of her obtaining the situation at once with the lady, for ladies are always more sensitive to personal attractions than men, even in domestics.

But presently a curious complication arose. The lady continually desired her young footman's presence, and by her peculiar manners it soon became evident that she was caught by Mary's grace, docility, and handsome presence.

Mary was some time in perceiving it; for it appeared such an extraordinary fancy that, even when it did force itself upon her, she could hardly believe it.

Yet the warm sentiments of the lady soon made themselves still more apparent, and Mary Read became, in consequence, not a little embarrassed.

She avoided her mistress as much as she possibly could; but, as is generally the case, the diffidence upon the part of the object of her passion only made the flame burn more fiercely; and, finally, the lady, overwhelmed with touching confusion and distress, openly avowed her feelings, and surrendered herself at discretion to her handsome footman!

This was a pretty job indeed!

Mary got out of the difficulty as best she could, without giving her mistress too much encouragement, and resolved to quit the house at once.

But, before she could fly, the lady, in a very singular manner, discovered her footman's real sex!

Mary Read fled from this house precipitately, and, falling in with some naval recruiting folk, she took the bounty and went before the mast on a man-of-war, bound upon active service.

Here she smelt powder, and showed herself as brave as she was intelligent and handsome.

But there was too little to be made in this career, and, her time being expired, she quitted the sea, and passed some time in Flanders.

Here, after awhile, her pecuniary resources were low, and, to recruit them, she enlisted in an infantry regiment.

During her period of service here, she distinguished herself greatly on many occasions; but, although she was always in the heat of the fight, she was never once wounded—a circumstance which must be looked upon as almost providential, seeing that the faintest scratch would have probably brought her under the doctor's hands, and then her real sex must have been inevitably discovered.

NAUTICAL TALES;

OR, ADVENTURES BY SEA AND LAND.

THE EXTRAORDINARY ADVENTURES OF
MARY READ, THE FEMALE PIRATE.

CONCLUDED.

This service she liked well enough, if one may put belief in her own confession; but, although she was so fortunate as to earn golden opinions in every direction, she was as far off promotion as the first day she enlisted.

This being the case, she exchanged into a cavalry regiment.

Here she performed prodigies of daring and of valour; and was soon the pet of the whole of the officers.

But a change was at hand.

While in the latter regiment, she fell in love with one of her comrades, a fine young Fleming; and, according to all accounts, she was heavily hit.

Until now one of the smartest soldiers on parade, Mary Read began to neglect her personal appearance, and her duties too.

Her arms and accoutrements were let go uncleaned for days together, and she was no longer ready at the first call to go upon any service to which she might be appointed.

But in all this there was a certain strangeness of manner, which her comrade, the object of her passion, could not fail to observe.

Mary Read lavished upon him a thousand cares, which even the soldiers, their comrades, observed, but without remotely suspecting the truth.

Love, however, is ingenious, and Mary soon hit upon a means of discovering her sex to her comrade.

The occasion she availed herself of was rather curious, and is worth noting.

They were seated together in a tent, playing at cards upon a drum, when she opened her uniform at the throat, with a pretence of being freer to lounge about.

The amazon knew that she had a neck and shoulders of snowy whiteness, and she fell into the tricks of her sex instinctively. No one, indeed, could have imagined she had passed all her life in breeches.

The Fleming saw the fair skin, looking yet fairer by contrast with the deep sun-tanned complexion above her collar, and he was dazzled.

He put down his pipe from his lips, and stared again.

Mary, seeing this, dropped her eyes in a way highly creditable to a bashful maiden, but looking very odd indeed in a soldier!

"What a white skin thou hast!" said the Fleming, feeling very unaccountably embarrassed.

Mary blushed up to the roots of her hair.

There was no affectation in this. Her maidenly distress was brought out as soon as she was known to be a woman.

The hypercritical may sneer at this, and pretend that a woman who passed her days in male attire could have no scruples of delicacy; but such a critic would be but a mere superficial observer, for the explanation shows that Mary Read had been habituated from her earliest recollections to this dress, and it is possible—nay, very probable—that she felt a good deal more at home in it than in her petticoats.

The further proof was that her comrade-lover courted her very assiduously, and finally offered to make her his wife.

This was the dearest wish of her heart.

They were engaged, and as soon as the regiment went into winter quarters she bought some garments more suited to her sex, and they were publicly married.

This extraordinary wedding of two cavaliers caused a great sensation. Many of the officers of the regiment attended the nuptials, and made them a number of presents, to set them up in housekeeping—the least they could do, they said, for a couple that had fought under them in many battles.

Then they procured their discharge easily enough, for the purpose of turning their attention to some more lucrative profession than soldiering.

They were soon enabled to hire a house near the Castle of Breda, which they converted into an inn.

The notoriety attached to their adventures and to their loves drew many customers to their house, and the officers of the garrison went there regularly to dine.

But this happiness did not last long, for her husband died soon after, and, the Peace of Ryswick being effected, the garrison was reduced at Breda. The number of the officers, of course, was reduced proportionately, and the widow found her business drop from her daily.

At length she was forced to abandon it, and her economies had dwindled to nothing, so that starvation stared her in the face.

Then Mary Read was forced to unsex herself once again.

She dressed herself as a man, and made for Holland, where she enlisted in a regiment of infantry, doing garrison duty in one of the frontier towns.

After she had been here some time, her active spirit chafed at resting idle, for the peace had spoiled all chance of promotion.

Therefore she embarked on board a ship bound for the West Indies.

Now, on the way, they fell in with a suspicious-looking craft, that hoisted the Dutch flag, and signalled them.

They drew nearer and nearer, until suddenly they lowered the Dutch flag and ran up the dreaded black ensign!

At the same instant their sham ports fell back, and discovered a whole range of heavy guns.

Now, the Dutchmen were not wanting in courage, but it would have been worse than madness to show fight against a vessel which could have sent them to the bottom, in all probability, with a single broadside.

So they let the pirates overhaul and pillage their vessel, being not a little pleased to escape with life itself; for, in all times, from those rascals whom I told you made Cæsar prisoner, when a youth, down to the wretches of the "Flowery

Land," that we strung up in front of Newgate a few years back, pirates have ever been the cruellest wretches.

In this adventure Mary became of great use, as she spoke English—for the pirates were of our nation, I am sorry to say—and when, after laying hands upon every article of value they could find, they left the Dutchman to its fate, they took Mary with them, because, as they said, "he was the only Englishman aboard."

Mary Read thus cruised with the pirates, until the King of England issued a proclamation in every island of the West Indies, offering to pardon all the pirates who should submit within a certain time.

The whole party to which Mary Read belonged availed themselves of the royal clemency, and retired to live peaceably upon their spoils.

Their money ran low very soon. "Lightly come, lightly go," you know, has ever been the rule.

They sought for further employment, and presently learned that the governor of the Isle of Providence, Captain Wood (or Woods, I am not sure which), was equipping some vessels to cruise against the Spaniards.

They sought employment here, therefore, and were at once engaged, Mary Read being amongst the number.

Now those vessels had barely put to sea, when several of their crews rose against their officers, and took possession of the ships, to go on a piratical excursion.

Mary Read was amongst them.

This was the gravest thing against her; but on the trial, it was urged in her behalf that she was but a member of the crew, and was forced to go with the mass, and that, moreover, she had only yielded after repeated solicitations of her comrades.

She, moreover, declared very often that she had a horror of this mode of life.

But then came the most contradictory evidence.

Two men declared, upon oath, that no pirate of the crew had shown such courage and resolution as Mary Read, and no one readier to board a vessel with which they were engaged.

That she, and another remarkable unsexed woman, Ann Bonny—of whom I shall give full particulars in another article—were the two that showed the greatest determination in the action in which they were taken prisoners.

They were the last to remain on deck, it was averred, and when the cowardly ruffians ran below, Mary Read, after urging them to fight the ship to the last, by threats, promises, menaces, ultimately carried out one of her threats and fired her pistols into the midst of the skulking cowards, killing one man and wounding several others.

This, at all events, is what was advanced against her, and it is in some degree borne out by the great courage the intrepid woman always displayed; yet she denied it entirely.

She urged, as I have said, that the mode of life was repugnant to her in the greatest degree; and, as true courage is rarely allied with brutality, there is a probability that she spoke only the truth.

But I am proceeding with the end of Mary Read's history before the time.

She was ever remarked for her great courage on board the vessel; and it is certain that her modesty was never to be called in question, for so did she conduct herself, that no one ever suspected her sex.

Now Mary, as I have said, made a very handsome man indeed, and, curiously enough, her good looks caught the fancy of another remarkable woman, Ann Bonny, to whom I have more than once alluded here.

Now came a very curious passage indeed.

Ann Bonny could not conquer her passion, and she chose a moment to discover her love to its object, and at the same time to acknowledge her real sex.

Can you imagine a situation more peculiar or diverting?

One woman, in male attire, acknowledges her sex to another woman in male attire!

Ann Bonny made no declaration in so many words; yet Mary Read was, after all, a woman, and knew the nature of her sex instinctively. She saw that she had inspired a fatal passion in the breast of the unlucky woman.

So there was no help for it but to declare her true sex to the woman who sought her as a lover.

Ann Bonny was filled with amazement at this.

Yet she got over the disappointment, and the two remarkable women became very fast friends henceforth.

But now arose a new and unforeseen complication.

Captain Rackham, who was in love with Ann Bonny, noticed them often together, and, far from suspecting Mary Read's true sex, he threatened Ann Bonny to cut her young swain's throat or knock him on the head and drop him overboard.

Ann Bonny was in a great fright at this, and so she confided, under promise of secrecy, the truth to Captain Rackham; and so well did the latter keep his word, that the truth was never suspected.

Some time after this, the pirates took a merchantman, on which they found a young man of certain personal advantages, besides being a skilled workman.

It was a rule with them to take any clever artizan, by fair means or foul, and keep him prisoner for their general good; so this young man was secured.

He had not been there very long when Mary Read fell hopelessly in love with him.

The young workman was not at all sorry to come across a friend amongst the pirates; but he was rather at a loss to account for the very warm nature of his "comrade's" attachment; but Mary soon found the means of discovering her sex to him, without appearing to do it with intent.

He was amazed. Every little attention that Mary now paid him had a double value in his eyes, and, in a word, he became violently in love with her.

Now, Mary soon gave him such proofs of her devotion that few women have done in any age.

Arriving near a port, the young carpenter had a quarrel with one of the pirates, and as fighting between the members of the crew was severely put down on board, a meeting was arranged to take place as soon as they landed.

This news was a terrible blow to poor Mary.

Not for worlds would she have had him decline the challenge; she had too much courage for this.

But she feared that he would be worsted against an adversary skilled in the use of arms.

In this difficulty, this extraordinary creature resolved generously to expose her own life, rather than risk her lover's.

So she sought the pirate, and picked a quarrel with him very easily, defying him to single combat.

The challenge was accepted.

They adjourned to the place of meeting as soon as they touched land, and Mary insisted upon the "first interview" with the pirate.

Sabre and pistol were the weapons selected, and Mary had the good fortune to overcome her adversary.

After this the lovers were solemnly betrothed, and, in a few months after this, came the chase of their vessel and their capture by the authorities.

This is but a brief outline of this wonderful woman's career.

I give you the leading facts; fill in the details with your fancy, and you will not assuredly exaggerate or romance.

Can you conceive a more extraordinary career?

When brought up for trial, she persisted in her statement that the life of a pirate was odious to her, and that she had only awaited a fitting moment to abandon the mode of life, together with several of the prisoners whom she named.

Amongst the latter was her husband, as she called him, for they regarded each other as husband and wife, although no church had sanctioned their union; but she forbore to mention this to the court, for fear of prejudicing the judges against him.

It was proved that he had not very long been made prisoner by the pirates, and this saved him.

Now there was much in Mary's case that prepossessed the court in her favour; and it is certain that they would have saved her, if they could.

But the law is formal, and cannot be put aside out of mere sympathy with a woman.

She was condemned, but a reprieve was granted, as it was discovered that she was about to become a mother.

But poor Mary Read profited little by her brief respite; for she cheated the law by dying in prison of a fever with which she was seized shortly after the trial.

THE DESERTER.

One autumn night, when the blue sky was clear and serene, and the moon was far on her western round, attended on her majestic throne by innumerable little legions of stars, Mrs. Greville, an officer's wife, stole from her little cottage, that slept, or rather hung, over the bosom of the dark wave, whose murmurings she could hear whenever the wind blew towards the shell-strewed beach.

She had retired early to rest; but, previous to that retirement, had offered up to Him on high the most solemn and pathetic prayer that ever affection drew from the bosom of devoted woman; but for whom? She had been married but one month, when his profession obliged him to bear arms in the support of the freedom of that land to which it was his pride and boast to say he belonged. The obedience was a cheerful one; for he, at all times, sacrificed all secular views in promoting the welfare and happiness of his native land; but this sudden separation from the object of his ardent attachment nearly overbalanced the brave officer's loyalty and zeal.

He looked at the awful mandate that directed him to join his corps, sighed, looked at his fond wife, whose arms had, on hearing the unwelcome news, encircled his neck.

At last, he broke silence in these words: "My beloved Mary, little did I consider, before I made you the participator of my all, that I should so soon be called upon to leave you; but I have one proposal to make."

His voice was interrupted by her asking,

"What is it, my love?" He was some time before he could proceed again. At last, he said,

"Mary, there are two things on which I would ask your advice; knowing that your answer would be actuated by the most honourable feelings, leaving self entirely out of the question. They are these:—We have a small competency to live on. I have waded through blood, toil, and hardships, in getting the rank I now hold in the army. To resign that now would be a painful task, and an injustice to you: besides, what would such a resignation at this critical juncture be attributed to? Not to affection—but to that which of all other surmises I could the least brook—that of cowardice: that I could not bear; yet, for love of thee, I could bear much—yes, Mary—very much; but I am sure your noble spirit would spurn as much at the idea as any one. What says my beloved? Shall I stay, branded by the vile name of coward, or go, and add another laurel to those I trust I have gained?"

"Go!" said the heroic wife; "go—I hate the timid and ignoble: go; and let this nerve you with fresh loyalty—new zeal—new strength—that you have a heart as constant as you are loyal; affectionate as you are brave; and as faithful as you are faithful."

It was on that spot on which she now stood that she had bidden him farewell, saying,

"Let these words console you in the battle's heat—that rather than I would hear the now dear name of Greville blighted by the tongue of scandal, or my dear husband taunted at as a coward, I would suffer his total loss; weep and mourn the residue of my life. Go, God be with thee!"

They parted. Greville hied to his ship; she to her solitude, to give vent to those griefs she had almost broken her young heart to smother. On the same eve she saw the white bosoms of those sails that bore him to Spain, the seat of contention.

He had now been absent twelve months; the period was long and trying to the bosom where love reigned.

She imagined that she saw her beloved husband standing on the side of a small ship, near the shore, calling her by name: and at last she saw him fall into the blue waters, and he seemed struggling to reach the shore; but, when within some few paces, he sunk to rise no more.

She screamed aloud and fainted; but the instant sweet recollection came to her aid, she rushed to the shore in her nightclothes, when, to her utter astonishment, she beheld something white floating on the sea, about ten yards from the white strand.

At last, a soft, but rising billow, placed it at her feet, and the wave then receded.

It was a youth, dressed in a sailor's blue jacket, and white trousers. She raised his head, and from his mouth gushed out a quantity of water, followed by a deep groan; his limbs became stiff; his hands seemed clenched in the cold embrace of death; again he threw up water,—there seemed a rattling in his throat.

She spoke to him, asked him if he was better—but not a word; at last he grasped her hand fast in his chilly embrace, which spoke the gratitude of his heart. His hands grew icy cold. He again became insensible; discharged more water.

By this time the wreck of the ship had reached the village, that stood about a mile off, and many of its benevolent inhabitants had left their warm beds to exercise their benevolence towards their distress. Her cries had reached some farming people on their return from market.

One assisted Mrs. Greville in conveying the poor stranger to her cottage, where everything was done that humanity could dictate, or a feeling heart devise, to restore him to animation. He was put to bed by her servants, who attended him the whole night, administering every kind of restorative that their benevolent mistress could think of.

On the following morning, the stranger was so much recovered as to open his eyes, and seemed to recognise everything about him with the greatest astonishment, but said nothing.

A medical gentleman was sent for, who pronounced him fast recovering. The next three days he laid in the same apathetic stupor, seemingly scrutinising everything around him with the most attentive solicitude; so much so, that it was feared his intellect had received a shock.

His pulse was regular, and denoted perfect ease and calmness. He ate and drank, but never spoke; seemed about twenty-two, handsome and well made—wore a gold chain round his neck—a ring on his finger; his hand was white and delicate, but his clothes denoted that he was a common sailor.

On the morning of the fifth day, when the servants arose, having left him perfectly well, their usual habit was to go into his bedroom to see him; but, imagine their astonishment and alarm, when they found that he was not there.

Every search was made for him in the vicinity, but in vain. The general conclusion was, that, in a fit of delirium, he had drowned himself; and the whole family were in the greatest distress. Money was offered to any person that found him, dead or alive.

On preparing for breakfast, they found all the plate missing, besides a small box containing Mrs. Greville's jewellery. The following note, written in plain English, was also found:—

"Strangers, start not. I have deserted my country in the day of her trouble; what are theft and ingratitude compared to that? When you have read this I shall be out of your reach. Search will be in vain. I loathe the very benevolent heart that rescued me from the grave.
"A SPANIARD."

From that day they heard nothing of him, although every search was made.

Amongst the property stolen was a miniature of Captain Greville, the loss of which wounded the affectionate Mrs. Greville. She did not, however, mention a syllable of this to her husband when she wrote to him, knowing it would only distress him, more particularly as the campaign was nearly ended.

Captain Greville, in one of the conflicts with the enemy, was severely wounded; his sword had been shot away. When a Spanish officer was in the act of cutting him to pieces, Captain Greville, who was a mason, made a masonic sign, and, fortunately for him, his opponent was also a mason. His uplifted hand was stayed; Greville was carried to a small hut. Putting a small tin box into the captain's hands, the officer said—

"Receive this, it may save your life, although it cost my brother his; he was executed for desertion, and on the day of his execution he gave me the contents of that box. Good bye, brother; heaven protect you."

Scarcely had he gone when a detachment of the English took possession of the hut, and the same evening Captain Greville was carried to the head-quarters of his regiment, and, when reposing on his bed, stained with his still bleeding body, he opened the tin box, and there saw his own portrait, the one he had exchanged with his wife for hers the day they separated.

This sad discovery opened a new wound—a wound in the heart; a wound which seemed to rob him of the power of reason. The identity was beyond doubt.

The desponding influence of loss of blood induced, perhaps, such queries as these—

"Hast thou forgot the magic tie
That once endeared thy soul to mine,
The impassioned gaze, the burning sigh,
That told me all my soul was thine?"

And he could not write so as to satisfy himself, such was the injury he had received.

At this period the affectionate letter from his Mary drove away suspicion, and awakened the tenderest emotions of his heart.

Still the mystery remained.

In six months, however, after this, he again presented her the picture; and his father having died, leaving him a considerable property, he sold out, and spent the residue of his days in domestic bliss—when the portrait became more valuable, from the strange events connected with it.

The ingratitude of the Spaniard thus did not prevent the heart of benevolence from rushing to the raging billows, when the cry of distress reached her pious ear; and their cottage ever retained the honourable appellation of the "Mariner's House," the door being always open to distress, and hearts and purse to those in need.

NOTICE.—*In deference to the wishes of numerous subscribers, the Supplements will be increased in size, and given monthly*

NAUTICAL TALES;

OR, ADVENTURES BY SEA AND LAND.

THE HARBOUR OF MARMORICE.

In the latter end of the month of January, 1801, the day dawned with every indication of bad weather—the mass of dense and heavy clouds, piled upon each other, occupied all space to the south-west—the sun in his course looked with a fiery aspect—and the sea-fowl, with the wonderful instinct that puzzles the wise, from their foreknowledge of the storm, came screaming in upon the land—the wind blew fiercely and in fearful gusts—the labouring clouds seemed preparing to discharge their over-loaded breasts, and distant thunder rolled along the horizon—the masses of clouds, as they sailed along the ocean, nearly shut out the light of day, and rose at opposite extremities into huge mountains of vapour; they were illuminated by fitful flashes of lightning, and looked like giant batteries erected in the heavens.

As they moved onwards from the south-west, they shot down vivid streams which, at times, pierced the waters like quivering blades of fire; again the electric fluid took an horizontal direction through the skies and its dazzling streak fluttered like a radiant streamer, until it lost itself among the clouds. Comparative darkness came on with a suddenness that I never before had observed, and the gusts were terrific.

During this elemental war, the British fleet, under Vice-Admiral Lord Keith, and the army under Sir Ralph Abercrombie, closely crammed in men-of-war (*armes en flute*), and transports to the number of two hundred sail, were carrying a heavy press of canvas to claw off a lee-shore—that shore was Caramania, in Asia Minor, a most mountainous, well-wooded, black-looking coast.

We were in search of Marmorice harbour, the appointed rendezvous of the Egyptian expedition; and the Asiatic pilots, frightened at the dangerous position of the fleet in this tremendous weather, lost the little knowledge they had formerly possessed of this unfrequented and frowning coast—whose mountains towered high above the clouds—on which no vestige of human life could be seen.

Every glass, in the clearance between the squalls, was eagerly turned upon the precipitous shore, upon which the heavy waves beat with the most horrific grandeur.

It was self-evident to the meanest capacity, that unless the harbour could be entered before night, the transports, filled with British warriors, would be wrecked on the lee-shore, with no chance of assistance.

The men-of-war, by dint of carrying sail, might claw off; but the great majority of this fine army would, in a few hours, become food for the monsters of the deep, or the ferocious and ravenous tenants of the vast forests that seemed interminable to our straining sight.

As each withdrew his glass, with a disappointed look, the longitude of their countenances increased, and the round-faced, laughing midshipman, lost his disposition for fun and frolic, and all at once became a reflecting, sedate personage.

The admiral, on whom all the responsibility rested, endeavoured to assume the calmness of tone and manner that the honesty of his open nature would not brook; his agitation was visible in the contortions of his venerable countenance, and the sudden starts of his nervous system.

"Fire a gun, and hoist a signal of attention to the fleet," said his lordship.

"They have all answered, my lord," said the officer of the signal department.

"Now, Mr. Stains, be particular; ask if any one is qualified to lead into Marmorice."

As the negative flag flew at the masthead of the men-of-war, every countenance proportionally fell. At length, with heartfelt joy, I proclaimed that one of our sloops had hoisted her affirmative.

"Who is she, youngster? D—n it, boy, do not keep me in suspense."

"The Petrel, my lord."

I saw an ejaculation of thankfulness rise warm from the heart on the lips of Lord Keith, as he piously raised his eyes and pressed his hand on his heart.

"Signal for the fleet to bear up, make more sail,

and follow the Petrel," said Lord Keith; "Captain Inglis may be depended on."

And we shook out a reef, and set the maintop-gallant sail, which soon closed our leader in the Petrel.

As we approached this mountainous and novel land, the idea (and it was an astounding one) seemed to dwell on and occupy the most unreflecting mind, that should Captain Inglis be wrong, every ship, with twenty-five thousand men, would be the sacrifice of such error. Lord Keith ordered the signal of attention with the Petrel's pendants.

"Captain Inglis, your responsibility is awful," said the telegraph. "Are you perfectly certain of the entrance of Marmorice?"

"Perfectly sure," was the answer, "and right ahead."

"Signal officers on the fore-yard, with their glasses," said the Admiral.

And, slinging our telescopes, we ascended; indeed, it was time, for now the roar of the waves, as they broke on the coast, throwing their spray on high, conveyed a dismal idea of our impending fate.

"A narrow entrance ahead," called the signal-lieutenant, Stains.

"Do the midshipmen make out the same?"

"We all of us discern it, my lord," shouted the whole at the very extent of their voices.

"God be praised for his great mercy!" ejaculated his lordship, uncovering and bowing his head with great devotion.

The entrance of Marmorice now became distinctly visible to all on deck, from the contrast of the deep still water to the creamy froth on the shore; and the signal for the fleet to crowd all sail for the port in view, and the men-of-war to haul their wind, until the merchantmen had entered the channel, was flying at the Foudroyant's mast-head, as she shot into the Gut of Marmorice.

The tremendous mountains overshadowed us, and seemed inclined, from their great height, to come thundering down upon us like the destructive avalanches in the mountains of Switzerland.

We now entered the spacious and splendid harbour, circular in its form, and more than twenty miles in circumference. It created great astonishment from its vast magnitude, being capable of containing all the ships in the world.

In so small a nook as to be nearly invisible, stands on a rock a fort, and a few wretched houses, surrounded by a high wall. This fortification displayed the crescent, and was saluted with eleven guns, as we took up anchorage, closely followed by our numerous fleet.

Scarcely had we moored, when the heavy masses of clouds that had rested on and capped the high land, now opened upon us in earnest, and the forked lightnings darted among the fleet with fatal effect. The gale increased to a perfect hurricane, and blew from all points of the compass; the flakes of ice—for they were too large to be called hail—came down with such prodigious force as to destroy man and beast; and whoever witnessed that storm, could entertain no doubt of a special Providence in the affairs of men. We were all safe moored, and the heart expanded in thankfulness to the Eternal Power that had watched over our safety.

The following night was beautifully serene—the watch, some of whom paced the deck, castle-building, and imagining scenes of bliss that never were to be realised, while others admired the starry vault of heaven, wondering with what sort of beings yon myriads of worlds were peopled.

Crombie, a grey-headed young gentleman (for all midshipmen are called *young* gentlemen, and with whom the youthful lieutenant of his watch commonly created some mirth by desiring him as youngster to sheer up to the mast-head and count the convoy,) now seized me by the button.

"I say, youngster, that was an ugly coast we ran down upon yesterday, and reminds me of an occurrence that was particularly mournful. You see, when I belonged to his Majesty's sloop—but it will be as well not to mention her name, as I cut and run one day without asking permission—well, we were cruising in the latitude, and by old Soundings' longitude (but that by dead reckoning could not always be depended upon), near where brother Jonathan said he had discovered a dangerous cluster of rocks, to which he had affixed the appropriate name of the 'Devil's Grip.'

"Well, I dined in the gun-room that day, and many a hearty laugh at the Yankee notion circulated with the bottle, for the master proved, to the satisfaction of all but one at the table, that rocks could not be in the open sea, so many hundred miles from any known land, and where the deep sea lead could not find bottom, and for which he had often tried in vain; so when the caterer bowed round to signify that the mess allowance of wine, viz., a pint each person, was drunk, the first luff proposed an extra bottle, while we listened to the most extraordinary youth I ever met with, as he, with fluency of speech and elegance of manner demolished the master's premises and inferences.

"This young gentleman was called the captain's nephew, and might, I think, have claimed nearer relationship; he was named Paulo, after his mother, Pauline, a Neapolitan countess, who fled from a nunnery, where she had been immured without asking her consent. She must have been a beauty, for her son, though of a very fragile and delicate make, was remarkably tall and handsome, with a most expressive countenance, generally clouded with a shade of melancholy: he was fond of gazing at the moon, and wrote a deal of poetry.

"Our doctor, who was a learned man, said he was a genius of the first order, full of susceptibility, and with nerves too finely strung for this coarse and bustling world; at all events, he was universally beloved for his gentleness and kindness of heart; at punishment you would see him with his hands clasped and his eyes suffused with tears, looking up in his uncle's face with such an imploring look to spare the culprit, while the muscles round his well-formed mouth used to work as the sharp lash fell on the tender skin of the sufferer.

"The captain was a stern, unbending man, but his iron countenance softened at the visible agony of this glorious youth, who frequently gained his point, and the last dozen was remitted.

"He said, as far as I could understand him, that the shell of the earth was trifling compared to its interior, which was supposed to be in a state of fusion, and hence arose volcanoes and earthquakes, the heaving up of lands that had been the bed of the ocean, and the submersion of others; that the vast Atlantic itself was supposed by some philosophers to have once been habitable, and a great continent.

"All this was too learned, and made no impression on any one but the doctor, so we drank the captain's toast, of good afternoon, and went to our usual duty; mine was to keep the first watch. Old Soundings, fortified by a nor'wester, was officer of the watch.

"The gale blew hard, right and aft, and we were dashing through a heavy sea in merry style. 'I think, Sir,' says I, addressing my officer without touching the hat, the night being too dark to notice the omission (a point on which he was very particular), 'I think, Sir, that the sea seems inclined to kick up a bobbery to night, and is rising fast.' 'I am of the same opinion, youngster; but what is that a-head?'

"At this moment the look-out man on the bowsprit sung out, 'Breakers a-head,' and was reiterated by the cat-headman, 'Breakers on both bows.'

"This terrific announcement woke even the sleepers, for in less time than I take to tell you, every man and boy was on deck, most of them in their shirts—poor dear Paulo, looking more like an aerial sprite than of mortal mould, ran after the captain, who went out on the end of the bowsprit, and looked steadily around, which required nerves of iron, for right a-head seemed a vast barrier of rocks, on which the sea was wildly breaking, throwing its white spray to the clouds, and on each side as the mad waves receded, were seen their black tops, peeping through the creamy froth that surrounded us, the gallant ship bounding like a greyhound, at the rate of ten knots, full upon them.

"It was a sight of such horror, youngster, that my hair turned perfectly white, and I shut my eyes with the sinner's last ejaculation, of 'God be merciful to me,' but not before I had seen Paulo, the beautiful and good Paulo, with the scream of a maniac, jump into the boiling surf.

"The manly tone of the captain's voice was heard high above the roar of the breakers, 'Port the helm, port! and silence all of you; your lives depend on your steadiness and prompt obedience. Master, take the weather-wheel, and steer for an opening, two points before the starboard beam: we may find water through the reef where it does not break so heavily—brace forward the yards;' and the lee-gunwale buried itself in the agitated water, as she sprung to the wind. 'Let fly the main-topgallant sheets;' the sail flew to ribbons, and saved the topmast. 'Now, master, hard up the helm, and square away the yards; send her between those high rocks where the sea does not break.'

"The noble ship leaped between them, while the spray from them washed some of the unnerved over the bulwarks, and their last despairing cry was drowned in the roar of the surf. She steered beautifully in the master's able hands, who had frequently declared he could turn her through the eye of a needle, and this channel between the breakers was like one, and very little wider than her mainyard.

"Nothing was heard from old Soundings but 'Port it is—starboard withal.' As I went to assist him at the wheel, after drawing in a long breath, I heard him mutter, 'Who would have thought the Yankee notion true, but it is the Devil's Grip, and a devilish ugly one it is for sartin.'

"'We are through the reef, thank Almighty God,' said the captain; and it came warm from the heart. 'Master, we will heave-to till daylight.'

"'Better take a larger offing,' said Soundings, 'the devil may have a young grip forming in the wake of his mother.'

"'Keep a good look out for breakers,' called the captain; 'and, Mr. Handsail, shorten sail for laying her to.'

"And we hove-to, a league to leeward of the most frightful cluster of rocks that ever reared their ugly heads above the wide and open sea.

"'But where is my boy, Paulo?' said the captain.

"I advanced, and gave my doleful story; his strong and pent-up feelings broke down in a torrent of grief, the big tears coursed each other down his weather-beaten cheeks, as he exclaimed, 'O! Paulo, my good and gentle son, Paulo, would to God that I had died for thee?'

"There is something so affecting in the grief of a strong mind like the captain's—so firm, that he retained his self-possession in the midst of scenes that paralysed the heart and blanched the boldest front—that all shed tears that heard him exclaim in the bitter accents of heartbroken misery that he was bereaved and desolate.

"I dearly loved the boy, who haunts me in my sleep. I saw him last night, plain as I saw you, and heard his maniac scream as he jumped into the agitated waters. Saying this, Crombie pulled off my button, and burst into tears.

"'The master,' said he, 'called for a nor'wester to comfort him, saying, 'Grief always made him dry.'

"The captain did his duty mechanically, but the elasticity of his step and his manly deportment had, like his son, left him for ever."

TARS OF THE OLD SCHOOL AND THE NEW.

When I shook hands with my messmates on board the "Victory" for a full due, sailors were sailors—our rig was as follows. If I'm wrong, Bob, you'll tell me of it.

First and foremost, our tails—they hung from our heads to our stern-post—all the ship's company wore them—and every boy in the ship greased his skull twice a-day, to give him a chance of getting a tail and a tidy set of ringlets.

Then, as to the tie, that was a regular affair between man and man—it used to be tie for tie, and hang all favour.

Then came the open neck, the checked shirt, and the black neckerchief tied in a running knot. If a man could sport a Guernsey frock, all the better for him.

Then there was a pair of trousers as tight across the hips as a lady's stays, with plenty of spare canvas in the legs; and on our shoes we had buckles as large as these things wore in the hospital, whilst the toe of the shoe was almost hid by the large broad ribbon, if the tar used a tie instead of a buckle.

Now, Bob, all that's altered; the head is cut as round as a skimming dish; there is not a fid of grease used in a twelvemonth; and if a man has a curl which he has nursed for his sweetheart, the ship's barber cuts it off, and gives it to the quartermaster to make the fly of a dogvane.

Then, bless your heart! the petty officers have got things on their arms like what our porters wear, only one is in the shape of an anchor, and the other like a plate; and, Bob, would you believe it? these new-factured seamen wear braces, have trousers cut close to the leg, and work in purser's shoes, which are large enough for jolly-boats for ten-gun brigs.

Instead of the regular fine old hairy tar, you may see a set of smock-face boys; instead of the knife stuck into the waist, or secured by a lanyard, bless your heart! some of them fasten it with a chain of hair, or a dandy-coloured ribbon.

Well, I looks at all this and shakes my head; for, says I, we did very well with tails and large trousers, and as it gave a certain distinction to our tars, I would rather they had been preserved.

NAUTICAL TALES;
OR, ADVENTURES BY SEA AND LAND.

THE LONE MAN OF THE OCEAN.

It was on the evening of her departure for a transatlantic voyage, that the quarter-deck of an English man-of-war, lying in the Tagus, was splendidly illuminated in honour of a farewell entertainment given by the British officers to a favoured selection of the residents of Lisbon.

No scene of gaiety presents a more picturesque appearance than that exhibited by the festive decorations of a full sized man-of-war; and, on the present occasion, the "Invincible" was not behind her sisters of the ocean in the arrangements of her marine festivities.

Her quarter-deck was covered by an awning of gay and party-coloured flags, whose British admixture of red glowed richly and gaily in the light of the variegated lamps, which, suspended on strings, hung in low rows from the masts and rigging of the vessel.

Below, the tables of the ward-room were spread with the most delicate and even costly refreshments.

All was mirth, and apparently reckless gaiety; and it seemed as if the sons of Neptune, in exercising their proverbial fondness for the dance, and acknowledged gallantry to their partners, had forgotten that the revolution of twenty-four hours would place a world of waters between them and the fair objects of their devotion, and would give far other employment for their limbs than the fascinating measures to which they now led them.

There were, however, two beings in that assembly whose feelings of grief, extending from the heart to the countenance, communicated to the latter an expression which consorted ill with the gaiety of the surrounding scene.

One of these countenances wore the aspect of an intense grief, which yet the mind of the possessor had strength sufficient to keep in a state of manly subjection; the other presented that appearance of unmixed, yet unutterable woe, which woman alone is capable either of feeling or meekly sustaining in silence.

Christian Loeffler and Ernestine Frederberg had been married but seven days, yet they were now passing their last evening together ere Loeffler sailed, a passenger in the "Invincible," to the Brazils.

Why circumstances thus severed those so recently united by the holiest ties, and why the devoted Ernestine was unable to accompany her husband, are queries that might be satisfactorily answered if our limits permitted. But the fact alone can here be stated.

The husband and wife joined the dance but once that evening, and then—publish it not at Almack's—they danced together!

Yet their hearts sickened ere the measure was ended; and retiring to the raised end of the stern, they sate apart from the mirthful crowd, their countenances averted from those faces of gladness, and their eyes directed towards the distant main, which showed dismal, dark, and waste, when contrasted with the bright scene within that gay floating house of pleasure.

The revels broke up; and ere the sun had set on the succeeding day, the so recent pleasure-vessel was ploughing her solitary way on the Atlantic; her festive decorations vanished like a dream, and even the shores that had witnessed them were no longer within sight.

On the second day of the voyage, the attention of Loeffler was forcibly arrested by the livid and almost indescribable appearance of a young seaman, who was mounting the mainshrouds of the vessel.

Christian called to him, inquired if he were ill, and, in the voice of humanity, counselled him to descend.

The young man did not, however, appear to hear the humane caution; and ere the lapse of a few seconds, he loosed his hold on the main-yards, which he had reached, and rushing, with falling violence, through sails and rigging, was quickly precipitated to the deck.

Loeffler ran to raise him; but not only was life extinct, even its very traces had disappeared, and—unlike vitality—the features of the youth had assumed the livid and straightened character of a corpse long deprived of its animating principle.

The log-book, however, passed a verdict of "accidental death, occasioned by a fall from the main-yard," on the youth's case; and as such it went down in the marine record, amidst notices of fair weather and foul, notwithstanding Loeffler's repeated representations of the young seaman's previous appearance.

Christian's testimony was fated ere long to obtain a fearful credence.

On the succeeding day several of the crew sickened; and ere the lapse of another twenty-four hours, death as well as sickness began to show itself.

The captain became alarmed; and a report was soon whispered through the vessel that the hand of some direful, base, or revengeful Portuguese had mingled poison with the festive viands which had been liberally distributed to the whole crew at the farewell entertainment of the "Invincible."

Loeffler, although a German, was no great believer in tales of mystery and dark vengeance. A more fearful idea than even that of poison once or twice half insinuated itself into his mind, but was forced from it with horror.

The wind, which had blown favourably for the

first ten days of the voyage, now seemed totally to die away, and left the vessel becalmed in the midway ocean.

But for the idle rocking occasioned by the under swell of the broad Atlantic waves, she might have seemed a fixture to those seas; for not even the minutest calculable fraction in her latitude and longitude could have been discovered, even by the nicest observer, for fourteen days.

All this while a tropical sun sent its burning, searching rays on the vessel, whose increasing sick and dying gasped for air; and unable either to endure the suffocation below, or the fiery sunbeams above, choked the gangways in their restless passage to and from deck, or giving themselves up in despair, called on death for relief.

The whole crew were in consternation; and they who had still health and strength left to manage or clear the ship, went about their usual duties with the feelings of men who might, at a moment's warning, be summoned from them to death and eternal doom.

Loeffler had shown much courage during these fearful scenes.

One night, after having for some time attended the beds of the sick and dying, he retired to his couch, and endeavoured to gain in slumber a brief forgetfulness of all the thoughts that weighed down his spirits.

But a death-like sickness came over him; his little cabin seemed to whirl round, as if moving on a pivot, while his restless limbs found no space for their feverish evolutions in his confined berth.

Christian began to think that his hour was coming, and he tried to raise his soul in prayer; but while he essayed to fix his thoughts on heaven, he felt that his reason was fast yielding to the burning fever which seemed almost to be consuming his brain.

He called for water, but none heard or answered his cries.

He crawled on deck, and, as the sun had now set several hours, hoped for a breath of the fresh air of heaven.

He threw himself down and turned his face towards the dark sky. But the atmosphere was sultry, heavy, oppressive. It appeared to lie like an insupportable weight on his chest.

He called for the surgeon, but he called in vain; the surgeon himself was no more, and his deputy found a larger demand on his professional exertions than his powers, either physical or mental, were capable of encountering.

A humane hand at length administered a cup of water.

Even the very element was warm with the heat of the vessel. It produced, however, a temporary sensation of refreshment, and Loeffler partially slumbered.

But who can describe that strange and pestilential sleep?

A theatre seemed to be "lighted up within his brain," which teemed with strange, hideous, and portentous scenes, or figures whose very splendour was appalling.

All the ship seemed lit with varied lamps; then the lamps vanished, and, instead of a natural and earthly illumination, it seemed as if the rigging, yards, and sails of the vessel, were all made of living phosphor, or some strange ignited matter, which, far and wide, sent a lurid glare on the waters.

Loeffler looked up long masts of bright and living fire, shrouds whose minutest interlacings were all of the same vivid element, yet clear, distinct, and unmixed by any excrescent flame which might take from the regular appearance of the rigging; while the size of the vessel seemed increased to the most unnatural dimensions, and her glowing top-masts—up which Loeffler strained his vision—seemed to pierce the skies.

He groaned, struggled, tried to thrust his arm violently from him, and awoke.

He found his neck distended to torture by a hard and frightful swelling, which almost deprived his head of motion, and caused the most excruciating anguish, while similar indications on his side assured him that disease was collecting its angry venom.

The thought he had often banished now rushed on Christian's mind; and a fearful test, by which he might prove its reality, now suddenly occurred to him. It seemed as if the delirium of his fever were sobered for a moment by the solemn trial he was about to make.

He was lying near one of the ship lights. He dragged himself, though with difficulty, towards it; he opened the breast of his shirt.

All was decided. Three or four purple spots were clustered at his heart.

Loeffler saw himself lost. He cast a languid and fevered glance toward the sullen waters which rolled onwards to the Portuguese shore, and murmured—

"Farewell! farewell! we meet not till the morning which wakes us to eternal doom."

He next called for the surgeon.

With difficulty that half-worn-out functionary was summoned to the prostrate German.

"Know you," said Loeffler, as soon as he saw him, "know you what fearful foe now stalks in this doomed vessel?"

He opened his breast and said solemnly—

"*The Plague* is amongst us! — warn your captain!"

The professional man stooped towards his pestilential patient, and whispered softly—

"We know all—have known all from the beginning. Think you that all this fumigation—this separation, as far as might be, of the whole from the sick, were remedies to arrest the spread of mortality from poisoned viands? But breathe not, for heaven's sake, your suspicions among this hapless crew. Fear is, in these cases, destruction. I have still hopes that the infection may be arrested."

But the surgeon's words were wasted on air. His patient's senses, roused only for an instant, had again wandered into the regions of delirious fancy, and the torture of his swollen members rendered that delirium almost frantic.

The benevolent surgeon administered a nostrum, looked with compassion on a fellow-being whom he considered doomed to destruction, and secure (despite his superior's fate), in what he had ever deemed professional exemption from infection, prepared to descend to the second deck.

He never reached it. A shivering fit was succeeded by deathly sickness.

All the powers of nature seemed to be totally and instantaneously broken up; the poison had reached the vitals, as in a moment—and the last hope of the fast-sickening crew was no more!

Those on deck rushed in overpowering consternation to the cabin of the captain. Death had been there, too! He was extended, lifeless.

The scenes that followed are of a nature almost too appalling, and even revolting, for description. Let the reader conceive (if he can without having witnessed such a spectacle) the condition of a set of wretched beings, pent within a scorching prison-house, without commander, without medical assistance, daily falling faster and faster, until there were not whole enough to tend the sick, nor living enough to bury the dead, while the malady became every hour more baneful and virulent, from the increasing heat of the atmosphere, the number of living without attendance, and dead without a grave.

It was about five days after the portentous deaths of the surgeon and commander that Loeffler awoke from a deep and lengthened, and, as all might well have deemed a last slumber, which had succeeded the wild delirium of fever.

He awoke like one returning to a world he had for sometime quitted. It was many minutes ere he could recollect his situation.

He found himself still above deck, but placed on a mattress, and in a hammock.

A portion of a cordial was near him. He drank it with the avidity, yet the difficulty, of exhaustion, and slightly partook of a sea-mess, which, from its appearance, might have been laid on his couch some days previously to the sleeper's awakening.

Life and sense now rapidly revived in the naturally strong constitution of our young German. But they brought with them the most fearful and appalling sensations.

With returned strength, Loeffler called aloud; but no voice answered him.

He began to listen with breathless attention; not a sound, either of feet or voices, met his ear.

A thought of horror, that for a moment half-stifled the pulsation at his heart, rushed on Loeffler's mind. He lay for a moment to recover himself, and then collecting his powers of mind and body, quitted his couch and stood on deck.

God of mercy! what a sight met Loeffler's eye!

The whole deck was strewed with lifeless corpses. The hand, fast stiffening in its fixed clasp on the hair; the set teeth, and starting eyeballs, showed where death had come as the reliever of those insupportable torments which attend the plague when it bears down its victim.

Others who had succumbed to its milder, more insidious, yet still more fatal (because more sudden and utterly hopeless) attack, lay in the helpless and composed attitude which might have passed for sleep.

The "Invincible," once the proudest and most gallant vessel which ever rode out a storm, or defied an enemy, now floated like a vast pest-house on the waters; while the sun of that burning zone poured its merciless and unbroken beams on the still and pestiferous atmosphere.

Not a sound, not a breeze, awoke the silence of the sullen and baleful air; not a single sail broke the desolate uniformity of the horizon: sea and sky seemed to meet only to close in that hemisphere of poisonous exhalations.

Christian sickened; he turned round with a feeling of despair, and burying his face in the couch he had just quitted, sought a moment's refuge from the scene of horror.

That moment was one of prayer; the next was that of stern resolution. He forced down his throat a potation, from which his long-confirmed habits of sobriety would formerly have shrunk with disgust; and, under the stimulus of this excitement, compelled himself to the revolting office of swallowing a food which he felt necessary to carry him through the task he contemplated.

First, he determined to descend to the lower decks, and see whether any convalescent, or even expiring, victim yet survived to whom he could tender his assistance; and, secondly, if all had fallen, he would essay the revolting, perhaps the impracticable office of performing their watery sepulture.

Loeffler made several attempts to descend into those close and corrupted regions ere he could summon strength of heart or nerve to enter them.

A profound stillness reigned there. He passed through long rows of hammocks, either the receptacle of decaying humanity, or—as was more often the case—dispossessed of their former occupiers, who had chosen rather to breathe their last above deck.

But a veil shall be drawn over this fearful scene. It is enough to say that not one *living* being was found amid the corrupted wrecks of mortality which tenanted the silent, heated, and pestiferous wards of the inner decks.

Loeffler was ALONE in the ship!

His task was then decided. He could only consign his former companions to their wide and common grave.

He essayed to lift a corpse; but—sick, gasping, and completely overcome—sunk upon his very burden. It was evident he must wait until his strength were further restored; but to wait amid those heaps of decaying bodies seemed impossible.

Night sunk upon the waters. He was alone—the stillness was so unbroken as to be startling.

Perhaps within a thousand miles there might be no living human being. He felt himself a solitary, vital thing among heaps of dead.

He started at every creak of the vessel, and sometimes fancied that he descried through the darkness the well-known and reanimate face of some departed shipmate.

Still he felt that his strength was returning in a manner that appeared almost miraculous; and that night saw many an appalling wreck of humanity consigned to decent oblivion.

On the evening of the following day but one human form tenanted that deserted ship.

As he saw the last of her gallant crew sink beneath the waves, Christian fell on his knees, and—well acquainted with the mother tongue of his departed companions—he took the sacred ritual of their church in his hand. The sun was setting, and by its parting beams Loeffler, with steady and solemn voice—as if there were those might hear the imposing service—read aloud the burial-rites of the Church of England.

Scarcely had he pronounced the concluding blessing ere the sun sunk, and the instantaneous darkness of a tropical night succeeded.

* * * * *

Week after week passed away, and still the Solitary Man of the Sea was the lone occupant of the crewless and now partially dismantled "Invincible."

A tropical equinox was, however, drawing near, though the lone seaman was not aware of its approach.

He listened, therefore, with an ear half fearful, half hopeful, to the risings of the blast. At first it began to whistle shrilly through the shrouds and rigging; the whistle deepened into a thundering roar, and the idle rocking of the ship was changed into the boisterous motion of a storm-beaten vessel.

Loeffler, however, threw himself as usual on deck for his night's repose; and, wrapped in his sea cloak, was rocked to slumber even by the stormy lullaby of the elements.

Towards midnight the voice of the tempest began to deepen to a tone of ominous and apparently concentrating force, which might have startled the most reckless slumberer.

Sheets of lightning—playing from one extremity of the sky to the other—showed wide-spread sheets of surge running towards the ship with a fury that half suggested the idea of malevolent volition on their part; while they dashed against the sides with a violence which seemed to drive in her timbers, and swamped the deck with foam and billows.

Whether any of these storm-tossed waves made their way below—or whether the ship, so long deprived of nautical examination, had sprung a leak in the first encounter of the tempest—Loeffler could not determine; but the conviction that she was filling with water forced itself on his mind.

He again cast his eyes to the north-eastern horizon, and again uttered aloud—

"Farewell! farewell!"

The storm subsided, and the moon, rising over dense masses of cloud, which dispersed from the mid heaven now cumbered the horizon, saw our young German lying in the sleep of confidence and exhaustion, on the still humid deck. He slumbered on, unconscious that the main deck was now almost level with the waves—unconscious of the dark gulf preparing to receive him.

The very steadiness which the waters, accumulating within her, had given to the ship, protracted the fatal repose of the sleeper. He awoke not until his senses were restored, too late, by the gushing of the waters over the deck.

Down, down, a thousand fathom deep, goes the gallant and ill-fated vessel; and with her, drawn into her dark vortex, sinks her lone and unpitied inhabitant!

———

It was in less than a month after this event that Loeffler awake in a spacious and beautiful apartment, the windows of which opened upon a garden of orange and lime trees, whose sweet scent filled the air, and whose bright verdure and golden fruit showed gay and cheerful in the sunshine.

Christian believed that his awakening was in Paradise; nor was the thought less easily harboured, that the object he best loved in life stood by his couch, while his head rested on her arm.

"And thou, too," he said confusedly; "thou too hast reached the fair land of peace, the golden of God!"

"His senses are returning—he speaks—he knows me!" exclaimed Ernestine, clasping her hands in gratitude to Heaven.

She had just received her husband from the hands of the stout captain of a Dutch galliot, whose crew had discovered and rescued the floating and senseless body of Christian on the very morning succeeding the catastrophe we have described.

The humble galliot had a speedier and safer passage than the noble man-of-war; and, in an unusually short time, she made the harbour of Lisbon, to which port she was bound.

It is needless to add that the German recovered both his health and intellects, and lived to increase the tender devotion of his bride, by his recital of the dangers and horrors of his Solitary Voyage.

www.ingramcontent.com/pod-product-compliance
Lightning Source LLC
Chambersburg PA
CBHW081912170426
43200CB00014B/2709